D0536015

PERSONAL TRAINER MANUAL

The Resource for Fitness Instructors

PERSONAL TRAINER MANUAL

The Resource for Fitness Instructors

MITCHELL SUDY

SUPERVISING EDITOR

AMERICAN
COUNCIL ON
EXERCISE

AMERICAN COUNCIL ON EXERCISE

PUBLISHER

San Diego, California

Library of Congress Cataloging-in-Publication Data

Personal trainer manual.

   Includes bibliographical references and index.
   1. Personal trainers — Certification.
I. Simon, Elliot. II American Council on Exercise.
GV428.7.P47 1991 613.7 — dc20 90-85510
ISBN 0-9618161-1-2

First edition, 1991
Reprinted, 1991
Reprinted, 1992

Published by
AMERICAN COUNCIL ON EXERCISE
5820 Oberlin Drive
Suite 102
San Diego, CA 92121-3787
(619) 535-8227

ISBN 0-9618161-1-2
Printed in the United States of America

Design: YAZZ GRAPHIC DESIGN
Production: COLE PUBLISHING CO.
Copy Editors: ELLIOT SIMON, ANNA K. MORGAN, NAN VAN GELDER
Proofreader: ANNA K. MORGAN
Anatomical Illustrations: JAMES STAUNTON
Photographer: WERNER KALBER
Models: EDDIE FITZGERALD, GREG FINLEY, KRYS GOLANSKI, JANE WEINZIERL

Acknowledgements: To the entire American Council on Exercise staff for their support and guidance throughout this lengthy process, and to NAN VAN GELDER for her editorial assistance with the rough manuscript.

Special thanks to BOB MARTIN of Polaris for providing the weight training equipment.

Special thanks to SHERYL MARKS, DEANNE DREIS, SHARON WELDY, MIKE YAZZOLINO, WERNER KALBER, and COLE PUBLISHING for their patience and encouragement.

To PETER DAVIS and ANGEL MARTINEZ for initial support for this project.

The **AMERICAN COUNCIL ON EXERCISE** gratefully acknowledges Reebok International Ltd. for their contribution to support the production of this book. Without their help, this project would not have been possible.

REVIEWERS

KATHY ALEXANDER, PH.D. Exercise physiologist; owner/operator of S.T.E.P.S., Inc., a personal fitness training facility in Nashville, Tennessee.

DOUGLAS BROOKS, M.S. Personal trainer; owner of The Training Edge, a private fitness studio in Southern California; author of *Going Solo—the Art of Personal Training*; distributor of exercise videos.

DONALD A. CHU, PH.D., R.P.T. Founder and director of ATHER'S Clinic, specializing in sports medicine; currently conducting research in the field of plyometrics.

KAREN CLIPPINGER-ROBERTSON, M.S., P.E. Director of Seattle Sports Medicine Seminars; consultant to the Pacific Northwest Ballet, U.S. Weightlifting Federation, the U.S. Men's Race Walking Team, and various sports medicine clinics and fitness studios.

SCOTT COULTER, M.S. Director of training for Sports Training Institute and its eight training facilities; served as a member of the American Council on Exercise Personal Trainer Certification Examination and role delineation committees.

ROD DISHMAN, PH.D. Professor of physical education and director of behavioral fitness laboratories for the University of Georgia, Athens; author of *Exercise Adherence: Its Impact on Public Health*.

DEBBIE ELLISON, R.P.T. Personal trainer; founder and president of A*PLUS* Workshops; consultant to Nike, Inc.; member of Nike's national fitness training and public speaking team, Body Elite.

KATHLEEN HARGARTEN, M.D., F.A.C.E.P Assistant professor at the Medical College of Wisconsin; board-certified in emergency medicine; fellow of the American College of Emergency Physicians; served on the American Council on Exercise Personal Trainer Certification Examination and role delineation committees.

WILLIAM L. HASKELL, PH.D. Associate professor, Stanford University School of Medicine; deputy director, Stanford Center for Research in Disease Prevention; past president, American College of Sports Medicine.

GWEN HYATT, M.S. Director of education for Desert Southwest Fitness; exercise physiologist at Logan Regional Hospital; American Council on Exercise-certified.

SHEILA KING, M.S. Clinical exercise physiologist; certified preventative and rehabilitation program director by American College of Sports Medicine; independent consultant for health promotion.

BRIAN KOEBERLE, J.D. Sports/fitness law attorney; American Council on Exercise Certified Personal Trainer; president of Personal Fitness Consultants, Inc., a sports/fitness consulting, marketing, and promotions company; author of *The Legal Aspects of Personal Training*.

SARA KOOPERMAN, J.D. Licensed attorney; professional dancer; judge for the Reebok/Crystal Light National Aerobic Championships competition; lecturer for the American College of Sports Medicine; American Council on Exercise-certified.

DANIEL KOSICH, PH.D. Private consultant serving as program director for the Jane Fonda Workout; consulting physiologist to the Jimmie Heuga Multiple Sclerosis Center in Vail, Colorado; active member of the American College of Sports Medicine; member of the American Council on Exercise Personal Trainer Certification Examination and role delineation committees.

ELAINE LAYDEN, M.A. Fitness specialist; health educator in weight loss, smoking cessation, and special populations; certified by the American Council on Exercise and the American College of Sports Medicine.

RICK PARKER, D.O. Practices Sports Medicine and Family Medicine at the San Diego Sports Medicine Center; serves on the board of directors of the American Osteopathic Academy of Sports Medicine; team physician for San Diego State University Athletics and the Men's and Women's U.S.A. (Olympic) Volleyball Teams; assistant team physician for the San Diego Chargers.

LEE RICE, D.O., F.A.A.F.P. Director of the San Diego Sports Medicine Center; on the faculty at University of California, San Diego, School of Medicine; team physician for the San Diego Chargers, Gulls, and Soccers; team physician for San Diego State University and the U.S.A. National Volleyball Teams.

BARRY ROSE, M.D. Board-certified orthopedic surgeon; chief of orthopedics, Sharp Rees-Stealy Medical Group; co-owner of Rose Fitness Connection, a personal training company, and Schliebes of California, a cross-training fitness club in Solana Beach, California.

IRV RUBENSTEIN, PH.D. Received his doctorate in the exercise sciences, specializing in kinesiology, from Peabody College-Vanderbilt University in Nashville, Tennessee; founder of S.T.E.P.S., Inc., a personal fitness training facility in Nashville, Tennessee.

CHRIS VEGA, M.P.H., R.D. Conducts Aerobic Training International in Puerto Rico; physical education teacher in sports and exercise for the last 20 years.

LARRY VERITY, PH.D. Associate professor of exercise physiology; director of the Adult Fitness Program and the American College of Sports Medicine Workshops at San Diego State University.

JAN WALLACE, PH.D. Associate professor of kinesiology and director of adult fitness at Indiana University; certified exercise specialist and program director by the American College of Sports Medicine; editor of *Certified News* for ACSM.

NEIL WOLKODOFF, M.A. Director of sport sciences at the Denver Athletic Club; trainer for Copper Mountain Ski School and U.S. Junior Olympic badminton team; certified by the American Council on Exercise, American College of Sports Medicine, National Strength and Conditioning Association, and the U.S. Weight Lifting Federation.

ARLEN ZWICKLER, M.S., A.T.C. General manager of the multi- recreational facility Sportset Syosset Club, New York, New York; member of the American Council on Exercise Personal Trainer role delineation committee.

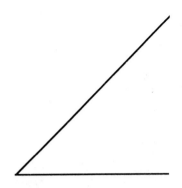

Contents

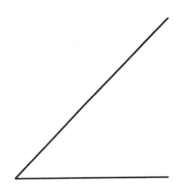

Foreword

The great interest in physical fitness and exercise today is the result of many factors and it provides professionals in the field many opportunities to be of service. The public has a better understanding than ever before of the importance of exercise in their lives and of appropriate ways to exercise. Even so, there remains much to be done in the way of public education to encourage more inactive people to become active. Also, many people start on a program but do not stay with it. That is an important reason the concept of a personal trainer has such significant potential. A personal trainer will be more available than group classes and can provide an individualized approach that gives that extra something to help a person stick with a program.

As a personal trainer, you have a moral and professional responsibility to prepare yourself to give quality programs to your clients. Your clients' understanding of exercise and fitness, ability to exercise properly, and motivation to carry out their programs will come, in large measure, from your leadership and professional expertise.

Just as important is the role model you can be. Your appearance, enthusiasm, and accuracy in what you say will be a large part of the message sent to your clients. Do not let them down!

The scientific information, teaching techniques, and methodology in this manual have been prepared by some of the most knowledgeable leaders in the fitness field. Study it carefully and refer to it regularly, and you will have a wealth of information to make your work as a personal trainer successful and rewarding.

ASH HAYES
Former Executive Director
President's Council on Physical
Fitness and Sports

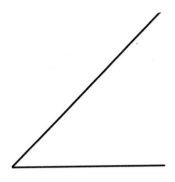

Introduction

Exercise enthusiasts are becoming more educated about fitness and health, more insistent on an exercise regimen that caters to their schedules, and more adventurous and versatile in the activities in which they participate. Emerging from the demands of these individuals is the need for fitness instructors conversant with a variety of sports and activities and willing to meet clients at the fitness center, in the home, or elsewhere to personally guide them through an exercise program designed specifically for them. This need has generated a new fitness niche, and we are witness to a new breed of fitness instructor—the personal trainer. This manual provides the background education and information needed by the personal trainer to work with clients safely and effectively.

The first challenge in developing this manual was to define the scope of practice of the personal trainer—what such instructors are required to do and what knowledge they need to do their job. Several hundred fitness professionals worked together with the American Council on Exercise and a professional testing service to accomplish this goal. They concluded that the major areas of responsibility and work activities include the abilities to (a) screen and evaluate prospective clients, (b) design safe and effective exercise programs, (c) instruct clients in correct exercise technique to avoid injury, and (d) be able to respond to the typical questions and problems that arise in a one-on-one setting.

Once it was clarified exactly what this new breed of exercise instructor should be able to do, it was necessary to identify the knowledge base required to accomplish the work tasks. Knowledge of anatomy, kinesiology, and exercise physiology were obvious fundamentals. But topics such as nutrition, principles of good communication, motivational techniques, and fitness testing were seen as equally important. This book, then, represents the minimum knowledge prerequisite to entering the fitness field as a personal trainer and working with apparently healthy adults.

In addition to providing background education and information to personal trainers, the Personal Trainer Manual was designed to serve as a companion and self-study aid to the American Council on Exercise's Personal Trainer Certification Examination. Launched in May 1990, the Personal Trainer Exam was patterned after the Council's successful Aerobics Certification Exam. Nearly 10,000 instructors take the aerobics certification test annually, making aerobics certification one of the most sought-after fitness certifications in the United States.

To bring you the latest scientific information available at the time of publication, the American Council on Exercise employed the help of 19 top experts in health, fitness, medicine, nutrition, and sports law to author this text. In addition, 24 reviewers were consulted to ensure the accuracy of the manual and to separate personal opinion from generally accepted standards. It is important to remember, however, that the field of knowledge on which this book is based will continue to change as research progresses. Therefore, it is the never-ending responsibility of all fitness professionals to continue their education and stay up to date on industry trends and research findings.

In summary, this book is a guide for teaching exercise to today's exercise enthusiasts, whether you work one-on-one with clients as part of a fitness center staff or as an independent personal trainer. As a professional, you have an abundance of information at your fingertips. Your challenge is to comprehend and apply this information in a way that is appealing, that brings results, and that ensures the long-term success of your clients.

A career in fitness can be long and rewarding. It offers an opportunity to creatively apply scientific information to help people achieve personal fitness goals. If you are considering a career in fitness, we hope this book entices you to pursue one. If you are already dedicated to fitness, we hope it aids you in your ongoing exploration and work in the fitness industry.

SHERYL MARKS
Executive Director
American Council on Exercise

PERSONAL TRAINER MANUAL

The Resource for Fitness Instructors

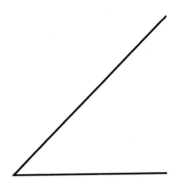

Exercise Science

PART I

The Personal Trainer Manual is a compilation of essays covering the broad range of information personal fitness trainers need to know to provide fun, high-quality, safe, and effective exercise programming. This first part presents the core, the fundamental sciences from which stem all program design. This complex and interrelated material is not easily learned and may well require more than one reading. However, the value of a full understanding of this material will become apparent as the reader moves through the remaining parts of the text. Part I's chapters on exercise physiology, anatomy, applied kinesiology, and nutrition explain in detail how and why the body responds to the stresses placed on it through exercise. Trainers should make this core material the cornerstone of their programs.

Exercise Physiology

DANIEL KOSICH

DANIEL KOSICH, PH.D., is a private consultant, serving as technical advisor to the Jane Fonda Workout, as well as consulting physiologist to the Jimmie Heuga Multiple Sclerosis Center in Vail, Colorado. He has developed numerous fitness and nutrition education programs for fitness center personnel and is an active member of the American College of Sports Medicine.

1

IN THIS CHAPTER:

- Physiology of the cardiopulmonary system: the heart, cardiac output, ejection fraction, oxygen extraction, cardiopulmonary responses to exercise.

- Energy production in the cells: ATP, aerobic and anaerobic energy systems, aerobic capacity.

- Guidelines for cardiovascular fitness: benefits of aerobic fitness; type, intensity, duration, and frequency of exercise; warm-up and cooldown; environmental concerns.

- Basic skeletal muscle anatomy and physiology: muscle fiber types; skeletal muscle anatomy; muscle contraction.

- Adaptations to strength training: muscle fiber adaptation; connective tissue adaptation; increased nervous system activity; decreased nervous inhibition.

- Guidelines for strength and flexibility training: types of strength overloads; muscle soreness and fatigue; slow, sustained, and ballistic stretching.

Interest in physical fitness training has grown rapidly in the past few years. Those involved with designing or supervising exercise programs must have a basic understanding of the principles of human physiology and anatomy. Physiology is the study of the myriad functions in a living organism, and exercise physiology is the study of the ways the cells and tissues of the body function during exercise. The study of exercise physiology challenges the fitness professional first to be familiar with how the body functions at rest, then to understand how the body responds and adapts to many different types of exercises.

How does the body respond to a gradually increasing pace of exercise? Does the body respond differently to a dramatic increase in pace compared with a gradual increase? What are the differences between the responses to lifting weights and running or cycling? Why is a slow, sustained stretch held with no pain much safer and generally more effective than rapid, bouncing stretches? These are all questions a personal trainer should be able to answer easily.

This chapter presents the fundamental concepts of exercise physiology any trainer should understand in order to design a safe and effective exercise program that will enable a healthy adult to achieve optimum fitness.

OPTIMUM FITNESS

There are many ways to define physical fitness. For a trainer, it is helpful to think about physical fitness in relation to the "specificity of training," which means that physiological adaptations to exercise are specific to the system worked during the stress of exercise. In other words, the type of exercise which develops cardiovascular endurance is not very effective for developing an optimum balance of muscular strength. Flexibility training usually increases the range of motion about a specific joint, such as the hip, but it is not effective for improving cardiovascular endurance or muscle strength. Resistance training, such as weight lifting, is the best way to increase strength, but it is not the most effective way to improve cardiovascular fitness.

The principle of training specificity defines optimum physical fitness as the condition resulting from a lifestyle that leads to the development of an optimal level of cardiovascular endurance, muscular strength, and flexibility, as well as the achievement and maintenance of ideal body weight.

Cardiovascular, or **cardiopulmonary endurance**, also referred to as cardiovascular/cardiopulmonary fitness or **aerobic** fitness, describes the ability of the cardiovascular/cardiopulmonary system (heart, lungs, blood vessels) to deliver an adequate supply of oxygen to exercising muscles. (Some exercise physiologists prefer to use the term cardiopulmonary rather than cardiovascular because cardiopulmonary includes the reference to the lungs—pulmonary. I will use the words interchangeably in this chapter; blood must flow from the heart through blood vessels—vascular—to the lungs to pick up oxygen which can be delivered to exercising muscles.)

Muscular strength is the maximum amount of force a muscle or muscle group can develop during a single contraction. **Muscular endurance** is the number of repeated contractions a muscle or muscle group can perform against a resistance without fatiguing, or the length of time a contraction can be held without fatigue.

Flexibility describes the amount of movement which can be accomplished at a joint (an articulation), such as the knee or shoulder, usually referred to as the "range of motion about a joint." Maintaining flexibility may help reduce the risk of injury and can also help improve performance in many activities.

Ideal body weight represents an ideal body composition. One's weight on a scale is comprised of two dimensions: (1) body-fat (adipose tissue) and (2) lean body mass. Body-fat, which is the body's primary reserve of stored energy, is stored as triglycerides both in fat (adipose) cells located between the skin and muscles all over the body, as well as within skeletal muscle. While the energy available from fat is used in many different cells in the body, exercising muscles can utilize a tremendous amount of fat to produce the energy necessary for muscle contraction. Percent body-fat represents the percentage of total body weight which is carried as fat. In general, ideal percent body-fat falls in the range of 17–25 percent for women and 10–16 percent for men. **Lean body mass** represents all the rest of the body's weight, excluding fat—muscles, bones, organs, and nervous tissue. Achieving and maintaining an ideal body composition is an important part of health and fitness.

It is possible to measure one's level of fitness in each of the areas of optimum fitness using a variety of fitness tests. The most important value of fitness testing, which will be discussed in detail in Chapter 6 and referred to throughout this manual, is to establish a baseline against which improvements can be measured over time. Using fitness tests to compare performance capabilities is generally best left to clinical experts doing research or developing programs for competitive athletes. Most fitness tests performed by personal trainers use equipment and techniques that are not sophisticated enough to assure clinical accuracy.

PHYSIOLOGY OF THE CARDIOPULMONARY SYSTEM

The cardiopulmonary system is primarily a transport network in the body. Blood serves as the vehicle to carry gases (like oxygen) and nutrients (like fat, amino acids, and carbohydrate) from where they are taken into the body to the cells where they are needed. Blood also picks up waste products (like lactic acid and carbon dioxide) from the cells where they are made and carries them to where they can be expelled or metabolized.

Cardio (as well as cardiac and coronary) refers to the heart. Pulmonary, as mentioned earlier, refers to the lungs. In the lungs, blood gives up carbon dioxide and picks up oxygen. Blood is transported in the body in an incredible network of blood vessels. Therefore, the cardiopulmonary system is composed of the heart, which pumps the blood; the lungs, where the blood picks up oxygen; and the blood vessels, which transport the blood throughout the body.

There are three kinds of blood vessels: arteries, capillaries, and veins. Generally, **arteries** carry blood with a fresh oxygen (O_2) supply away from the heart to be delivered to the various cells and tissues. **Capillaries** are very narrow, thin-walled vessels across which the exchange of gases, nutrients, and cellular waste products occurs between the blood and the cells of the body. After passing through the capillaries, blood enters the **veins**. The venous system provides the network of vessels through which the blood, now lower in oxygen content than arterial blood but with a much higher content of carbon dioxide, flows back to the heart to continue the cyclic blood flow.

The Heart

The heart muscle is divided into right and left sides, and each side is further divided into upper and lower chambers, making a total of four separate chambers. The upper chambers are called **atria**; the lower chambers are called **ventricles**. As depicted in Figure 1–1, the right side of the heart receives the venous blood (blood coming back to the heart through the veins), then pumps this blood to the lungs. All of the blood from the venous system enters the right atrium, then flows to the right ventricle. When the heart muscle contracts, the right ventricle squeezes against the volume of blood that has filled into the chamber and sends this blood to the lungs through the pulmonary arteries.

In the lungs the blood picks up a fresh supply of oxygen and gives off carbon dioxide (CO_2) in the pulmonary capillaries. Oxygen and, to a limited extent, carbon dioxide are carried in red blood cells on a protein called hemoglobin. The freshly oxygenated blood returns to the left atrium through the pulmonary veins, then flows to the left ventricle. Simultaneous with contraction of the right ventricle, the left ventricle contracts and pumps the blood in its chamber through the largest artery in the body—the aorta—to be delivered to the rest of the body.

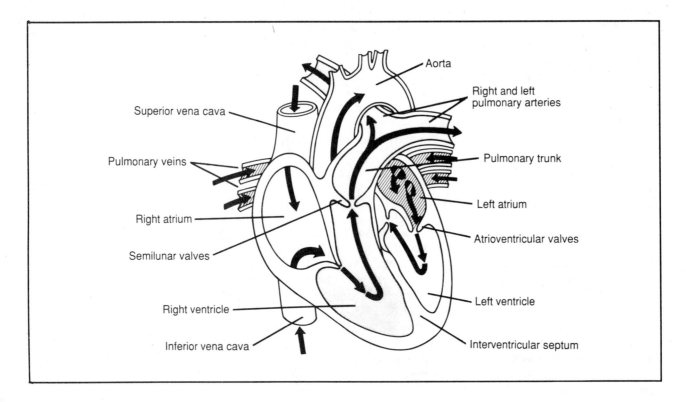

Figure 1–1 Anatomy of the heart, and pattern of blood flow through the heart.

In essence, the cardiovascular system has two circulatory patterns: one is pulmonary circulation—from the heart to the lungs and back; the other, often referred to as systemic circulation, is the flow of blood from the left ventricle to the rest of the body and back. Remember, the right and left ventricles contract at the same time, and each side pumps the same amount of blood per contraction.

There are two phases in the rhythmic pattern of cardiac contraction and relaxation called the cardiac cycle: systole and diastole. **Systole** refers to the contraction phase; **diastole** refers to the relaxation phase of the cardiac cycle. During systole, the atria contract first, pumping blood to the ventricles. A fraction of a second later, the ventricles contract, pumping blood to the lungs and the body. Remember, the left and right sides of the heart contract at the same time, so at the same time blood from the right ventricle is pumped (ejected) to the lungs through the pulmonary arteries, blood from the left ventricle is ejected to the rest of the body through the aorta.

As the heart muscle relaxes during diastole, blood fills the left and right chambers of the heart in preparation for the next contraction. Note that during diastole the heart muscle itself is supplied with its blood flow (therefore its oxygen supply) through the coronary arteries. One of the many benefits of having a high level of cardiopulmonary fitness is that the heart spends more time resting (in diastole) at any submaximal exercise intensity, including rest, than when the system is poorly trained. We'll discuss the reasons for this later.

Cardiac Output

The amount of blood that is pumped out of each ventricle each minute is described by the term **cardiac output**. In other words, cardiac output (Q) is the amount of blood that flows from each ventricle in a minute's time. The cardiac output from the left and right ventricles is exactly the same. However, the blood in the left ventricle is ejected with significantly greater force than the blood in the right ventricle because the blood from the right ventricle goes just to the lungs and back, whereas the blood from the left ventricle has to be pumped with enough force to send it throughout the rest of the body.

Cardiac output is a product of two factors. One is heart rate (HR), the number of times the heart beats per minute (bpm). The other is stroke volume (SV), the amount of blood pumped from each ventricle each time the heart beats. Stroke volume is measured in milliliters (ml) per beat (1 ounce = 29.6 ml). If heart rate is multiplied by stroke volume, or the number of beats per minute is multiplied by the amount of blood pumped from each ventricle per beat, the resulting volume represents the cardiac output. Cardiac output can be expressed by the following equation:

$$Q = HR \times SV$$

For example, if the heart beats 60 times per minute (HR = 60), and 70 milliliters of blood are pumped each beat (SV = 70 ml), the cardiac output would be

$$60 \text{ bpm} \times 70 \text{ ml/beat} = 4200 \text{ ml/min}$$

This equals about a gallon of blood per minute, a fairly typical cardiac output at rest.

Ejection Fraction

The amount of blood that fills the ventricles during diastole is not always completely ejected (pumped out) during systole. The percentage of the total volume of blood in the ventricle at the end of diastole that is subsequently ejected during contraction is called the **ejection fraction**.

The ejection fraction at rest is only about 50 percent because there is minimal need for oxygen in the muscle cells at rest, so the heart can supply adequate oxygen with minimal effort. But during work, when there is great increase in the need for oxygen in the muscles, the heart is able to completely empty the ventricles during contraction. So, during exercise the ejection fraction can increase to 100 percent of the blood in the ventricles at the end of diastole. (The ejection fraction is also higher when one is lying down because of the effect of gravity, but it is not of major importance here.) The importance of the increase in ejection fraction, which clearly increases cardiac output, as one goes from rest to increasingly higher exercise intensities will soon be clear.

Oxygen Extraction at the Muscles

As mentioned earlier, a primary purpose of the cardiovascular system during exercise is to deliver oxygen and other nutrients to the exercising muscle cells and to carry carbon dioxide and other waste products away from the muscles. Cardiac output represents the volume of blood (therefore, oxygen) flowing toward the muscles each minute. But another critically important factor, especially in exercise performance, is the amount of oxygen taken from the hemoglobin (remember, this occurs in the capillaries of the muscles) and subsequently used in the exercising muscle cells. This process is referred to as oxygen extraction.

Normally, all of the oxygen delivered to the cells via the arteries is not extracted in the capillaries. So, while the amount of oxygen in venous blood is certainly less than the amount of oxygen in arterial blood, there is some oxygen in the blood which returns back to the heart. In other words, we are able to load the blood with more oxygen in the lungs than our body is able to use at the cellular level. Therefore, in a healthy person, the inability to breathe fast enough is not the limiting factor in performance. The major limitation to exercise performance is the capacity of the muscles to extract oxygen from the bloodstream to produce energy.

ENERGY PRODUCTION IN THE CELLS

Why is oxygen so important? An understanding of the functions of the cardiopulmonary system in oxygen delivery and extraction can help explain energy production in the cells, and particularly in muscle cells.

ATP, The Energy Molecule

When a muscle contracts and exerts force, the energy used to drive the contraction comes from a special substance in the cell known as **ATP**, **adenosine triphosphate**. For our purposes, ATP is the body's energy source, just as gasoline is the energy source in an automobile engine. How quickly and efficiently a muscle cell produces ATP determines how much work the cell can do before it fatigues. While there is some ATP stored in a muscle cell, the supply is limited. Therefore, muscle cells must produce more ATP in order to continue working. Muscle cells replenish the ATP supply using three distinct biochemical pathways, or separate series of chemical reactions.

Aerobic and Anaerobic Energy Systems

The word "aerobic" means "with oxygen." The aerobic energy system for producing ATP is dominant when adequate oxygen is delivered into the cell to meet energy production needs, such as when the muscle is at rest. Most cells, including muscle cells, contain structures called **mitochondria**. The mitochondria are the site of aerobic energy (ATP) production. The greater the number of mitochondria in a cell, the greater the aerobic energy production capability of that cell.

The other two energy systems are the primary sources of ATP when an inadequate supply of oxygen is available to the cell to meet its energy needs. In the absence of sufficient oxygen, as when a muscle cell needs to generate a lot of force very quickly to lift a heavy weight, the cell shifts into the **anaerobic** energy systems, which provide a rapidly available source of ATP. "Anaerobic" means "without oxygen." The anaerobic production of ATP occurs inside the cell, but outside the mitochondria.

Many cells, such as those in the heart, brain, and other organs, have an extremely limited anaerobic capability. Therefore, these cells must be continuously supplied with oxygen, or they will die. For example, if a coronary artery (which supplies blood and oxygen to the heart muscle) becomes clogged with a build-up of cholesterol deposits, there will be a diminished flow of blood through that artery, referred to as **ischemia**. The decreased blood flow can lead to an insufficient oxygen supply to the heart muscle, during either rest or exercise, which often leads to a sensation of pain and/or pressure in the chest called **angina pectoris**.

If the oxygen supply is cut off, such as when a blood clot forms where the coronary artery has become clogged, the area of the heart muscle (myocardium) beyond the blockage suffers a **myocardial infarction**, often called a heart attack. If enough of the myocardium is involved, the result is a fatal heart attack. In the brain, ischemia can lead to a stroke.

Unlike the heart and brain, however, skeletal muscles, such as triceps, and quadriceps, have a significant anaerobic capability. A personal trainer must understand aerobic and anaerobic energy production in relation to what substances are used to produce ATP, as well as to exercise intensity, with rest and maximum effort representing the two extremes of possible intensity. The body uses an extremely complex chemical process to produce ATP. However, just a basic understanding of the process will assist the trainer in designing effective exercise programs.

Fat (**fatty acids**) and a carbohydrate (**glucose**) are the two substances (**substrates**) the body's cells use to produce most of the ATP supply. Proteins, which are comprised of various combinations of **amino acids**, are not a preferred energy source; in an adequately nourished client, proteins play a minor role in energy production. However, when a diet does not supply sufficient calories, the body is capable of using protein stored in tissues like muscle to produce the energy it needs. This is certainly not an ideal process.

At rest, when the cardiopulmonary system is easily able to supply adequate oxygen to the mitochondria of muscle cells, both fatty acids and glucose are used to produce ATP. In other words, at rest, most of the needed ATP is produced aerobically, using both fatty acids and glucose. In fact, the body produces about one calorie per minute at rest. About 50 percent of this one cal/min comes from fat, even in an untrained person. In a well-trained endurance athlete, fats provide as much as 70 percent of the resting caloric expenditure.

With increasing exercise intensity, the cardiovascular system makes every attempt to increase its delivery of oxygen into the mitochondria of exercising muscles to produce enough ATP aerobically. At some point in increasing intensity, determined both by a client's level of aerobic fitness and by genetics, the cardiovascular system becomes unable to supply enough oxygen to the exercising muscles, so they switch to the anaerobic systems to produce ATP rapidly. The intensity at which adequate oxygen is unavailable is referred to as the **anaerobic threshold**. As illustrated in Figure 1-2, the anaerobic threshold is reached before maximum effort, generally somewhere in the range of 50-85 percent of maximum effort.

The anaerobic systems, however, cannot be used for a prolonged period. The primary source of anaerobic ATP production is glucose, which is stored in muscles and the liver as **glycogen**, a large molecule made up of chains of glucose. A second source of anaerobic ATP production is **creatine phosphate**, a molecule which can be broken apart quickly to help produce ATP. However, as with the muscles' store of ATP, there is an extremely limited supply of creatine phosphate. Research done nearly 20 years ago (J. Bergstom et al., 1971) has shown that even in a well-trained athlete, the muscles store only enough creatine phosphate and ATP, together referred to as **phosphagens**, to last for about 10 seconds of maximal effort.

To summarize, as long as a muscle cell is aerobic, it uses both fat and glucose to produce ATP. The aerobic system produces much more ATP than the anaerobic systems, primarily because fat yields 9 calories of energy per gram, while glucose and protein yield only 4 calories of energy per gram. Further, the waste products of aerobic ATP production are water and carbon dioxide (CO_2). Both are relatively easy for the body to deal with, so that aerobic energy production does not lead to muscle fatigue. Since water is a waste product of aerobic ATP production, it is crucial to replace this eliminated water by

Figure 1–2   Energy production and relative intensity in an exercising muscle.

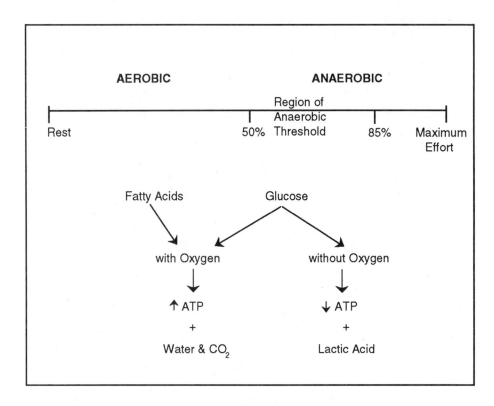

drinking plenty of fluids every day. The more one exercises, the more water is necessary.

When an exercising muscle becomes anaerobic it relies on glucose (and to a limited extent the phosphagen system) to produce ATP. However, not only is much less ATP produced anaerobically than aerobically per molecule of substrate used, the waste products of anaerobic ATP production include lactic acid. As the level of lactic acid and other waste products increases in a muscle, continued contraction of that muscle is soon inhibited. Lactic acid is thought to be the principal cause of the immediate soreness (the "burn") in an exercising muscle.

In addition to lactic acid build-up, muscles give other signals when they can no longer produce enough ATP aerobically. One is **hyperventilation**, defined as "breathing faster than is necessary at a given pace," an indication that anaerobic ATP production is predominating. When inadequate oxygen is available, the muscle signals the brain to increase the rate and depth of breathing. However, since the limiting factor is not breathing but oxygen extraction at the muscle, hyperventilation is a futile process. Figure 1-3 summarizes the essential elements of the biochemistry muscles use to produce the ATP needed for contraction.

The chemistry that the body uses to produce ATP depends on proteins in the body called **enzymes**. Enzymes are needed to start the chemical reactions which produce ATP both aerobically and anaerobically. The fat-metabolizing enzymes are different from the carbohydrate-metabolizing enzymes. Further, separate enzymes are used to metabolize carbohydrate aerobically than are used to metabolize carbohydrate anaerobically. So when we exercise at an intensity below the anaerobic threshold, the aerobic enzymes which metabolize fat and carbohydrate are dominating in the production of ATP. But when exercise is done above the anaerobic threshold, the anaerobic enzymes take over the dominant role in producing ATP.

Energy System	Substance(s) used to produce ATP	Limitation to ATP production	Primary Use
ANAEROBIC 1. Phosphagen	Creatine Phosphate (CP) Stored ATP	Muscle stores very little CP and ATP	High intensity, short duration activities; less than 10 seconds to fatigue
2. Breakdown of Glucose	Glucose and Glycogen	Lactic acid buildup causes rapid fatigue	High intensity, short duration activities; from 1-3 minutes to fatigue
AEROBIC	Fatty acids, Glucose, and Glycogen	Depletion of muscle glycogen and sugar; insufficient oxygen delivery	Long duration, sub-anaerobic threshold activities; longer than 3 minutes to fatigue

Aerobic training will lead to an increased capacity in the aerobic system, but has little effect on anaerobic enzymes. Aerobic training, therefore, significantly increases our ability to burn fat. Anaerobic training, on the other hand, will lead principally to an improved function in the anaerobic enzyme system—another application of the principle of specificity of training.

Figure 1–3 Energy systems available to an exercising muscle.

Aerobic Capacity (Maximal Oxygen Consumption)

The total capacity to consume oxygen at the cellular level is referred to as **maximal oxygen consumption** or $\dot{V}O_2$ **max**. This phrase represents our maximum aerobic capacity. $\dot{V}O_2$ max depends on two factors: (1) the delivery of oxygen to the working muscle by the blood, or the cardiac output, and (2) the ability to extract the oxygen from the blood at the capillaries and use the oxygen in the mitochondria. Maximum oxygen consumption is represented by the following formula:

$$\dot{V}O_2 \text{ max} = \text{cardiac output}_{max} \times \text{oxygen extraction}_{max}$$

$\dot{V}O_2$ (the volume of oxygen consumed) is measured as either milliliters of oxygen consumed per kilogram of body weight per minute (ml O_2/kg/min), or as liters of oxygen consumed per minute (l O_2/min).

We can illustrate how much oxygen is actually used at rest when compared with a hypothetical maximum aerobic capacity of a client who weighs 70 kilograms (154 lbs). If his resting heart rate is 60 bpm, stroke volume is 70 ml/beat (remember cardiac output = heart rate x stroke volume), and oxygen extraction is 6 ml O_2/100 ml of blood, then his resting $\dot{V}O_2$ is

$$\dot{V}O_2 = 60 \text{ bpm} \times 70 \text{ ml/beat} \times 6 \text{ ml } O_2/100 \text{ ml blood}$$

Which equals 252 ml O_2/min. Divided by 70 kg, his resting $\dot{V}O_2$ is about 3.5 ml/kg/min. During maximal exercise our man has a heart rate of 180 bpm, a stroke volume of 115 ml/beat, and an oxygen extraction of 15 ml O_2/100 ml blood. So his maximum $\dot{V}O_2$ is

$$\dot{V}O_2 \text{ max} = 180 \text{ bpm} \times 115 \text{ ml/beat} \times 15 \text{ ml } O_2/100 \text{ ml blood}$$

which equals 3,105 ml O_2/min, or 44.4 ml/kg/min.

While the example represents a hypothetical client in average condition, it clearly illustrates that our bodies have a tremendous capacity to increase oxygen consumption, in this case by more than 12.5 times. While increases in both heart rate and stroke volume account for the increased cardiac output during exercise, the increase in oxygen extraction (referred to as arterio-venous oxygen difference, or A-$\dot{V}O_2$ diff.) results from different stimuli. During exercise, several changes occur which make it easier for oxygen to be taken off the hemoglobin molecule for use in aerobic energy production in the muscles. The changes include increases in the temperature, acidity, and level of carbon dioxide in the bloodstream.

The resting $\dot{V}O_2$ of 3.5 ml/kg/min is often referred to as one Metabolic Equivalent, or 1 MET. Activities are sometimes described in terms of METS; for example, volleyball has a range of 3–6 METS and aerobic dancing has a range of 6–9 METS. To determine the $\dot{V}O_2$ equivalent of any MET value, simply multiply the MET value times 3.5. Physicians often prescribe exercise by MET values for patients in cardiac rehabilitation programs, determining the MET capacity of the patient as the rehabilitation progresses.

Not only does $\dot{V}O_2$ max increase with aerobic training, the percentage of maximum effort at which the anaerobic threshold occurs also increases. Practically speaking, this means that a client is able to produce ATP aerobically at increasingly greater intensities in response to aerobic training. Further, the aerobically trained person generally can perform more intense activities than the untrained person and still be working aerobically.

CARDIOVASCULAR/CARDIOPULMONARY RESPONSES TO EXERCISE

Since maximal aerobic capacity is actually a function of cardiac output times extraction, the trainer must know how these factors change in response to aerobic training and the rules for effective cardiovascular (aerobic) training.

Changes in Oxygen Delivery

As one begins an exercise session, heart rate and stroke volume (therefore, cardiac output) increase in order to increase the delivery of oxygen to working muscles. Blood flow is also shunted from the abdominal area to the exercising muscles. This redistribution results from a dilation, or an increase in diameter, in the arterial vessels which supply blood to the exercising muscles along with a decrease in the diameter of the vessels which supply the abdominal area. The breathing rate also increases.

Blood pressure also changes. Systolic blood pressure is the amount of pressure generated by the contraction of the left ventricle (systole). Systolic pressure provides the driving force which propels blood through the system. Diastolic blood pressure represents the amount of pressure left in the system when the heart muscle relaxes between beats (diastole). Blood pressure of 120/80 means that the left ventricle generates 120 millimeters (of mercury) of pressure during contraction and 80 millimeters of pressure remain in the vascular system when the heart is relaxing between beats.

Blood pressure response is one of the important measures taken during a clinical stress test to evaluate cardiovascular fitness and health. During exercise, systolic pressure should increase as the cardiovascular system attempts to increase oxygen delivery to the muscles. Diastolic pressure, on the other hand, should stay the same or even decrease a little because the dilation of blood vessels in the muscles (and in the skin to help get rid of heat as exercise continues) decreases the amount of residual pressure in the vascular system.

All of these changes occur in an attempt to deliver more oxygen to the exercising muscles. It is clear that when the muscles need to produce more ATP to meet the increased energy needs of exercise, oxygen consumption also increases. As long as enough oxygen can be delivered into the mitochondria to meet this increased energy need, ATP production will proceed aerobically.

Changes in Cardiac Output

In response to proper aerobic training, several adaptations occur in the cardiopulmonary system which lead to a significantly increased aerobic capacity. Resting heart rate decreases in part because the interior dimension of the ventricles increases; that is, the ventricles can hold more blood—the heart gets larger inside. Since the ventricles can fill with a greater volume of blood during diastole, stroke volume at rest also increases. The same cardiac output can be maintained at a lower heart rate. Because a given intensity of activity requires a given amount of oxygen, the cardiac output at a given intensity—such as rest— is essentially the same whether one is trained or untrained. Since more blood is pumped with each contraction, the heart beats fewer times per minute to achieve the necessary oxygen delivery. This increased efficiency is certainly a benefit to the heart.

In response to aerobic training, the stroke volume during exercise also becomes greater. Since a given intensity requires a given amount of oxygen, the heart rate at any given submaximal intensity will be lower following as few as three months of regular aerobic exercise. If a given work effort (say, a 10-minute mile pace) raised the heart rate to 150 bpm before training, then the same work effort after training may raise the heart rate to only 130 bpm. In order to get to 150 bpm, the trained client will need to exercise at a greater intensity, perhaps an 8-minute mile.

Maximum cardiac output is significantly greater following training because of the increase in stroke volume. Maximum heart rate is determined by age, not by state of training, but a greater maximum stroke volume times the same maximum heart rate yields a greater maximal cardiac output.

Changes in Oxygen Extraction

In addition to increased stroke volume and maximum cardiac output, other changes occur which enable us to sustain exercise at a much greater intensity and still be "aerobic" following training (see Figure 1-4). Recall that the other factor responsible for $\dot{V}O_2$ is the extraction of oxygen from the blood and its subsequent use in the muscle cells' mitochondria. The exchange of gases and nutrients between blood and tissues occurs in the capillaries. One change in response to aerobic training is that new capillaries are produced in the active skeletal muscles, increasing the area for the exchange of oxygen. The other major change in response to aerobic training is a significant increase in the mitochondrial density, so that more of the muscle cell is occupied by mitochondria. This also leads to a significant increase in the amount of aerobic

Figure 1–4 Summary of adaptations to cardiovascular training.

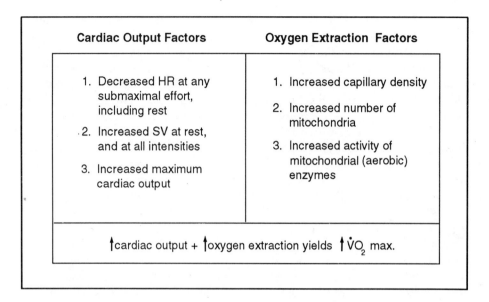

Cardiac Output Factors	Oxygen Extraction Factors
1. Decreased HR at any submaximal effort, including rest 2. Increased SV at rest, and at all intensities 3. Increased maximum cardiac output	1. Increased capillary density 2. Increased number of mitochondria 3. Increased activity of mitochondrial (aerobic) enzymes

$\uparrow$cardiac output + $\uparrow$oxygen extraction yields $\uparrow\dot{V}O_2$ max.

enzyme activity in the cell, since the mitochondria are the site of aerobic ATP production. The increased aerobic enzyme capacity allows a greater use of oxygen; thus, exercising at greater intensities can still be accomplished "aerobically."

The increased maximum cardiac output combined with the increased extraction capability yields not only a greater maximum aerobic capacity, but also an elevated anaerobic threshold. The greater the ability to make ATP aerobically at higher exercise intensities, the more "fit" a client becomes, and the greater the ability to "burn" fat.

Aerobic training also produces a number of other changes that influence performance during submaximal exercise. First, we use more fat for energy at any submax intensity. Second, during submaximal exercise we store more glycogen in trained muscles and produce less lactic acid, both of which lead to improved endurance. Aerobic training also makes us more tolerant of the lactic acid that is produced during exercise. Finally, training also often increases one's tolerance for stressful situations and improves the ability to deal more effectively with such stress. It is clear that aerobic exercise is beneficial. So let's briefly define the specific guidelines for cardiovascular training.

GUIDELINES FOR CARDIOVASCULAR FITNESS

Any type of fitness training, whether it be aerobic training, strength training, or flexibility training, is based on what exercise physiologists call the overload principle. Overload means that in order to train one of the body's systems, such as the cardiopulmonary system or the skeletal muscle system, that system must be made to work harder than it is accustomed to working. The overload to cause significant improvement in the cardiovascular system is an increased venous return sustained for a prolonged period. In other words, the exercise(s) must cause a sustained increase in the amount of blood returning to the heart.

In order to maximize overload, aerobic training should follow four rules. The exercise should (1) be the correct type, (2) be done at the proper intensity, (3) be of sufficient duration, and (4) occur with adequate frequency. Please refer to Chapter 7 for a detailed discussion of the variables to be considered when developing a cardiovascular training program.

TYPE OF EXERCISE.   The type of exercise is related to the principle of specificity of training. For maximum effectiveness, aerobic exercises need to be rhythmic and continuous and involve the large muscle groups. Generally, the hip flexors and extensors (iliopsoas, rectus femoris) and the knee flexors and extensors (hamstrings, quadriceps) should be involved. Walking, jogging, cycling, aerobic dance, and stair climbing are examples of activities that use these muscle groups. Activities combining upper and lower extremity movements, such as cross-country skiing, rowing, and swimming, can lead to high levels of aerobic capacity. However, for those with physical challenges, such as spinal cord problems which prohibit lower extremity movement, using large upper body muscles—such as in upper body ergometry—will clearly enhance aerobic fitness.

Rhythmic, large muscle movements are essential for an effective increase in blood flow back to the heart. The rhythmic squeezing action of the large muscles against the veins within these muscles is called the muscle pump. This muscle pump leads to a significant increase in venous return, which is required for effective aerobic conditioning.

INTENSITY OF EXERCISE.   The intensity rule is critical. The principles of aerobic and anaerobic energy production make it clear that exercise at too great an intensity for a client's level of fitness will use the anaerobic systems, not the aerobic systems. Research shows that optimum exercise intensity for fitness improvement is in the range of about 50–85 percent of maximum oxygen consumption. This corresponds to about 60–90 percent of maximum heart rate. The ranges are broad because of the effects of the level of fitness, as well as genetic factors. The higher a client's level of fitness, the higher the appropriate exercise intensity.

Heart rate during exercise can provide an excellent monitor of intensity. Keep in mind that many factors will cause an increase in heart rate, and that an elevated heart rate is not necessarily an indication of an effective aerobic training pace. However, if the increased heart rate is accomplished by the correct type of activity, then the cardiovascular training potential is substantial.

Monitoring a target heart rate (THR) training zone provides an excellent indication of correct exercise intensity. Clients also monitor intensity by learning to recognize their anaerobic threshold. Exercising above the anaerobic threshold leads to hyperventilation, lactic acid build-up, and rapid fatigue. The talk test takes advantage of the hyperventilation response. The client should be able to carry on comfortable conversation while exercising. If breathing is labored and difficult, the intensity is too great. Hyperventilation during exercise is normally accompanied by a burning, sometimes painful sensation in the active muscles because of the lactic acid accumulation.

Another excellent way to monitor intensity is to use Borg's Ratings of Perceived Exertion (RPE). Clients can use this scale as a subjective way of measuring how hard they are exercising. For most people, exercising at a level of 13–15 (somewhat strong to hard) correlates well with an appropriate training heart rate. Please refer to Chapter 6 for a discussion of these and other heart rate monitoring techniques.

DURATION OF EXERCISE.   The third rule is that aerobic exercise must last for at least 15–20 minutes per session to lead to substantial fitness improvements over time. Once a client reaches the proper intensity, the activity must be sustained for the minimum time in order to cause adequate aerobic overload.

Because aerobic training is related to the oxygen cost of activity, there is an inverse relationship between intensity and duration. If intensity is increased, the duration can be decreased and yet achieve a similar training effect. Conversely, if the intensity is decreased, the duration must be increased to achieve the same training effect. In general terms, when the cells of the body consume one liter (about one quart) of oxygen per minute, about five calories per minute have been expended (1 liter O_2/min = 5 cal/min). If two liters per minute are consumed, the expenditure would rise to ten calories per minute. For example, walking costs approximately 5 cal/min.; jogging costs approximately 10 cal/min. So walking for 60 minutes would use about 300 calories (5 x 60 = 300). Jogging for 30 minutes would also use about 300 calories (10 x 30 = 300). Therefore, walking for twice as long as jogging will cause approximately the same training effect. This is an especially important consideration for the untrained client.

A method of training which is increasingly being applied to the general public is **interval training**. There are two types of interval training: (1) performance interval training—a very high intensity effort designed to enhance competitive performance in a specific sport; and (2) fitness interval training—a modest to high intensity effort designed to improve general fitness.

Interval training has been used for many years by competitive athletes. In performance training, interval training often involves periods of maximal or near-maximal effort followed by short periods of rest. Such a method of training leads to significant performance benefits, in great measure due to an increased tolerance to the build-up of lactic acid. However, only well-trained athletes should do performance intervals. Because of the high intensity, an untrained person is at an increased risk for injury, not to mention quick fatigue, if performance intervals are attempted.

However, trainers can encourage clients to do fitness intervals. In fitness interval training, the client periodically increases intensity throughout a workout. The intervals are not rigidly defined as in performance interval training. Most importantly, the increase in intensity is capped when the anaerobic threshold is reached. At this point, the intensity is decreased. Figure 1-5 illustrates how interval training might look in a fitness training application.

FREQUENCY OF EXERCISE. The fourth rule for cardiovascular training is that the proper type of activity, done at correct intensity and continued for sufficient duration, must be done at least three days per week. While training three days per week may be sufficient, especially for those just beginning an exercise program, more frequent exercise, such as a brisk, daily walk, is certainly acceptable. However, keep in mind that it is most important to allow adequate rest and recovery to minimize the risks associated with over-training. Most experts encourage even competitive athletes to take at least one day a week for rest or a low intensity recreational activity, like a round of golf.

WARM-UP AND COOL-DOWN. Both a warm-up and a cool-down period are an essential part of any exercise session (not just aerobic exercise). Warming up accomplishes important changes which reduce the risk of injury, as well as make the exercise session more comfortable: (1) it causes an actual increase in the temperature of the muscle and connective tissue, thereby reducing the risk of soft tissue injury, and (2) it allows the cardiovascular system to adjust blood flow effectively from the abdominal area to the active muscles where the need for oxygen is increasing in response to the exercise, while maintaining adequate venous return. This blood shunt is accomplished by constriction in

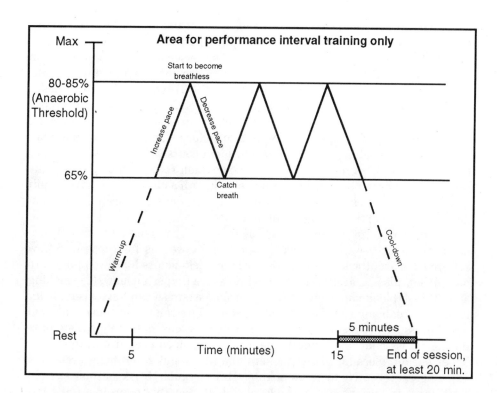

Figure 1–5   Fitness interval training.

arteries which supply blood to the gut and dilation in arteries which deliver blood to the active muscles. Heart rate will quickly rise to near maximum in an attempt to supply adequate oxygen if the necessary 3 to 5 minutes of warm-up is not done, especially if an intense pace is attempted too soon. Cool down to 18–20 beats per 10 seconds (108-120 bpm) to allow the system to reverse the blood shunt.

It is often difficult for the trainer to impress the need for warm-up and cool-down on a client. The best activities for both are simply to work at a much lower pace in whatever activity the client is using for training. Examples include slow cycling for cycling, walking for jogging, and slow swimming for swimming. A trainer should impress on the client that warm-up and cool-down not only reduce the potential for fatigue, but they reduce the risk of exercise-related injuries as well.

Benefits of Regular Aerobic Exercise

Research has shown that regular aerobic exercise has a number of significant health benefits, both for those who are apparently healthy and for those who suffer from various health problems. In addition to the highly positive body composition benefits, aerobic exercise has been reported to actually decrease appetite in many people. But even if it doesn't decrease appetite, the calorie-burning effects of regular aerobic exercise allow for a substantial daily calorie intake. In fact, competitive endurance athletes often consume 3,000–5,000 calories per day, and yet remain lean. Clearly, long-term aerobic training (combined with a sensible diet) leads to a decrease in percent body-fat and an increase in lean body tissue.

Weight-bearing exercises, such as jogging and brisk walking, have been shown to help strengthen the skeletal system. This is a benefit not only in helping reduce the risk for developing osteoporosis, but also for helping stop further progress of the condition in those whose physicians recommend exercise.

Since aerobic exercise training increases the sensitivity of the cells to insulin, aerobic exercise is often part of the treatment program for diabetics whose blood sugar is well controlled. Berger (1979) reported that less insulin is required to regulate blood sugar levels effectively in diabetics who exercised regularly. In several reported cases, adult-onset diabetics who were medicated with drugs other than insulin were able to reduce significantly, or eliminate completely, medications by following a prudent course of exercise and healthy eating habits. The American Diabetes Association recommends that any diabetic considering an exercise program consult with a physician to have insulin and glucose levels carefully monitored. Further, eating a carefully designed diet is essential in the management of diabetes.

Aerobic exercise is often part of the therapy for reducing the risk of coronary artery disease in high-risk individuals, as well as for those who have suffered a heart attack. Three of the primary risk factors for developing coronary artery disease are: (1) high blood pressure (hypertension), (2) smoking, and (3) high blood cholesterol levels. Aerobic exercise can have a significant impact on reducing risk for several reasons. First, many of those with high blood pressure are also overweight. Aerobic exercise definitely assists in reducing excess body-fat, generally helping lower blood pressure in those with hypertension. Second, many smokers find that regular aerobic exercise provides a great incentive to quit smoking. Third, regular, brisk, aerobic exercise often leads to an increase in the level of high density lipoprotein (HDL), or "good" cholesterol.

Aerobic exercise is also frequently part of the therapy for those with arthritis. One of the primary benefits is that it helps maintain ideal body weight. However, appropriate exercise also helps maintain joint range of motion.

It is essential to keep in mind that the role of the personal trainer in working with clients with significant health risk is to help implement the physician's recommendations. It is illegal, unethical, and certainly not in the client's interest for the trainer ever to attempt to diagnose a problem or suggest an exercise prescription for high-risk clients. See Chapter 12 for a discussion of considerations for working with clients' physicians to implement exercise programs for those with specific health problems.

Environmental Concerns

ALTITUDE.   Because there is less oxygen in the air at progressively higher altitudes, even well-trained athletes need to work at reduced intensity levels until they become acclimated to other than normal altitudes. While the acclimating process depends on the new altitude compared with the altitude the person is accustomed to, it takes about two weeks to acclimate significantly to altitudes up to about 8,000 feet, but can take up to four to five weeks to adapt to altitudes over 12,000 feet. However, noticeable improvements are generally observed within four to five days.

Since there is less oxygen in the air at higher altitudes, the heart will beat faster in order to deliver adequate oxygen to the muscles, even at rest. During exercise, the heart rate at any given intensity may be as much as 50 percent higher than normal, so pay particularly close attention to the onset of hyperventilation when beginning an exercise program at altitude. Decrease exercise pace to an intensity which allows the client to complete the session without being exhausted.

There are a number of potential problems associated with high altitude, including headache, insomnia, irritability, weakness, dizziness. Be sure to report any such symptoms to a physician to reduce the risk of more severe complications. It might seem reasonable to assume that training at higher altitudes would enhance aerobic capacity upon return to lower altitude. In reality, the changes the body makes to enhance oxygen carrying and delivery capacity to muscles owing to the lower pressure at higher altitudes are lost within three to four weeks of return to lower altitude.

HEAT. When we exercise in a hotter-than-normal environment, blood vessels near the skin open to facilitate the transfer of body heat to the environment so the body's internal temperature can be maintained. This causes a reduction in both venous return and stroke volume. At any given exercise pace, heart rate will be higher than usual as the cardiovascular system attempts to maintain cardiac output to meet oxygen needs in the muscles.

Because sweating is one of the body's most effective means of regulating internal temperature, exercising in hot, humid conditions is especially stressful to the unacclimated person. In order for sweat to dissipate heat, it must evaporate. When the humidity is high, sweat does not evaporate. So even though your client may be sweating profusely, there is a risk of severe heat problems. See Chapter 17 for a discussion of the signs and symptoms of heat-related problems.

The main concerns in exercising in the heat and humidity are replenishment of water and allowing the maximum amount of sweat evaporation. To replenish water, drink at least 3-6 ounces every 10-15 minutes during exercise—the cooler the water the better because cooler water empties more rapidly than warm water from the stomach into the intestines where it can be absorbed. Drink 8 ounces of water 20-30 minutes before exercise, and another 8-10 ounces of water in the 30 minutes following the exercise session. To allow evaporation of sweat, wear lightweight clothing. Light colors—white is best—reflect heat better than darker colors. Wear a light colored hat to keep from absorbing heat through the top of the head. Never wear rubberized or waterproof garments which prevent the evaporation of sweat. Such a practice could lead to severe heat stress. Most experts recommend 100 percent cotton garments, rather than synthetics, for exercising in the heat, although there are now a number of specialized fabrics on the market that wick perspiration away from the body. See Chapter 15 for more information on these newer fabrics. Be sure to have your clients use sunscreen to reduce the risk of skin cancer.

COLD. It surprises some to learn that replenishment of body fluids is just as important when exercising in a cold environment as it is when exercising in the heat. Not only is water lost as vapor in exhaled air, but the kidneys increase urine production in the cold. Exercising in the cold generally produces enough body heat so that few problems occur during the exercise session. However, risks can become apparent when exercise is stopped, when the possibility of losing too much body heat increases.

The easiest way to be certain that the body doesn't overheat during exercise or lose too much heat during a rest period is to dress in layers. As the body temperature increases during higher intensity exercise, successive layers of clothing can be removed to allow the heat to dissipate. Layers can be replaced during rest or periods of low intensity effort to help maintain body heat.

Be certain than the layers near the client's skin are made from fabrics such as wool or polypropylene (a synthetic material that wicks moisture away from the skin) which allow sweat to pass through. During a period of rest or low intensity effort, a layer of wet clothing next to the skin will cause the body to lose heat. If the day is windy, the outer layer should provide wind protection to reduce the chilling effects during a rest period. It is important to wear a hat when exercising in the cold, especially during periods of rest, since a significant amount of heat can be lost through the scalp.

BASIC SKELETAL MUSCLE ANATOMY AND PHYSIOLOGY

In addition to basic knowledge of function and training in the cardiopulmonary system, the trainer must give similar attention to the skeletal muscle system. There are three primary types of muscle cells in the body:

1. Cardiac cells are muscle cells unique in structure and function and found only in the heart.

2. Smooth muscle cells are found in the walls of arteries, which allow for the blood shunt—the constriction and dilation in blood vessels—to redistribute blood flow, and in the walls of the intestines.

3. Skeletal muscle cells are the ones trainers are most concerned with in fitness programs.

Muscle Fiber Types

There are two primary types of skeletal muscle fibers (cells): **slow-twitch** (Type I) and **fast-twitch** (Type II) fibers. The determination of the different muscle fiber types has been made possible by a laboratory technique known as muscle biopsy. In a muscle biopsy, a sample of muscle tissue is excised (taken out) using a needle which is inserted directly into the muscle. The section of tissue which is taken is mounted on a slide and stained for microscopic analysis. Based on the results of the biopsy technique, the slow- and fast-twitch types of muscle cells have been clearly identified.

Each type of fiber has several unique characteristics. The slow-twitch fiber contracts more slowly than does the fast-twitch fiber. The slow-twitch has many mitochondria, has a high aerobic capacity, and therefore is fatigue-resistant. Slow-twitch fibers, also referred to as red fibers, are also smaller in cross section than fast-twitch fibers. Fast-twitch fibers, also called white fibers, are not only larger than slow-twitch, but are also divided into two major sub-groups—type IIa and type IIb. Type IIa fibers are called fast-twitch oxidative because they have more mitochondria than the type IIb, which are referred to as fast-twitch glycolytic. However, type IIa fibers do not have the aerobic capability of slow-twitch fibers.

In terms of the distribution of fast- and slow-twitch fibers, there are two general considerations. First, in a given client, the distribution of fast- and slow-twitch fibers is different in different muscles. For example, there is a different percentage of fast- and slow-twitch fibers in the biceps compared to the quadriceps and in the deltoids compared to the triceps. Second, in the same muscle of different clients there is very likely a different percentage of fast- and slow-twitch fibers. For example, one person may have a high percentage of fast-twitch fibers in the quadriceps muscles; whereas another person will have a lower percentage of fast-twitch in the quadriceps muscles.

As a general rule, those people who are world-class power athletes, such as power weightlifters, have a distribution of approximately 60–90 percent fast-twitch fibers in those muscles which are used in their activity. In comparison, world-class endurance athletes, such as long distance runners and cross-country ski racers, would likely have 60–90 percent slow-twitch fibers in the muscles used in their events.

Trainers need to understand that while short-term endurance training does not change fast-twitch fibers (type II) to slow-twitch fibers (type I), research does show that it is possible to increase the aerobic capacity of the type II fast-twitch fibers. Likewise, power training does not change slow-twitch fibers to fast-twitch fibers. Fiber type characteristics and responses to training are very complex, involving more than is necessary for the purposes of this manual. As long as it is clear that a client's fiber type distribution is apparently genetically determined, and training will not change one fiber type to the other, trainers can design individual programs and understand the reasons that different clients respond differently to the same training program.

There are no differences between males and females with respect to fiber type distribution. In fact, there is no physiological difference between the muscle fibers in a male and a female; there is no such thing as a "male muscle cell" and a "female muscle cell." A muscle fiber is a muscle fiber, and fast- and slow-twitch fibers are found in both females and males, with the same distribution and fiber performance characteristics.

Skeletal Muscle Anatomy

Muscle cells, whether fast- or slow-twitch fibers, contract by the same basic mechanism. Functionally, the fast-twitch fibers simply contract to maximum force more rapidly than the slow-twitch fibers, but the process of contraction is the same. A fast-twitch fiber is a single muscle cell, as is a slow-twitch fiber. The contractile process and anatomy are the same for both. Refer to Figure 1–6 for an illustration of basic skeletal muscle anatomy.

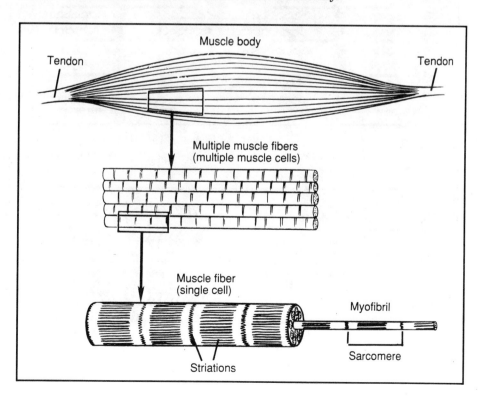

Figure 1–6 Anatomy of skeletal muscle: muscle, muscle fiber, myofibrils, sarcomere.

Muscles are composed of many individual muscle fibers. Running the length of each muscle fiber are strands of protein known as **myofibrils**. There are several proteins in a myofibril, but the two that need to be considered in relation to the process of muscle contraction are the proteins **actin** and **myosin**, also known as contractile proteins.

Looking at a muscle fiber under a microscope shows the muscle fiber to be made of several repeating units along the length of the muscle cell. Each of the repeating units is called a **sarcomere**. A muscle cell has many sarcomeres along its length. Again, the fiber is made of repeating units called sarcomeres, and running through all the sarcomeres, from one end of the cell to the other end, are the myofibrils (of which actin and myosin are a part). Within each sarcomere of the muscle cells, the proteins actin and myosin are located in different areas. The myosin protein is located in the middle of each sarcomere; each actin portion of the myofibril overlaps a portion of one end of the myosin, and extends through the sarcomere boundary into the adjacent sarcomere, where it overlaps one end of the myosin in that sarcomere.

Muscle Contraction

In order for muscle contraction to occur, there must be sufficient ATP present near the actin and myosin proteins, and there must be a nervous impulse from the central nervous system. According to the **sliding filament theory** of muscle contraction, when these two factors are present, the tiny projections from the myosin (myosin heads) attach to the actin, forming an actin-myosin cross bridge. Figure 1–7 illustrates this process.

Figure 1–7 Anatomy of a muscle: (a) resting myofibril (b) contracted myofibril.

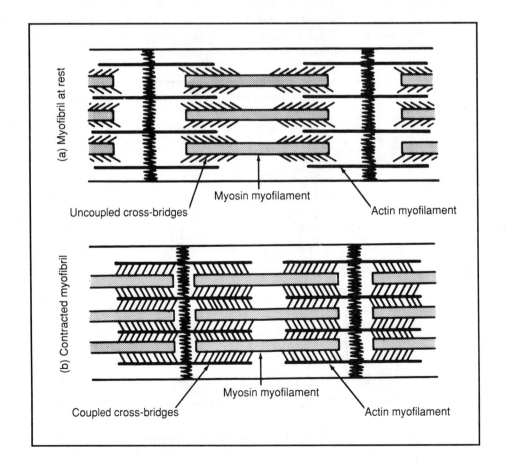

The energy from ATP causes the myosin heads on each end of the myosin to swivel toward the center of the sarcomere, pulling on the attached actin filament so that the actin slides inward toward the center of the sarcomere. This process causes each sarcomere along the entire length of the muscle fiber to shorten. Since all of the sarcomeres shorten at the same time, the overall length of the muscle fiber is decreased. When a multitude of fibers contract, the result is muscle contraction, which is really nothing more than the simultaneous shortening of many of the fibers in the whole muscle.

Even though individual fibers shorten when they contract, muscle contraction does not always involve a shortening in the length of the whole muscle. A **concentric contraction** does involve a shortening of the muscle. However, an **eccentric contraction** occurs when individual fibers contract, but the resistance is greater than the force generated, so the muscle actually lengthens. **Isometric contraction** describes a contraction of individual fibers, but no change in the length of the whole muscle.

To review, muscle contraction is an interaction between the actin and myosin proteins causing a shortening of individual muscle fibers. It is important to remember that sufficient ATP (energy) must be present, as well as a continued nervous impulse, in order to sustain this contraction process.

FORCE OF CONTRACTION (STRENGTH).   When a muscle fiber shortens, it exerts force. Skeletal muscle tissue functions according to an all-or-none principle. This means that when a single muscle fiber shortens, it generates its maximum force capability. A skeletal muscle fiber has no ability to grade its force of contraction (as cardiac muscle cells do); when it is stimulated to contract, it does so maximally. The amount of force that is generated during contraction in the whole muscle depends on two factors: (1) the size of the individual fibers contracting (a larger fiber is a stronger fiber), and (2) the number of muscle fibers which contract simultaneously (to generate more force, more fibers are recruited).

The force generated by muscle contraction is also related to the speed of movement at the associated joint, as well as the initial length of the muscle belly. The "force-velocity" relationship suggests that, in general, the faster the speed of movement, the lower the force generated by the contracting muscle. For example, the biceps muscle will generate more force during a maximal contraction when the elbow joint is flexing at 60 degrees of movement per second than when the elbow is flexing at 180 degrees of movement per second. The "length-tension" relationship demonstrates that a muscle generates maximum force when it begins its contraction at 1.2 times its resting length. This relationship helps explain why athletes such as baseball batters and golfers slightly stretch the appropriate muscles before beginning the swinging movement.

MUSCLE FIBER SIZE.   The force the fiber generates is related to its cross-sectional area. A larger fiber exerts more force than a smaller one. Note that the strength of a given cross-sectional area of muscle tissue from males and females is the same. Males are generally stronger because of a greater amount of muscle tissue. Women respond to a strength-training program in many of the same ways that men do. Therefore, strength training is an important part of a physical fitness program for both genders.

MOTOR UNITS.   In a given muscle, muscle fibers are stimulated in units, or groups. A single motor nerve (from the spinal cord) and all the muscle fibers it stimulates is called a **motor unit**. Motor units come in different sizes.

Motor units in which one nerve stimulates only 5–10 fibers are responsible for fine, delicate movements like moving the eye, blinking the eyelid, and drawing intricate detail in a picture. On the other hand, motor units consisting of one motor nerve and 500–1,000 fibers are called on for forceful tasks like lifting, kicking, or jumping. Regardless of the size, motor units are made of either all fast-twitch fibers or all slow-twitch fibers. When the fibers of a motor unit are called on to contract, all of the muscle fibers in the unit contract together, and they contract with maximum force (remember the all-or-none law). So the amount of force generated at any one time depends on how many motor units are called on to contract simultaneously.

To exert minimal force—like picking up a pencil—only a few motor units in the forearm muscles are recruited. To pick up a dumbbell, many more motor units in these muscles would be stimulated to contract. To exert maximum muscle force, the nervous system will attempt to contract as many motor units in the muscle as possible. Since the number of motor units (fibers) and the size of the fibers in those contracting motor units determine how much force will be generated on contraction, what happens in the muscle fiber in response to a strength-training program?

ADAPTATIONS TO STRENGTH TRAINING

Describing the adaptations to strength training is not as straightforward as the discussion of the adaptations to aerobic training. There are many variables which influence the strength-training adaptations, including the relationship of resistance and repetitions in the lifting program, the distribution of fast- and slow-twitch fibers in the muscles being trained, and the level of the naturally occurring hormone testosterone. But we can discuss general adaptations with the understanding that individual differences in the above-mentioned variables can dramatically influence specific response in a given client.

The specific overload to cause strength gains is a progressive increase in the amount of resistance (weight) used in the training program. To continue to increase strength, one must continue to increase the overload. This section describes those changes that occur in the body as a result of weight training that account for an increased ability to generate force.

Muscle Fiber Adaptation

The most obvious adaptation to strength training is usually an increase in the size of the muscle itself. This is known as muscle **hypertrophy**. Hypertrophy is the result of an increase in the number and size of myofibrils inside muscle fibers, or more simply, an increased amount of actin and myosin, which are responsible for force generation. Within the muscle, this is probably the most important adaptation leading to an increase in strength. When men and women are exposed to the same strength-training program, men will generally hypertrophy to a greater extent than will women. This is primarily because of higher levels of the hormone testosterone (which plays an important role in the production of the contractile proteins such as actin and myosin) in men than in women. Greater muscle size is one reason most men are capable of greater absolute strength than most women.

While hypertrophy will generally result as an adaptation to strength training, the relationship of repetitions (rep) and resistance to hypertrophy is clear. A high-resistance, low-repetition program will usually lead to significant hypertrophy in most males. Most females, because of naturally low levels of testosterone, will not generate significant hypertrophy even in this type of program. Conversely, a low-resistance, high-rep program will generally lead to little hypertrophy, even in males. Many women shy away from strength training because of a fear of the "body builder" hypertrophy. Trainers can allay their fears by using low-resistance, high-rep programs.

Besides increasing fiber size, training will also increase the number of sarcomeres in trained fibers. The increase in size also enhances the amount of contractile protein in the fiber, adding to the strength potential of the fiber. Further, some research with animals suggests that the use of extremely high resistance might possibly increase the number of muscle fibers (hyperplasia) in the muscle. Evidence for muscle fiber hyperplasia in humans has not been found. For now the conclusion is that the change in the muscle is an increase in protein content, and often in diameter, of existing fibers, not an increase in the number of muscle fibers.

Connective Tissue Adaptation

In addition to changing muscle tissue itself, training also changes the connective tissues of the body. There are three basic types of connective tissue: **cartilage**, which serves as a padding between the bones that meet at a joint in the skeleton; **ligaments**, which connect bones to bones at a joint; and **tendons**, which connect skeletal muscles to the bones, transmitting the force of muscle contraction to the bones. The tendons are an extension of tendinous connective tissue which weaves a network of support around and between the muscle fibers of a muscle, giving strength and stability to the belly of the muscle by holding the fibers of the motor units together.

In response to strength training, the connective tissues associated with muscle become stronger by becoming thicker, and are thus able to withstand the increase in force of contraction generated by the strength-trained muscle. The increased strength of connective tissue is thought to play a highly significant role in the total strength gain which results from a regular resistance training program.

Increased Nervous System Activity

A third change in response to strength training is the stimulation of motor units which were previously inactive. Part of strength generation depends on the number of motor units contracting. When untrained, and not working against much resistance, some fibers (motor units) are never used. But the need to generate more force in a strength training program stimulates activation of some inactive fibers (motor units).

When an untrained client begins a carefully designed strength program, gains in strength can often be noted in just a couple of weeks. Clearly, there will not be noticeable hypertrophy in such a short period. What accounts for the initial gains? Most likely the recruitment of previously inactive motor units is responsible for much of the initial increase in strength.

Decreased Nervous Inhibition

One of the most important adaptations to strength training is that we can overcome, or decrease, nervous inhibition to the muscles. Nervous inhibition is both psychological and physiological. In a psychological sense, confidence increases, allowing lifts never before thought possible. This is especially true in non-athletes who think themselves weaker than they actually are.

Physiological (functional) adaptation is also important. In the tendons, which connect the muscle to the bones, there is a sensor called a muscle tendon organ, or a **Golgi tendon organ**. This tendon organ is a part of the nervous system, a protection against generating too much contractile force. When the muscle tendon organ is stimulated by too much contractile force, its associated muscle will relax to prevent injury to the muscle itself or to its associated connective tissues. Under normal circumstances, maximal contraction is prevented; that is, all of the motor units in a muscle will not contract simultaneously because of the inhibitory protection of the muscle tendon organ.

It is possible, however, to override psychologically the physiological Golgi protective inhibition. Two examples can illustrate the consequences of overriding the Golgi inhibition. One is that of a woman who finds that the jack has slipped while her husband was working under the car, so the car has fallen on him. She reaches under the bumper of the car, generates a maximum muscular contraction in several muscle groups, and miraculously lifts the car off her husband's body. In so doing, however, she undoubtedly has suffered severe injury to much of her connective tissue because she overrode the threshold protection of the Golgi tendon organs.

A second example is the weightlifter who attempts to lift more weight than he has trained himself to lift, and physiologically (or pharmacologically) pumps himself up to the point that he is able to overcome the threshold protection of the tendon organ. In attempting the lift, the weightlifter can actually tear the tendon, causing severe injury. The biceps tendon and the quadriceps tendon are two connective tissue structures often injured by overriding their associated tendon organ protection.

Strength training raises the threshold of force generation at which the Golgi tendon organ is stimulated, probably because the overload of training causes more connective tissue protein to be added to the tendon. Its associated muscle can then generate greater contractile force before the tendon organ is stimulated.

In summary, the ability to exert more force after strength training is not solely owing to muscle fiber adaptations, but involves extremely important adaptations in connective tissue and the nervous system as well. Many scientists argue that the connective tissue and nervous system adaptations are probably more important to overall strength gains than the changes in the muscle fibers. Clearly many successful strength athletes train using significant variability in training protocols. Without doubt it will take continued research in the area of strength adaptations to elucidate the specific details of the current theories.

GUIDELINES FOR STRENGTH TRAINING

With an idea about how the body adapts to the progressive overload of a strength training program, the trainer needs general concepts to establish a knowledge base for developing a strength-training program. (Please refer to Chapter 8 for a detailed discussion of the variables to be considered when developing and supervising such programs.) Strength training is a highly individualized procedure. Well-trained and highly successful power and endurance athletes have all established their own most effective training regimens. And frequently two equally successful strength athletes will have very different training routines. However, as with any aspect of fitness development, the trainer must assist the client to challenge the factors responsible for strength with an appropriate and specific overload.

Types of Strength Overloads

For many years strength training programs have been described as being isometric, isotonic, or isokinetic, based on the type of muscle contraction involved during the exercise. (The prefix "iso" means "same".)

Isometric (same length) refers to exercises which develop high intensity contractions in the muscle with no change in muscle length. Generally, isometric exercises call for a maximal effort against an immovable object, like a wall or a desk. Isometric training clearly increases muscle strength, but unfortunately only at the joint angle where the contraction occurs.

Isotonic (same tone or tension) refers to exercises which use a given amount of external resistance which is challenged through the movement's entire range of motion. It is not correct to assume that the tension in the muscle is constant throughout the range of motion. The actual amount of force generated by a muscle will change throughout the movement because of the biomechanics at the joint or joints involved. For example, even though a 10-pound dumbbell is obviously a constant weight throughout a biceps curl, the biceps does not generate a constant 10 pounds of force throughout its entire contraction. (The biomechanics of this concept are presented in Chapter 3.)

Several exercise physiologists now suggest that strength exercises using a fixed amount of external resistance be referred to as "**dynamic constant external resistance**" training, not isotonic training. Exercises which use machines with a shaped cam can be called "**dynamic variable** external resistance." These descriptions accurately suggest that even though the free weight is constant, or the pin on the machine stays in the same plate, throughout the movement, the amount of force generated by the overloaded muscles changes throughout the movement.

Isokinetic (same speed) refers to a type of resistance exercise that causes the exercising muscles to generate a maximum amount of force throughout the entire range of movement by keeping the speed of movement constant. Isokinetic and dynamic resistance exercises are performed with either concentric or eccentric muscle contractions, or both. Concentric (shortening) movements are often referred to as the positive phase of a lift. Eccentric (lengthening) movements, on the other hand, are referred to as the negative phase. The type of contractions involved during strength training appears to have an impact on the degree of muscle soreness which occurs one to three days after training.

Muscle Soreness and Fatigue

MUSCLE SORENESS.   There are two general types of exercise-related muscle soreness. One is the immediate soreness felt while exercising or immediately after exercising. The other type of soreness is that which persists for one to three days following a session.

Immediate soreness appears to be most directly related to the build-up of **lactic acid** (and other waste products) in the muscle that have leaked out of the muscle cells and stimulated sensitive nerve endings near the muscle cells. This excess lactic acid is removed quite rapidly when the exercise session is completed, generally within 30–60 minutes. Much of the excess lactic acid is metabolized in the muscle cell in which it was produced during exercise. The lactic acid not used is carried to the liver where it is metabolized. Immediate soreness may also involve minor muscle or connective tissue tears, so don't ignore it. Refer to Chapter 16 for a discussion of a wide range of exercise-related injuries and sources of soreness during exercise.

The explanation of latent soreness, the soreness unnoticed during exercise but present from one to three days following exercise, is the subject of much research and some controversy. The most current research seems to indicate that delayed soreness is most likely the result of very small tears in the connective tissues that hold individual muscle fibers together within the belly of the muscle, as well as some tearing of the membrane of the muscle cells.

Furthermore, research suggests that this latent soreness is closely associated with the eccentric, or negative, phase of muscular effort. During negative work, the muscle fibers are contracting and attempting to cause a shortening of the muscle. But the resistance is greater than the force developed so the muscle and associated connective tissue is actually lengthening. This lends credibility to theories that implicate microscopic tears within the muscle belly or in the muscle-tendon areas during aggressive negative effort. Studies investigating concentric overloads report little or no delayed soreness compared with the significant soreness usually reported with heavy eccentric work.

MUSCLE FATIGUE.   The reasons for fatigue are also varied, but they relate primarily to the intensity and duration of the exercise bout. For instance, the fatigue felt when performing a power event or other maximum effort which lasts 0–30 seconds to exhaustion occurs because the active muscle cells run out of ATP at the site of the actin-myosin crossbridge, which is part of the mechanism of muscle fiber contraction. Without ATP present, the fibers can no longer contract.

Muscle fatigue which results during heavy exercise lasting anywhere from about 30 seconds up to about 40–60 minutes to exhaustion is generally thought to be related to lactic acid accumulation. Clearly this is a broad range, and several other factors may be involved in varying degrees, but lactic acid accumulating from intense effort ultimately inhibits the ability of the muscle cell to contract.

Finally, the fatigue felt in prolonged endurance activities lasting 60–180 minutes or longer occurs primarily because glycogen—the storage form of glucose—becomes depleted in the exercising muscles. Without a source of glucose, muscle cells cannot contract even with an adequate supply of oxygen and fat. In other words, when glycogen is depleted (a marathoner calls this "hitting the wall"), the muscles being used are unable to maintain the required intensity. Other factors also implicated in fatigue during prolonged activities include dehydration, increased body temperature, waste products other than lactic acid, and boredom.

FLEXIBILITY TRAINING

Flexibility is defined as the range of motion about a joint. Therefore, flexibility training is designed to increase the range of motion in a specific area, such as the low back, the hamstrings, or the shoulder girdle. Flexibility is limited by four factors: (1) the elastic limits of the ligaments and tendons crossing the joint, (2) the elasticity of the muscle tissue itself, (3) the bone and joint structure, and (4) the skin.

Many types of exercises can increase flexibility. As every system must be overloaded to generate specific gains, so must the connective and skeletal muscle be overloaded to generate increased flexibility. The safest overload for flexibility training is a slow, sustained stretch. Bobbing and bouncing activities are not only potentially detrimental to increases in range of motion, but can lead to injury in the muscle fibers and connective tissues being aggressively overstretched.

Only general guidelines for stretching are presented here. A detailed discussion of specific guidelines for increasing flexibility is presented in Chapter 9. Slowly stretch to the point where tension (tightness) is felt in the muscles being stretched. Do not stretch to the point of pain. Hold the stretch for at least 10 seconds, but 30–60 seconds is preferable, being sure not to hold the breath.

Just as the Golgi tendon organ serves as a protection against generating too much contractile force, fibers in the muscle tissue protect against too much stretch. These fibers are called **muscle spindles**. In **ballistic** (rapid, bouncing) stretching, the muscle spindle is stimulated, causing the muscle in which it is located to contract as a protection against the excessive stretch. On the next rapid bob or bounce, when we stretch against a contracted muscle, there is a high risk of tearing in the muscle and/or connective tissues. Slow, sustained stretching that does not cause pain does not stimulate the muscle spindle. A daily program of slow, sustained stretching exercises leads to a substantial increase in flexibility and joint range of motion, because the stretches are not done against protectively contracted muscles.

SUMMARY

This chapter gives the personal trainer a basic introduction to the principles of exercise physiology. First, the trainer must develop a sound understanding of the relationships between exercise intensity and energy production in exercising muscles. Then, the trainer can apply the principles of specificity and overload to design the most appropriate program for any client. It is the responsibility of all fitness professionals to develop enough of a foundation of knowledge to write safe and effective programs for any client.

The amount of information in exercise physiology is growing at a rapid pace. This chapter is by necessity geared to present the basics of many areas of the science of exercise. All fitness professionals must recognize the responsibility of becoming students of the literature in this field to keep abreast of the constant flow of information.

REFERENCE

Bergstrom, J., Harris, R.C., Hultman, E., & Nordensjo, L.O. (1971). Energy-rich phosphagens in dynamic and static work. In B. Pernow & B. Saltin (Eds.), *Muscle metabolism during exercise* (p. 341). New York: Plenum Press.

SUGGESTED READING

Alter, M.J. (1988). *The science of stretching*. Champaign, IL: Human Kinetics.

Katch. F.I., & McArdle, W.D. (1983). *Nutrition, weight control and exercise* (2nd ed.). Philadelphia: Lea & Febiger.

McArdle, W.D., Katch, F.I., & Katch, V.L. (1986). *Exercise physiology: Energy, nutrition and human performance* (2nd ed.). Philadelphia: Lea & Febiger.

Rejeski, W.J., and Kenny, E.A. (1988). *Fitness motivation: Preventing participant dropout*. Champaign, IL: Human Kinetics.

Sharkey, B.J. (1984). *Physiology of fitness* (2nd ed.). Champaign, IL: Human Kinetics.

Wilmore, J.H. (1986). *Sensible fitness* (2nd ed.). Champaign, IL: Human Kinetics.

Anatomy

ROD A. HARTER

2

ROD A. HARTER, PH.D., A.T.,C., is currently assistant professor and program director of athletic training education in the Department of Exercise and Sport Science at Oregon State University in Corvallis. His areas of specialization are athletic-training/sports medicine and biomechanics. Dr. Harter has been a certified athletic trainer for more than a decade. He currently serves on the editorial board of *Athletic Training, Journal of the National Athletic Trainers' Association.*

IN THIS CHAPTER:

- Anatomical terminology.
- Cardiovascular system.
- Respiratory system.
- Nervous system.

- Skeletal system, including the axial and appendicular skeletons, joints, and joint motion.
- Muscular system, including the muscles of the lower extremity, the trunk, and the upper extremity.

Anatomy is the broad science concerned with the study of the structure of the body and the relationships of the body parts to one another. A fundamental understanding of human anatomy is essential for the personal trainer whose professional responsibilities include the identification of appropriate activities and exercises that help clients ultimately achieve their personal fitness goals. This chapter provides a brief description of the functional anatomy of five major systems operating within the human body: the cardiovascular system, the respiratory system, the nervous system, the skeletal system, and the muscular system.

ANATOMICAL TERMINOLOGY

When studying anatomy for the first time, you may encounter descriptive terms that are unfamiliar. It is essential to learn and use the correct anatomical terms for position, location, and direction when describing a particular movement, exercise, or activity.

Most anatomical terms have their roots in Latin and Greek, and are usually quite descriptive. For example, many muscle names tell of the muscle's location, shape, or action. To illustrate, let's use the *anterior tibialis* muscle.

Table 2–1   ANATOMICAL, DIRECTIONAL AND REGIONAL TERMS

Anterior (ventral)	Toward the front
Posterior (dorsal)	Toward the back
Superior	Toward the head
Inferior	Away from the head
Medial	Toward the midline of the body
Lateral	Away from the midline of the body
Proximal	Toward the attached end of the limb, origin of the structure, or midline of the body
Distal	Away from the attached end of the limb, origin of the structure, or midline of the body
Superficial	External; located close to or on the body surface
Deep	Internal; located further beneath the body surface than the superficial structures
Cervical	Regional term referring to the neck
Thoracic	Regional term referring to the portion of body between the neck and the abdomen; also known as the chest (thorax)
Lumbar	Regional term referring to the portion of the back between the abdomen and the pelvis
Plantar	The sole or bottom of the foot
Dorsal	The top surface of the foot and hand
Palmar	The anterior or ventral surface of the hands
Sagittal plane	An imaginary longitudinal line that divides the body or any of its parts into right and left parts, gives rise to medial and lateral aspects of the body
Frontal plane	An imaginary longitudinal line that divides the body into anterior and posterior parts; lies at a right angle to the sagittal plane, gives rise to anterior and posterior aspects of the body
Transverse plane	Also known as horizontal plane; an imaginary line that divides the body or any of its parts into superior and inferior parts, gives rise to superior (upper) and inferior (lower) aspects of the body

Table 2–2   COMMON ANATOMICAL (MEDICAL) TERMINOLOGY

Root	Meaning	Term	Definition
arthro	joint	arthritis	Inflammation in a joint
bi	two	biceps	Two-headed muscle
brachium	arm	brachialis	Muscle of the arm
cardio	heart	cardiology	The study of the heart
cephalo	head	cephalic	Pertaining to the head
chondro	cartilage	chondroectomy	Excision of a cartilage
costo	rib	costochondral	Pertaining to a rib and its cartilage
dermo	skin	dermatitis	Inflammation of the skin
hemo, hemat	blood	hemorrhage	Internal or external bleeding
ilio	ilium	ilium	The wide, upper part of the pelvic bone
myo	muscle	myocitis	Inflammation of a muscle
os, osteo	bone	osteomalacia	Softening of the bone
thoraco	chest	thorax	Chest
tri	three	triceps brachii	The three-headed muscle on arm

For our purposes, **anterior** means "toward the front", the *tibia* is the larger of the two bones between the knee and the ankle. In this case, by knowing the meanings of the root words, the reader understands both the anatomical term and the location of the muscle—the anterior tibialis muscle is found on the front of the tibia. Other important terms that describe the anatomical position are defined in Table 2–1. To help the reader avoid having continually to refer to a medical dictionary to define the terms used throughout this chapter, a summary of commonly used anatomical (medical) terms is presented in Table 2–2. A representation of anatomical position is given in Figure 2–1, along with the anatomical planes of motion.

There are five major systems of the human body most pertinent to physical activity: the cardiovascular system, the respiratory system, the nervous system, the skeletal system, and the muscular system.

CARDIOVASCULAR SYSTEM

Oxygen, the breath of life, is required for energy production, and thus it sustains cellular activity (cellular metabolism) in the human body. A by-product of this activity is carbon dioxide. Because high levels of carbon dioxide in the cells produce acidic conditions that are poisonous to cells, excess CO_2 must be rapidly eliminated. The cardiovascular and respiratory systems are primarily responsible for this function. The cardiovascular system is comprised of the blood, the blood vessels, and the heart. It distributes oxygen and nutrients to the cells, carries carbon dioxide and metabolic wastes from the cells, protects against disease, helps regulate body temperature, and prevents serious blood loss after injury through the formation of clots.

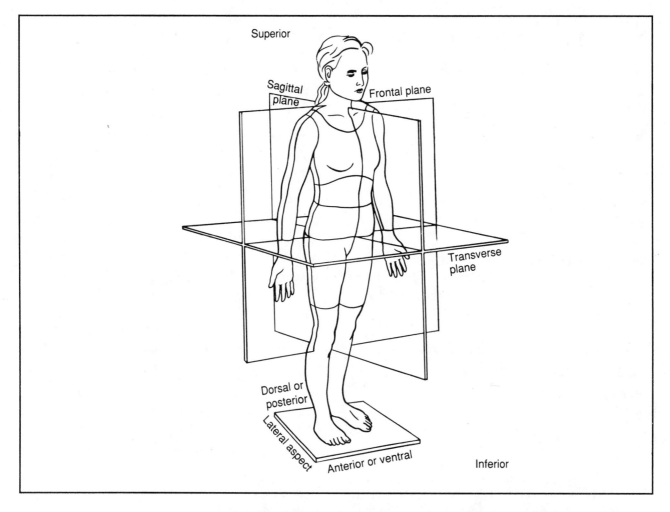

Figure 2–1   Anatomical position.

Blood is composed of two parts, *formed elements*, which include white blood cells, red blood cells, platelets, and *plasma*, the liquid portion of blood. Plasma is about 92 percent water and 8 percent dissolved solutes. Blood volume in an average-size woman is about four to five liters (approximately four to five quarts), while an average-size man has about five to six liters of blood.

There are two types of blood vessels—**arteries** carry blood *away* from the heart, whereas **veins** carry blood *toward* the heart. Arteries are stronger and thicker than veins, and their muscular walls help propel blood. Unlike arteries, veins contain valves to prevent the blood from flowing backward. The largest arteries are those nearest the heart; as blood flows further away from the heart, the arteries branch into smaller arteries called **arterioles** that deliver the blood to the even smaller **capillaries** which are microscopic blood vessels that branch to form an extensive network throughout the distal tissues. It is in the capillary beds that the critical exchange of nutrients and metabolic waste products takes place. Depleted of its oxygen and nutrients on the way from the heart to the periphery, capillary blood now begins the journey back to the heart via small vessels called **venules**. The venules are a continuation of the capillaries, and join together to form **veins**. As the blood is transported back to the heart, the veins become larger, carrying a greater volume of blood.

The human *heart*, a hollow, muscular organ that pumps blood throughout the blood vessels, is the "center" of the cardiovascular system. In the adult, the heart is about the same size as the closed fist, and lies to the left of center, behind the sternum and between the lungs. The heart itself is divided into four

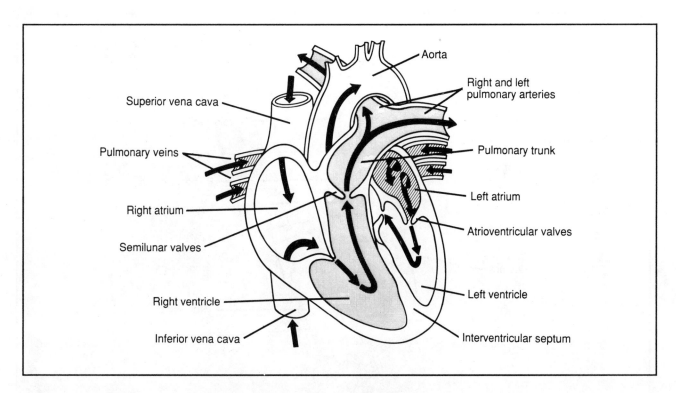

Figure labels:
Aorta, Right and left pulmonary arteries, Pulmonary trunk, Left atrium, Atrioventricular valves, Left ventricle, Interventricular septum, Superior vena cava, Pulmonary veins, Right atrium, Semilunar valves, Right ventricle, Inferior vena cava

Figure 2–2 Structure of the heart and pattern of blood flow through it.

spaces (*chambers*) that receive circulating blood. The two upper chambers are called the *right* **atrium** and *left* **atrium**; the two lower chambers of the heart are known as the *right* and *left* **ventricles** (Fig. 2-2). The heart is in reality a series of four separate pumps: two primer pumps, the atria, and two power pumps, the ventricles. Knowledge of the sequence of blood flow through the heart is fundamental to understanding the cardiovascular system. The right atrium receives blood from all parts of the body, except the lungs. The *superior vena cava*, which drains blood from body parts superior to the heart (head, neck, arms), and the *inferior vena cava*, which brings blood from the parts of the body inferior to the heart (legs, abdominal region), transport blood to the right atrium. During contraction of the heart, blood accumulates in the right atrium. With relaxation of the heart, blood from the right atrium flows into the right ventricle, which during contraction pumps it into the *pulmonary trunk*. The pulmonary trunk then divides into *right* and *left pulmonary arteries*, which transport blood to the lungs, where carbon dioxide is released and oxygen is acquired. This newly oxygenated blood returns to the heart via four *pulmonary veins* which empty into the left atrium. The blood then passes into the left ventricle, which during contraction pumps the blood into the *ascending aorta*. From this point the blood is distributed to all body parts (except the lungs) by several large arteries.

RESPIRATORY SYSTEM

The respiratory system supplies oxygen, eliminates carbon dioxide, and helps regulate the acid–base balance (pH) of the body. The respiratory system is comprised of the lungs and the series of passageways leading to and from the lungs (mouth, throat, trachea, bronchi). Respiration is the overall exchange of gases (oxygen, carbon dioxide, nitrogen) between the atmosphere, the blood, and the cells. There are three general phases of respiration: external, internal, and cellular. *External respiration* is the exchange of oxygen and carbon dioxide between the atmosphere and the blood within the large capillaries in the lungs.

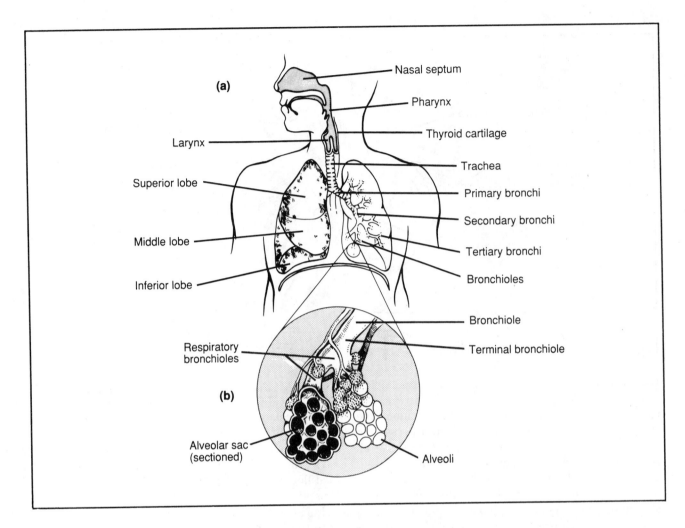

Figure 2–3 (a) Upper and lower respiratory pathways; (b) terminal bronchiole into alveoli (enlarged view).

Internal respiration involves the exchange of those gases between the blood and the cells of the body. *Cellular respiration* involves the utilization of oxygen and the production of carbon dioxide by the metabolic activity within cells.

When the body is at rest, air enters the respiratory system via the nostrils of the nose, and is warmed as it passes through a series of nasal cavities lined by mucous membrane covered with *cilia* (small hairs) that filter out small particles. From the nasal cavity, inspired air next enters the *pharynx* (throat), which lies just posterior to the nasal and oral (mouth) cavities. The pharynx serves as a passageway for air and food, and also provides a resonating chamber for speech sounds. During vigorous physical activity, mouth breathing tends to predominate, and air taken in via the mouth is not filtered to the same extent as air taken in through the nostrils.

The *larynx* (the organ of voice) is the enlarged upper (proximal) end of the *trachea* (windpipe). It conducts air to and from the lungs via the pharynx. An easy landmark for locating the larynx is the *thyroid cartilage*, or Adam's apple. The *trachea* extends from the larynx to approximately the level of the fifth thoracic vertebra, where it divides into the *right* and *left primary bronchi*. The trachea is a tubular airway about 12 centimeters (4.5 inches) long. It is kept open by a series of C-shaped cartilages that function in a manner similar to the wire rings in the hose of a vacuum cleaner. After the trachea divides into the right and left primary bronchi, each primary bronchus then enters a lung and divides into smaller *secondary bronchi*, one for each lobe of the lung (five in total). The secondary bronchi branch into many tertiary bronchi, and these branch several times further, eventually forming tiny *terminal* **bronchioles**. The terminal bronchioles have microscopic branches called *respiratory* bronchioles that, in turn, subdivide into several *alveolar ducts* (plural = *alveoli*). The actual exchange of respiratory gases, such as oxygen and carbon dioxide, between the lungs and the blood occurs at this anatomic level. It is estimated that the lungs contain 300 million alveoli that provide an extremely large surface area (approximately 70 square meters or 230 square feet) for the exchange of gases. The continuous branching of the trachea resembles a tree trunk and branches and is commonly referred to as the *bronchial tree* (Fig. 2-3).

The final components of the respiratory system are the *lungs*, paired, cone-shaped organs lying in the thoracic cavity. The right lung has three lobes; the left lung has only two. The *diaphragm*, the muscle that forms the floor of the thoracic cavity, contracts during inspiration and relaxes to allow expiration. The lungs are separated by a space known as the *mediastinum*, which contains, most notably, the heart, the *esophagus* (foodpipe), and part of the trachea.

NERVOUS SYSTEM

The nervous system is the body's control center and network for internal communication. Of primary importance to the personal trainer is the nervous system's function of stimulating and controlling movement. Skeletal muscle cannot contract until it is stimulated by a nerve impulse. Without central control, coordinated movements are impossible. For readers who seek more detailed information than provided by the following overview, see the references listed at the conclusion of this chapter.

Although there is only a single nervous system, it may be divided into two parts according to location, the central nervous system and the peripheral nervous system. The *central nervous system (CNS)*, consisting of the brain and the spinal cord, is totally enclosed within bony structures. That is, the brain is protected by the skull, while the spinal cord is protected by the vertebral canal of the spinal column, The CNS is the control center of the nervous system, since it receives input from the peripheral nervous system, integrates this information, and formulates appropriate responses to the input. The *peripheral nervous system* is made up of nerves that connect the outlying parts of the body (the extremities) and their receptors within the CNS. The peripheral nervous system includes: 12 pairs of *cranial nerves*, of which 2 pairs arise from the brain and 10 pairs originate in the brain stem; and 31 pairs of *spinal nerves* that arise from the spinal cord. The spinal nerves include 8 cervical pairs, 12 thoracic pairs, 5 lumbar pairs, 5 sacral pairs, and 1 coccygeal pair (Fig. 2-4). These nerves are named and numbered according to region and the vertebral level at which they emerge from the spinal cord. For example, the fourth lumbar nerve (written L4) exits the spinal cord at the level of the fourth lumbar vertebra.

The anterior (ventral) branches of the second through twelfth thoracic spinal nerves (written T2 through T12) individually supply muscles and other structures. In all other cases the anterior branches of the spinal nerves join with adjacent nerves to form a *plexus*, or a network of nerve branches. There are four main plexuses in the human body: the *cervical plexus*, whose nerves supply the head, neck, upper chest, and shoulders; the *brachial plexus*, supplying the shoulder and down to the fingers of the hand; the *lumbar plexus*, innervating the abdomen, groin, genitalia, and anterior and lateral thigh; and the *sacral plexus*, which supplies the large muscles of the posterior thigh and the entire lower leg, ankle, and foot (see Fig. 2-7).

The nerve cells that comprise the nervous system carry messages called *nerve impulses* that originate in either the central nervous system (brain or

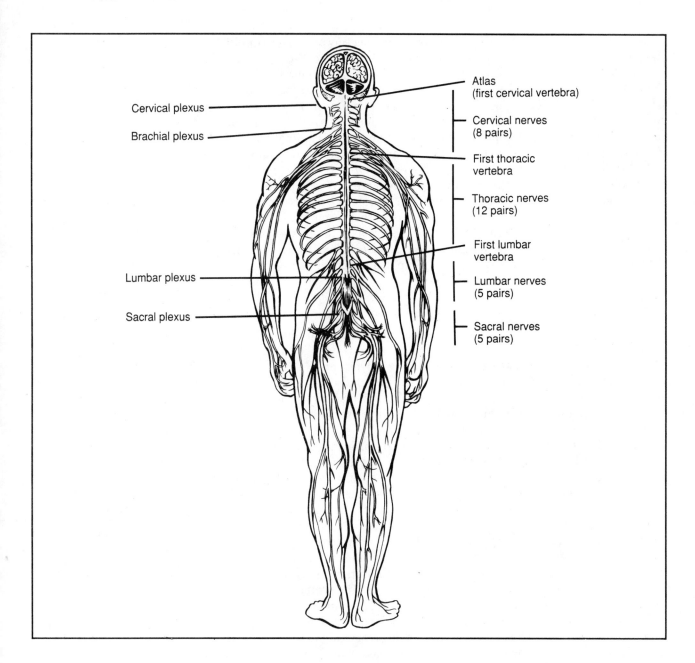

Cervical plexus

Brachial plexus

Lumbar plexus

Sacral plexus

Atlas
(first cervical vertebra)

Cervical nerves
(8 pairs)

First thoracic
vertebra

Thoracic nerves
(12 pairs)

First lumbar
vertebra

Lumbar nerves
(5 pairs)

Sacral nerves
(5 pairs)

Figure 2–4   Spinal cord and spinal nerves (posterior view).

spinal cord) or in specialized nerve cells called *receptors*. Receptors are located throughout the body; different types of receptors are sensitive to pain, temperature (hot and cold), pressure, and changes in body position. *Sensory* nerve cells carry the impulses from the peripheral receptors to the spinal cord and brain. *Motor* nerve cells carry impulses away from the CNS to respond to the perceived changes in the body's internal or external environment.

An example of how this system works is the *withdrawal*, or *flexion*, *reflex*. If the hand encounters a very hot stimulus, e.g., an open flame, receptors in the skin of the hand send impulses to the spinal cord that communicate extreme heat and pain. In a matter of milliseconds, the appropriate muscles are activated to withdraw the hand from the fire. Similarly, when performing a complex physical activity, e.g., an inclined bench press, the central and peripheral nervous systems work in unison to initiate, guide, and monitor all aspects of the specific activity. Assuming we already know how to perform an inclined bench press, we may also assume that the CNS has stored in memory a "computer program" of specific muscles in which to send impulses in order to safely perform the bench press. In this example, the nerve receptors in the periphery, located in the arm and shoulder region, continually provide information (feedback) to the CNS regarding the amount of resistance encountered, limb position, pressure sensed on the palms of the hands, and so on. This communication between central and peripheral nervous systems utilizing the motor and sensory nerves is essential for us to learn, modify, and successfully perform both simple and complex physical activities. Feeling the "burn" of fatigue in a muscle or group of muscles being heavily exercised is another example of how the feedback provided by our nervous system functions to protect us. While many individuals judge the quality or quantity of a workout by the "burn" they feel in their muscles, a more appropriate interpretation of the intense burning sensation that often accompanies muscle fatigue would be as warning of the increased risk of muscle or tendon injury through overexertion, as well as a clear signal to modify (lower) the intensity level of the particular activity or workout.

SKELETAL SYSTEM

The human skeletal system (Fig. 2-5) consists of 206 bones that can be divided into two sections: the *axial* skeleton, the 80 bones that comprise the head, neck, and trunk; and the *appendicular* skeleton, the 126 bones that form the extremities (Table 2-3).

The bones that form the skeleton combine to provide five basic, very important functions. First, the skeletal system provides *protection* for many of the vital organs, such as the heart, brain, and spinal cord. Second, the skeleton provides *support* for the soft tissues so that erect posture and the form of the body can be maintained. Third, the bones provide a framework of *levers* to which muscles are attached. When particular muscles contract, long bones typically act as levers to produce movement. Fourth, the red marrow of bone is responsible for the *production* of certain blood cells, namely, red blood cells, some types of white blood cells, and platelets. Fifth, bones serve as *storage areas* for calcium, phosphorus, potassium, sodium, and other minerals. Due to their high mineral content, bones remain intact for many years after death. Fat is also stored within the middle section of long bones, in the *medullary cavity* (see Fig. 2-6). The current prevalence of *osteoporosis* (increased porosity of bone) among certain woman who are *amenorrheic* (absent or suppressed menstruation) and many women who are postmenopausal (after the permanent cessation of menstrual activity) is a very important reason why the unique ability of bone to respond to the stresses (or lack thereof) placed on it should be of particular interest to the personal trainer.

Bone is composed of two main ingredients—an *organic* component made of **collagen**, a complex protein that is found in various forms within other connective tissues; and an *inorganic* component comprised of mineral salts, primarily calcium and potassium. According to *Wolff's Law*, bone is capable of adjusting its strength in proportion to the amount of stress placed on it. If heavy loads, such as in resistance training, are applied over long periods of time, bones with ample blood supply will become more dense, with increased collagen fibers and mineral salts. On the other hand, if bone is not subjected to stress, as in individuals with a sedentary lifestyle or in the absence of gravity (as in space flight), bones will become less dense over time as mineral salts are withdrawn from bone. An easy way to remember this important law is with the dictum "Form follows function." Simply stated, the *form* that bone will take (strong or weak) is in direct response to the recent *function* of that

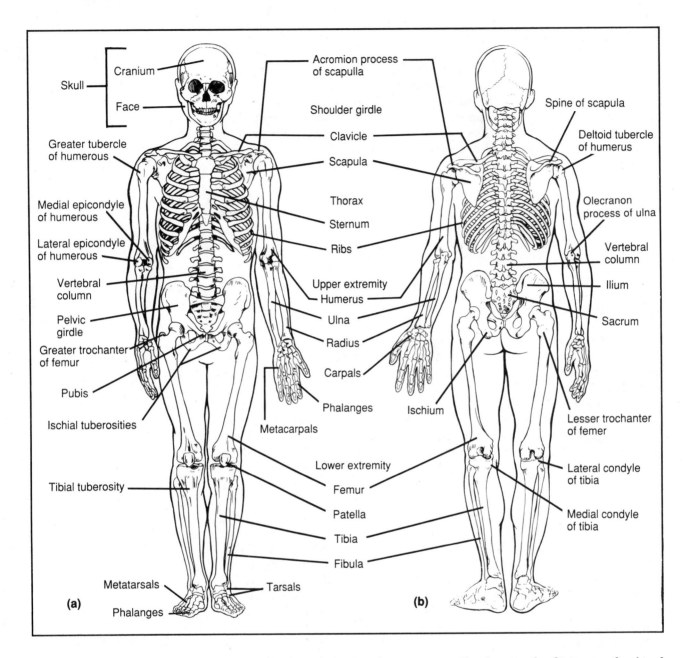

Figure 2–5   Skeletal system. (a) Anterior view; (b) posterior view.

bone. This knowledge has important applications to the fitness professional who must have the bone health of his/her client in mind when prescribing specific conditioning and training exercise programs.

Bones may also be classified according to their shape: long, short, flat, or irregular. *Long* bones are those in which the length exceeds the width and the thickness. Most of the bones in the lower and upper extremities are long bones, including the femur, tibia, fibula, and metatarsals in the lower limb, and the humerus, radius, ulna, and metacarpals in the upper extremity. Each long bone has a shaft called a *diaphysis* and two ends that are usually wider than the shaft, known as *epiphyses* (singular = *epiphysis*). The diaphysis of a long bone is surrounded by a connective tissue sheath called *periosteum* (Fig. 2–6). The periosteum has two layers, an outer layer that serves as an attachment site for muscles and tendons, and an inner layer that, when disrupted by fracture, signals the release of *osteoblasts* (bone-forming cells) to repair the fracture.

Short bones have no long axis but are approximately equal in length and width. They are found in the hands (carpals) and the feet (tarsals). *Flat* bones

Table 2–3   BONES IN THE AXIAL AND APPENDICULAR SKELETONS (N = 206)

AXIAL SKELETON	NUMBER OF BONES
Skull	
Cranium	8
Face	14
Hyoid	1
Vertebral Column	26
Thorax	
Sternum	1
Ribs	24
(Auditory ossicles)*	6
Total	80

APPENDICULAR SKELETON	
Lower Extremity	
Phalanges	28
Metatarsals	10
Tarsals	14
Patella	2
Tibia	2
Fibula	2
Femur	2
Pelvic Girdle	
Hip or pelvic bone (os coxae=	
ilium, ischium, pubis)	2
Shoulder Girdle	
Clavicle	2
Scapula	2
Upper Extremity	
Phalanges	28
Metacarpals	10
Carpals	16
Radius	2
Ulna	2
Humerus	2
Total	126

*The auditory ossicles, three per ear, are not considered part of the axial or appendicular skeleton, but rather a separate group of bones. They are here placed in the Axial skeleton group for convenience.

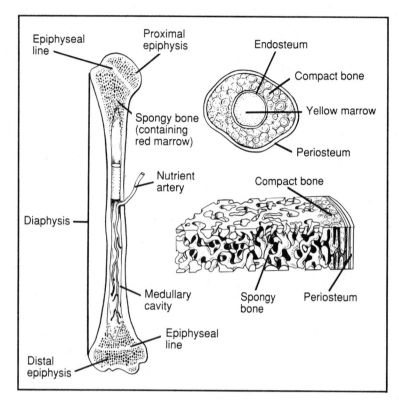

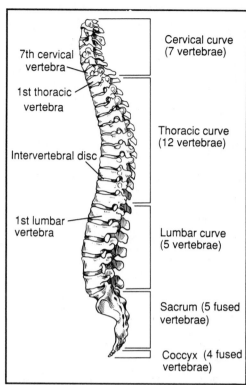

Figure 2–6 Long bone gross anatomy.

Figure 2–7 Vertebral column (lateral view).

are somewhat described by their name, for they are thin but usually bent or curved rather than flat. Examples include the bones of the skull, the ribs, the sternum, and the scapulae (shoulder blades). *Irregular* bones are bones of various shapes that do not fall into the other three categories of bones. The hip bones (os coxae), the vertebrae, and many of the bones of the skull are examples.

Axial Skeleton

As previously stated, the axial skeleton consists of the 80 bones that form the skull, the vertebral column, and the thorax (chest). This portion of the skeletal system provides the main structural support for the body while also protecting the central nervous system and vital organs of the thorax (heart, lungs, and so on). Of primary importance is the adult vertebral column, consisting of 33 vertebrae divided into five groups, according to the region of the body in which they are located. The upper seven are **cervical vertebrae**, followed by 12 **thoracic vertebrae**, five **lumbar vertebrae**, five *sacral* vertebrae fused into one bone known as the *sacrum*, and four *coccygeal* vertebrae fused together into one bone called the *coccyx*. The sacral vertebrae and coccygeal vertebrae become fused in the adult, so there are only 26 movable vertebrae (Fig. 2-7).

Appendicular Skeleton

The appendicular skeleton is comprised of the bones of the lower and upper limbs and the bones by which the legs and arms attach to the axial skeleton—the *pelvic* (hip) and *pectoral* (chest) girdles. The pelvic girdle consists of two large hip bones known collectively as the *os coxae*, each side being comprised of an *ilium*, an *ischium*, and a *pubis* (see Fig. 2-5). Much of the weight supported by the os coxae is transferred to the bones of the lower limbs. Conversely, the two pectoral girdles, each consisting of a clavicle (collarbone) and scapula (shoulder

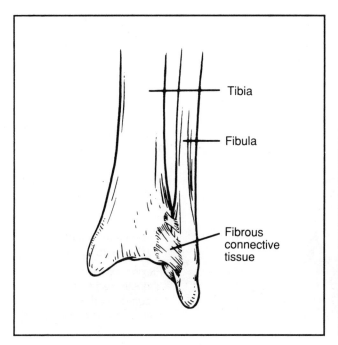

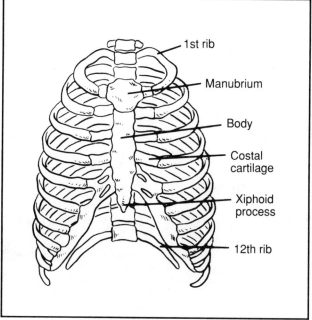

blade), attach the bones of the upper extremities to the axial skeleton at the sternum. Since this is the only attachment or link of the upper extremities to the axial skeleton several tradeoffs exist from this configuration. Most important, the pectoral girdle does not provide very strong support for the upper extremity; however, the girdle does permit a wide range of movements at the shoulder, making the shoulder the most mobile joint in the body.

Figure 2–8   Example of a fibrous (syndesmoses) joint.

Articulations (joints)

An *articulation*, or *joint*, is the point of contact or connection between bones, or between bones and cartilage. The stability and integrity of all joints are maintained by **ligaments**, that is, dense, fibrous strands of connective tissue that link together the bony segments. Some joints permit a large range of motion in several directions, whereas other joints permit virtually no motion at all. The various joints in the body can be classified into two general categories according to (1) the structure of the joints, and (2) the type of movement allowed by the joints.

Figure 2–9   Example of a cartilaginous (synchondroses) joint.

STRUCTURAL CLASSIFICATION OF JOINTS.   When classifying joints according to their structure, two main characteristics differentiate the types of joints: (1) the type of connective tissue that holds the bones of the joint together, and (2) the presence or absence of a joint cavity. There are three major structural categories of joints—fibrous, cartilaginous, and synovial. *Fibrous* joints (*syndesmoses*) have no joint cavity and include all joints in which the bones are held tightly together by fibrous connective tissue. Very little space separates the ends of the bones of these joints; as a result, little or no movement occurs. Examples include the joints, or *sutures*, between the bones of the skull, the joint between the distal tibia and fibula, and the joint between the radius and ulna (Fig. 2–8).

In *cartilaginous* joints (*synchondroses*), the bones are united by cartilage. No joint cavity exists and, as with fibrous joints, little or no motion occurs. Familiar examples include the joints formed by the *hyaline cartilages* that connect the ribs to the sternum (breastbone), and *fibrocartilages* that separate the bodies of vertebrae in the spinal column (Fig. 2–9).

Table 2–4   MAJOR JOINTS IN THE BODY

REGION/JOINT	TYPE	NUMBER OF AXES OF ROTATION	MOVEMENT(S) POSSIBLE
LOWER EXTREMITY			
Metatarsophalangeal	Synovial (condyloid)	2	Flexion-extension; abduction-adduction; circumduction
Ankle	Synovial (hinge)	1	Plantarflexion-dorsiflexion
Between distal tibia and fibula	Fibrous	0	Slight movement possible
Knee (tibia and femur)	Synovial (modified hinge)	2	Flexion-extension; medial-lateral rotation
Hip	Synovial (ball and socket)	3	Flexion-extension; abduction-adduction; circumduction; medial-lateral rotation
UPPER EXTREMITY			
Metacarpophalangeal	Synovial (condyloid)	2	Flexion-extension; abduction-adduction; circumduction
Thumb	Synovial (saddle)	3	Flexion-extension; abduction-adduction; circumduction opposition
Wrist	Synovial	2	Flexion-extension; abduction-adduction; circumduction
Proximal radioulnar	Synovial (pivot)	1	Pronation-supination
Elbow (ulna and humerus)	Synovial (hinge)	1	Flexion-extension
Shoulder	Synovial (ball and socket)	3	Flexion-extension; abduction-adduction; circumduction; medial-lateral rotation
Ribs and sternum	Cartilaginous	0	Slight movement possible

Most of the joints in the body are *synovial* joints (*diarthroses*). These joints have a space, or *joint cavity*, between the bones forming the joint. The movement of synovial joints is limited only by the shapes of the bones of the joint and the soft tissues (ligaments, joint capsules, tendons, muscles) that surround the joint. Synovial joints have four distinguishing features that set them apart structurally from the other types of joints. First, the ends of the bones in synovial joints are covered with a thin layer of *articular cartilage*. The articular cartilage of synovial joints is hyaline cartilage, and although it covers the surfaces of the articulating bones, the hyaline cartilage does not attach the bones together. Second, all synovial joints are surrounded by an *articular*, or *joint, capsule* made of dense, fibrous connective tissue. Third, the inner surface of the joint capsule is lined with a thin *synovial membrane*. The synovial membrane's primary function is the secretion of *synovial fluid*, the fourth distinguishing characteristic of synovial joints. Synovial fluid acts as a lubricant for the joint, and provides nutrition to the articular cartilage. Normally, only a very small amount of synovial fluid is present in even the largest joints, such as the knee and shoulder. However, acute injury to or overuse of a synovial joint can stimulate the synovial membrane to secrete excessive synovial fluid, typically producing swelling and decreased pain-free motion.

In addition to these four features, some synovial joints have articular discs called *meniscii* (singular = meniscus) made of fibrocartilage. The meniscii (**cartilages**) divide the joint cavity into two separate spaces. Particularly in a weight-bearing joint like the knee, the cartilages help to absorb shock, increase joint stability, and aid in joint nutrition by directing the flow of synovial fluid. A torn cartilage or meniscus, one of the most common knee injuries in athletics, is simply a tearing of one of the articular discs in the joint.

FUNCTIONAL CLASSIFICATION OF JOINTS.   The functional classification of joints is based on the degree and type of movement they allow. Fibrous joints are classified as *synarthroses* (*syn* = together, *arthro* = joint; "an immoveable joint") (see Fig. 2-8). Cartilaginous joints, which fall into the category of *amphiarthroses* (*amphi* = both sides, *arthro* = joint; "cartilage on both sides of the joint"), are slightly moveable (see Fig. 2–9). Finally, the largest functional category of joints, *diarthrodial* (*di* = apart, *arthro* = joint; "apart joint") is that of the synovial joints. Diarthroses are freely moveable joints; typically, many different movements are possible at these joints.

Unlike joints classified according to the material that connects the bones together, synovial joints are classified by the movements they allow. Typically, the shapes of the bony structures forming a synovial joint are the primary factors limiting that joint's movement. Other factors that limit motion in synovial joints are: (1) ligament/capsule tension, (2) muscle/tendon tension, and (3) apposition (touching) of the soft tissues, e.g., the calf against the hamstrings. A summary of the main joints in the body, classified by type and movements possible at each, is presented in Table 2–4.

MOVEMENT OF SYNOVIAL JOINTS.   Recall the earlier discussion of the anatomical planes of motion used to describe the actions of the body (see Fig. 2-2). In order for a joint to move in a given plane, there must be an axis of rotation. An *axis of rotation* is an imaginary line perpendicular to (at right angles to) the plane of movement about which a joint rotates. Due to their configuration, many joints have several axes of rotation, enabling bones to move in the various planes.

Joints with one axis of rotation can only move in one plane, and are known as *uniaxial* joints. Uniaxial joints are also known as "hinge" joints, since hinges only work in one plane. The ankle joint proper and the elbow (ulnohumeral) joint are examples of uniplanar joints. Some joints have two axes of rotation, permitting motion in two planes that are at right angles to one another. These *biaxial joints*, common throughout the body, include the knee (tibiofemoral) joint, a modified hingejoint; the joints of the hand and fingers (metacarpal-phalangeal), condyloid joints; and the joints of the foot and toes (metatarsal-phalangeal joints), also condyloid joints. *Multiaxial* joints have at least three axes of motion and permit movement in three planes. Examples include the hip joint and the shoulder (glenohumeral), both of which are ball-and- socket joints, and the thumb (first metacarpal-phalangeal joint), which is a saddle joint (Fig. 2-10).

There are two basic types of movements in the various synovial joints: angular and circular. *Angular* movements increase or decrease the angle between bones, and include primarily **flexion**, **extension**, **abduction**, and **adduction**.

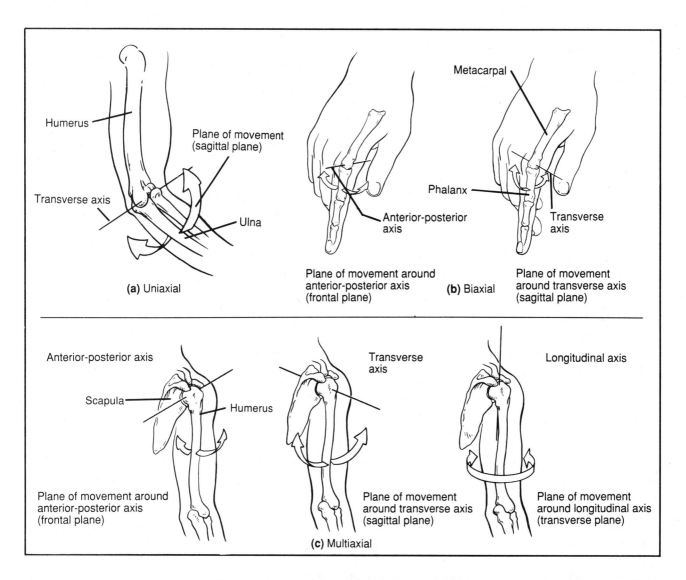

Figure 2–10 Movement of synovial (diarthrodial) joints. (a) uniaxial; (b) biaxial; (c) multiaxial.

Flexion and extension occur in the **sagittal** (anterior–posterior) **plane**. Flexion usually involves a decrease in the angle between the **anterior** surfaces of articulating bones, whereas extension most often describes an increase in this angle. Exceptions are the knee and toe joints, where the reference points for flexion and extension are the **posterior** articulating surfaces of the joints (Fig. 2–11).

Abduction and adduction movements always occur in the **frontal** (medial-lateral) **plane**, and are defined with respect to the midline of the body. When an arm or leg is moved away from the midline of the body, abduction occurs. Adduction is the return motion from abduction, and involves movement of the body part toward the midline of the body, to regain anatomical position. Abduction and adduction movements are possible at many joints, some of which are presented in Figure 2–12.

In addition to the four primary angular movements, there are four circular movements possible at some of the synovial joints. Forearm supination and pronation are motions in the transverse, or horizontal, plane. Supination is a term that specifically describes the lateral (outward) rotation of the forearm which causes the palm to face anteriorly. The radius and the ulna are parallel in this position, which is the *anatomical*, or *reference*, *position* for the

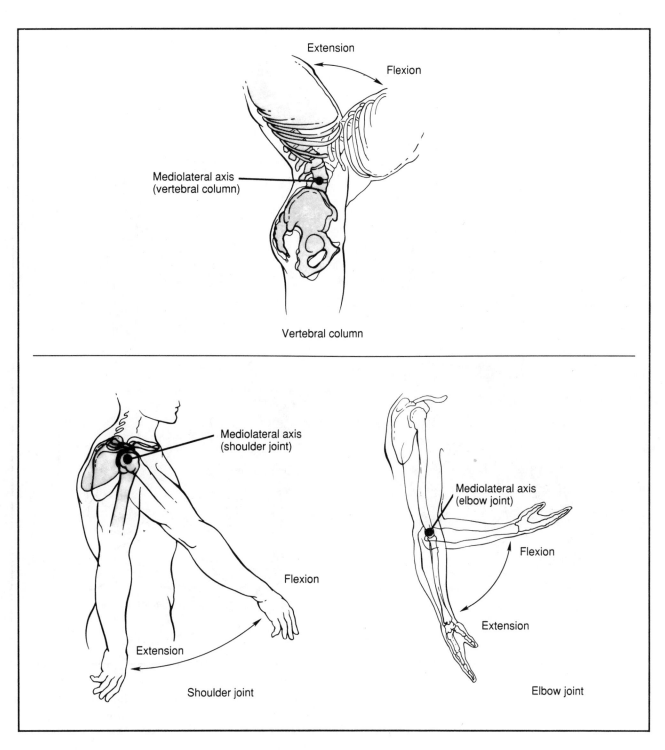

Vertebral column

Shoulder joint

Elbow joint

forearms (see Fig. 2-1). Pronation describes the medial (inward) rotation of the forearm that causes the radius to cross diagonally over the ulna and the palms to face posteriorly. *Rotation* is the motion of a bone around a central axis, and is described as being either **medial** (inward) or **lateral** (outward) rotation of the anterior surface of the bone involved. The femur at the hip joint and the humerus at the shoulder (glenohumeral) joint are among the most frequently rotated bones. The fourth circular movement, *circumduction*, is a sequential combination of flexion, abduction, extension, and adduction.

Figure 2–11 Segmental movements in the sagittal plane. (Redrawn from Kreighbaum and Barthels, 1985, pp 43-44)

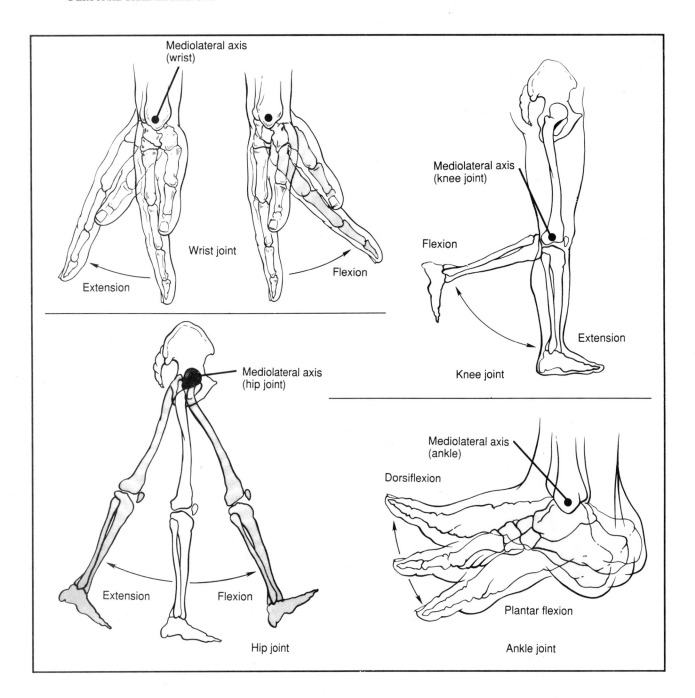

Figure 2–11 (cont.) Segmental movements in the sagittal plane. (Redrawn from Kreighbaum and Barthels, 1985, pp 43–44.

Similar to rotation, circumduction commonly occurs at the hip and shoulder joints (Fig. 2–13). At some synovial joints, the fundamental movements are given specialized names in order to clarify their action. These, together with the primary angular and circular movements, are summarized in Table 2–5.

MUSCULAR SYSTEM

Although knowledge of the major anatomical systems is important for the personal trainer, the anatomical system most directly affected by exercise is the muscular system, for although bones and joints provide the framework for the body, it is the contraction (and relaxation) of specific muscles that enables us to move. There are three types of muscle tissue: skeletal, cardiac, and visceral.

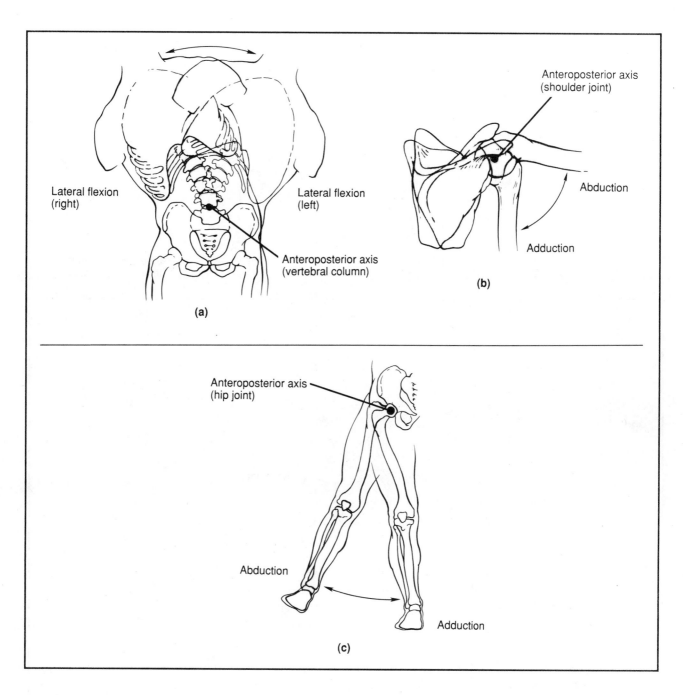

Figure 2–12 Segmental movements in the frontal plane. (Redrawn from Kreighbaum and Barthels, 1985, pp 45-46)

Skeletal muscle tissue is attached to bones by tendons, and is typically named according to its location. Skeletal muscle is voluntary muscle; that is, it can be made to contract by conscious effort. *Cardiac* muscle tissue forms the walls of the heart and is involuntary by nature. The third type of muscle, *visceral* muscle, is found in the walls of internal organs like the stomach and intestines and in blood vessels. The contraction of visceral muscle is also involuntary, and thus it is not under conscious control. While all three types of muscle have vital functions, the structure and function of skeletal muscles warrant further discussion. Both ends of a skeletal muscle are attached to bone via **tendons** (a cord of connective tissue). In some cases, skeletal muscles are attached to bone by an *aponeurosis*, a broad, flat type of tendon. The wide, flat insertion of the rectus abdominis is an excellent example of an aponeurosis.

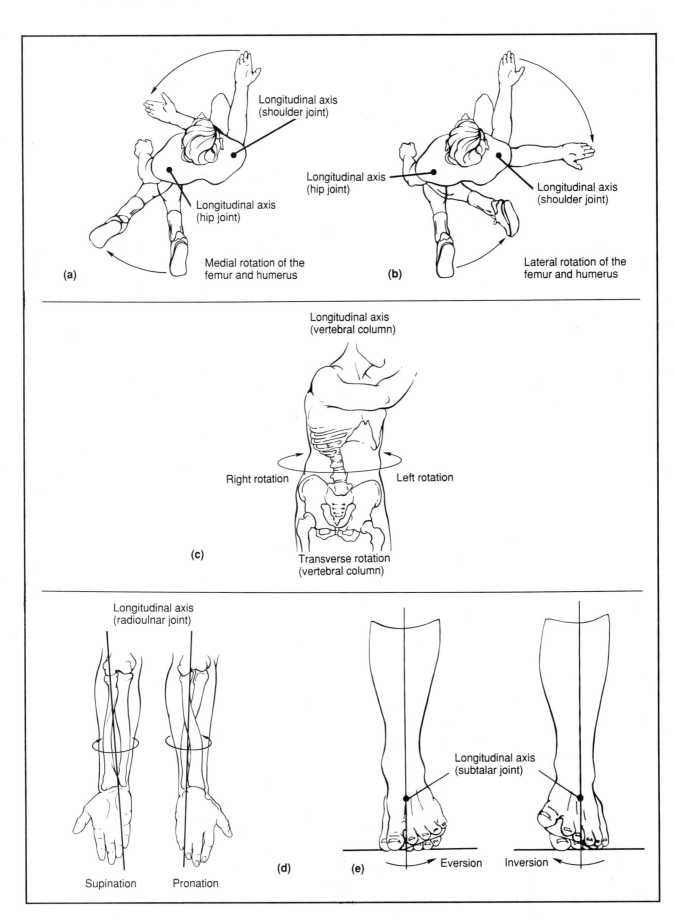

Table 2–5 FUNDAMENTAL MOVEMENTS (FROM ANATOMICAL POSITION)

PLANE	ACTION	DEFINITION
Sagittal	Flexion	Decreasing the angle between two bones
	Extension	Increasing the angle between two bones
	Dorsiflexion	Moving the top of the foot toward the shin (ankle only)
	Plantarflexion	Moving the sole of the foot downward; "pointing the toes" (ankle only)
Frontal	Abduction	Motion away from the midline of the body (or part)
	Adduction	Motion toward the midline of the body (or part)
	Elevation	Moving to a superior position (scapula)
	Depression	Moving to an inferior position (scapula)
	Inversion	Lifting the medial border of the foot (subtalar joint only)
	Eversion	Lifting the lateral border of the foot (subtalar joint only)
Transverse	Rotation	Medial (inward) or lateral (outward) turning about the vertical axis of bone
	Pronation	Rotating the hand and wrist medially from the elbow
	Supination	Rotating the hand and wrist laterally from the elbow
	Horizontal flexion	From a 90° abducted arm position, the humerus is flexed in toward the midline of the body in the transverse plane
	Horizontal extension	The return of the humerus from horizontal flexion
Multiplanar	Circumduction	Motion that describes a "cone"; combines flexion, abduction, extension, and adduction in sequential order
	Opposition	Thumb movement unique to primates and humans

Figure 2–13 Segmental movements in the transverse (horizontal) plane. (Redrawn from Kreighbaum and Barthels, 1985, pp 47-48)

Table 2–6   ACTIONS OF MAJOR LOWER EXTREMITY MULTIJOINT MUSCLES

MUSCLE	HIP	KNEE	ANKLE
Rectus femoris	Flexion	Extension	—
Biceps femoris	Extension (long head); lateral rotation	Flexion; lateral rotation	—
Semitendinosus	Extension; medial rotation	Flexion; medial rotation	—
Semimembranosus	Extension; medial rotation	Flexion; medial rotation	—
Gracilis	Adduction; medial rotation	Flexion; medial rotation	—
Sartorius	Flexion; lateral rotation	Flexion; medial rotation	—
Gastrocnemius	—	Flexion	Plantarflexion

There are over 600 muscles within the human body—only the major muscles will be discussed in this chapter. Muscles are named according to their:

- *Location* (e.g., posterior tibialis, rectus abdominis)

- *Shape* (deltoid, trapezius, serratus anterior, rhomboid)

- *Action* (various muscle names include the terms extensor, flexor, abductor, adductor)

- *Number* of divisions (biceps brachii, triceps brachii, quadriceps femoris)

- *Bony attachments* (coracobrachialis, iliocostalis)

- *Size relationships* (pectoralis major, pectoralis minor; in addition, several muscles include the terms longus—"long"—and brevis—"short"—in their names

Muscle tissue has the ability to receive and respond to input from the nervous system that may cause the muscle to contract (shorten and thicken) or relax. Muscle tissue also has *elasticity*, so that with proper techniques muscles may be safely stretched. From a functional perspective, it is important to understand that most muscles of the trunk and extremities are arranged in opposing pairs. That is, when one muscle is contracting to achieve a desired movement (the **agonist**), its opposite muscle (the **antagonist**) is being stretched. For example, when the abdominal muscles contract during a bent-knee sit-up, the erector spinae muscles are stretched. At most joints several muscles help (combine) to perform the same anatomical function; these muscles are functionally known as **synergists**. For example, the synergistic contractions of the gastrocnemius, soleus, and posterior tibialis muscles of the leg produce plantarflexion at the ankle joint.

Muscular contraction results in human motion, the maintenance of posture, and heat production. Locomotion (walking, running) is the result of the complex, combined functioning of the bones, joints, and muscles attached to the bones. Muscle contraction also enables the maintenance of posture in stationary positions, e.g., sitting, standing. Through regular contraction, muscles produce heat; this plays an important role in maintaining normal body temperature.

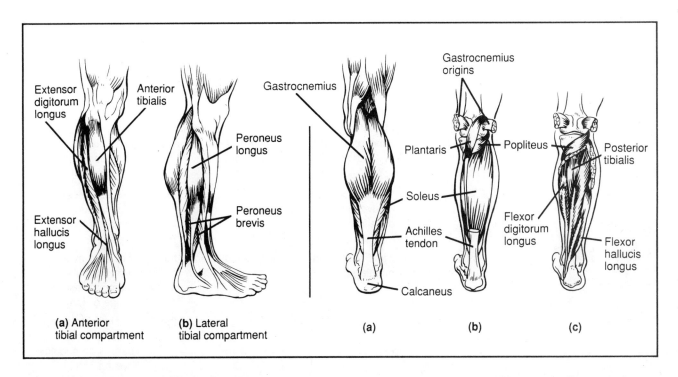

(a) Anterior tibial compartment   **(b) Lateral tibial compartment**   **(a)**   **(b)**   **(c)**

Muscles of the Lower Extremity

The major links of the lower extremity are the: (1) *ankle joint*, formed by the distal tibia, distal fibula, and talus; (2) *knee joint*, comprised of the tibiofemoral and patellofemoral joints; and (3) *hip joint*, linking the femur with the hip (coxal) bone. When compared to the muscles of the upper extremity, the muscles of the lower extremity tend to be larger and more powerful. Many of the muscles of the lower extremity cross two joints (either the hip and the knee, or the knee and the ankle). The major muscles of the lower extremity that act at more than one joint are listed in Table 2-6.

MUSCLES THAT ACT AT THE ANKLE AND THE FOOT.   The muscles of the leg are grouped into three compartments that are divided by an *interosseous membrane* (inter = between, os = bone) between the tibia and fibula, and the *fascia*. The *anterior tibial compartment* muscles contract to extend the toes and dorsiflex (flex) the ankle. These muscles include the *anterior tibialis, extensor digitorum longus*, and *extensor hallucis longus* (Fig. 2-14a). The muscles of the *lateral tibial compartment* are known as the *peroneals* (peroneus longus and brevis), and act to cause **eversion** (abduction) of the foot and plantarflexion of the ankle (Fig. 2-14b). The seven muscles of the *posterior tibial compartment* can be further divided into three superficial muscles (*gastrocnemius, soleus, plantaris*) and four deep muscles (*popliteus, posterior tibialis, flexor hallucis longus, flexor digitorum longus*) (Fig. 2-15). The primary functions of these posterior muscles include **plantarflexion** (extension) of the ankle, flexion of the toes, and **inversion** (adduction) of the foot. The *Achilles tendon*, found in the posterior compartment, attaches the gastrocnemius and soleus via one common tendon to the calcaneus (heel bone). The origins of, insertions of, primary function(s) of, and examples of exercises to develop the muscles that act at the ankle and the foot are presented in Table 2-7.

Figure 2–14   Muscles of the lower leg. (a) Anterior; (b) lateral.

Figure 2–15   Posterior calf muscles that plantarflex the ankle. (a) Gastrocnemius; (b) soleus: (c) flexor hallucis and digitorum longus.

Table 2–7   MAJOR MUSCLES THAT ACT AT THE ANKLE AND THE FOOT

MUSCLE	ORIGIN	INSERTION	PRIMARY FUNCTION(S)	SELECTED EXERCISES
Anterior tibialis	Proximal two-thirds of lateral tibia	Medial aspect of first cuneiform and first metatarsal	Dorsiflexion at the ankle; inversion at the foot	Cycling with toe clips, resisted inversion (with dorsiflexion)
Peroneus longus	Head of fibula + proximal two-thirds of lateral fibula	Inferior aspects of medial tarsal (first cuneiform) and first metatarsal	Plantarflexion at the ankle; eversion at the foot	Resisted eversion of foot, walking on inside of foot
Peroneus brevis	Distal two-thirds of lateral fibula	Base of the fifth metatarsal	Plantarflexion at the ankle; eversion at the foot	Resisted eversion of foot with rubber tubing, walking on inside of foot
Gastrocnemius	Posterior surfaces of femoral condyles	Posterior surface of calcaneus via Achilles tendon	Plantarflexion at the ankle	Hill running, jumping rope, toe raises with barbell on shoulder, cycling
Soleus	Proximal two-thirds of posterior surfaces of tibia and fibula	Posterior surface of calcaneus via Achilles tendon	Plantarflexion at the ankle	Virtually the same as for gastrocnemius, bent-knee toe raises with resistance
Posterior tibialis	Posterior surface of tibia-fibular interosseous membrane	Lower medial surfaces of medial tarsals and metatarsals	Plantarflexion at the ankle; inversion at the foot	Resisted inversion of foot with surgical tubing, with plantarflexion

MUSCLES THAT ACT AT THE KNEE JOINT.   The muscles that cross the knee joint to act on the leg (tibia and fibula) can be divided into three separate groups. The four major muscles on the front of the thigh are located in the anterior, or extensor, compartment. The primary function of these muscles is to extend the leg. These muscles are typically grouped together and referred to as the *quadriceps femoris*, although each muscle has its own individual name—*rectus femoris, vastus medialis, vastus intermedius,* and *vastus lateralis* (Fig. 2–16). The quadriceps insert via a common tendon known as the *patellar tendon,* which attaches to the tibial tuberosity (see Fig. 2–5).

The muscles in the posterior, or flexor, compartment of the thigh are the *biceps femoris, semitendinosus,* and *semimembranosus.* These muscles, collectively known as the *hamstrings,* cross the knee joint and cause flexion of the leg. This large group of muscles has a common origin at the ischial tuberosity (see Fig. 2–5). Below the knee, the biceps femoris attaches laterally, while the semitendinosus and semimembranosus attach on the medial aspect of the tibia. Between these tendons lies the *popliteal space,* a triangular area on the posterior aspect of the knee joint (Fig. 2–17).

The third major group of muscles that act on the leg is the *pes anserine* group, which includes the previously mentioned *semitendinosus* as well as the *sartorius* and the *gracilis* (see Figs. 2–16 and 2–17). These muscles are grouped together because of their common site of insertion on the medial tibia, just below the knee. The sartorius, the longest muscle in the body, originates on the ilium and courses diagonally across the anterior aspect of the thigh to

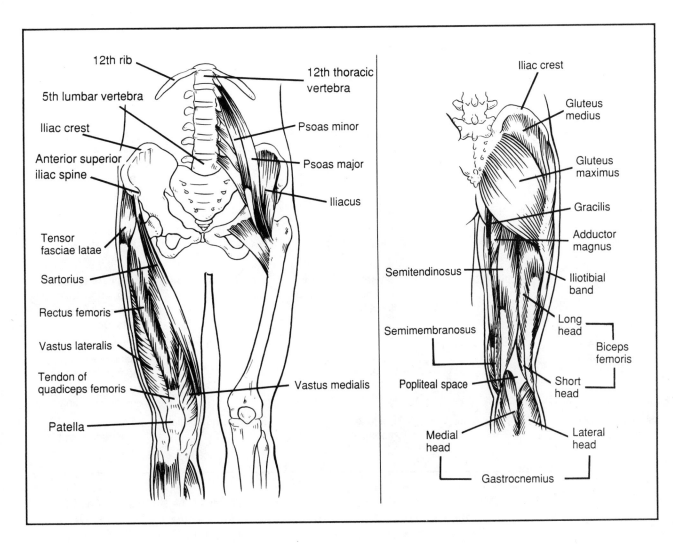

its insertion on the proximal tibia. Even though the sartorius is an anterior muscle, its contraction causes flexion of the leg. As a group, the three pes anserine muscles medially rotate the leg (tibia) when the knee is flexed. The origins of, insertions of, primary function(s) of, and examples of exercises to develop the major muscles that act on the leg are presented in Table 2–8.

MUSCLES THAT ACT AT THE HIP.   Most of the muscles that cross the hip joint and act on the thigh (femur) have their origins on the pelvis. Located on the anterior aspect of the hip, the *psoas major* and the *psoas minor* muscles arise from the five lumbar vertebrae. These two muscles, along with the *iliacus*, have a common attachment on the lesser trochanter of the femur and work together as powerful flexors of the thigh. This group of three muscles is commonly referred to as the *iliopsoas* muscle. The rectus femoris is the only muscle of the quadriceps femoris group that crosses the hip joint; it also causes flexion of the thigh (see Fig. 2–16).

Posteriorly, three large muscles combine to give shape to the buttocks and serve as powerful mobilizers of the hip joint. The *gluteus maximus*, the largest and most superficial of the three gluteals, extends and laterally (outwardly) rotates the thigh. Underlying the gluteus maximus are the *gluteus medius* and the *gluteus minimus*, which combine to abduct and medially (inwardly) rotate the femur. Also on the posterior aspect of the thigh are the *hamstring muscles* (biceps femoris, semitendinosus, semimembranosus), whose action at the hip joint is to extend the thigh (see Fig. 2–17).

Figure 2–16   Musculature of the anterior hip and thigh (femur).

Figure 2–17   Superficial musculature of the posterior hip and thigh.

Table 2–8   MAJOR MUSCLES THAT ACT AT THE KNEE JOINT

MUSCLE	ORIGIN	INSERTION	PRIMARY FUNCTION(S)	SELECTED EXERCISES
Rectus femoris	Anterior-inferior spine of ilium	Superior aspect of patella and patellar tendon	Extension (most effective when hip is extended)	Cycling, leg press machine, squats, vertical jumping, stair climbing, jumping rope
Vastus medialis, intermedius, and lateralis	Proximal two-thirds of anterior femur at midline	Patella and tibial tuberosity via the patellar tendon	Extension (particularly when hip is flexed)	Same as for rectus femoris; resisted knee extension, straight leg raises
Biceps femoris	Ischial tuberosity	Lateral condyle of tibia and head of fibula	Flexion and lateral rotation	Jumping rope, hamstring curls with knee in lateral rotation
Semitendinosus	Ischial tuberosity	Proximal anterior-medial aspect of tibia	Flexion and medial rotation	Essentially the same as for biceps femoris; hamstring curls with knee in medial rotation
Semimembranosus	Ishial tuberosity	Posterior aspect of medial tibial condyle	Flexion and medial rotation	Same as for semitendinosus

The muscles located on the medial aspect of the thigh are named for both their function and their size. The *adductor magnus, adductor longus,* and *adductor brevis* work in concert to adduct the femur (Fig. 2–18). The adductors are also synergists for medial and lateral rotation of the thigh. The origins of, insertions of, primary actions of, and examples of exercises to develop the major muscles that act on the thigh (femur) are presented in Table 2–9.

Muscles of the Trunk

For our discussion, the muscles of the trunk will include only the major muscles associated with the spinal column and the wall of the abdomen. Contraction of these muscles, in their agonist/antagonist relationships, results primarily in sagittal plane motion, i.e., flexion and extension of the trunk. There are three major muscles responsible for movement of the vertebral column: the *iliocostalis,* the *longissimus,* and the *spinalis,* better known by their functional group name—*erector spinae.* Each of the three muscles in this group has a subdivision name based on the particular portion of the spinal column in which it inserts. For example, there are three divisions of the iliocostalis muscle: the *iliocostalis lumborum, iliocostalis thoracis,* and *iliocostalis cervicis.* In addition to extending the vertebral column, unilateral contraction of the iliocostalis muscle will produce *lateral flexion* to that side (Fig. 2–19).

The walls of the abdominal cavity are supported entirely by the strength of the muscles located there, for there are no bones that provide support for this region. To make up for the lack of skeletal support, the three layers of muscles in the abdominal wall run in different directions, thus providing additional

Table 2–9   MAJOR MUSCLES THAT ACT ON THE HIP JOINT

MUSCLE	ORIGIN	INSERTION	PRIMARY FUNCTION(S)	SELECTED EXERCISES
Iliacus	Inner surface of the ilium and base of sacrum	Lesser trochanter of femur	Flexion and lateral rotation	Straight-leg sit-ups, running with knees lifted up high, leg raises
Psoas major and minor	Transverse processes of all five lumbar vertebrae	Lesser trochanter of femur	Flexion and lateral rotation	Essentially same as for iliacus
Rectus femoris	Anterior-inferior spine of ilium	Superior aspect of patella and patellar tendon	Flexion	Running, leg press, squats, jumping rope
Gluteus maximus	Posterior one-fourth of iliac crest and sacrum	Gluteal line of femur and iliotibial band	Extension and lateral rotation	Cycling, jumping rope, squats, stair climbing
Biceps femoris	Ischial tuberosity	Lateral condyle of tibia and head of fibula	Extension	Cycling, hamstring curls with knee in lateral rotation
Semitendinosus	Ischial tuberosity	Proximal anterior-medial aspect of tibia	Extension	Essentially the same as for biceps femoris; hamstring curls with knee in medial rotation
Semimembranosus	Ischial tuberosity	Posterior aspect of medial tibial condyle	Extension	Same as for semitendinosus
Gluteus medius and minimus	Lateral surface of ilium	Greater trochanter of femur	Abduction	Side-lying leg raises, walking, running
Adductor magnus	Pubic ramus and ischial tuberosity	Medial aspects of femur	Adduction and lateral rotation	Side-lying bottom leg raises, manually resisted adduction exercises
Adductor brevis and longus	Pubic ramus and ischial tuberosity	Medial aspects of femur	Adduction, flexion, and medial rotation	Side-lying bottom leg raises, resisted adduction

support (Fig. 2–20). In the outermost (superficial) layer is the *external oblique* muscle, whose fibers run anteriorly downward and toward the midline. In the second layer, the fibers of the *internal oblique* muscle run posteriorly and downward. An easy way to remember the orientations of these two muscles is to picture the fibers of the external oblique running into the front pockets of your slacks and the fibers of the internal oblique running diagonally into the rear pockets. Unilateral (one side) contraction of the lateral fibers of the obliques (external and internal) produces lateral flexion of the spinal column on that side. Trunk rotation is produced by contraction of an external oblique and an internal oblique muscle on opposite sides. Bilateral (both sides) contraction of the external and internal obliques compresses the abdominal cavity; these muscles are commonly activated during forced exhalation, defecation, and urination.

Table 2–10   MAJOR MUSCLES THAT ACT ON THE TRUNK

MUSCLE	ORIGIN	INSERTION	PRIMARY FUNCTION(S)	SELECTED EXERCISES
Rectus abdominis	Pubic crest	Cartilage of fifth through seventh ribs and xiphoid process	Flexion and lateral flexion of the trunk	Bent-knee sit-ups, partial curl-ups, good posture, pelvic tilts
External oblique	Anteriolateral borders of lower eight ribs	Anterior half of ilium, pubic crest, and anterior fascia	Lateral flexion of the trunk	Twisting bent-knee sit-ups (rotation opposite), and curl-ups
Internal oblique	Iliac crest	Cartilage of last three to four ribs	Lateral flexion of the trunk	Twisting bent-knee sit-ups (rotation same side), and curl-ups
Transverse abdominis	Iliac crest, lumbar fascia, and cartilages of last six ribs	Xiphoid process of sternum, anterior fascia, and pubis	Compresses abdomen	—
Erector spinae	Posterior iliac crest and sacrum	Angles of ribs, transverse processes of all ribs	Extension of trunk	Squats, prone back-extension exercises, good standing posture

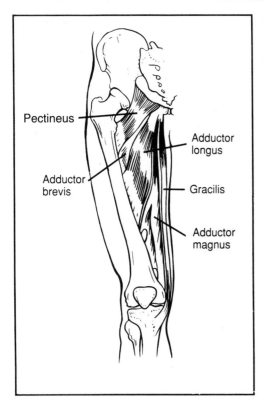

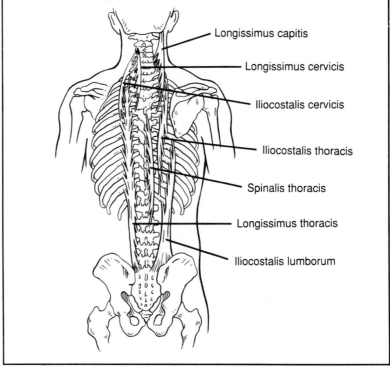

Figure 2–18 Adductors of the femur.

Figure 2–19 The erector spinae muscles.

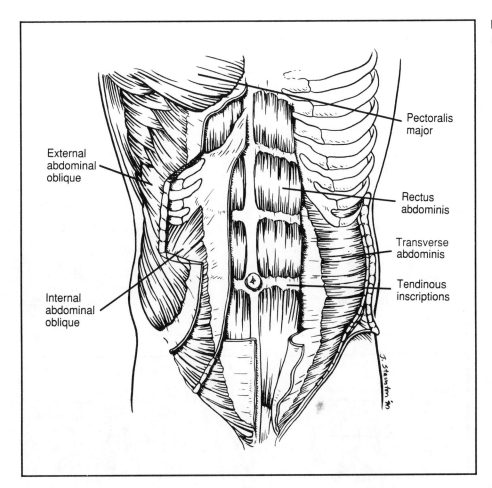

Figure 2–20 Muscles of the abdominal wall.

In the deepest muscular layer in the abdominal wall lies the *transverse abdominis* muscle. The fibers of this thin muscle run horizontally, encircling the abdominal cavity. Contraction of this muscle also compresses the abdomen (see Fig. 2–20). The *rectus abdominis* is a narrow, flat muscle on the anterior aspect of the abdominal wall that flexes the vertebral column. Its fibers run vertically from the pubis to the rib cage. The rectus abdominis is crossed by three transverse fibrous bands called *tendinous inscriptions* (see Fig. 2–20). The origins of, insertions of, primary function(s) of, and examples of exercises to develop the muscles that act on the trunk are presented in Table 2–10.

Muscles of the Upper Extremity

In studying the musculature of the upper extremity, the personal trainer should concentrate on understanding the motions (and muscles responsible for producing motion) at the four major links: the *wrist joint*, comprised of the distal radius and ulna and proximal carpal bones; the *elbow joint*, formed by the union of the olecranon process of the ulna and the distal humerus; the *shoulder joint*, consisting of the proximal humerus and the glenoid fossa of the scapula; and the *scapulothoracic "joint"*. The connection between the scapula and the thorax is not a bony joint, per se, but more an important functional, soft tissue (muscle and fascia) link between the scapula and the trunk. Similar to the lower extremity, there are many muscles that act at two joints. These muscles are identified in Table 2–11.

Table 2–11   ACTIONS OF MAJOR UPPER EXTREMITY MULTIJOINT MUSCLES

MUSCLE	SHOULDER	ELBOW	FOREARM	WRIST
Biceps brachii	Flexion	Flexion	Supination	—
Brachioradialis	—	Flexion	Pronation and supination	—
Triceps brachii	Extension (long head)	Extension	—	—
Flexor carpi radialis	—	Flexion	—	Flexion; abduction
Flexor carpi ulnaris	—	Flexion	—	Flexion; adduction
Extensor carpi radialis (longus and brevis)	—	Extension	—	Extension
Extensor carpi ulnaris	—	Extension	—	Extension; adduction

Figure 2–21   Major muscles acting at the wrist.

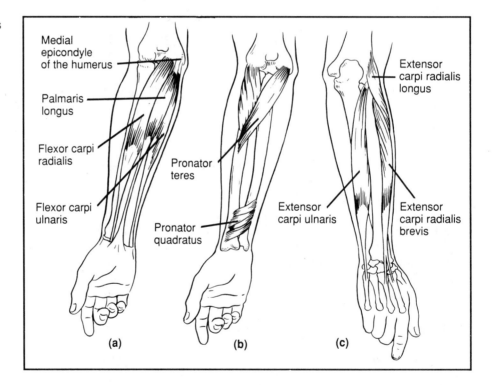

MUSCLES THAT ACT AT THE WRIST.   The muscles that act at the wrist joint can be grouped according to their origin and function.   The *flexor-pronator* muscles originate on the medial epicondyle of the humerus, and cause flexion of the wrist and pronation of the forearm (radius and ulna).   The major wrist flexors include the *flexor carpi radialis, palmaris longus,* and *flexor carpi ulnaris* (Fig. 2–21a).   The major pronators of the forearm are the *pronator teres* at the elbow and the *pronator quadratus* at the wrist (Fig. 2–21b).   The antagonist muscles to the flexor-pronators are the *extensor-supinators,* which arise from a common tendon on the lateral humeral epicondyle and, as their names indicate, cause extension of the wrist and supination of the forearm.   The major wrist

Table 2–12   MAJOR MUSCLES THAT ACT AT THE WRIST

MUSCLE	ORIGIN	INSERTION	PRIMARY FUNCTION(S)	SELECTED EXERCISES
Flexor carpi radialis	Medial epicondyle of humerus	Second and third metacarpals	Flexion	Wrist curls against resistance; grip-strengthening exercises; baseball/softball; racquet sports, particularly racquetball and badminton
Flexor carpi ulnaris	Medial epicondyle of humerus	Fifth metacarpal	Flexion	Same as for flexor carpi radialis
Extensor carpi radialis longus	Lateral epicondyle of humerus	Second metacarpal	Extension	"Reverse" wrist curls, racquet sports (particularly tennis)
Extensor carpi ulnaris	Lateral epicondyle of humerus	Fifth metacarpal	Extension	Same as for extensor carpi radialis longus

extensors are the *extensor carpi radialis longus* and *brevis* and the *extensor carpi ulnaris* (Fig. 2–21c). Simply enough, the *supinator* muscle (with synergistic help from the *biceps brachii*) is responsible for supination of the forearm (Fig. 2–21b). The origins of, insertions of, primary functions of, and examples of exercises to develop the muscles that act at the wrist and forearm are presented in Table 2–12.

MUSCLES THAT ACT AT THE ELBOW.   The muscles that act at the elbow joint produce motion of the forearm (radius and ulna), and are easily remembered by the motions that their contractions produce. As you recall, the elbow (ulnohumeral) joint is a hinge joint, and as such permits motion in only one plane. In the case of the elbow, that one plane is the sagittal plane, and the only motions in the sagittal plane are flexion and extension. The flexors of the elbow, the *biceps brachii, brachialis,* and *brachioradialis,* are located on the anterior aspect of the arm (humerus) (Fig. 2–22). The *triceps brachii* is the major extensor of the elbow joint, and is located on the posterior aspect of the arm. As its name suggests, the triceps has three heads, or origins: one on the scapula and two on the proximal humerus. All three heads converge and insert via a common tendon into the *olecranon* process of the ulna (see Fig. 2–23). The origins of, insertions of, primary functions of, and examples of exercises to develop the muscles that act at the elbow joint are listed in Table 2–13.

MUSCLES THAT ACT AT THE SHOULDER.   As mentioned previously, the *shoulder* (glenohumeral) joint is the most mobile joint in the body. Accordingly, nine muscles cross the shoulder joint and act on the arm (humerus). We will concern ourselves here with only the major muscles of the shoulder. The two largest muscles, the *pectoralis major* and the *latissimus dorsi,* have their origins on the thorax. The pectoralis major has several important functions at the shoulder: flexion in the sagittal plane, adduction in the frontal plane,

Table 2–13   MAJOR MUSCLES THAT ACT ON THE ELBOW AND FOREARM

MUSCLE	ORIGIN	INSERTION	PRIMARY FUNCTION(S)	SELECTED EXERCISES
Biceps brachii	Long head from tubercle above glenoid cavity; short head from coracoid process of scapula	Radial tuberosity and bicipital aponeurosis	Flexion at elbow; supination at forearm	"Curling" with barbell, chin-ups, rock climbing, upright "rowing" with barbell
Brachialis	Anterior humerus	Ulnar tuberosity and coronoid process of ulna	Flexion at elbow	Same as for biceps brachii
Brachioradialis	Distal two-thirds of lateral condyloid ridge of humerus	Radial styloid process	Flexion at elbow	Same as for biceps brachii
Triceps brachii	Long head from lower edge of glenoid cavity of scapula; lateral head from posterior humerus; short head from distal two-thirds of posterior humerus	Olecranon process of ulna	Extension at elbow	Push-ups, dips on parallel bars, bench press, military press
Pronator teres	Distal end of medial humerus and medial aspect of ulna	Middle third of lateral radius	Flexion at elbow; pronation at forearm	Pronation of forearm with dumbbell

Figure 2–22 Superficial musculature of the anterior chest, shoulder, and arm (humerus).

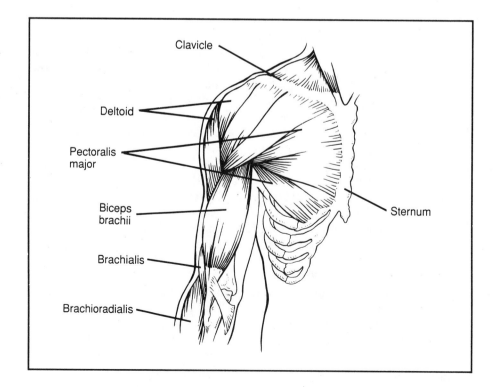

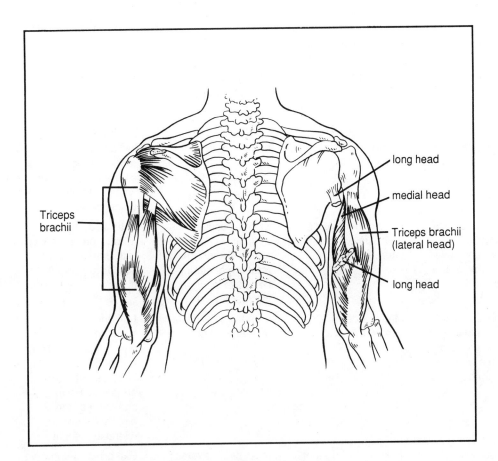

Figure 2–23 Major muscles of the posterior arm that effect the elbow.

long head

medial head

Triceps brachii (lateral head)

long head

Triceps brachii

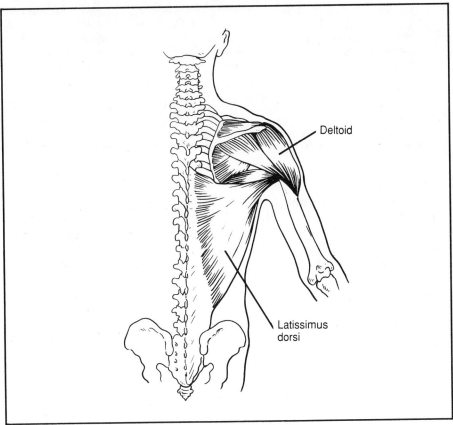

Figure 2–24 Superficial musculature of the posterior trunk.

Deltoid

Latissimus dorsi

Table 2–14   MAJOR MUSCLES THAT ACT AT THE SHOULDER

MUSCLE	ORIGIN	INSERTION	PRIMARY FUNCTION(S)	SELECTED EXERCISES
Pectoralis major	Clavicle, sternum, and first six costal cartilages	Greater tubercle of humerus	Flexion; adduction; medial rotation	Push-ups, pull-ups; incline bench press; regular bench press; climbing a rope; all types of throwing; tennis serve
Deltoid	Anterolateral clavicle, border of the acromion, and lower edge of spine of the scapula	Deltoid tubercle of humerus on mid-lateral surface	Entire muscle: abduction; anterior fibers: flexion, medial rotation; posterior fibers: extension, lateral rotation	Lateral "butterfly" (abduction) exercises with dumbbells; similar to pectoralis major
Latissimus dorsi	Lower six thoracic vertebrae, lumbar vertebrae, crests of ilium and sacrum, lower four ribs	Medial side of humerus	Extension; adduction; medial rotation	Pull-ups; rope climbing; dips on parallel bars; rowing; any exercise that involves pulling the arms downward against resistance, e.g., "lat" pulls on exercise machine
Rotator cuff	Various aspects of scapula	All insert on greater tubercle of humerus except for the subscapularis, which inserts on lesser tubercle of humerus	Infraspinatus teres minor: lateral rotation; subscapularis: medial rotation; supraspinatus: abduction	Exercises that involve medial and lateral rotation, e.g., tennis serve, throwing a baseball, medial and lateral rotation exercises from prone position with dumbbells

and medial (inward) rotation in the transverse plane (see Fig. 2–22). The latissimus dorsi arises posteriorly from the pelvis and lumbar and lower thoracic vertebrae. Interestingly, due to its medial insertion on the arm, the latissimus shares two functions with the pectoralis major. While the latissimus dorsi is a prime extensor of the shoulder joint, it complements the pectoralis as an adductor and medial rotator of the arm (Fig. 2–24).

The remaining muscles that act at the shoulder joint have their origins on the scapula itself. The *deltoid* muscle, a superficial muscle located on the superior aspect of the shoulder joint, resembles its name in several ways. The deltoid is shaped like a triangle (Greek letter delta = Δ), and it is also divided in three functional sections. The *anterior* deltoid fibers flex and medially (inwardly) rotate the arm. The *middle* portion of the deltoid is a primary abductor of the arm. The *posterior* deltoid fibers extend the arm as well as cause lateral (outward) rotation (see Figs. 2–22 and 2–24).

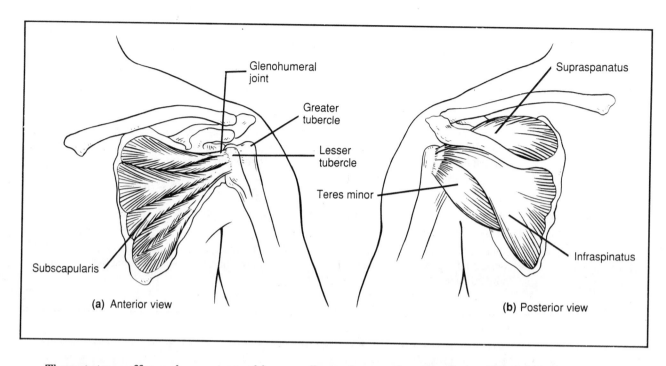

The **rotator cuff** muscles, a group of four small muscles, are functionally very important. These muscles act against the pull of gravity to hold the arm in the shoulder joint, as well as cause medial and lateral rotation of the arm (in the transverse plane). These muscles are frequently injured due to errors in training, e.g., general overuse, improper or insufficient warm-up, excessive repetitions of shoulder abduction with medial rotation. Inflammation of the rotator cuff muscles commonly results in a painful condition known as *impingement syndrome,* in which the swollen rotator cuff muscles and the bursa are "pinched" by the scapula when the arm is abducted. The personal trainer who recommends exercise regimens that include repeated overhead arm motions, e.g., swimming, weight training, racquet sports, and gymnastics, should closely monitor client performance in order to avoid inducing shoulder impingement syndrome. The rotator cuff muscles are easily remembered as the SITS muscles: the **s**upraspinatus, which abducts the arm; the **i**nfraspinatus and **t**eres minor, which laterally rotate the arm; and the **s**ubscapularis, which as its name describes, is located on the inferior surface of the scapula, and medially rotates the arm (Fig. 2-25). The origins of, insertions of, primary function(s) of, and examples of exercises designed to develop the muscles that cross the shoulder joint are presented in Table 2-14.

Figure 2–25 Muscles of the rotator cuff.

MUSCLES THAT ACT AT THE SCAPULOTHORACIC "JOINT." The primary function of the muscles and fascia that make up the soft tissue "joint" between the scapula and the trunk is to stabilize the scapula during movement of the arm (humerus). The four major muscles that anchor the scapula are named according to their shape (*trapezius, rhomboid major* and *minor*) and function (*levator scapulae*) (Fig. 2-26). Due to its shape and the varied directions of pull of its fibers, the superficial trapezius has several different functions. The *upper* portion of the trapezius is responsible for elevation of the scapula (example: shrugging the shoulders). The *middle* section of the trapezius has horizontally directed fibers, resulting in adduction of the scapula when contracted. The fibers of the *lower* portion of the trapezius angle downward toward their attachment on the thoracic vertebrae. Contraction of the lower trapezius primarily results in depression and adduction of the scapula. Deep to the trapezius are the *rhomboids* (major and minor), which work in unison to produce adduction

Table 2–15   MAJOR MUSCLES THAT ACT AT THE SHOULDER GIRDLE

MUSCLE	ORIGIN	INSERTION	PRIMARY FUNCTION(S)	SELECTED EXERCISES
Trapezius	Occipital bone, spines of cervical and thoracic vertebrae	Acromion process and spine of scapula	Upper: elevation of scapula; middle: adduction of scapula; lower: depression of scapula	Upright rowing, shoulder shrugs with resistance
Levator scapulae	Upper four or five cervical vertebrae	Vertebral border of scapula	Elevation of scapula	Shoulder shrugs with resistance
Rhomboids (major and minor)	Spines of seventh cervical through fifth thoracic vertebrae	Vertebral border of scapula	Adduction and elevation of scapula	Chin-ups, supported dumbbell bentover rows

Figure 2–26   Muscles that act on the scapulothoracic "joint."

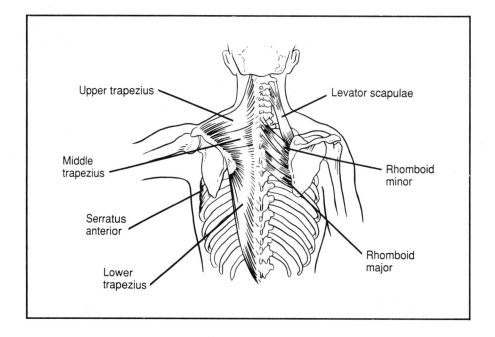

and slight elevation of the scapula (see Fig. 2-26). Good muscle tone in the rhomboids will help maintain good upper back posture, and thereby avoid the "rounded shoulders" posture. The *levator scapulae* muscle runs from the upper cervical vertebrae to the medial border of the scapula, and, together with the upper part of the trapezius, elevates the scapula. The origins of, insertions of, primary functions(s) of, and examples of exercises to develop the muscles of the scapulothoracic "articulation" are listed in Table 2-15.

SUMMARY

Personal trainers are required to design programs that are safe and effective and that accomplish the desired fitness and/or personal goals of clients. Without a fundamental understanding of human anatomy, this task is nearly impossible. Anatomical terminology and the five major anatomical systems—cardiovascular, respiratory, nervous, skeletal, and muscular— were presented. With this information, personal trainers have at their disposal sufficient information to identify specific exercises and physical activities that will efficiently accomplish the fitness goals of clients.

REFERENCES

Gardner, E., Gray, D.J., O'Rahilly, R. (1975). *Anatomy: A regional study of human structure*, (4th ed.). Philadelphia: Saunders.

Guiton, A. C. (1991) *Textbook of medical physiology*, (8th ed.). Philadelphia: Saunders

Hay, J.G. & Reid, J.G. (1988). *Anatomy, mechanics, and human motion*, (2nd ed.), pp. 3-108, Englewood Cliffs, NJ: Prentice Hall.

Kreighbaum, E. (1987). *Anatomy and kinesiology*. In Van Gelder, N. & Marks, S. (Eds.), *Aerobic dance-exercise instructor manual* (pp.35-88), San Diego: American Council on Exercise.

Rush, P. J. (1989). *Kinesiology and applied anatomy*, (7th ed.). Philadelphia: Lea & Febiger.

Spence, A.P. & Mason, E.B. (1979). *Human anatomy and physiology*. Menlo Park, CA: Benjamin/Cummings.

Thompson, C.W. (1979). *Manual of structural kinesiology*, (11th ed.). St. Louis: Times Mirror/Mosby.

Tortora, G.I. (1983). *Principles of human anatomy*, (3rd ed.). New York: Harper & Row.

SUGGESTED READING

Clemente, C.D. (1975). *A regional atlas of the human body*. Philadelphia: Lea & Febiger.

Drinkwater, B.L., Bruemner, B., & Chestnut, C.H. III. (1990). Menstrual history as a determinant of current bone density in young athletes. *Journal of the American Medical Assoc.* 263(4) 545-548.

Pansky, B. & Allen, D.J. (1980). *Review of neuroscience*. New York: Macmillan.

Snow-Harter, C., Bouxsein, M., Lewis, B., et al. (June, 1990). Muscle strength as a predictor of bone mineral density in young women. *Journal of Bone & Mineral Research.* 5(6), 589-595.

Snow-Harter, C. & Marcus, R. (November 1989). Exercise and regulation of bone mass. *Bone* 6(4), 45-48.

Biomechanics and Applied Kinesiology

3

DEBORAH L. ELLISON

DEBORAH ELLISON, P.T., is a registered physical therapist and personal trainer and is founder and president of A*plus*Workshops. Through her company she serves as a fitness consultant, frequent convention speaker and an international fitness instructor trainer. She chairs the Accreditation Commission of the American Council on Exercise, participated as an item writer for the personal trainer certification exam, and has served on the American Council on Exercise staff as the first director of education. Having published numerous articles on exercise technique, she is now writing her first book on the subject.

IN THIS CHAPTER:

- Concepts of biomechanics, including center of gravity, line of gravity and base of support, and forces and motion.
- Physical laws affecting motion: inertia, acceleration and momentum, impact and reactive forces, linear and rotary motion, levers and torque.
- Musculoskeletal considerations, including kinds of muscular contraction.
- Applied kinesiology.
- Muscles and movements of the upper extremity: shoulder girdle, rotator cuff, and shoulder joint.

- Injury prevention.
- Muscles and movements of the pelvis and lower extremity, including pelvic tilt, hip, deep external rotators, hamstrings, knee joint, ankle, and foot.
- Posture and muscle imbalance.
- Examples of movement analysis.
- Examples of exercise analysis.

Kinesiology is the study of the principles of mechanics and anatomy in relation to human movement. It's one of the fun parts of exercise science because it's here that trainers can really *use* their knowledge of anatomy and biomechanics to do something creative with clients. Trainers need to understand the physical principles governing objects in motion and how the body responds to gravity (mechanics). They also need to know where the muscles attach and how they cross the joints (anatomy). It isn't necessary to memorize a long list of muscle functions. Rather, by simply visualizing the muscles' attachments and the fiber directions and employing a knowledge of biomechanics, the trainer can logically determine what the muscle does, in any position and against any kind of resistance. By mastering the principles in this chapter, trainers can critique the exercises they see and decide for themselves how effective they are. They can create their own exercise programs and design more mechanically safe and effective forms of traditional exercises. They will also understand why certain movements are unsafe, and therefore avoid them.

BIOMECHANICS

Motion is a change of an object's position or place in relation to another object. Thus, whether an object is moving or at rest depends on reference point. For example, a sleeping baby in a car travelling 30 mph is at rest if the car seat is the reference point. If the road is the reference point, however, the baby is in motion.

To analyze body movement, it is necessary to choose a reference point; otherwise the analysis becomes confusing.

Center of Gravity

To track the motion of an object, we look at its **center of gravity**—the center of its **mass**. For something rigid and of uniform density, like a baseball, this point is at its geometric center. But the location of the center of gravity in the ever-changing human body is more difficult to find. The body's center of gravity is the point at which its mass balances out in all planes (frontal, sagittal, transverse). It is the point at which its mass is considered to concentrate. We also consider gravity as acting through this point in its constant downward pull. Thus, a body's center of mass is its center of gravity.

Although finding a person's center of gravity in varying positions can get complicated (it changes from person to person, depending on build), it is generally located at the level of the second sacral vertebra. The center of gravity also changes with a person's position in space and whether he/she is supporting external weight. For example, when a client is standing erect, the center of gravity is within the pelvis (second sacral vertebra). With exercise such as the trunk curl, the center of gravity shifts toward the chest as the arms are raised toward the head (see Fig. 3-1). This shift will affect the **range of motion** during the curl and the muscular force required to lift the upper body.

Line of Gravity and Base of Support

Gravity acts in a straight line through the body's center of gravity and toward the center of the earth. This line of gravitational pull is the **line of gravity**. To stay balanced without moving, a person's line of gravity must fall within the **base of support**, that is, the area beneath the body that is encompassed when you connect, via one continuous line, all points of the body that are in contact with the ground (e.g., the position of the feet if the person is standing). A large, wide base of support is more stable than a small, narrow one. Thus, standing with one's feet apart and toes turned out is more stable than with them very close together and parallel. As an example, when performing side-lying leg raises, one is more stable when bending the bottom leg because the base of support is broader. To remain balanced while standing, without excessive muscular effort or strain, the body must be equally distributed about the line of gravity (within the base of support). This is what we call good posture. Such balanced alignment prevents excessive stress on muscles and ligaments.

Forward locomotion such as walking or running is actually the process of losing and catching one's balance. The line of gravity moves beyond the base of support, then the feet are moved to reestablish the base of support underneath

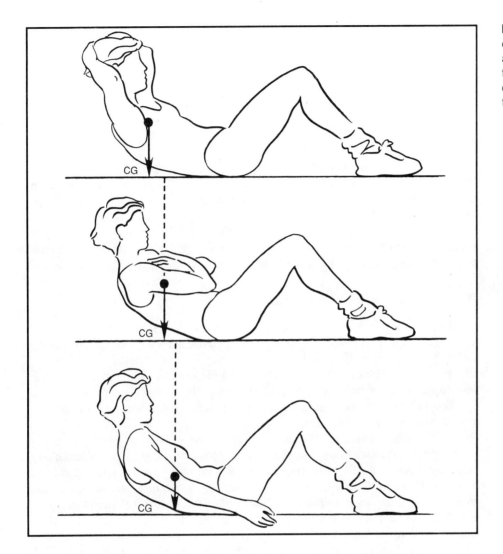

Figure 3–1 Trunk curls with changing arm positions. The arrow indicates the point in the body at which the center of gravity (CG) is acting as the arm position is changed.

it. The muscles exert forces to counteract the force of gravity and propel the body forward.

Forces and Motion

A **force** is something that causes motion. There are many kinds of force: internal, external, motive, resistive, and applied. A force is either internal or external, depending on the reference point chosen. When we speak of the hip joint, the force of muscle contraction is external to the joint. When we speak of the whole body, muscle contraction is an internal force. Internal forces acting alone cannot cause movement.

Motive and resistive forces are external forces. A **motive force** is an external force that causes an increase in speed or change in direction. A **resistive force** is an external force that resists the motion of another external force. Motion occurs when the motive and resistive forces acting on a body or segment are unequal.

Generally, forces outside the human body are referred to as **applied forces**. They may be motive, such as being pushed off balance by someone, or resistive such as free weights, variable-resistance machines, elastic bands or tubing, and manual resistance.

PHYSICAL LAWS AFFECTING MOTION

In order to understand forces and their effects on human movement, it is first necessary to understand the physical laws that apply to the motion of all objects, namely, inertia, acceleration and momentum, and impact and reactive forces.

Inertia

Sir Isaac Newton formulated three laws regarding motion. His first law is the **law of inertia**: A body at rest stays at rest, and a body in motion stays in motion with the same velocity and direction unless acted on by unbalanced forces. A body's inertia is proportional to its mass. For example, a lead weight has more inertia than a piece of plastic of the same dimensions. Therefore it is harder to start moving a denser object than a lighter one. It is also harder to stop the denser object than the lighter one moving at the same velocity.

Acceleration and Momentum

Newton's second law is the **law of acceleration**. It states that the force (F) acting on a body in a given direction is equal to the body's mass (m) multiplied by the body's acceleration (a) in that direction: $F = ma$. Another way to state this is that the acceleration of a body is proportional to the magnitude of the force applied: $a = F/m$. The acceleration occurs in the direction of the force.

The second law also relates to a moving body's momentum. **Linear momentum** is the force with which a body moves, and is equal to its mass times its velocity. Momentum will increase if the mass of the body increases. As momentum increases, stopping the motion requires more force. Momentum can play a positive role in human movement and plays an important role in sports such as football and judo. However, excessive momentum can cause injury, especially when working with weights. Weightlifting should occur at speeds that are under complete muscular control. If momentum, rather than muscular control, is used to lift a weight that's too heavy, the acceleration and the resulting force may exceed the muscles' ability to stop the motion. This exposes the connective tissues and joint structures to risk of injury.

Impact and Reactive Forces

Newton's third law states that for every force applied by one body to a second, the second applies an equal force on the first, but in the opposite direction. Thus, for every action there is an equal and opposite reaction. This law has bearing on the impact forces that the body must absorb during activities such as running, jumping, and high-impact aerobics. According to Newton's third law, the earth exerts a force against the body equal to the force applied to the earth as one runs or jumps. Combine Newton's second law (force equals mass multiplied by acceleration) with this third law and you begin to understand the magnitude of the impact on feet and body: mass multiplied by downward acceleration equals the reactive force from the earth that the body must dissipate. Such forces can multiply quickly in high-impact activities. Thus we see why overuse and stress injuries can be a problem with high-impact activities.

Linear and Rotary Motion

There are two basic types of movement, linear and rotary. When an object in motion is not tied down anywhere, it moves in **linear motion**. It can move either in a straight line (*rectilinear motion*) or in a curved line (*curvilinear motion*), such as the path of a ball thrown through the air. If the object is tied down at some point, it turns around the fixed point in **rotary** (or angular) **motion**, such as a tetherball or most joints of the body. We experience linear motion when we ride a bicycle or an elevator. On the bicycle, some body parts also experience rotary motion (hips, knees, ankles). The body as a whole undergoes rotary motion around the center of gravity during a somersault or a cartwheel. At the same time, we are in linear motion across the floor. Thus it is possible to be in linear and rotary motion simultaneously.

Levers and Torque

The body's skeletal structure is constructed as a system of levers. A **lever** is a rigid bar with a fixed point around which it can rotate when an external force is applied. The fixed point (joint) is its **fulcrum**. The **axis of rotation** is the imaginary line or point about which the lever rotates. This imaginary line is perpendicular to the plane of movement. In the body, a joint is a fulcrum for rotary motion of the bones. The axis of rotation intersects the center of the joint (see Fig. 3–2).

For rotation to occur, the motive force must contact the lever at some distance from the axis of rotation. It also must be great enough to overcome any resistive force (remember, the external forces must be unbalanced). The perpendicular distance from the axis to the line of the force is called a **lever arm**. The lever arm length of the motive force (F) is the **force arm** (Fa). The lever arm length of the resistance (R) is the resistance arm (Ra). The lever is in balance if the force times the force arm equals the resistance times the resistance arm. (F×Fa = R×Ra).

The turning effect of a force operating on a lever at some distance from the axis of rotation is called **torque**. The amount of torque is found by multiplying the amount of force by the length of the lever arm (perpendicular distance from the axis of rotation). Therefore, F×Fa is the torque of the motive force, and R×Ra is the torque of the resistance. If the force and resistance torques are equal, no rotation occurs and the system is balanced. When one torque is greater, rotation occurs in the direction of the greater torque.

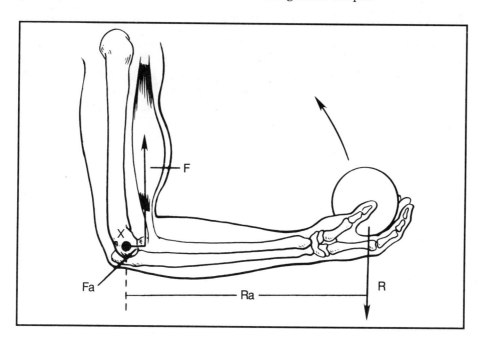

Figure 3–2 Example of a lever system in the human body. X = axis of rotation, F = motive force, R = resistance, Fa = lever arm of the motive force, Ra = lever arm of the resistance.

Figure 3–3 The three classes of levers. X = axis of rotation (fulcrum), R = resistance load, F = effort force, Fa = lever arm distance from the force to the axis (force arm), Ra = lever arm distance from the resistance to the axis (resistance arm). The product of force and force lever arm balances the product of the resistance and resistance lever arm in this example (F x Fa = R x Ra); therefore, the resulting torques (turning effects) are equal.

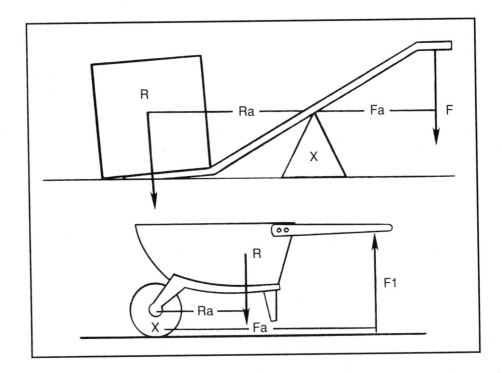

Lever Classes

There are three classes of levers, determined by the relative locations of the axis, force, and resistance. The first two classes are demonstrated primarily outside the body (tools such as the crow bar [I] and the wheelbarrow [II]; see Fig. 3–3). The third class of levers is seen inside the body. The body operates primarily as a series of third-class levers when the muscles shorten as they contract. In third-class levers, the force (F) acts between the axis (X) and the resistance (R), as in the example of the biceps action at the elbow in Figure 3–2. Note the locations of the axis, force, and resistance.

Musculoskeletal Considerations

Levers such as the crow bar and the wheelbarrow enable us to lift heavy weight with a relatively small force. However, the levers in the human body do not usually give the muscles a mechanical advantage for lifting weight. The attachments are typically close to the joint and therefore must use a short lever arm. Since the bones are relatively long, with resistance applied at the end (long lever arm), the forces necessary to lift even small weights are larger than we might imagine. For example, to abduct the arm to 80° with a 10-pound weight in the hand may require up to 300 pounds of tension in the deltoid. If the deltoid connected one inch farther down (longer lever arm for the force) and the arm were two inches shorter (shorter lever arm for the resistance), it would take much less muscular force to lift the same weight. Also, if we shortened the lever arm of the resistance by bending the elbow or attaching the weight at the elbow, we could move it with much less tension in the deltoid.

Although the body's lever system presents mechanical disadvantages to the muscles, it's very conducive to speed. With a small force of contraction of the deltoid, the hand can move a great distance. With tools that extend the lever arm beyond the hand, such as a tennis racquet, great acceleration can be achieved. Remembering that force equals mass times acceleration, we

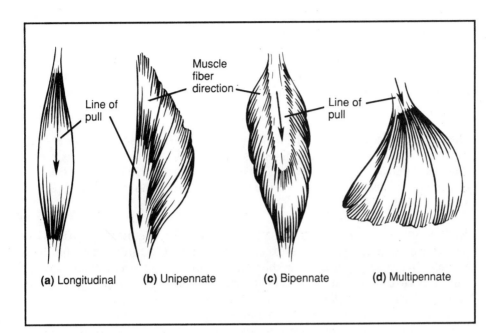

Figure 3–4 Muscle fiber arrangements.

realize that the human form can create significant striking or throwing forces but relatively small lifting forces.

There are anatomical factors, however, that increase a muscle's ability to create force. The muscle's fiber arrangement is one such anatomical factor. There are several kinds of fiber arrangements, including penniform (unipennate, bipennate, multipennate) and longitudinal (see Fig. 3-4). Most muscles in the body are *penniform* muscles, in which the fibers lie diagonally to the line of pull. (The line of pull is generally thought of as a straight line between the muscle's two points of attachment.) This type of muscle is thicker (greater cross section); therefore, more fibers can contribute to force production. The quadriceps is an example of a penniform muscle that can produce significant amounts of force. *Longitudinal* muscles are long and thin and have parallel fibers running in the same direction as the length of the muscle. This type of fiber arrangement allows for speed of contraction. However, since the cross section is small, the force of contraction is small. The sartorius is an example of a longitudinal fiber arrangement.

There are, of course, additional physiological factors that affect muscle strength, such as the number and size of muscle fibers, fiber type, and neurological training and recruitment. However, it is always important to consider the biomechanical factors when designing a client's conditioning program.

Kinds of Muscular Contraction

When a muscle contracts it develops tension or force. However, the verb *contract* can be misleading when it refers to muscles, since it means "to come together." When a muscle contracts, it actually may shorten (come together), lengthen (away from the middle), or remain the same.

STATIC (ISOMETRIC) CONTRACTION.   When resistance is greater than or matches the tension in a muscle and no visible movement occurs, this is called **isometric contraction**. The resistance may come from the opposing muscle group (cocontraction) or from another force such as gravity, an immovable object, or weight-training equipment. Bodybuilders use isometric cocontraction when striking a pose to show their muscle development. Physical therapists use isometrics in rehabilitation following an injury when the joint must not move. Personal trainers may use isometrics in certain stretching techniques, such as a PNF hold-relax (See Ch. 9). They can also be included in strengthening programs, for example, brief holds in the up-phase of a trunk curl or pushup. (See Ch. 8 for pros and cons of isometric exercise.)

CONCENTRIC (SHORTENING) CONTRACTION. When the force generated by a muscle is greater than an applied resistance, the muscle shortens as it contracts and moves the resistance. This is called **concentric contraction**. For example, the biceps contracts concentrically in the up-phase of a biceps curl with a dumbbell.

ECCENTRIC (LENGTHENING) CONTRACTION. An **eccentric contraction** occurs when an external force exceeds the contractile force generated by a muscle. In eccentric contraction the muscle is producing force but also returning to its resting length from a shortened position. The muscle "gives in" to or is overwhelmed by the external force. For example, the biceps contracts eccentrically in the return phase of a biceps curl with a dumbbell.

An understanding of muscle contractions is crucial to exercise analysis. Joint motion alone does not accurately reveal the muscle causing that motion. For example, hip abduction and adduction could occur by the concentric or the eccentric contractions of different muscles, depending on the circumstances.

The body's position and the direction of gravity's pull often are clues to which muscle is contracting and how. If the movement occurs against the pull of gravity, the agonist normally performing that joint action is contracting concentrically. If the movement is slow and controlled and occurs in the same direction as the pull of gravity, the antagonist muscle is contracting eccentrically. (The motion must be slower than the segment in free fall with no muscle action. An eccentric contraction, then, provides a "braking" action on the movement.) If the motion occurs in the direction of gravity but is faster than the acceleration of gravity or occurs against external resistance, the cause is a concentric contraction of the agonist. When the movement occurs perpendicular to the pull of gravity, it is usually due to alternating concentric contractions of the expected muscle groups.

As an illustration, let us consider hip abduction and adduction (Fig. 3-5). In Figure 3-5a (side-lying leg raise), the initial action is hip abduction

Figure 3–5 Hip abduction and adduction. (a) Side-lying leg raise; (b) supine with feet toward ceiling, legs pulled apart and together.

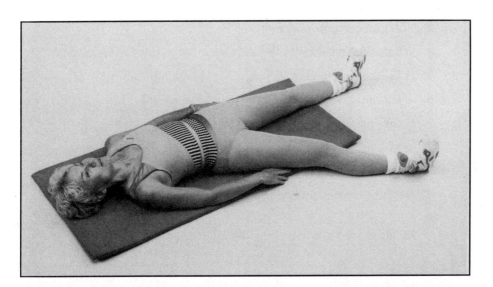

Figure 3–5 (c) Supine. with legs extended on the floor.

occurring against gravity. Therefore, the agonists (the hip abductors) are contracting concentrically. In the return phase of the side leg raise, the joint action is hip adduction. However, since the motion occurs slowly in the same direction as gravity, hip adduction is controlled by the hip abductors contracting eccentrically. However, performing a side leg raise and then bringing the leg down very fast, or pushing against some type of external resistance, involves a concentric contraction of the hip adductors (agonists for the joint action). In Figure 3–5b (lying supine, feet toward ceiling), the first action is horizontal abduction of the hip as the legs move apart. However, since the movement occurs in the same direction as gravity, the hip adductors control the motion by eccentric contraction. In bringing the legs together again, the hip adduction is occurring against gravity, by concentric contraction of the adductors. In Figure 3–5c (lying supine, legs extended on the floor), the joint actions are hip abduction and adduction. The actions occur neither against nor in the same direction as gravity. They occur in the plane perpendicular to the pull of gravity; therefore, the effect of gravity is not a factor. The hip abductors contract concentrically as the hip abducts, and the hip adductors contract concentrically as the hip adducts.

APPLIED KINESIOLOGY

At the heart of kinesiology is the analysis of movement and exercise. To perform such analysis, the personal trainer must understand motion and the forces that cause and resist motion. In addition, he/she must know human anatomy. An understanding of the mechanical principles of levers, lever arms, and torque; the center and line of gravity; and muscular contractions and gravity's effect on those contractions is also necessary.

The Goal: Exercise Analysis

To analyze and design effective exercise programs, the personal trainer first has to know what muscles are working during the various movements. In order to break down a movement or exercise into understandable parts, it helps to ask ourselves the following questions:

> **1.** What is the goal of the exercise?

2. What movements occur at each joint?

3. What is the position of the body segment in relation to gravity?

4. Is the movement slow or fast, against resistance or not?

5. What muscles are causing the joint movement?

6. Is the contraction concentric, eccentric, or isometric?

7. Which muscles are movers and which are stabilizers?

8. Does the movement achieve the stated goal of the exercise?

9. Does the movement compromise the safety of other body parts?

10. How can the exercise be adapted to meet the specific needs of the client (made more difficult or less difficult)?

These questions should be used as a guideline in analyzing old exercises and developing new ones. Keep these questions in mind as we examine the muscles and movements of the human body, including joint and muscle function.

There are several factors to consider in accurately assessing muscle function: joint movement, muscle attachment, line of pull or fiber direction, and biomechanical influences. We need to look at each muscle's location, the line of pull, and its attachment in relation to the axis of the joint—in front (**anterior**), behind (**posterior**), above (**superior**), below (**inferior**), to the inside (**medial**), or to the outside (**lateral**). If we know the location of a muscle and its attachments and can visualize the muscle's line of pull as the fibers come together, we can deduce what the muscle does as it contracts concentrically. We can figure out what movements occur, and the muscles that cause those movements, without memorizing a long list of muscle functions. Although electromyographic studies have demonstrated some exceptions, this method of determining muscle function is quite adequate for general training purposes.

As a muscle contracts concentrically, the two attachments (origin and insertion) move closer together. Both ends of the muscle move toward the middle. An easy example to visualize is the abdominal crunch pictured in Figure 3–6a. If one attachment (the origin) is stabilized, the other will move toward it in a concentric contraction as in a reverse abdominal curl. In a reverse curl (see Fig. 3–6b), the head and shoulders stay on the ground, the feet are in the air, and the abdominal muscles contract to tilt the pelvis and lift the hips from the floor. The insertion (the more distal attachment) can also be stabilized. Then as the muscle contracts, the "other end" will move. For

Figure 3–6   Assessing muscle function. (a) Abdominal crunch; (b) reverse abdominal curl.

Figure 3–6 (c)   Standard abdominal curl.

example, see the standard abdominal curl shown in Figure 3–6c. Performing a posterior pelvic tilt prior to the curl stabilizes the insertion of the abdominal muscle. Utilizing these variations for each muscle group, when possible, can help the trainer develop more exercise alternatives for any particular muscle group.

Also, the location of the muscle's attachment in relation to the joint will influence its function at a particular time. A muscle's line of pull may change as the position of the joint changes. For example, the biceps muscle crosses the shoulder joint anteriorly (in front). Therefore, when the shoulder is in a neutral position, the biceps participates in shoulder flexion. But, when the shoulder is externally rotated, the long head of the biceps moves laterally. The line of pull is then superior to the joint; so, with the shoulder externally rotated, the biceps is a shoulder abductor.

MUSCLES AND MOVEMENTS OF THE UPPER EXTREMITY

The shoulder (glenohumeral) joint is the articulation between the glenoid fossa of the scapula and the humerus. As a multiaxial joint, it allows movement in three planes. Therefore, many motions are possible: flexion and extension in the saggital plane, abduction and adduction in the frontal plane, external and internal rotation and horizontal flexion and extension in the transverse plane, and circumduction in a combination of planes. Movements of the upper arm are actually the result of motion at several joints. However, only movements of the scapula and the glenohumeral joint will be discussed here.

The scapula and glenohumeral joints work together and use highly co-ordinated, synchronized movements to perform most functions of the upper extremities. One such coordinated effort is called scapulo-humeral rhythm. Studies have shown that in a 90° shoulder abduction, 30° of that motion is scapular motion and 60° is glenohumeral joint movement.

Posterior Shoulder Girdle Muscles

In activities of daily living, the scapular muscles usually function as stabilizers. That is, they hold the upper body in position so that we can reach, flex, push, or pull with arms and hands. Some also stabilize the humerus in its socket. Their stabilizing function has earned them the name *posterior shoulder girdle* muscles. Scapular movements controlled by the posterior shoulder girdle muscles are pictured in Figure 3-7. They include adduction and abduction (sometimes called retraction and protraction), elevation and depression, and upward and downward rotation.

TRAPEZIUS.   Shoulder girdle muscles generally run from the spine to the scapula. The largest and most superficial of these is the trapezius (see Fig. 3-8) which attaches along the base of the skull, at all the cervical vertebrae, and at all the thoracic vertebrae. At the other end, it attaches to the scapular spine. Because the muscle's origin is very broad, the fibers actually travel in three very different directions; as such, they function as three different muscles. As can be seen from the fiber direction of the upper trapezius in Figure 3-8, if the upper fibers contracted while the head stayed still, the scapula would move up and toward the spine; that is, it would elevate and adduct. The fibers of the middle trapezius are horizontal between the spine and the scapula. Thus, when they contract, the scapula adducts, or moves toward the spine (since the spine is stable).

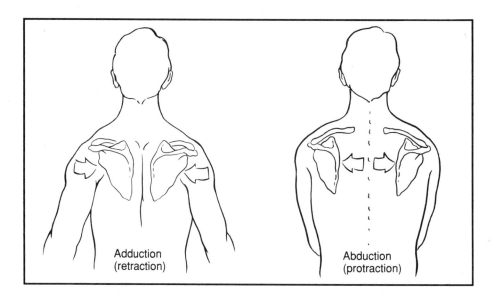

Figure 3-7   Scapular movements.

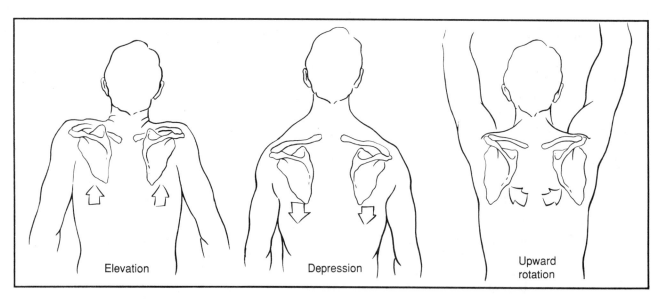

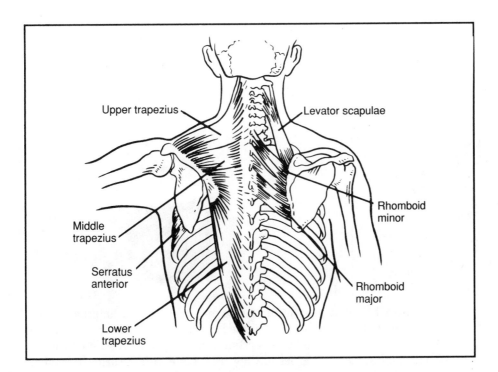

Figure 3–8 Posterior shoulder girdle muscle.

The lower trapezius fibers are on a diagonal, with the origin along the lower thoracic spine moving up and outward to the scapula. Thus, when they contract, the scapula moves down (depresses) and in (adducts). The lower trapezius fibers also participate in downward rotation of the scapula. If the arms are raised in front, or out to the side, the shoulder blades rotate, with the lower corner moving upward and away from the spine. This upward rotation of the scapula occurs as the upper and middle trapezius, rhomboids, and serratus anterior pull on different edges of the scapula (see Fig. 3-8). The lower trapezius fibers return the scapula to neutral position (downward rotation), assisted by the rhomboids and the levator scapulae.

Let us now use the different parts of the trapezius to apply the biomechanical principles presented thus far. To effectively strengthen a muscle, it must contract against external resistance, such as a variable-resistance machine, or the body must be positioned so the muscle is contracting against gravity. In this *antigravity position*, the body segment (either the limb or the whole body) is lifted against gravity.

Here are the antigravity positions required to effectively strengthen the three parts of the trapezius muscle. For the upper fibers, it is necessary to perform a shoulder shrug: the client stands erect and brings the scapulae up and together toward the spine. The origin of the muscle is stabilized and the scapulae are moving upward against gravity. To achieve muscle balance, the upper trapezius muscle typically needs strengthening through the full range of motion. However, it is advisable to avoid exercises that require the upper trapezius to contract isometrically for long periods of time, such as many little arm circles with the arms extended at shoulder level. During this endeavor, the upper trapezius contracts isometrically to maintain the scapular position. Then as the deltoid muscle fatigues, the upper trapezius elevates the scapula to maintain the appearance of the arm at the horizontal (90°). There are many other ways to effectively exercise the other shoulder and arm muscles without putting the upper trapezius under such strain.

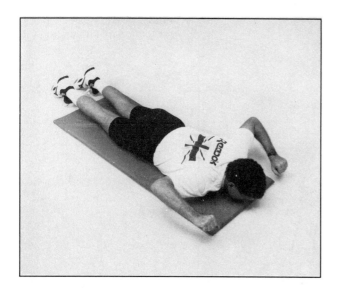

Figure 3–9   Scapular adduction. (a) Prone; (b) standing.

The upper trapezius also needs stretching. Because of habitual forward head posture, with the cervical vertebrae hyperextended, the upper trapezius muscles contract isometrically and eccentrically in a very restricted range of motion throughout the day, especially if work is done with the arms in front and unsupported. Over time, the muscles adapt to this position, often becoming shortened and tight.

To effectively stretch a muscle, the muscle must be placed so that the origin and insertion of the muscle are pulled away from each other, opposite to the primary motion of the muscle when it contracts concentrically. To effectively stretch the upper trapezius, the muscle should be positioned opposite to a shoulder shrug, with the shoulder depressed and the head tilted slightly forward and to the opposite side.

To put the middle trapezius in an antigravity position, the client should lie face down with arms out to the sides and elbows bent. Then the client should squeeze the shoulder blades together and lift the arms, keeping them parallel to the floor (see Fig. 3-9a). However, performing this same movement upright (Fig. 3-9b) is much less effective, since the middle trapezius would contract, but with virtually no resistance. The primary muscular overload in that position would be the isometric contraction of the middle deltoid and

Figure 3–10   Applying resistance to bilateral scapular adductors. (a) Elastic resistance; (b) manual resistance.

upper trapezius required to hold the arms abducted at 90°, which can reinforce existing tightness in the upper trapezius.

However, if another external force is applied as resistance, such as elastic bands or tubing, the options expand. The client could then effectively resist the middle trapezius in an upright position because the muscle would be contracting against the resistance of the elastic band or tubing (Fig. 3–10a). One could also apply manual resistance at the elbow (Fig. 3–10b). The trainer should, however, still consider limiting the time spent with the upper trapezius and deltoid in isometric contraction.

An advanced exercise for the lower and middle fibers would be a pull-up. (See Fig. 3–11). In the starting position for a pull-up, the scapulae are abducted and upwardly rotated because of the arm position. To accomplish a pull-up, the lower and middle fibers of the trapezius must contract strongly to stabilize the scapulae (adduct, depress, and downwardly rotate) so that the arms can adduct and lift the body to clear the chin over the bar. In the case of the pull-up exercise, the muscles are having to lift the body weight against gravity.

RHOMBOIDS.   Another posterior shoulder group is the rhomboids (major and minor). They are located beneath the middle and upper trapezius (see Fig. 3–8). The fiber direction is not horizontal like the middle trapezius. Rather, the fibers run diagonally from the spine to the scapula like the upper trapezius, but at more of an angle, that is, closer to the vertical. Their function, then,

Figure 3–11   From the hanging position, the initial stage of a pull-up requires strong attraction of scapular adductors and depressors.

Figure 3–12 Rotator cuff muscles.

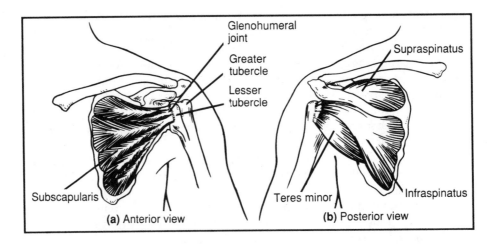

judging from the fiber direction, is to adduct and elevate the scapula. They also participate in downward rotation of the scapula.

LEVATOR SCAPULAE.   A third posterior shoulder girdle muscle is the levator scapulae. Its line of pull (see Fig. 3-8) is more vertical. Its contraction, then, would primarily elevate the scapula; hence, its name. It also participates in downward scapular rotation, and, to a lesser extent, scapular adduction.

Rotator Cuff Muscles

The other posterior muscles originate on the scapula and act at the gleno-humeral joint. They serve primarily as stabilizers and rotators. They are known as the rotator cuff muscles, because they rotate the shoulder joint. Their tendons form a cuff around the upper and posterior part of the joint. You may remember them better as the SITS muscles: *s*upraspinatus, *i*nfraspinatus, *t*eres minor, and *s*ubscapularis. They attach to the humerus in that order, start-ing at the top of the humerus and moving toward the back and then around underneath to the front (See Fig. 3-12). Their names tell us where they are located. The supraspinatus is above (supra) the spine (spinatus) of the scapula. The infraspinatus is below (infra) the scapular spine. The name *teres minor* doesn't tell us much, but it is located inferior to the infraspinatus. The subscapularis is located on the anterior side, or beneath (sub) the scapula (scapularis), and crosses anterior to the joint, attaching to the front of the humerus.

Knowing that the supraspinatus attaches high on the humerus, above (su-perior to) the joint, and considering the line of pull, we can tell that the muscle serves to abduct the humerus. It is also an effective stabilizer of the humerus in its socket, actively and passively resisting the downward pull of gravity that tends to pull the humerus out of its socket. Since it crosses the joint right on top, neither in front nor behind, it is the only one of the cuff muscles that does not actually rotate the humerus.

The infraspinatus and teres minor muscles attach in a cuff behind the supraspinatus, and their line of pull passes behind the joint on a slight diag-onal. Thus, when they contract, the humerus externally rotates. One way to strengthen these muscles is pictured in Figure 3-13. The line of pull of the subscapularis crosses anterior and slightly inferior to the joint, attaching in front of the supraspinatus. When it contracts, then, the humerus will rotate internally.

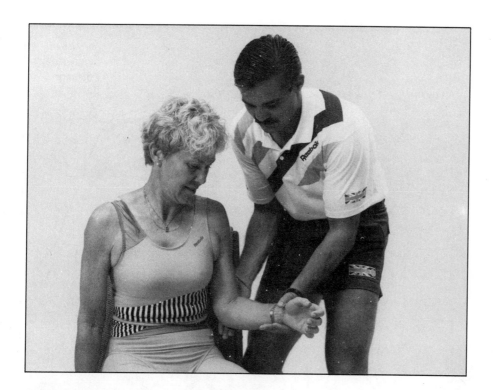

Figure 3–13   One way to strengthen the infraspinatus and teres minor muscles is via manual resistance.

Anterior Shoulder Girdle Muscles

The anterior shoulder girdle muscles, like the posterior girdle, attach the scapulae to the thorax. The primary ones are the serratus anterior and the pectoralis minor (see Fig. 3-14). The serratus anterior, already mentioned for its part working with the trapezius and rhomboids to upwardly rotate the scapula, gets its name because the front edge is serrated like a knife. The muscle enables forceful forward motion of the arm, such as a boxer's knockout punch. It also

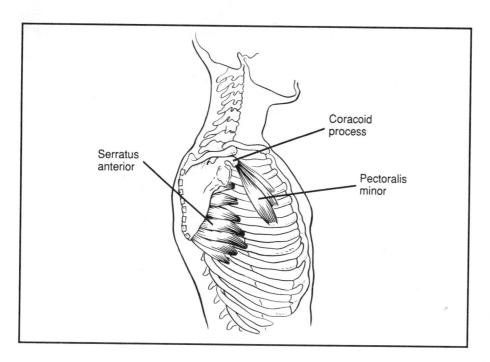

Figure 3–14   Anterior shoulder girdle muscle.

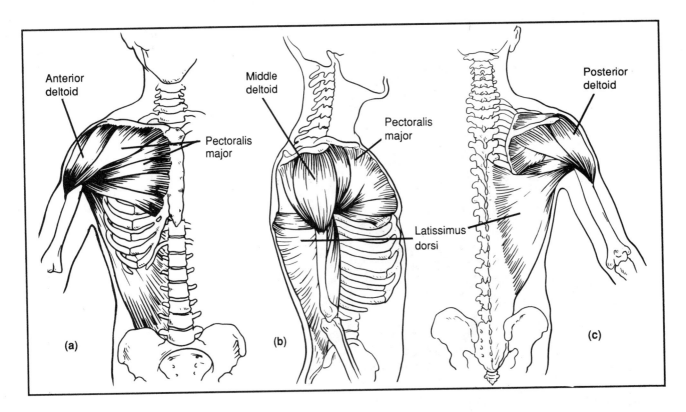

Figure 3–15 Muscles of the shoulder joint.

helps to keep the scapulae flat on the back, so when it is weak the scapulae may wing out, especially during an exercise such as a push-up. If winging occurs, the muscle should be strengthened individually before using push-ups. This can be done by having the client lie supine with the shoulder flexed and elbow extended while pushing a held weight toward the ceiling without bending the elbow.

The pectoralis minor can pull the scapula forward and down. When it is too short it contributes to a round-shouldered posture. Therefore, the primary concern in an exercise program would be to stretch this muscle. The only way to effectively stretch it is manually.

Muscles of the Shoulder Joint Proper

DELTOID.   The deltoid is easy to spot. Similar to the trapezius, the deltoid has fibers running in three different directions, and is identified by three names, according to fiber location relative to the joint (see Fig. 3–15). The muscle is multipenniform and attaches a good distance from the joint, making it a powerful mover of the shoulder joint in certain points of the range of motion.

Since the anterior deltoid attaches in front of the joint (anteriorly), contracting it concentrically in an antigravity position will flex the shoulder, raising the arm overhead. It will also participate in horizontal adduction and internal rotation of the shoulder.

In an antigravity position for shoulder flexion, such as sitting or standing, the anterior deltoid is a shoulder flexor. Look at what happens, though, if shoulder flexion occurs while lying on the back: Half of the motion, upward to the vertical, is against gravity, so the first half is accomplished by a concentric contraction of the anterior deltoid. However, once past the vertical, the motion occurs in the same direction as gravity, so the resisting force is an eccentric contraction of the antagonists (shoulder extensors—posterior deltoid and latissimus). These are important considerations when recommending positions in which to perform exercises and making the best use of limited time with a client. The middle deltoid's line of pull passes above (superior to) the joint, like the supraspinatus. Concentrically, then, its function is shoulder abduction. An eccentric contraction would lower the arm into adduction, such as when the arm is held out to the side and then returned to the resting position. Again, body position in relation to gravity is important. Eccentric contractions occur when the movement happens slowly in the same direction as gravity.

Because the fibers of the posterior deltoid pass behind the joint, it functions as a shoulder extensor and horizontal abductor. To effectively strengthen the posterior deltoid, use the principles of antigravity positioning and eccentric contraction. With the weight of the arm as resistance or holding weights as external resistance, position the client's body so the muscle must contract concentrically to extend or horizontally abduct the shoulder against gravity, then contract eccentrically to return the shoulder to the resting position. This could be achieved by having the client lie face down (prone) on a bench, stand in a supported forward lunge position, or half-kneel with the chest supported on the forward thigh. Alternately, the client could use elastic bands or tubing as resistance or manual resistance in any position because then gravity would not be an important factor.

LATISSIMUS DORSI AND TERES MAJOR. The teres major and latissimus dorsi would be effectively strengthened in the same way as the posterior deltoid. They both participate in shoulder extension against resistance. Figure 3–15 shows the position and fiber directions of the latissimus dorsi and teres major muscles. Their fiber directions are very similar, though the teres major attaches to the lower corner of the scapula, whereas the latissimus has a much broader attachment along the lower thoracic spine and the entire lumbar spine. The latissimus is more active in extension when the arm is raised between 30° and 90°. They both cross the shoulder joint interiorly, so they would act to adduct the shoulder. The teres major participates only against resistance or when the arm is already behind the back. The attachments of these muscles to the humerus also place them in a position to internally rotate the arm, though there is controversy about their participation in this movement.

In the absence of variable-resistance equipment, a good way to provide progressive resistance to these muscles is to have clients perform a lat pull-down against elastic bands or tubing held by the opposite hand. Swimming, rowing, and lifting the body up on parallel bars will also strengthen these muscles.

PECTORALIS MAJOR. Another muscle that shares at least one common function with the latissimus dorsi is the pectoralis major (see Fig. 3–15). Note that its insertion on the humerus is very close to the latissimus and that it has a broad origin along the sternum and the clavicle. The fibers of the clavicular portion are similar in direction and function to the anterior deltoid. The fibers of the sternal portion are more horizontal, and may actually oppose the function of the clavicular portion at certain angles. Therefore, it must be considered as more than one muscle to effectively strengthen and stretch it. As a whole, the muscle serves to flex and horizontally adduct the shoulder. It also adducts and internally rotates the arm against resistance.

There are several common training errors related to the latissimus dorsi and pectoralis major. One is seen commonly in swimmers and bodybuilders who work hard to build up their pectorals and latissimus but fail to stretch those muscles. They have a gorilla-like standing posture in which their shoulders are

Figure 3–16 Faulty posture resulting from shortness of shoulder adductors and internal rotators. The palms face backward, instead of toward the body as in good posture.

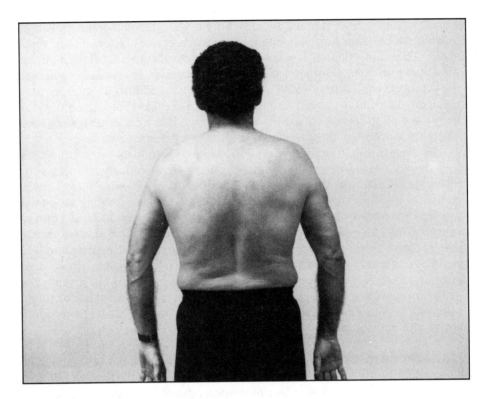

always internally rotated (Fig. 3–16). This may be because the pecs and lats are too short. A less severe version of this standing posture is also seen in some untrained clients whose shoulders are rounded forward and whose hands face backward instead of toward each other in relaxed standing. In an undeveloped individual, this is often due to weak, overstretched scapular adductors that allow the shoulder to fall passively into internal rotation. The external rotators may also show weakness. The scapular adductors become overstretched because, in habitually poor sitting and standing posture, the scapulae passively slide away from the spine, maintaining the muscles that connect the scapulae to the spine in a state of perpetual stretch. This may be accompanied and accentuated by a tight pectoralis minor that exerts a downward pull on the upper front part of the scapula.

Many clients exhibit a slight round-shouldered posture with a forward head. If a client has a noticeably rounded posture and/or complains of pain in this area, he/she should be referred to a physician for evaluation. However, personal trainers can help to create muscle balance in the shoulder area of clients with mild round-shouldered posture. To effectively assist such a client, the trainer must first assess whether the client has tight adductors and internal rotators (lats and pecs) or weak, overstretched scapular adductors (trapezius and rhomboids), or tight pectoralis minors. To help make this distinction, the trainer should note whether the palms face backward or face each other in relaxed standing. If backward, there is a component of shoulder internal rotation to the posture. Then the trainer should be sure there is no structural kyphosis of the spine. (Any rounding of the thoracic spine is not structural if the client can lie on the back, knees bent, feet flat on the floor, perform a pelvic tilt, and have the spine and head flat on the floor.) Next the client should be checked for tightness of the shoulder adductors and internal rotators (see Fig. 6–30 and 6–31). If shortness exists, the trainer should emphasize stretches for the pecs and lats. (Remember, an effective stretch is designed by positioning the muscle opposite to its concentric function.) If pecs and lats exhibit normal length,

Figure 3–17 Minimally effective pectoral stretch.

trainers should emphasize strengthening the posterior shoulder girdle muscles (rhomboids, mid and lower trapezius) and the external rotators (infraspinatus and teres minor). Utilizing the principles discussed here, trainers can design very specific stretches and strengtheners for each muscle group.

Clients often want to spend most of their training time strengthening the anterior muscles, and very little time strengthening the posterior muscles or stretching. Trainers must be sure to consider muscular balance when planning time with a client.

Sometimes the motion shown in Figure 3–17 is recommended as a pectoral stretch. We now know, however, that this is a less effective stretch for this muscle, since the position opposes only one of the muscle's functions. The primary stretch here is to the anterior capsule of the joint and some clavicular fibers. For a better stretch, the arm position should be a combination of abduction, external rotation, and some hyperextension as in Figure 3–18. Varying the angle of abduction would stretch different parts (sternal and clavicular) of the muscle.

Another frequent training error occurs when inexperienced trainers want to strengthen the pectorals. The client stands or sits holding dumbbells for resistance and brings the arms together and apart at chest level (Fig. 3–19). However, in this position the deltoids, upper trapezius, and biceps are contracting isometrically against the resistance to maintain the arm position; the pectorals encounter very little resistance. In contrast, the client could have the same body position on a "pec deck" weight machine and strengthen the pectoralis major because a resistive force is now applied appropriately (Fig. 3–20). Note that the elbows should remain in a position of slight flexion during these movements.

A similar error in position involves the latissimus dorsi muscle. Inexperienced clients copy the motion of the lat pulldown machine, but without the machine. Starting with the arms overhead, they adduct the arms, sometimes with weights in the hands. As we know, such a movement would be controlled by

Figure 3–18 Recommended pectoral stretch.

Figure 3–19 Ineffective way to strengthen the pectorals.

an eccentric contraction of the shoulder abductors, not the latissimus. Clients can use the motion in that position, however, if manual resistance is applied beneath the arm, above the elbow (Fig. 3–21a), or by using elastic resistance (Fig. 3–21b).

CORACOBRACHIALIS AND BICEPS BRACHII. The coracobrachialis (Fig. 3–22) has a line of pull and an attachment that are anterior to the joint, so it flexes the shoulder. The biceps brachii is a two-joint muscle. It crosses the shoulder joint as well as the elbow. Note where the long and short heads of the muscle cross the shoulder joint. As we consider their line of pull, we can see that the degree of shoulder rotation affects the position of the long head. In external rotation, the long head moves from an anterior to a superior and lateral position, so its function changes from flexion to abduction. The biceps

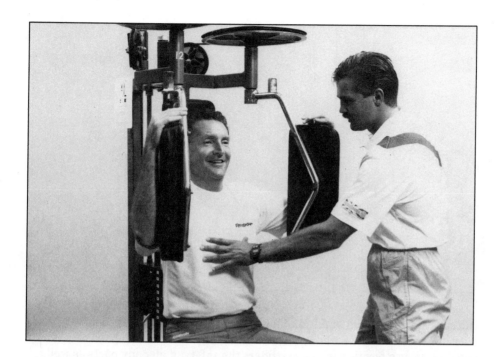

Figure 3–20 One recommended way to strengthen the pectorals.

will participate more as a shoulder abductor when there is applied external resistance.

Trainers should remember the biceps' two-joint function, especially in regard to injury prevention. The long head of the biceps lies in a shallow groove in the humerus as it crosses the shoulder. With repeated long lever movement of the arms, either in flexion or abduction, especially at a fast tempo, the biceps in many clients is quite susceptible to tendinitis.

The biceps also flexes the elbow and supinates the forearm. However the biceps does not participate in unresisted elbow flexion when the forearm is pronated (palms face down). That motion is performed by the brachialis muscle. We can demonstrate this by feeling the biceps muscle as we first flex the elbow with the palm up, then with the palm down. Feeling it once more as we pull up against the bottom of a table with the back of the hand (resisted elbow flexion with pronation), we see that the biceps does assist when there is resistance.

TRICEPS. The triceps is also a two-joint muscle, crossing posterior to the shoulder and elbow (Fig. 3–23). Therefore, its concentric function is extension at both joints. This muscle can be placed into an antigravity position in several ways. For example, the client could stand in a slight forward lunge and hold the shoulder in hyperextension, then extend the elbow. Or lying supine with the shoulder flexed to 90°, the client could begin with the elbow flexed and then extend it while pressing the hand toward the ceiling. The client could also stand with the shoulder flexed to about 150° or abducted to about 135° and extend the elbow. The trainer must take care in progressing the resistance in this position so that the client can maintain the neck and spine in neutral alignment. Another position often utilized by trainers is to have the client stand with the shoulder abducted to 90° and extend the elbow out to the side. This is an antigravity position for the triceps, but it requires a sustained isometric contraction of the deltoid and upper trapezius and often causes a lateral deviation of the spine. It also usually involves internal rotation at the shoulder, which at 90° of abduction

PERSONAL TRAINER MANUAL

Figure 3–21 Strengthening the lattisimus dorsi muscle. (a) Using manual resistance; (b) using elastic resistance.

can cause impingement at the shoulder joint. If the arm is dropped just 10°, the position is much safer without loss of effectiveness to the triceps. The trainer should choose a position which considers the safety of all body parts as well as effective strengthening of the triceps.

Injury Prevention Through Neutral Alignment

Injury prevention should be a major consideration when designing exercise programs. Other body parts, such as the neck and low back, should not be put at risk for injury in order to gain an advantage for another muscle group. Progressive resistance should be added gradually and weight decreased if form degrades. Spotting is very important when working with large amounts of resistance. Personal trainers should be able to recognize muscle substitution patterns that occur as muscles fatigue and approach failure. This will be noticed as body positions change, for instance, at the neck and low back, either to gain an advantage for the muscle that is beginning to fail or sometimes to substitute other muscles that have a slightly different line of pull. The client is more interested in a few more reps than in maintaining proper form or using precisely the right muscle, so the temptation is great for the client to substitute less safe positions. However, this should not be allowed, since the spine and surrounding structures are more easily injured in these positions.

The spine, in particular the neck and low back, should be maintained in a neutral position. *Neutral position* refers to maintaining the natural curves of the back without flexion, extension, rotation, or excessive anterior pelvic tilt. For example, Figure 3–24a shows unsafe alignment of the neck and low back while performing a push-up. Figure 3–24b shows safe alignment with the neck and low back in neutral position, using the abdominals to stabilize the pelvis.

Summary of the Muscles and Movements of the Upper Extremity

See Table 3–1 for a summary of the muscle location and functions for the upper extremity.

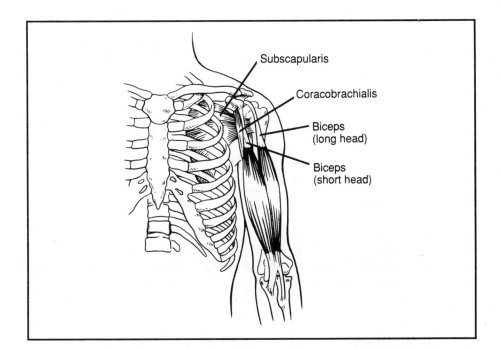

Figure 3–22 Biceps brachii and coracobrachialis muscles.

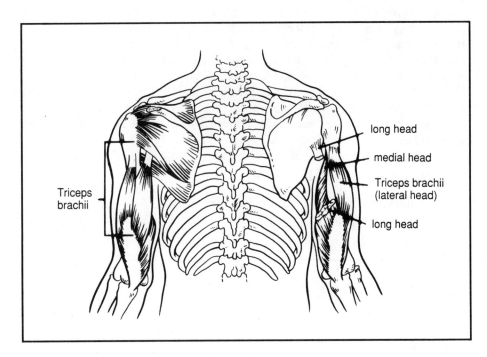

Figure 3–23 Triceps muscle.

MUSCLES AND MOVEMENTS OF THE PELVIS AND LOWER EXTREMITY

The hip joint is a triaxial joint, like the glenohumeral joint, allowing motion to occur in several planes. Unlike the glenohumeral joint, the hip has inherent stability in its bone and ligament structure. Like the shoulder, the hip connects to a bony and muscular girdle that provides a stable base for lower-extremity function and that rotates to position the femur and to provide improved angles

Figure 3–24 Performing a push-up. (a) Unsafe alignment of neck and low back; (b) safe (neutral position) alignment.

of pull for the hip muscles. It is different from the shoulder in that the pelvic girdle functions as a single unit and so the right and left sides cannot operate as independently as the shoulders can. The movements that occur at the hip joint are flexion and extension, hyperextension, abduction and adduction, circumduction, internal and external rotation, and the hybrid horizontal abduction and adduction.

The pelvic movements are known as *tilts* and can be anterior (forward), posterior, or lateral (Fig. 3–25). If we think of the pelvis as a bucket, then the anterior pelvic tilt (Fig. 3–25b) is like tipping the bucket forward and spilling the water in front. It is associated with increased hip flexion and low-back hyperextension. The posterior tilt (Fig. 3–25c) is tipping the bucket backward and spilling the water behind. It is associated with hip hyperextension and flexion of the low back at the lumbosacral joint. A lateral tilt (Fig. 3–25d) is like lifting the hip to walk with a stiff knee. In a neutral pelvis (Fig. 3–25a), the bucket would be straight up, not tipped in any direction. The pelvis can also rotate, which is very important to normal walking. Pelvic rotation is like grasping the rim of the bucket and twisting back and forth.

Figure 3–25 Pelvic inclinations. (a) Neutral pelvis; (b) anterior tilt; (c) posterior tilt; (d) lateral tilt.

Muscles Acting to Tilt the Pelvis

Active anterior pelvic tilt is achieved by contraction of the iliopsoas muscle (see anterior hip muscles, Fig. 3–27). The fact that it originates on the lumbar

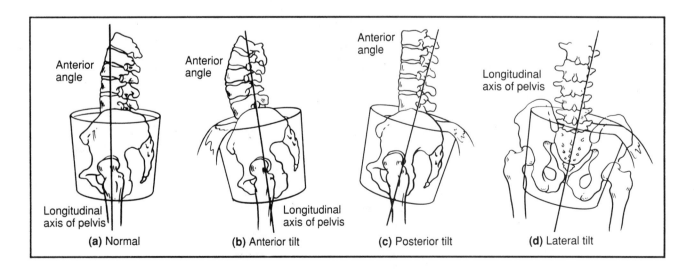

vertebrae tells us that it exerts a force on the pelvis as well as on the hip joint. When this muscle is too short, it passively pulls the pelvis into an anterior tilt.

The antagonists to the iliopsoas at the pelvis are those that tilt the pelvis posteriorly. Posterior pelvic tilt is performed by concentric contraction of the rectus abdominis and bilateral contraction of the external obliques (Fig. 3–26). The fibers of the rectus abdominis travel vertically. You can remember the direction of the external oblique fibers: They run in the same direction as putting your hands in your front pockets. Lateral tilts are performed by

Table 3–1   MUSCLES USED TO PRODUCE SPECIFIC MOVEMENTS OF THE JOINTS IN THE UPPER EXTREMITY

MOVEMENT	MUSCLE	ARTICULATION	ACTION
Shoulder flexion	Biceps brachii	Shoulder	Flexion
		Elbow	Flexion
		Radioulnar	Supination
	Anterior deltoid	Shoulder	Flexion
			Transverse flexion
	Coracobrachialis	Shoulder	Flexion
			Transverse flexion
	Pectoralis major (clavicular)	Shoulder	Flexion
			Transverse flexion
Shoulder extension	Posterior deltoid	Shoulder	Extension
	Triceps	Shoulder	Extension
		Elbow	Extension
	Latissimus dorsi	Shoulder	Extension
	Teres major		Medial rotation
Shoulder abduction	Middle deltoid	Shoulder	Abduction
	Supraspinatus		
Shoulder adduction	Pectoralis major	Shoulder	Adduction
		Sternoclavicular	Protraction
	Latissimus dorsi	Shoulder	Adduction
	Teres major		Medial rotation
Shoulder medial rotation	Latissimus dorsi	Shoulder	Medial rotation
	Teres major		
Shoulder lateral rotation	Infraspinatus	Shoulder	Lateral rotation
	Teres minor		
Shoulder transverse adduction	Pectoralis major	Shoulder	Transverse adduction
		Sternoclavicular	Protraction
	Coracobrachialis		Flexion
	Anterior deltoid		
Shoulder transverse abduction	Triceps	Shoulder	Transverse abduction
	Posterior deltoid		Extension
Elbow flexion	Biceps Brachii	Elbow	Flexion
		Shoulder	Flexion
		Radioulnar	Supination
	Brachialis	Elbow	Flexion
	Brachioradialis	Elbow	Flexion
		Radioulnar	Supination and pronation to midposition
Elbow extension	Triceps	Elbow	Extension
		Shoulder	Extension

Figure 3–26 Muscles acting to tilt the pelvis.

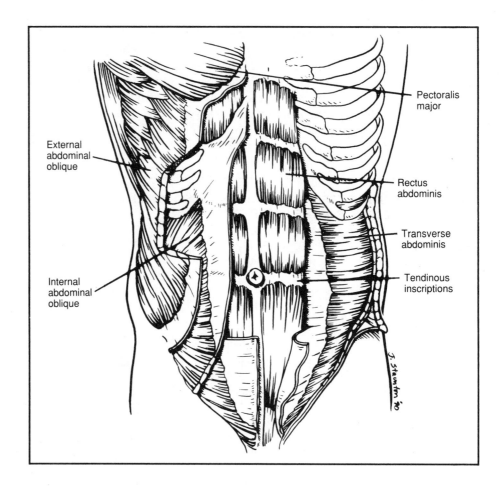

varying combinations of contractions by the internal and external obliques. The internal oblique fibers form an *inverted V*. The transverse abdominis fibers travel horizontally and act in forced expiration.

Abdominal exercises should be included in any well-rounded conditioning program. Utilizing the principle of increased lever arm of the resistance, the trainer can progress the difficulty by having the client first extend the arms by the sides, then cross the arms on the chest, then support the head with the hands. The difficulty can also be varied by incorporating more eccentric contractions, for instance, by making the down-phase of a trunk curl slower than the up-phase. The trainer must take care to progress the resistance gradually and have the client breathe throughout the exercise.

Because of possible tightness in the hip flexors in performing abdominal strengthening exercises such as trunk curls, it is advisable for beginners to position the hips in some degrees of flexion (knees bent and feet on the floor), so the pelvis is stabilized passively in a position of posterior tilt. If the legs are held straight (not bent at the knee) and the hip flexors are tight, the pelvis would be passively pulled into an anterior tilt. In this position the client with weak abdominals would be unable to tilt the pelvis posteriorly and perform a trunk curl. When then attempting to curl the trunk forward from a position of anterior tilt, the client could strain the low back. One way to progress clients is to instruct them to gradually use their abdominals to tilt the pelvis back actively instead of passively as in the position with the knees bent and feet flat on the floor.

Another effective exercise series for the untrained client would be performing posterior pelvic tilts without the trunk curl, progressively straightening the

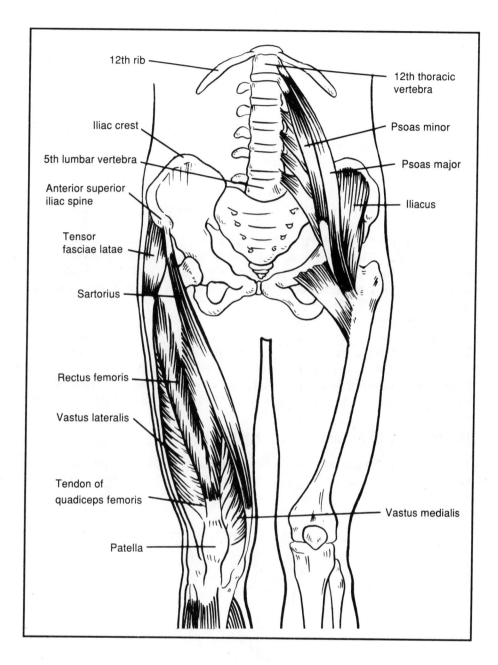

12th rib

Iliac crest

5th lumbar vertebra

Anterior superior
iliac spine

Tensor
fasciae latae

Sartorius

Rectus femoris

Vastus lateralis

Tendon of
quadiceps femoris

Patella

12th thoracic
vertebra

Psoas minor

Psoas major

Iliacus

Vastus medialis

Figure 3–27   Anterior hip
muscles: hip flexors.

legs. However, the trainer should first make sure that the client's hip flexors
are of normal length.

Anterior Muscles: Hip Flexors

The anterior hip muscles contribute to flexion at the hip. They are primarily the
iliopsoas and the rectus femoris, but also include the sartorius, tensor fasciae
latae, and pectineus (see Fig. 3-27).

ILIOPSOAS.   The iliopsoas is actually two muscles—the psoas major and the
iliacus—that function as one. It flexes the hip when the lumbar spine is stabilized, such as in a straight leg raise when lying face up on the floor. It moves
the trunk toward the thighs if the femur is stabilized, such as in a sit-up when
the legs are held down.

However, as we know, another condition must be met for the iliopsoas to move the trunk toward the thighs: The movement must occur against gravity or against another external resistance. Bending forward from the standing position would not involve the hip flexors but would instead be an eccentric contraction of the low back and hip extensors. Considering the weight of the upper body and the closeness of the attachments of the muscles and supporting ligaments to the joints of the low back, we recognize that potentially harmful torque and shearing stresses are put on the low back in this position. The situation is made much worse if additional weight is being lifted with the arms while the knees are straight. The potential harm is even greater if trunk rotation stress is added. Not only are the muscles and ligaments maximally stressed, but the internal pressure of the intervertebral discs rises significantly.

RECTUS FEMORIS AND OTHER HIP FLEXORS. Another hip flexor is the rectus femoris. The rectus femoris is one of the four quadriceps muscles of the anterior thigh (Fig. 3-27). It is the only one to cross the hip joint and contribute to hip flexion. Other hip flexors include the tensor fasciae latae and the sartorius (see Fig. 3-27).

A common postural imbalance is related to the hip flexors. They are shortened in many clients, perhaps as a result of many hours of sitting. The shortness in the front of the hip may also be a shortness of the iliofemoral ligament, which is difficult to stretch. (For a simple test of hip flexor length, see Figs. 6-27 and 6-28.) Stretching hip flexors is a priority in a well-balanced exercise program. Figure 3-28 presents an effective hip flexor stretch that is safe for most clients.

Posterior Hip Muscles: Hip Extensors

The muscles of the posterior hip include the gluteus maximus, hamstrings (biceps femoris, semimembranosus, and semitendinosus), and six deep external rotators.

Figure 3–28 Safe, effective hip flexor stretch.

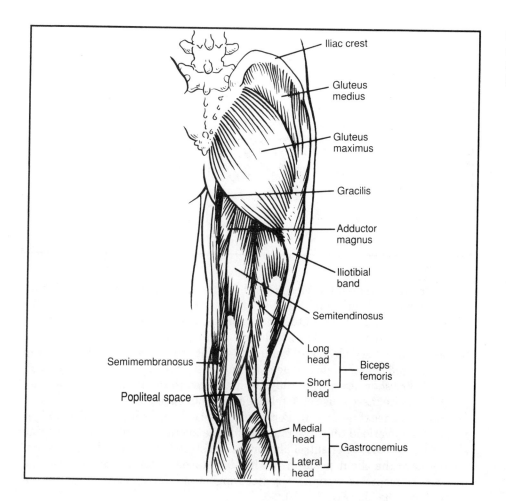

Figure 3–29 Fiber direction of the gluteus maximus in relation to the hip joint (posterolateral view).

GLUTEUS MAXIMUS.   The largest and most superficial of the posterior hip muscles is the gluteus maximus. It attaches to the pelvic rim at one end and broadly along the iliotibial tract (IT band) at the other (Fig. 3–29). This muscle is a good example of why we can seldom assign a single function to a muscle. Remember, a muscle's function depends on the line of pull of its fibers across a joint. Looking at the fibers of the gluteus maximus, we can see that for the most part it crosses behind the hip; therefore, it extends the hip. But some of the fibers cross superior to the center of the joint and others cross inferior to the joint, which means that those fibers contribute to abduction and adduction, respectively, but only against strong external resistance. The attachment into the IT band is lateral to the joint, with the line of pull across the back, making it also an external rotator of the hip when the hip is extended.

In addition to extension, abduction, and adduction against resistance, the greatest activity of the gluteus maximus, researchers have found, is during the activities of walking up an inclined plane, stair climbing, jumping, hyperextending the hip against resistance from the erect standing position, and isometric contraction.

Deep External Rotators

Not much time is devoted to the development of the hip external rotators. However, there does seem to be some confusion about their role and what exercises are best for this group.

Figure 3–30 Deep rotators of the hip.

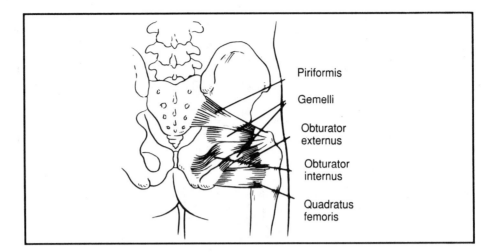

There are six small muscles located **deep** to the gluteus maximus (Fig. 3–30). Their order, top to bottom, is: piriformis, gemelli superior, obturator internus, gemelli inferior, obturator externus, and quadratus femoris. Their fibers are directed *horizontally*, and cross behind the joint. Their attachment to the femur is very close and behind the joint, meaning they rotate the hip externally and help the femoral head to stay in its socket. With their very small size and very short lever arm, they are not suited to resist large forces alone.

To exercise these muscles safely, clients should keep the lever arm short by bending the knee (Fig. 3–31a). Performing this exercise with the knee straight is too much overload on these muscles for the average client. Also, the spine should be supported in neutral alignment. To stretch and relax these muscles, simply have the client position the hip in internal rotation (opposite to the muscles' concentric function). Greater range of motion can be achieved if the client flexes the hip (Fig. 3–31b).

Hamstrings

Figure 3–31 Deep rotator of the hip. (a) An exercise to strengthen. (b) An exercise to stretch.

Another posterior muscle group of the hip is the hamstring group. Note their origin (except the short head of the biceps femoris) is on the pelvis (specifically the ischial tuberosity, or "sitz" bone) (Fig. 3–32). They also cross the knee joint, the "semis" attaching medially; the biceps, laterally. Observing their

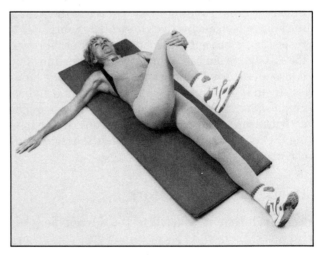

fiber direction, we can see that their function is mainly hip extension and knee flexion. They are also considered to be important in stabilization of the knee joint.

The hamstrings are a group that often contracts eccentrically in activities of daily life. For example, when we bend forward at the hip in standing, the hips are flexing in the same direction as gravity. As we learned earlier, the hip extensors (hamstrings) are contracting eccentrically. Since the hamstrings are contracting strongly in this position, it is only logical that it would not be the most effective position for stretching the muscles. Also, as mentioned earlier, the rotational stresses and the torque created by the weight of the upper body in this position, if unsupported, is potentially harmful to the low back.

The hamstrings are short in many clients. (For a simple test of hamstrings flexibility, see Figs. 6–24 through 6–27.) To stretch the hamstrings effectively, the client should assume a position of hip flexion and knee extension. An effective trainer-assisted stretch for the hamstrings is pictured in Figure 3–33.

Hamstrings are relatively weak in many clients. Some researchers have suggested a muscle balance of 2:3 between the hamstrings and quadriceps as advisable for injury prevention in sports. It is wise for the trainer to design exercises that call for hip extension and knee flexion, making sure the client's low back is stabilized, especially when using external resistance.

Medial Hip Muscles: Adductor Group

There are several muscles located medial to the hip joint, all of them adductors: big (magnus), little (minimus), long (longus), and short (brevis). One more also crosses the knee joint: the gracilis, a long, slender muscle, as its name suggests (Fig. 3–34). They also internally rotate the hip.

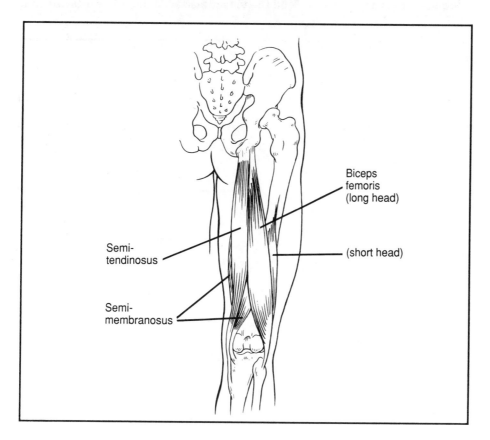

Figure 3–32 Hamstring muscles.

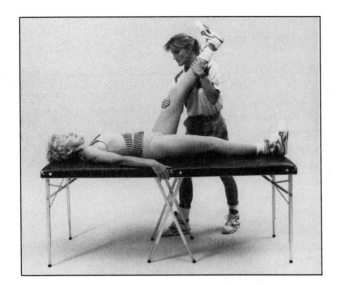
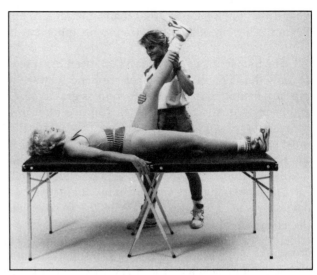

Figure 3–33 Effective PNF hamstrings stretch (trainer-assisted). (a) Isometric contraction; (b) Relax hamstring while trainer assists with stretch.

A suggestion for an antigravity exercise for the hip adductors is given in Figure 3-35. Many female clients consistently want to lose the fat deposits that often are located along the medial thigh, and want to "tone" the adductors. It is important for the trainer to educate such clients that spot reducing does *not* work. To decrease body fat stores, clients must exercise aerobically.

Lateral Hip Muscles: Hip Abductors

The lateral group of muscles causing motion of the hip joint consists of the gluteus medius and minimus, and the tensor fasciae latae. Their attachments

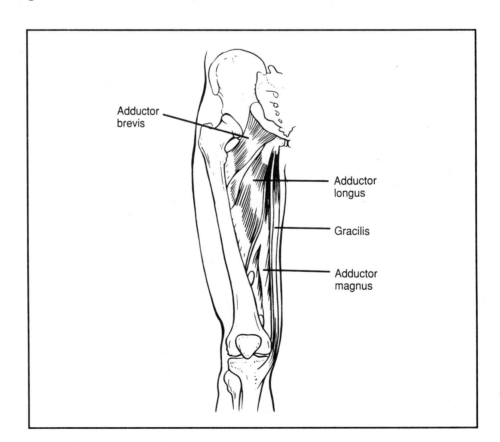

Figure 3–34 Adductor muscles of the hip.

Figure 3–35 Antigravity exercise for the hip.

and fiber directions are shown in Figure 3–36. It is easy to see that the attachments are superior to the joint; therefore, one function is hip abduction. More difficult to see from the angle portrayed is that the attachments of the gluteus medius and minimus are also slightly anterior to the joint, so these muscles also internally rotate the hip. Note that these muscles are located high on the hip, not on the outer thigh.

Many clients are also interested in reducing the fat deposits along the outer thigh. As with the hip adductors, specific exercises for the hip abductors will not diminish body fat. Only systematic aerobic exercise and proper nutrition will accomplish that goal.

If we consider the muscles' locations carefully, we see that the angle of hip flexion should be no more than 45° flexed to utilize the gluteus medius effectively. The tensor fasciae latae participates more in a side-lying leg raise when the hip is slightly flexed.

In addition to the common side-lying leg raise, another effective position for exercising the abductors is lifting the leg to the side in the standing position. Even though the lift is not antigravity through the full range of motion, this position actually works the left and right abductors at the same time. The abductors of the leg being lifted contract concentrically and eccentrically to raise and lower the leg. The abductors of the standing leg contract isometrically to stabilize the pelvis.

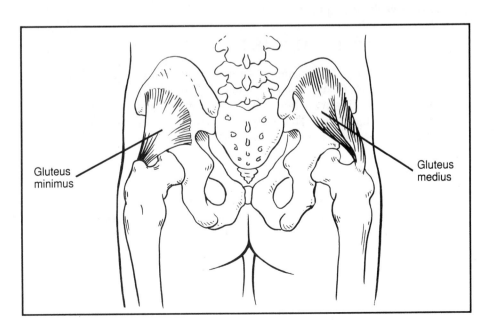

Figure 3–36 Lateral hip muscles: abductors (posterior view).

Gluteus minimus

Gluteus medius

The abductors play an important role in normal walking, as will be seen in the next section, so they should be included in a general strengthening program.

Example of Movement Analysis: the Hip During Walking

Because the hip is a weight-bearing joint, many of the muscles we have been talking about function at least part of the time with their insertions stabilized and the origins moving. To demonstrate a correct analysis of movement about the hip when the client is weight-bearing, let's go through an example.

As we have already said, when the hips flex as the trunk leans forward in the standing position, the hip extensors contract eccentrically. What happens at the right hip during walking? When we step on the left foot and swing the right leg through, first the right hip is flexing against gravity, which indicates concentric contraction of the hip flexors. Of course, when the right leg is no longer in contact with the ground, gravity pulls down on the right side of the pelvis. To resist the lateral drop of the pelvis, the antagonists must contract eccentrically. The tricky part here is figuring out the antagonists to a lateral pelvic tilt to the right. They might be the lateral trunk flexors on the right side, if each side of the pelvic girdle functioned independently, like the shoulder girdle. But the pelvis is a single unit, so the muscle group acting to resist the lateral pelvic tilt to the right when we walk is actually the left hip abductors. Their insertion on the femur of the standing leg is stabilized; they pull down on the rim of the pelvis on the left. That keeps the pelvis from drooping on the right. As we did when we considered pelvic tilts, we can think of the pelvis as a bucket that is balanced on two sticks. When we remove one stick from under the bucket, we must do something to keep it from tipping sideways. What happens is, the muscles connected to the other stick contract to keep the bucket level.

Once the right heel hits the ground in walking, the ground exerts an "impact" (reactive force) that the body must absorb and dissipate. As we shift all our weight to the right foot and the left foot leaves the floor, the right hip abductors contract to keep the pelvis level. Then as the upper body shifts forward, the right hip moves into extension. However, the extension occurs passively as the body moves forward with momentum. Consequently, the gluteus maximus participates very little in normal walking.

MUSCLES ACTING AT THE KNEE JOINT

The knee, like the elbow, is primarily a hinge joint, so the primary motions, for our purposes, are flexion and extension (although it does allow for minimal rotation). The knee is supported medially and laterally by ligaments, with no musculature located there. The muscles controlling knee motion are located anteriorly (the extensors) and posteriorly (the flexors).

Anterior Muscles: Knee Extensors

The anterior muscles of the knee joint include the four muscles making up the quadriceps: rectus femoris, vastus medialis, vastus intermedius, and vastus lateralis. As penniform muscles, they have a large cross section and are capable of producing high amounts of force. The fibers run diagonal to each muscle's line of pull, converging at the patella, wrapping around it, and attaching to the tibia by way of the patellar ligament, sometimes called the patellar tendon

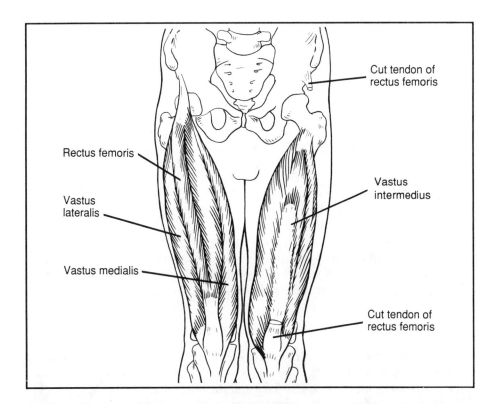

Figure 3–37   Anterior thigh muscles; knee extensors (quadriceps)

(Fig. 3–37). The patella acts like a pulley, enabling the muscle to have a favorable angle of pull, even when the knee is flexed past 90°.

There is controversy among the experts regarding safe strengthening exercises for the quadriceps. Safety at the knee involves the kinesiology of the quadriceps and knee joint, specifically the stability of the knee when performing a squat or deep knee bend. To analyze the movement, let's consider what occurs at the knee and hip during a squat. Since hip and knee flexion occur in the same direction as gravity, antagonists to the movement contract eccentrically (primarily hamstrings at the hip and quadriceps at the knee). The motive forces are the weight of the upper body segments; the resistive forces are the eccentric contractions of the antagonists (Fig. 3–38). Clearly, there are large forces involved. And although the muscles here are suited to sustain large forces, the inherent instability of the knee joint, especially in the flexed position, can be a problem. As the angle of knee flexion increases, the angle of pull changes such that the forces created by the muscles tend to dislocate rather than stabilize the joint. There is also potential for the patella to slip out of its track, because of the quadriceps' line of pull. This is more of a problem for women with wide pelvises. Perhaps the best solution (short of avoiding all squats) is to limit the degree of knee flexion to no more than 90° in a weight-bearing exercise such as a parallel squat. Also, the speed of descent should be carefully controlled.

Posterior Muscles: Knee Flexors

The primary knee flexors are the hamstrings, which were discussed previously with the hip extensors. Secondary knee flexors include the sartorius, gracilis, and popliteus. The popliteus is a stabilizer, helping to prevent dislocation when a squatting position is maintained. The gastrocnemius, though primarily an ankle muscle, acts in certain instances to stabilize or flex the knee.

Figure 3–38   Safe position for a parallel squat: knee flexion <90 degrees.

Posterior Muscles Acting at the Ankle: Plantarflexors

GASTROCNEMIUS AND SOLEUS GROUP. The gastrocnemius and soleus group make up the bulk of muscle on the posterior calf (Fig. 3–39). They both cross posterior to the ankle joint; therefore, they plantarflex the ankle.

The gastrocnemius, a two-joint muscle, is penniform and has a large angle of pull. It is capable of creating large forces. Because the gastrocnemius is meant to support body weight, one of the best ways to provide resistance is to use body weight against gravity. It can be overloaded by performing multiple sets of heel raises on both feet, progressing to one foot. The range of motion can be increased by dropping the heel, such as over the edge of a step.

The gastrocnemius and soleus muscles are often shortened, particularly in clients who wear high heels. To help clients stretch the gastrocnemius effectively, and bearing in mind that it is a two-joint muscle, have them extend the knee and dorsiflex the ankle, preferably in a position that does not require the muscle to support body weight. The soleus does not cross the knee; therefore, it is better stretched with the knee flexed. That way, any tightness of the gastrocnemius will not interfere with the soleus stretch.

Anterior Muscles Acting at the Ankle: Dorsiflexors

Figure 3–40 shows the anterior muscles of the lower leg, the primary one being the tibialis anterior. Its line of pull operates anterior to the ankle joint, so its function is to dorsiflex the ankle. This and the other muscles located along the shin are your first line of defense with regard to shock absorption in high-impact activities. Together they also control foot movements important to balance in walking and running, particularly on uneven ground. It is important that they be adequately prepared for the job with a thorough warm-up prior to impact activities. A common warm-up method is toe-tapping, straight and side to side.

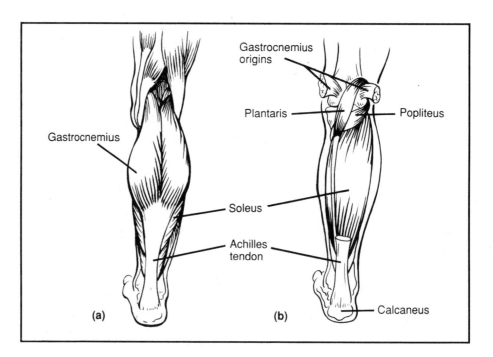

Figure 3–39 Posterior calf muscles that plantarflex the ankle. (a) Gastrocnemius; (b) soleus.

Table 3–2   MUSCLES USED TO PRODUCE SPECIFIC MOVEMENTS OF THE JOINTS IN THE PELVIS AND LOWER EXTREMITY

MOVEMENT	MUSCLE	ARTICULATION	ACTION
Hip flexion	Iliopsoas	Hip	Flexion
		Vertebral column	Flexion
	Rectus femoris	Hip	Flexion
		Knee	Extension
	Sartorius	Hip	Flexion
		Knee	Flexion
Hip extension	Gluteus maximus	Hip	Extension
	Biceps femoris	Hip	Extension
		Knee	Flexion
			Lateral rotation
	Semitendinosus	Hip	Extension
	Semimembranosus		Medial rotation
Hip abduction	Tensor fasciae latae	Hip	Abduction
	Gluteus medius		
	Gluteus minimus		
Hip adduction	Pectineus	Hip	Adduction
	Adductor longus		
	Adductor magnus		
	Adductor brevis		
	Gracilis		
Hip lateral rotation	Six internal rotators		Lateral rotation
	Gluteus maximus		
Hip medial rotation	Iliopsoas	Hip	Medial rotation
		Vertebral column	Flexion
	Tensor fasciae latae	Hip	Medial rotation
Knee flexion	Biceps femoris	Knee	Flexion
			Lateral rotation
		Hip	Extension
	Semitendinosus	Knee	Flexion
	Semimembranosus		Medial rotation
		Hip	Extension
	Sartorius	Knee	Flexion
		Hip	Flexion
Knee extension	Rectus femoris	Hip	Flexion
		Knee	Extension
	Vastus lateralis	Knee	Extension
	Vastus medialis		
	Vastus intermedius		
Ankle dorsiflexion	Tibialis anterior	Ankle	Dorsiflexion
		Subtalar	Inversion
	Extensor digitorum longus	Ankle	Dorsiflexion
		Subtalar	Eversion
Ankle plantar-flexion	Gastrocnemius	Ankle	Plantar flexion
		Knee	Flexion
	Soleus	Ankle	Plantar flexion
	Tibialis posterior	Ankle	Plantar flexion
		Subtalar	Inversion
	Flexor digitorum longus	Ankle	Plantar flexion
		Subtalar	Inversion
	Flexor hallucis longus	Ankle	Plantar flexion
		Subtalar	Inversion
	Peroneus longus and brevis	Ankle	Plantar flexion
		Subtalar	Eversion
	Peroneus tertius		

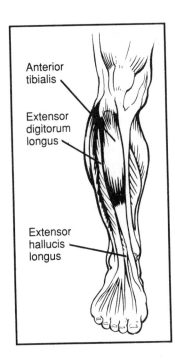

Figure 3–40 Anterior muscles of the lower leg.

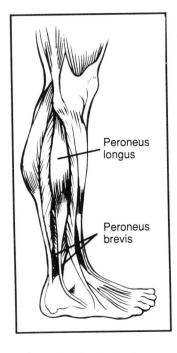

Figure 3–41 Lateral muscles of the lower leg.

Lateral Muscles Acting at the Ankle and Foot

The peroneus longus and brevis are the muscles that compose the lateral compartment of the lower leg (Fig. 3–41). Their tendons curve around the lateral malleolus of the ankle and attach to the first and fifth metatarsal, respectively. Their common functions are plantarflexion and eversion. They are active in walking and are also important in maneuvering on uneven ground. Toe-tapping side to side is a warm-up for these muscles also.

Summary of the Muscles and Movements of the Pelvis and Lower Extremity

Table 3-2 summarizes the locations and functions for the muscles of the pelvis and lower extremity.

POSTURE AND MUSCLE IMBALANCE

Much has been written about posture—"ideal," good, and bad. There is considerable disagreement among the "experts" about what ideal posture is, since there are several variables involved, body type being one. There does seem to be a general alignment that minimizes stress on the spine (Fig. 3–42).

There is much to learn about clients through observing and assessing their posture. Muscular imbalances often manifest themselves in a person's standing posture. They are frequently influenced by a person's work and his/her habits of standing and sitting. For example, if a person sits most of the day (working, eating, driving, watching TV) and then sleeps in a fetal position, many hours have been spent overstretching ligaments and shortening particular muscle groups. It is no wonder that anterior muscles at the hip and shoulder tend to be tight.

A person's **kinesthetic awareness** also manifests itself and is influenced by habitual postures. Kinesthetic awareness is a person's ability to know where his/her body is in space without looking. For example, a large percentage of Americans exhibit a forward head in sitting and standing (Fig. 3–43b). When taught correct head and neck alignment, most say the position feels funny. That is, their head has been forward so long, it feels right, and any other position feels unnatural. Their kinesthetic awareness of their body in space and how it is aligned has changed. Allowing clients to observe their movement in a mirror or on video will help increase their awareness of correct and incorrect postures. Exaggerated movements repeated several times, followed by the assumption of the correct, more neutral position, has been used by some therapists to sharpen kinesthetic awareness.

There are three classic postural deviations that a personal trainer should be able to recognize and describe—lordosis, kyphosis, and scoliosis. **Lordosis** (Fig. 3–43a) is an increase in the normal inward curve of the low back, often accompanied by a protruding abdomen and buttocks, rounded shoulders, and forward head. **Kyphosis** (Fig. 3–43b) is an increase in the normal outward curve of the thoracic spine. It is often accompanied by rounded shoulders and a sunken chest, and forward head with neck hyperextension. **Scoliosis** (Fig. 3–43c) is a lateral curve of the spine. There are usually two curves, on opposite sides of the spine, one compensating for the other. If any of these conditions typifies a client, especially if associated with pain or discomfort, the trainer should refer him/her to a physician.

There are some common muscle imbalances of which trainers should be aware. One is due to shortness of the hip flexors. Here, the person stands with a habitual lordosis. Slight kyphosis, rounded shoulders, forward head, and possibly hyperextended knees and pronated feet may also be observed.

Another common primary muscle imbalance is between the abdominals and hip flexors. These muscle groups act as antagonists within the pelvis because the abdominals tilt the pelvis posteriorly while the hip flexors, if too short, act passively to tilt the pelvis anteriorly. In this case, the abdominal muscles are probably weak and perhaps overstretched. The hip flexors may be shortened. A balanced exercise program would include stretches for all the hip flexors (iliopsoas, rectus femoris) and progressive resistive exercise for the abdominals. When strengthening the abdominals in this case it is advisable for trainers to include only abdominal exercises that minimize hip flexor involvement (positions where the hip flexors must contract eccentrically). The pelvis should be stabilized in a posterior tilt using abdominal action.

EXAMPLES OF EXERCISE ANALYSIS

Having reviewed the locations and functions of most of the major muscles of the trunk and extremities, and having applied biomechanical principles pertinent to each muscle group and analyzed the type of muscle contractions involved in many joint movements, let's put it all together to analyze two exercises commonly employed by personal trainers: the push-up and the seated lat pull-down.

Push-Up

Let's look at the push-up in Figure 3-24.

UP-PHASE. In the up-phase, the body is raised by extending the elbows. The prime motion occurs at the shoulders, shoulder girdle, elbows, and wrists. And, though no movement occurs, critical stabilization happens at the neck, lumbar spine, and hips.

Shoulders: The joint movement is horizontal flexion and internal rotation. The movement occurs against gravity, so it is controlled by concentric

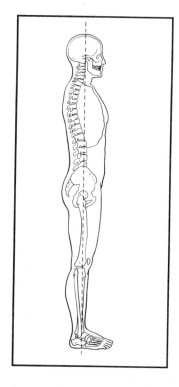

Figure 3–42 Body alignment that minimizes stress on the spine.

Figure 3–43 Postural deviations. (a) Lordosis; (b) kyphosis; (c) scoliosis.

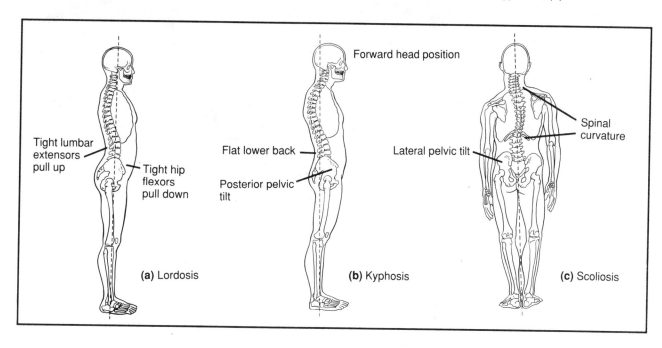

Tight lumbar extensors pull up

Tight hip flexors pull down

(a) Lordosis

Forward head position

Flat lower back

Posterior pelvic tilt

(b) Kyphosis

Spinal curvature

Lateral pelvic tilt

(c) Scoliosis

contractions of the shoulder flexors and internal rotators: pectoralis major, anterior deltoid, coracobrachialis, and subscapularis.

Shoulder girdle: The motion is scapular abduction, and upward rotation controlled by concentric contraction of the agonists: pectoralis minor, serratus anterior as a force coupled with the upper and middle trapezius and rhomboids.

Elbows: The movement is extension against gravity; so muscular action is concentric contraction of the extensors: triceps.

Wrists: Hyperextension occurs here by concentric contraction of the wrist extensors.

Head and neck: Cervical vertebrae are maintained in neutral alignment by isometric contraction of the cervical extensors. (When there is no movement, we can imagine what would happen if all muscles relaxed, then decide which muscles are contracting to prevent that motion.)

Lumbar spine: A neutral spine is maintained by isometric contractions of the abdominals.

Hips: No movement occurs, but the joint is stabilized by isometric contraction of the flexors, since gravity acting unresisted would tend to cause hip extension.

DOWN-PHASE.   In the down-phase of the movement, the opposite movements occur at the shoulder, shoulder girdle, elbows, and wrists. Since the down-phase movements occur in the same direction as gravity, they are controlled by eccentric contractions of the muscles just listed. The head, spine, and hips are maintained in a neutral position by the same muscles contracting isometrically.

Figure 3–44   Lat pull-down.

Lat Pull-Down

Now let's look at the lat pull-down pictured in Figure 3-44.

DOWN-PHASE.   In the down-phase the resistance of the machine is lifted by adducting and extending the shoulders. The prime motion occurs at the shoulders, shoulder girdle, and elbows. Stabilization occurs at the wrist, neck, lumbar spine, and hips. In the analysis of an exercise performed against an external resistance other than gravity, the direction of the movement in relation to gravity is a lesser consideration.

Shoulders: The primary joint movements are adduction and extension. The movement occurs against the external resistance of the machine, so it is controlled by concentric contractions of the agonists: shoulder adductors (pectoralis major, latissimus dorsi, and teres major) and extensors (latissimus, teres major, posterior deltoid, and triceps). Also, some internal rotation may occur depending on the exact start and end positions, so the subscapularis also contracts concentrically.

Shoulder girdle: The motion is scapular adduction, depression, and downward rotation occurring against the external resistance of the machine (the resistance is being lifted against gravity). Therefore, it is controlled by concentric contraction of the agonists: primarily the lower and middle trapezius muscles, and the rhomboids.

Elbows: The movement is flexion against the resistance of the machine. (It occurs in the same direction as gravity, but we must remember that the resistance is being lifted against gravity.) The muscular action is concentric contraction of the biceps, and because the forearm is pronated, the brachialis also contracts concentrically.

Wrists: Ideally, the wrists should be stabilized in neutral by isometric cocontraction of the flexors and extensors.

Head and neck: Cervical vertebrae are maintained in neutral, with minimal muscle contraction if they are properly aligned.

Lumbar spine: In sitting, gravity tends to pull the pelvis into a posterior tilt. Neutral position is achieved by isometric contraction of the spinal extensors.

Hips: No movement occurs ordinarily, though a slight forward lean at the hip may occur, controlled by eccentric contraction of the hip extensors.

RETURN PHASE.   In the return phase of the exercise, the opposite motions occur at the shoulder, shoulder girdle, and elbows. They are controlled by eccentric contractions of the muscles just listed for those three joints.

CREATING PROGRESSIVE EXERCISE PROGRAMS

In working with individual clients, it is important for the trainer to begin the exercise program at the level appropriate for each client. It is also imperative to progress the client in such a way that he/she feels successful yet challenged, without threat of injury. Of course, with variable-resistance machines, we can simply move the pin to the next notch to progress the resistance. But what if the client is not ready to use such equipment, or what if we do not have access to it?

Experience will have to teach the trainer the appropriate beginning level for clients. But there is a series of modifications that can be used for each exercise in order to progressively overload the muscle, using the principles of biomechanics presented earlier in this chapter. First, the body position can be changed from one in which gravity is not a factor to an antigravity position. Second, the trainer can utilize a series of concentric, eccentric, and (when appropriate) isometric contractions of the same muscle group. Third, the lever arm of the resistance can be increased, such as by lifting the leg with the knee extended instead of flexed. Finally, additional external resistance can be added in the form of either the trainer's own manual resistance, elastic bands or tubing, or free weights.

SUMMARY

This chapter has discussed the tools needed to tailor an exercise program for individual clients. It has presented the principles of how and why the body moves, showing how muscles and outside forces such as gravity and other applied resistance affect movement. It has examined the main categories of muscles and their functions in varying positions and during numerous exercise alternatives. It has described the mechanical principles necessary to create a progressive exercise program.

It is recommended that trainers develop a file or list of exercises found to be most effective for each muscle group. It would also be helpful for them to develop a graded series for each exercise movement, using the principles discussed here. That should provide trainers all they need to design safe, effective exercise programs to help clients achieve their goals.

SUGGESTED READING

Luttgens, K., & Wells, K. (1982). *Kinesiology: Scientific basis of human motion.* New York: Saunders.

Kapit, W., & Elson, L. (1977). *The anatomy coloring book.* New York: Harper & Row.

Kendall, H., Kendall, F., & Wadsworth, G. (1971). *Muscles: Testing and function.* Baltimore: Williams & Wilkins.

Kreighbaum, E., & Barthels, K. (1981). *Biomechanics.* Minneapolis, MN: Burgess.

Rasch, P. (1989). *Kinesiology and applied anatomy.* Philadelphia: Lea & Febiger.

Van Gelder, N., & Marks, S. (eds.) (1987). *Aerobic dance-exercise instructor manual.* San Diego: American Council on Exercise.

Nutrition

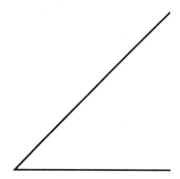

BY JACQUELINE R. BERNING

JACKIE BERNING, M.S., R.D., is currently working on her Ph.D. in nutrition at Colorado State University. Her specialty is sports nutrition. Presently, she is nutrition consultant for the Denver Broncos, the U.S. Olympic Swim Team, and the University of Colorado Athletic Department. She sits on the Denver Mayor's Council on Physical Fitness, and has published on the subject of sports nutrition, writing chapters in two sports medicine books. She is currently chair-person of the Sports and Cardiovascular Nutritionists (SCAN) Practice Group of the American Dietetic Association.

4

IN THIS CHAPTER:

- Nutrients: water, carbohydrates, protein, fat, vitamins, and minerals

- Food group eating plans, nutrient density, and vegetarianism.

- Recommended daily allowances (RDA) and vitamin/mineral supplementation.

- The relation of calcium and iron to growth and maturity.

- Dietary guidelines, including tips about fats and oils.

- Heart disease and its relation to cholesterol, lipoproteins, and triglycerides.

- Nutrition and exercise, including carbohydrate loading.

- Dispelling sports nutrition myths.

Eating well and making wise food choices is not difficult, in principle. All that is needed is to eat a selection of foods that supplies appropriate amounts of the essential nutrients and energy. Yet to master the principle and put it into practice may be extremely difficult for some. The personal trainer can help clients make appropriate food selections for good health. As a personal trainer you should guide clients by becoming more knowledgeable about nutrition and providing them with a meal pattern they can understand and follow, as well as knowing when to refer them to a **registered dietitian** or physician.

This chapter provides up-to-date information about diet and its role in providing good health. It's the first step in becoming more knowledgeable about nutrition. Personal trainers can go beyond its scope by obtaining the suggested readings and keeping up with nutrition articles written by nutritional professionals. Being a role model and practicing healthy eating habits will show commitment to good, sound nutrition. Lastly, find a local resource in nutrition, a dietitian capable of giving sensible responses to your questions. A group of

Table 4.1   THE SIX NUTRIENT CATEGORIES AND THEIR PHYSIOLOGIC FUNCTIONS WITHIN THE BODY

Nutrient	Functions
Protein	Builds and repairs body tissue
Carbohydrates	Provide energy for the body
Fat	Necessary part of every cell; protects internal organs; carries fat-soluble vitamins
Vitamins/minerals	Regulate body processes
Water	Important for the many chemical reactions in the body

dietitians who practice in sports and cardiovascular nutrition (SCAN) can be used as a local resource. To locate local SCAN dietitians, contact the American Dietetic Association and ask for the SCAN referral list.

NUTRIENTS

Nutrients fall into six categories, all found in most foods. The nutrient water is the most predominant: 60 percent of the body is made up of water. The three energy nutrients—carbohydrates, fat, and protein—are next in abundance. Last come the vitamins and minerals, in smaller, yet significant, amounts. Table 4-1 lists the nutrient categories and their functions.

Water

Water is such an integral part of us, yet we seldom are aware of its importance—deprived of it, the body can survive only a few days. The body fluids, made up mostly of water, bring to each system all the exact ingredients required and also carry away the body's by-products. Water is also an important, active participant in many chemical reactions in the body. It can act as a lubricant around joints and also protect sensitive tissues and organs from shock.

Energy Nutrients

The energy nutrients—**carbohydrates (CHO)**, **protein**, and **fat**—all contain calories. Their energy can be used by the body in several ways: for heat, to build its structures, to move its parts, or to be stored as body-fat. The energy values of these nutrients are:

    1 gm carbohydrate = 4 calories
    1 gm fat = 9 calories
    1 gm protein = 4 calories

Practically all foods contain a mixture of the three energy nutrients, although they are sometimes classified by the predominant nutrient. A protein-rich food like beef actually contains a lot of fat as well as protein. A carbohydrate-rich food like corn also contains fat (corn oil) and protein. Thus it is incorrect to say we are eating a protein when we eat meat; we are actually eating a protein-rich food that also contains other nutrients, such as fat. Only a few foods are exceptions to this rule, the common ones being sugar (almost pure carbohydrate) and oil (almost pure fat).

Essential Nutrients

The body can make certain nutrients from other nutrients. For example, it can convert some amino acids into carbohydrates, if need be. It can manufacture one of the vitamins, niacin, from a certain amino acid. There are, however, certain compounds absolutely indispensable to bodily functions that the body cannot make for itself; these are termed **essential nutrients**. In this context, *essential* means the nutrient is needed in the diet because the body cannot make it for itself. There are about 40 nutrients to be concerned about. It may be a relief to discover that diet planning can be reduced to a few simple principles to ensure that we take in all the nutrients in the appropriate amounts without having to count and weigh each one. The use of a food group plan makes it possible to design a diet that meets all the nutrient needs.

FOOD GROUP PLANS

The "Four Food Groups" make up the most widely used eating plan. This plan is simple and has great flexibility. Most Americans were taught the Four Food Groups back in elementary school and it remains the best model to teach nutrition principles. This plan specifies that a certain quantity of food must be consumed from each group. For the adult, the number of servings recommended is two, two, four, and four (see Table 4-2). Most selections of food based on this plan will supply 100 percent of the recommended amounts of all nutrients for men and all except iron for women. (By using the Four Food Group approach, women miss getting the full daily recommended amount of iron by only 10 percent.)

The personal trainer can use the Four Food Group plan to teach clients how to make wise food choices, to plan menus for nutritious meals, to grocery shop, and to assess a diet to determine if it's nutritionally sound. By advising clients to follow the three easy steps, the personal trainer can help them make better food choices using the Four Food Groups:

Step 1: *Eat foods from all Four Food Groups every day.* Foods from the milk, meat, fruit and vegetable, and grain groups supply the more than 40 nutrients the body needs to stay healthy.

Step 2: *Include a variety of foods.* Foods within a food group are usually good sources of the same nutrients. By eating different foods within each food group, clients have a good chance of getting all the nutrients they need. Each food group provides **leader nutrients**.

- Try low-fat milks and low-fat cheeses and yogurts from the Milk Group. They supply the body with calcium, protein, and riboflavin as leader nutrients.

- Experiment with new recipes for chicken, fish, beef, egg, dried beans, and peas from the Meat Group. These supply leader nutrients such as protein, niacin, iron, and thiamine.

- Find creative ways to include foods from the Fruit and Vegetable Group. Add spinach, carrots, broccoli, mushrooms, and green peppers to salads and casseroles. This group provides vitamins A and C as leader nutrients.

- Enjoy new tastes from the Grain Group. Try bagels, tortillas, and rye, pita or cracked-wheat bread for sandwiches. The Grain Group supplies these leader nutrients: carbohydrates, thiamine, iron, and niacin.

Step 3: *Practice moderation.* By practicing moderation, individuals can get the nutrients they need without getting additional, unnecessary amounts of fat and/or sodium.

- Eat at least the recommended number of servings from each food group every day.

- Watch how many servings you have from the "other" category. (see below)

- Eat foods in the serving sizes listed in Table 4–2.

Many foods do not fit into any of the Four Food Groups, for example, butter, margarine, cream, sour cream, salad dressing, mayonnaise, jam, jelly, broth, coffee, tea, and alcohol. These items are grouped together into the *"others" category.* Although some of them do contribute nutrients; either they are not foods or their nutrient content is not significant enough to characterize them as a food group. Many years ago health professionals labeled these "other" foods as empty calories, meaning they contain more calories than nutrients. Today most nutritionists use the concept of **nutrient density**. This is a measure of nutrients per calorie. A nutrient-dense food provides more nutrients at a low-caloric cost. Therefore, a non-nutrient-dense food is one that contains more calories and/or fat and fewer nutrients, such as potato chips, cake, cookies, and soda pop.

At first, the Four Food Group plan appears quite rigid, but it can be used with great flexibility once its intent is understood. For example, personal trainers can suggest to clients that yogurt be substituted for milk because it supplies protein, calcium, and riboflavin in about the same amounts. Dried beans and peas, as well as nuts, are alternative choices for meats. The plan can be adapted to casseroles and other mixed dishes and to different national and cultural cuisines. Many cultural cuisines can be analyzed or assessed by using the Four Food Group approach. Oriental dishes that have vegetables, chicken, and rice supply three of the four groups. Spanish and Mexican dishes, such as tamales with beans, rice, and cheese, may have all four food groups, if they use a tomato salsa or sauce. The Four Food Group plan can also be used for clients who exercise or train regularly. Eating more servings from the groups that provide carbohydrates (Fruit and Vegetable Group and Grain Group) will help athletes and active individuals meet their requirements for energy foods.

Teaching the Four Food Groups not only helps individuals learn the number of servings required from each group but also helps them realize which foods will provide the leader nutrients. For example, clients who want to know food sources of vitamin C need only review the Four Food Groups chart (Table 4–2) to see which foods will provide that nutrient. The Four Food Groups method of diet planning is a simple and an educational means of assuring an adequate, well-balanced diet for most clients.

Table 4–2   THE FOUR FOOD GROUPS

Milk Group

Key nutrients provided:
  calcium
  protein
  riboflavin

2 servings daily for adults
3 servings daily for children
4 servings daily for teenagers

One serving equals:
  1 cup milk
  1 cup yogurt
  1 oz cheese
  ½ cup cottage cheese
  ½ cup ice cream

Meat Group

Key nutrients provided:
  protein
  niacin
  iron
  thiamine

2 servings daily for all ages

One serving equals:
  2–3 oz lean meat, fish, poultry
  1 egg
  2 Tb peanut butter
  ¼ cup nuts, seeds
  ½ cup peas, beans

Fruit and Vegetable Group

Key nutrients provided:
  vitamin A
  vitamin C

4 servings for all ages
8 servings for athletes in
  heavy training

One serving equals:
  ½ cup juice
  ½ cup vegetable, fruit
  1 medium apple, banana, orange
  ½ grapefruit
  ¼ cantaloupe
  ¼ cup dried fruit

Grain Group

Key nutrients provided:
  carbohydrate
  thiamine
  iron
  niacin

4 servings for all ages
8 servings for athletes in
  heavy training

One serving equals:
  1 slice bread
  ½ English muffin
  1 oz ready-to-eat cereal
  ½ cup pasta, rice, cooked cereal
  ½ flour tortilla
  1½ corn tortillas

Food Groups for Vegetarians

The vegetarian faces a special problem in diet planning—that of obtaining the needed nutrients from fewer food groups. There are two major classes of vegetarians (with many variations): the **lacto-ovo vegetarian** eats milk and eggs but excludes meat, fish, and poultry from the diet, whereas a pure vegetarian, or **vegan**, excludes all of these foods and eats only foods from plant

Table 4–3   VITAMINS: SOURCES AND ADULT RDA

VITAMIN	SOURCES	ADULT RDA
Fat Soluble		
A	Liver, fortified milk and margarine, butter, egg yolk, leafy green and yellow vegetables, dried apricots, cantaloupe, peaches	800–1,000 I.U.*
D	Fortified milk, egg yolk, fish, and sunlight (absorbed through the skin)	400 I.U.
E	Vegetable oils, wheat germ and whole grains, nuts	30 I.U.
K	Leafy green vegetables, cabbage and cauliflower, tomatoes, wheat bran, milk (adults also produce vitamin K in their intestines)	70–80 mcg†
Water Soluble		
C	Citrus fruits, tomatoes, strawberries, melons, potatoes, broccoli, green peppers	50–60 mg‡
B_1 (Thiamine)	Pork, organ meats, legumes, whole-grain and enriched cereals and breads, wheat germ	1.0–1.5 mg
B_2 (Riboflavin)	Organ meats, milk and dairy products, whole-grain and enriched cereals and breads, eggs, fish, leafy green vegetables	1.2–1.8 mg
Niacin	Fish, liver, meat, poultry, eggs, peanuts, grains, legumes	13–19 mg
B_6 (Pyridoxine)	Meat, cereal bran and wheat germ, egg yolk, legumes	1.6–2.0 mg
B_{12}	Liver, kidney, meat, fish, milk, cheese (only in foods of animal origin)	3.0 mcg
Folic Acid (Folacin)	Green vegetables, organ meats, lean beef, eggs, fish, dry beans, lentils, asparagus, yeast	180–200 mcg
Pantothenic acid	Whole-grain cereals, organ meats, eggs, vegetables (found in most plant and vegetable foods)	2.0 mcg
Biotin	Liver, egg yolk, peanuts, yeast, milk, legumes, bananas, cereal	100–200 mcg

*International Units
†micrograms
‡milligrams

sources. For both types of diet, it is necessary to know how to combine foods to obtain the nutrients non-vegetarians get from the Meat and Milk groups. Foods derived from animal sources like chicken, fish, beef, milk, and eggs contain all the essential amino acids. These incomplete proteins can be made complete by combining them either with other foods that are complete proteins, such as cereal with milk, and rice with cheese, or with other incomplete proteins, such as beans with rice, and peanut butter with bread.

Many cultures have dishes or food combinations that meet the requisite amino acid combinations. In most cases, these dishes have been served for many generations. For example, Mexicans serve beans and tortillas and/or rice; Indians eat lentils and rice; Lebanese prepare humus tahini (garbanzo beans and sesame seed paste) with pita bread; and cornbread and beans are served in the southern United States.

For the lacto-ovo vegetarian, the Four Food Groups plan can be adapted by making a change in the meat group and by using non-meat proteins like eggs, dairy products, legumes, and nuts. The strict vegetarian, who doesn't use dairy products, should take a vitamin B_{12} supplement or use soy milk fortified with vitamin B_{12}.

NUTRIENT NEEDS

RDA (Recommended Dietary Allowances)

The United States government publishes recommendations concerning appropriate nutrient intakes for the people in this country. These are **Recommended Dietary Allowances (RDA)**. As Table 4-3 shows, the RDAs include recommendations for protein, ten vitamins, and six minerals, while additional tables include three more vitamins and nine more minerals as well as energy (calories). **USRDA**, which stands for United States Recommended Dietary Allowances, is used in food labeling to express the nutrients of the RDA in percentages.

The RDA have been much misunderstood. The following facts should help put them into perspective.

- The RDA are published by the government, but the study group that recommends them is composed of nutritionists and other scientists.

- They are recommendations, not requirements, and certainly not minimum requirements. They include a margin of safety (Fig. 4-1) that is so substantial that two-thirds of the RDA is often deemed adequate except for calorie intake.

- They recommend a range within which most of a healthy person's intake of nutrients probably should fall. Individuals' needs differ. While two-thirds of the RDA may be adequate for the general public, it may not be adequate for some. A physician who can provide a complete blood chemistry test should make an assessment.

- They are for healthy people only. Medical problems may alter nutrient needs.

Figure 4–1   Most people wrongly view the RDA as a minimum requirement (naive view). They are not requirements; they are recommendations. They include a margin of safety so that two-thirds of the RDA is often deemed adequate except for calorie intake.

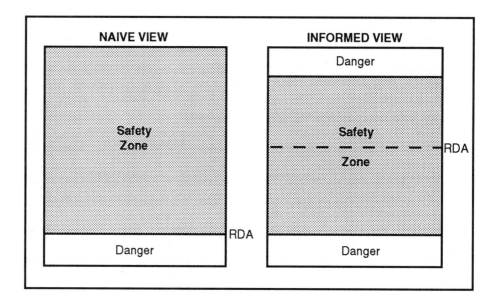

With the understanding that they are approximate, flexible, and generous, we can use the RDA as a yardstick to measure the adequacy of diets in whole populations. Personal trainers should not be assessing a client's diet using the RDA. This should be left to the client's physician and/or a registered dietitian. The personal trainer can, however, make the dietary suggestions by using the Four Food Groups approach, suggesting variety and moderation.

Vitamin/Mineral Supplementation

Because there is a lot of confusion in consumer's minds over what makes up a nutritionally balanced diet, and because most individuals don't understand the RDA, many Americans turn to **vitamin** and **mineral** supplementation as nutritional insurance. The question that arises is, should most people be taking a supplement? Generally, no. The consumer who takes a simple one-a-day type of vitamin or mineral supplement that does not exceed the nutrient levels of the RDA is probably not doing any harm. Most consumers do not need to take the supplement; however, this type of one-a-day supplementation does little harm even to the pocketbook. The consumer or client who limits food selection and calories may have a difficult time getting the recommended levels of nutrients. A multiple one-a-day could be recommended. Of greater concern is the supplement taker who has a whole cabinet full of supplements. These individuals take a handful of supplements for breakfast, perhaps several tablespoons of nutritional yeast and assorted pills containing trace minerals, powdered protein, and herbs. These consumers are asking the pills and supplements to play a role that is better delegated to food. Takers of self-prescribed supplements need a warning about the risks of overdosing. Concern should be expressed if individuals are taking high doses of fat-soluble vitamins (A, D, E, and K). These particular vitamins are stored within the body, and toxic levels have been found in people who take megadoses of these nutrients.

The water-soluble vitamins (B complex and C) are not stored within the body, and any excesses are excreted in the urine. It was once thought that a toxic level of water-soluble vitamins was impossible. But recent research shows that if consumers ingest megadoses of water soluble vitamins, those vitamins, too, can reach toxic levels.

Vitamin toxicity usually affects the nervous system. Both vitamins A and B_6 are known to produce adverse neurologic reactions (such as nerve transmission) when ingested in megadoses rather than the recommended nutritional doses. The symptoms of vitamin or mineral toxicity are vague at best; diarrhea, vomiting, skin rashes, and overall "just not feeling right" have been reported. Because these symptoms could describe any disease or illness, it is best for the personal trainer not to make recommendations about vitamin toxicity to clients. The personal trainer should, however, suggest that such clients seek professional medical advice about the symptoms. Encourage them to take their supplements to the physician and/or dietitian for assessment.

Because consumers may have strong beliefs in their vitamin supplement program, several strategies can be used to avoid upsetting them. Acknowledge their feelings and the values that underlie their practices, and then distinguish between practices that are dangerous and those that are not. For example, clients using supplements at pharmacological doses (greater than 100 times the RDA) are headed for toxic levels, unlike those who are just taking a multivitamin/mineral supplement once a day. Confront only the dangerous practices and ignore the harmless practices. Try to wean such clients gradually instead of allowing them to quit all at once. Encourage them to get their nutrients from foods. Educate your clients to the fact that there is a lot of information that scientists have not yet discovered about nutrients and the effect of their combinations in foods, and that it is most important to attain nutritional adequacy and balance by adopting the Four Food Groups plan.

Most individuals can meet the recommendation of the RDA by making wise food selections from the Four Food Groups. However, for women the nutrients most often lacking are calcium and iron.

CALCIUM. The need for calcium is greater during adolescence than in either childhood or adulthood. Approximately 45 percent of an adult's skeletal mass is formed during the pubertal growth spurt. The RDA for calcium for females 11 to 24 years of age is 1,200 mg. If calcium intake is inadequate during peak adolescent growth, it may predispose some individuals to osteoporosis in later life. Consumption of low-fat dairy products rich in calcium should be encouraged. There are many ways to incorporate calcium foods into the diet in order to meet the daily requirements of 1,200 mg. For example, two glasses of skim milk and two ounces of low-fat mozzarella cheese contain the recommended dietary allowance for young women. A combination of skim milk, low-fat cottage cheese, and frozen nonfat yogurt is also appropriate. To incorporate more calcium into the diet, clients might try the following tips:

- Prepare canned soup with skim milk instead of water.

- Add nonfat dry milk to soups, stews, casseroles, and even cookie recipes.

- Add grated low-fat cheese to salads, tacos, and pasta dishes.

- Have yogurt as a snack, or use it to make low calorie dressings.

- Choose calcium-rich desserts such as low-fat cheese and fruit, frozen nonfat or low-fat yogurt, and puddings made with skim milk.

- Drink hot chocolate made with skim milk.

It has also been reported that decreased physical activity reduces the efficiency of calcium utilization and may also contribute to bone loss. It would therefore

Table 4–4 FOODS HIGH IN CALCIUM

Milk and Milk Products	Calcium (in mg)
Whole milk (8 oz)	291
Low-fat milk, 1% (8 oz)	300
Low-fat milk, 2% (8 oz)	297
Skim milk (8 oz)	302
Low-fat chocolate milk (8 oz)	287
Lactaid, lactose-reduced low-fat milk (8 oz)	300
Low-fat yogurt, plain (1 cup)	415
Low-fat yogurt, fruit flavored (1 cup)	314
Hot chocolate prepared with milk (1 cup)	298
Milkshake, vanilla (8 oz)	457
Instant breakfast prepared with milk (8 oz)	470
Cheese	
American (1 oz)	124
Brick (1 oz)	191
Cheddar (1 oz)	204
Colby (1 oz)	194
Low-fat cottage cheese (1 cup)	138
Cream cheese (2 Tb)	23
Edam (1 oz)	206
Gouda (1 oz)	198
Havarti (1 oz)	176
Monterey Jack (1 oz)	212
Mozzarella (1 oz)	207
Muenster (1 oz)	203
Provolone (1 oz)	214
Ricotta (1 oz)	337
Romano (1 oz)	302
Swiss (1 oz)	272
Cheese spread (1 oz)	159

Fruits and Vegetables	
Figs, dried (10 figs)	269
Baked beans (1 cup)	155
Broccoli, cooked (1 cup)	178
Collards, cooked (1 cup)	148
Kale, cooked (1 cup)	172
Kidney beans, red, cooked (1 cup)	116
Navy beans, cooked (1 cup)	128
Okra, cooked (1 cup)	100
Spinach, frozen, boiled (½ cup)	139
Tofu (½ cup)	258

seem prudent to encourage women to have a lifelong exercise program in addition to consuming calcium-rich foods.

IRON.   Iron is present in all cells of the body and plays a key role in numerous reactions. It plays a vital role in the transport and activation of oxygen and is present in several pathways that create energy. Various studies have found the diets of women to be low in iron. One of the problems with dieting and limiting calories is that a woman may not be able to meet her iron requirements while trying to cut calories and lose weight. Because women face a potentially greater chance of lacking iron because of low caloric intakes and increased iron loss through menstruation, it has been suggested that they consider routine use of iron supplements, particularly during periods of heavy training. Iron supplementation in non-anemic women has not been shown to be useful, and may be potentially harmful. Clearly, there is some hazard from prolonged administration of large doses of iron to persons who are not iron-deficient. The hazard of serious iron overload resulting from supplementation exposes them needlessly to *hemosiderosis*, a disorder of iron metabolism in which large deposits of iron are made in the liver (Fairbanks & Bentherk, 1988). Routine screening tests of women should be performed by medical professionals, such as physicians and medical clinics to detect early stages of iron depletion. Those women found to be iron-deficient or anemic should receive professional dietary counseling from a physician or dietitian. Supplemental iron may be indicated in individual cases; however, routine use of iron supplements by all females is not warranted.

To ensure adequate intake of iron, trainers should encourage the following:

- At each meal, eat foods high in vitamin C to help the body absorb iron. For example, drink orange juice with an iron-enriched cereal, or combine pasta with broccoli, tomatoes, and green peppers, or salsa and/or chili peppers with a bean burrito.

- Include meat, preferably lean red meat, and the dark meat of chicken and turkey, as part of the training diet. These foods provide the body with a form of iron called heme-iron that is more readily absorbed than the type of iron found in vegetables and grains.

- To enhance the absorption of non-heme-iron (vegetable and grain sources of iron), combine vegetable proteins with meat. For example, split pea soup with ham, tuna noodle casserole, turkey vegetable soup, chicken soup with lentils, or chili beans with lean ground turkey or hamburger.

- To increase iron as well as carbohydrates, eat cereals, breads, and pastas labeled "enriched" or "fortified".

Women should be encouraged to make daily selections of calcium and iron-rich foods. Tables 4-4 and 4-5 list foods that are excellent sources of these two nutrients and will help trainers and clients make wiser food choices.

DIETARY GUIDELINES

In the 1960s a select committee on nutrition and human needs was formed to study the nutritional status of the United States population. For about 17 years the committee held hearings on malnutrition, hunger, obesity, nutrition, and heart disease. Seeing many connections, the committee published Dietary Goals for the United States, which emphasized sugar, fat, **cholesterol**, and salt as items to avoid. In the three years that followed, critics reacted violently against the goals. The committee published a revised edition that suggested weight reduction, if necessary, and the avoidance of alcohol overuse. The committee disbanded in the late '70s, and the Department of Health and Human Services and the Department of Agriculture jointly published *Dietary Guidelines*

Table 4–5   IRON-RICH FOODS

Meats	Iron (in mg)
Beef brisket, lean (3½ oz)	2.2
Pot roast, lean (3½ oz)	3.1
Flank steak, lean (3½ oz)	2.5
Hamburger, lean (3½ oz)	2.4
Beef ribs, BBQ (3½ oz)	2.5
T-Bone steak (3½ oz)	3.0
Sirloin steak (3½ oz)	3.5
Pork chop (3 oz)	4.0
Hot dog (1)	1.0
Chicken, dark meat (3½ oz)	1.4
Chicken, light meat (3½ oz)	1.3
Turkey, dark meat (3½ oz)	2.3
Turkey, light meat (3½ oz)	1.4

Fruits and Vegetables	
Apricots, dried (10 halves)	1.5
Dates, dried (10)	1.0
Figs, dried (10)	4.2
Peaches, dried (10 halves)	5.3
Raisins (⅔ cup)	2.0
Strawberries, frozen (1 cup)	1.5
Baked beans (1 cup)	3.0
Refried beans (1 cup)	4.5
Black beans (1 cup)	3.6
Broccoli (½ cup)	.9
Brussel sprouts (½ cup)	1.0
Garbanzo beans (chick-peas) (1 cup)	4.7
Black-eyed peas (1 cup)	4.3
Green beans (1 cup)	1.0
Kidney beans (1 cup)	3.0
Lima beans (1 cup)	4.5
Navy beans (1 cup)	4.8
Peas, green (½ cup)	1.3
Pinto beans (1 cup)	4.5
Potato, baked (1 large)	2.8
Spinach, boiled (½ cup)	2.6

Grains	
Bagel (1)	1.5
Cornbread (1 square)	1.5
English muffin (1)	1.7
Bran muffin (1)	1.3
Pancakes made from mix (3 pancakes)	1.5
Enriched pasta (1 cup)	2.0

Cereal	Iron (in mg)
Ready-to-Eat	
Apple Jacks (1 cup)	4.5
Cheerios (1¼ cup)	4.5
Corn Bran, Quaker (⅔ cup)	8.1
Crispy Wheats and Raisins (¾ cup)	4.5
Fruit and Fiber (½ cup)	4.4
Golden Grahams (¾ cup)	4.5
Grape-nut Flakes (⅞ cup)	8.0
Honey Nut Cheerios (¾ cup)	4.5
Life, Quaker (⅔ cup)	8.1
Cinnamon Life, Quaker (⅔ cup)	8.1
Most (⅔ cup)	18.0
Product 19 (¾ cup)	18.0
Raisin Bran (¾ cup)	4.5
Special K (¾ cup)	4.5
Total (1 cup)	18.0
Trix (1 cup)	4.5
Wheaties (1 cup)	4.5
Hot Cereal	
Cream of Wheat, Instant (¾ cup)	9.0
Cream of Wheat, Mix and Eat (1 packet)	8.1
Malt-o-Meal (¾ cup)	7.1
Quaker Instant Oatmeal	
plain (1 packet)	8.1
apples and cimmamon (1 packet)	6.1
bran and raisins (1 packet)	4.5
cinnamon and spice (1 packet)	8.1
honey and graham (1 packet)	4.5
maple and brown sugar (1 packet)	8.1
peaches and cream (1 packet)	4.5
raisins and spice (1 packet)	4.5
raisins, dates and walnuts (1 packet)	4.5
strawberries and cream (1 packet)	4.5
Wheatena (¾ cup)	1.0

for Americans (Human Nutrition Information Service, 1986). This document lists somewhat different goals, but does emphasize that all Americans should:

1. Eat a wide variety of foods.
2. Maintain ideal body weight.
3. Avoid too much fat, saturated fat, and cholesterol.
4. Eat adequate amounts of starch and fiber.
5. Avoid too much sugar.
6. Avoid too much sodium.
7. Consume alcohol in moderation, if at all.

There have been many different reactions to the goals and guidelines; however, most health professionals seem to think that some of the guidelines are desirable, especially the one that emphasizes reducing fat, saturated fat, and cholesterol. Figure 4–2 expresses the Dietary Goals in quantitative amounts and compares them to our current dietary pattern.

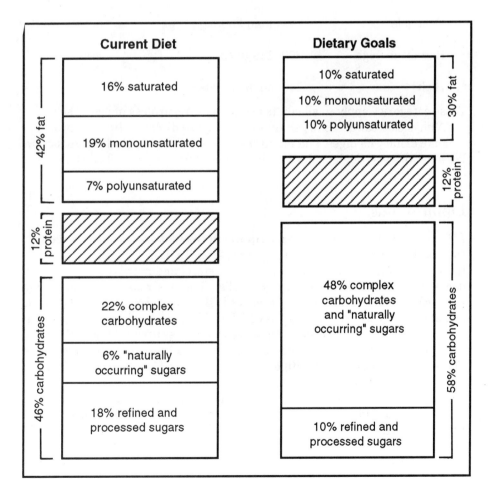

Figure 4–2 Dietary goals of the United States.

HEART DISEASE

Almost 30 percent of the nearly 2 million deaths in this country each year are the result of coronary heart disease. Most coronary heart disease is due to blockages in the arteries that supply blood to the heart muscle. Fat, saturated fat, and cholesterol, circulating in the blood, are deposited on the inner walls of the arteries. Over the years, scar tissue builds up as more fat and cholesterol are deposited. The arteries become narrower and narrower. This process is known as **atherosclerosis**.

Cholesterol

Genetic and animal studies have shown that elevated levels of blood **cholesterol** lead to early development of coronary heart disease. Research studies have shown that individuals with high blood cholesterol have more of a chance of developing heart disease than do people with lower levels of cholesterol, and that the chances of developing coronary heart disease increase in proportion to the amount the cholesterol is elevated, especially for cholesterol values over 200 mg/dl. Recently, the National Cholesterol Education program classified blood cholesterol levels for adults:

Desirable	Less than 200 mg/dl
Borderline–high	200–239 mg/dl
High	240 mg/dl and above

These categories apply to all adults over age 20, regardless of age or sex.

A physician can assess a person's risk for heart disease, offer advice on how to make dietary changes, and monitor progress toward cholesterol reduction. Persons with very high cholesterol levels might need a prescribed cholesterol-lowering drug.

Lipoproteins

LDL and *HDL* refer to two types of **lipoproteins** that are made by the body to transport fat and cholesterol through the blood. **LDLs**, or low-density lipoproteins, contain the greatest amounts of cholesterol and may be responsible for depositing cholesterol on the artery walls. For this reason they are sometimes called "bad" cholesterol. Levels of LDL cholesterol that are 160 mg/dl and above are classified as high risk LDL. LDL cholesterol can be lowered by exercise, weight loss, incorporating more **monounsaturated** and **polyunsaturated** fats into the diets, and decreasing the overall percentage of fat calories. Those clients with extremely high levels of LDL may have to go on medication to control LDL cholesterol.

HDLs, or high-density lipoproteins, contain more protein than cholesterol. They are responsible for removing cholesterol from the cells in the arteries and transporting it back to the liver for repackaging and removal from the body. Studies have shown that individuals with higher levels of HDL have less heart disease. Thus, HDLs have become known as the "good" cholesterol. HDL cholesterol below 35 mg/dl is considered a risk factor for coronary heart disease. Several factors have been found to raise HDLs. For example, regular, consistent exercise will raise HDL. One study showed that persons who ran just eight miles per week saw an increase in HDL. Moderate alcohol consumption

Table 4–6   RISK FACTORS FOR CORONARY HEART DISEASE

- **Being Male.** Males have higher blood cholesterol than premenopausal women. After menopause, however, the cholesterol level of women usually increases to a level higher than that of men.

- **Family History of Heart Disease.** Genetic factors play a major role in determining blood cholesterol level. Some people have an inherited tendency towards high blood cholesterol.

- **Being Overweight.** Being overweight may increase blood cholesterol levels. Most overweight patients with high levels of cholesterol can help lower their levels through weight reduction.

- **Lack of Exercise.** Regular exercise may help control weight, lower blood pressure, and increase the level of HDL cholesterol.

- **High Cholesterol.** Persons with high blood cholesterol have a significantly higher risk of developing heart disease.

- **Being a Smoker.** Cigarette smoking increases the risk for coronary heart disease. Advice to quit smoking is particularly important because it has the potential not only to reduce heart disease by 50 percent but also to prevent cancer and chronic lung disease.

Note: See Chapter 5 for more details

also appears to raise HDLs; however, most health professionals recommend exercise as a better method of raising HDL cholesterol.

Clients with desirable blood cholesterol levels (<200 mg/dl) are advised to have another serum cholesterol test within three years. Clients with cholesterol levels of 200 mg/dl or greater should have the value confirmed by repeating the test, and the average used as a guide.

Those who have high blood cholesterol (240 mg/dl or greater) should undergo lipoprotein analysis, as should those with borderline high blood cholesterol (200–239 mg/dl), who are at high risk because they have definite coronary heart disease, or those with two other risk factors. See Table 4–6 for a discussion of risk factors. A more detailed discussion of risk factors appears in Chapter 5.

Clients with confirmed borderline high cholesterol with no symptoms of heart disease or those with two other risk factors need no further evaluation and should be given the dietary information designed for the general population. However, clients may still request a lipoprotein analysis. Personal trainers, with the technology available today, can provide initial cholesterol screening. However, if lipoprotein analysis is desired, this must be done by a medical professional using a 12-hour fast and a venipuncture blood draw. All patients with an LDL cholesterol greater than 160 mg/dl, and those with a level of 130–159 mg/dl and high-risk status should be evaluated clinically by a physician.

Triglycerides

The bulk of fat consumed in the diet is ingested in the form of **triglycerides**. Triglycerides are made up of a glycerol backbone with three **fatty acids** attached (Fig. 4–3). The fatty acids attached to the glycerol may differ from one another in two ways: in chain length, and in degree of saturation. *Saturation* refers to the chemical structure. A **saturated fatty acid** is one that carries

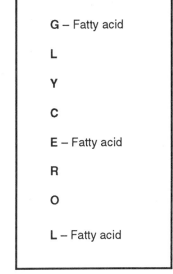

G – Fatty acid

L

Y

C

E – Fatty acid

R

O

L – Fatty acid

Figure 4–3   Structure of a triglyceride.

the maximum number of hydrogen atoms, leaving no points of unsaturation. Unsaturated fatty acids can be divided into two kinds: monounsaturated and polyunsaturated. Food fats contain a mixture of the three kinds of fatty acids.

When a fat contains predominantly saturated fatty acids, it is said to be a saturated fat. Similarly, when a fat or oil contains a large proportion of monounsaturated or polyunsaturated fatty acids, it is called a monounsaturated fat or a polyunsaturated fat, respectively. Saturated fat will increase blood levels of cholesterol. The more saturated fat an individual eats, the higher the cholesterol will go. The major sources of saturated fatty acids in the diet are the fats from animal products, such as meats and whole milk dairy products. Low-fat dairy products are lower in saturated fats and should be recommended for adults who need to lower saturated fats and cholesterol. A few vegetable fats are quite high in saturated fatty acids: coconut oil, palm kernel oil, palm oil, and the cocoa fat found in chocolate. These four oils are not available for consumer purchase; however, they are often used in commercial baked goods and other processed foods.

Since saturated fats raise blood cholesterol, eating less saturated fat is recommended. Key points to remember about eating less saturated fats are:

- Reducing total fat can reduce saturated fat as well.

- Most animal fats contain high proportions of saturated fat, whereas vegetable foods provide a higher proportion of polyunsaturated fatty acids.

- The vegetable oils from palm kernel, coconut, and palm, as well as cocoa fat, contain large proportions of saturated fat.

- Some margarines are lower in saturated fat and higher in unsaturated fats than butter.

Tips for Clients About Fats and Oils

- Choose low-fat dairy products, lean cuts of meat, chicken, and fish.

- Choose low-fat baked goods made with oils high in unsaturated fat and low in saturated fat.

- When using fats and oils, use only small amounts, and replace those high in saturated fat with items high in polyunsaturates or high in total unsaturates.

- Read the nutrient section of food labels to choose items low in saturated fatty acids.

- When buying margarines, read the list of ingredients. Choose the brands that list liquid vegetable oils first.

Remember, the key to nutrition is to eat a wide variety of foods from the Four Food Groups and be moderate with foods that are high in fat, saturated fat, and calories.

NUTRITION AND EXERCISE

People who exercise are usually aware of nutrition but unfortunately they don't always know how to apply that knowledge, or they fall prey to the myths and fallacies that surround nutrition.

Water

Water is by far the most important nutrient for the athlete. For optimal performance, fluids must be replaced before, during, and after exercise. Most people rely on thirst as an indicator of how much water is lost. Unfortunately, thirst is *not* an accurate indicator of how much fluid the body has lost. Water losses can and must be monitored by one of two methods:

- The client weighs in before and after a workout. For each pound of body weight lost, *two* cups of fluid must be consumed.

- Check the color of their urine. A dark gold color means the client is dehydrated. A pale yellow or no color means that the client is headed toward a state of hydration.

GUIDELINES FOR FLUID REPLACEMENT.

- Consume 3–6 ounces every 10–15 minutes during a workout.

- Consume cold fluids since they empty from the stomach most quickly.

- If the exercise or workout lasts longer than 90 minutes of continual work, then sports drinks can be used because muscle glycogen has depleted and the body needs a source of carbohydrates.

- If the exercise workout is less than 90 minutes, then water is the experts' choice for fluid replacement.

- Sports drinks need not be diluted, as long as the sugar concentration is no higher than 6 percent. Beverages that supply more than 9 percent carbohydrates lengthen the time it takes water to empty from the stomach, thereby compounding dehydration.

Carbohydrates

Another area of confusion to the exercising population is how much carbohydrate food to eat. Generally, consumers have no idea how many calories they need, let alone the percentage of carbohydrates from the total calories they consume. Advice like "Eat 50–70 percent carbohydrates" means little to most people. Grams of carbohydrate mean more and are easier to calculate than percents. Give a list of common foods in grams of carbohydrates to the client (Table 4–7). Recommend between 400 and 500 grams of carbohydrates daily for optimal **glycogen** storage. The list also serves to show which foods contain a high proportion of carbohydrates and should therefore be included in the daily diet.

CARBOHYDRATE LOADING. Muscle glycogen depletion is a well-recognized limitation to endurance exercise that exceeds 90 minutes. Athletes using glycogen supercompensation techniques (*carbohydrate loading*) can nearly double their muscle glycogen stores. Obviously, the greater the pre-exercise glycogen content, the greater the endurance potential.

The classic study on carbohydrate loading (Bergstrom et al., 1967) compared exercise time to exhaustion at 75 percent of VO_2 max after three days of three diets varying in carbohydrate content—a low carbohydrate diet, a normal

Table 4–7   HIGH CARBOHYDRATE FOODS (WITH GRAM WEIGHT)

	Calories	Carbohydrate (in gm)
Milk Group		
Low-fat (2%) milk (1 cup)	121	12
Skim milk (1 cup)	86	12
Chocolate milk (1 cup)	208	26
Pudding, any flavor (½ cup)	161	30
Frozen yogurt, low-fat (1 cup)	220	34
Fruit-flavored low-fat yogurt (1 cup)	225	42
Meat Group		
Blackeyed peas (½ cup)	134	22
Pinto beans (1 cup)	235	44
Navy beans (1 cup)	259	48
Refried beans (½ cup)	142	26
Meat loaf (3 oz)	230	13
Fruit and Vegetable Group		
Fruits		
Apple (1 medium)	81	21
Apple juice (1 cup)	111	28
Applesauce (1 cup)	232	60
Banana (1)	105	27
Canteloupe (1 cup)	57	14
Cherries, raw (10)	49	11
Cranberry juice cocktail (1 cup)	147	37
Dates, dried (10)	228	61
Fruit cocktail, packed in own juice (½ cup)	56	15
Fruit rollups (1 roll)	50	12
Grapes (1 cup)	114	28
Grape juice (1 cup)	96	23
Orange (1)	65	16
Orange juice (1 cup)	112	26
Pear (1)	98	25
Pineapple (1 cup)	77	19
Prunes, dried (10)	201	53
Raisins (⅔ cup)	302	79
Raspberries (1 cup)	61	14
Strawberries (1 cup)	45	11
Watermelon (1 cup)	50	12
Vegetables		
3-Bean salad (½ cup)	90	20
Carrots (1 medium)	31	8
Corn (½ cup)	89	21
Garbanzo beans (chick-peas) (1 cup)	269	45
Lima beans (1 cup)	217	39
Peas, green (½ cup)	63	12
Potato (1 large)	220	50
Sweet potato (1 large)	118	28
Water chestnuts (½ cup)	66	15
White beans (1 cup)	249	45

Table 4–7 HIGH CARBOHYDRATE FOODS (WITH GRAM WEIGHT)(CONT.)

	Calories	Carbohydrate (in gm)
Grain Group		
Bagel (1)	165	31
Biscuit (1)	103	13
White bread (1 slice)	61	12
Whole wheat bread (1 slice)	55	11
Breadsticks (2 sticks)	77	15
Cornbread (1 square)	178	28
Cereal, ready-to-eat (1 cup)	110	24
Oatmeal (½ cup)	66	12
Cream of rice (¾ cup)	95	21
Cream of wheat (¾ cup)	96	20
Malto-Meal (¾ cup)	92	19
Flavored oatmeal, Quaker instant (1 packet)	110	25
Graham crackers (2 squares)	60	11
Saltines (5 crackers)	60	10
Triscuit crackers (3 crackers)	60	10
Pancake (4" diameter)	61	9
Waffles (2, 3.5" x 5.5")	130	17
Rice (1 cup)	223	50
Rice, brown (1 cup)	232	50
Hamburger bun (1)	119	21
Hot dog bun (1)	119	21
Noodles, spaghetti (1 cup)	159	34
Flour tortilla (1)	85	15

diet, and a high carbohydrate diet. The low carbohydrate diet sustained only an hour of exercise; the mixed diet sustained 115 minutes of exercise; and the high carbohydrate diet sustained 170 minutes of the high intensity exercise.

Following additional research, the carbohydrate loading sequence developed into a week-long regimen, starting with an exhaustive training session one week before competition. For the next three days, the athlete consumed a low carbohydrate diet, yet continued exercising, to lower muscle glycogen stores even further. Then for three days prior to competition, the athlete rested and consumed a high carbohydrate diet to promote glycogen supercompensation. For many years, this week-long sequence was considered the optimal way to achieve maximum glycogen storage. However, this regimen has many drawbacks. The three days of reduced carbohydrate intake can cause **hypoglycemia** (low blood sugar) and **ketosis** (increased blood acids) with associated nausea, fatigue, dizziness, and irritability. The dietary manipulations prove to be too cumbersome for many athletes, and an exhaustive training session the week before competition may predispose the athlete to injury.

A revised method of carbohydrate loading has been proposed that eliminates many of the problems associated with the old regimen. Six days before the competition, the athlete exercises hard (70–75 percent of aerobic capacity for 90 minutes) and consumes a normal diet providing 50 percent carbohydrate. On the second and third days, training is decreased to 40 minutes at 70–75 percent of aerobic capacity and again the athlete consumes a normal diet. On the next two days, the athlete consumes a high carbohydrate diet providing 70 percent carbohydrate (about 550 gm, or 10 gm per kg) and reduces training to 20 minutes at 70–75 percent of aerobic capacity. On the last day,

Table 4–8   CARBOHYDRATE LOADING REGIME

Day	Exercise Duration	Dietary Carbohydrate (percentage)
1	90 minutes	50
2	40 minutes	50
3	40 minutes	50
4	20 minutes	70
5	20 minutes	70
6	Rest	70
7	Competition	

the athlete rests while maintaining the high carbohydrate diet. The modified regimen results in muscle glycogen stores equal to those provided by the classic low carbohydrate regimen (See Table 4–8).

Protein

Recent research (Lemon, 1987) suggests that protein may play a greater role in providing energy for exercise than previously thought. However, protein intakes of most exercising individuals are adequate, if not excessive. When assessing protein intakes for clients, guidelines must be used. Generally, for adolescents, 1.0 gm protein/kg of body weight is used. For adults involved in very heavy weight training (1 hour or more) or those involved in endurance training, the recommendation is 1.5 gm protein/kg of body weight (see Table 4–9). This added quantity is still very easily attained in the average diet, and no protein or amino acid supplements should be encouraged. Potential problems with excessive protein or amino acid intakes include excessive weight gain, dehydration, and excessive loss of urinary calcium. High protein intakes may impose a heavy burden on the liver and kidney to secrete excess nitrogen.

Amino acid imbalances and toxicities are possible if single amino acid supplements such as arginine and ornithine are consumed in large quantities to achieve growth hormone release and muscle development. Because single amino acid supplements have not been routinely consumed by humans in the past, little scientific data is available. Athletes should be informed that single amino acid supplements in large doses have not been tested in human subjects, and therefore no margin of safety is available. Amino acids taken in large doses are essentially drugs with unknown physiologic effects.

Vitamins and Minerals

Like all consumers, the exercising population is bombarded with information about what to eat, what not to eat, and what supplement they should or should not be taking. Food records from exercising individuals show that they get more than enough of the leader vitamins from food. For the most part, athletes who use supplements have adequate diets; those with less adequate diets, generally due to calorie restriction or dieting, do not use supplements.

When counseling clients who use supplements, remember that consideration should be given to nutrient deficiencies, toxic levels, and unnecessary supplementation. Deficiencies of vitamins and minerals can be damaging to work performance and growth in young adolescents because of their role in releasing energy from food. However, this does not mean that vitamin or

Table 4–9   PROTEIN CALCULATIONS FOR EXERCISING INDIVIDUALS

To calculate protein requirements, take:
1. Weight (in pounds) and divide by 2.2 = _____ (weight in kg)
2. Weight in kg _____ × 1.5 gm protein per kg = _____ gm protein/day

For example, a 154-lb male needs 105 gm protein/day:
154 ÷ 2.2 = 70 kg
70 × 1.5 = 105 gm protein/day

Remember, there are:
8 gm protein/serving dairy products
7 gm protein/ounce meat
2 gm protein/serving carbohydrates

Most protein sources in the Four Food Groups plan are found in the Meat Group and the Milk Group:
3 oz chicken × 7 gm protein/oz = 21 gm protein
1 cup low-fat milk × 8 gm protein/serving = 8 gm protein

mineral supplementation will further improve performance for fit people who are already well nourished. There is a consensus among sports nutritionists that when clients consume less than 70 percent of the RDA in their diet, diet modification is indicated, and perhaps a multiple one-a-day supplement should be considered. Fit individuals consuming megadoses of vitamins and minerals may be at risk for toxicity.

DISPELLING SPORT NUTRITION MYTHS

1. Large amounts of protein will increase strength and size. There is no evidence to show that consuming excess amounts of protein will increase muscle strength or size. In fact, protein consumed in excess of what the body needs will be converted to fat. It is true athletes in heavy training (muscular endurance training lasting 60–90 minutes) may need 18–24 percent of their calories from protein, while non-athletes require only 12 percent. The reason is that during heavy training periods the body may have a reduction in protein stores. However, this increased requirement can be met with a well-balanced diet and by selecting protein-rich foods more often during the periods of heavy training.

2. Eating honey, candy bars, soft drinks, or sugar before competing will provide a quick burst of energy. Since these foods have a high sugar content, eating them an hour or less before competition causes the amount of insulin in the blood to rise, and the sugar in the blood is removed too quickly. Low blood sugar results, and the exerciser may feel tired and weak. However, more recent evidence suggests that high carbohydrate foods taken 2–3 hours prior to competition may improve performance. Does this mean that endurance athletes should load up on soft drinks and candy bars before they exercise? Comparison of the results of the old and new studies suggests that individuals differ in susceptibility to a lowering of blood glucose during exercise. The physiological basis for this difference has not been determined. At this time, athletes should be advised that consuming sugar-containing foods

30–45 minutes prior to exercise could harm their performance if they are sensitive to a lowering of their blood glucose level.

3. Drinking water prior to and during exercise causes upset stomach and cramps. Water is the most important nutrient to an exercising individual. Restricting fluids during exercise, especially in hot weather, can cause severe dehydration and limit performance. Exercising individuals should drink one-half cup of water every 10–15 minutes during exercise to help replace body fluids lost through perspiration. The exercising individual should monitor water losses, and rehydrate with the appropriate amount (see earlier section on fluid).

4. Drinking milk causes cotton mouth and reduces speed. There is no evidence that cotton mouth results from drinking milk. Cotton mouth seems to result from emotional stress and loss of body fluids. Milk consumption should not be restricted because milk is an important source of calcium, which is necessary for the proper development of bones and teeth, and should be consumed as part of a daily meal plan.

5. Muscle cramps are caused by inadequate salt intake. Cramps are caused by excess water loss through perspiration. Water should be consumed before, during, and after exercise to prevent dehydration. Ingesting salt tablets can aggravate existing dehydration by drawing water out of body tissues and into the stomach.

6. Taking vitamin and mineral supplements will give more energy. Not one of the 14 vitamins has been shown to supply energy. Their role is to release the energy from food. While some vitamins are involved in energy production, taking excess amounts of these vitamins will not give the individual more energy. Additionally, all 14 vitamins are supplied by a well-balanced diet. Megadoses of vitamins and minerals do not supply extra energy.

7. Tea and coffee are the best precompetition beverages. Tea and coffee contain caffeine, a stimulant. While some research has found caffeine can improve endurance performance by increasing the use of fat as an energy source, thus sparing muscle glycogen, not all individuals will get this effect. In fact, a hypersensitive response resulting in increased heart rate and anxiety may occur in many people. There is also increased urine production, which can lead to dehydration.

8. Crash diets are the fastest, most effective way to lose weight. While large amounts of weight can be lost by following a crash diet, the weight lost is muscle mass, glycogen stores, and water, not excess body-fat. As a result, the individual's endurance is impaired. There are other problems associated with crash diets, including electrolyte imbalances, calcium deficiency, iron deficiency anemia, and other vitamin and mineral deficiencies. A person should lose no more than two pounds per week. The fastest way to lose weight is with a combination of diet and exercise. If one eats 500 calories less per day and burns 500 calories more per day through exercise, by the end of one week one might lose two pounds. It is important to be sensible about diet—any crash diet results in poor performance. (See Chapter 10 for more information on weight control.)

9. Special supplements such as aspartic acid, brewer's yeast, ginseng, bee pollen, and strawberry extract improve athletic performance. There is no scientific evidence to show these compounds contribute anything to performance. Some of these supplements may even be harmful. Since many of them are expensive, it is wise for most people not to purchase them at all.

SUMMARY

Fortunately, the same diet that enhances health also maximizes performance for most clients. Because carbohydrates are the main fuel for the exercising muscle, it is extremely important to consume at least 55–70 percent of the total calories from carbohydrates. Probably the most important nutrient concern is water. A 2 percent decrease in body weight due to sweat will decrease performance. Additional decreases can lead to heat-related problems. Exercising people must monitor their water losses. It is important to keep a close watch on calcium and iron intake, especially for female athletes and adolescent male athletes; performance can be impaired with even a mild iron deficiency. The dietary intakes of consumers are usually above the RDA for most nutrients (except iron and calcium in women). Megadoses of vitamins or minerals do not enhance performance. If a person still feels the need to take a supplement, then a multiple type vitamin is recommended, although it's probably not needed.

REFERENCES

Bergstrom, J., Hermanson, L., Hultman, E., & Saltin, B. (1967). Diet muscle glycogen and physical performance. *Acta Physiol. Scand.*, 71, 140–150.

Fairbanks, V.F., & Beutler, E. (1988). Iron. In M.E. Shils & V.R. Young (Eds.), *Modern nutrition in health and disease*. Philadelphia: Lea & Febiger.

Human Nutrition Information Service. (1986). *Dietary guidelines for Americans*. Washington, D.C.: U.S. Department of Agriculture.

Lemon, P.W.R. (1987). Protein and exercise: Update 1987. *Med. Sci. Sports Exercise*, 19, S179–S190.

SUGGESTED READING

Clark, N. (1990). *Nancy Clark's sports nutrition guidebook*. Champaign, IL: Leisure Press.

Hamilton, E.M., & Whitney, E.N. (1985). *Nutrition: Concepts and controversies* (3rd ed.). St. Paul, MN: West.

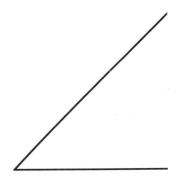

Screening and Evaluation   PART II

Any successful client/trainer relationship starts with the gathering of valuable baseline data. The trainer is responsible for screening clients to determine if their health status and goals are matched with the trainer's capabilities. It is not uncommon for the trainer to refer the potential client to a more qualified medical professional for initial clearance based on information gathered in the screening process. The evaluation of the client's beginning fitness level and the establishment of quantifiable goals are crucial to the development of any successful exercise program. The chapters on screening and evaluation are designed to help the trainer through these important first steps. Sample screening forms and detailed descriptions of common fitness evaluation exercises are provided. The importance of these first two steps cannot be overemphasized.

Health Screening

JEFF ANTHONY, D.O.

5

JEFF ANTHONY, D.O., is a team physician at San Diego State University and for the USA Men's and Women's Olympic Volleyball teams. He is staff physician at the San Diego Family Practice & Sports Medicine Center and lectures on sports medicine at colleges and medical conferences, as well as for IDEA. He is also a member of the IDEA Advisory Board.

IN THIS CHAPTER:

- Medical disorders and conditions that may make exercise unsafe.

- The effects of medications on the heart-rate response to exercise.

- Importance of a physical evaluation for blood pressure, heart rate, flexibility, and strength.

- When to refer clients for medical clearance or further evaluation.

Health screening is a means for the personal trainer to: (1) identify medical conditions that may place the client at risk when participating in certain activities; (2) identify possible contraindicated activities; (3) assist in designing an exercise program that includes safe activities and/or appropriate modifications, and (4) fulfill legal and insurance requirements for the personal trainer or health club. This chapter will identify some of the more common conditions a personal trainer may encounter requiring modifications in an exercise program and/or physician participation.

If the purpose of an exercise program is to improve one's quality of life, aggravating an existing medical condition is, of course, counterproductive to the goal. To set up the most effective program, personal trainers need to evaluate their clients' medical conditions and their goals. If a significant medical condition or risk factor for injury exists, a client may need medical clearance or recommendations from a physician. The need for medical clearance should not deter a trainer from working with a client. With proper modifications, almost everyone can and should engage in exercise. In these cases, the personal trainer, client, and physician act in harmony to coordinate the most effective program, giving careful consideration to the risks, benefits, and goals of exercise.

Is exercise worth the trouble? If so, why doesn't the physician prescribe it? There is no doubt that appropriate exercise is beneficial, but many physicians don't have the training or the time to provide the education, encouragement, and motivation most people need. Only in the last two decades has exercise truly been appreciated as a medical necessity. In the early 1900s, the average life expectancy was 50 years, and most people died of infections and acute diseases. With the advent of antibiotics, immunizations, and better health care, people are now living much longer. The average life expectancy is now approaching 80 years. People today die primarily from chronic diseases, which are largely a result of the way they live.

Statistics tell us that in the 1990s, 80 percent of the deaths in the United States will be from diseases that are largely a result of life-style (Rosenstein, 1987). That's good news because we now have a say in how we die, by taking responsibility for how we live. It becomes obvious that we have to take care of ourselves even better than our parents did. We can compare our bodies with our automobiles: the ones that are taken care of and not abused last longer with better performance. With the human body, the key ingredients to a healthy life are:

- Exercise.

- Good nutrition.

- Stress alleviation/management.

- Psychological and spiritual balance.

- Routine check-ups.

A personal trainer specifically addresses the importance of exercise, which positively influences the other components. A sedentary life-style is now recognized as a health hazard, and everyone can benefit from some form of exercise. However, before beginning to work with a client, a trainer must take a medical history, assess client goals for and commitment to exercise, and assess the client's fitness level.

HEALTH SCREENING FORMS

The health history is a personal trainer's primary tool for setting up a safe and effective training program. The sample health history form in Figure 5-1 can serve as a model for trainers to modify as needed. Listing common conditions that affect the ability to exercise enables a trainer to identify the major health risks for clients beginning a program. The information on the form should be updated every 6-12 months or when new conditions arise.

Clients who answer "yes" to any one of the questions (1-16) may be at increased risk for injury during exercise. These clients should obtain a physician's release before starting an exercise program. In addition, men over 40 years of age, women over 45, and any client with a medical condition the trainer is not thoroughly equipped to handle should obtain clearance from a physician. The physician's release serves several purposes: (1) it minimizes the client's risk, (2) it reduces the trainer's liability, and (3) it enables the physician to direct modifications in the exercise program. Figure 5-2 provides a sample release form, which identifies the planned exercise program to the physician and enables the physician to return his/her consent and recommendations.

MEDICAL CONDITIONS THAT AFFECT EXERCISE

Are there risks to exercise? Yes, and identification of these risks is the first step to preventing them. Injuries in sport usually come from:

NAME _____ DATE _____

Sex M F

Physician's Name _____

Physician's Phone # _____

Person to Contact in Case of Emergency

Name _____ Relationship _____ Phone # _____

Are you taking any medications or drugs? What?

Does your physician know you are participating in this exercise program?

Describe your exercise program now.

Do you now, or have you had in the past:	Yes	No
1. History of heart problems, chest pain or stroke.	—	—
2. Increased blood pressure.	—	—
3. Any chronic illness or condition.	—	—
4. Difficulty with physical exercise.	—	—
5. Advice from physician not to exercise.	—	—
6. Recent surgery (last 12 months).	—	—
7. Pregnancy (now or within last 3 months).	—	—
8. History of breathing or lung problems.	—	—
9. Muscle, joint, or back disorder, or any previous injury still affecting you.	—	—
10. Diabetes or thyroid condition.	—	—
11. Cigarette smoking habit.	—	—
12. Obesity (more than 20 percent over ideal body weight).	—	—
13. Increased blood cholesterol.	—	—
14. History of heart problems in immediate family.	—	—
15. Hernia, or any condition that may be aggravated by lifting weights.	—	—
16. Please explain any yes answers on back.	—	—

Comments _____

_____

_____

_____

Figure 5–1 Sample Health History Form

Date _____

Dear Doctor:

Your patient _____ wishes to start a personalized training program. The activity will involve the following:

   (type, frequency, duration and intensity of activities)
_____

_____

If your patient is taking medications that will affect his or her heart rate response to exercise, please indicate the manner of the effect (raises, lowers, or has no effect on heart rate response):

Type of medication _____

Effect _____

Please identify any recommendations or restrictions that are appropriate for your patient in this exercise program:

_____

_____

Thank you.

Sincerely,

Fred Fitness
Personalized Gym
Address
Phone

_____ has my approval to begin an exercise program with the recommendations or restrictions stated above.

Signed _____ Date _____ Phone _____

Figure 5–2   Sample Medical Release Form

- Aggravating an existing condition (either known or unknown by the client).

- Precipitating a new condition.

The primary organ systems injured with exercise are the cardiovascular (heart disease, stroke, heat illness) and the musculoskeletal (sprains, strains, overuse injuries) systems. Having a client complete the health history form (Fig. 5-1) provides a personal trainer needed information in these areas.

Cardiovascular Disease

Atherosclerosis is a process whereby fatty deposits of cholesterol and calcium accumulate on the walls of the arteries, causing them to harden, thicken, and lose elasticity. When this process affects the arteries that supply the heart, it is called **coronary artery disease** (CAD). As with other muscles, the heart contracts when we exercise. The increased contraction of the heart muscle is made possible by an increased supply of oxygen-rich blood to provide the necessary nutrients. The greater the exercise load, the larger the demand for blood and oxygen to the heart muscle. If the vessels that supply the heart with this blood are narrowed from atherosclerosis and are not able to stretch, the blood supply is limited, and the increased oxygen demand by the heart cannot be met. This can result in chest discomfort, called **angina**, and, potentially, a **myocardial infarction** or "heart attack."

Angina is usually described as a "pressure or tightness" in the chest, but can also be experienced in the arm, shoulder, or jaw. This pain may be accompanied by shortness of breath, sweating, nausea, and palpitations (pounding or racing of the heart). Although mild exercise may be part of the treatment and rehabilitation for CAD, vigorous exercise is contraindicated. Anyone with a history of CAD or chest pain should have a physician's release, along with a description of any specific limitations, before beginning an exercise program.

RISK FACTORS.   Unfortunately, many people with CAD have no known symptoms and are unaware of their potential for heart attack. Long term studies have helped researchers identify several factors which correlate with an increased risk for CAD. The American College of Sports Medicine has identified the following as major coronary risk factors (ACSM, 1991 pp 6-7):

1. Diagnosed hypertension or systolic blood pressure $\geq$ 160 mmHg or diastolic blood pressure $\geq$ 90 mmHg on at least 2 separate occasions, or on antihypertension medication

2. Elevated total cholesterol $\geq$ 240 mg/dl

3. Cigarette smoking

4. Diabetes mellitus

5. Family history of coronary or other atherosclerotic disease in parents or siblings prior to age 55

The more of these **risk factors** a person has, the greater the chance of either having or developing CAD. The goal of any exercise program should be to minimize these risk factors as much as possible to reduce the risk for heart disease. Any client with two or more of these risk factors should be referred to a physician before the trainer begins a fitness evaluation or the client starts a vigorous (intensity > 60% VO_2 max) exercise program. In addition the ACSM recommends that males age 40 and above and females age 50 and above have a medical evaluation including a maximal exercise test before beginning vigorous exercise programs. The physician and the personal trainer can then work together to set up the ideal program.

CEREBROVASCULAR ACCIDENT. The process of atherosclerosis can affect not only the coronary arteries, but all the vessels of the body. Another vital area affected by atherosclerosis is the brain. Sudden and dramatic development of a neurologic deficit due to compromise in the circulation of the brain results in **cerebrovascular accident** (CVA), commonly called a stroke. A stroke can result not only from atherosclerotic changes within the vessel wall, but also from a rupture in the cerebral (brain) vessel.

All the risk factors for atherosclerotic heart disease (ASHD) apply to strokes as well, particularly **hypertension** (high blood pressure). Approximately 90 percent of those who have strokes have a history of hypertension. This is important information for the personal trainer, since we know blood pressure increases with exercise, especially in activities involving heavy resistance, such as weight lifting and isometric exercises. If a person's resting blood pressure is already high, the blood pressure may elevate to dangerous levels during exercise, increasing the likelihood of a stroke. Therefore, a client with uncontrolled hypertension should receive medical treatment and bring a signed release including recommendations from a physician before starting an exercise program.

Pulmonary

The lungs (respiratory system) extract oxygen from the air we breathe and deliver it to the body's tissues via the cardiovascular system. As mentioned previously, oxygen is essential to all the tissues of the body for survival. A problem occurring in the respiratory system will interfere with the body's ability to provide enough oxygen for the increasing demand occurring during exercise. Bronchitis, asthma, and chronic obstructive pulmonary disease are some of the more common respiratory problems that would necessitate a physician's clearance before designing an exercise program for a new client.

Bronchitis refers to a condition with inflammation (-itis) and excessive mucous production of the bronchial tubes (air passages to the **alveoli** in the lungs) resulting in reduced airflow. Acute bronchitis is commonly caused by a bacterial or viral infection. Prolonged cigarette smoking is the most common single factor leading to chronic bronchitis (a productive cough for at least three months of the year for more than two consecutive years). **Asthma** is a reversible narrowing or constriction of these same airway passages. Typically, most attacks are manifested by periods of **dyspnea**, (difficult breathing), coughing, and wheezing. Both of these conditions reduce the effective oxygen delivered to the blood and tissues. Asthma may spontaneously resolve in some people, but it is generally classified as a chronic obstructive pulmonary disease.

Exercise increases the body's oxygen demand, which may not be met if the person exercising suffers from these conditions. **Chronic obstructive pulmonary disease** (COPD) is a condition in which there is obstruction of air flow from chronic asthma, bronchitis and/or emphysema. This is a more serious and permanent condition affecting the oxygen delivery system and is most commonly the result of years of smoking. Exercise is usually possible in all of these cases but must be modified after clearance by a physician. Exercise tolerance in these clients may be markedly reduced.

Metabolic

There are many metabolic diseases that may interfere with the **metabolism**, or utilization, of energy. Two of the more common types are diabetes and thyroid disorders. **Diabetes mellitus** is the inability to metabolize blood glucose properly. All of the cells in the body require sugar, or glucose, to function. **Insulin** is a hormone, produced in the pancreas, which acts to help blood glucose move into the cells.

There are two types of diabetes. Type I diabetics are insulin-dependent, meaning they require injections of insulin for cellular survival. Type II diabetics are able to produce insulin, but not in sufficient quantities to regulate the cellular need for glucose. Type II diabetes is closely linked to obesity and is first treated with proper diet and exercise. However, these persons may progress to the point in their disease where they require either oral medication or insulin to control their glucose.

Exercise, both as a means to regulate blood glucose and to facilitate fat loss, is an important component of a diabetic's life-style. Along with a specific diet and medication, it is the mainstay of treatment. However, the diabetic must take care to meet the varying demands for glucose and insulin during exercise. If the glucose supply to the cells is not met, the imbalance may lead to dizziness, coma, or even death. To avoid complications, diabetics need to understand thoroughly the effects of diet, exercise, and medication on their blood sugar.

The thyroid is a small gland in the neck that secretes a hormone that regulates the rate of metabolism, including the heart rate. **Hyperthyroid** persons have an increased level of this hormone and have a higher metabolic rate. **Hypothyroid** persons have a reduced level of this hormone and require thyroid medication to increase their metabolism to normal. Because exercise also increases the metabolism, it could be dangerous in a person with uncontrolled thyroid disease. A client with either diabetes or thyroid disease requires physician approval before initiating an exercise program.

Musculoskeletal

The musculoskeletal system consists of the muscles, bones, tendons and ligaments that function to support and move the body. This system is also the most commonly injured during exercise. Aside from the pain and discouragement of an injury, there are other factors to contend with. Changes or modifications in the exercise program are necessary to accommodate the injury. Motivation is also a big factor to contend with in these circumstances. Furthermore, a trainer may be legally liable for a client's injury. For these reasons, it is important to be cognizant of potentially hazardous situations before they happen. Most minor sprains and strains are easily managed, but a persistent problem or a more serious injury requires referral to a physician and appropriate treatment. Medical referral is not only for a client's protection, but for the trainer's as well.

The screening evaluation is crucial to identifying both old injuries and risk factors for potential new injuries. The most common type of injury sustained by persons participating in aerobic activity is the **overuse injury**. These injuries are usually the result of poor training techniques, poor body mechanics, or both. Essentially, overuse injuries are caused by exercise that is too much, too soon, or too fast for a particular tissue involved in the activity to adapt. The result is repetitive stress in the tissue without time for recovery, thus overwhelming the body's ability to heal itself. During repetitive activity, the body is in a dynamic balance of breakdown and repair of tissue. The overuse mechanism tips the balance in favor of breakdown. Examples of overuse injuries include runner's knee (a painful knee condition), swimmer's shoulder (pain in the shoulder), and iliotibial (IT) band syndrome (pain along the outside of the thigh). To avoid aggravating the existing injury and to allow for healing to occur, a trainer must help clients with overuse injuries to modify their exercise programs. Cross training may be required for a period of time.

Another common type of injury is the **sprain** (ligament) or **strain** (muscle or its tendon), which is a tearing (partial or complete) of the respective tissue. Again, these must be recognized before implementation of an exercise program so as not to worsen the condition. A client with an injury more severe than a simple sprain or strain must have a physician's approval before beginning a program. If specific weakness of the muscle or looseness of the joint exists, medical referral is also indicated.

A herniated nucleus pulposus (HNP) or **herniated disc** is a condition in which the disc between two vertebrae of the spine bulges backward (posteriorly) and compresses a nerve root, compromising the function of that nerve. The HNP can be identified by specific signs or symptoms in the back or legs. The most common neurologic signs and symptoms are pain and/or numbness, radiating down the leg with accompanying weakness of the extremity. These findings are usually aggravated by hip or back flexion. A client with a history of a herniated disc, or neurologic symptoms into the legs, must be evaluated by a physician.

A much more common condition of the back is the strain or sprain of the low back. The pathophysiology will not be discussed here, but it is extremely important to design an exercise program that will not aggravate a back injury. Good biomechanics, posture, and technique are paramount to good back care, especially with a history of back pain. Please refer to Chapter 12 for a more detailed discussion of this issue.

Arthritis is a general term for inflammation of a joint. There is usually accompanying pain, stiffness, swelling, or limitation of motion. There are many different types, the most common being **osteoarthritis**, or the "wear and tear" form of arthritis. An arthritic or degenerative back, hip, or knee may be aggravated by high impact activities such as running or jumping, but may respond favorably to the lower impact of cycling or stair climbing machines, and better still to non-weight bearing activities like swimming or water aerobics. Knowing that a client has an arthritic condition, and which joints are affected, will enable a trainer to tailor an appropriate workout. A trainer who has doubts about the appropriate exercise advice for an arthritic client should seek assistance from the client's physician.

A client who has had recent orthopedic surgery may not be ready for a standard exercise program. Depending on the surgery performed, it may take up to one year (in the case of knee reconstruction, for example) for the tissues to heal completely. Also, disuse atrophy of the muscles surrounding an injury may begin after only two days of inactivity. Therefore, it is extremely important to strengthen and stabilize the weakened area before beginning a generalized fitness program. To properly rehabilitate the weakened area requires knowledge of the type of surgery as well as the indicated rehabilitation program. This information can be gained from the client's surgeon and physical therapist. A client may perform strengthening exercises of non-involved muscle groups in conjunction with the rehabilitation program. The important point is that the trainer needs to address the client's weakened area primarily, before designing a generalized program. Beginning a fitness program before complete rehabilitation may lead to biomechanical imbalances predisposing the client to other injuries. Communication with the physician is paramount, and recommended for a trainer whose client has a history of surgery within the last year.

Other Conditions

Another condition that needs consideration, especially with weight lifting, is history of an inguinal or abdominal **hernia**. This is a protrusion of the abdominal contents into the groin or through the abdominal wall, respectively. Pain is usually present, but may not be in some cases. During an activity involving increased abdominal pressure, as with the **Valsalva maneuver**, the hernia may be further aggravated. A hernia is a relative contraindication for weight lifting until cleared by a physician. If there is a history of a hernia, it is very important to instruct and educate the client on proper breathing and lifting techniques.

Age is also a factor to consider, although people mature at different rates secondary to their lifestyles and their genetic make up. One person who is actually 55 may have the body of a 40-year-old, and vice versa. However, it's best for the trainer to follow current ACSM guidelines (1991). A male client over 40 years (or a female over 45) should obtain a physician's consent before beginning an exercise program. Referral is also recommended for a male 35–40 years (40–45 for females) with a sedentary lifestyle and any positive risk factors.

Optimum fitness levels during *pregnancy* are beneficial for the health of the mother as well as for the unborn infant. Back strengthening and stabilization and cardiovascular fitness are the primary concerns for the mother. During the later stages of pregnancy and during delivery, a strong back is vital to reduce low back fatigue and strains. Cardiovascular endurance is beneficial during the labor period and facilitates the delivery process. Maintenance of self-esteem is another benefit of exercise during pregnancy. There are restrictions, however, as to the type and intensity of exercise during pregnancy, especially in the last trimester. This is not the time to achieve maximum fitness goals, but rather to maintain a good fitness level. For both her optimum care and the trainer's own liability, a client should have a physician's approval during pregnancy and until three months after delivery. Please refer to Chapter 12 for more information on modifying an exercise program during pregnancy.

Another factor that may impair a client's ability to exercise is recent history of *illness* or *infection*. Moderate exercise may be of benefit to a mild illness such as a resolving cold. A more serious condition requires more of the body's energy reserves, and exercise would be contraindicated until the client improves. Our bodies have a given amount of energy available, which must be balanced between the body's physiological requirements, including fighting infections, and a person's emotional need or desire to exercise. This balance varies from person to person but, generally speaking, it is not advisable to start a new exercise program during an illness. To distinguish between a minor and a major illness, a trainer may need to talk to the client and the client's physician.

MEDICATIONS

The last important health history question pertains to medications or drugs. These substances alter the biochemistry of the body and may alter a client's ability to perform or respond to exercise. The properties of these drugs must be understood and discussed with a physician.

In designing and supervising an exercise program, it is important to re-

Table 5–1   EFFECTS OF MEDICATIONS ON HEART-RATE AND BLOOD PRESSURE

MEDICATIONS	RESTING HR	EXERCISE HR	MAXIMAL EXERCISING HR	BP REST	COMMENTS
Beta-adrenergic blocking agents	↓	↓	↓	↓	Dose-related response
Calcium-channel blockers	↑, ↔, or ↓	↑, ↔, or ↓	↓ or ↔	↓	Variable and dose-related responses
Diuretics	↔	↔	↔	↓	
Other Anti-hypertensives including ACE inhibitors	↑, ↔, or ↓	↑, ↔, or ↓	usually ↔	↓	Many antihypertensive medications are used. Some may decrease, a few may increase, and others do not affect heart rates. Some exhibit dose-related response.
Decongestants	↔ or ↑	↔ or ↑	↔	↑	
Antihistamines	↔	↔	↔	↔	
Tranquilizers	↔ or if anxiety reduced may ↓	↔	↔	↔ or ↓	
Alcohol	↔ or ↑	↔ or ↑	↔	↔, ↑, or ↓	Exercise prohibited while under the influence; effects of alcohol on coordination increase possibility of injuries.
Antidepressants	↔ or ↑	↔	↔	↔ or ↓	
Bronchodilators	↑ or ↔	↔ or ↑	↔	↔ or ↑	Inhalers, pills or liquid

Table 5–1(cont.)   EFFECTS OF MEDICATIONS ON HEART-RATE AND BLOOD PRESSURE

MEDICATIONS	RESTING HR	EXERCISE HR	MAXIMAL EXERCISING HR	BP REST	COMMENTS
Diet Pills					
With sympathetomimetic activity (SA)	↑or ↔	↑ or ↔	↔	↑	Discourage as a poor approach to weight loss; acceptable only with physician's written approval
Containing amphetamines	↑	↑	↔	↑ or ↔	
Without sympathomimetic activity or amphetamines	↔	↔	↔	↔	
Caffeine	↔ or ↑	usually ↔	↔	↔ or ↑	
Nicotine	↔ or ↑	↔ or ↑	↔	↔ or ↑	Discourage smoking; suggest lower target heart rate and exercise intensity for smoker.

↑= increase   ↔= no significant change   ↓= decrease

Adapted from Van Camp, S. (1987). Health Screening. In N. Van Gelder (Ed.) *Aerobic dance-exercise instructor manual* (pp. 117-126). San Diego: American Council on Exercise.

alize that many over-the-counter medications, prescriptions, or illicit drugs affect the heart's response to exercise. Medications may be referred to by the manufacturer's brand name (e.g., Inderal) or by the scientific general name (propranolol). There are hundreds of thousands of different drugs on the market. In order to understand each specific drug's effect, the trainer can look at the general category under which each drug is grouped, such as beta blockers, antihistamines, or antihypertensives. The drugs in each group have similar properties, and each group is thought to have a similar effect on the average person, although there may be individual variations.

Table 5-1 lists many of the medications that may affect a person's response to exercise. The particular response is dose dependent: the larger the dose, the greater the response. The effect also depends on when the medication is taken; as the medications are metabolizing, their effects diminish. If a trainer has any questions concerning a client's medications, it is advisable to discuss them with a physician.

ANTI-HYPERTENSIVES.   High blood pressure or hypertension is common in our society, and there are many medications used for treatment. Most anti-hypertensives have their primary effect on one of three different sites: the heart, to reduce its force of contraction; the peripheral blood vessels, to open or dilate them to allow more room for the blood; or the brain, to reduce the sympathetic nerve outflow. The site the medication acts upon helps to determine its effect on the individual as well as the potential side effects. The following are common anti-hypertensives:

- *Beta blockers.* **Beta blockers** are commonly prescribed for high blood pressure, migraine headaches, and heart dysrhythmias (rapid or irregular heart rate). These medications bind at the beta receptor of the sympathetic nervous system (primarily the heart) and therefore prevent the stimulating effect of catecholamines (specific hormone produced in the adrenal gland) at these sites. This blockade lowers the heart rate and blood pressure both at rest and during exercise, thus invalidating the usual method of recommending and monitoring a target heart rate. Modifications in determining exercise intensity, using the Borg Scale of Perceived Exertion, for example, must be made for a safe and effective aerobic exercise program.

- *Calcium channel blockers.* Calcium channel blockers block calcium dependent contraction of the smooth muscles in the arteries, causing vasodilation of the arteries, which lowers the blood pressure. These agents are also used for angina and heart dysrhythmias. There are several types of calcium blockers on the market, and the effect on the blood pressure and heart rate depends on the specific agent.

- *ACE inhibitors.* ACE inhibitors block an enzyme secreted by the kidneys, thereby preventing formation of a potent hormone that constricts blood vessels. If this enzyme is blocked, the vessels dilate, and the blood pressure will decrease.

- *Diuretics.* **Diuretics** are medications that increase the excretion of water and electrolytes through the kidneys. They are usually prescribed for high blood pressure, or when a person is accumulating too much fluid, as with congestive heart failure. They have no primary effect on the cardiovascular system, but they can cause water and electrolyte imbalances, which may lead to dangerous cardiac dysrhythmias. It is also important to monitor for dehydration and heat exhaustion in clients taking diuretics, especially when exercising in hot or humid environments. Diuretics are also used by athletes to try to lose weight for sport, which is a dangerous practice.

BRONCHODILATORS. Asthma medications (e.g. bronchodilators) are medications that relax or open the air passages in the lungs, allowing better air exchange. There are many different types, but the primary action is to stimulate the sympathetic nervous system. In addition to opening the airways, these medications increase the heart rate and may cause a transient shaky feeling, similar to an "adrenaline rush."

DECONGESTANTS. Decongestants act directly on the smooth muscles of blood vessels to stimulate vasoconstriction. In the upper airways, this constriction reduces the volume of the swollen tissues and results in more air space. Because vasoconstriction in the peripheral vessels may raise blood pressure, clients taking decongestants should perform exercise, especially heavy resistance exercise, with caution.

ANTIHISTAMINES. Antihistamines block the histamine receptor, which is involved with the mast cells and the allergic response. These medications do not have a direct effect on the heart rate or blood pressure. They do, however, produce a drying effect in the upper airways and may cause drowsiness. Most cold medications are a combination of decongestants and antihistamines and so have the combined effects.

GOALS AND COMMITMENT

Probably the most important component of the health history is to identify the *clients' goals* and *level of commitment.* Is their primary objective to lose excess fat or to build muscle? Are they engaging in the exercise program to "look good" or has their physician recommended it to reduce their cardiac risk factors? Answers to these questions will allow the trainer to set up the best type of program for them. Next, identify their level of commitment. Do they want to start now or on New Year's Day? Are they already in an exercise program but lack sufficient motivation? Are they willing to commit to a one-hour session three times a week? Are their goals realistic in view of their degree of commitment? Do they understand what success in achieving their goals will require? Frank consideration of these questions will provide both the trainer and client with a clear understanding of the best program and reduce many misunderstandings in the future.

It is very important that the trainer's goals coincide with the client's. For example, a trainer may notice that a client has underdeveloped arms and could use an upper extremity strengthening program. However, if the client does not want strong arms, the trainer cannot force his/her objectives on the client. Instead, a trainer needs to (1) acknowledge the clients' goals (if they are realistic and attainable) and (2) motivate them to achieve these goals. Chapters 13 and 14 provide information on motivating and working effectively with clients.

PHYSICAL SCREEN

The medical history is very important, but it has the limitation of defining only the conditions that a client is aware of and remembers to report. A client may be completely unaware of a significant risk factor. The purpose of a physical evaluation is to identify these unknown conditions and to further delineate a known condition. The physical screen is also important to establish an initial baseline and to discover specific areas that need work. Finally, it communicates to clients that a trainer is interested in them and is designing an individualized program for them.

Two important components of the exam are **blood pressure** and heart rate. Normal blood pressure in our society is 120/80. The top number (systolic) is the maximum pressure in the vessels during contraction of the heart. The bottom number (diastolic) is the pressure during relaxation of the heart. There are many factors that can elevate blood pressures, including atherosclerosis, medications, obesity, and stress. Exercise, which also raises blood pressure, can be a form of treatment if performed correctly. However, exercise in a person with uncontrolled high blood pressure can be dangerous and should be postponed until the condition is treated. A blood pressure greater than 140/90 in an adult is high and needs the attention of a physician. Blood pressure normals for children vary depending on age and body mass (Kaplan, 1986).

The normal heart rate is usually 60–100 beats per minute and is regular in rhythm. Well-trained endurance athletes have developed an efficient cardiovascular system and often have heart rates in the low 40s. If a client's resting heart rate is greater than 100, or less than 60 in an untrained person, or if the heart rate is irregular, medical clearance is recommended.

Observation is the next part of the physical screen. Observation should actually begin as soon as a trainer meets a client. Is he/she short of breath at rest? How is his/her posture? Does he/she walk with a limp? The trainer must be aware of any physical characteristics or limitations that may influence the design of the program.

Flexibility

The next part of the physical screen is the hands-on evaluation to determine a client's flexibility and strength. Fitness is defined by flexibility, strength, and endurance; however, most people neglect flexibility training. A trainer's job is to help a client develop total fitness while reducing risk for injury. Good flexibility is of prime importance to overall success. Loss of flexibility is associated with:

1. Reduced performance of the muscle.

2. Increased incidence of injuries, both strained muscles, and overuse injuries from altered biomechanics.

3. Reduced circulation and therefore longer tissue healing and warm-up times.

The purpose of the flexibility evaluation is to identify areas of restriction that are at risk for injury. This information alerts the trainer to areas needing concentrated stretching as well as to modifications required in the client's strength and endurance programs because of poor flexibility. For example, a client with tight pectoral muscles may not be able to use the pectoral deck machine. Clients with reduced hamstring flexibility are at risk for low back injuries, especially during weight lifting. Biomechanics and posture are of utmost importance in these cases, and back stabilization exercises may be indicated. Chapter 6 provides more detailed information on assessing a client's flexibility.

Strength

Strength testing is important to establish a baseline and to determine muscular imbalances which would have a negative impact on performance. For example, weak rotator cuff muscles of the shoulder will offset the muscular balance and biomechanics of the shoulder. This may not normally be a problem, but with the increased use during exercise, this imbalance will predispose the shoulder to injury.

The type and completeness of strength testing depends on the client's goals and the individual exercise program. Chapter 11 provides specifics on designing an exercise program. Strength and flexibility are mentioned here to emphasize the importance of evaluation before beginning the exercise program.

SUMMARY

Exercise is a vital component of health. The goal of a good exercise program is to improve a client's quality of life without aggravating or precipitating an injury or illness. This goal requires the trainer to recognize any significant medical conditions or risk factors for injury and modify the program accordingly.

The medical history is an important component of the health screening and should give particular attention to the cardiovascular and musculoskeletal systems. It is important also to address risk factors for different diseases because the client may not be aware of a potential or underlying problem. Finally, medications should be evaluated because they can alter exercise performance as well as increase risk factors.

In many cases a safe and appropriate exercise program requires a coordinated effort by the trainer, physician, and client to safely achieve the desired goals.

REFERENCES

American College of Sports Medicine (1991). *Guidelines for exercise testing and prescription* (4th ed.). Philadelphia: Lea & Febiger.

Kaplan, N. (1986). *Clinical Hypertension* (4th ed.). Baltimore: Williams & Wilkins.

Rosenstein, A. (1987). The benefits of health maintenance. *The Physician and Sportsmedicine, 15,* 57–69.

Van Camp, S. Health screening. In N. Van Gelder (ed.), *Aerobic dance-exercise instructor manual* (pp. 117–126). San Diego: American Council on Exercise.

Physician's Desk Reference (1990). Oradell, NJ: Medical Economics Company.

SUGGESTED READING

ACSM Position Papers are released periodically, all providing an excellent resource for current industry standards.

American College of Sports Medicine (1991). *Guidelines for exercise testing and prescription* (4th ed.). Philadelphia: Lea & Febiger.

Isselbacher, K. (ed.) (1981). *Harrisen's principle of internal medicine* (9th ed.). New York: McGraw-Hill.

Physician and Sportsmedicine. (Monthly journal).

Physician's Desk Reference (1990). Oradell, NJ: Medical Economics Company.

Roy, S., & Irvin, R. (1983). *Medicine: Prevention, evaluation, management, and rehabilitation.* Englewood Cliffs, NJ: Prentice-Hall.

Van Gelder, N., & Marks, S. (Eds.). (1986). *Aerobic dance-exercise instructor manual.* San Diego: American Council on Exercise.

Testing and Evaluation

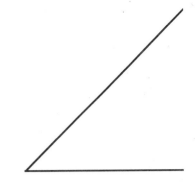

By Richard T. Cotton

6

Richard T. Cotton, M.A., is the Senior Director of Education for the American Council on Exercise in San Diego, California. He is an ACE certified Personal Trainer and is certified as both an Exercise Program Director and Exercise Specialist by the American College of Sports Medicine.

IN THIS CHAPTER:

- Required vs. optional evaluation components.
- Cardiorespiratory testing and evaluation, including the measurement of blood pressure, heart rate, and endurance (via bicycle test, step test, field test).
- Body composition testing and evaluation, via hydrostatic weighing, skinfold measurement, bioelectrical impedance, and girth measurements.

- Flexibility testing and evaluation, including tests of trunk flexion and extension, hip flexion, and shoulder flexibility.
- Muscular strength and endurance testing and evaluation, via the sit-up test, push-up test, and bench-press test.
- Follow-up consultation and testing.

The testing and evaluation of a client is an important early step in the training process. A sound testing and evaluation package provides valuable information for both trainer and client. Additionally, it complements the trainer's exercise leadership skills, adds to the trainer's professional image, and is an additional revenue-generating service a trainer can provide. The specific tests administered in an assessment may vary from client to client. A comprehensive assessment measures the following four components:

- Cardiorespiratory efficiency (resting and exercise).
- Muscular strength and endurance.
- Muscle and joint flexibility.
- Body composition.

The testing and evaluation process offers an opportunity to gather information related to a client's current level of physical fitness. Its purpose may be any or all of the following:

- To assess current fitness levels relative to age and sex.

- To aid in the development of an exercise program.

- To identify areas of health/injury risk and possible referral to the appropriate health professional.

- To establish goals and provide motivation.

- To evaluate progress.

A sound fitness testing battery should assess the function of the heart, blood vessels, lungs, and muscles, all with respect to the physical demands of an individually defined optimal life-style. Many clients desire a level of fitness that supports daily activities, an active life-style, and the confronting of unforeseen emergencies, not only without undue fatigue but at a level of optimal human functioning. Others will desire a level of physical fitness that is more athletic. Clients with such goals will want more competitive levels of cardiovascular endurance, muscular strength, muscular endurance, flexibility, and body composition. Still others may have strong feelings about not being tested at all.

Required vs. Optional Evaluation Components

Not all clients need or desire comprehensive exercise testing, but some form of evaluation is necessary for all clients, its primary purpose being to determine cardiovascular risk, as well as to aid in exercise program development. The *required* component in such evaluation is to gain health-screening information needed to assess cardiovascular risk and determine a client's suitability for any level of testing and training.

Cardiovascular risk and the necessity for pre-exercise physician follow-up are determined by applying a **cardiovascular risk factor** assessment to the guidelines developed by the American College of Sports Medicine; these are explained in detail in Chapter 5. Additionally, a client's exercise history, attitudes toward exercise, and fitness goals must be considered. Figure 6-1 is an example of a pre-exercise assessment tool. Along with gathering health-screening information, it can be used as a minimum evaluation for the client who, for whatever reason, is not being tested.

While many and perhaps most of a personal trainer's clients look forward to testing and evaluation, it is important to understand that some are very uncomfortable with the process, and it actually may be counterproductive to the success of an exercise program. Some may be embarrassed with their physical condition and would rather be tested at a later date or perhaps not at all. Others are extremely competitive with themselves and understand that poor test results might be too much to tolerate when attempting to make such an important life-style change. The minimum evaluation a trainer should require is the assessment of cardiovascular risk factors (covered in Ch. 5) and completion of an Exercise History and Attitude questionnaire (Fig. 6-1). The risk factor assessment must be completed in order to determine the necessity of physician clearance and/or physician- supervised exercise testing. The history and attitude questionnaire is necessary to help the trainer design a program for each client's habits and motivation.

Name: _____ Date: _____

General Instructions: Please fill out this form as completely as possible. If you have any questions, DO NOT GUESS; ask your trainer for assistance.

1. Please rate your exercise level on a scale of 1 to 5 (5 indicating very strenuous) for each age range through your present age:

   15–20 _____   21–30 _____   31–40 _____   41–50+ _____

2. Were you a high school and/or college athlete?

   Yes _____   No _____   If yes, please specify: _____

3. Do you have any negative feelings toward or have you had any bad experience with physical activity programs?

   Yes _____   No _____

   If yes, please explain: _____

4. Do you have any negative feelings toward or have you had any bad experience with fitness testing and evaluation?

   Yes _____   No _____

   If yes, please explain: _____

5. Rate yourself on a scale of 1 to 5 (1 indicating the lowest value and 5 the highest). Circle the number that applies the most.

   Characterize your present athletic ability:

   1   2   3   4   5

   When you exercise, how important is competition?

   1   2   3   4   5

   Characterize your present cardiovascular capacity:

   1   2   3   4   5

   Characterize your present muscular capacity:

   1   2   3   4   5

   Characterize your present flexibility capacity:

   1   2   3   4   5

Figure 6–1 Exercise History and Attitude Questionnaire

6. Do you start exercise programs but then find yourself unable to stick with them?

Yes _____ No _____

7. How much are you willing to devote to an exercise program?

minutes/day _____ days/week _____

8. Are you currently involved in regular endurance (cardiovascular) exercise?

Yes _____ No _____ If yes, specify the type of exercise(s) _____

days/week _____ minutes/day _____

Rate your perception of the exertion of your exercise program (circle the number):

(1) Light   (2) Fairly light   (3) Somewhat hard   (4) Hard

9. How long have you been exercising regularly?

_____ months _____ years

10. What other exercise, sport, or recreational activities have you participated in?

In the past 6 months? _____

In the past 5 years? _____

11. Can you exercise during your work day?

Yes _____ No _____

12. Would an exercise program interfere with your job?

Yes _____ No _____

13. Would an exercise program benefit your job?

Yes _____ No _____

14. What types of exercise interest you?

Walking _____	Stationary biking _____
Jogging _____	Rowing _____
Swimming _____	Racquetball _____
Cycling _____	Tennis _____
Dance exercise _____	Other aerobic _____
Strength training _____	Stretching _____

Figure 6–1(cont.) Exercise History and Attitude Questionnaire

15. Rank your goals in undertaking exercise: What do you want exercise to do for you? Use the following scale to rate each goal separately.

						Somewhat important						
Extremely important	1	2	3	4	5	6	7	8	9	10	Not at all important

_____   a.   Improve cardiovascular fitness

_____   b.   Body-fat weight loss

_____   c.   Reshape or tone my body

_____   d.   Improve performance for a specific sport

_____   e.   Improve moods and ability to cope with stress

_____   f.   Improve flexibility

_____   g.   Increase strength

_____   h.   Increase energy level

_____   i.   Feel better

_____   j.   Enjoyment

_____   k.   Other

16. By how much would you like to change your current weight?

(+) _____ lbs   (-) _____ lbs

Figure 6–1(cont.)   Exercise History and Attitude Questionnaire

CARDIORESPIRATORY TESTING AND EVALUATION

Measuring Blood Pressure

Blood pressure is the force of the blood against the walls of the arteries when the heart pumps blood to the body. The upper and lower numbers that represent the blood pressure are the **systolic** and **diastolic blood pressures**, respectively. Blood pressure is measured in millimeters of mercury (mmHg). The systolic blood pressure represents the pressure created by the heart as it pumps blood (via ventricular contraction) to the body; this is the maximum pressure created by the heart during a complete cardiac cycle. The diastolic blood pressure represents the pressure that remains in the arteries during the filling phase of the cardiac cycle, when the heart relaxes; it is the minimum pressure within the arteries during a complete cardiac cycle.

Ideally blood pressure should be 120/80 or less. A physician will diagnose systolic **hypertension** when the measurement of 140 mmHg or greater is made on two or more separate visits. Similarly, diastolic hypertension is medically diagnosed when diastolic blood pressure is measured greater than or equal to 90 mmHg on two or more separate occasions.

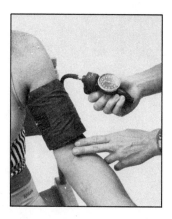

Figure 6–2 Correct cuff position for measuring blood pressure.

The causes of hypertension are numerous and complex, with both life-style and genetics playing major roles in its development. At least 90 percent of all hypertension is classified as "essential," meaning it has no known cause. Exercise improves blood pressure primarily by enhancing cardiovascular efficiency, lowering body-fat weight, and reducing both the physical and emotional manifestations of stress.

Blood pressure is measured with a sphygmomanometer and stethoscope. The sphygmomanometer consists of a rubber bladder enclosed in a nylon cuff and connected to an inflating bulb and manometer from which the pressure is read. The three most frequently used cuff sizes are child, adult, and large adult.

Since blood pressure assessment often is affected by the client's anxiety over the unfamiliar surroundings within which testing may be conducted, measurements should be taken in quiet, comfortable surroundings to obtain a reasonable estimate of resting blood pressure. Thus, each client should be allowed to sit quietly for 10–15 minutes *before* a measurement is obtained. Then, with the subject seated, the cuff should be placed on the upper portion of a bare arm about one inch above the crease in the elbow joint (Fig. 6–2). The middle of the bladder should be over the brachial artery on the inner part of the upper arm. The arm, slightly flexed, should be resting comfortably on a table or arm of a chair at heart level. The bell of the stethoscope is placed firmly on the brachial artery (inner portion of the elbow joint). The brachial artery is located by feeling for a pulse before placing the stethoscope. To avoid unnecessary sounds, the stethoscope should come in contact with only the arm and not be touching any of the cuff or tubing surfaces at the test site. While listening carefully through the stethoscope, pump the cuff. The pulse should be heard then should disappear as the cuff is pumped to approximately 20–30 mmHg above the point at which the sound disappeared. Release the pressure at a rate that will cause the pressure to fall about 2–3 mmHg/second. If the pressure is released too fast, it is difficult to obtain an accurate reading. If the pressure is released too slowly, pressure builds within the arm, causing discomfort and yielding inaccurate readings. The blood pressure assessment should be performed within 60 seconds, or else there is the likelihood of falsely elevating the blood pressure.

As the pressure falls, the sounds can be heard in four and sometimes five distinct phases, called **Korotkoff sounds**. The first sound heard is the first phase and represents the systolic blood pressure reading. As the mercury continues to fall, this sound will change in quality to a louder, more sharp tapping, representing the second and third phases, which are of no particular significance. At rest, the fourth and fifth phases usually coincide and involve the disappearance of sound, which is the diastolic blood pressure. During exercise, the fourth phase may be a muffling of the sound, representing the diastolic blood pressure. Although during exercise the fifth phase (muffled sound) sometimes disappears shortly thereafter, it may actually last until the pressure is completely released.

If a blood pressure measure needs to be repeated on the same arm, allow 30–60 seconds between trials so normal circulation can return. Record the results for comparison with subsequent measurements. If abnormal readings result, take a repeated measurement on the opposite arm. If there is significant discrepancy with readings from arm to arm, the client should be referred to his/her personal physician for medical evaluation, for such discrepancy may represent a significant circulatory problem.

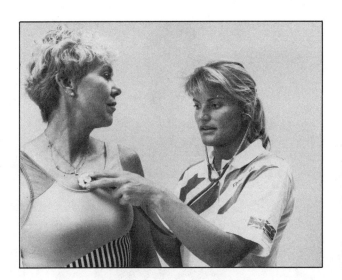

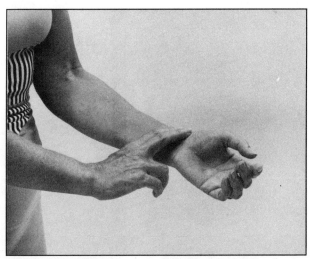

Figure 6–3 Correct stetho-scope position for measuring resting and exercise heart rates.

Figure 6–4 Radial pulse is palpated with two fingers on the wrist, at the base of the thumb.

Measuring Heart Rate

The resting heart rate is usually measured indirectly by placing the fingertips on a pulse site (**palpation**), or directly by listening through a stethoscope (*auscultation*) (Fig. 6-3). Resting heart rate is most accurately measured just before the client gets out of bed in the morning. Accuracy is further enhanced by averaging three separate morning readings. Resting pulse can be taken for a full minute, or for 30 seconds and then multiplied by two, to determine the number of beats per minute. Resting pulse can also be accurately measured by palpation of the radial pulse on the wrist, in line with the base of the thumb (Fig. 6-4). Place the tips of the index and middle fingers (not the thumb, which has a pulse of its own) over the artery and apply light pressure.

Exercise pulse is most accurately palpated from the larger carotid artery just to the side of the larynx (Fig. 6-5). Heavy pressure should not be applied to the carotid arteries, because they contain baroreceptors that sense increases in pressure and respond by slowing the heart rate. Exercise pulse should be taken for 10 seconds, counting the first pulse beat as 0 at the start of the 10-second period. When measuring by auscultation, place the bell of the stethoscope on the third intercostal space to the left of the sternum (Fig. 6-3).

Another very accurate and easy method of measuring heart rate both for testing and training uses one of the portable heart-rate monitors currently on the market. These consist of a chest strap containing electrodes that pick up the actual heart rate (not pulse rate) and transmit the signal to a digital readout on a wrist receiver (Fig. 6-6). These monitors currently cost from $150 to $350 and have become an indispensable tool for many personal trainers.

Interpretation of resting heart rate as it relates to cardiovascular fitness is difficult at best. A normal resting heart rate can vary from as low as 40 beats per minute to as high as 100 beats per minute, with an average of 70 beats per minute for men and 75 beats per minute for women. Usually, endurance-trained persons have a lower resting heart rate due to the increased amount of blood the heart pumps with each beat (**stroke volume**). Resting heart rate can vary widely for both endurance-trained athletes and deconditioned subjects. Resting heart rate can be used as an index to improved cardiovascular fitness, because as cardiovascular fitness improves, especially in a previously sedentary client, resting heart rate usually decreases.

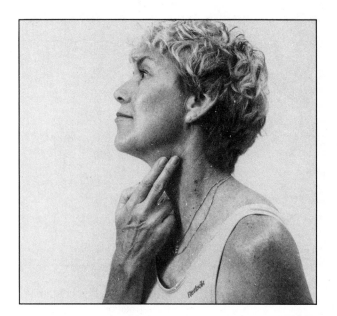

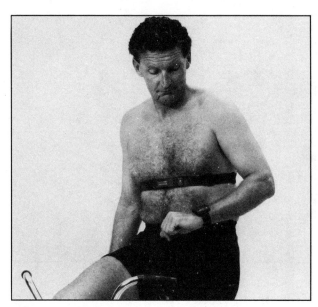

Figure 6–5 To palpate the carotid pulse, place the fingertips on the neck, just to the side of the larynx.

Figure 6–6 Chest-strap heart-rate monitor.

Cardiorespiratory Endurance Testing

The assessment of cardiorespiratory endurance is made by either direct measurement of oxygen consumption during a maximal graded exercise test or indirectly by estimating oxygen consumption from the heart rate response to a progressive increase in sub-maximal workloads. The direct measurement of **maximal oxygen consumption** is by far the most accurate method, but it requires specialized equipment in addition to a maximal aerobic challenge. Depending on the age and cardiovascular risk of the subject, this method is often limited to either clinical or research facilities and is usually performed in the presence of a physician trained in advanced cardiac life support. The sub-maximal exercise test provides a reasonably accurate prediction of maximal work capacity and estimation of maximal oxygen consumption (±12 percent) and therefore is one of the more professional methods a personal trainer can employ to evaluate cardiovascular endurance. This method is based on the assumption that oxygen consumption increases at the same rate as heart rate and workload; therefore, maximal work capacity and maximal oxygen consumption can be estimated from the rate at which heart rate increases with progressively increasing workloads.

The limitation of the sub-maximal estimation method lies in the prediction of the maximal heart rate from the following formula:

Estimated maximal heart rate = 220 – Age

which is accurate to approximately ±15 bpm (beats per minute). Estimations of maximal work capacity and maximal oxygen consumption are both based on the prediction of maximal heart rate. Therefore, if maximal heart rate is over- or under-predicted, so are maximal work capacity and maximal oxygen consumption. While there may be some error in the estimation of maximal oxygen consumption, the heart rates collected at the sub-maximal workloads are very accurate and reproducible. Therefore, it is the comparison of the heart rates at equivalent workloads during follow-up testing that will show a relative change in aerobic fitness. If the heart rates are accurate and used to estimate maximal oxygen consumption, a change in oxygen consumption will be valid as a measure of relative change in aerobic fitness.

Pretest Procedures and Safety Procedures

While the sub-maximal aerobic exercise test and other tests outlined in this chapter carry relatively low risk of cardiovascular and other medical complications, it is essential that a trainer follow accepted standards of procedure in the assessment of cardiovascular and other medical risks before testing or training a client. Before a client is tested, the cardiovascular risk assessment should be administered and reviewed. The American College of Sports Medicine guidelines recommend that anyone 35 years or older with one or more major risk factors and everyone over 45 years should undergo a physician-supervised maximal graded exercise test before any test or training takes place. The cardiovascular risk assessment given to the client before testing should include questions related to all the major risk factors recognized by the ACSM and outlined in Chapter 5.

WRITTEN EMERGENCY PROCEDURES. All trainers and exercise facilities should have written emergency procedures that include everything from how to report and what to do for minor injuries in the gym to how to respond to an apparent cardiovascular event. All procedures should include a detailed delineation of responsibilities in the event of an incident and appropriate documentation of such incidents.

WRITTEN CONSENT. All test subjects should read and sign an informed consent before being tested. This consent should explain the purpose and process of the testing, including a statement of the potential for discomfort, pain, or even death associated with the implementation of testing. While this may sound extreme, it is the legal responsibility of a trainer to inform clients adequately of even the most unlikely occurrences that could take place during a procedure. In the event of an incident, proper written emergency procedures and consents may help to protect the trainer or exercise facility, as long as the procedures were properly administered.

YMCA Sub-maximal Bicycle Test

The YMCA has developed a sub-maximal bicycle ergometer test by adapting the tests developed by Sjostrand (1947) to evaluate physical working capacity and Astrand and Rhyming (1954) to estimate maximal oxygen uptake. The bicycle ergometer is used by the YMCA instead of the treadmill because it is less expensive, requires little space, is easily transported, makes it easier to take heart rate, and requires little or no training or practice, because its external work is known (treadmill workload must be calculated from rate and grade). The ergometer used should be accurate, easily calibrated, have constant torque, and have a range of 1–2,100 kilogram-meters per minute (kgm/min). Additional equipment is required:

- A metronome set at 50 or 100 bpm (It works well to borrow a metronome and record about 15 minutes of the correct rhythm).

- A timer to time test duration.

- A stopwatch to time heart rate, or a heart-rate monitor.

- A stethoscope to count heart rate.

- Testing forms to record data.

The YMCA test is meant to establish the relationship between heart rate and workload. In order to maintain the validity of the test, the two heart rates used in the estimation of maximal exercise capacity must be greater than 110 bpm and less than 85 percent of age-predicted maximal heart rate. The YMCA uses an upper limit of 150 bpm, which encompasses most age groups likely to be tested.

The workloads on bicycle ergometers are usually expressed in kgm/min, an expression of work rate. The kilogram–meters portion of the expression is consistent with the formula for work, Work = Force × Distance, that is, the force, in kilograms, applied to the wheel, and the distance the wheel travels. For exercise testing the distance is always calculated for one minute. The wheel of the Monark bicycle travels six meters for every complete turn of the pedals. The required pedal rate for the sub-maximal bicycle test is 50 RPM; therefore, the wheel will travel 300 meters in one minute (50 rpm × 6 meters/revolution). For example, if the force applied is 1.5 kg, the work will be:

1.5 kg × 300 m/min = 450 kgm/min

To simplify the process of deciding workload progression, a guide to setting workloads has been developed (Fig. 6–7). All subjects begin at 150 kgm/min and progress according to their heart rate response at the first workload. The metronome is set to either 100 bpm (two beats/pedal cycle) or 50 bpm (one beat/pedal cycle) to maintain a constant pedal rate throughout the test, or the client maintains a 50-rpm pedal rate using the bike's speedometer (if available). Check the calibration of the bicycle, with the belt tension released and the flywheel stationary. On the Monark ergometer the red line of the pendulum weight should line up with the zero line on the workload scale. This is achieved by adjusting the wing nut attached to the screw that rests against the workload scale. Adjust the seat height so the leg is straight when the heel is in contact with the pedal on the down stroke or lowest point of rotation and/or the knee is slightly bent when the ball of the foot is placed on the pedal at the same low

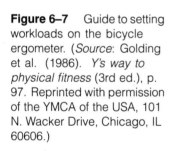

Figure 6–7 Guide to setting workloads on the bicycle ergometer. (*Source*: Golding et al. (1986). *Y's way to physical fitness* (3rd ed.), p. 97. Reprinted with permission of the YMCA of the USA, 101 N. Wacker Drive, Chicago, IL 60606.)

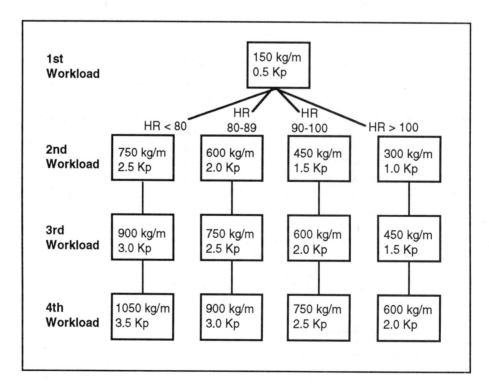

Figure 6–8 Basic positioning for bicycle ergometer submaximal testing.

point of rotation. Record the seat position on the data sheet so that it may be used for retesting.

In order to familiarize clients with the 50-rpm pedal rate, start the metronome and have them pedal with very little or no resistance. Start the test by setting the first workload to 150 kgm/min and then starting the time clock. Take a 10-second exercise heart rate near the end of the second and third minutes of the first stage and multiply by 6 for the minute value (Fig. 6–8). A steady-state heart rate must be achieved before progressing to the next stage. If the difference between the second-minute heart rate and the third-minute heart rate is greater than 5 bpm, the heart rate has not yet reached a steady stage and a fourth minute should be added. It may even take five minutes for the heart rate to stabilize, especially in less conditioned subjects.

CAUTIONS. Before the test begins, the client should be warned to stop exercising if he/she experiences dizziness or lightheadedness, nausea, or severe shortness of breath, or otherwise feels the need to stop. Throughout the test, watch for exertional intolerance or other signs of undue fatigue or unusual response such as profuse sweating, a very red face, or the inability to speak in response to a question. Once each minute, use the Perceived Exertion Scale (Fig. 6–9) to assess the client's subjective assessment of the exercise intensity. Given the upper-limit heart rate of 150 bpm, 16 or greater on the scale is the maximum exertion a subject should reach.

To continue testing, use the guide to setting workloads to determine the workload of stage 2. Be conservative in the progression of the workload in order to avoid driving the heart rate too high. There is no need to hurry the test; each state is timed independent of the others, so be careful to measure and

6	
7	Very, very light
8	
9	Very light
10	
11	Fairly light
12	
13	Somewhat hard
14	
15	Hard
16	
17	Very hard
18	
19	Very, very hard
20	

Figure 6–9 Perceived Exertion Scale.

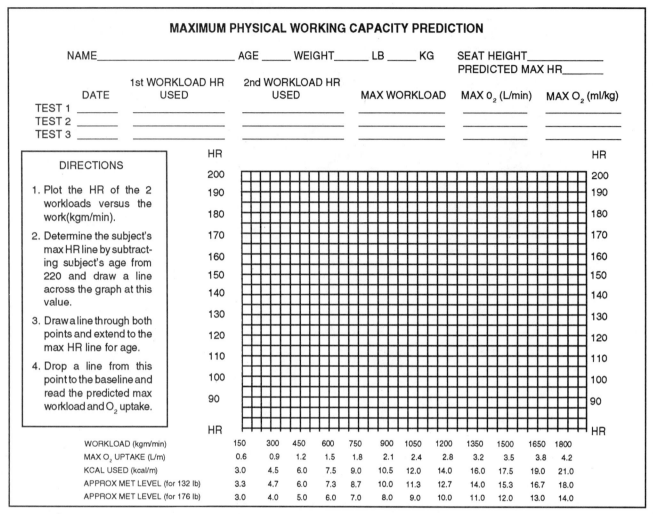

Figure 6–10 Sample graph for plotting two heart rates and two workloads in predicting maximal work capacity and estimating maximal oxygen consumption.

record all data accurately. Repeat the heart-rate monitoring guidelines used in the first stage for subsequent stages. Continue the test until two steady-state heart rates between 110-150 bpm have been recorded for two different stages. End the test by releasing all but 0.5-1.0 kg of resistance on the ergometer, allowing the client time to cool down.

The following is an example of a typical test.

This subject required three workloads to complete the test because the first workload did not elicit a heart rate of greater than 110 bpm. The third workload required a fourth minute to reach a steady-state heart rate, since the difference between the second- and third-minute heart rates was greater than 5 bpm.

The results of the second and third workloads and corresponding heart rates are used to estimate exercise capacity and maximal oxygen consumption (Fig. 6-10). Each workload/heart-rate pair is plotted on the graph and connected to determine a line segment. This line segment is then extended upward to the point of intersection with the horizontal line extending from the predicted maximal heart rate (220 – age). A vertical line perpendicular to the heart-rate line is then drawn from that point down to the baseline. The point of intersection with the baseline marks the predicted maximal working capacity and estimated maximal oxygen consumption.

Using the following formula, absolute oxygen consumption, expressed in liters/minute (l/min), is converted to relative oxygen consumption, expressed in milliliters of oxygen/kilogram of bodyweight/minute (ml/kg/min).

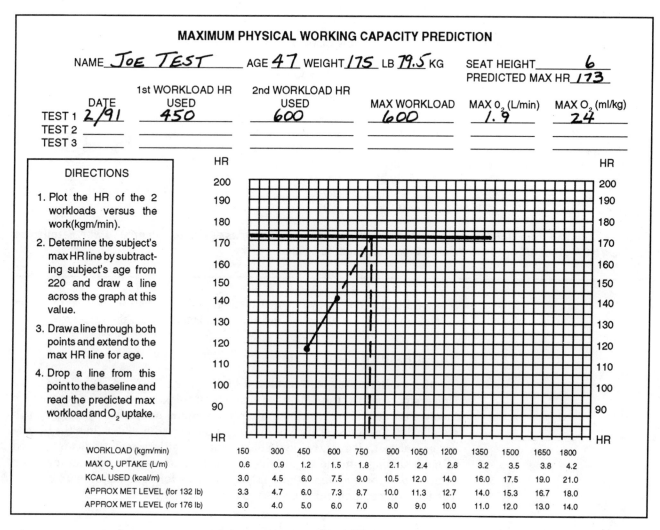

MAXIMUM PHYSICAL WORKING CAPACITY PREDICTION

NAME _JOE TEST_ AGE _47_ WEIGHT _175_ LB _79.5_ KG   SEAT HEIGHT _____ **6**
PREDICTED MAX HR _173_

	DATE	1st WORKLOAD HR USED	2nd WORKLOAD HR USED	MAX WORKLOAD	MAX O$_2$ (L/min)	MAX O$_2$ (ml/kg)
TEST 1	2/91	450	600	600	1.9	24
TEST 2						
TEST 3						

DIRECTIONS

1. Plot the HR of the 2 workloads versus the work(kgm/min).

2. Determine the subject's max HR line by subtracting subject's age from 220 and draw a line across the graph at this value.

3. Draw a line through both points and extend to the max HR line for age.

4. Drop a line from this point to the baseline and read the predicted max workload and O$_2$ uptake.

WORKLOAD (kgm/min)	150	300	450	600	750	900	1050	1200	1350	1500	1650	1800
MAX O$_2$ UPTAKE (L/m)	0.6	0.9	1.2	1.5	1.8	2.1	2.4	2.8	3.2	3.5	3.8	4.2
KCAL USED (kcal/m)	3.0	4.5	6.0	7.5	9.0	10.5	12.0	14.0	16.0	17.5	19.0	21.0
APPROX MET LEVEL (for 132 lb)	3.3	4.7	6.0	7.3	8.7	10.0	11.3	12.7	14.0	15.3	16.7	18.0
APPROX MET LEVEL (for 176 lb)	3.0	4.0	5.0	6.0	7.0	8.0	9.0	10.0	11.0	12.0	13.0	14.0

$$\text{Relative } O_2 \text{ consumption} = \frac{O_2 \text{ consumption (l/min)} \times 1{,}000}{\text{bodyweight (kg)}}$$

Oxygen consumption in ml/kg/min is calculated by multiplying the oxygen consumption in l/min by 1,000 to convert to ml/min. This figure is then divided by the subject's weight, in kilograms, to determine oxygen consumption in ml/kg/min (relative oxygen consumption).

The calculation of relative oxygen consumption allows for comparison to others of different body weights. A very heavy person may have a somewhat high absolute maximal oxygen consumption (l/min) when compared to a lighter person, but when expressed in relative terms (ml/kg/min), the lighter person may be shown to have a higher level of cardiovascular fitness.

Figure 6–11 Form for plotting the prediction of maximal work capacity. (*Source*: Golding et al. (1986). *Y's way to physical fitness* (3rd ed.), p. 100. Reprinted with permission of the YMCA of the USA, 101 Wacker Drive, Chicago, IL 60606.)

Subject X	**Subject A**	**Subject B**
Weight	231 lb (105 kg)	132 lb (60 kg)
Absolute maximal O$_2$ consumption	3.8 l/min	3.2 l/min
Relative O$_2$ consumption	3.8 ×1,000/105 = 36.1 ml/kg/min	3.2 ×1,000/60 = 53.3 ml/kg/min

Table 6–1   NORMS FOR RELATIVE MAXIMAL OXYGEN CONSUMPTION (MEN)

Relative Maximal O₂ Concentration	Age (years)					
	18–25	26–35	36–45	46–55	56–65	65+
Excellent	>60	>56	>51	>45	>41	>37
Good	52–60	49–56	43–51	39–45	36–41	33–37
Above average	47–51	43–48	39–42	35–38	32–35	39–32
Average	42–46	40–42	35–38	32–35	30–31	25–28
Below average	37–41	35–39	31–34	29–31	26–29	22–25
Poor	30–36	30–34	26–30	25–28	22–25	20–21
Very poor	<30	<30	<26	<25	<22	<20

Source: Adapted from Golding, et al. (1986). *The Y's way to physical fitness* (3rd ed.). Reprinted with permission of the YMCA of the USA, 101 N. Wacker Drive. Chicago, IL 60606.

Use Figure 6–11 for your own testing. The norms for relative maximal oxygen consumption are given in Table 6–1 for men and Table 6–2 for women.

Sub-maximal Step Test

The three-minute step test developed by Dr. Fred Kasch of San Diego State University is used by the YMCA for mass testing of participants. The procedure involves the delivery of a measured aerobic stimulus controlled by stepping to a standardized cadence. This type of test is easier to administer than the bicycle ergometer test. It requires less equipment and at less cost, and can be used in mass testing situations. Its disadvantage is its relative inaccuracy when compared to the bicycle test and the lack of data for comparison with retests. The following equipment is needed to administer the test:

- A 12-inch high step bench.

- A metronome for accurate pacing (96 bpm) (It works well to borrow a metronome and record three minutes of the correct rhythm and one minute recovery).

- A timer for timing the three-minute test and the one-minute recovery.

- Test forms to record data.

The test is preceded by a demonstration of the stepping procedure by the test administrator. With the metronome set to 96 bpm (24 stepping cycles per minute), start stepping to a four-beat cycle—up, up, down, down (Fig. 6–12). It does not matter which foot begins the cycle, although both feet must contact the top of the bench on the up portion of the cycle, and both feet must contact the floor during the down portion. The lead foot may change during the test. Give the client a short practice session in which to step in place without the bench or, if necessary, with the bench with adequate recovery afterward.

To begin the test itself, have the client face the bench, and then remind him/her that the stepping will be for three minutes and that he/she will be seated immediately afterward for a one-minute pulse count. Have the client step in place in time with the metronome. Start the timing of the three minutes when the client begins stepping. Check stepping rhythm throughout the test, announcing when one minute, two minutes, and two minutes and 40 seconds

Table 6–2   NORMS FOR RELATIVE MAXIMAL OXYGEN CONSUMPTION (WOMEN)

Relative Maximal O₂ Concentration	Age (years)					
	18–25	26–35	36–45	46–55	56–65	65+
Excellent	>56	>52	>45	>40	>37	>32
Good	47–56	45–52	38–45	34–40	32–37	28–32
Above average	42–46	39–44	34–37	31–33	28–31	25–27
Average	38–41	35–38	31–33	28–30	25–27	22–24
Below average	33–37	31–34	27–30	25–27	22–24	19–22
Poor	28–32	26–30	22–26	20–24	18–21	17–18
Very poor	<28	<26	<22	<20	<18	<17

Source: Adapted from Golding, et al. (1986). *The Y's way to physical fitness* (3rd ed.), p. 112. Reprinted with permission of the YMCA of the USA, 101 N. Wacker Drive. Chicago, IL 60606.

have elapsed. To further assist the client, the trainer may want to provide additional verbal cues by clapping the hands or saying "up, up, down, down" in cadence with the metronome. At the end of the three-minute stepping period, immediately begin counting the heart rate of the seated subject for one minute. The one-minute post-exercise heart rate is used to score the test and can be compared to both the norms in Tables 6–3 and 6–4 and previous test results if appropriate.

The Rockport® Fitness Walking Test™ (1 Mile Walk)

The Rockport Fitness Walking Test is routinely used to assess cardiovascular fitness. The test involves a timed 1 mile walk and run on a smooth and level surface (preferably a ¼-mile running track). The only other equipment necessary is a timing device and a form for recording results.

An advantage of this test over the lab tests is that it evaluates performance, whereas the lab tests measure parameters (e.g., estimated $\dot{V}O_2$, workload, or heart rate) that give a very good indication of how well an individual will perform during aerobic activity, This test is also excellent for mass testing. Limitations to the test lie in the fact that pacing ability and body-fat weight may adversely affect performance. The test is designed for 170-pound men and 125-pound women. If the client weighs substantially less, the relative cardiovas-

Figure 6–12   Three-minute step test.

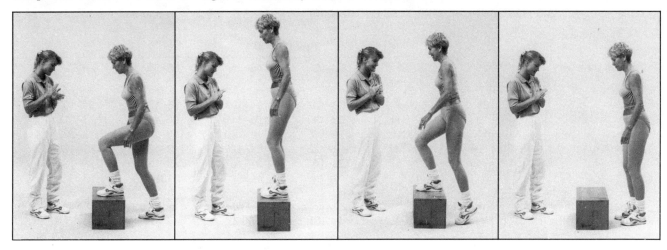

cular fitness level will be slightly underestimated. Conversely, if he/she weighs substantially more, cardiovascular fitness will be slightly overestimated. Since the test requires the mile to be walked as fast as possible, lack of motivation may result in an underestimation of cardiovascular fitness.

The test should begin with a warm-up consisting of walking and light stretching. After the warm-up, it should be explained to all participants that this test requires a near maximal effort. For reasons of safety, however, it should be made clear that clients should not walk to exhaustion and should stop at any time if necessary. All participants should start at the same time. Elapsed times should be announced with every lap. Immediately upon completion of the mile, each subject or test administrator/assistant should take a 10-second exercise pulse. This 10-second value and its corresponding per minute pulse (the 10-second pulse times 6) should be recorded along with the time it took to complete the mile walk. After test completion, all participants should walk for at least 5 minutes to cool down.

In addition to completion time and immediate post-exercise heart rate, a maximal perceived exertion could also be recorded to provide an indication of effort and for comparison to subsequent tests. Completion time and minute pulse rate are used to score the test using the proper chart for age and sex in Figure 6-13a. Find the point on the chart defined by each client's walking time

Table 6–3   NORMS FOR 3-MINUTE STEP TEST (MEN)

Fitness Category	Age (years)					
	18–25	26–35	36–45	46–55	56–65	65+
Excellent	<79	<81	<83	<87	<86	<88
Good	79–89	81–89	83–96	87–97	86–97	88–96
Above average	90–99	90–99	97–103	98–105	98–103	97–103
Average	100–105	100–107	104–112	106–116	104–112	104–113
Below average	106–116	108–117	113–119	117–122	113–120	114–120
Poor	117–128	118–128	120–130	123–132	121–129	121–130
Very poor	>128	>128	>130	>132	>129	>130

Source: Adapted from Golding, et al. (1986). *The Y's way to physical fitness* (3rd ed.), p. 613. Reprinted with permission of the YMCA of the USA, 101 N. Wacker Drive. Chicago, IL 60606.

Table 6–4   NORMS FOR 3-MINUTE STEP TEST (WOMEN)

Fitness Category	Age (years)					
	18–25	26–35	36–45	46–55	56–65	65+
Excellent	<85	<88	<90	<94	<95	<90
Good	85–98	88–99	90–102	94–104	95–104	90–102
Above average	99–108	100–111	103–110	105–115	105–112	103–115
Average	109–117	112–119	111–118	116–120	113–118	116–122
Below average	118–126	120–126	119–128	121–126	119–128	123–128
Poor	127–140	127–138	129–140	127–135	129–139	129–134
Very poor	>140	>138	>140	>135	>139	>134

Source: Adapted from Golding, et al. (1986). *The Y's way to physical fitness* (3rd ed.), p. 114. Reprinted with permission of the YMCA of the USA, 101 N. Wacker Drive. Chicago, IL 60606.

and heart rate at the end of the walk. This will allow you to compare the client's performance to that of others in his/her age and sex categories.

The Rockport Fitness Treadmill Test™

Another effective test for use in a home or health club is the Rockport Fitness Treadmill Test. While the principles of the test remain the same, the techniques of administration are slightly different. An accurate result is obtained by having the client walk one mile on a level treadmill at a fixed rate.

After stretching, but before begining the timed mile, have the client warm up on the treadmill, then establish an exact pace that can be held for one mile. With the pace established, the client should walk for the time necessary to complete the mile at the fixed rate. After finishing the mile immediately take and record the client's pulse rate for 10 seconds. Have the client cool down by walking slowly for at least 5 minutes.

In addition to walking pace and immediate post-exercise heart rate, a maximal perceived exertion could also be recorded to provide an indication of effort and for comparison to subsequent tests. Walking pace and minute pulse rate are used to score the test using the proper chart for age and sex in Figure 6-13b. Find the point on the chart defined by each client's walking pace and heart rate at the end of the walk. This will allow you to compare the client's performance to that of others in his/her age and sex categories.

BODY COMPOSITION TESTING AND EVALUATION

Excess body-fat has been associated with a number of health risks, including heart disease, diabetes, hypertension, arthritis, gall bladder disease, cirrhosis of the liver, hernia, intestinal obstruction, and sleep disorders. It is also associated with reduced endurance performance and increased risk for injury. The most prevalent reason adults begin exercise programs is to reduce body weight. Therefore, it is important to be able to assess body composition in order to determine an accurate ideal body weight and develop a sound exercise program. **Body composition** refers to the quality or makeup of total body mass. Total body mass can be divided into lean body mass and fat mass. Lean body mass is composed of bone, muscle and organs, and fat mass is composed of adipose tissue. The assessment of body composition determines the relative percentages of lean body mass and fat mass.

Ideal body weight has historically been determined without concern for body composition. This method most commonly has involved the use of the standardized height–weight tables. Ideal body weight is estimated from height and frame size without consideration of the composition of the weight. Therefore, a well-muscled bodybuilder would most likely be considered overweight, while another person could fall within the accepted range and actually be over-fat by body composition standards. It is not uncommon for an exerciser to lose fat weight and gain muscle weight without any change in total body weight. Without an assessment of body composition, this favorable change could go undetected and lead to frustration on the part of the exerciser.

The three most common methods of assessing body composition are hydrostatic weighing, bioelectrical impedance, and measurement of skinfolds.

Hydrostatic Weighing

Hydrostatic weighing, also known as underwater weighing, is considered the "gold standard" of body composition assessment. The test involves suspending a client, seated in a chair attached to a scale, in a tank of water. Body density is

172

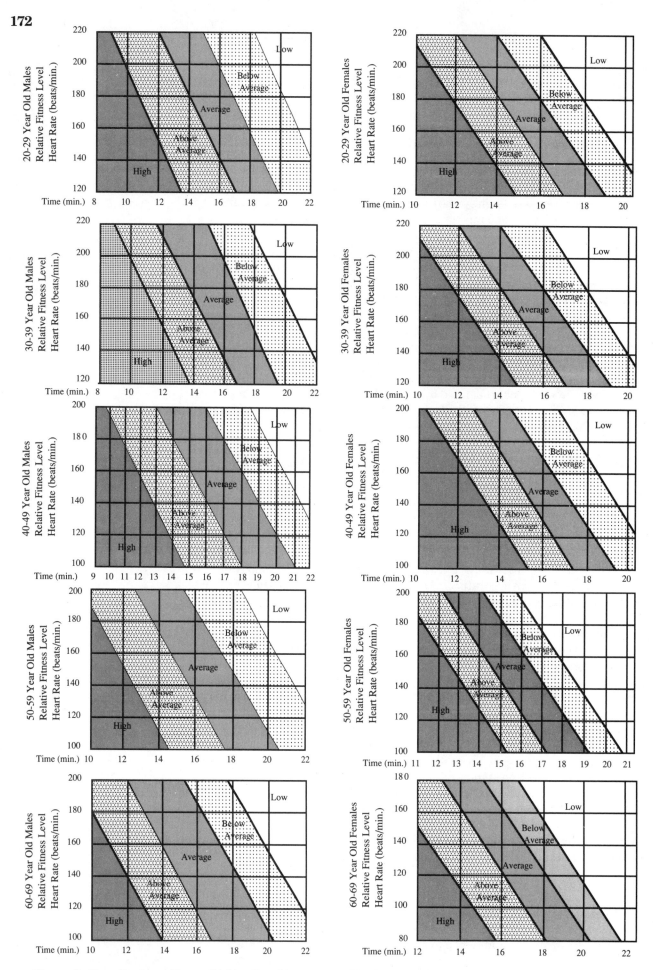

Figure 6–13a Rockport Fitness Walking Test Charts ©1991 The Rockport Company. All rights reserved. Reprinted by permission of the Rockport Company.

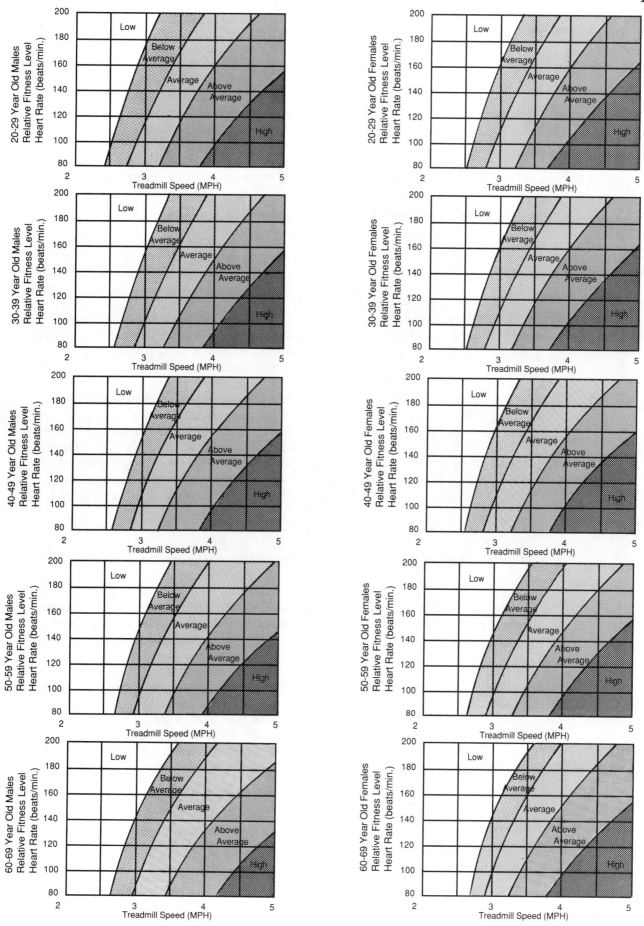

Figure 6–13b Rockport Fitness Treadmill Test Charts © 1991 The Rockport Company. All rights reserved. Reprinted by permission of the Rockport Company.

calculated from the relationship of normal body weight to underwater weight. From body density the percentage of body-fat is calculated. This method is most accurate when combined with a measurement of *residual volume* (the amount of air left in the lungs after a complete expiration). When residual volume is estimated via formula, the accuracy of the hydrostatic method can be significantly decreased. Although accurate, a properly administered hydrostatic weighing is impractical in terms of expense, time, and equipment.

Bioelectrical Impedance

The measurement of bioelectrical impedance is an increasingly popular method for determining body composition. It is based on the principle that the conductivity of an electrical impulse is greater through lean tissue than through fatty tissue. Pairs of electrodes, through which an imperceptible electrical current is passed, are placed on the hand and foot. The analyzer, essentially an ohmmeter and a computer, measures the body's resistance to electrical flow, in ohms, and from that computes body density and percent body-fat. This method requires the subject to lie still, with the wrist and ankle electrodes accurately placed. The subject should be well-hydrated and not have exercised in the past 6 hours or consumed any alcohol in the past 24 hours. Some recent research has shown the impedance method to be as accurate as the skinfold method, depending on the manufacturer of the analyzer, the formula used to compute body density, and the adherence of the client to the aforementioned restrictions. Assessing body composition via bioelectrical impedance is both fast and easy and requires minimal technical training. The cost of the analyzers ranges from $300 to $5,000, depending on design and report-generation capabilities (from simple digital readout of impedance to elaborate multi-page reports).

Skinfold Measurements

Measurement of skinfolds provides a relatively inexpensive way to assess body composition. The results are both valid and reliable if the measurements are taken properly. The standard error of the method is 3.5 percent or more fat, depending on the equation applied. This is compared to a 2.7 percent error for a hydrostatically determined measurement. The method, based on the notion that approximately 50 percent of total body-fat is under the skin, involves measuring the thickness of the skinfolds at standardized sites. These measurements are summed and applied to one of many equations available. For the most part, the equations calculate body density, with percent fat being calculated from the same formula used for hydrostatic weighing. Calculation is often simplified through the use of a table or nomogram. Calipers specifically designed for skinfold measurement are the only equipment needed for this method of body-fat assessment. The calipers range in cost from $20 to $300.

The procedure for measuring skinfolds is as follows:

1. Identify the anatomical location of the skinfold. All measurements are taken on the right side of the body. (Optional: Mark the site with a common eyebrow pencil to expedite site relocation in repeated measures.)

2. Grasp the skinfold firmly with the thumb and index finger of the left hand.

3. Holding the calipers perpendicular to the site, place the pads of the calipers approximately one-quarter inch from the thumb and forefinger.

4. Read the dial to the nearest 0.5 millimeter approximately one or two seconds after the trigger has been released.

5. A minimum of two measurements should be taken at each site, with a minimum of 15 seconds between measurements to allow the fat to return to normal thickness.

6. If the first two measurements vary by greater than one millimeter, others should be taken until two measurements vary by less than one millimeter.

Improper site determination and measurement are the two primary sources of error in skinfold measurement. The technique is best learned by locating and measuring the standard sites numerous times and comparing results with those of a well-trained associate. Skinfold measurements should not be taken after exercise, because the transfer of fluid to the skin could result in overestimations.

Of the many equations for estimating body composition, two of the equations developed by Jackson and Pollock (1985) result in the least likelihood of error for a general population. These equations are based on the sum of measurements taken at three sites. For men the skinfold sites are as follows (Fig. 6-14):

1. *Chest* (Fig. 6-15): a diagonal skinfold taken halfway between the anterior axillary line (crease of the underarm) and the nipple.

2. *Abdomen* (Fig. 6-16): a vertical skinfold taken one inch lateral to the umbilicus.

3. *Thigh* (Fig. 6-17): a vertical skinfold taken midway between the hip and knee joints on the front of the thigh.

For women the skinfold sites are as follows (Fig. 6-18):

1. *Triceps* (Fig. 6-19): a vertical fold on the back of the upper arm taken halfway between the acromial (shoulder) and olecranon (elbow) processes.

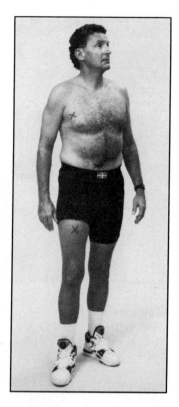

Figure 6–14   Skinfold sites for men: chest, abdomen, and thigh.

Figure 6–15   Chest skinfold for men. (a) Locate the site midway between the anterior axillary line and the nipple. (b) Grasp a diagonal fold and pull it away from the muscle.

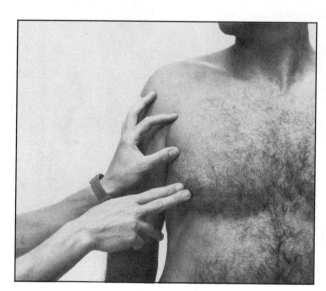

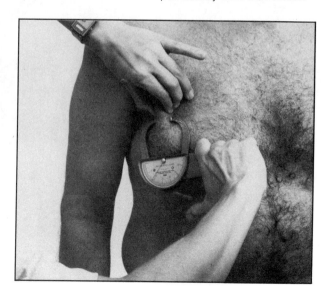

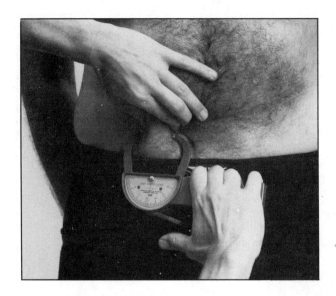

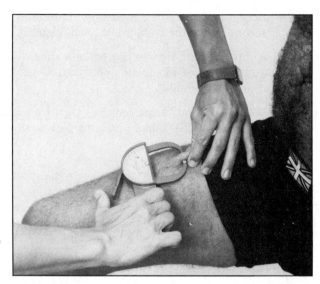

Figure 6–16 Abdominal skinfold for men: Grasp a vertical skinfold one inch to the left of the umbilicus.

Figure 6–17 Thigh skinfold for men: Grasp a vertical skinfold and pull it away from the muscle.

2. *Suprailium* (Fig. 6–20): a diagonal fold taken at or just anterior to the crest of the ilium.

3. *Thigh* (Fig. 6–21): a vertical skinfold taken midway between the hip and knee joints on the front of the thigh.

After obtaining three satisfactory measurements, add them and refer to Table 6–5 for men and Table 6–6 for women.

For example, for a 47-year-old man with measurements of 20 for the chest, 30 for the abdomen, and 17 for the thigh, the sum of measurements is 67. In Table 6–5, at the intersection of the row corresponding to the sum of the skinfolds and the column corresponding to the age, is the estimated body-fat percentage of 21.3 percent. Figures 6–22 and 6–23 contain various ranges of

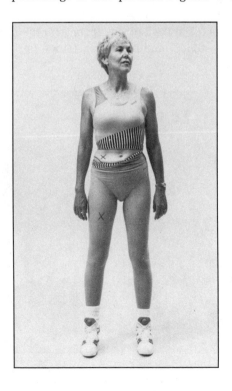

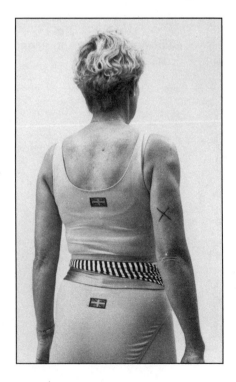

Figure 6–18 Skinfold sites for women. (a) Supraillium and thigh; (b) triceps.

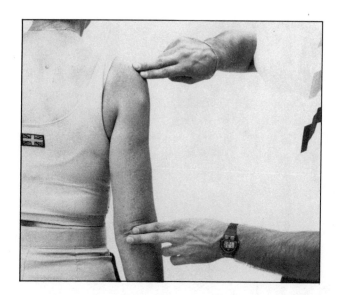 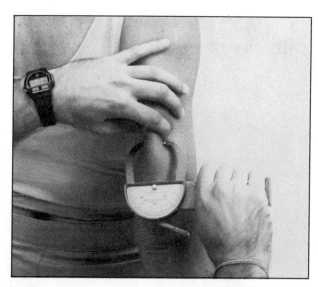

body-fat for optimal health, fitness, or competitive athletics. This man is 5 percent above the upper limit of the 12–18 percent range for men desiring optimal fitness. In order to calculate this man's weight for the desired range, his lean body weight must first be calculated. Since 23 percent of his body weight is fat weight, then 100 percent – 23 percent = 77 percent of his weight is lean body mass. Assuming a total body weight of 212 pounds, we then use the decimal form of the percentage figure to derive a lean body weight of 163 pounds. To summarize:

Figure 6–19 Triceps skin-fold for women. (a) Locate the site midway between the acromial (shoulder) and olecranon (elbow) processes. (b) Grasp a vertical fold on the posterior midline and pull it away from the muscle.

Step 1: 100% – Fat percentage = Lean body percentage
100% – 23% = 77%
Step 2: Body weight × Lean body percentage = Lean body weight
212 × .77 = 163 lb

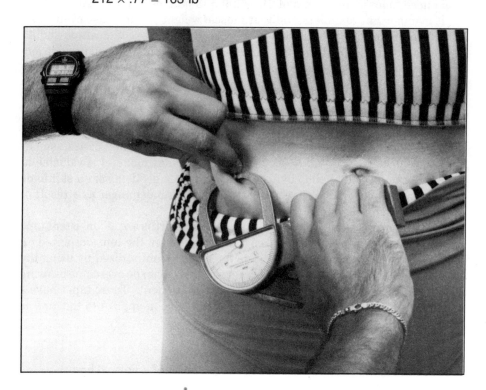

Figure 6–20 Supraillium skinfold for women: Grasp a diagonal skinfold just above and slightly forward of the crest of the ilium.

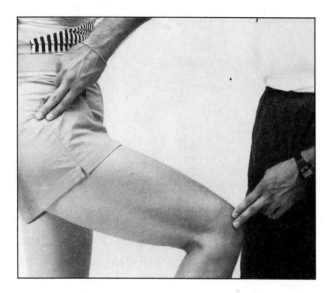

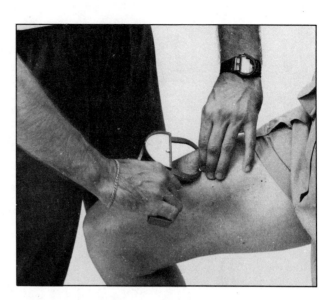

Figure 6–21 Thigh skinfold for women. (a) Locate the hip and the knee joints and find the midpoint on the top of the thigh. (b) Grasp a vertical skinfold and pull it away from the muscle.

A body weight for a desired percent fat is then calculated by first subtracting the desired percent fat from 100% and then dividing the lean body weight by the decimal form of this percentage:

Step 3: 100 – Desired percent fat = Desired lean percent
Upper limit: 100% – 18% = 82%
Lower limit: 100% – 12% = 88%
Step 4: Lean body weight / Desired lean percentage = Desired body weight
163/0.82 = 199 lb
163/0.88 = 185 lb

The weight range corresponding to a desired body-fat of 12–18 percent is 185–199 pounds. With regular aerobic activity and dietary management, this man would need to lose a minimum of 212 – 199 = 13 pounds of fat weight.

It is important to understand that muscle weight can increase even when exercise participation is limited to aerobic activity. Body composition should be assessed periodically throughout an exercise program. This can provide motivating information, especially when fat weight loss appears to have plateaued.

Girth Measurements

Girth measurements have been used alone and in combination with skinfold measurements to assess body composition. While this method of assessment has been shown to be no more accurate than skinfolds alone, it is valuable in the evaluation of body build changes and provides a good check on skinfolds and other methods of assessment as body composition changes as a result of exercise-induced weight changes.

The two primary sources of error in measuring girths are inconsistent tape placement during repeated measures and variations in the tension placed on the tape during the measurement. The first error is minimized by using the standardized sites described below. The second error can be overcome by using a cloth tape specifically designed for girth measurement. These tapes have a tension scale that allows standardization of the tension applied to the tape as each site is measured.

Take the measurements at these sites:

1. *Chest*–at the nipple line during the midpoint of a normal breath.

2. *Waist*—at the narrowest point, below the rib cage and just above the top of the hip bones.

3. *Hips*—with feet together, at the level of the sysphisis pubis in front, at the maximal protrusion of the buttocks in the back.

4. *Thigh*—at the crotch level and just below the fold of the buttocks.

5. *Calf*—at the maximal circumference.

6. *Ankle*—at the minimal circumference, usually just above the ankle bone.

7. *Upper arm*—at the maximal circumference; arm extended, palm up.

Table 6–5

**PERCENT FAT ESTIMATE FOR MEN:
SUM OF CHEST, ABDOMEN, AND THIGH SKINFOLDS**

Age Groups

Sum of Skinfolds (mm)	Under 22	23–27	28–32	33–37	38–42	43–47	48–52	53–57	Over 57
8–10	1.3	1.8	2.3	2.9	3.4	3.9	4.5	5.0	5.5
11–13	2.2	2.8	3.3	3.9	4.4	4.9	5.5	6.0	6.5
14–16	3.2	3.8	4.3	4.8	5.4	5.9	6.4	7.0	7.5
17–19	4.2	4.7	5.3	5.8	6.3	6.9	7.4	8.0	8.5
20–22	5.1	5.7	6.2	6.8	7.3	7.9	8.4	8.9	9.5
23–25	6.1	6.6	7.2	7.7	8.3	8.8	9.4	9.9	10.5
26–28	7.0	7.6	8.1	8.7	9.2	9.8	10.3	10.9	11.4
29–31	8.0	8.5	9.1	9.6	10.2	10.7	11.3	11.8	12.4
32–34	8.9	9.4	10.0	10.5	11.1	11.6	12.2	12.8	13.3
35–37	9.8	10.4	10.9	11.5	12.0	12.6	13.1	13.7	14.3
38–40	10.7	11.3	11.8	12.4	12.9	13.5	14.1	14.6	15.2
41–43	11.6	12.2	12.7	13.3	13.8	14.4	15.0	15.5	16.1
44–46	12.5	13.1	13.6	14.2	14.7	15.3	15.9	16.4	17.0
47–49	13.4	13.9	14.5	15.1	15.6	16.2	16.8	17.3	17.9
50–52	14.3	14.8	15.4	15.9	16.5	17.1	17.6	18.2	18.8
53–55	15.1	15.7	16.2	16.8	17.4	17.9	18.5	19.1	19.7
56–58	16.0	16.5	17.1	17.7	18.2	18.8	19.4	20.0	20.5
59–61	16.9	17.4	17.9	18.5	19.1	19.7	20.2	20.8	21.4
62–64	17.6	18.2	18.8	19.4	19.9	20.5	21.1	21.7	22.2
65–67	18.5	19.0	19.6	20.2	20.8	21.3	21.9	22.5	23.1
68–70	19.3	19.9	20.4	21.0	21.6	22.2	22.7	23.3	23.9
71–73	20.1	20.7	21.2	21.8	22.4	23.0	23.6	24.1	24.7
74–76	20.9	21.5	22.0	22.6	23.2	23.8	24.4	25.0	25.5
77–79	21.7	22.2	22.8	23.4	24.0	24.6	25.2	25.8	26.3
80–82	22.4	23.0	23.6	24.2	24.8	25.4	25.9	26.5	27.1
83–85	23.2	23.8	24.4	25.0	25.5	26.1	26.7	27.3	27.9
86–88	24.0	24.5	25.1	25.7	26.3	26.9	27.5	28.1	28.7
89–91	24.7	25.3	25.9	26.5	27.1	27.6	28.2	28.8	29.4
92–94	25.4	26.0	26.6	27.2	27.8	28.4	29.0	29.6	30.2
92–97	26.1	26.7	27.3	27.9	28.5	29.1	29.7	30.3	30.9
98–100	26.9	27.4	28.0	28.6	29.2	29.8	30.4	31.0	31.6
101–103	27.5	28.1	28.7	29.3	29.9	30.5	31.1	31.7	32.3
104–106	28.2	28.8	29.4	30.0	30.6	31.2	31.8	32.4	33.0
107–109	28.9	29.5	30.1	30.7	31.3	31.9	32.5	33.1	33.7
110–112	29.6	30.2	30.8	31.4	32.0	32.6	33.2	33.8	34.4
113–115	30.2	30.8	31.4	32.0	32.6	33.2	33.8	34.5	35.1
116–118	30.9	31.5	32.1	32.7	33.3	33.9	34.5	35.1	35.7
119–121	31.5	32.1	32.7	33.3	33.9	34.5	35.1	35.7	36.4
122–124	32.1	32.7	33.3	33.9	34.5	35.1	35.8	36.4	37.0
125–127	32.7	33.3	33.9	34.5	35.1	35.8	36.4	37.0	37.6

8. *Wrist*—at the minimal circumference; arm extended, palm up.

Record the measurements, and repeat each time body composition is assessed.

FLEXIBILITY TESTING AND EVALUATION

Flexibility is defined as the range of motion of a given joint. It is often associated with only **muscular flexibility**, which is the extent to which range of motion is limited by muscles and tendons surrounding the joint. But flexibility is also influenced by the amount of freedom allowed by the ligaments connecting the bones that make up a given joint.

Table 6–6

PERCENT FAT ESTIMATE FOR WOMEN:
SUM OF TRICEPS, SUPRAILIUM, AND THIGH SKINFOLDS

Age Groups

Sum of Skinfolds (mm)	Under 22	23–27	28–32	33–37	38–42	43–47	48–52	53–57	Over 57
23–25	9.7	9.9	10.2	10.4	10.7	10.9	11.2	11.4	11.7
26–28	11.0	11.2	11.5	11.7	12.0	12.3	12.5	12.7	13.0
29–31	12.3	12.5	12.8	13.0	13.3	13.5	13.8	14.0	14.3
32–34	13.6	13.8	14.0	14.3	14.5	14.8	15.0	15.3	15.5
35–37	14.8	15.0	15.3	15.5	15.8	16.0	16.3	16.5	16.8
38–40	16.0	16.3	16.5	16.7	17.0	17.2	17.5	17.7	18.0
41–43	17.2	17.4	17.7	17.9	18.2	18.4	18.7	18.9	19.2
44–46	18.3	18.6	18.8	19.1	19.3	19.6	19.8	20.1	20.3
47–49	19.5	19.7	20.0	20.2	20.5	20.7	21.0	21.2	21.5
50–52	20.6	20.8	21.1	21.3	21.6	21.8	22.1	22.3	22.6
53–55	21.7	21.9	22.1	22.4	22.6	22.9	23.1	23.4	23.6
56–58	22.7	23.0	23.2	23.4	23.7	23.9	24.2	24.4	24.7
59–61	23.7	24.0	24.2	24.5	24.7	25.0	25.2	25.5	25.7
62–64	24.7	25.0	25.2	25.5	25.7	26.0	26.7	26.4	26.7
65–67	25.7	25.9	26.2	26.4	26.7	26.7	27.2	27.4	27.7
68–70	26.6	26.9	27.1	27.4	27.6	27.9	28.1	28.4	28.6
71–73	27.5	27.8	28.0	28.3	28.5	28.8	29.0	29.3	29.5
74–76	28.4	28.7	28.9	29.2	29.4	29.7	29.9	30.2	30.4
77–79	29.3	29.5	29.8	30.0	30.3	30.5	30.8	31.0	31.3
80–82	30.1	30.4	30.6	30.9	31.1	31.4	31.6	31.9	32.1
83–85	30.9	31.2	31.4	31.7	31.9	32.2	32.4	32.7	32.9
86–88	31.7	32.0	32.2	32.5	32.7	32.9	33.2	33.4	33.7
89–91	32.5	32.7	33.0	33.2	33.5	33.7	33.9	34.2	34.4
92–94	33.2	33.4	33.7	33.9	34.2	34.4	34.7	34.9	35.2
95–97	33.9	34.1	34.4	34.6	34.9	35.1	35.4	35.6	35.9
98–100	34.6	34.8	35.1	35.3	35.5	35.8	36.0	36.3	36.5
101–103	35.3	35.4	35.7	35.9	36.2	36.4	36.7	36.9	37.2
104–106	35.8	36.1	36.3	36.6	36.8	37.1	37.3	37.5	37.8
107–109	36.4	36.7	36.9	37.1	37.4	37.6	37.9	38.1	38.4
110–112	37.0	37.2	37.5	37.7	38.0	38.2	38.5	38.7	38.9
113–115	37.5	37.8	38.0	38.2	38.5	38.7	39.0	39.2	39.5
116–118	38.0	38.3	38.5	38.8	39.0	39.3	39.5	39.7	40.0
119–121	38.5	38.7	39.0	39.2	39.5	39.7	40.0	40.2	40.5
122–124	39.0	39.2	39.4	39.7	39.9	40.2	40.4	40.7	40.9
125–127	39.4	39.6	39.9	40.1	40.4	40.6	40.9	41.1	41.4
128–130	39.8	40.0	40.3	40.5	40.8	41.0	41.3	41.5	41.8

Source: Jackson and Pollack, 1985. Reprinted from the May 1985 issue of *The Physician and Sportsmedicine* by special permission from McGraw-Hill, Inc. Copyright 1990 by McGraw-Hill, Inc.

Flexibility affects both health and fitness. Inflexibility increases risk for joint and muscle injury. The most frequent example is low-back inflexibility, which relates to low-back pain and injury. In order for an athlete to perform at optimal levels, he/she must be able to move through motions specific to the sport with ease and fluidity. Limitations to movement in sports affect both performance and musculoskeletal health.

As with strength testing, there is no single flexibility test that predicts the range of motion of other joints of the body. Each joint must be assessed individually with a specifically designed test. While it is not the purpose of this chapter to explain the assessment of multiple joints throughout the body, tests of shoulder, hip, and low-back range of motion will be highlighted.

Trunk Flexion

Trunk flexion is measured with the sit-and-reach test (the same test is used by the YMCA). It is administered with a yardstick and tape and has well-established norms for comparison. There is a limited risk of muscle strain or pull if a forward movement is attempted that is too vigorous. Therefore, all participants should warm up with gentle stretching of the low back and hamstrings, and the test should be performed slowly and cautiously. Place the yardstick on the floor, and put a piece of tape at least 12 inches long at a right angle to the stick at the 15-inch mark. The client should remove his/her shoes and sit with the stick between the legs, with the zero mark toward the body. The feet should be approximately 12 inches apart and the heels aligned with the tape at the 15-inch mark on the yardstick (Fig. 6–24). Have the client place

Figure 6–22 Body-fat content for men. (*Source*: Goethal, p. (1989). Winning over the overweight. *Fitness Management, 5(11)*, p. 26. Reprinted with permission of Leisure Publications, Inc., Los Angeles.)

Figure 6–23 Body-fat content for women. (*Source*: Geothal, p. (1989). Winning over the overweight. *Fitness Management, 5(11)*, p. 27. Reprinted with permission of Leisure Publications, Inc., Los Angeles.)

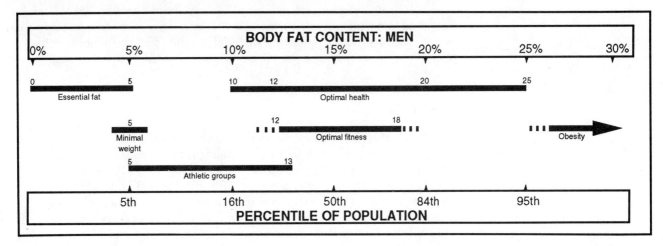

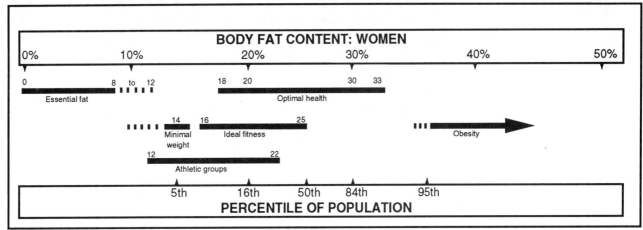

Figure 6–24 Sit-and-reach flexibility test.

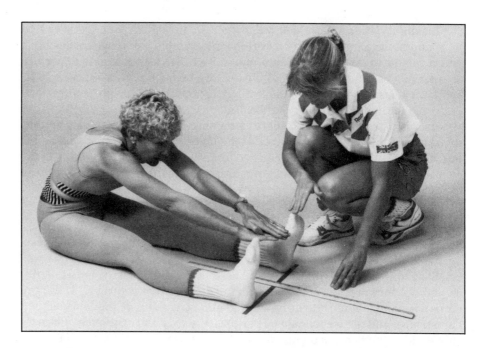

one hand on top of the other, with the tips of the fingers aligned, and then exhale and slowly lean forward by dropping the head toward or between the arms. The fingers should be kept in contact with the yardstick, and the knees should be kept straight by the test administrator.

The score is the longest point reached after three trials. Scores can be compared to norms in Tables 6–7 and 6–8. The quality of the trunk flexion can be evaluated further by observing where along the spine the bending is taking place while the subject is in the flexed position. Use Table 6–9 for comparison to norms.

Trunk Extension

The trunk-extension test evaluates the amount of backward bend (extension) available to the lumbar spine. As flexibility in the lumbar spine is lost, the risk for low-back pain and injury increases significantly. Have your client lie face down with the hands in a position for a push-up (Fig. 6–25). The client then pushes the upper body up while letting the lower back relax as much as possible and attempting to keep the hip bones in contact with the floor. Although this movement is commonly used as a therapeutic exercise for low-back-pain patients, it is important to avoid injury by making sure the extension is not forced and the movement stops when the hip bones begin to lose contact with the floor. Note the location along the spine where the bending is taking place. Evaluate trunk extension using Table 6–10.

Hip Flexion

Hip-flexion tests evaluate the amount of flexibility in the hips and hamstring. Limitations to hip flexion place increased stresses on the low back, increasing risk for low-back pain and injury. To assess hamstrings flexibility, have the client lie flat on his/her back. The trainer's right hand is used to hold the left leg down, thus stabilizing the pelvis, while the trainer's left hand passively raises the client's right leg to an angle of 80°–85°. Normal hamstring length will allow for this amount of hip flexion (Fig. 6–26). Tight hamstring flexibility

Figure 6–25 Final position for trunk-extension assessment. Note where the bending is taking place.

Table 6–7   **NORMS FOR TRUNK FLEXIBILITY TEST (MEN)**

	Age (years)					
Flexibility	**18–25**	**26–35**	**36–45**	**46–55**	**56–65**	**65+**
Excellent	>20	>20	>19	>19	>17	>17
Good	18–20	18–19	17–19	16–17	14–17	13–16
Above average	17–18	16–17	15–17	14–15	12–14	11–13
Average	15–16	15–16	13–15	12–13	10–12	9–11
Below average	13–14	12–14	11–13	10–11	8–10	8–9
Poor	10–12	10–12	9–11	7–9	5–8	5–7
Very poor	<10	<10	<8	<7	<5	<5

Source: Adapted from Golding, et al. (1986). *The Y's way to physical fitness* (3rd ed.), p. 114. Reprinted with permission of the YMCA of the USA, 101 N. Wacker Drive. Chicago, IL 60606.

Table 6–8   **NORMS FOR TRUNK FLEXIBILITY TEST (WOMEN)**

	Age (years)					
Flexibility	**18–25**	**26–35**	**36–45**	**46–55**	**56–65**	**65+**
Excellent	>24	>23	>22	>21	>20	>20
Good	21–23	20–22	19–21	18–20	18–19	18–19
Above average	20–21	19–20	17–19	17–18	16–17	16–17
Average	18–19	18	16–17	15–16	15	14–15
Below average	17–18	16–17	14–15	14–15	13–14	12–13
Poor	14–16	14–15	11–13	11–13	10–12	9–11
Very poor	<13	<13	<10	<10	<9	<8

Source: Adapted from Golding, et al. (1986). *The Y's way to physical fitness* (3rd ed.), p. 115. Reprinted with permission of the YMCA of the USA, 101 N. Wacker Drive. Chicago, IL 60606.

is demonstrated when the client's leg raises to approximately 50° of hip flexion without pain in the back of the leg or bending of the knee (Fig. 6-27).

To test for hip flexor length, have the client maintain a flat low back on the table while grasping behind the knee and pulling the left leg toward the chest. Normal length is demonstrated when the right leg stays flat to the table (Fig. 6-28). Shortened hip flexors are indicated when the right leg raises off the table (Fig. 6-29).

Shoulder Flexibility

Swimming and racquet and throwing sports all require flexibility in the shoulders for good performance and avoidance of injury. The purpose of the test of shoulder flexibility is to measure the multi-rotational components of the shoulder joints. Test the left shoulder by having the client sit or stand and place his/her right arm straight up, letting the elbow bend so the hand comes to rest palm down between the shoulder blades. Then the client should reach back with the left arm so the palm is up. Have the client attempt to touch hands with his/her fingers (Fig. 6-30). Evaluate shoulder flexibility using Table 6-11. Repeat the procedure for the opposite shoulder.

Table 6-9   EVALUATION OF TRUNK FLEXION

Flexion	Characteristics
Good	The trunk is able to move forward onto the thighs, and motion is occuring at the hips and low back.
Fair	Bending forward causes some restriction in the low back so that bending occurs more in the lumbar spine.
Poor	Bending forward results in the lumbar spine remaining straight, and the bending occurs in the upper areas of the spine.

Source: Adapted from Krepton, D., and Chu, D. (1984). *Everybody's aerobics book* (1st ed.). Oakland, CA: Star Rover House. Reprinted with permission.

Table 6-10   EVALUATION OF TRUNK EXTENSION

Extension	Characteristics
Good	The hips remain in contact with the floor while the arms are fully extended.
Fair	The hips come up from the ground up to two inches.
Poor	The hips come up from the ground two inches or more.

Source: Adapted from Krepton, D., and Chu, D. (1984). *Everybody's aerobics book* (1st ed.). Oakland, CA: Star Rover House. Reprinted with permission.

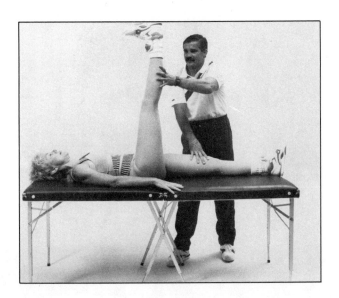

Figure 6–26   Hamstrings flexibility test: normal flexibility.

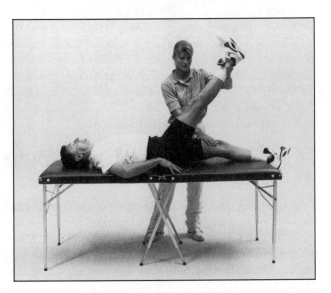

Figure 6–27   Hamstrings flexibility test: tight flexibility.

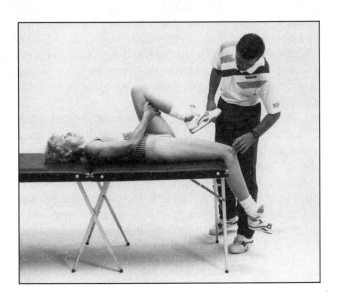

Figure 6–28   Test for hip flexor length: normal length.

Figure 6–29 Test for hip flexor length: shortened length.

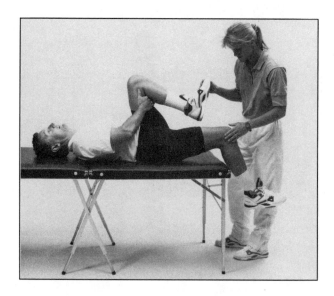

Poor shoulder flexibility can also affect a client's postural alignment. If the shoulder adductors are excessively tight, the client may assume a posture with the shoulders depressed and forwardly rotated and the arms medially rotated, often called the "gorilla stance." To test for poor shoulder adductor flexibility, have the client lie on his/her back with knees bent, back flat, and arms overhead. Adequate flexibility is demonstrated if the arms lie flat overhead (Fig. 6–31). If the arms do not lie flat (Fig. 6–32), a shortness in the pectoralis major, teres major, and latissimus dorsi is indicated.

MUSCULAR STRENGTH AND ENDURANCE TESTING AND EVALUATION

Two components of muscular fitness testing are muscular strength and muscular endurance. **Muscular strength** is the greatest amount of force that muscles can produce in a single maximal effort. **Muscular endurance** refers to the ability to exert a sub-maximal force either repeatedly or statically over time. Adequate muscular strength and endurance are necessary for both optimal health and optimal athletic performance. From a health perspective, adequate strength and endurance facilitate participation in activities of daily living without injury or undue fatigue, and also enhance life at an optimal level of human functioning. Strength and muscular endurance requirements for athletics vary significantly according to the requirements of the sport. Both are necessary for optimal performance in most recreational sports, and, in fact, muscular strength training is even a subject of increased interest among distance runners.

While the assessment of muscular strength can be made independent of muscular endurance, the assessment of muscular endurance also measures strength to some degree. Careful consideration of client health and fitness should be made before the specific muscular strength tests are chosen. The lower-weight/higher-repetition muscular endurance tests are more appropriate for less fit clients and those with more health-related exercise strength goals, especially for those who have been previously inactive. Two muscle endurance tests that are both reliable and easy to administer are the one-minute timed sit-up test and the push-up test. Both test relative muscular endurance, because results are relative to body weight. Another endurance test that will

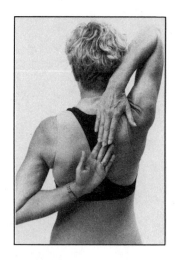

Figure 6–30 Assessing flexibility of the left shoulder.

Table 6–11   EVALUATION OF SHOULDER FLEXIBILITY

Flexibility	Characteristics
Good	The fingers can touch.
Fair	The fingertips are not touching, but are less than two inches apart.
Poor	The fingertips are more than two inches apart.

Source: **Adapted from Krepton, D., and Chu, D. (1984).** *Everybody's aerobics book* **(1st ed.). Oakland, CA: Star Rover House. Reprinted with permission.**

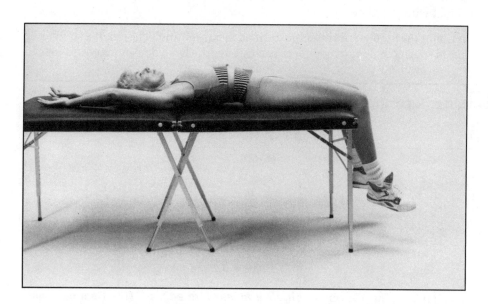

Figure 6–31 Test for shoulder flexibility: adequate flexibility.

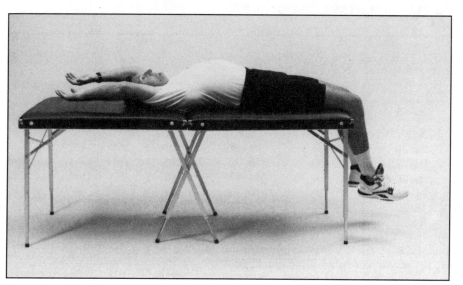

Figure 6–32 Test for shoulder flexibility: muscle shortness.

be presented is the bench-press test. This is an absolute muscular endurance test. The weight used is standardized, and therefore results do not vary as a function of body weight.

Sit-up Test

The equipment requirements for the sit-up test are a stopwatch and an exercise mat. The sit-up method for the test is not the same as that recommended for training; but in order to maintain the reliability of the test, the sit-ups should be performed as follows:

1. Have the client lie face up with knees bent at right angles and heels about 18 inches from the buttocks, fingers next to the ears (Fig. 6–33).

2. In order to avoid neck discomfort and injury, each client should be warned not to pull on the neck and head and to keep the buttocks on the mat.

3. The test administrator should hold the ankles firmly to keep the feet in contact with the floor.

4. Count the number of sit-ups performed in one minute. The client's shoulders should touch the floor to complete each sit-up; the head does not need to touch.

Table 6–12 NORMS FOR ONE-MINUTE TIMED SIT-UPS (MEN)

	Age (years)					
Fitness	**18–25**	**26–35**	**36–45**	**46–55**	**56–65**	**65+**
Excellent	>49	>45	>41	>35	>31	>28
Good	44–49	40–45	35–41	29–35	25–31	22–28
Above average	39–43	35–39	30–34	25–28	21–24	19–21
Average	35–38	31–34	27–29	22–24	17–20	15–18
Below average	31–34	29–30	23–26	18–21	13–16	11–14
Poor	25–30	22–28	17–22	13–17	9–12	7–10
Very poor	<25	<22	<17	<13	<9	<7

Source: Adapted from Golding, et al. (1986). *The Y's way to physical fitness* (3rd ed.), p. 116. Reprinted with permission of the YMCA of the USA, 101 N. Wacker Drive. Chicago, IL 60606.

Table 6–13 NORMS FOR ONE-MINUTE TIMED SIT-UPS (WOMEN)

	Age (years)					
Fitness	**18–25**	**26–35**	**36–45**	**46–55**	**56–65**	**65+**
Excellent	>43	>39	>33	>27	>24	>23
Good	37–43	33–39	27–33	22–27	18–24	17–23
Above average	33–36	29–32	23–26	18–21	13–17	14–16
Average	29–32	25–28	19–22	14–17	10–12	11–13
Below average	25–28	21–24	15–18	10–13	7–9	5–10
Poor	18–24	13–20	7–14	5–9	3–6	2–4
Very poor	<18	<13	<7	<5	<3	<2

Source: Adapted from Golding, et al. (1986). *The Y's way to physical fitness* (3rd ed.), p. 117. Reprinted with permission of the YMCA of the USA, 101 N. Wacker Drive. Chicago, IL 60606.

Figure 6–33 Sit-up test, up position.

5. Score the number of sit-ups performed in one minute. Refer to Tables 6–12 and 6–13 for comparison to norms.

Push-up Test

The push-up test assesses the endurance and strength of the triceps, anterior deltoids, and pectoralis major. The push-up position is different for men than for women. Men use the standard push-up position with only the hands and toes in contact with the floor (Fig. 6–34a). Women use the modified bent-knee position (Fig. 6–34b). The rest of the procedure is the same for both sexes.

1. The client should assume the appropriate up-position with the body rigid and the hands about a shoulder-width apart.

2. Make sure the client's body remains rigid throughout the motion, and that the chest comes within three inches of the floor. The test administrator's fist placed beneath the chest can serve as a general guide.

3. Score the total number of push-ups performed to exhaustion. Refer to Table 6–14 for comparison to norms.

Bench-press Test

The bench-press test developed by the YMCA using a standardized weight is a good method of testing the endurance and strength of the chest and shoulders. The disadvantage of the test is the use of the fixed weight, which places lighter clients at a disadvantage. The bench-press test goes as follows:

1. Use a 35-pound barbell for women or an 80-pound barbell for men. A spotter should be present during the test. If one spotter is unable to safely lift the weight used, two spotters should be present.

2. Set a metronome to 60 bpm. (It works well to borrow a metronome and record about two minutes of the correct rhythm.)

3. A spotter should hand the weight to the client in the down position. In this position the elbows should be flexed and hands a shoulder-width apart (Fig. 6–35).

Figure 6–34 Push-up test. (a) Standard push-up position. (b) Modified bent-knee position.

4. A repetition is counted when the elbows are fully extended (Fig. 6–35). After each extension the bar should be lowered to touch the chest.

5. An up or down movement should be in time to the 60-bpm rhythm, which would be 30 lifts per minute.

6. The test is terminated when the client is unable to come to full extension or falls behind the 60-bpm rhythm. Count the number of successful repetitions. Use Table 6–15 or 6–16 for comparison to norms.

FOLLOW-UP

Consultation

Figure 6–35 Bench press test. (a) Starting (down) position. (b) Completion of one repetition.

Following testing, the trainer should present the results to the client. Ideally, this consultation should take place in a private area with comfortable seating around a desk or table. The communication of test results is an art in and of itself. The trainer should get to know the client and should utilize this knowledge to convey the results in a manner that is both individualized and effective.

Table 6–14   NORMS FOR PUSH-UP TEST

Fitness	Age (years)					
	17–19	20–29	30–39	40–49	50–59	60–65
Males: Standard position						
Excellent	>51	>43	>37	>31	>28	>27
Good	35–50	30–42	25–36	21–30	18–27	17–26
Minimum	19–34	17–29	13–24	11–20	9–17	6–16
Below Minimum	4–18	4–16	2–12	1–10	0–8	0–5
Poor	<3	<3	<1	0		
Females: Modified position						
Excellent	>32	>33	>34	>28	>23	>21
Good	21–31	23–32	22–33	18–27	15–22	13–20
Minimum	11–20	12–22	10–21	8–17	7–14	5–12
Below Minimum	0–10	1–11	0–9	0–7	0–6	0–4
Poor		0				

Source: *Canadian Public Health Association Project*. (1977). Reprinted with permission.

Table 6–15   NORMS FOR BENCH-PRESS TEST (MEN)

Fitness	Age (years)					
	18–25	26–35	36–45	46–55	56–65	65+
Excellent	>37	>33	>29	>23	>21	>17
Good	29–37	26–33	23–29	19–23	14–21	10–17
Above average	24–28	22–25	19–22	14–18	10–13	8–9
Average	21–23	18–21	15–18	10–13	7–9	5–7
Below average	15–20	13–17	11–14	7–9	4–6	3–4
Poor	9–14	6–12	6–10	3–6	1–3	1–2
Very poor	<9	<6	<6	<3	<1	0

Source: Adapted from Golding, et al. (1986). *The Y's way to physical fitness* (3rd ed.), p. 118. Reprinted with permission of the YMCA of the USA, 101 N. Wacker Drive. Chicago, IL 60606.

Table 6–16   NORMS FOR BENCH-PRESS TEST (WOMEN)

Fitness	Age (years)					
	18–25	26–35	36–45	46–55	56–65	65+
Excellent	>35	>32	>27	>25	>21	>17
Good	27–35	24–32	21–27	19–25	16–21	12–17
Above average	22–26	19–23	16–20	13–18	11–15	9–11
Average	17–21	15–18	12–15	10–12	8–10	5–8
Below average	13–16	11–14	9–11	6–9	4–7	2–4
Poor	7–12	4–10	3–8	2–5	1–3	0–1
Very poor	<7	<4	<3	<2	0	0

Source: Adapted from Golding, et al. (1986). *The Y's way to physical fitness* (3rd ed.), p. 118. Reprinted with permission of the YMCA of the USA, 101 N. Wacker Drive. Chicago, IL 60606.

Testing

The frequency of follow-up testing will depend on the quality and quantity of the exercise training and on the design of the testing and training packages offered by the personal trainer or fitness center. While many clients will begin to feel the positive effects of training in as little as one week, measurable changes will usually take about four weeks; therefore, the first follow-up tests will usually be administered four to twelve weeks following the onset of training.

SUMMARY

The foundation of a well-designed fitness program is in part determined by the acquisition and analysis of baseline fitness information. This chapter has provided the trainer with a number of ways to test and evaluate a client's fitness status. The trainer should assess the client's cardiorespiratory efficiency, muscular strength and endurance, flexibility, and body composition in order to design a quality fitness program and, most important, to evaluate the effectiveness of the program over time by retesting the client.

REFERENCES

Astrand, P.O., & Rhyming, J. (1954). A nomogram for calculation of aerobic capacity (physical fitness) from pulse rate during submaximal work. *Journal of Applied Psychology*, 7, 218–221.

Berger, R.A. (1982). *Applied exercise physiology*. Philadelphia: Lea and Febiger.

Cooper, K.H. (1982). *The aerobics program for total well-being*. New York: Bantam Books.

Golding, L.A., Meyers, C.R., & Sinning, W.E. (Eds.) (1986). *The Y's way to physical fitness* (3rd ed.) Champaign, IL: Human Kinetics.

Jackson, A.S., & Pollock, M.L. (1985). Practical assessment of body composition. *The Physician and Sports Medicine*, May, 76–90.

Sjostrand, T. (1947). Changes in the respiratory organs of workmen at an ore melting works. *Acta Medica Scandinavia, 128*, (suppl. 196), 687–699.

SUGGESTED READING

American College of Sports Medicine (1991). *Guidelines for exercise testing and prescription* (4th ed.). Philadelphia: Lea & Febiger.

Getchell, B. (1983). *Physical fitness: A way of life* (3rd ed.). New York: Wiley.

Howley, E., & Franks, D. (1986). *Health fitness instructor's handbook*. Philadelphia: Lea & Febiger.

Van Gelder, N., & Marks, S. (Eds.). (1987). *Aerobic dance-exercise instructor manual*. San Diego: American Council on Exercise.

Krepton, D., & Chu, D. (1984). *Everybody's aerobic book*. Oakland, CA: Star Rover House.

Lamb, D.R. (1984) *Physiology of exercise, responses and adaptations* (2nd ed.) New York: Macmillan.

Nieman, D.C. (1990). *The sports medicine fitness course*. Palo Alto, CA: Bull Publishing.

Powers, S., & Howley, E. (1990). *Exercise physiology: Theory and application to fitness and performance*. Dubuque, IA: W.C. Brown.

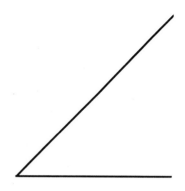

Principles and Methods of Training

PART III

The fitness consumer is inundated with misleading and incorrect information. The trainer must develop the client's program based on established exercise principles and methodology and not on the endless supply of exercise gimmicks. To assist the client, the trainer should consider all components of fitness. The chapters on cardiorespiratory fitness, muscle strength and endurance, flexibility, and weight control expand on the core sciences, demonstrating how the combination of different training methods and modalities affect the body. Applying and adhering to these principals when designing an exercise program is the trainer's best strategy for success.

Cardiorespiratory Fitness

RALPH LA FORGE

7

RALPH LA FORGE, M.S., teaches exercise physiology and health management at the University of California, San Diego, Extension, where he is the Fitness Instruction and Health Promotion Professional Certificate Program coordinator. He is also director of health promotion at the San Diego Cardiac Center and has designed and managed numerous programs in exercise science, cardiac rehabilitation, and preventive medicine.

IN THIS CHAPTER:

- Benefits of cardiorespiratory fitness.
- Components of a cardiorespiratory exercise program: warm-up and cool-down, aerobic activity criteria, supportive conditioning exercise, fitness goals, progression plan, safety.
- Training methods: continuous training, interval training, Fartleck training, circuit training, aerobic composite training.

- Activity guidelines: walking, jogging and running, cycling, swimming, rowing, aerobic dance, stair climbing, racquet sports, hiking and backpacking.
- Monitoring cardiorespiratory exercise: monitoring exercise intensity by METS, percent of maximal heart rate, and the Karvonen formula; ratings of perceived exertion; the talk test method; laboratory techniques.

Cardiorespiratory fitness has received high acclaim for the last two decades as a centerpiece of physical fitness and cardiovascular health. For health and fitness applications, the terms cardiorespiratory fitness, cardiovascular fitness, and aerobic endurance are synonymous. Cardiorespiratory fitness seems to be the current standard in textbooks, and it best describes the health and function of the heart, lungs, and circulatory system. Cardiorespiratory fitness is also related to **cardiorespiratory endurance**, the ability to persist or sustain an activity for an extended period. It also refers to the ability of the lungs to provide oxygen to the blood and of the circulatory system to transport blood and its nutrients to tissues for sustained periods without undue fatigue.

BENEFITS OF CARDIORESPIRATORY FITNESS

The numerous benefits of cardiorespiratory fitness (see Table 7-1) are related to a variety of adaptive physiologic responses to aerobic exercise. Physiologic responses to training—such as an increase in body-fat utilization, a decrease in peripheral vascular resistance, and an increase in maximal oxygen

---

Table 7–1   REPORTED BENEFITS OF CARDIORESPIRATORY FITNESS

Cardiovascular Health Benefits	Adaptive Physiologic Responses
Reduction in blood pressure	Decreased resting heart rate
Increased HDL-cholesterol	Increased heart volume
Decreased total cholesterol	Increased resting and maximum stroke volume
Decreased body fat stores	Increased maximum cardiac output
Increased aerobic work capacity	Increased maximum oxygen consumption
Decreased clinical symptoms of anxiety, tension, and depression	Increased capillary density and blood flow to active muscles
Reduction in glucose-stimulated insulin secretion	Increased total blood volume
Increased heart function	Increased maximal ventilation
Possible reduction in mortality in post myocardial infarction patients	Increased lung diffusion capacity
	Increased mobilization and utilization of fat

Sources: **McArdle, et al. 1986; Brown, 1990; and Froelicher, 1990.**

---

consumption—combine to help decrease the risk of cardiovascular disease by helping to favorably modify risk factors like obesity, hypertension, and high blood cholesterol. When such risk factors are removed from clients' health profiles, they attain an acceptable level of cardiorespiratory fitness, or cardiovascular health. Cardiovascular health goes beyond merely attaining aerobic fitness. It defines the status of the heart muscle, its blood vessels, and the circulatory system it serves. Acquiring and maintaining cardiorespiratory fitness is one of the primary pathways to cardiovascular health.

Likewise, aerobic endurance activities have been effective in other conditioning and clinical therapies, such as cardiac and pulmonary rehabilitation, sleep disorder treatment, diabetic treatment therapy, prenatal/post-partum and renal dialysis conditioning, and stress and anxiety reduction programs. In such clinical settings, aerobic exercise must be prescribed and managed very carefully by trained exercise specialists. For referrals, the personal trainer must know the available clinical rehabilitation programs using medically monitored cardiorespiratory endurance activities.

Cardiorespiratory fitness also serves as a foundation for other fitness programs. The conditioning and health of the heart and blood vessels are prime ingredients in the safety and performance of nearly all sports and conditioning. Activities such as tennis, golf, skiing, dancing, skating, basketball, volleyball, boxing, and all muscular strength training programs will benefit from cardiorespiratory fitness. Clients with adequate cardiorespiratory fitness generally have more stamina, which translates to less fatigue and fewer risks for certain types of injuries.

COMPONENTS OF A CARDIORESPIRATORY (AEROBIC) EXERCISE PROGRAM

It is imperative for the personal trainer to understand the physiologic rationale and the application of each of the components of the cardiorespiratory exercise program. The essential components of the written plan are:

1. Warm-up and cool-down

2. Primary cardiorespiratory activity criteria

    a. Mode of exercise

    b. Frequency of exercise session

    c. Duration of exercise session

    d. Intensity of exercise session

3. Supportive conditioning exercise (e.g., strength and flexibility)

4. Cardiorespiratory fitness goals

5. Progression plan

6. Safety and cautions

Each of these components must be discussed with the client and presented in a legible and succinct written form. Chapters 11 and 12 will provide examples of different formats to use in various settings.

Warm-up and Cool-down

Although most fitness professionals teach a variety of techniques for warm-up and cool-down, few fully understand their psychological and physiological rationales. Table 7-2 shows the psychological and physiological reasons for warm-up and cool-down. Graduated low-level aerobic exercise is essential for maximizing safety and **economy of movement** during the cardiorespiratory conditioning phase of an exercise session. The warm-up should increase the heart rate, blood pressure, oxygen consumption, dilation of the blood vessels, elasticity of the active muscles, and the heat produced by the active muscle groups in a graduated fashion. The warm-up should consist of two distinct components:

1. Graduated aerobic warm-up activity (e.g., walking, or slow tempo rhythmic dance movements)

2. Flexibility exercise commensurate with the biomechanical nature of the primary conditioning activity (e.g., calf and Achilles stretching prior to running)

Because a warm muscle is more easily stretched than a cold muscle, the flexibility component should be preceded by 5 to 8 minutes of low-level aerobic activity using the same muscle groups. For instance, a five-minute walk will

---

Table 7–2   PHYSIOLOGICAL AND PSYCHOLOGICAL RATIONALE FOR WARM-UP AND COOL-DOWN

Warm-up

1. Permits a gradual increase in metabolic requirements (e.g., oxygen consumption), which enhances cardiorespiratory performance (e.g., a higher maximum cardiac output and oxygen consumption).

2. Prevents the premature onset of blood lactic acid accumulation and fatigue in higher level aerobic exercise.

3. Causes a gradual increase in muscle temperature which decreases the work of contraction and reduces the likelihood of muscle injury.

4. Facilitates neural transmission for motor unit recruitment.

5. Improves coronary blood flow in early stages of the conditioning exercise, lessening the potential for myocardial ischemia.

6. Provides a screening mechanism for potential musculoskeletal or metabolic problems that may increase at higher intensities.

7. Provides a psychological warm-up to higher levels of work. (i.e., increases arousal and focus on exercise).

Cool-down

1. Prevents post-exercise venous blood pooling and too rapid a drop in blood pressure, thereby reducing the likelihood of post-exercise lightheadedness or fainting.

2. Reduces the immediate post-exercise tendency for muscle spasm or cramping.

3. Reduces the concentration of exercise hormones (e.g., norepinephrine) that are at relatively high levels immediately after vigorous aerobic exercise. This reduction will lower the probability of post-exercise disturbances in cardiac rhythm.

Sources: Giese, 1988; McArdle et al., 1986.

---

increase muscle temperature and circulation of the thigh and leg, thereby promoting easier and safer stretching of the same muscle groups.

Table 7–3 lists example warm-up activities for a variety of aerobic exercises. These examples are simplistic; however, the one chosen for the client must provide a graduated level of activity mechanically similar to the primary conditioning activity, and intensity should be well below that of the primary conditioning activity. Duration of the warm-up depends on the activity in the primary conditioning phase and the level and intensity of those activities, as well as the level of fitness of the client (Giese, 1988).

Cool-down instructions are also an integral part of the exercise program. The purpose of the cool-down is to slowly decrease the cardiac work (i.e., the heart rate) and overall metabolism that have been elevated during the conditioning phase. Low-level aerobic exercise similar to that of the conditioning exercise is recommended (see Table 7–3). Walking, slow jogging, cycling with little or no resistance, and slow aquatic activity or swimming are good examples. Cool-down helps prevent the sudden pooling of blood in the veins and ensures adequate circulation to the skeletal muscles, heart, and the brain. Cool-down aids in preventing delayed muscle stiffness and reduces any tendency toward post-exercise fainting and dizziness. For high cardiovascular risk clients, a gradual decrease in the intensity of exercise is crucial. Sudden

Table 7–3 SAMPLE WARM-UP AND COOL-DOWN ACTIVITIES (INCLUDING STRETCHING EXERCISE)

Primary Conditioning Exercise	Warm-up/Cool-down Activity
Dance aerobics	Graduated low-level aerobic activity utilizing same muscle groups
Jogging and running	Walking, walk-jogging, or jogging at slower pace
Sprinting	Jogging and graduated pace in running intervals
Outdoor cycling	Begin with relatively flat terrain in lower gears; gradually shift to higher gears and steeper terrain
Stationary cycling	Start with cycling against little or no resistance at $\frac{2}{3}$ of the pedal crank rpm used in the conditioning phase
Lap swimming	Begin with slow crawl and gradually increase arm stroke, pace, and/or begin with short 1- or 2-lap slow intervals
Mountain hiking	Graduate from relatively flat terrain at minimal altitudes to steeper terrain and higher altitudes
Stationary exercise devices (e.g., Stairmaster, rowing)	Begin with 50–60% of intended conditioning workload or speed; the duration of submaximal graduated warm-up should be proportional to the peak intensity of the conditioning work load
Rope skipping	Graduated walking or walk-jogging pace and/or slow tempo rope skipping pace
Racquetball, handball, or squash	Walk-jog and/or graduated tempo volleying
Competitive tennis	Walk-jog and/or graduated tempo volleying proportional to the level of the game

cessation of exercise without cool-down may adversely affect cardiac function because a relatively high concentration of adrenalin and other exercise hormones remains in the blood from the conditioning exercise. The length of the cool-down phase is proportional to the intensity and length of the conditioning phase. A typical 30–40 minute conditioning phase at 70 percent of maximum heart rate would warrant a 5–10 minute cool-down. The aerobic component of the cool-down phase should be followed by several minutes of stretching of those muscle groups active in the conditioning phase.

Primary Cardiorespiratory Exercise Criteria

For maximum effectiveness and safety, the cardiorespiratory exercise program must have specific instruction on the mode, frequency, duration, and intensity of exercise. Most of these criteria originate from the American College of Sports Medicine exercise guidelines and position statements to ensure standardization and validity in the broad field of exercise science (ACSM, 1989; ACSM, 1991).

To avoid confusion, the exercise criteria stated in the sections below relate to the criteria for measurable improvements in *cardiorespiratory fitness* (e.g., increase in $\dot{V}O_2$ max, reduction in body-fat composition). This is a very important clarification, since the exercise criteria for "health enhancement" are generally at a lower threshold (ACSM, 1991). For instance, the minimum duration and intensity of exercise required for "health enhancement" are 15 minutes and 40 percent of max $\dot{V}O_2$, respectively.

EXERCISE MODE.   Selection of the exercise mode is made on the basis of the client's functional capacity, interests, time availability, equipment and facilities, and personal goals and objectives. Any activity that uses large muscle groups, that can be maintained continuously, and is rhythmical and cardiorespiratory in nature can be used. The American College of Sports Medicine classifies cardiorespiratory endurance activities into three groups:

GROUP 1: Physical activities in which exercise intensity is easily sustained with little variability in heart rate response: walking, aerobic dancing, swimming, jogging, running, cycling, cross-country skiing, and skating.

GROUP 2: Physical activities in which energy expenditure is related to skill: figure skating, swimming, highly choreographed dance exercise, etc.

GROUP 3: Physical activities that are quite variable in intensity: soccer, basketball, racquetball, etc.

Group 1 activities are recommended when precise control of the exercise intensity is necessary, as in the beginning stages of a conditioning program. These activities can be performed in a continuous or discontinuous (interval) format, depending upon the client's fitness level and personal preference. Group 1 activities expend the most energy per unit of time and are useful during all stages of conditioning. Group 2 activities are useful because of the enjoyment provided by settings other than an exercise gym. Adding Group 2 exercise helps foster compliance and reduce boredom. Because of the variable intensity nature of Group 3 activities, they should require a base-level conditioning in Group 1 or similar activities. Group 3 activities tend to be group- or team-sport oriented and therefore provide greater interest and compliance for many individuals.

EXERCISE FREQUENCY.   **Frequency** refers to the number of exercise sessions per week included in the program. The frequency of exercise depends on the duration and intensity of the exercise session. Lower intensity exercise done for shorter periods of time can warrant more sessions per week. To improve both cardiorespiratory fitness and maintain body-fat at near optimum levels, a client should exercise at least three days a week with no more than two days between sessions. The American College of Sports Medicine recommends three to five days a week for most aerobic programs. When a client is starting an aerobic exercise program for the first time, a frequency of every other day for at least the first eight weeks is appropriate. For those with a poor functional capacity, one to two daily sessions may be recommended. Those with an average functional capacity should exercise at least three times a week on alternate days. In general, clients who are just beginning weight bearing exercise such as aerobic dancing and jogging should have at least 36 to 48 hours of relative rest between workouts to prevent early overuse and promote adequate bone joint stress recovery. This is especially true with those who are overweight.

EXERCISE DURATION.   **Duration** refers to the number of minutes of exercise during the conditioning period. The conditioning period, exclusive of the warm-up and cool-down, may vary from 20 to 60 minutes to gain significant cardiorespiratory benefits. The duration required to achieve cardiorespiratory benefits is dependent upon exercise intensity. This relationship can be visualized by taking a given intensity of exercise, for example, 75 percent of functional capacity, and comparing an exercise duration of 5 minutes versus 20 minutes at this intensity. Obviously, more total energy is expended during the 20-minute exercise session, making it more intense than the 5-minute bout. The conditioning response to an exercise program is the result of the product of the intensity and duration of exercise (total energy expenditure). Beginners who are in the lower cardiorespiratory fitness classifications should begin with 10 to 20 minutes of aerobic conditioning; those in the average classification should go for 15 to 45 minutes, and those in the high classification can go for 30 to 60 (ACSM, 1991; Pollock 1984).

INTENSITY OF EXERCISE. **Intensity** refers to the speed or workload (resistance) of exercise. As a rule, the American College of Sports Medicine (ACSM, 1991) recommends a range of 60 to 90 percent of **maximal heart rate** (MHR)*. This range approximates 50 to 85 percent of **maximal oxygen consumption** (functional capacity or $\dot{V}O_2$ max) and 50 to 85 percent of **heart rate maximum reserve (Karvonen formula)**. From a strict physiologic point of view, this 50 to 85 percent range is the goal for cardiorespiratory training benefits. Intensity is probably the most important and most involved determinant of the program. Lower intensities such as 50 to 60 percent of maximal oxygen consumption and heart rate maximum reserve are advised for beginners in the lower cardiorespiratory fitness levels, although persons with very low fitness levels can benefit from training intensities as low as 40 to 50 percent of maximal oxygen consumption. Exercise intensities as high as 75 to 85 percent of maximal oxygen consumption and heart rate reserve may be more appropriate for those who are apparently healthy and in the higher fitness classifications. Overall, the average exercise intensity for apparently healthy adults is usually between 60 and 70 percent of their maximum oxygen consumption.

Monitoring Exercise Intensity

Of numerous methods for monitoring exercise intensity, five have been somewhat standardized and are recommended for the personal trainer. The method chosen will depend on the client's exercise program and level of fitness, the trainer's access to referral test data (e.g., stress test heart rates and work loads), and the trainer's experience. The following are the primary methods of monitoring exercise intensity:

1. By METS

2. As a percentage of maximal heart rate

3. By the Karvonen formula (heart rate maximum reserve)

4. As measured by perceived exertion

5. Using the "talk test" method

INTENSITY MEASURED BY METS. Exercise intensity can be assessed by a graded exercise test (bicycle or treadmill). Based on the time the client stays

---

* These recommendations are similar to but not identical to those stated in the 1991 ACSM guidelines. The two sets are slightly different because the 1990 ACSM position stand focuses primarily on fitness enhancement (i.e., personal trainer focus), whereas the 1991 guidelines are designed to include activity that may enhance health without having a major impact on fitness.

on the treadmill or bicycle ergometer, the maximal oxygen consumption (i.e., functional capacity) can be estimated and converted to a **MET** equivalent. A MET is a multiple of resting oxygen consumption. One MET equals a person's oxygen consumption at rest, which is equal to approximately 3.5 milliliters of oxygen per kilogram of body weight per minute (3.5ml/kg/min). The intensity of exercise may be determined as a specified percentage of the client's maximal oxygen consumption or functional capacity (e.g., 50–85%) and then choosing activities that are known to require energy expenditure at the desired level (see Table 7-4). For example, if a client has a functional capacity ($\dot{V}O_2$ max) of 10 METS and the trainer recommends the client start at 60 percent of functional capacity, then 60 percent times 10 METS equals 6 METS beginning intensity.

10 METS (functional or
aerobic capacity) × .60 (60% lower
intensity range) 6 METS (beginning exercise intensity)

Using METS to determine exercise intensity is important for those clients selecting specific activities like sailing or horseback riding (see Table 7-4) who want an approximate energy cost of those activities. The personal trainer may receive referral from physicians for clients who require a supervised conditioning program (e.g., for weight loss). Frequently, the personal trainer may receive written results from a stress EKG from the physician or sports medicine exercise laboratory including exercise heart rate and MET level data. Here the MET level achieved (estimated maximal oxygen consumption) will be useful in determining initial cardiorespiratory fitness level.

However, exercise determined by METS has some disadvantages. Environmental influences such as wind, hills, heat, humidity, altitude, air pollution, and a variety of mechanical factors, such as the mechanical efficiency of a bicycle, can alter the energy cost of the activity. In addition, as the client improves cardiorespiratory endurance, higher MET levels will be required to ensure an adequate training stimulus. As a rule, training by heart rate may be an easier and more accurate method for determining effective aerobic exercise.

INTENSITY BY PERCENTAGE OF MAXIMAL HEART RATE. Another method of monitoring the intensity of exercise is calculated as a percentage of maximal heart rate. Maximal heart rate can be determined by a maximal functional capacity test, using a bicycle or treadmill ergometer, or by age-predicted maximal heart rate tables which frequently use the 220 – age formula for determining maximal heart rate. If this method of estimating maximal heart rate is used, the following formula applies:

Training Heart Rate Range = Maximal measured or predicted heart rate × 70–85% × 1.15

For example:

a 40-year-old man for whom an intensity of 70–80% of maximal heart rate is desired:

180 (age-determined maximal heart rate, 220 – age)
× .70 (70% low intensity range)
126 (70% lower limit exercise heart rate)

180 (age-determined maximal heart rate, 220 – age)
× .80 (80% upper intensity range)
144 (80% upper limit exercise heart rate)

or a target heart rate range of 126–144 beats per minute × 1.15 = 145–165 bpm.

Over the years, taking a straight percentage of maximal heart rate has been shown to be conservative when compared to the other heart rate methods and a more appropriate percentage of maximal oxygen uptake. If this method is used, the personal trainer should add 10 to 15 percent to the above calculated training heart rate (Pollock & Wilmore, 1990). For many fitness professionals, adding the 15 percent conversion factor will be new. With this conversion, the percentage of maximal heart rate will better reflect the percentage of functional aerobic capacity. As a final caution, the personal trainer should use caution when using age group average maximal heart rate tables because these tables only estimate a "rule of thumb" maximal heart rate, usually from the 220 – age formula. This method has a variability of ± 10-12 beats per minute (Durstine, 1988).

It is essential to understand the relationship between exercise heart rate and aerobic capacity (maximal oxygen consumption). A necessary point often overlooked in aerobic exercise is that for nearly all levels of submaximal exercise, the percentage of heart rate maximum does not equal the same percentage of aerobic capacity unless the heart rate maximum reserve method (Karvonen formula) is used. As described in Table 7-5, for any given percent maximal heart rate, the corresponding percentage of maximal oxygen consumption (aerobic capacity) is 5 to 10 percent less.

INTENSITY BY THE KARVONEN FORMULA. The Karvonen Formula (heart rate maximum reserve method) is similar to the percentage of maximal heart rate method, except resting heart rate is factored in:

Training Heart Rate = Maximum heart rate
  – Resting heart rate
  × Desired intensity (50–85%)
  + Resting heart rate

For example: What is the Target Heart Rate for a 40 year old client with a resting heart rate of 80 bpm at an intensity of 70%?

(T.H.R. = (Max H.R.–R.H.R.) × Intensity + R.H.R.)

220–40 = 180 (Predicted max H.R.)

180 (Predicted maximal heart rate)
– 80 (Resting heart rate)
100 (Heart rate reserve)
× .70 (70% intensity)
70
+ 80 (Resting heart rate)
150 (Target heart rate at 70% of heart rate reserve)

The physiological basis for this method of determining exercise heart rate is that the difference between resting and maximal heart rates for a given client represents the reserve of the heart for increasing cardiac output. Like the percentage of maximal heart rate method, the accuracy of the Karvonen Formula is somewhat compromised when the predicted maximal heart rate is estimated from tables or 220 – age rather than determined from an actual functional capacity test. Still, this method is one of the most popular for determining exercise heart rates.

INTENSITY BY PERCEIVED EXERTION. Exercise intensity can also be measured by assigning a numerical value (6–20) to subjective feelings of exercise exertion. The popular name for this method is **ratings of perceived exertion**. Originally designed by Dr. Gunnar Borg, it is sometimes called the Borg

Table 7–4 APPROXIMATE ENERGY EXPENDITURE, IN METS, OF VARIOUS SPORTS, EXERCISE CLASSES, AND GAMES

	Mean	Range
Archery	3.9	3–4
Back Packing	—	5–11
Badminton	5.8	4–9+
Basketball		
Gameplay	8.3	7–12+
Nongame	—	3–9
Billiards	2.5	—
Bowling	—	2–4
Boxing		
In-ring	13.3	—
Sparring	8.3	—
Canoeing, rowing, kayaking	—	3–8
Conditioning exercise	—	3–8+
Climbing hills	7.2	5–10+
Cricket	5.2	4.6–7.4
Croquet	3.5	—
Cycling		
Pleasure or to work	—	3–8+
10 mph	7.0	—
Dancing (social, square, tap)	—	3.7–7.4
Dancing (aerobic)	—	6–9
Fencing	—	6–10+
Field hockey	8.0	—
Fishing		
from bank	3.7	2–4
wading in stream	—	5–6
Football (touch)	7.9	6–10
Golf		
Power cart	—	2–3
Walking (carrying bag or pulling cart)	5.1	4–7
Handball	—	8–12+
Hiking (cross-country)	—	3–7
Horseback riding		
Galloping	8.2	—
Trotting	6.6	—
Walking	2.4	—

Table 7–4(cont.)   APPROXIMATE ENERGY EXPENDITURE, IN METS, OF VARIOUS SPORTS, EXERCISE CLASSES, AND GAMES

	Mean	Range
Horseshoe pitching	—	2–3
Hunting (bow or gun)		
Small game (walking, carrying light load)	—	3–7
Big game (dragging carcass, walking)	—	3–14
Judo	13.5	—
Mountain climbing	—	5–10+
Music playing	—	2–3
Paddleball, racquetball	9.0	8–12
Rope jumping	11.0	—
60–80 skips/min	9.0	—
120–140 skips/min	—	11–12
Running		
12 min per mile	8.7	—
11 min per mile	9.4	—
10 min per mile	10.2	—
9 min per mile	11.2	—
8 min per mile	12.5	—
7 min per mile	14.1	—
6 min per mile	16.3	—
Sailing	—	2–5
Scubadiving	—	5–10
Shuffleboard	—	2–3
Skating, ice and roller	—	5–8
Skiing, snow		
Downhill	—	5–8
Cross-country	—	6–12+
Skiing, water	—	5–7
Sledding, tobogganing	—	4–8
Snowshoeing	9.9	7–14
Squash	—	8–12+
Soccer	—	5–12+
Stairclimbing	—	4–8
Swimming	—	4–8+
Table Tennis	4.1	3–5
Tennis	6.5	4–9+
Volleyball	—	3–6

Source: **From ACSM (1990).** *Guidelines for exercise testing and prescription* **(4th ed.). Philadelphia: Lea and Febiger. Reprinted with permission.**

Scale. The ratings of perceived exertion (RPE) takes into account all that the exercising client is perceiving in terms of exercise fatigue, including psychological, musculoskeletal, and environmental factors. This level of perceived physical effort is assigned a rating from either of the two rating scales in Table 7–6. For instance, using the Borg Scale, an RPE of 12 to 13 corresponds to approximately 60 to 79 percent of maximal heart rate or 50 to 74 percent of

Table 7–5   RELATIONSHIP BETWEEN PERCENT MAXIMAL AEROBIC CAPACITY (MAX $\dot{V}O_2$) AND PERCENT MAXIMAL HEART RATE

Percent Max Heart Rate	Percent Max $\dot{V}O_2$
50	28
60	42
70	56
80	70
90	83
100	100

Source: McArdle, W., Katch, F., and Katch, V. (1986). *Exercise Physiology* (2nd ed.). Philadelphia: Lea and Febiger. Reprinted with permission.

Table 7–6   RATINGS OF PERCEIVED EXERTION

RPE		New Rating Scale	
6		0	Nothing at all
7	Very, very light	0.5	Very, very weak
8		1	Very weak
9	Very light	2	Weak
10		3	Moderate
11	Fairly light	4	Somewhat strong
12		5	Strong
13	Somewhat hard	6	
14		7	Very strong
15	Hard	8	
16		9	
17	Very hard	10	Very, very strong
18			Maximal
19	Very, very hard		
20			

Source: Gorg, G.V. (1982). Psychological basis of perceived exertion. *Medicine and Science in Sports and Exercise*, *14*, 377–381. American College of Sports Medicine.

maximal oxygen consumption or heart rate maximum reserve (Table 7-7). An RPE of 16 would correspond to about 90 percent of maximal heart rate or 85 percent of maximal oxygen consumption or heart rate reserve. Thus, as a rule, most clients would exercise between 12 and 16 on the Borg Scale. The Borg Scale begins at 6 because originally it was to approximate exercise heart rate. For example, an RPE of 6 would approximate a heart rate of 60; an RPE of 15 would approximate a heart rate of 150. The RPE response correlates very well with cardiorespiratory and metabolic factors such as heart rate, breathing rate, oxygen consumption, and, certainly, overall fatigue.

In recent years, a revision of the Borg Scale (see New Rating Scale in Table 7-6) makes it easier to use because of its simpler 0-10 rating. On this revised RPE Scale, a client should exercise between an RPE of 4 (somewhat strong) and an RPE of 5 or 6 (strong) (Carlton, 1985). Perhaps the most appropriate use of ratings of perceived exertion is as an adjunct to heart-rate monitoring. Ideally, the client will monitor and record both intensities to ensure close observation of the cardiac and physiological exercise response.

INTENSITY BY THE TALK-TEST METHOD.   Another means of evaluating intensity of exercise is the **talk test**. Like the RPE method of measuring exercise intensity, the talk test is subjective, but it is also quite useful in determining a "comfort zone" of aerobic intensity. Clients should be able to breathe comfortably and rhythmically throughout all phases of a workout to ensure a safe and comfortable level of exercise, especially for those just beginning an exercise program. Those who progress to higher functional capacities and higher level workouts may find this technique somewhat conservative, especially at intensities greater than 80 percent of functional capacity.

In summary, the personal trainer can modify criteria such as the mode, frequency, duration, and intensity of exercise to suit the client's level of fitness, program goals, and schedule. As a rule, building a foundation of endurance at relatively low to moderate intensity before higher intensity workouts or competition is clearly justified for safety and comfort. This may mean moving the client for the first few weeks through gradual increases in duration while

Table 7-7   CLASSIFICATION OF INTENSITY OF EXERCISE BASED ON 30-60 MINUTES OF ENDURANCE TRAINING

| Relative Intensity (%) | | Rating of Perceived Exertion | Classification of Intensity |
HR max*	$\dot{V}O_2$ max* or HR max reserve		
<35%	<30%	<10	Very light
35-59%	30-49%	10-11	Light
60-79%	50-74%	12-13	Moderate (somewhat hard)
80-89%	75-84%	14-16	Heavy
≥90%	≥85%	>16	Very Heavy

Source: Pollock, M.L., and Wilmore, J.H. (1990). *Exercise in health and disease: Evaluation and prescription for prevention and rehabilitation* (2nd ed.). Philadelphia: W.B. Saunders. Reprinted with permission.

*HR max = maximum heart rate; $\dot{V}O_2$ max = maximum oxygen uptake.

holding intensity nearly constant until an acceptable level of endurance, such as 20 to 30 minutes, has been achieved. Within each of these criteria, the personal trainer has an enormous range of choices, such as variations in modes and intensities, with which to vary the exercise stimulus and maximize the client's interest and adaptation to increasing levels of exercise.

Supportive Conditioning Exercise

All cardiorespiratory exercise programs must be supported by flexibility, strength, and even neuromuscular fitness exercise in order to enhance the efficiency of aerobic exercise (exercise economy) and minimize musculoskeletal injury. Although some of this supportive exercise, such as stretching, can be part of the warm-up and/or cool-down, it is prudent to add several separate sessions per week that improve the strength of the back, legs, and abdomen. Stretching and range-of-motion exercises to ensure flexibility of muscle groups that become tight from aerobic exercise are fundamental to a successful cardiorespiratory fitness program. Incorporating various neuromuscular relaxation activities into the cool-down phase of the program is appropriate for those coming from high-stress work environments who need more than just aerobic exercise. The trainer can help the client relax both mentally and physically by teaching easy stretching and mental relaxation skills simultaneously. Chapters 8 and 9 describe strength and flexibility exercises in more detail.

Cardiorespiratory Fitness Goals

The goals and personal objectives of cardiorespiratory fitness must be clearly stated in the written exercise plan to reinforce compliance and motivation and for assessment during follow up. The client's implementation and progression plan must reflect these goals and depict means of achieving them safely and realistically. The following goals and objectives are examples:

1. Overall acquisition and maintenance of cardiorespiratory fitness

    a. Desired objectives (e.g., Kcal/day energy expenditure, mastery of jogging, 20 pound weight loss)

    b. Interim targets

2. Cardiovascular risk factor modification

    a. Weight control

        (1) Desired body weight and body-fat percentage

        (2) Interim body weight and body-fat targets

    b. Blood pressure reduction

        (1) Desired blood pressure given blood pressure history

        (2) Interim target blood pressure (e.g., 1 month, 3 months)

    c. Cholesterol control

        (1) Desired total cholesterol, LDL, and HDL cholesterol

        (2) Interim target cholesterol, LDL, and HDL cholesterol

d. Stress and anxiety reduction

    (1) Desired behavioral response to workplace and domestic stressors

    (2) Interim accomplishments in coping with stress (e.g., relaxation response skills)

3. Performance objectives

    a. Personal accomplishment (e.g., 10K run or mile swim)

        (1) Target goal (e.g., 10K run in six months)

        (2) Interim target goal (e.g., 5K run with four months of training)

    b. Increase physical stamina

        (1) Desired level of physical energy for particular assignment

        (2) Interim perceived energy levels (scale 0–10)

Progression Plan

A written progression plan with periodic reevaluation is crucial. This plan must provide details for a graduated progression in the frequency, duration, and intensity of exercise. There must be sufficient flexibility in the rate of progression so that the plan comfortably adjusts to the client's cardiorespiratory and musculoskeletal response. The rate of progression depends upon a number of factors:

- Individual level of fitness (aerobic capacity)
- Age
- Health status
- Cardiorespiratory response to exercise
- Individual needs and goals
- Social and family support
- Level of exercise initiative and motivation
- Access to appropriate facilities and equipment

There are three stages of progression for the cardiorespiratory endurance exercise plan identified by the American College of Sports Medicine guidelines (ACSM, 1991): the initial conditioning stage, the improvement conditioning stage, and the maintenance conditioning stage.

INITIAL CONDITIONING STAGE. This stage usually lasts four to six weeks or longer and usually includes low-level aerobic activities, stretching, and light calisthenics. Exercise frequency should begin with every other day. Depending upon initial level of fitness and functional capacity, duration should start with 12 to 15 minutes and gradually increase according to the client's cardiorespiratory and musculoskeletal response. For those with low functional capacity (4–7 METS or less), it may be appropriate to prescribe low-level aerobic interval exercise of two to five minutes' duration. The most important thing to remember during the initial conditioning stage is to be conservative with the intensity of exercise. For example, if the individual has a 9 MET functional capacity (31.5 ml/kg/min $\dot{V}O_2$ max), begin at a conservative 50 to 60 percent of this value or at about 5 METS. Here, exercise heart rate should begin at approximately 50 to 60 percent of heart rate maximum reserve (Karvonen).

IMPROVEMENT CONDITIONING STAGE. This is the primary conditioning stage for most aerobic training programs. It may last from 8 to 20 weeks, and the rate of progression in intensity is more rapid. The exercise intensity can be increased to the next higher level than that completed in the initial conditioning stage and within the 60 to 90 percent of maximal heart rate (50 to 85 percent of maximal oxygen consumption or heart rate maximum reserve) depending on fitness level and age. Exercise duration should be increased every two to three weeks, according to the client's response and goals. It is important to periodically review progress at two to four week intervals during this stage either by direct monitoring or by assessing self report data (RPE, heart rate, symptoms, caloric expenditure).

MAINTENANCE CONDITIONING STAGE. When clients reach their target functional capacity or primary goals, the maintenance stage begins. This stage is usually reached after the first six months of training, but may be delayed as long as 12 months, depending upon goals. In any case, it is important to reassess goals at the beginning of this stage. Maintenance of a particular level of cardiorespiratory fitness may require slightly less frequency, duration, and intensity of exercise. Cardiorespiratory fitness can often be maintained by regularly engaging in a variety of endurance related sports and activities.

Cautions

The last component of an exercise plan is individual information to ensure each client's exercise safety with specific precautions. List any personal or environmental information that reduces the risk of exercise injury or that may compromise exercise safety. Individualized comments such as those about hot, humid environments or avoiding orthopedic symptoms specific to the client are included. Another useful format is to enumerate several cautions that are standard for nearly all exercise programs:

Do not exercise for at least 90 minutes after a meal.

Avoid continuing exercise with chest discomfort, lightheadedness, or dizziness.

Reduce exercise intensity in response to very hot or humid environments or to altitudes above 5,000 feet.

Avoid exercise with tenderness in a joint, for example, a knee or foot, that tends to worsen with activity.

Avoid strenuous aerobic exercise during viral infections such as flu or upper respiratory tract infection.

TRAINING METHODS

Once the mode, frequency, duration, and intensity of exercise has been established, the trainer must choose an appropriate training method. The choice provides the foundation for the exercise progression plan. Selection requires understanding of the physiological response to various training methods and, preferably, personal experience with each of those methods. As with exercise intensity and progression, the training method depends on the functional fitness level and the goals of the participant. There are five major training methods (Heyward, 1984; Wells & Pate, 1988):

1. Continuous training

   a. Intermediate slow distance

   b. Long slow distance

2. Interval training

   a. Aerobic interval training

   b. Anaerobic interval training

3. Fartlek training

4. Circuit training

5. Aerobic composite training

Continuous Training

Continuous training involves conditioning stage exercise such as walking, jogging, cycling, swimming, and aerobic dancing. The prescribed intensity is maintained continuously between 50 and 85 percent of functional capacity (maximal oxygen consumption). For those with initially low functional capacities, continuous training is usually preceded by four to six weeks of interval training in the initial conditioning stage. In practice, continuous training is divided into two types:

- Intermediate slow distance: Generally from 20 to 60 minutes of continuous aerobic exercise, the most common type of sustained aerobic exercise for fitness improvement. Body-fat reduction, improvement in cardiorespiratory fitness, and cardiovascular risk factor management all are responsive to this type of continuous training.

- Long slow distance: 60+ minutes of continuous aerobic exercise, usually employed for athletic training in such sports as cycling and long distance running. Cardiorespiratory and metabolic demands are great for LSD training. At least six months of successful intermediate slow distance training must precede LSD training. Increased risk of musculoskeletal injury (e.g., Achilles tendinitis) accompanies this type of prolonged aerobic training.

Interval Training

Interval training consists of repeated intervals of exercise (e.g., jogging or running) interspersed with intervals of relatively light exercise (e.g., walking). Interval training has useful applications for beginners of aerobic exercise as well as experienced, conditioned clients wishing to improve aerobic power. Personal trainers can use two types, aerobic and anaerobic interval training.

Table 7–8   CARDIORESPIRATORY FITNESS LEVEL CLASSIFICATIONS

Fitness Level	Oxygen Consumption ml/kg/min	METS
Poor	3.5–13.9	1.0–3.9
Low	14.0–24.9	4.0–6.9
Average	25.0–38.9	7.0–10.9
Good	39.0–48.9	11.0–13.9
High	49.0–56.0	14.0–16.0

Source: ACSM. (1986). *Guidelines for exercise testing and prescription* (4th ed.). Philadelphia: Lea and Febiger. Reprinted with permission.

*For 40-year-old males. Adjustments are appropriate for those over 65 years and those with cardiovascular disease.

AEROBIC INTERVAL TRAINING.   Aerobic interval training is best suited for those beginning in the poor or low cardiorespiratory fitness classification (Table 7–8) because it is less intense. Generally, aerobic interval training uses exercise bouts of 2 to 15 minutes and the intensity is between 60 and 80 percent of functional capacity (modified from Wells & Pate, 1988). Those with poor or low functional capacity should start with two to three minute exercise intervals at 60 to 70 percent of functional capacity. Rest intervals should take approximately the same time as a complete exercise interval. Intervals can be repeated five to ten times depending on the client's response and program goals; for example, stationary bicycling for three minutes at work load intensity of 60 to 70 percent of functional capacity with a two minute "rest period" of cycling at zero resistance or load. Hypothetically, this would be repeated five to ten times or for a total workout of 25 to 50 minutes. Higher intensity and longer duration aerobic interval training (e.g., 5- to 15-minute bouts at 70 to 80 percent of functional capacity) should be reserved for those in higher cardiorespiratory fitness classifications seeking increased aerobic endurance and speed.

ANAEROBIC INTERVAL TRAINING.   Anaerobic interval training is primarily reserved for those in the higher cardiorespiratory fitness classifications who desire to increase speed and overall aerobic power. It usually results in greater concentrations of muscle lactic acid accompanied by greater muscular discomfort. Because of the relatively high metabolic and cardiorespiratory demands, beginners or those below a 10-MET aerobic capacity should refrain from anaerobic interval training. Although there are many derivations of anaerobic interval training, the training stimulus is usually between 30 seconds and 4 minutes long at an intensity of 85 to 100+ percent of functional capacity (maximal oxygen uptake). The probability of musculoskeletal injury is greater because of high muscle contraction velocities and forces. The client, usually an athlete, should engage in substantial aerobic warm-up and stretching before vigorous activity.

Fartlek Training

Fartlek training is similar to interval training; however, the work-rest intervals are not systematically or accurately measured. Work-rest intervals and intensity are usually determined by how the participant feels. Over the years, Fartlek training has blossomed in many aerobic training regimens, primarily to prevent boredom and to enhance aerobic endurance. One of its most useful applications is in running, where the runner warms up by running for 10 to 20 minutes, then significantly varies the pace every 5 to 10 minutes. Like long slow distance aerobic training, this form should be reserved for those at the average or higher cardiorespiratory fitness levels because of the relatively high demand on the cardiorespiratory system.

Circuit Training

Circuit training takes the participant through a series of exercise stations, with relatively brief rest intervals between each station. The number of stations may range from four to ten. Historically, circuit training was designed for enhancing muscular endurance and therefore incorporated mostly muscular endurance exercises such as sit ups, the bench press, and the leg press. A circuit of four to ten stations with an aerobic warm-up station, for example the stationary bicycle, could be followed mostly by exercise stations using either free weights and/or single station weight machines. A good example of circuit training in a more natural environment is par course exercise. This method intersperses walking or jogging with a variety of flexibility, muscular endurance, and strength exercises.

In the last few years, aerobic circuit training programs have become popular. Between four and eight aerobic exercise stations with one to three minutes per station and a 15-second rest break between stations constitute a circuit. Depending on the number of stations, the number of circuits completed would be equivalent to 20 to 45 minutes of aerobic exercise. The key to success is to set the workload at each station to 50 to 70 percent of the client's functional capacity. Circuit training is a form of interval training. Depending on the mode, duration, and intensity of each exercise station as well as the entire session, this form of training can significantly improve cardiorespiratory endurance. The benefits of circuit training are that it breaks the monotony of sustained long slow distance aerobic exercise and it can be performed inside, at night, or in inclement weather.

Aerobic Composite

Aerobic composite training is an individualized combination or composite of all training methods and is characterized by a variety of intensities and modes. It is primarily for those in the maintenance phase of conditioning who want variety and an intensity corresponding to how they feel during a given exercise workout. A good example is a 50-minute workout where the client warms up by jogging 15 minutes to a pool, swims for 20 minutes, and then jogs 15 minutes back home. Another example is bicycling 20 minutes to a track or running course and, after 20 minutes of running, cycling back home. Combining a group of aerobic activities over one sizable circuit at steady or various intensities is an excellent method of cross-training in the same workout and fighting the boredom of a workout with the same mode and intensity every day. This method can also be applied to circuit training in a gym by combining a continuous relatively low-level aerobic session, such as 20 minutes of stationary cycling, with 10 to 20 minutes of a variety of higher intensity aerobic intervals on a variety of aerobic ergometers, and concluding with a 5-10 minute cool-down cycle. The many obvious permutations of this method all should begin with a continuous low-level cardiorespiratory exercise effort for effective physiological warm-up. This method instills variety and is a mini-version of a "training triathalon."

GUIDELINES FOR CARDIORESPIRATORY ACTIVITY

The best resources for detailed aerobic activities are those that adopt American College of Sports Medicine progression guidelines (Greenberg & Pargman, 1989; Franks & Howley, 1989; and Nieman, 1990). The following are guidelines for popular aerobic and sport activities.

Walking

Walking is the simplest aerobic conditioning activity and is often preferred because of its low injury rate, relative simplicity, and adaptability to busy schedules. Several kinds of clients will respond well to a graduated walking program:

- Those with low functional capacity (2–7 METS) who need an initial low-intensity workout.

- Those over 60 years of age who have been sedentary and are just beginning an exercise program.

- Those who are 20 or more pounds overweight.

The energy cost of walking is relatively low when compared to jogging because of slower speeds; however, at walking speeds of five miles per hour and faster, the oxygen and/or caloric cost per minute of walking approaches that of jogging or running (see Table 7–9). Because walking is generally less intense than jogging or running, longer sessions can be maintained with less likelihood of musculoskeletal injury. When hilly terrain is gradually added to the walking

Table 7–9   ENERGY COSTS OF WALKING (KCAL/MIN)

Body weight (lb)	Miles per hour/METS						
	2.0/2.5	2.5/2.9	3.0/3.3	3.5/3.7	4.0/4.9	4.5/6.2	5.0/7.9
110	2.1	2.4	2.8	3.1	4.1	5.2	6.6
120	2.3	2.6	3.0	3.4	4.4	5.6	7.2
130	2.5	2.9	3.2	3.6	4.8	6.1	7.8
140	2.7	3.1	3.5	3.9	5.2	6.6	8.4
150	2.8	3.3	3.7	4.2	5.6	7.0	9.0
160	3.0	3.5	4.0	4.5	5.9	7.5	9.6
170	3.2	3.7	4.2	4.8	6.3	8.0	10.2
180	3.4	4.0	4.5	5.0	6.7	8.4	10.8
190	3.6	4.2	4.7	5.3	7.0	8.9	11.4
200	3.8	4.4	5.0	5.6	7.4	9.4	12.0
210	4.0	4.6	5.2	5.9	7.8	9.9	12.6
220	4.2	4.8	5.5	6.2	8.2	10.3	13.2

Source: Franks, D., and Howley, E. (1989). *The fitness leader's handbook*, p. 149. Champaign, IL: Human Kinetics. Copyright 1989 by B. Don Franks, Edward T. Howley, and Susan Metros. Reprinted by permission.

program, greater energy expenditures occur. Perhaps the safest and most effective cardiorespiratory weight control exercise for those who are 20 to 30 pounds overweight is progressive variable terrain walking. This walking protocol graduates from walking approximately two miles on flat terrain to walking up to five miles over a variety of grades such as those found in many urban and rural trails. It is not difficult to achieve and maintain the walking intensity and duration necessary for acceptable cardiorespiratory fitness. However, this often will require 20 or more minutes of fast-paced, flat-ground walking or slightly slower variable terrain walking. When prescribing walking exercise, three things are important:

1. When walking is the primary activity, footwear is very important. Specialized walking shoes are available from many stores, although many walkers will prefer a good pair of running shoes.

2. Always warm up and cool down. Begin each session by walking for about five minutes and then stretch Achilles tendon, calf, and low back muscles. After the primary conditioning phase, cool down by both walking at a slower pace and then easy stretching of the same muscles that were stretched before.

3. Give special emphasis to graduating the duration—for example, from 15 to 60 minutes—over the length of the program. Intensity progression should follow successful duration progression. Emphasize duration first, then gradually add faster paced walking. Keep in mind that adding hilly terrain is adding intensity but ensure that the terrain is within the client's capacity.

Jogging and Running

Jogging and running are superb cardiorespiratory endurance activities. The essential difference between the two is that jogging is "slower running," or as some authorities define it, jogging is running slower than eight minutes per mile. For beginners, a natural sequence of progression would be:

1. Walk/jog intervals: walk 50 yards, jog 50 yards, repeat 10–20 times; over time gradually increase the jogging interval to two or more miles.

2. Jogging: gradually increase jogging distance to desired distance or energy expenditure.

3. Running: as jogging endurance improves, increase stride frequency and stride length to a comfortable running style.

It is not necessary to graduate to running if desired goals can be achieved by jogging. However, running is a natural progression for those who orthopedically and psychologically respond well to jogging. Table 7–10 shows the energy cost in calories per minute for jogging or running, and that the energy cost increases proportionately with increasing speed. These proportional increases in energy cost mean that a client who runs a mile at 9 miles an hour (6.6 minutes per mile) will finish the mile twice as fast as when jogging 4.5 miles per hour (13.3 minutes per mile), but energy cost per mile is about the same. Numerous benefits can be obtained from successful jogging and running programs which are adequately balanced with appropriate muscular strength and flexibility exercises. They include increased oxygen consumption capacity, improved body composition (decrease in body-fat stores), coronary risk reduction, increased bone strength, and enhanced psychological well-being.

When prescribing jogging or running exercise, four things are important:

1. Wear appropriate footwear. A comfortable pair of running shoes designed for distance jogging/running should have adequate sole cushion, good heel support, and sufficient mid sole flexibility. (See Chapter 15)

2. Always accompany jogging or running exercise with appropriate flexibility exercise. Stretching of the Achilles tendon, calf and hamstring muscle groups, quadriceps muscles, foot, and even the low-back muscles will help improve jogging and running efficiency (see Chapter 9).

3. For beginners, jog every other day or no more than four days per week with a day of rest between workouts to allow for adequate recovery of the weight-bearing joints, ligaments, and tendons. Limit the initial duration to no more than 25 to 30 minutes per workout for the first six to eight weeks.

4. Increase jogging pace and add hills only gradually. First, emphasize a gradual increase in distance at a relatively slow pace, and then slowly increase pace or speed. Aerobic interval training will facilitate a safe and gradual increase in distance.

Cycling

Cycling is another excellent cardiorespiratory activity with benefits similar to jogging and running. It is a good alternative for those who do not like to jog or run or who have orthopedic limitations to weight-bearing exercise. Two types are outdoor cycling and indoor stationary cycling. Both have advantages and disadvantages; however, with sufficient frequency, duration, and intensity, either can be an excellent stimulus to cardiorespiratory fitness.

OUTDOOR CYCLING. Advantages of outdoor cycling are the benefits of sunlight, fresh air and adequate cooling, variety of terrain and scenery, and that it can be a good source of inexpensive transportation. Most clients find cycling

Table 7–10 ENERGY COSTS OF JOGGING AND RUNNING (KCAL/MIN)

	Miles per hour/METS							
Body weight (lb)	**3.0/5.6**	**4.0/7.1**	**5.0/8.7**	**6.0/10.2**	**7.0/11.7**	**8.0/13.3**	**9.0/14.8**	**10.0/16.3**
110	4.7	5.9	7.2	8.5	9.8	11.1	12.3	13.6
120	5.1	6.4	7.9	9.3	10.6	12.1	13.4	14.8
130	5.5	7.0	8.6	10.0	11.5	13.1	14.6	16.1
140	5.9	7.5	9.2	10.8	12.4	14.1	15.7	17.3
150	6.4	8.1	9.9	11.6	13.3	15.1	16.8	18.5
160	6.8	8.6	10.5	12.4	14.2	16.1	17.9	19.8
170	7.2	9.1	11.2	13.1	15.1	17.1	19.1	21.0
180	7.6	9.7	11.8	13.9	15.9	18.1	20.2	22.2
190	8.1	10.2	12.5	14.7	16.8	19.1	21.3	23.5
200	8.5	10.8	13.2	15.4	17.7	20.1	22.4	24.7
210	8.9	11.3	13.8	16.2	18.6	21.1	23.5	25.9
220	9.3	11.8	14.5	17.0	19.5	22.2	24.7	27.2

***Source*: Franks, D., and Howley, E. (1989). *The fitness leader's handbook*, p.150. Champaign, IL: Human Kinetics. Copyright 1989 by B. Don Franks, Edward T. Howley, and Susan Metros. Reprinted by permission.**

outdoors makes it easier to prolong duration of exercise because of distances between destinations and more interesting environments. Disadvantages include inclement weather, nightfall, and some unsafe city environments. However, convenient outdoor cycling combined with indoor stationary cycling make for a stimulating year long program.

Guidelines for outdoor bicycling include the following:

1. Use a bicycle with at least 10 speeds so that the cyclist can easily adapt to nearly any change in grade or wind.

2. For beginners, keep a relatively constant pedal crank speed by appropriately adjusting gears to variable grades and headwinds. This pedal crank speed can vary depending on fitness and comfort but will usually be between 70 and 90 rpm per leg. This will help minimize fatigue and maximize blood flow and nutrient supply to the legs.

3. Bicycle seat height should be high enough so that the leg that is on the bottom of the downstroke is not quite completely extended when the ball of the foot is on the pedal.

4. Use toe clips, especially with significant hill climbing. Toe clips improve pedaling efficiency by delivering more muscular power to the pedal crank axis throughout the entire revolution of the pedal crank.

5. Wear bicycling apparel. Always wear a cycling helmet. Padded shorts and gloves will increase comfort for longer distance cycling lasting more than 45 minutes.

INDOOR STATIONARY CYCLING. Advantages are its convenience and relative safety. Most health clubs and fitness centers have two types of stationary cycles, those with manually braked flywheels and those that are electronically braked. Either type will provide a good aerobic or anaerobic workout; however, the electronically controlled bicycles generally display digital work-load information which may be helpful to motivate clients. On electronically controlled cycles, some beginners do not always get adequate warm-up when selecting certain exercise programs on the display monitor. Regardless of the type of cycle, always warm up to higher pedal crank resistance loads by cycling against very low pedal crank resistances for at least six to eight minutes. Many stationary bicycles are not accurately calibrated, so there may be noticeable differences in pedal crank resistances for similar indicated work loads between cycles.

The following guidelines apply to stationary cycling machines:

1. Ensure proper ventilation. If necessary, a fan gives adequate cross ventilation. This will enable good evaporative heat loss. Cooling and evaporation of sweat are necessary to prevent rapid rise in body temperature. Unlike outdoor bicycling, indoor cycling may not receive adequate ventilation for prolonged exercise.

2. As in outdoor bicycling, adjust seat height for a slight bend in the knee at the down position.

3. Adjust handlebars so that the client is relaxed and leaning slightly forward.

4. Hold pedal crank speed relatively constant for beginners in the range of 70 to 90 rpm per leg.

5. Always warm up and cool down with 5 to 10 minutes of low resistance cycling.

Swimming

Aquatic activities are another excellent form of cardiorespiratory endurance exercise. Swimming is a very good alternative for those with chronic orthopedic problems or with a recent musculoskeletal injury. Relatively experienced swimmers generate a lower heart rate response for any level of effort compared to cyclists and runners. The diminished cardiac work is due to the prone position and the effect of immersion in a relatively cool environment. This is important when determining a target heart rate range, which may be as much as 10 beats per minute lower with lap swimming than with cycling or running. This does not mean that swimming is not a significant cardiorespiratory stimulus. However, swimming generally requires a higher level of motor skill which may take significantly longer to learn than cycling or running. Several factors determine swimming efficiency and early success with any swimming program. These include body buoyancy, swimming skill and style, and body dimensions. As a rule, women are more efficient swimmers than men, partly because of greater body-fat stores as well as more even distribution of body-fat, which improves buoyancy.

The following guidelines should be followed for swimming:

1. Assess swimming or aquatic exercise skill by evaluating exercise history or by observation. If skill level (i.e., stroke efficiency and style) is low, supervision and swimming lessons should precede swimming as a cardiorespiratory conditioning exercise.

2. Keep pool temperature for lap swimming at 76 to 84°.

3. Ideally use a lap pool with, at the most, 80 laps per mile to enable the swimmer to attain a reasonable stroke rhythm before turning.

4. For the beginner, use interval training. For example, swimming either the width of the pool one to two times or the length of the pool one to two times may be appropriate. Each of these would constitute a set with a rest interval of walking one or two widths in waist high water. This could be repeated four to ten times, depending on skill and cardiorespiratory fitness.

5. For the beginner, include a good warm-up and cool-down exercise such as walking the width of the pool in waist- or chest-high water for 5 to 10 minutes.

Rowing

Rowing machines have become popular in gyms and fitness centers for cardiorespiratory exercise as well as for attaining a reasonable degree of arm, back, and thigh muscular endurance. As with any stationary aerobic exercise device, a fan should provide air circulation to facilitate evaporation of sweat and prevent overheating. There are numerous manufacturers of rowing machines, some very basic and some quite sophisticated with hydraulic action of the arm movement and work load display monitors. However, most operate on the principle of coordinated effort of lower extremity muscular work with arm rowing action. Rowing intensity (rowing motion resistance) can be varied in most machines by changing the force angle of the rowing arm of the machine or by changing the hydraulic pressure in the pressure cylinder, or via electronic programming. Intensity can also be varied by increasing the rowing rate or number of rows per minute. Those just learning should note that all rowing machines require several sessions to learn how to perform repetitive efficient rowing motions which require synchronizing the arms, back, and legs. Several guidelines may be helpful:

1. Secure feet to anchors in the front part of the machine.

2. Ensure a smooth rowing action (coordinate arm and back rowing movements with leg extensions).

3. Begin with a relatively low intensity (low resistance) with approximately 8 to 10 rows per minute for 5 to 10 minutes.

4. Graduate the speed to approximately 15 to 30 rows per minute and gradually increase duration to 15 to 30 minutes.

5. Gradually increase intensity according to heart rate and perceived exertion response.

Aerobic Dance

Recent studies on the effects of aerobic dance show it to be an excellent form of cardiorespiratory endurance exercise. Aerobic dance and aerobic movement exercise provide a good alternative for those who do not like to jog, run, or swim. To gain significant benefits, the client must maintain the dancing for at least 20 to 30 minutes three to four times a week. The tempo (speed or pace) should be adjusted to fit the desired intensity of heart rate range. Like swimming, aerobic dance requires a degree of motor skill and coordination, and may take more time to learn than cycling or running. For those significantly overweight or with a history of orthopedic injuries, this type of exercise may create undue demands on the cardiorespiratory and/or musculoskeletal systems.

For aerobic dance exercise the following guidelines apply:

1. Wear appropriate footwear. Of many specialized aerobic dance shoes, the one chosen should follow the four standards of cushion, support, flexibility, and traction compatibility set by the *Exercise Standards and Malpractice Reporter* (Richie, 1989).

2. For beginners, recommend low-impact aerobics, a form of aerobic dance which features one foot on the ground at all times, reducing the risk of musculoskeletal injury, and may include the use of light weights.

3. For beginners, recommend a class which will adapt appropriately to the beginner's functional capacity and skill level.

4. Adjust the target heart rate slightly because aerobic dance exercise may elicit heart rates 10 to 15 beats per minute higher than running or cycling for the same percentage of aerobic capacity (Parker, et al., 1989). This disproportionate relationship between oxygen consumption and heart rate is generally true for most aerobic exercise routines using upper body muscle groups.

The personal trainer has an excellent reference for dance exercise—*Aerobic Dance-Exercise Instructor's Manual*, (American Council on Exercise, 1987).

Stair Climbing

Stair climbing can be a very effective means of attaining cardiorespiratory fitness. The client may use either a staircase or one of the sophisticated electrically braked stair climbing machines increasingly popular in fitness centers. Because the energy cost of stair climbing is largely dependent upon body weight, a large anaerobic component is possible for those overweight or unaccustomed to regular stair climbing. Because of the potentially large energy costs, an adequate warm-up and cool-down period must be incorporated. Walking for 5 to 10 minutes on relatively flat terrain, either on a track or treadmill, usually provides adequate warm-up or cool-down. Interval training methods are best when beginning a program with regular stairs or steps in a stadium. After warm-up, walking four flights of stairs and a 60-second walk on flat ground, and repeating this sequence four to ten times is an example of an interval approach.

The advent of computer-interactive, electrically braked stair climbing machines has brought more effective and better controlled stair climbing exercise to the health club and fitness center. Because most of these devices regulate the intensity of climbing based on body weight and training method chosen, they allow for more effective warm-up and cool-down as well as a variety of training intensities. A fan or other means of convective air circulation should always be used. The personal trainer should also note that many people support their weight by holding on to guard rails, so the actual work performed is less than indicated on the monitor. Most people find these machines fun, and they can provide an interesting addition to circuit training programs or be a primary means of attaining cardiorespiratory fitness.

Tennis, Racquetball, and Handball

Tennis, racquetball, and handball are all popular sports and deserve special attention for their potential to induce cardiorespiratory fitness. Each requires various motor skills and neuromuscular coordination, and the level and duration of play will depend on these skills. For the beginner, these racquet sports demand more from anaerobic energy systems than aerobic. However, as one becomes more skilled and efficient with movement and play, it is easier to prolong the activity and obtain more cardiorespiratory benefits. The degree with which one obtains cardiorespiratory benefits thus is dependent upon several factors:

Skill level and style of the player

Level of competition (intensity)

Total duration of each volley

Time interval between volleys and games

Total duration of entire session

For these sports, as the intensity and duration meet the criteria for cardiorespiratory endurance fitness (that is, 50 to 85 percent of maximal oxygen consumption for 20 to 60 minutes), they become more of a cardiorespiratory stimulus. Because of the stop and start nature of these court activities, they are not ideal aerobic exercise. Racquetball and handball tend to require more cardiorespiratory endurance because of the prolongation of each volley or game, as the walls of the court keep the ball in play. Racquetball and handball often are played in hot, unventilated environments, and thus require more attention to regular fluid intake and to signs of dehydration. Generally, these racquet sports require at least average cardiorespiratory fitness and are, therefore, excellent activities for fitness and maintenance.

Hiking and Backpacking

Hiking and backpacking activities can require high levels of cardiorespiratory endurance. Although most clients do not engage in these activities more than once a week, they are an excellent adjunct to a cardiorespiratory fitness program using more fundamental aerobic activities such as jogging, bicycling, or aerobic dance. The energy cost (oxygen consumption and calories expended) per minute is lower for hiking and backpacking, depending on grade, pack loads, and altitude. However, often the duration of such activity is prolonged (2–8 hours), and the total energy cost is well above most routine aerobic workouts. It is important to be in at least average cardiorespiratory fitness, preferably the "good" classification (Table 7–8), before attempting prolonged variable terrain hiking. One of the most important concerns with prolonged hiking is dehydration. Ensure that adequate water and glucose replacement is included in trips longer than 60 minutes.

Many factors govern the cardiorespiratory level of hiking and backpacking. The following are among the most important:

Duration of the hike

Number and size of the grades

Altitude of the hike

Speed of movement

Pack load

Air temperature

Cardiorespiratory Benefit of Other Activities

Numerous other activities such as rope skipping and cross-country skiing have a large aerobic component and, therefore, induce cardiorespiratory benefit. There is no doubt that many activities such as golf, bowling, volleyball, tennis and martial arts exercise, because of their stop- and start- and often low-intensity nature, do not induce a significant cardiorespiratory benefit. To determine an activity's potential for generating cardiorespiratory benefits, follow these guidelines:

1. Sustain rhythmic muscular activity, ideally using large muscle groups (legs).

2. Sustain for at least 20 minutes non-stop.

3. Maintain an intensity between 50 and 85 percent of functional capacity.

4. Schedule exercise for 3 to 5 days per week to obtain cardiorespiratory benefits.

Activity Selection

The cardiorespiratory activity should be chosen based on a number of factors, such as the participant's cardiorespiratory fitness level, goals and objectives of the program, musculoskeletal health, motivation, and availability of facilities. The cardiorespiratory fitness level of the client is the most fundamental criterion. It best relates aerobic capacity to the overall aerobic requirements of the method. Table 7–11 describes the relationship between fitness classification and recommended training methods for aerobic exercise programs. For example, an apparently healthy 35-year-old man who is beginning a jogging program and is in the low cardiorespiratory fitness classification would best begin by aerobic interval training at an intensity around four to five METS, which is within his functional capacity. Interval training has the advantage of relatively short work-rest periods, which adapts well to those beginning a new training program and unaccustomed to sustained aerobic exercise. As higher cardiorespiratory fitness levels develop over several months, the client should progress to continuous aerobic exercise. Higher level aerobic interval training, anaerobic interval training, Fartlek, and aerobic composite training are appropriate for those in higher fitness classifications who either wish to increase speed and/or endurance in a particular aerobic sport like running, or simply want variety.

The personal trainer should also recognize a variety of other indications that may influence or defer progress within any training method for any aerobic activity. Table 7-12 lists a number of these conditions and indications that have been modified from the American College of Sports Medicine (Painter & Haskell, 1988).

MONITORING CARDIORESPIRATORY EXERCISE

Monitoring cardiorespiratory exercise performance is necessary for assessing exercise response, regulating exercise intensity, documenting progress, and assuring safety. Essentially, three techniques are used to monitor cardiorespiratory exercise: heart rate, ratings of perceived exertion, and laboratory monitoring techniques.

Table 7–11   TRAINING METHOD SELECTION

Cardiorespiratory Fitness Level	Aerobic Capacity (METS)	Training Method
Poor	1–3.9	Low-level (2–3 METS) aerobic interval training
Low	4–6.9	Aerobic interval training at 3–5 METS
Average	7–10.9	Aerobic interval training at 6–8 METS; continuous training at 5–8 METS
Good	11–13.9	Aerobic interval training at 9–12 METS; continuous training at 8–12 METS; aerobic composite training at 8–12 METS; moderate anaerobic interval training
High	14+	Aerobic interval training at 10–13+ METS; continuous training at 9–13+ METS; aerobic composite training at 9–13+ METS; anaerobic or Fartlek training

Source: ASCM (1986): *Guidelines for exercise testing and prescription*. (4th ed.). Philadelphia: Lea and Febiger.

Table 7-12   REASONS TO TEMPORARILY DEFER EXERCISE

Recurrent illness
Progression of cardiac disease
Abnormally elevated blood pressure
Recent changes in symptoms
Orthopedic problem
Emotional turmoil
Severe sunburn
Alcoholic hangover
Cerebral dysfunction—dizziness or vertigo
Sodium retention—edema or weight gain
Dehydration
Environmental factors
    Weather (excessive heat or humidity)
    Air pollution (smog or carbon monoxide)
Overindulgence
    Heavy, large meal within 2 hours
    Coffee, tea, Coke (xanthines and other stimulating beverages)
Drugs
    Decongestants
    Bronchodilators
    Atropine
    Weight-reduction agents

Source: ACSM (1990). *Resource manual for guidelines for exercise testing and prescription*, p. 260 (as modified from the American Heart Association). Philadelphia: Lea and Febiger. Reprinted with permission.

Measuring Heart Rates

As mentioned earlier, heart rate is a good guide for exercise intensity and cardiorespiratory responsiveness. The heart rate can be obtained by palpating (feeling) the pulse or by using a cardiotachometer or electrocardiogram. From a practical standpoint, palpation or feeling the pulse is the easiest method to assess heart rate. The pulse may be palpated in the neck (carotid artery), the head (temporal artery), the wrist (radial artery), or the shoulder area (apical artery) (see Figure 7-1). For example, the carotid pulse may be felt by gently placing the index or middle finger over either of the carotid arteries in the lower neck just above the collarbone. It is important not to apply too much pressure as there are carotid sensors in these arteries that are sensitive to pressure and may induce a sudden drop in heart rate. Assessing the radial pulse in the wrist is done by placing the first two fingers (index and middle) on the underside and thumb side of the wrist.

Computerized heart rate monitors are called cardiotachometers. These digital readout devices are made for mounting on the wrist or on stationary exercise machines and measure the heart rate with special electrode sensors on the chest or arms. Cardiotachometers reduce the need to stop exercise to take a pulse and are reasonably accurate. However, because these devices are subject to motion artifact created by excessive electrode movement, they can sometimes produce erroneous readings.

Figure 7–1a   The carotid
pulse site.

Figure 7–1b   The temporal
pulse site.

Figure 7–1c   The radial
pulse site.

Figure 7–1d   The apical
pulse site.

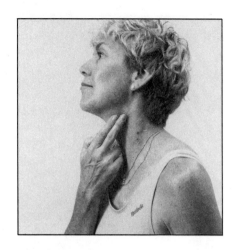
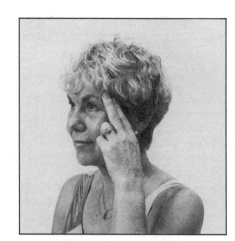
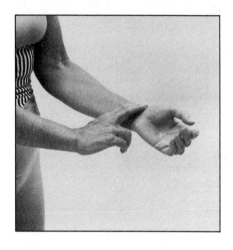
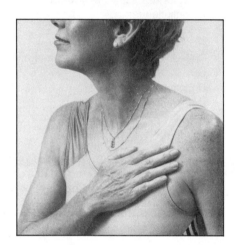

The longer the time interval used to measure the pulse, the more accurate the result. For instance, while on a stationary bicycle, measuring the pulse for 30 seconds and multiplying by two will give a slightly more accurate reading than measuring for 10 seconds and multiplying by six. Still, shorter heart rate measurement times may be more convenient, and in the case of running, dancing, or swimming, the client will spend less time stopping to find and count the pulse. Whichever time interval is used, be consistent with that method. Resting heart rate measurement is probably best standardized by taking either a 30-second count and multiplying by two or by a 60-second count. When measuring resting heart rate, it is imperative to be truly at rest. Resting heart rate should be measured after the client has rested quietly for at least four or five minutes either sitting or recumbent. Digestion, mental activity, environmental temperature, biological rhythms, body position, and cardiorespiratory fitness all affect resting heart rate, and to some extent, exercise heart rate. Because of the number of factors influencing heart rate, it should not be the only guide when assessing cardiorespiratory fitness.

HEART RATE RESPONSE TO TRAINING.   There are basically two trends to look for when monitoring the heart rate response to cardiorespiratory exercise training. First is the tendency of the heart rate, for any given level of exercise, to decrease with training. This tendency primarily applies to submaximal exercise, such as that between 60 and 80 percent of maximum functional capacity. For example, expect a decrease in heart rate for the same submaximal work load on a stationary bicycle after several weeks of training. The actual decrease in exercise heart rate and the length of time required to elicit this change is variable between clients but is primarily dependent upon age, initial level of fitness, length of the training program, and the exercise program intensity. Expect to see a decrease of four to ten beats per minute for any given level of exercise after six to eight weeks, assuming consistent progressive training. Resting heart rate also tends to decrease with training along with the decrease in submaximal exercise heart rate.

As a final word on heart rate response to exercise, note that swimming generally elicits a lower maximal heart rate response (10-13 beats per minute) versus running or cycling (McArdle et al., 1986). On the other hand, aerobic dance activity tends to stimulate higher heart rate responses for any given percentage of aerobic capacity (i.e., oxygen consumption) compared to running and cycling (Parker et al., 1989). In the case of swimming, the prone body position and submersion effects of water combine to lower exercise heart rate slightly. Aerobic dance activity uses upper extremity muscle groups and is upright, which combine to increase heart rate slightly compared to running and cycling. This may mean adjusting the target heart rate range for each of these activities depending on the client's age, functional capacity, and program goals.

RATINGS OF PERCEIVED EXERTION (BORG SCALE).   Table 7-6 illustrates the traditional Borg scale and a new, simplified version of ratings of perceived exertion (RPE). This subjective method of rating exertion is valuable and is a relatively accurate gauge of cardiorespiratory exercise fatigue. Many fitness professionals find it easier to use the revised scale in Table 7-6 because of its simple 0-to-10 scale. For those who do not have typical heart rate responses to graded exercise, RPE becomes the primary means of measuring exercise intensity. Such clients are those on beta blocking medications, some cardiac and diabetic patients, pregnant women, and others who may have an altered heart rate response.

To teach the use of RPE scales, the following general guidelines may be helpful:

1. Teach heart-rate measurement first for direct monitoring of the cardiovascular response to exercise.

2. Teach the use of either RPE scale by associating each numerical rating with a particular subjective feeling, such as seven being very, very light on the Borg scale, and then relate this rating to the associated exercise heart rate.

3. Attempt to relate each numerical rating to a particular level of work performed, such as speed of walking or tempo of a dance routine; for example, a rating of seven or eight on the Borg scale might be walking at 2.5 mph or the equivalent of a warm-up.

4. Unless the client falls into one of the atypical heart rate response categories mentioned above, do not use RPE as the sole source of exercise intensity measurement.

LABORATORY TECHNIQUES.   Although the personal trainer may not practice in a laboratory setting, knowledge of the variety of laboratory techniques for monitoring exercise is needed when laboratory data accompanies a client referral. A number of reliable techniques for monitoring cardiorespiratory endurance exercise exist in an exercise laboratory setting. In general, there are three laboratory cardiorespiratory monitoring techniques available:

1. Exercise blood pressure evaluation. The blood pressure response to exercise reflects the stage of the blood vessels throughout the body and the function of the heart. Blood pressure measurement with a sphygmomanometer is recorded before, during, and after graded cardiorespiratory exercise to evaluate cardiac work (the product of heart rate and blood pressure), the potential for exercise hypertension, and overall blood pressure response to exercise.

2. Exercise electrocardiography. A multi-lead electrocardiogram is recorded during graded cardiorespiratory exercise, usually on a treadmill or bicycle ergometer. The exercise electrocardiogram records the electrical activity of the heart and focuses primarily on the heart rate, electrical rhythm, and the potential for blood flow restrictions in the coronary arteries.

3. Exercise metabolism (oxygen consumption). Exercise expired-air analysis is performed to assess oxygen consumption and carbon dioxide production. This procedure is necessary for more accurate assessment of aerobic capacity or maximum oxygen consumption. This information will quantify a client's maximal cardiorespiratory capacity as well as determine exercise fuel utilization (i.e., respiratory quotient and protein, carbohydrate, and fat utilization).

These techniques and procedures should always be performed in medically supervised settings by certified exercise or sports medicine specialists. Laboratory cardiorespiratory evaluation can be a valuable resource to the personal trainer when screening for exercise cardiovascular risk (exercise electrocardiogram) or accurately assessing aerobic capacity before and after a training program. The following classification scheme may help to simplify the various types of cardiorespiratory exercise tests:

Category I: Submaximal cardiorespiratory fitness assessments administered by the personal trainer within the scope of the personal trainer's expertise and certification. Examples: timed mile walk, 1.5-mile run, submaximal bicycle ergometer test.

Category II: Submaximal and maximal cardiorespiratory exercise tolerance tests administered by an exercise science laboratory such as that in a university or sports medicine setting for the purpose of assessing aerobic capacity. Examples: maximum treadmill or bicycle ergometer test with expired air analysis (measured oxygen consumption).

Category III: Maximal graded exercise tolerance testing (GXT) with a multi-lead electrocardiogram administered in a clinical setting under physician supervision for the purpose of evaluating the exercise electrocardiogram and/or exercise cardiac symptoms. Examples: maximal or near maximal Bruce treadmill test for cardiac screening and diagnosis.

Required Time for Expected Increases in Aerobic Capacity

For young and middle-aged adults, the usual improvement in aerobic capacity will be 15 to 20 percent over 10 to 20 weeks of training (Pollock, 1973). However, aerobic capacity may increase up to 45 to 50 percent depending upon the following factors:

Initial level of fitness (aerobic capacity)

Age

Frequency of training

Intensity of training

Duration of exercise and total training programs

Those who begin a cardiorespiratory conditioning program with a relatively high maximal oxygen consumption (aerobic capacity) with moderate training can expect relatively little improvement in aerobic capacity compared to those with initially low capacities. Age is not a detriment to increasing aerobic capacity in itself; however, training generally shows smaller improvements in aerobic capacity because of lower exercise intensities.

Overall, the personal trainer can expect greater improvements with greater intensity and/or duration of exercise up to a point. This range for aerobic improvement is reflected in the mode, frequency, duration, and intensity standards set by the American College of Sports Medicine previously mentioned. For most clients, cardiorespiratory changes, including aerobic capacity, continue to take place over many months, perhaps up to 24, as depicted in Figure 7-2. This figure illustrates the relationship between initial functional capacity

Figure 7–2 Hypothetical relationship between training program duration and improvements in aerobic capacity for cardiorespiratory fitness levels (in healthy individuals).

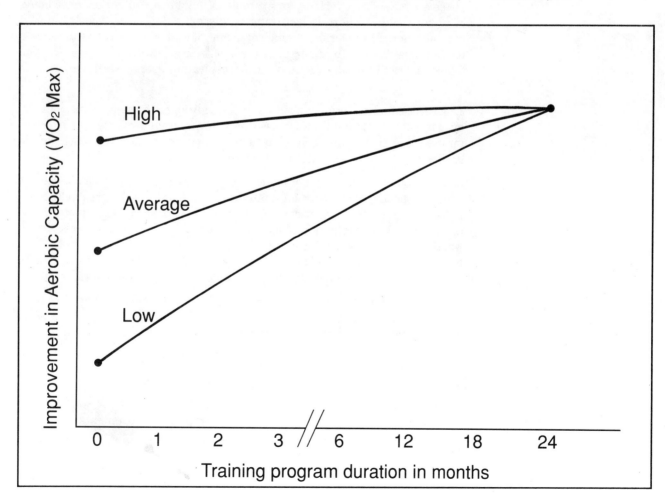

represented by three cardiorespiratory fitness levels and approximate times required to increase aerobic capacity (Pollock, 1973; Saltin et al., 1977; & McArdel et al., 1986). This will provide the personal trainer a general estimate of expected aerobic capacity changes compared to program duration. Note that endurance performance (increasing exercise duration) may increase with little or no further increase in aerobic capacity. This is more likely to occur during the latter stages of training, such as the maintenance stage. The time required for other changes to occur, such as body-fat reduction and coronary risk modification, will generally be related to improvements in aerobic capacity, although the rate of change may vary.

SPECIAL CONSIDERATIONS AND SAFETY

The personal trainer will be responsible for determining current health status, developing an exercise program, and following up on a variety of clients. Two areas of special importance are understanding and differentiating the various sources of cardiorespiratory exercise fatigue and maximizing exercise safety.

This ability is especially helpful when evaluating self-report progress and teaching exertion limitation and safety precautions. Chapter 1 covers the physiology of aerobic and anaerobic capacity. This chapter will discuss only basic sources of endurance exercise fatigue and list their basic characteristics. These sources often overlap. For example, often during longer exercise bouts in warm weather, there is heat fatigue, glycogen depletion, and lactic acid accumulation. However, becoming cognizant of each source will better enable the personal trainer to understand the spectrum of exercise responses. The following are five basic sources of cardiorespiratory exercise fatigue:

1. Exercise fuel depletion. Liver and muscle glycogen (storage forms of carbohydrate) are at relatively low levels after 60 to 80 minutes of intense cardiorespiratory exercise. This form of fatigue is focused in the exercising muscle groups and, if exercise continues, leads to increasing anaerobic work.

2. Anaerobic accumulation of lactic acid. This form of fatigue usually comes with over-pacing at too high an intensity, usually at levels of greater than 80 percent of maximal oxygen consumption or as a result of inadequate warm-up. Anaerobic accumulation of lactic acid may also occur with exercise in hot weather or exercise at relatively high altitudes (more than 5,000 feet). This fatigue has a relatively fast onset. It is characterized by the inability to sustain the previous pace or intensity and by transient muscular weakness.

3. Hyperthermia-dehydration. A gradual increase in body temperature from prolonged aerobic exercise in hot, humid conditions and/or inadequate water replenishment during prolonged exercise. Elevated body temperatures, high heart rates, inability to sustain usual aerobic exercise intensities, and mental confusion can characterize this form of exercise fatigue.

4. Musculoskeletal (orthopedic). Although not considered fatigue, per se, musculoskeletal discomfort exhibits "fatigue-like" qualities. This discomfort is often the result of overuse, with prolonged repetitive movements or unusual stress on a joint or bone from weight-bearing exercise such as jogging. This form of fatigue is nearly always focused on the muscle, ligament, tendon, or joint that is stressed and is characterized by increasing joint or muscular tenderness that tends to worsen with repeated activity.

5. Abnormal cardiac symptoms or chest discomfort (angina). Although uncommon, this form of "fatigue" would represent a contraindication to continued

CHAPTER SEVEN **229**

exercise and justify a physician referral. This symptom usually characterizes coronary artery disease and someone who is prone to heart attack. Symptoms include chest discomfort (aching, pressure, burning, or tightness), that tends to come with physical effort and is relieved by rest. The personal trainer should always make sure the client understands the seriousness of the symptoms and discontinues exercise, and should require the client to report these symptoms to a physician.

Maximizing Exercise Safety

The personal trainer should be aware of and understand the behavioral and environmental factors that can either alter the response to exercise or pre-dispose the client to increased risk of injury or cardiovascular complications. These factors include post-meal exercise, thermal stress, air pollutants, drugs and other substances, and the presence of unusual symptoms.

POST-MEAL EXERCISE. Vigorous aerobic exercise soon after a full meal can cause the heart to work harder, compromise oxygen and nutrient delivery to the working muscles, and cause gastric discomfort. Consequently, the personal trainer should advise waiting at least 90 minutes after a full meal before beginning to engage in moderate and higher level aerobic exercise. The level of exercise and the amount and type of food ingested both affect the amount of time required for digestion to be completed before beginning exercise. The higher the exercise level and/or the greater the number of calories of food ingested, the longer should be the time between eating and exercise.

THERMAL STRESS. Exercise in hot, humid environments can place the client at risk for heat injury as well as affect the usual intensity of exercise. Heat injury treatment is discussed in Chapter 17. Methods recommended by the American College of Sports Medicine and others (Vogel et al., 1988) can prevent thermal or heat stress.

1. Allow 10 to 14 days for acclimatization to a hot, humid environment.

2. Defer exercise if the heat index is in the "high risk" zone. (See Vogel et al., 1988, p. 92).

3. Avoid training in the hottest part of the day, usually between 10 a.m. and 2 p.m., during summer months.

4. Drink water or diluted 5–6 percent glucose solutions before, during and after exercise in the heat. During prolonged aerobic exercise, drink four to six ounces of fluids (preferably water) at approximately 20-minute intervals.

5. Wear loose-fitting clothing that will allow for the evaporation of sweat.

6. Decrease training intensity by monitoring heart rate.

7. Incorporate compulsory rest periods of at least 10 minutes for every 45 to 50 minutes of physical activity.

8. Give special consideration to and use caution with the following heat-susceptible persons: those unacclimatized to the heat, the obese, the unfit (low cardiorespiratory fitness classifications), the dehydrated, and those with a previous history of heat stroke.

AIR POLLUTANTS. The principal air pollutants that may concern those who exercise outdoors in or near big cities are ozone, carbon monoxide, and sulfur dioxide. The major factors in determining the dose are the concentration of the pollutant, the duration of the exposure, and the volume of air inhaled. Since ventilation increases with the level of exercise, the effects of the pollutant will also depend on the intensity of exercise. See ACSM Resource Manual (ACSM, 1988) for a more detailed description of air pollution hazards and exercise.

Perhaps the most problematic of these pollutants is ozone or smog (not stratospheric ozone) which is formed by the reaction of a combination of ultraviolet light and emissions from internal combustion engines. The level of ozone we breathe is a function of weather patterns, traffic density, and industrial output. Ozone exposure may impair lung function during moderate aerobic exercise at concentrations as low as .08 parts per million, which is at or below most air quality standards.

Carbon monoxide is another common air pollutant that can substantially reduce aerobic capacity. A 10 percent increase in carbon monoxide in the blood results in an approximate 10 percent reduction in maximal oxygen consumption. Moderate submaximal exercise in healthy individuals does not appear to be significantly affected by a 10 to 15 percent increase in blood carbon monoxide. Cardiac and pulmonary patients are generally affected by as little as a 5 percent increase in this pollutant. It is also noteworthy that because of the relatively slow removal of carbon monoxide from the blood (the clearance half-time is two to four hours), exposures that occur hours before an exercise session, on crowded freeways or in smoke-filled rooms, could influence aerobic performance.

Sulfur dioxide is most frequently produced in smelters, refineries, and other stationary sources and is not a major irritant for most apparently healthy individuals. However, those persons with asthma or bronchospasm tendencies tend to be quite sensitive to sulfur dioxide.

The personal trainer should be cognizant of the environmental air quality in his or her county. An excellent resource for local trends and standards of air quality is the county Air Quality Board or local Environmental Protection Agency. In most cities, one of these agencies or the weather bureau will periodically measure these pollutants and combine them into a Pollution Standards Index (PSI) that ranges from 0 to 500. Generally, PSI levels above 100 will affect those who are very unfit or who have cardiovascular or pulmonary disease, while levels of 200 to 300+ are required to impair cardiorespiratory performance in healthy normal clients. By understanding environmental air quality standards and resources for more information, the personal trainer can minimize unnecessary fatigue and respiratory distress in clients.

DRUGS AND OTHER SUBSTANCES. There are a number of substances that, when combined with moderate to high level aerobic exercise, can increase the risk of cardiovascular complications and/or affect the response to exercise. These substances are certain prescription medications, alcohol, tobacco, strong stimulants, and over-the-counter medications. Although each is briefly discussed here, the personal trainer is referred to an excellent and comprehensive review of drugs and substances and their effects on exercise performance in the ACSM Resource Manual (Van Camp, 1988).

Virtually all beta-blocking drugs and some of the calcium-channel blocking medications prescribed for a variety of hypertensive and cardiac disorders lower the heart rate response to exercise (see Chapter 5). Although these medications may, in fact, increase the client's ability to perform safe exercise, it is important to understand that the heart rate response to both submaximal and maximal exercise will be blunted.

Alcohol consumption before, during, or after exercise can impair normal exercise heat exchange in prolonged exercise in hot weather. Smoking tobacco in any form increases blood carbon monoxide levels, which will decrease the oxygen consumption of the heart and skeletal muscles. Stimulants such as nicotine, amphetamines, and especially cocaine all have the potential to induce abnormal cardiac rhythms and decrease the oxygen consumption of the heart. These substances also may mask important signs of exercise fatigue which are important for the client to discern in order to adjust exercise intensity. Mixing these or combining any of these substances with near maximal or maximal aerobic exercise markedly increases risk of cardiovascular complications.

Over-the-counter medications such as decongestants, antihistamines, and aspirin products are not contraindications to exercise by themselves but warrant attention because of the infections or ailments for which they are taken. The personal trainer should caution clients who have viral infections to abstain from prolonged and/or intense aerobic exercise because of the potential for complications and cardiac rhythm disturbances.

UNUSUAL SYMPTOMS. There are several symptoms which would be an indication to discontinue exercise, and, in some cases, consult a physician. These include chest discomfort, musculoskeletal pain, dizziness, light-headedness, or malaise. Exceptional chest discomfort (not necessarily chest "pain") such as aching, pressure, tightness, or burning in the chest is always an indication to consult a physician. The client should never exceed the exercise threshold necessary to cause chest discomfort without physician referral.

Musculoskeletal pain or tenderness in a muscle or joint which tends to increase with increasing exercise intensity or duration is an indication to discontinue that particular mode and/or intensity of exercise (see Chapter 16). The beginner should be told to expect some minor muscle soreness and general post-exercise fatigue. These minor symptoms usually resolve themselves in several weeks; however, those musculoskeletal symptoms which tend to reproduce themselves over the course of several weeks warrant special attention.

Exercise during viral infections, such as the flu and upper-respiratory infections, may lead to complications including worsening of the infections, increase in body temperature, and cardiac rhythm disturbances. The personal trainer should advise rest and the usual recuperative recommendations as long as malaise, congestion, or fever persist.

SUMMARY

Cardiorespiratory fitness, or the ability of the lungs to provide oxygen to the blood and of the heart and circulatory system to transport blood and its nutrients to the tissues, is basic to all fitness programs. The personal trainer must understand the physiology and application of each component of a cardiorespiratory exercise program: warm-up and cool-down; the mode, frequency, duration, and intensity of an exercise session; the importance of supporting cardiorespiratory exercise with flexibility and strength exercise; the development of a written exercise progression plan that is updated on a regular basis; and the information and guidance necessary to ensure each client's safety.

The trainer has a variety of training methods and cardiorespiratory activities with which to develop an exercise program that meets the needs of each client. The trainer needs to be familiar with the application of and the physiological response to five basic training methods; continuous training, interval training, Fartleck training, circuit training, and aerobic composite training. The trainer also must provide guidelines for such popular aerobic and sport activities as walking, jogging, indoor and outdoor cycling, swimming, rowing, aerobic dance, stair-climbing, and hiking. These guidelines include teaching clients to monitor their exercise intensity using one or more heart rate and/or ratings of perceived exertion techniques. Finally, the trainer must understand the various sources of cardiorespiratory exercise fatigue and take steps to maximize exercise safety for each client.

REFERENCES

American College of Sports Medicine. (1991). *Guidelines for exercise testing and prescription* (4th ed.). Philadelphia: Lea & Febiger.

American College of Sports Medicine. (1988). *Resource manual for guidelines for exercise testing and prescription.* Philadelphia: Lea & Febiger.

American College of Sports Medicine. (1990). The recommended quantity and quality of exercise for developing and maintaining fitness in healthy adults. ACSM position statement. *Medicine and Science in Sports and Exercise, 22,* 265–274.

American College of Sports Medicine. (1984). Prevention of thermal injuries during distance running. ACSM position statement. *Medicine and Science in Sports and Exercise, 16,* (2).

Astrand, P.O., & Rodahl, K. (1977). *Textbook of work physiology.* New York: McGraw-Hill.

Borg, G.V. (1982). Psychological basis of perceived exertion. *Medicine and Science in Sports and Exercise, 14,* 377–381.

Brown, D. (1990). Exercise, fitness, and mental health. In C. Brochard, R. Shepard, T. Stephens, J. Sutton, and B. McPherson (Eds.), *Exercise fitness and health* (pp. 607–620). Champaign, IL: Human Kinetics.

Carlton, R., & Rhodes, E. (1985). A critical review of the literature on the ratings scales of perceived exertion. *Sports Medicine, 2,* 198–222.

Durstine, L., & Pate, R. (1988). Cardiorespiratory responses to acute exercise. In American College of Sports Medicine, *Resource manual for guidelines for exercise testing and prescription* (pp. 48–54). Philadelphia: Lea & Febiger.

Folinsbee, L. (1990). Exercise and the environment. In C. Brochard, R. Shepard, T. Stephens, J. Sutton, & B. McPherson (Eds.), *Exercise fitness and health* (p. 179). Champaign, IL: Human Kinetics.

Franks, D., & Howley, E. (1989). *The fitness leader's handbook.* Champaign, IL: Human Kinetics.

Froelicher, V. (1990). Exercise, fitness, and coronary heart disease. In C. Brochard, R. Shepard, T. Stephens, J. Sutton, and B. McPherson (Eds.), *Exercise fitness and health* (pp. 429–453). Champaign, IL: Human Kinetics.

Giese, M. (1988). Organization of an exercise session. In American College of Sports Medicine, *Resource manual for guidelines for exercise testing and prescription* (pp. 244–247). Philadelphia: Lea & Febiger.

Greenberg, J., & Pargman, D. (1989). *Physical fitness: A wellness approach* (2nd ed.). Englewood Cliffs, NJ: Prentice-Hall.

Heyward, V.H. (1984). *Designs for fitness.* Minneapolis: Burgess Publishing.

McArdle, W., Katch, F., & Katch, V. (1986). *Exercise physiology* (2nd ed.). Philadelphia: Lea & Febiger.

Nieman, D. (1990). *Fitness and sports medicine: An introduction.* Palo Alto, CA: Bull Publishing.

Painter, P., & Haskell, W. (1988). Decision making in programming exercise. In American College of Sports Medicine, *Resource manual for guidelines for exercise testing and prescription* (pp. 256–262). Philadelphia: Lea & Febiger.

Parker, S., Hurley, B., Hanlon, D., & Vaccaro, P. (1989). Failure of target heart rate to accurately monitor intensity during aerobic dance. *Medicine and Science in Sports and Exercise, 21,* 230.

Pollock, M. (1973). The quantification of endurance training programs. *Exercise and Sport Science Reviews, 1,* 155–188.

Pollock, M., Wilmore, J., & Fox, S. (1984). *Exercise in health and disease.* Philadelphia: Saunders.

Pollock, M., Wilmore, J. (1990). *Exercise in health and disease.* Philadelphia: Saunders.

Richie, D. (1989). Medical and legal implications of dance exercise leadership: The role of footwear. *Exercise Standards and Malpractice Reporter, 3,* 61.

Saltin, B, et al. (1977). Fiber types and metabolic potentials of skeletal muscles in sedentary man and endurance runners. *Annals of the New York Academy of Science, 301,* 3.

Shapiro, Y., & Seidman, D. (1990) Field and clinical observations of exertional heat stroke patients. *Medicine and Science in Sports and Exercise, 22,* 6–14.

Van Camp, S. (1988). Pharmacologic factors in exercise and exercise testing. In American College of Sports Medicine, *Resource manual for guidelines for exercise testing and prescription.* Philadelphia: Lea & Febiger.

Vogel, J., Jonge, B.H., & Rock, P.P. (1988). Environmental considerations in exercise testing and training. In American College of Sports Medicine, *Resource manual for guidelines for exercise testing and prescription.* Philadelphia: Lea & Febiger.

Wells, C., & Pate, R. (1988). Training for performance in prolonged exercise. In D. Lamb & R. Murray (Eds.), *Prolonged exercise* (Vol. 1), pp. 357–389. Carmel, IN: Benchmark Press.

SUGGESTED READING

American College of Sports Medicine. (1988). *Resource manual for guidelines for exercise testing and prescription.* Philadelphia: Lea & Febiger. (Excellent technical reference for ACSM guidelines.)

American Heart Association, Exercise standards: A statement for health professionals from the American Heart Association. *Circulation*(Vol. 82)6, December 1990.

Bouchard, C., Shepard, R., Stephens, T., Sutton, J., & McPherson, B. (1990). *Exercise fitness and health: A consensus of current knowledge.* Champaign, IL: Human Kinetics. (Superb research support for cardiorespiratory fitness.)

Franks, D., & Howley, E. (1989). *The fitness leader's handbook.* Champaign, IL: Human Kinetics.

Franks, D., & Howley, E. (1989). *Fitness facts.* Champaign, IL: Human Kinetics.

Greenberg, J., & Pargman, D. (1989). *Physical fitness: A wellness approach* (2nd ed.). Englewood Cliffs, NJ: Prentice-Hall.

Herbert, W., & Herbert, D. *The Exercise Standards and Malpractice Reporter,* 1987 to present. (A quarterly journal with good information on the legalities of training methods.)

Neiman, D. (1990). *The sports medicine fitness course.* Palo Alto, CA: Bull Publishing.

Pollock, M., & Wilmore, J. (1990). *Exercise in health and disease.* Philadelphia: Saunders.

Van Gelder, N., & Marks, S. (Eds.). (1987). *Aerobic dance-exercise instructor manual.* San Diego: American Council on Exercise.

Muscular Strength and Endurance

WAYNE L. WESTCOTT

8

WAYNE L. WESTCOTT, PH.D., is fitness director for the South Shore YMCA in Quincy, Massachusetts, strength consultant for the National YMCA, former strength consultant for the President's Council on Physical Fitness and Sports, and a member of both the Strength Training Certification Committee of the National YMCA and the American Council on Exercise Personal Trainer Certification Exam Committee. He is the author of five texts and numerous articles on strength fitness, and he writes a weekly newspaper column on fitness.

IN THIS CHAPTER:

- Strength benefits: Physical capacity, appearance, metabolic function.

- Strength production: isometric, concentric, and eccentric contractions; prime mover, antagonist, and stabilizer muscles.

- Strength factors: gender, age, limb length, muscle length, tendon insertion, muscle fiber type, motor learning.

- Strength training equipment: isometric resistance, isokinetic resistance, dynamic constant resistance, and dynamic variable resistance equipment.

- Strength training: exercise selection, sequence, speed, sets, resistance and repetitions, range, progression, and frequency.

- Strength program considerations: mistakes; warm-up and cool-down; body-weight, free-weight, and machine exercises; spotting; strength plateaus; motivation; program discontinuation.

Every movement we make involves our muscular system. Muscles are unique in their ability to relax, contract, and produce force. In addition, this metabolically active tissue is highly responsive to training stimuli. With appropriate exercise muscles become larger and stronger, and without appropriate exercise muscles become smaller and weaker. This chapter presents information about the benefits of sensible strength training and the recommended procedures for safe, effective, and efficient muscle development.

STRENGTH BENEFITS

Strength training is the process of exercising with progressively heavier resistance for the purpose of strengthening the musculoskeletal system. Physiologically the positive adaptations that result from regular strength training include:

- Increased muscle fiber size.
- Increased muscle contractile strength.
- Increased tendon tensile strength.
- Increased bone tensile strength.
- Increased ligament tensile strength.

These beneficial changes within the musculoskeletal tissue have a profound influence on our physical capacity, physical appearance, metabolic function, and injury risk.

Physical Capacity

Physical capacity may be loosely defined as one's ability to perform work or exercise. Muscles utilize energy to produce movement power, functioning as the engines of our bodies. Specifically, strength training increases the size and strength of our muscle fibers, resulting in a greater physical capacity to perform work. Stronger muscles enable us to lift a heavier weight one time (muscle strength), and to lift lighter weight more times (muscle endurance).

Research indicates that previously untrained men and women gain about 2–4 pounds of muscle and 20–40 percent more strength after two months of regular strength exercise. The rate of muscle gain and strength development slows down after the initial training period.

Physical Appearance

Our skeletal muscles have a lot to do with our overall physique. Consequently, strength training can play a major role in enhancing our body composition and physical appearance. Consider a 114-pound woman who is 24 percent fat (27 pounds fat weight, 87 pounds lean weight). If she loses 4 pounds of fat and adds 4 pounds of muscle she will still weigh 114 pounds but will be only 20 percent fat (23 pounds fat weight, 91 pounds lean weight). Although her body weight remains the same she has less fat and more muscle for a leaner, firmer, and fitter appearance.

Our physical appearance and physical capacity can be positively influenced by muscle gain or negatively influenced by muscle loss. Unfortunately, unless we perform regular strength exercise, we lose up to one-half pound of muscle every year of life after age 25. Without an appropriate training stimulus, our muscles gradually decrease in size and strength (**atrophy**). Strength training is therefore important for preventing the muscle loss that normally accompanies the aging process.

Metabolic Function

Muscle is very active tissue with high energy requirements for maintenance and rebuilding processes. Even when we are asleep, our skeletal muscles are responsible for over 25 percent of our calorie use. An increase in muscle tissue causes a corresponding increase in our metabolic rate, and a decrease in muscle tissue causes a corresponding decrease in our metabolic rate.

The gradual loss of muscle tissue means that non-training adults will experience a ½ percent reduction in metabolic rate every year of life. This gradual decrease in metabolism is closely related to the gradual increase in body-fat that typically accompanies the aging process. When less energy is required for daily metabolic function, calories that were previously necessary may end up in fat storage. Although our metabolism eventually slows down with age, this and other degenerative processes can be markedly delayed through regular strength training.

Injury Risk

In addition to being the engines of the body, our muscles also serve as shock absorbers and balancing agents. Strong muscles help dissipate the repetitive landing forces experienced in weight-bearing activities such as running and aerobic dance. Balanced muscle development reduces the risk of overuse injuries that result when one muscle group is much stronger than its opposing muscle group.

For example, jogging places more stress on the posterior leg muscles than the anterior leg muscles, creating a muscle imbalance that often leads to knee injuries. Similarly, tight low-back muscles and weak midsection muscles are predisposing factors for low-back pain. To reduce the risk of unbalanced muscle development, trainers should address opposing muscle groups such as the gastrocnemius and anterior tibialis muscles of the leg, and quadriceps and hamstrings muscles of the thigh, the low-back and abdominal muscles of the midsection, the pectoralis, latissimus and deltoid muscles of the torso, the biceps and triceps muscles of the arm, and the neck flexor and neck extensor muscles.

A comprehensive strength training program that addresses all of the major muscle groups may be the most effective means for reducing injury risk. Although four out of five Americans experience low-back discomfort, 80 percent of low-back problems are muscular in nature and probably preventable. The sensible strength training programs that work so well for injury rehabilitation may be even more useful for injury prevention.

STRENGTH PRODUCTION

When a muscle is used to contract, it develops tension and attempts to shorten. The resulting movement, or lack of movement, depends on the relationship between muscular forces and resistive forces.

ISOMETRIC CONTRACTION. When the muscular force is equal to the resistive force, there is no movement. This is known as an **isometric contraction** and is most representative of one's actual strength production. For example, if Ralph can hold a maximum weight of 50 pounds at 90 degrees of elbow flexion, his effective isometric force output is 50 pounds.

CONCENTRIC CONTRACTION. When the muscular force is greater than the resistive force, the muscle shortens, resulting in a **concentric contraction**. Concentric contractions are not so strong as isometric contractions because internal muscle friction decreases effective concentric force output by about 20 percent. For example, Ralph can hold a maximum weight of 50 pounds at 90 degrees of elbow flexion (isometric contraction), but he can lift a maximum weight of only 40 pounds in the biceps curl exercise (concentric contraction).

Ralph's actual strength production is still 50 pounds, but internal muscle friction subtracts about 20 percent from his effective concentric force output.

ECCENTRIC CONTRACTION.   When the muscular force is less than the resistive force, the muscle lengthens, resulting in an **eccentric contraction**. Eccentric contractions are stronger than isometric contractions because internal muscle friction increases effective eccentric force output by about 20 percent.   For example, Ralph can hold a maximum weight of 50 pounds at 90 degrees of elbow flexion (isometric contraction), but he can slowly lower a maximum weight of 60 pounds in the biceps curl exercise (eccentric contraction). Ralph's actual strength production is still 50 pounds, but internal muscle friction adds about 20 percent to his effective eccentric force output.

PRIME MOVER MUSCLES.   Muscles that are principally responsible for a given joint movement are called **prime mover muscles**. For example, the biceps muscles are prime movers for elbow flexion exercises such as the biceps curl. The biceps muscles contract concentrically during the lifting phase and eccentrically during the lowering phase of this exercise.

ANTAGONIST MUSCLES.   Muscles that produce the opposite joint movement are referred to as **antagonist muscles**. For example, the triceps muscles responsible for elbow extension serve as antagonists to the biceps muscles. Antagonist muscles work cooperatively with prime mover muscles to produce smooth and controlled joint movements.

STABILIZER MUSCLES.   Muscles that stabilize one joint so that the desired movement can occur at another joint are known as **stabilizer muscles**. For example, during the biceps curl exercise, the pectoralis major and latissimus dorsi muscles contract isometrically to stabilize the shoulder joint so that controlled movement can occur at the elbow joint.

STRENGTH FACTORS

There are a number of factors that affect our strength performance over which we have little control. These include gender, age, limb length, muscle length, tendon insertion, muscle fiber type, and motor learning.

GENDER.   Gender does not affect the quality of our muscle, but it does influence the quantity of our muscle. Although male and female muscle tissue is essentially the same, men typically have more muscle than women because muscle size is positively influenced by the presence of testosterone, a male sex hormone. Because most human muscles produce approximately 1–2 kilograms of force per square centimeter cross-sectional area, larger muscles are stronger muscles. However, when evaluated on a pound-for-pound basis, men and women demonstrate similar strength performance. For example, one study evaluated quadriceps strength in more than 900 men and women. The average male performed 10 strict leg extensions with 62 percent of his body weight, and the average female completed 10 strict leg extensions with 55 percent of her body weight. If lean body weight were substituted for total body weight the average performance scores would have been even closer.

AGE.   Recent research has revealed that men and women of all ages can increase their muscle size and muscle strength as a result of progressive strength training. However, the rate of strength gain appears to be greater during the years of normal growth and development, which may generally be considered from ages 10 to 20. After reaching maturity, muscular improvements usually come more slowly, necessitating a more patient approach toward strength training.

LIMB LENGTH.   There are several reasons for avoiding strength comparisons with other individuals. One of these is related to limb length. Other things being equal, persons with short limbs may use more exercise resistance than persons with long limbs because favorable leverage factors enhance effective force output. For example, Jim and John have identical strength capacity in their biceps muscles. However, because Jim has a shorter forearm he can hold more weight at 90 degrees of elbow flexion because of the leverage advantage.

MUSCLE LENGTH.   Muscles are attached to bones by connective tissue called tendons. Relative to bone length, some people have long muscles with short tendon attachments, and some people have short muscles with long tendon attachments. Other things being equal, **muscle length** will affect strength development; persons with relatively long muscles have greater potential for developing size and strength than persons with relatively short muscles.

TENDON INSERTION.   Another factor that influences effective muscle strength is the point of **tendon insertion**. For example, Susan and Gayle both have the same forearm length, biceps length, and biceps strength. However, Susan's biceps tendon attaches to her forearm a little farther from her elbow joint than Gayle's. This gives Susan a biomechanical advantage that enables her to use more resistance than Gayle in elbow flexion exercises.

MUSCLE FIBER TYPE.   Humans have two basic types of skeletal muscle fibers, generally referred to as slow twitch and fast twitch. **Slow-twitch muscle fibers** are best suited for aerobic energy use. They have the ability to produce lower levels of force for longer periods of time. Conversely, **fast-twitch muscle fibers** are best suited for anaerobic energy utilization. They have the ability to produce higher levels of force for shorter periods of time.

Most men and women have a fairly even mix of slow-twitch and fast-twitch muscle fibers. However, some persons inherit a high percentage of slow-twitch muscle fibers that enhances their performance potential for endurance exercise. For example, world-class distance runners are born with a preponderance of slow-twitch muscle fibers that enables them to be successful in their events given appropriate training programs. Other persons inherit a high percentage of fast-twitch muscle fibers that enhances their performance potential for power activities. For example, world-class sprinters are born with a preponderance of fast-twitch muscle fibers that enables them to be successful in their events given appropriate training programs.

Although both fiber types respond positively to progressive resistance training, the fast-twitch fibers experience greater increases in size and strength (**hypertrophy**). Consequently, persons with a preponderance of fast-twitch muscle fibers may obtain better results from their strength-training program.

MOTOR LEARNING.   It should be noted that much of the apparent strength gain observed during the early stages of training is due to neurological factors. That is, the muscle-fiber recruitment pattern becomes significantly more efficient during the first several exercise sessions. This is referred to as the motor-learning factor, and is responsible for much of the initial strength improvement experienced by new exercisers. The smaller strength increments observed later in the training program are mostly due to the development of new muscle tissue.

STRENGTH/ENDURANCE RELATIONSHIPS

Muscle strength is generally defined as one's ability to perform a single repetition with maximum resistance. Muscle endurance is usually understood as one's ability to perform many repetitions with a sub-maximum resistance. Muscle endurance may be evaluated at any point beyond the first repetition on the strength endurance continuum.

Although one may train specifically for muscle strength or muscle endurance, there is an inherent relationship between these abilities. Research indicates that most people can perform about 10 repetitions with 75 percent of their maximum resistance. For example, if Kim's maximum bench press is 100 pounds, she will be able to complete 10 repetitions with 75 pounds. If she increases her maximum bench press to 120 pounds, she will be able to complete 10 repetitions with 90 pounds. In other words, Kim's 10-repetition resistance changes in direct proportion to her 1-repetition resistance.

Persons with a high percentage of fast-twitch (low endurance) muscle fibers typically perform fewer repetitions with 75 percent of their maximum resistance, whereas persons with a high percentage of slow-twitch (high endurance) muscle fibers typically perform more repetitions with 75 percent of their maximum resistance. Because the ratio of fast-twitch to slow-twitch muscle fibers is apparently unaffected by training protocol, genetics largely determines our muscle endurance with a given percentage of maximum resistance.

STRENGTH-TRAINING EQUIPMENT

There are basically four categories of strength training equipment. These include devices that provide isometric resistance, isokinetic resistance, dynamic constant resistance, and dynamic variable resistance.

Isometric Equipment

Although **isometric** (static) **equipment** is frequently used for testing muscle strength, it is seldom recommended for developing muscle strength because isometric muscle contractions restrict blood flow and may trigger unacceptable increases in blood pressure. Whenever possible, it is best to avoid isometric (static) forms of strength training. However, if isometric exercises are used, encourage the client to breathe continuously during each contraction.

Advantages of isometric exercise include little equipment, low cost, space efficiency, and time efficiency. Disadvantages include blood pressure escalation, strength increase only at specifically exercised positions in the movement range, training monotony, and lack of performance feedback.

Isokinetic Equipment

Isokinetic equipment is characterized by a constant movement speed and a matching resistive force. That is, the amount of muscle force applied determines the amount of resistive force encountered. More muscle force produces more resistive force, and vice versa. There are various types of isokinetic equipment, including hydraulic resistance machines and electronic resistance machines. Hydraulic machines provide resistance only during concentric muscle contractions. Some electronic machines provide resistance only during concentric muscle contractions, while others offer resistance during both the concentric and eccentric movements.

Advantages of isokinetic exercise include accommodating resistance forces, speed regulation, and detailed performance feedback. Disadvantages include cost of equipment, force regulation, need for training motivation, and lack of accessibility.

Dynamic Constant Resistance Equipment

Barbells are an example of **dynamic** (isotonic) **constant resistance equipment**. First, the amount of resistive force encountered determines the amount of muscle force applied. More resistive force requires more muscle force, and vice versa. Second, the resistive force remains constant throughout the exercise movement. However, due to the mechanics of human movement, the effective muscle force is higher in some positions and lower in other positions. As a result, the muscle effort varies throughout the exercise movement.

Advantages of dynamic constant resistance exercise include low cost of equipment, similarity to most work and exercise activities, variety of training movements, tangible evidence of improvement, and easy accessibility. Disadvantages include the inability to train through a full range of joint motion in many exercises, and inconsistent matching of resistive forces and muscular forces throughout the exercise movements.

Dynamic Variable Resistance Equipment

Dynamic (isotonic) **variable resistance equipment** is similar to dynamic constant resistance equipment in that the amount of resistive force encountered determines the amount of muscle force applied. It is different in that the resistive force changes throughout the exercise movement. By means of moving levers, cams, or linkage systems, dynamic variable resistance machines provide proportionally less resistive force in weaker muscle positions and proportionally more resistive force in stronger muscle positions. Consequently, the muscle effort remains relatively constant throughout the exercise movement. Dynamic variable resistance may be provided by specially designed weightstack machines and air pressure equipment.

Advantages of dynamic variable resistance exercise include the ability to train through a full range of joint motion on most exercises, reasonably consistent matching of resistive forces and muscular forces throughout the exercise movements, and (in most cases) tangible evidence of improvement. Disadvantages include equipment expense, limited number of training movements, and lack of accessibility.

STRENGTH EVALUATION

One reason for performing fitness evaluations is to compare a client's physical ability to established standards of performance. A more useful application is to determine a client's appropriate exercise starting point and to show progressive personal improvement as a result of the training program. A basic premise of fitness assessment is to use similar exercise modes for testing and training. Although this should generally be the case, strength testing may offer occasional exceptions to the rule.

Isometric Strength Testing

Any strength test that involves movement will either underestimate or overestimate maximum force output. This is because internal muscle friction decreases effective force output during concentric muscle contractions and increases effective force output during eccentric muscle contractions. To complicate matters further, faster movement produces more **internal muscle friction**. Consequently, isometric (static) strength testing is the most accurate means for assessing actual muscle strength.

One disadvantage of isometric strength testing is that it tends to elicit a higher blood pressure response. It also requires testing at a variety of positions because effective muscle strength varies throughout the range of joint movement.

Isokinetic Strength Testing

Isokinetic strength testing can be recorded by graphic computer printouts of effective muscle force output at every point in the movement range. However, for isokinetic strength comparisons to be valid, the tests must be performed with identical technique and movement speed. Even then, the damping controls smooth out the actual force recording curves. While the data collected from isokinetic strength assessments may provide more information, the computerized testing equipment is very expensive. Consequently, the accessibility of isokinetic strength evaluations may be a practical consideration.

Dynamic Strength Testing

Perhaps the most popular form of strength testing is dynamic (isotonic) assessments using free-weights or weight stack machines. Examples include the one-repetition-maximum (1 RM) bench press, squat, overhead press, and deadlift. Although these are reasonably good indicators of strength performance, it may not be advisable to test beginners with maximum resistance lifts. Because most people can complete 10 repetitions with 75 percent of their maximum resistance, the 10-repetition-maximum (10 RM) test may be a safer means for evaluating muscle strength.

Because of momentum, isotonic strength tests must be conducted with strict form and slow movement speed. While not as comprehensive as isokinetic assessments, properly performed isotonic tests can provide valid strength comparisons at considerably less cost.

STRENGTH TRAINING GUIDELINES

There are as many ways to develop muscle strength as there are strength trainers. In fact, almost any form of progressive resistance exercise will stimulate some degree of strength gain. Unfortunately, many strength training programs have a high rate of injury and a low rate of muscle development. The following exercise guidelines are basic to safe, effective, and efficient strength training. While they may not be fully representative of advanced bodybuilding or weightlifting routines, they provide a sensible approach for achieving high levels of strength fitness.

EXERCISE SELECTION. It is important to select at least one exercise for each major muscle group to ensure comprehensive muscle development. Training only a few muscle groups leads to muscle imbalance and increases the risk of injury. The major muscle groups include the quadriceps, hamstrings, hip adductors, hip abductors, low-back, abdominals, pectoralis major, latissimus dorsi, deltoids, biceps, triceps, neck flexors, and neck extensors. Other muscle groups that should be trained regularly are the gluteals, obliques, gastrocnemius, anterior tibialis, forearm flexors, and forearm extensors.

EXERCISE SEQUENCE. When performing a circuit of strength exercises, it is advisable to proceed from the larger muscle groups of the legs to the smaller muscle groups of the torso, arms, and neck. This permits performance of the most demanding exercises when fatigue levels are lowest.

EXERCISE SPEED. Exercise speed plays a major role with regards to injury risk and strength development. Fast lifting places high levels of stress on the muscles and connective tissue at the beginning of each movement. Slow lifting requires a more even application of muscle force throughout the movement range. In addition, slow movement speeds are characterized by less momentum and less internal muscle friction. Although control is the major objective, a reasonable training recommendation is 1–2 seconds for each lifting movement (concentric contraction) and 3–4 seconds for each lowering movement (eccentric contraction).

EXERCISE SETS. An exercise set is usually defined as a number of successive repetitions performed without resting. The number of sets per exercise is largely a matter of personal preference. Several studies have shown similar strength gains from one, two, or three sets of exercise. Clients who prefer single-set exercise usually continue to the point of **momentary muscle failure**, which is referred to as high-intensity training. Those who choose multiple-set exercise typically rest 1–3 minutes between sets. Multiple-set training may be advisable for clients who cannot consistently push themselves hard enough on single-set exercise routines. Regardless of the number of sets performed, each repetition should be done in proper exercise form and under control.

An advantage of multiple-set strength training is the additional calorie use of the longer exercise session. An advantage of single-set strength training is the efficient use of time of the shorter exercise session.

EXERCISE RESISTANCE AND REPETITIONS. There is an inverse relationship between exercise resistance and exercise repetitions. When exercising to the point of momentary muscle failure, most clients can complete about 6 repetitions with 85 percent of maximum resistance, 8 repetitions with 80 percent of maximum resistance, 10 repetitions with 75 percent of maximum resistance, 12 repetitions with 70 percent of maximum resistance, and 14 repetitions with 65 percent of maximum resistance.

Training with 85 percent of maximum resistance increases the injury risk, and training with 65 percent of maximum resistance decreases the strength stimulus. Consequently, 8–12 repetitions with 70 to 80 percent of maximum resistance is a sound training recommendation for safe and effective strength development. When performed in a controlled manner, 8–12 repetitions with 70 to 80 percent of maximum resistance require about 50 to 70 seconds of high intensity (anaerobic) muscle effort.

EXERCISE RANGE. It is important to perform each exercise through a full range of joint movement, with emphasis on the completely contracted position. Full-range exercise movements are advantageous for strengthening the prime-mover muscles and for stretching the antagonist muscles, thereby enhancing both muscle strength and joint flexibility.

EXERCISE PROGRESSION. The key to strength development is **progressive resistance**. As the muscles adapt to a given exercise resistance, the resistance must be gradually increased to stimulate further strength gains. Of course, the increase in resistance is usually accompanied by a decrease in the number of repetitions that can be performed.

A double progressive program, in which the client alternately increases repetitions and resistance, is recommended for safe and systematic muscle strengthening. The client begins with a resistance that can be performed at least 8 times. When 12 repetitions can be completed, the resistance is increased by 5 percent or less. For example, when Mary works up to 12 repetitions with 50 pounds, she increases the resistance to 52.5 pounds. When she achieves 12 repetitions with 52.5 pounds, she adds another 2.5 pounds. Under some circumstances it may not be practical in increase the resistance by 5 percent or less. Although each case must be evaluated individually, it is not advisable to increase the resistance by more than 10 percent between successive training sessions.

EXERCISE FREQUENCY. High-intensity resistance exercise may produce tissue microtrauma that temporarily reduces strength output and causes varying degrees of muscle soreness. It is therefore desirable to provide ample rest time between successive training sessions. During this recovery period, the muscles synthesize proteins and build to slightly higher levels of strength. Because the muscle rebuilding process generally requires about 48 hours, strength workouts should be scheduled every other day. Clients who prefer to train more frequently should avoid working the same muscle groups on consecutive days.

STRENGTH PROGRAM CONSIDERATIONS

The strength training guidelines above address those factors most essential for a safe and productive exercise session. However, there are additional considerations that may affect the overall training program.

Common Training Mistakes

The most common and critical training mistakes have to do with exercise technique. The tendency to use too much resistance typically results in poor form, which decreases the training stimulus and increases the risk of injury. Examples of poor form that are not acceptable are bouncing the bar off the chest in the bench press, bouncing at the bottom of the squat, using hip/back extension to initiate barbell curls, bending backward under barbell presses, using momentum in any exercise, and training at faster speeds than the exerciser can control. See Table 8–4 for a list of high-risk strength exercises and suggested alternatives.

Warm-Up

It is always prudent to warm up prior to a strength-training workout. A few minutes of progressive warm-up exercise provide physiological and psychological preparation for higher levels of effort and energy utilization. Although warm-up routines may take many forms, it is advisable to include some aerobic activity such as stationary cycling or stairclimbing. It is also important to perform static stretching exercises for the major muscle groups, with particular attention to the low back area.

Because many clients are pressed for time, they often eliminate or abbreviate the warm-up exercises. Personal trainers should encourage clients to take full advantage of a progressive warm-up session to reduce injury risk and enhance training responsiveness.

Cool-Down

Whenever a vigorous exercise session is stopped abruptly, blood tends to accumulate in the lower body. With reduced blood return, cardiac output decreases and lightheadedness may occur. Because muscle movement helps squeeze blood back to the heart, it is important to continue some muscle activity after the last exercise set is completed. Easy cycling and walking are appropriate cool-down activities. A few stretching exercises are recommended at the conclusion of the cool-down. Because of possible cardiovascular complications, trainers must not permit clients to omit the cool-down portion of their workout. As a general guideline the last 10 minutes of the training session should be dedicated to cool-down activity.

Circuit Training

Circuit training is a form of strength training in which the exerciser performs a series of strength exercises with little rest between exercise stations. One popular system of circuit training involves a line of 10-12 exercise machines that work each major muscle group in order from larger to smaller. This type of training is effective for strength development and efficient in terms of time commitment. Generally, a 10-12 station strength circuit can be completed in 20-25 minutes. Although not the recommended means of aerobic conditioning, circuit strength training may provide some cardiovascular benefits. These adaptations result from maintaining a target zone heart rate throughout the 20-25 minute circuit strength training session.

Bodybuilding Routine

Some clients have the genetic potential and personal motivation to pursue competitive bodybuilding. The major objective in bodybuilding is to develop larger muscles. **Bodybuilders** typically perform several sets (4-6) of moderate repetitions (8-12) in each exercise, with brief rests (15-45 seconds) between sets. This produces blood accumulation within the muscles and is referred to as a muscle pump. Furthermore, bodybuilders generally perform 3-5 exercises per muscle group to maximize fiber involvement. Because bodybuilding routines are very demanding in terms of time and energy, many bodybuilders follow a 6-day training schedule. To provide ample rebuilding time they may train their legs, low back, and abdominals on Mondays and Thursdays, their chest, shoulders, and triceps on Tuesdays and Fridays, and their upper back, biceps, and neck on Wednesdays and Saturdays.

Weightlifting Routine

Some clients have the genetic potential and personal motivation to pursue competitive weightlifting. The main objective in weightlifting is to develop stronger muscles, particularly those involved in the competitive lifts. **Olympic lifters** compete in two explosive lifts—the clean and jerk, and the snatch. **Power lifters** compete in three slow lifts—the squat, the bench press, and the deadlift.

Because strength maximization and sport specificity necessitate the use of relatively heavy weightloads, weightlifters usually take long rests (3–6 minutes) between sets. They generally perform several sets (6–8) of low repetitions (2–6) in the competitive lifts and a few sets of supplementary exercises. Because the training programs may be very demanding and time consuming, some weightlifters perform different exercises on different days with ample rebuilding time for individual muscle groups.

Spotting

In terms of performance enhancement, few things work as well as a conscientious **spotter** (partner) who demands proper technique and full effort on every exercise set. An effective spotter gives plenty of encouragement and just enough assistance to permit completion of a final repetition. Perhaps the most important function of a spotter is to provide protection in high-risk barbell exercises such as squats, bench presses and incline presses. These lifts should not be performed without a spotter, because failure to complete the final repetition could trap the exerciser under a heavy barbell. During the squat, the spotter should stand behind the client ready to wrap his/her arms around the client's chest and help him/her to a standing position if necessary. During the bench press and incline press, the spotter should stand behind the bench ready to grasp the barbell and help lift it back to the standards when needed. Spotting recommendations are included in Tables 8-1, 8-2, and 8-3, at the back of the chapter.

In addition to reducing the risk of injury, spotters assist by observing and modifying the client's training technique. Consequently, spotters provide an essential service for both free-weight and machine strength training.

Supplements

Muscle tissue is approximately 70 percent water and 22 percent protein. Protein has been emphasized as a muscle-building nutrient, and numerous protein supplements are available for the purpose of enhancing muscle growth. This is unfortunate for several reasons:

- The normal diet in modern nations provides considerably more protein than the relatively small amount required for muscle development. In fact, a 175-pound adult requires only 80 grams of protein per day (1 gram protein for every 2.2 pounds bodyweight), which is less than 3 ounces of protein daily.

- Protein consumption does not increase muscle size. After the growth years, muscles must be stimulated by progressive resistance exercise to increase their size and strength. In fact, even though American adults ingest plenty of proteins, they lose about one half pound of muscle every year unless they perform regular strength training.

- Too much protein consumption can be physically harmful. Extra protein must be broken down, and the waste products must be excreted from the body, placing additional work on the kidneys.

With regards to vitamins and minerals, a balanced daily diet again provides an abundance of these nutrients, with the possible exceptions of calcium and iron. However, like protein, calcium is abundant in low-fat dairy products, and iron is obtained in lean meats, poultry, and fish. Although a little extra protein and a daily 100 percent RDA vitamin/mineral pill may be advisable in some situations, a balanced daily diet (15–20 percent proteins, 20–25 percent fats, 60–65 percent carbohydrates) is the best recommendation for meeting our nutritional needs. See Chapter 4 for further discussion of exercise and nutrition.

Steroids

Anabolic steroids are synthetic derivatives of the male sex hormone testosterone and are taken for the purpose of increasing muscle size and strength. When combined with strength exercise, anabolic steroids may enhance the protein synthesis and tissue-building processes. However, the physical and psychological harm that may result from anabolic steroid use far outweighs all possible benefits. The potential consequences of anabolic steroid use include increased blood pressure, decreased levels of HDL ("good") cholesterol, liver enzyme leakage, liver cancer, testicle atrophy, sterility, breast shrinkage, uterus shrinkage, and uncontrolled mood swings from depression to aggression. It is strongly recommended that anabolic steroid use be avoided for medical reasons. Sensible strength training and proper nutrition are the keys to muscle development, and they have no harmful side effects.

Program Discontinuation

If for some reason it is necessary to discontinue strength training, one result is certain, and others may be anticipated. In the absence of a strength stimulus the muscles gradually become smaller and weaker. Although the rate of decrease may vary among individuals, strength loss is usually similar to strength gain. For example, during a 12-week training program Natalie gained strength at the rate of 5 percent per week. If Natalie discontinues her training, she will most likely lose strength at the rate of 5 percent per week until she is slightly above her pre-training level of strength. Because eating habits tend to remain rather consistent, calories that were previously utilized during strength workouts are stored as fat. Less muscle mass results in a lower metabolic rate, further reducing calorie use and increasing fat stores. Without careful attention to diet, program discontinuation may be followed by simultaneous muscle loss and fat gain for a disappointing change in body composition, physical capacity, and personal appearance. Fortunately, one or two brief workouts per week are sufficient to maintain strength levels for extended periods of time. It is therefore better to schedule an abbreviated strength-training program than to discontinue strength exercise altogether.

STRENGTH PLATEAUS

After an initial period of strength gain, most clients experience a **strength plateau** during which their strength level remains essentially the same. Appropriate changes in the training program usually enable the exerciser to make further progress and attain progressively higher levels of strength. The following eight strategies have proved useful in overcoming strength plateaus.

TRAINING FREQUENCY.   As we become stronger, we typically perform more demanding workouts. However, more stressful training sessions may require longer recovery periods for tissue-building to be completed. Consequently, it is often helpful to reduce the training frequency. For example, a person who normally rests two days between training sessions may obtain better results by taking three recovery days. A person who typically trains all of the major muscle groups three days per week may make further improvement by exercising the lower body muscles on Mondays and Thursdays, and upper body muscles on Tuesdays and Fridays.

TRAINING EXERCISES. Because our **neuromuscular system** adapts to specific movement patterns, it is advisable to change the training exercises occasionally. For example, if progress comes to a halt in the bench press exercise, then the bar dip, incline press, or chest cross exercise can serve as excellent substitutes. Although all of these exercises target the pectoralis major muscles, the different movements require different muscle-fiber recruitment patterns that may stimulate further strength development.

TRAINING SETS. When strength development reaches a plateau, it may be helpful to vary the number of sets performed. Persons who have been training with multiple sets may benefit by switching to a single-set program. Conversely, single-set trainees may benefit from a multiple-set or a super-set protocol. Super-set training involves two or more successive exercises for a given muscle group. For example, a set of triceps extensions followed immediately by a set of bar dips may provide a more effective training stimulus for the triceps muscles.

RESISTANCE/REPETITIONS RELATIONSHIPS The neuromuscular system adapts to specific training workloads. Changes in the resistance/repetitions relationship may therefore be beneficial. For example, if 8 repetitions with 80 pounds becomes a strength plateau, perhaps 12 repetitions with 70 pounds will produce additional strength gains. Conversely, if 12 repetitions with 140 pounds becomes a strength plateau, perhaps 8 repetitions with 160 pounds will stimulate further muscle development. Although some resistance/repetitions relationships may be more effective than others, the main objective is to avoid prolonged periods of training with the same workload.

BREAKDOWN TRAINING. Sometimes the training stimulus must be intensified to maximize muscle development. One means for recruiting additional muscle fibers during an exercise set is referred to as breakdown training. For example, Claudia normally experiences momentary muscle failure after 10 leg extensions with 75 pounds. By immediately reducing the weightload to 65 pounds, Claudia can complete 2 or 3 more repetitions. Breakdown training, although uncomfortable, enables Claudia to reach momentary muscle failure twice and to fatigue more muscle fibers.

ASSISTED TRAINING. Assisted training is similar to breakdown training in that the resistance is reduced in accordance with the muscle's momentary contractile capacity. However, with assisted training a partner actually helps the client perform two or three post-failure repetitions. For example, Donna normally encounters momentary muscle failure after 12 leg curls with 70 pounds. By receiving a little partner assistance during the lifting movement, Donna can complete a few more repetitions and fatigue additional muscle fibers. Also, by not receiving assistance during the lowering movement, Donna can emphasize the eccentric muscle contractions.

NEGATIVE TRAINING. Because effective muscle force output is greater during eccentric contractions, negative training is useful for increasing muscle strength. However, lowering weights that are too heavy to lift creates a higher injury risk for both the muscles and the connective tissue. It is therefore recommended that all negative training be carefully controlled and supervised by a conscientious spotter. As indicated in the previous section, assisted training is an excellent means for emphasizing eccentric muscle contractions. Another safe approach to negative training is body weight exercises such as bar dips and chin ups. For example, Ellen steps to the top position of a bar dip (elbows extended) and slowly lowers her body to the bottom position (elbows flexed). This exercise produces controlled eccentric contractions in the pectoralis major and triceps muscles with little risk of injury, as the downward movement may be stopped at any time by the spotter.

TEN-SECOND TRAINING. Another means for making the muscles work harder is to slow the movement speed. Slower movement speeds reduce the role of momentum and require more muscle effort. A general guideline is to take a full 10 seconds for each lifting movement. It will require only a few slow repetitions to produce muscle failure, and the increased muscle tension will be obvious. As with other methods for enhancing the exercise intensity, 10-second training should not be practiced every workout session. It will also be more productive when supervised by an attentive spotter.

TRAINING MOTIVATION

In spite of its simplicity, **exercise-recording** is an effective means for maintaining a consistent training schedule. The personal trainer who carefully records each workout will have a written progress account that provides the client with added incentive to continue training. Record-keeping is even more motivational when the workout charts are routinely reviewed with an interested trainer and appropriate modifications are implemented.

It is hard to overestimate the value of a concerned and communicative fitness trainer. One of the best forms of motivation is **performance feedback**, especially when pertinent exercise information is shared in a personal and positive manner. Encouragement and **positive reinforcement** are highly motivational, particularly for beginners who may be unsure of themselves. To be most meaningful, reinforcing comments should contain specific information emphasizing those things that the client is doing well. Perhaps the most powerful means of motivation is the strength-fitness model presented by the trainer. The physical appearance, training regularity, exercise technique, and personal attitude of the trainer provide an example that can significantly reduce or enhance the client's enthusiasm for strength training. See Chapter 14 for an in-depth discussion of teaching techniques for the personal trainer.

An important aspect of training motivation is maximizing the rate of improvement and minimizing the risk of injury. Fitness trainers should therefore monitor each client's exercise intensity and recovery capacity to ensure optimum training results. On the one hand, clients should be encouraged to attain momentary muscle failure during each exercise set. On the other hand, clients should be discouraged from doing too much, and observed for signs of overtraining. Persistent muscle soreness, prolonged fatigue, and performance inconsistency are indications that the workload should be reduced or the recovery period should be increased, or both.

STRENGTH EXERCISES

BASIC BODY-WEIGHT EXERCISES. Table 8-1 presents some basic exercises for the major muscle groups utilizing body weight resistance. The major advantages are no equipment, low cost, and easy accessibility. The major disadvantages are lack of progressive resistance and difficulty in targeting specific muscle groups.

BASIC FREE-WEIGHT EXERCISES. The major advantages of free-weight training are progressive resistance, wide variety of exercises, unlimited movement patterns, and the incorporation of assisting muscle groups for balance and stability. The major disadvantages are training time, exercise control, and injury risk. Some basic free-weight exercises and performance recommendations are presented in Table 8-2. All free-weight exercises should be performed through a full movement range, with controlled movement speed and continuous breathing.

BASIC MACHINE EXERCISES. The major advantages of machine training are supportive structure, variable resistance, rotary movement, and direct resistance. These features contribute to exercise safety and muscle isolation. Some basic machine exercises and performance recommendations are presented in Table 8-3. All machine exercises should be performed through a full movement range, with controlled movement speed and continuous breathing in accordance with the manufacturer's technique recommendations.

HIGH-RISK EXERCISES. There are hundreds of strength training exercises, and each one is effective to some degree. However, many exercises commonly performed by bodybuilders and weightlifters pose a high risk of injury for average strength-training clients. Some of these exercises and the major injury risks are shown in Table 8-4.

Table 8–1   BODY-WEIGHT EXERCISES

MUSCLE GROUP	EXERCISE	PERFORMANCE RECOMMENDATIONS	SPOTTING RECOMMENDATONS
Gastrocnemius	Heel raise	Stand with balls of feet on step and hand on railing for balance. Slowly rise onto toes, pause briefly, and lower as fast as comfortable.	Emphasize full muscle contraction on each repetition.
Anterior tibialis	Toe raise	Sit on stool with feet relaxed. Dorsiflex the ankle, bringing the toes as close to the shins as possible.	Emphasize full muscle contraction on each repetition.
Quadriceps	Lunge	Stand with feet together. Take a long step forward with one foot and bend the knee to a fencer's lunge position. Push back to a standing position. Repeat exercise with other leg.	Begin with small steps and progress gradually. Make sure each lunge is performed in a controlled manner, with the head held upright. Do not let the knee pass in front of the forward foot.

Table 8–1(cont.) BODY-WEIGHT EXERCISES

MUSCLE GROUP	EXERCISE	PERFORMANCE RECOMMENDATIONS	SPOTTING RECOMMENDATONS
Hamstrings	Squat	Place hands on hips, with feet about shoulder width apart. Slowly lower body until the thighs are parallel to the floor, and rise to a standing position.	Be alert to balance. Make sure each squat is performed in a controlled manner, with the head held upright.

MUSCLE GROUP	EXERCISE	PERFORMANCE RECOMMENDATIONS	SPOTTING RECOMMENDATONS
Hip abductors	Side lying leg lift	Lying on side, slowly lift the top leg as high as possible and return to the starting position.	This movement must be performed slowly in order to be productive.

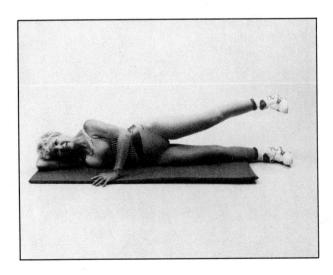

Table 8–1(cont.) BODY-WEIGHT EXERCISES

MUSCLE GROUP	EXERCISE	PERFORMANCE RECOMMENDATIONS	SPOTTING RECOMMENDATONS
Hip adductors	Side lying leg lift	Lying on side, slowly lift the bottom leg as high as possible and return to the starting position. Do not let the hips drop back.	This movement must be performed slowly in order to be productive. Due to the short movement range, a momentary pause in the top position may be beneficial.

MUSCLE GROUP	EXERCISE	PERFORMANCE RECOMMENDATIONS	SPOTTING RECOMMENDATONS
Gluteals	Front lying leg lift	Lying face down, lift one leg as high as possible, pause momentarily, and return to the starting position. Repeat with other leg.	Be cautious: this exercise can place stress on the low back. Do not let the exerciser simultaneously lift the chest.

Table 8–1(cont.)   BODY-WEIGHT EXERCISES

MUSCLE GROUP	EXERCISE	PERFORMANCE RECOMMENDATIONS	SPOTTING RECOMMENDATONS
Low Back (spinal erectors)	Front lying chest lift	Lying face down, lift the chest off the floor by contracting the low-back muscles and assisting slightly with the arms. Pause briefly and return to the starting position.	Do not let the exerciser throw the head back nor overextend the low back. Use as much arm assistance as necessary to assist the low-back muscles.

Abdominals	Trunk curl	Lying face up with the knees bent and the hands loosely placed along the head, slowly curl the upper back off the floor while pressing the low back against the floor. Pause briefly and repeat.	The exerciser should not put much hand pressure on the head. Should be performed slowly, and the low back should not be lifted off the floor as in a sit-up.

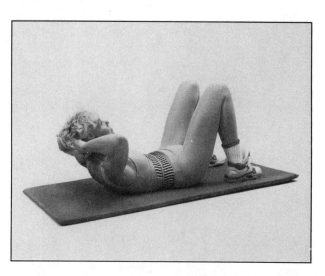

Table 8–1(cont.)   BODY-WEIGHT EXERCISES

MUSCLE GROUP	EXERCISE	PERFORMANCE RECOMMENDATIONS	SPOTTING RECOMMENDATONS
Obliques	Twisting trunk curl	Similar to the basic trunk curl, but bring the opposite elbow and knee together on alternate repetitions.	Do not let the exerciser move quickly, but insist on a controlled curling and twisting movement.

Pectoralis major	Push-up (variations include working off the knees, wide hand spacing, narrow hand spacing, and hands on a chair)	Begin on the floor with the hands slightly wider than the shoulders and legs together. Press a straight body to full arm's extension and slowly lower until the chest contacts the floor. Repeat.	The exerciser should not sag in the midsection nor let the head drop.

Table 8–1(cont.)   BODY-WEIGHT EXERCISES

MUSCLE GROUP	EXERCISE	PERFORMANCE RECOMMENDATIONS	SPOTTING RECOMMENDATONS
Latissimus dorsi	Chin-up (variations include wide hand spacing, narrow hand spacing, palms-facing, and palms-away)	Start with a shoulder-width, palms-away grip. Pull chin to bar, pause briefly, and return to arms-extended position.	Manual assistance necessary.

MUSCLE GROUP	EXERCISE	PERFORMANCE RECOMMENDATIONS	SPOTTING RECOMMENDATONS
Deltoids	Decline push-up	Place the feet on a chair, with the hands slightly wider than the shoulders on the floor. Slowly lower, in a straight body position, until the chin contacts the floor, then press up to the starting position.	The exerciser should not sag in the midsection nor let the head drop.

Table 8–1(cont.)   BODY-WEIGHT EXERCISES

MUSCLE GROUP	EXERCISE	PERFORMANCE RECOMMENDATIONS	SPOTTING RECOMMENDATONS
Biceps	Chin-up	Start with a shoulder-width, palms-facing grip. Pull chin to bar, pause briefly, and return to arms-extended position.	Help the exerciser maintain a relatively straight body position, and provide a little manual assistance if necessary.

Triceps	Chair dip	Sit on a chair with the hands gripping the front edge. With legs together, move forward until the hips are off the seat. Slowly lower the hips toward the floor, and press up to full arm's extension. Repeat.	The exerciser should keep the hips a few inches in front of the chair, with the legs straight during each repetition.

Table 8–2   FREE-WEIGHT EXERCISES

MUSCLE GROUP	EXERCISE	PERFORMANCE RECOMMENDATIONS	SPOTTING RECOMMENDATIONS
Gastrocnemius	Weighted heel raise	Stand with the barbell across the rear shoulders. slowly rise onto the toes, pause briefly, and return heels to floor.	Assist with balance if necessary, and emphasize full muscle contraction on each repetition. 
Anterior tibialis	Weighted toe raise	Sit on a high stool with a small weight plate attached to the toes of one foot by means of a thin rope. Dorsiflex the ankle, bringing the toes as close to the shin as possible. Return to relaxed foot position. Repeat.	Emphasize full muscle contraction on each repetition.
Quadriceps	Squat	Stand with the barbell behind the shoulders, hands gripping the barbell and feet about shoulder-width apart. Slowly lower the body until the thighs are parallel to the floor, and rise to a standing position.	Stand behind the exerciser and provide assistance if needed. This is best accomplished by wrapping the arms around the lifter's torso and helping him/her to an erect position. Make sure each squat is performed in a controlled manner, with the head held upright. 

Table 8–2(cont.)   FREE-WEIGHT EXERCISES

MUSCLE GROUP	EXERCISE	PERFORMANCE RECOMMENDATIONS	SPOTTING RECOMMENDATIONS
Hamstrings	Squat	Same as for quadriceps.	Same as for quadriceps.
Gluteals	Dead lift	Assume a squat position above the barbell. With the arms extended, back straight, and head up, pull the barbell to the upper thighs in an erect body position by extending the hip, low back, and knee joints.	Make sure each dead lift is performed in a controlled manner, with the head held upright.

MUSCLE GROUP	EXERCISE	PERFORMANCE RECOMMENDATIONS	SPOTTING RECOMMENDATIONS
Low back (spinal erectors)	Dead lift	Same as for gluteals.	Same as for gluteals.
Abdominals	Weighted trunk curl	Lying face up with the knees bent and the hands holding a weight plate either behind the neck or on the chest, slowly curl the upper back off the floor while pressing the low back against the floor. Pause briefly and repeat.	Should be performed slowly, and the low back should not be lifted off the floor as in a sit-up. It is more difficult to hold the wieght plate behind the neck than on the chest.

Table 8–2(cont.)   FREE-WEIGHT EXERCISES

MUSCLE GROUP	EXERCISE	PERFORMANCE RECOMMENDATIONS	SPOTTING RECOMMENDATIONS
Obliques	Weighted side bend*	Stand erect with a dumbbell in the left hand. Bend sideways to the right, pause briefly, and return to an erect position. After several repetitions, place the dumbbell in the right hand and bend sideways to the left.	Must be performed in a slow and controlled manner, one side at a time. Make sure the exerciser bends directly to the side.

Pectoralis major	Bench press (variations include wide grip, narrow grip, incline bench, and decline bench)	Lie face up on the bench and grasp the barbell, with hands slightly wider than shoulders. Slowly lower the barbell to chest and press up to elbow extended position.	Stand behind the exerciser and provide assistance if needed. This is best accomplished by evenly grasping the bar and lifting it to the standards with the exerciser. Make sure the hips remain on the bench at all times and that the bar is never bounced off the chest.

*The obliques actually assist the abdominals in this exercise.

Table 8–2(cont.)   FREE-WEIGHT EXERCISES

MUSCLE GROUP	EXERCISE	PERFORMANCE RECOMMENDATIONS	SPOTTING RECOMMENDATIONS
Latissimus dorsi	Supported dumbbell bentover row	Bend at the waist with the back parallel to the floor. Grasp a dumbbell with one hand, and place the other hand and knee on a bench for back support. Pull the dumbbell to the chest, pause momentarily, and lower slowly to elbow-extended position.	Make certain the exerciser's back is supported, and that the dumbbell is lifted and lowered in a controlled manner.

MUSCLE GROUP	EXERCISE	PERFORMANCE RECOMMENDATIONS	SPOTTING RECOMMENDATIONS
Deltoids	Upright row	Stand erect and hold the barbell at waist level with a very narrow overhand grip. Leading with the elbows, pull the barbell to the chin, pause briefly, and slowly lower to the starting position.	The exerciser should maintain an erect body position throughout each repetition. Make sure the elbows lead the upward movement.

Table 8–2(cont.)   FREE-WEIGHT EXERCISES

MUSCLE GROUP	EXERCISE	PERFORMANCE RECOMMENDATIONS	SPOTTING RECOMMENDATIONS
Biceps	Curl (variations include seated dumbbell curl and preacher bench curl)	Stand erect and hold the barbell at waist level with a shoulder-width underhand grip. Keeping the elbows at the sides, curl the barbell to the chin, pause briefly, and slowly lower to the starting position.	Make sure the exerciser does not lean backwards or move the elbows away from the sides.

Triceps	Triceps extension	Hold a dumbbell in both hands with the arms extended overhead. keeping the elbows high, slowly lower the dumbbell behind the neck. Lift the dumbbell to the starting position. Repeat.	The exerciser should keep the elbows high throughout each repetition, and should never rebound from the bottom position.

Table 8–3   MACHINE EXERCISES

MUSCLE GROUP	EXERCISE	PERFORMANCE RECOMMENDATIONS	SPOTTING RECOMMENDATIONS
Gastrocnemius	Standing heel raise (variation: seated heel raise)	Stand erect. Slowly rise onto toes, pause briefly, and return heels to floor.	Assist with balance if necessary, and emphasize full muscle contraction on each repetition.

| Quadriceps | Leg extension | Align knee joints with machine axis of rotation, and place the ankles under the roller pad. Lift the roller pad to knee-extended position, pause briefly, and slowly lower to starting position. | Make sure the exerciser attains the fully contracted position, moves slowly, and does not let the weight stack touch between repetitions. Maintain a back-supported position throughout. |

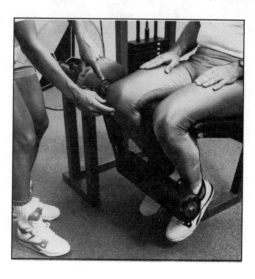

Table 8–3(cont.) **MACHINE EXERCISES**

MUSCLE GROUP	EXERCISE	PERFORMANCE RECOMMENDATIONS	SPOTTING RECOMMENDATIONS
Hamstrings	Leg curl	Align knee joints with machine axis of rotation, and place the ankles under the roller pad. Lift the roller pad to knee-flexed position, pause briefly, and slowly lower to starting position.	Make sure the exerciser attains the fully contracted position, moves slowly, and does not let the weight stack touch between repetitions. Do not let the hips lift more than a few inches off the bench.

Hip adductors	Hip adduction	Align hip joints with machine axis of rotation, and place inside knees against the movement pads. Squeeze the movement pads together, pause momentarily, and return slowly to starting position.	Have the exerciser maintain a slight bend at the knee joints, and maintain a back-supported position throughout.

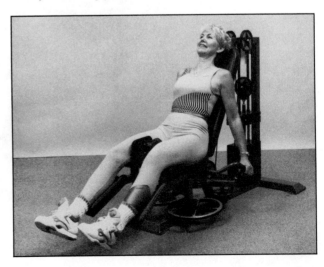

Table 8–3(cont.) **MACHINE EXERCISES**

MUSCLE GROUP	EXERCISE	PERFORMANCE RECOMMENDATIONS	SPOTTING RECOMMENDATIONS
Hip abductors	Hip abduction	Align hip joints with machine axis of rotation, and place outside knees against the movement pads. Push the movement pads apart as far as possible, pause briefly, and return slowly to starting position.	Have the exerciser maintain a slight bend at the knee joints, and maintain a back-supported position throughout.

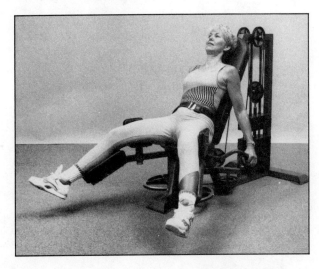

MUSCLE GROUP	EXERCISE	PERFORMANCE RECOMMENDATIONS	SPOTTING RECOMMENDATIONS
Low back	Low back	Sit on seat with legs secured and upper back in contact with the roller pad. Move backwards into a position of hip-back extension, pause briefly, and return slowly to starting position.	The exerciser must move slowly and work within a comfortable range of movement. The legs should be anchored securely. The arms should remain relaxed and the head maintained in a neutral position throughout.

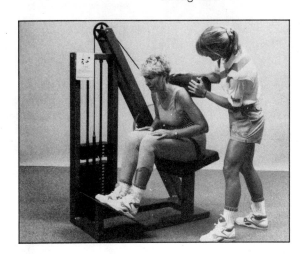

Table 8–3(cont.)   MACHINE EXERCISES

MUSCLE GROUP	EXERCISE	PERFORMANCE RECOMMENDATIONS	SPOTTING RECOMMENDATIONS
Gluteals	Leg press	Adjust movable sled so the knees are bent at 90° in the bottom position. Place the feet shoulder-width apart, relax the neck, and grasp the hand grips. Slowly extend the knees and hips, but do not lock the knees. Slowly return to starting position without letting the weights touch.	Make sure the feet are secure and the back is not arched. Do not lock the knees.

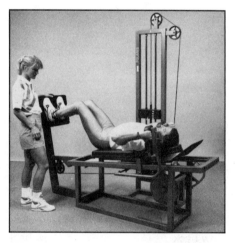

MUSCLE GROUP	EXERCISE	PERFORMANCE RECOMMENDATIONS	SPOTTING RECOMMENDATIONS
Abdominals	Abdominal curl	Sit on seat with feet under the anchor pads and shoulders against the movement pads. Squeeze movement pads downward until abdominals are fully contracted, pause briefly, and slowly return to starting position.	The exerciser must move slowly, and work within about 30° of trunk flexion to target the abdominal muscles. The head should be maintained in a neutral position throughout.

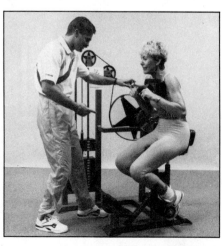

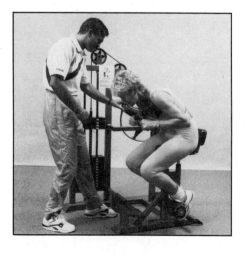

Table 8–3(cont.)   MACHINE EXERCISES

MUSCLE GROUP	EXERCISE	PERFORMANCE RECOMMENDATIONS	SPOTTING RECOMMENDATIONS
Pectoralis major	Pec deck	Align shoulders with machine axis of rotation, and place arms under roller pads. Squeeze roller pads together, pause momentarily, and slowly return to starting position.	Do not permit the head or hips to lift off the bench. For better back support, the feet may be placed on a stool or the end of the bench.
		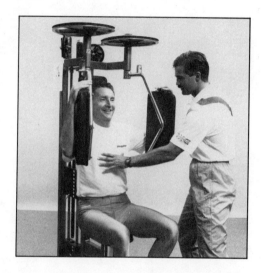	
Latissimus dorsi	Lat pull-down	Grasp the bar with an overhand grip slightly wider than the shoulders. Align the head directly under the pully. Slowly pull the bar down behind the neck and return to starting position.	Be careful not to hit the top of the head or the back of the neck with the bar. When pulling the pin on the weight stack, make sure the bar doesn't fall.

Table 8–3(cont.)   MACHINE EXERCISES

MUSCLE GROUP	EXERCISE	PERFORMANCE RECOMMENDATIONS	SPOTTING RECOMMENDATIONS
Deltoids	Lateral raise	Align shoulder joints with machine axis of rotation, and place the arms against the movement pads. Raise the movement pads until the arms are parallel to the floor, pause briefly, and slowly return to starting position.	It is important to maintain a supported low-back position and a neutral head position throughout. It is not advantageous to raise the arms above a horizontal position.

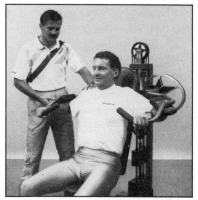

MUSCLE GROUP	EXERCISE	PERFORMANCE RECOMMENDATIONS	SPOTTING RECOMMENDATIONS
Biceps	Biceps curl	Align elbows with machine axis of rotation, and loosely grip the handles. Lift the handles until the biceps are fully contracted, pause briefly, and slowly return to starting position.	Do not permit the elbows to fully extend. For best results, the elbows should be slightly higher than the shoulders.
Triceps	Triceps extension	Align elbows with machine's axis of rotation, and place side of hands against the movement pads. Push the movement pads downward until the triceps are fully contracted, pause briefly, and slowly return to starting position.	Do not permit the elbows to lift off the support pad. For best results, the elbows should be slightly higher than the shoulders.

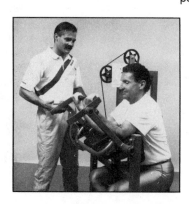

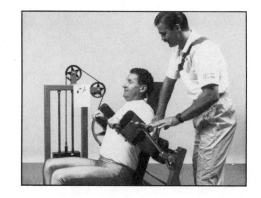

Table 8–4   HIGH-RISK STRENGTH EXERCISES

EXERCISE (MUSCLE GROUPS)	TYPICAL PERFORMANCE	MAJOR INJURY RISK	SUGGESTED ALTERNATIVES
Barbell bentover row (latissimus dorsi, biceps)	Bend at the waist. Grasp the barbell with an overhand grip and pull to chest.	Due to the unfavorable biomechanical position, may place excessive stress (several times the barbell weight) on the low back.	• Supported dumbbell bentover row • Pull down

Cheat bench press (pectoralis major, triceps)	Lie on bench with the feet on the floor and the hips held above the bech, raising the chest in an arched position.	Bouncing the barbell off the chest may damage the sternum. Arching the back (bridging) may place unacceptable stress on the low back and neck.	• Bench press (proper form) • Incline bench press

Table 8–4(cont.)   HIGH-RISK STRENGTH EXERCISES

EXERCISE (MUSCLE GROUPS)	TYPICAL PERFORMANCE	MAJOR INJURY RISK	SUGGESTED ALTERNATIVES
Cheat curl (biceps)	Bend forward at hips while holding the barbell with an underhand grip. Initiate the upward movement by forcefully extending the hips. Bend backward to "catch" the barbell at the top of the curling movement.	Using the hip and back extensors to produce barbell momentum subjects the low back to considerable stress. Bending backwards to "catch" the barbell further increases injury risk to the low back.	• Curl (proper form) • Incline dumbbell curl

Dumbbell fly (pectoralis major)	Lie on bench with feet on floor and a dumbbell in each hand. Beginning with the dumbbells held above the chest, lower the arms until parallel to floor, and return to starting position.	Rebounding the dumbbells from the bottom (stretched) position places great stress on the chest muscles due to the mismatch of strength vs. resistive forces, and unfavorable leverage.	• Chest cross • 10° chest

Table 8–4(cont.)   HIGH-RISK STRENGTH EXERCISES

EXERCISE (MUSCLE GROUPS)	TYPICAL PERFORMANCE	MAJOR INJURY RISK	SUGGESTED ALTERNATIVES
Good morning (low back)	Stand with the barbell behind the shoulders. Bend forward until back is parallel to floor and return to erect position.	Bending forward with a barbell across the shoulders places significant stress on the low back and the neck.	• Seated rowing • Low back

Cheat overhead press (deltoids, triceps)	Begin with the barbell at shoulder level. Bending backwards, press the barbell to full arm's extension overhead, and return to shoulder level.	May place the low back in a stressful position. Seated presses may place excessive compression forces on the vertebral column.	• Upright rowing • Lateral raise • Overhead press (proper form)

Table 8–4(cont.)   HIGH-RISK STRENGTH EXERCISES

EXERCISE (MUSCLE GROUPS)	TYPICAL PERFORMANCE	MAJOR INJURY RISK	SUGGESTED ALTERNATIVES
Power clean (quadriceps, hamstrings, low back, deltoids, trapezius)	Assume a squat position above the barbell, with the arms extended, back straight, and head up. Forcefully extend the knees, hips, and back while pulling the barbell as high as possible. Drop under the barbell and catch it at shoulder level.	The explosive forces that must be generated to produce barbell momentum may subject the low back to excessive stress. The vulnerable arm position used to catch the barbell presents high injury potential to the wrist, elbow, and shoulder joints.	• Squat • Leg press • Upright rowing

Stiff leg dead lift (low back, hamstrings, gluteals)	Assume a straight-legged position above the barbell. Grasp the barbell by bending at the hips. Pull the barbell to the upper thighs in an erect body position by extending the hips and low back.	Unfavorable leverage may place excessive stress on the low- back and hip areas.	• Squat • Leg press • Low back

Table 8–5   EXERCISE MODE

MUSCLE	BODY WEIGHT	FREE WEIGHT	MACHINE
Gastrocnemius	Heel raise	Weighted heel raise	Standing heel raise
Anterior tibialis	Toe raise	Weighted toe raise	—
Quadriceps	Lunge	Squat	Leg extension
Hamstrings	Squat	Squat	Leg curl
Hip adductors	Side lying leg lift	—	Hip adduction
Hip abductors	Side lying leg lift	—	Hip abduction
Gluteals	Front lying leg lift	Dead lift	Lower back
Low back	Front lying chest lift	Dead lift	Lower back
Abdominals	Trunk curl	Weighted trunk curl	Abdominal curl
Obliques	Twisting trunk curl	Weighted side bend	Rotary torso
Pectoralis major	Push-up	Bench press	Pec deck
Latissimus dorsi	Chin-up	Dumbbell bentover row	Lat pull
Deltoids	Decline push-up	Upright row	Lateral raise
Biceps	Chin-up	Curl	Biceps curl
Triceps	Chair-dip	Triceps extension	Triceps extension
Neck flexors	—	—	Neck flexion
Neck extensors	—	—	Neck extension

SUMMARY

Strength training improves our ability to perform work or exercise, improves our physical appearance, increases our metabolic rate, and reduces the risk of injury. To design safe and effective strength training programs, a trainer must understand the relationship between muscular forces and resistive forces, as well as the factors that affect strength performance. The trainer must also be knowledgeable about the four categories of strength training equipment—isometric, isokinetic, dynamic constant resistance, and dynamic variable resistance.

Almost any form of progressive resistance exercise will stimulate some degree of strength gain; however, many strength training programs have a high rate of injury and a low rate of muscle development. The trainer needs to employ guidelines that are basic to safe, effective, and efficient strength training for the average client. To that end, this chapter includes basic body weight, free-weight, and machine exercises for the major muscle groups (summarized in Table 8–5) and provides performance and spotting recommendations for each exercise. Finally, the trainer must be prepared to address the dangers of using anabolic steroids (and to a lesser degree, protein supplements), know how to overcome strength plateaus, and know how to monitor and motivate clients to achieve optimal training results.

SUGGESTED READING

Brzycki, M. (1989). *A practical approach to strength training*. Grand Rapids, MI: Masters Press.

Fleck, S., & Kraemer, W. (1987). *Designing resistance training programs*. Champaign, IL: Human Kinetics.

Sienna, P. (1988). *One rep max: A guide to beginning weight training*. Indianapolis, IN: Benchmark Press.

Westcott, W. (1989). *Strength fitness: Physiological principles and training techniques* (3rd ed.). Dubuque, IA: William C. Brown.

Flexibility

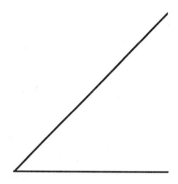

MARI CYPHERS

9

MARI CYPHERS, P.T., is a physical therapist with an extensive background in physical medicine, including a 12-year emphasis in sports medicine. She is director and co-founder of SporTec Physical Therapy Center in Livermore, California, and frequently lectures for IDEA conventions, ACSM Aerobic and Fitness instructor certifications, Fitness Associates network, and California State University, Hayward.

IN THIS CHAPTER:

- The benefits of flexibility: exercises for major muscle groups.
- Mechanics of stretching: elastic deformation and plastic (viscous) deformation.

- Types of stretching: static, ballistic, and PNF.
- Factors affecting flexibility: age, activity, gender, body type, warm-up.

Most professionals agree that **flexibility** is an important component of fitness and a critical factor in achieving peak physical potential. However, flexibility has often been overlooked or misused. Some runners and weightlifters, for example, stress their cardiovascular or strength training and pay little attention to their flexibility. Athletes and trainers who do stress flexibility often have different systems of flexibility training, and the scientific data is not strong enough to support the value of one over another. Although controversies still exist, and the arguments for flexibility training are not as strong or well-supported as those for cardiovascular and strength training, it is important for personal trainers to take a conservative approach and include flexibility training in all fitness programs. To assist the trainer, this chapter presents an overview of the substantial body of knowledge about flexibility training that can help clients attain fitness goals and decrease the risk of injury.

FLEXIBILITY: A DEFINITION

Flexibility is a joint's ability to move freely in every direction, or more specifically, through a full and normal **range of motion** (ROM). Within each joint, and for each activity, there is an optimum ROM essential to peak performance. A number of factors can limit joint mobility, including genetic inheritance; the joint structure itself; connective tissue elasticity within muscles, tendons, or skin surrounding a joint; and neuromuscular coordination. Flexibility training minimizes the factors that limit flexibility and helps balance muscle groups that might be overused during physical training sessions or as a result of poor posture.

There are two basic types of flexibility: static flexibility and dynamic flexibility. **Static Flexibility** is the ROM about a joint, with little emphasis on speed of movement. For example, a gymnast holding a split is demonstrating static flexibility. On the other hand, **dynamic flexibility** is resistance to motion at the joint and therefore involves speed during physical performance. A major league pitcher must have sufficient dynamic flexibility of the shoulder joint to throw a baseball at 90 mph. Although static and dynamic flexibility might be achieved using different training methods, both are important in promoting overall fitness. The benefits derived from each—full, normal ROM—are numerous and include the following:

1. *Increased physical efficiency and performance.* A flexible joint has the ability to move farther in its range and requires less energy to do so.

2. *Decreased risk of injury.* Although there is insufficient data to support this conclusion, most professionals agree that increasing ROM decreases the resistance in various tissues, and a client is therefore less likely to incur injury by exceeding tissue extensibility, or maximum range of tissues, during activity.

3. *Increased blood supply and nutrients to joint structures.* Flexibility training increases tissue temperature, which in turn increases circulation and nutrient transport, thus allowing greater elasticity of surrounding tissues.

4. *Increased quality and quantity of joint synovial fluid.* Increasing the quantity and decreasing the viscosity, or thickness, of **synovial fluid** enables more nutrients to be transported to the joint articular cartilage. This allows more freedom of movement and has a tendency to decelerate joint degenerative processes.

5. *Increased neuromuscular coordination.* Studies have shown that nerve impulse velocity (the time it takes an impulse to travel to the brain and return) is enhanced with flexibility training. In attuning the central nervous system (CNS) to the physical demands placed upon it, opposing muscle groups work in a more synergistic or coordinated fashion.

6. *Reduced muscular soreness.* There is still controversy over why muscle soreness occurs and the role of flexibility in soreness. However, recent studies have indicated that slow, static stretching is extremely effective in reducing localized delayed muscular soreness after exercise.

7. *Improved muscular balance and postural awareness.* Flexibility helps realign soft tissue structures which may have adapted poorly to the effects of gravity and postural habits. Realignment consequently reduces the effort it takes to achieve and maintain good posture in activities of daily living.

8. *Decreased risk of low-back pain.* Strong clinical evidence indicates that lumbo-pelvic flexibility, including hamstrings, hip flexors, and muscles attaching to the pelvis, is critical in decreasing stress to the lumbar spine.

9. *Reduced stress.* In general, stretching promotes muscular relaxation. A muscle in a constant state of contraction or tension may require more energy to accomplish activities. Muscular relaxation encourages healthy nutrition directly to the muscle, which decreases the accumulation of toxins, reduces the potential for adaptive shortening, and diminishes fatigue.

10. *Enhanced enjoyment.* A physical training program must be enjoyable if a client is to stick with it. Many trainers find that by relaxing both mind and body, flexibility training increases a client's sense of well-being and personal gratification during exercise.

Although flexibility is a valuable aspect of physical training, it is important for the trainer to be aware of potential disadvantages associated with this type of conditioning. How much joint flexibility is necessary is still not clearly understood and, in fact, is highly specific to each client. Most experts believe excessive flexibility will overstretch ligaments, thus increasing the likelihood of injury. Instability caused by over-stretched ligaments may lead to decreased joint-protective reflexes and neuromuscular coordination, and ultimately predispose a person to degenerative (arthritic) joint changes. Additional studies have determined negative tissue adaptations after prolonged stretch. A muscle that has been overstretched for an extended period of time has a tendency to develop **stretch weakness** (Kendall, et al., 1971). A stretch weakness may increase vulnerability to injury during even less intense daily activities. These potential changes only magnify the need for well-balanced programs in muscular strength *and* flexibility to achieve greater joint stability and thus minimize the incidence of injury.

THE MECHANICS OF STRETCHING

Flexibility is enhanced by using a variety of stretching methods. It is accomplished by applying a force (stretch or tension) to the involved limb in order to overcome a resistance within the joint, hence increasing the available ROM. Stretch refers literally to the process of elongation, and it is widely accepted that the most resistance to stretch is not from the more elastic muscle fiber itself, but rather from the connective tissue framework in and around the muscle. Therefore, understanding the mechanical properties of **connective tissue** under tension is essential in determining the best methods of increasing ROM and flexibility.

Connective tissue is composed of a series of collagen fibers within a protein matrix that ultimately creates various soft tissue structures including tendons, ligaments, and fascia (Fig. 9-1). It has a very high **tensile strength** and therefore has a greater ability to support and protect these soft tissue structures. Organized connective tissue has a combination of two mechanical properties relating to obtaining normal flexibility: it is **elastic**, and it is **plastic** (viscous). An elastic stretch is an elongation of tissues which recovers when the tension is

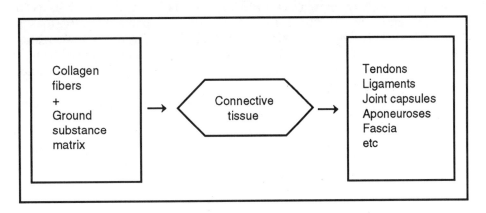

Figure 9-1   Organization of connective tissue structures.

Figure 9–2 The "spring" model, representing recoverable (elastic) deformation.

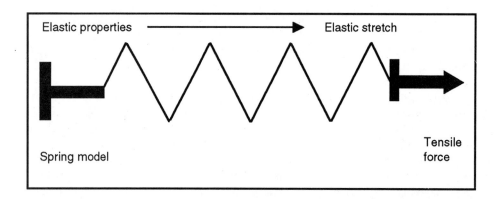

Figure 9–3 The "hydraulic cylinder" model, representing permanent (plastic) deformation.

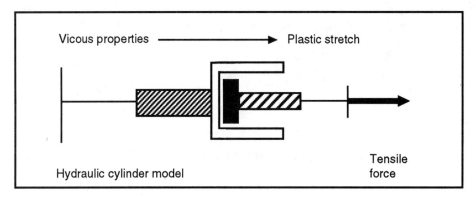

Figure 9–4 Viscoelastic connective tissue has both plastic and elastic elements connected in series.

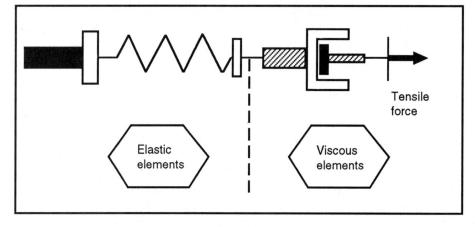

removed. It is often called temporary or recoverable elongation (deformation) and is frequently compared to a string-like model (Fig. 9-2). A plastic stretch is an elongation in which the deformation to tissue remains even after tension is removed. This property is termed permanent or nonrecoverable elongation and is likened to a hydraulic cylinder (Fig. 9-3). If a hydraulic cylinder is pulled out, it will usually stay in the end position until another force acts upon it to return it to the original state.

To obtain maximum results, it is imperative to realize that connective tissue behaves in a **viscoelastic** manner when stretched. That is, connective tissue exhibits both viscous (plastic) and elastic tendencies during elongation (see Fig. 9-4). So, when a soft tissue structure is stretched and the force is removed, elastic tissue (largely consisting of muscle fibers) recovers quickly, while plastic deformation of the connective tissue framework may remain. Because of this, ROM or stretching techniques must be designed to gain plastic elongation (deformation).

The amount of viscoelastic elongation during stretch can vary widely and frequently depending on how one stretches and under what conditions. Two predominant factors in assuring proper stretch are the force and the duration of the stretch. The degree of tissue lengthening remaining after a force is removed is greatest when incorporating a low-force, long-duration stretch (static) rather than a high-force, short-duration stretch (ballistic). Furthermore, a high-force, short-duration stretch favors recoverable or elastic tissue deformation, while a lower force, sustained over a longer period of time, encourages permanent or plastic deformation.

Although different stretching methods may be appropriate in different instances, most professionals agree that a static stretch is the safest and most effective means of obtaining flexibility. Partial support for this practice is provided by the S.A.I.D. principle (Specific Adaptation to Imposed Demands) in athletic training. Simply stated, the body, or in this case connective tissue, has the ability to adapt to the stresses placed upon it during physical activity in a positive or negative way. Tissues can accommodate in a healthy manner by becoming stronger, sustaining increased and progressive levels of exercise intensity; or, if training conditions exceed the ability to adjust to the current level of intensity, tissues will fail. Connective tissue that is stretched too vigorously and/or for an excessive length of time will weaken structurally, leading to serious injury.

Another factor influencing connective tissue extensibility during stretch is an elevation of tissue temperature. Exercise physiologists DeVries (1980) and Astrand (1970) concur that an elevation in core body temperature of as little as $1°-3°$ produces greater aerobic metabolism on a cellular level (O_2 transport) and reduced muscle fiber viscosity, increasing muscle elasticity, and generally diminishing stiffness. Additional studies have shown that by raising tissue temperature, a thermal transition takes place within collagen microstructures, further augmenting viscous relaxation, and thus permitting enhanced flexibility (Sapega, 1981).

To summarize:

- A high-force, short-duration stretch performed when the tissue temperature is near normal or below will produce maximum structural weakness and elastic deformation, or temporary, recoverable elongation.

- A low-force, long-duration stretch at slightly elevated tissue temperature will produce minimum structural weakness and viscous (plastic) deformation, or permanent, non-recoverable elongation.

THE STRETCH REFLEX

A primary component associated with the effects of stretching has a neurophysiologic basis involving reflex activity and is termed the **myotatic stretch reflex**. The sense organs or neural receptors responsible for the stretch reflex are the **muscle spindles** lying parallel to the muscle fiber, and the **Golgi tendon organs** (GTO), found deep within the musculotendinous junctions. Each of these receptors is sensitive to stretch and ultimately aids in protecting a muscle against unnecessary injury.

In general, the muscle spindle passively mimics, or follows, the movements of its adjacent muscle fibers. That is, as the muscle fiber stretches, so does the spindle. If the stretch is extreme enough, the muscle spindle responds by sending a signal to the spinal cord, which then returns an order to create a sudden, protective muscular contraction. The spindle ceases to fire when this

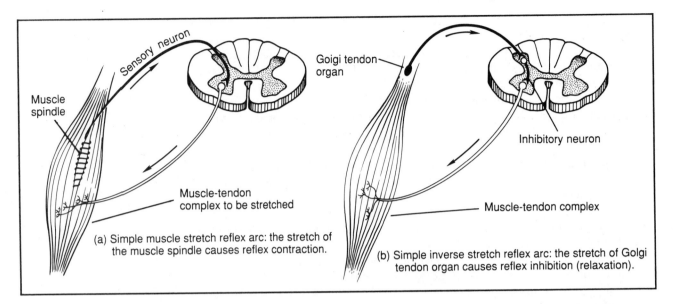

(a) Simple muscle stretch reflex arc: the stretch of the muscle spindle causes reflex contraction.

(b) Simple inverse stretch reflex arc: the stretch of Golgi tendon organ causes reflex inhibition (relaxation).

Figure 9–5 The stretch reflex and autogenic inhibition. (a) *Simple muscle stretch reflex arc*: The stretch of the muscle spindle causes reflex contraction. (b) *Simple inverse stretch reflex arc*: The stretch of Golgi tendon organ causes reflex inhibition (relaxation).

shortening begins, "unloading" as the muscle fiber contracts, and preventing potential tissue damage (Fig. 9–5).

The reflex evoked by the physician when he/she taps the patellar ligament directly below the kneecap during an examination is a classic example of the stretch reflex. By striking this ligament with a rubber mallet, the physician causes a quick stretch in the quadriceps mechanism. In turn, the muscle spindles react to this unexpected stretch by contracting the quadriceps, resulting in the knee-jerk reflex. Another example is falling asleep in a seated position. As the head relaxes and droops forward, the muscle spindle experiences a sudden stretch, sending a message to the cervical muscle fibers, causing contraction and a sudden jerk to the upright position.

It is also important to note that as the stretch reflex occurs, antagonizing muscle action is inhibited. So, when the quadriceps are stimulated with a reflex tap, the antagonistic action of the hamstrings group is automatically inhibited. This inhibitory response is called **reciprocal innervation** or reciprocal inhibition.

Up to a point, the harder a muscle is stretched, the stronger the reflex contraction. However, when tension becomes great enough to risk rupture, contraction abruptly stops, and the muscle relaxes. This relaxation response to extreme stretch is called **autogenic inhibition** and is chiefly dependent on the GTO. The GTO receptor is actually a weaker and non-dominating system of muscular inhibition. Nevertheless, if all systems are overloaded as a result of excessive stretch, the GTO transmits impulses to an inhibitory neuron within the spinal cord which finally overrides input from the muscle spindle, causing an immediate relaxation of the entire muscle (Fig. 9–5). A greater understanding of the stretch reflex and autogenic and reciprocal inhibition will assist the trainer in determining the effectiveness of various types of stretching techniques used today.

TYPES OF STRETCHING

There are numerous variations in flexibility exercises, but most types can be placed into two main categories: **passive stretching** and **active stretching**. During a passive stretch, the elastic components of the muscle are usually relaxed, and the portion of muscle most likely to be loaded is the connective tissue structures mentioned earlier as important in plastic elongation. The static stretch method is an excellent example of passive stretching. On the other hand, active or dynamic stretching has greater effects upon the elastic components—muscles, tendons, and musculotendinous junctions (Hubley-Kozey and Stanish, 1984). Because active stretching requires muscle contraction through a range of motion, it has a tendency to load, strengthen, and thus prepare these structures for functional activities at hand. As one can see, for maximum benefits in flexibility, it is vital to include both active and passive stretching methods in one's training program.

Three basic techniques used to increase flexibility are popular today: **static stretching, ballistic stretching**, and **proprioceptive neuromuscular facilitation** (PNF) stretching. Of these, the static stretching method is advocated by professionals as the most effective in achieving results and the least likely to cause injury.

Static Stretching

Static stretching involves a slow, gradual, and controlled elongation through a full range of motion. For example, a client stretching the calf (gastrocnemius) would lean (with back straight) over the forward knee until feeling a pull (without pain) in the calf and hold the position for 15–30 seconds (Fig. 9-6). This low-intensity, long-duration technique imposes less microtrauma to tissues and results in superior flexibility. Stretching in this manner also physiologically suppresses the stretch reflex. As muscle spindles and the central nervous system (CNS) adapt slowly to a lengthened position, spindle discharge is diminished and GTOs are activated to further depress muscular contraction, allowing greater relaxation. Another reason for static stretching is to prevent so-called **delayed muscle soreness**. Delayed muscle soreness, occurring 24–48 hours after strenuous exercise, has been attributed to numerous theories.

One popular explanation is that exercise creates an accumulation of waste products, such as lactic acid or other metabolites, within the muscle. A resulting increase in pressure may in effect irritate sensory nerves to initiate a painful episode (Alter, 1988). A second theory maintains that as we exercise, microscopic ruptures take place within the muscle, generating soreness just as any muscular strain might (Schultz, 1979). The last, and felt by many to be the most likely, reason for delayed soreness is the "spasm theory." DeVries (1980), as well as other researchers, postulated that soreness after prolonged exercises resulted from a tonic, localized spasm of individual muscle motor units. DeVries professed that sustained exercise above a minimum level temporarily cuts off blood supply to the active muscle, creating an ischemic reaction that may produce subsequent soreness. Electromyographic (EMG) studies determined that recorded electrical muscular activity and symptomatic muscle soreness were significantly decreased in subjects using static stretching. Therefore, trainers working with clients to enhance flexibility and decrease muscular soreness and risk of injury should include static stretching as part of the training program.

Ballistic Stretching

Ballistic or dynamic stretching employs rapid, uncontrolled, bouncing or bobbing motions (Fig. 9-7). This technique incorporates a high-force, short-duration action, stimulating muscle spindle activity and therefore greater reflex muscular contraction. It is obvious that uncontrolled or excessive movements can also easily overload soft tissue structures beyond normal elastic capabilities. Consequently, most trainers, physical therapists, and physicians

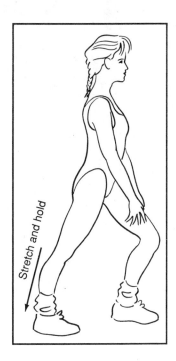

Figure 9–6 Static stretching: slow, controlled elongation held for 15–30 seconds.

Figure 9–7 Ballistic stretching: rapid bouncing or bobbing motions.

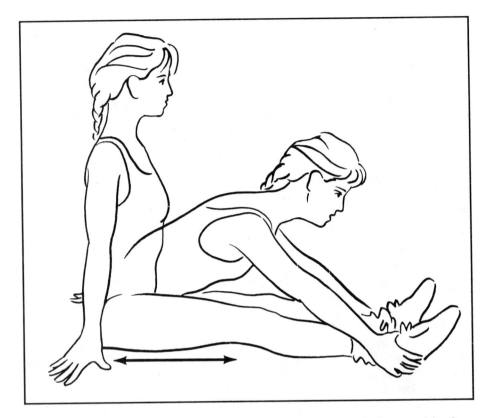

feel ballistic stretching is the least beneficial stretching technique and is also often unsafe.

While ballistic stretching may appear contradictory to the aim of flexibility training, there are still some who believe there is a practical advantage to the use of this method of stretch—that it may in fact promote dynamic flexibility and decrease potential injury by preparing tissues for high-speed, volitional type exercise. Since many movements in sport and exercise are ballistic in nature, a dynamic stretching technique may be appropriate when specifically training for sport competition. Technically, dynamic stretching should consist of rhythmic actions meant to mimic a training activity, initially small and gradually increasing to larger ranges of motion. However, this method of stretching is not generally recommended for the general population because control may be compromised and risk of injury increased.

Proprioceptive Neuromuscular Facilitation (PNF)

PNF, another common stretching procedure, was first developed by physicians and physical therapists for use in rehabilitation. As described by its developers, PNF is a method of hastening neuromuscular responses by stimulating neural **proprioceptors** (Voss, et al., 1985). Although PNF is extremely complicated and composed of many strategies to promote a variety of results, the aspect most commonly used in training is the contract-relax sequence of PNF. Based on the principle of reciprocal inhibition, this method requires an initial isometric contraction against maximum resistance at the end of the limb's range of motion for approximately six seconds, followed by relaxation and a slow, passive stretch to the point of limitation (Fig. 9–8). This sequence is usually repeated several times, and the summation of maximum neural excitations to the muscle being stretched theoretically allows for a greater reflex inhibition and thus a greater stretch. Proponents of this method claim that individuals experience more passive mobility. However, researchers Moore and Hutton (1980) concluded that the more complicated PNF technique was no more effective than conventional stretching techniques, and that contract-relax was often perceived as more uncomfortable when compared to static stretching. Since pain is one of the body's mechanisms to protect us from further insult, PNF stretching may actually produce excessive rather than gradual tissue deformation and thus at times be dangerous. In addition, because PNF exercises were designed to be done with a partner for the best results, they should be performed with a knowledgeable and experienced professional.

FACTORS AFFECTING FLEXIBILITY

Clearly, different stretching techniques produce different results. There are also a number of additional factors specific to each client that contribute to the success or failure of a fitness program.

Age and Inactivity

Several studies have indicated there is a distinct relationship between age and degree of flexibility. Developmentally, the greatest increase in flexibility usually occurs up to and between the ages of 7 and 12. During early adolescence, flexibility tends to level off and thereafter begins to decline. After the age of 25, normal aging tends to accelerate, causing significant changes in connective tissue and eventually decreased extensibility. Aging increases both the diameter of collagen fibers and the number of intermolecular cross-links (Alter, 1988)

Figure 9-8 Proprioceptive neuromuscular facilitation (PNF): contraction followed by relaxation and slow, passive stretch.

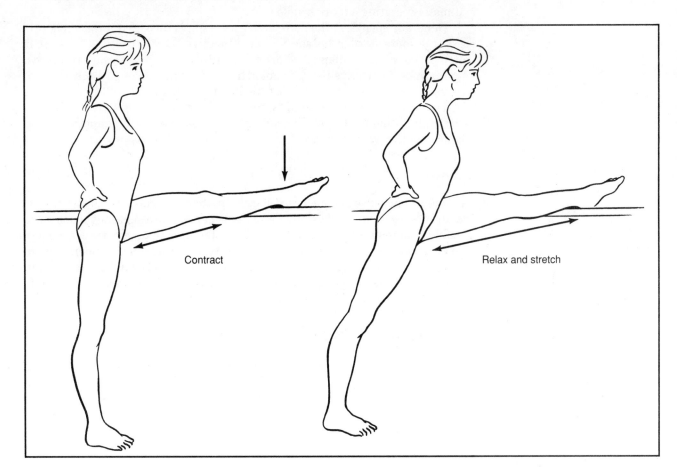

Contract

Relax and stretch

PERSONAL TRAINER MANUAL

Figure 9–9 Age-related changes in collagen fibers. (a) Normal collagen fiber; (b) Age-related collagen fiber crosslinks; (c) Newly synthesized fiber, the result of aging.

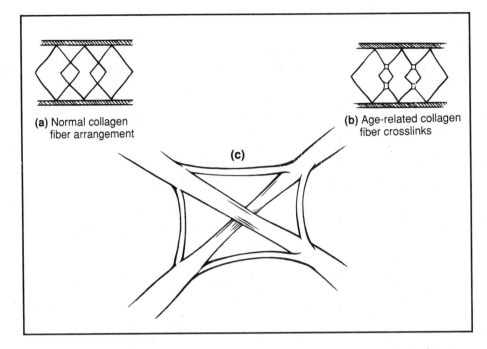

(a) Normal collagen fiber arrangement

(b) Age-related collagen fiber crosslinks

(c)

(Fig. 9–9). This age-related effect strengthens connective tissue bonds, further increasing the resistance to deformation. A fair amount of dehydration in and around soft tissue structures also occurs as one ages. This lack of water to soft tissue structures diminishes lubrication and the flow of nutrients to the site, ultimately creating a more fragile unit.

Generally speaking, the more active a person is throughout the aging process, the more flexible he/she will be. Inactivity, or **hypokinesis**, as it is often called, permits adaptive shortening within connective tissue structures. Again, when connective tissue is not actively stretched through a full range of motion, it becomes shorter and less resilient, making it difficult to obtain the good muscular balance essential for proper alignment during activity. Regular stretching throughout one's life can enhance positive tissue adaptability and reduce natural wear and tear.

Gender

Although conclusive evidence is still lacking, there appears to be a strong gender difference related to flexibility potential. Females are generally much more flexible than males. One hypothesis for this factor is that, genetically, women are designed for a greater range of flexibility, especially in the pelvic region, in order to accommodate childbearing. A second aspect may be attributed to circulation of the hormone relaxin during pregnancy, which relaxes ligaments for greater range of motion (Alter, 1988).

Body Type and Strength Training

Many attempts have been made to relate body type and flexibility. For example, an underweight fragile body type (**ectomorph**) would have greater flexibility than a heavier, over-developed, or massive body type (**endomorph**). However, in recent studies, there has been little correlation between weight and body type and the ability to achieve range of motion.

Strength training is an area where misconceptions concerning flexibility continue to exist. Many still believe that weight training causes a muscle-bound body type that lacks overall flexibility. It is true that overdeveloping muscles may encourage muscular imbalances if stretching is not incorporated into the training program, but the perception that strength training independently decreases flexibility remains a myth. The 1976 U.S. Olympic weightlifting team ranked second only to gymnasts in joint range of motion testing.

It is important to remember that flexibility has been consistently shown to be highly specific to the individual, to the activity, and to each joint. Since each person has different musculature, joint structure, and genetic composition, trainers must create programs that are individual to each client. Flexibility is not necessarily an underlying characteristic of each person, but it is an essential component of physical fitness.

Warm-up

A warm-up is a slow, rhythmic exercise of larger muscle groups done before an activity, which provides the body with a period of adjustment between rest and performance of that activity. Generally, warm-up prepares the body for what is about to come. Scientists agree that by imitating an exercise activity for a period of 5–15 minutes before high-intensity involvement, overall performance will be heightened. This technique gradually warms tissues, increasing blood flow and nutrients to active structures. Warm-up may also fine-tune CNS receptors to improve **kinesthetic awareness** during activity. (That is, sensory organs within muscles, tendons, and joints facilitate our ability to know where we are in space during an activity.) This kinesthetic awareness helps prepare our bodies for activity, so that we gain a certain amount of protection and psychological readiness necessary for reducing potential injuries. Warm-up can be used to prepare soft tissue structures for the flexibility necessary for any particular activity.

PRINCIPLES OF STRETCHING

Although there is continuing controversy over which flexibility exercises are best, whether to stretch before or after exercise, or just how much to stretch, professionals currently agree on certain guidelines which should be incorporated into a client's fitness program. Most experts recommend stretching both before and after intense activity, but each for different reasons. In preparation for activity, pre-stretch is primarily active and aimed at improving dynamic flexibility. As body temperature increases and tissues offer less resistance, passive stretching of the muscles used most in an activity, and thus most likely to be injured, should be emphasized. For example, an aerobic dance participant would statically stretch hamstrings and calves during warm-up, while a tennis player might stretch forearm and shoulder muscles.

After more intense exercise, muscles may adapt to a shortened position due to repetitive contractions. Stretching after exercise will ensure muscle relaxation, facilitating normal resting length, circulation to structures, and removal of unwanted waste products. Body core temperature is also found to be highest just after the aerobic or more intense portions of training programs. For these reasons and in order to achieve maximum gains in range of motion, it is logical and highly recommended to include static stretching exercises at this stage.

How often one should stretch is still not fully understood. Professionals seem to agree, however, that daily stretching is best, or at least before and after activity sessions. In a Swedish study, Wallin et al. (1985) found that once subjects had attained optimal flexibility, stretching just one to two times per week would maintain those ranges. However, when stretching was incorporated three to five times per week after attainment, range of motion was augmented further. In other words, frequent stretching increases the likelihood of avoiding muscular imbalances created by daily activities or exercise.

A trainer designing a stretching program for a client should keep the following in mind:

1. Connective tissue elongation (plastic deformation) is the primary target when stretching.

2. The two most important factors influencing stretching are intensity and duration. A low-intensity, long-duration stretch favors more lasting plastic tissue deformation. A high-intensity, short-duration stretch favors a more temporary elastic tissue deformation.

3. Elevated tissue temperature facilitates range of motion.

4. Flexibility is specific; therefore exercises must be specific to each joint and/or muscle group.

5. Proper alignment for each stretch is critical in achieving maximum effectiveness in any one specific muscle group. In addition, creating a good relationship of one joint to another during exercise and emphasizing postural balance places muscles in positions to absorb shock effectively, ultimately decreasing stress to underlying soft tissue structures.

FLEXIBILITY EXERCISES

A client would benefit most by regularly performing all 16 exercises in Figures 9-10 through 9-15, which emphasize major muscle groups important in postural correction as well as individual sports activities. Figure 9-16 indicates contraindicated exercise that should be avoided. If there are time constraints, the trainer's first priority should be to target a client's individual needs based on flexibility assessments (see Chapter 6). In addition, if a client has overworked a specific muscle group during exercise or daily activities, include a series of stretches addressing that area at the end of the session. Finally, it is important to include exercises addressing a client's chronically tight areas, such as hamstrings, calves, posterior neck, anterior shoulder, and low-back musculature.

Figure 9–10 Stretches for the neck or cervical spine. (a) *Neck extensor stretch*: Slowly bend head forward, bringing chin to chest. Clasp hands behind the head and allow the weight of the hands to stretch the back of the neck. (b) *Neck sidebend/rotation combination stretch*: With left arm at side and shoulder depressed, slowly bend the chin to chest and turn toward right shoulder. Using only the weight of the hand, stretch away from left shoulder. Repeat for left side.

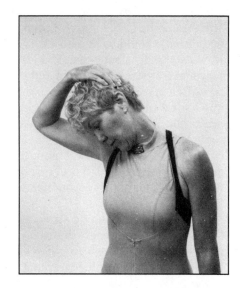

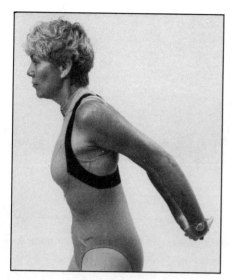

Figure 9–11   Stretches for the shoulder. (a) *Anterior shoulder stretch (pectoralis stretch)*: Grasp hands behind back. Keeping elbows slightly bent, gently push arms upward. (b) *Posterior shoulder stretch*: Place left hand on right sholder. With elbow up and parallel to the floor, use the right hand to apply gentle pressure above the elbow and toward the body. Repeat for right side.

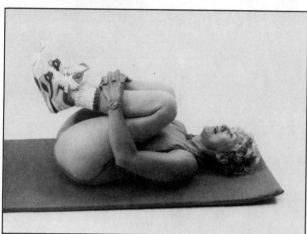

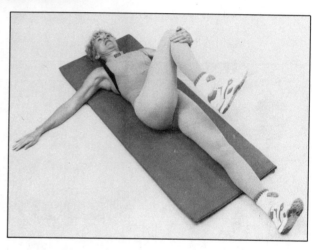

Figure 9–12   Stretches for the low back. (a) *Double knee to chest:* On back, with knees bent, gently pull both knees toward chest, lifting feet off the floor, hold and relax. This exercise may also be done using one leg.

Figure 9–12   (b) *Figure-four stretch (piriformis stretch):* On back, with head down, flex right knee across the body and pull toward left shoulder. Repeat for left side.

Figure 9–12   (c) *Cat/cow stretch:* On hands and knees, sag back, lifting head up. Arch back, head down. Keeping head down, lean back onto heels and hold.

Figure 9–12 (cont.) (c) *Cat/cow stretch*

Figure 9–12   (d) *Press-up:* On stomach, place hands as if to do a push-up. Lift upper body, keeping hips and lower body on the floor. Perform this exercise in a pain-free range only, do not cause pain.

Figure 9–13   Stretches for the hip and groin. (a) *Hip flexor stretch (lunge):* Assume lunge position, making sure front knee is directly over the foot and ankle. With weight supported by both hands, press hips toward floor.

Figure 9–13   (b) *Groin stretch (butterfly):* Sitting erect with soles of feet together, gently pull heels toward groin and press inside of knees toward floor.

Figure 9–14   Stretches for the knee.   (a) *Quadriceps stretch (prone):* On stomach, reach back with right hand and grasp ankle. Repeat on left. May use a towel to insure alignment.

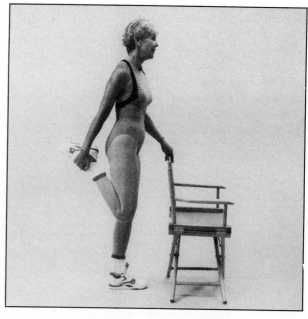

Figure 9–14   (b) *Quadriceps stretch (standing):* Using a wall or chair as support, reach back with the right hand and grasp right ankle. Be sure hips are forward and knees are adjacent to each other. Repeat on left.

Figure 9–14   (c) *Hamstrings stretch (straight leg raise):* On back, with knees bent and feet flat on floor, raise the right leg without lifting hips from the floor. Repeat on the left. Grasp the leg below the knee to increase the stretch.

Figure 9–14 (d) *Hamstrings stretch (standing)*: With right leg on raised surface and back straight, lean chest toward the right knee, keeping back straight.

Figure 9–15 Stretches for the calf. (a) *Gastrocnemius stretch*: Using the wall or a chair as support, place one foot behind the other. With front knee slightly bent, back knee straight and heel down, lean hips forward, stretching back leg. Repeat on opposite side. (b) *Soleus stretch*: Using the wall or a chair as support, place one foot behind the other. With both knees bent and heels down, lean hips forward, stretching back leg. Repeat on opposite side.

Figure 9–16   Contraindicated exercises. (a) *Yoga plow* places excessive stress on cervical spine. (b) *Spinal flexion, legs straight with twist*, places excessive stress on lumbar structures. (c) *Low-back hyperextension (standing position)* compresses lumbar discs.

Figure 9–16 (cont.)
(d) *Deep squat* increases wear and tear on knee joint. (e) *Hurdler's stretch* overstretches ligaments on bent knee. (f) *Kneeling quadriceps stretch* causes excessive pressure to knee joint. (g) *Neck hyper-extension (full neck rotations)* increases compression to cervical discs and may accelerate wear and tear to the spine.

SUMMARY

Although its role in fitness is not as well-documented scientifically as that of other components, flexibility is an essential part of a well-balanced exercise program. To understand the effects of various stretching techniques, a trainer needs to understand the mechanics and neurophysiology of flexibility. Most professionals agree that of the three major types of stretching—static, ballistic, and PNF—static stretching is most beneficial and least likely to cause injury. A static stretch is a low-intensity, long-duration stretch that favors more lasting connective tissue elongation (plastic deformation). Ideally, a client should stretch daily. The trainer can at least see that the client stretches both before and after an exercise session. Because age, gender, level of activity, and type of activity play a role in achieving and maintaining full and normal range of motion, it is important that the trainer design a stretching program to meet the assessed needs of each client.

REFERENCES

Alter, M.J. (1988). *Science of stretching*. Champaign, IL: Human Kinetics.

Astrand, O., & Rodahl, K. (1970). *Testbook of work physiology*. New York: McGraw-Hill.

DeVries, H.A. (1980). *Physiology of exercise for physical education* (3rd ed.). Dubuque, IA: William C. Brown.

Hubley-Kozey, C., & Stanish, W. (1984). Can stretching prevent athletic injuries? *Journal of Musculoskeletal Medicine, 9,* 25-32.

Kendall, H., Kendall, F., & Wadsworth, G. (1971). *Muscles: Testing and function* (2nd ed.). Baltimore: Williams & Wilkins.

Moore, M., & Hutton, R. (1980). Electromyographic investigation of muscle stretching techniques. *Medicine and Science in Sports and Exercise, 12,* 322- 329.

Sapega, A., Quedenfeld, T., Moyer, R., & Butler, R. (1981). Biophysical factors in range-of-motion exercise. *Physician and Sportsmedicine, 9,* 57-64.

Schultz, P. (1979). Flexibility: Day of the static stretch. *Physician and Sportsmedicine, 7,* 109-117.

Voss, D., Ionta, M., & Myers, B. (1985). *Proprioceptive neuromuscular facilitation: Patterns and techniques* (3rd ed.). Philadelphia: Harper & Row.

Wallin, D., Ekblom, B., Grahn, R., & Nordenberg, T. (1985). Improvement of muscle flexibility: A comparison betwen two techniques. *American Journal of Sports Medicine, 13,* 263-268.

SUGGESTED READING

Anderson, B. *Stretching*. (1980). Bolinas, CA: Shelter Publications.

Francis, P., & Francis, L. (1988). *If it hurts, don't do it*. Rocklin, CA: Prima Publishing.

Wirhed, R. (1984). *Athletic ability and the anatomy of motion*. London: Wolfe Medical Publications.

Weight Control

Dorie Krepton

10

Dorie Krepton, M.S., is an exercise nutritionist and professor in the Kinesiology–Physical Education Department at California State University, Hayward. She teaches courses in nutrition and performance and a wide spectrum of aerobic classes. Professor Krepton has written numerous articles on health and fitness and is the co-author of *Everybody's Aerobic Book* and the author of *Aqua Aerobics: The Ultimate Workout*. As the founder of the Health and Fitness Institute, she conducts certification clinics and educational seminars.

IN THIS CHAPTER:

- Energy balance: including factors determining basal metabolic rate (BMR), and how to determine it.

- The energy requirements of physical activity: including formulas for estimating caloric needs of activity, and the thermic effect of food (TEF).

- Understanding body weight: the use of height–weight charts and bathroom scales; body composition and methods for measuring it.

- Obesity: genetic, psychological, and physiological factors.

- Extreme approaches to weight loss: anorexia nervosa, bulimia, fasting, special clothing and body wraps, spot reducing, cellulite, diet pills/drugs, surgery, vibrating belts and muscle stimulators, and fad diets.

- Planning a successful weight-control program.

- Planning a successful weight-gain program.

Energy is essential to all forms of life. The human body continually uses energy, even during rest, to digest food, to form hormones, to create nerve impulses, to regenerate tissues, to aid enzyme function, and in a host of other physiological processes. Just as gasoline (fuel) provides energy for a car, so food (fuel) provides energy for the body.

Food energy, both in its consumption and in its expenditure, is measured in terms of heat equivalents, called **calories**. One *small calorie* represents the amount of heat energy needed to raise the temperature of one gram of water by 1°C; it is sometimes called the *gram calorie*. A *large calorie*, or *kilocalorie* (kcal) equals 1,000 small calories and is the amount of heat energy needed to raise the temperature of 1,000 grams of water by 1°C (*calor* means "heat"; *kilo* means "1,000").

295

ENERGY BALANCE

The amount of energy a particular food has depends on how much carbohydrate, protein, and fat it contains. Practically all foods contain mixtures of all three of these nutrients, although they are sometimes classed by the predominant nutrient. A protein-rich food such as beef actually contains a lot of fat as well as protein; a carbohydrate-rich food such as corn also contains fat and protein. One gram of each of the following three nutrients yields the following calories:

1 gram of carbohydrate = 4 kcal
1 gram of protein = 4 kcal
1 gram of fat = 9 kcal

Like any well-designed machine, the body can store energy for future use. The primary means of storage is fat, or adipose tissue, which lies under the skin and surrounds the internal organs. Think of fat and its potential calories as the body's gas tank. But unlike a gas tank, the body's capacity to accumulate an energy reserve is almost limitless. Calories consumed in excess of the body's immediate needs are stored in fat deposits.

Weight control is a question of energy balance. For body weight to remain stable, there must be a balance between intake and output of calories. During the growth and development years of childhood and adolescence, intake predominates slightly, creating a positive energy balance and a growth of body mass. As the adolescent enters young adulthood, the major growth processes are just about complete, and so dietary intake and metabolic output must be equal to maintain body weight. If output predominates, the client will lose weight—a condition of negative caloric balance. If intake is greater, a positive caloric balance exists, and the client will gain weight.

Energy in = Energy expended = Weight stable
Energy in > Energy expended = Weight gain
Energy in < Energy expended = Weight loss

Trainers need to be aware that small, regular increases in daily caloric intake can markedly affect a client's weight. For example, an extra doughnut a day (125 calories) can lead to an increase of about 13 pounds of body weight in a year. As little as 25 extra calories consumed a day—the amount in a tablespoon of ice cream or one plain graham cracker—adds up to 175 calories a week, or a total of 9,100 calories a year. That's enough to add 2.6 pounds a year, or 26 pounds in a decade. Every 3,500 calories consumed above and beyond energy needs equals a gain of one pound of body-fat, and every 3,500 calories spent beyond energy intake equals a loss of one pound of body-fat. Trainers with a clear understanding of (1) basal metabolic rate (BMR), (2) physical activity, and (3) food digestion (thermic effect of food) will be able to assist clients in designing effective weight-control programs.

BASAL METABOLIC RATE (BMR)

Most of the body's energy, about 60–70 percent, goes to support the ongoing metabolic work of the body's cells, the **basal metabolic rate**, or simply the BMR. This continual work of the body includes the beating of the heart, respiration, and the maintenance of body temperature. The energy needs for these processes must be met before any calories can be used for physical activity or food digestion. A client who needs a total of 2,000 calories a day will expend as many as 1,200–1,400 of them to support the BMR.

Factors Affecting Basal Metabolic Rate

A person's BMR is influenced by a number of factors, including age, height, gender, environmental temperature, exercise, and diet.

AGE.   In general, the younger the client, the higher the BMR. Because of the increased activity of cells undergoing division, the BMR is highest during the growth spurts that take place during childhood, adolescence, and pregnancy. The BMR peaks at age 20 for both males and females, then decreases by 2 percent per decade throughout life. For example, at age 30 the BMR operates at 98-percent efficiency; at age 40, at 96 percent. The decline in BMR in adults may also be partially attributed to inactivity and the subsequent loss of muscle tissue (Williams, 1988).

HEIGHT.   The greater a client's amount of body surface the faster the metabolism. Tall, thin people have higher BMRs. For example, for two people of different shape but of the same weight, the shorter, stocky person will have a slower metabolic rate than the taller, thinner person. The lean client metabolizes 1.26 calories per minutes (cal/min), the plump one 1.16 calories per minute. Assuming their caloric consumption is the same, this difference of 0.10 calories yields an excess of six calories per hour, 144 calories per day, 1 pound every 24 days, and 15 pounds per year.

GENDER.   Because of the greater percentage of lean tissue in the male body, men generally have a 10–15 percent faster metabolic rate than women. Lean tissue uses more calories than fat tissue. Muscle tissue is metabolically highly active even when at rest, whereas fat tissue is comparatively inactive metabolically. An increase in muscle mass, for both males and females, elevates the BMR. Conversely, the more fat tissue, the lower the BMR. Thus, the lean mass of the body is the major influence on the body's energy requirements and nutrient needs. Recent research (Williams, 1989) has shown that gender is not a significant factor in determining the BMR in well-trained athletes. When body weight is made up of a higher proportion of muscle mass, the energy requirement for the body increases. When body weight is made up of a higher proportion of fat or bone, the energy requirement decreases. The fact remains that women do exhibit a lower BMR. However, this is due to a smaller proportion of muscle mass to fat rather than gender. This direct relationship between lean body mass and the elevation of the BMR points to the importance of strength training for a weight-loss program. Regular strength training can have a positive effect on the development and the protection of lean body mass.

FASTING AND DIETING.   A client's metabolic rate can drop as low as 20 percent during fasting or dieting. This drop is due to the loss of lean tissues as well as to the body's effort to conserve energy by slowing down the BMR. This slowing down of the metabolism seems to be a protective mechanism to conserve fat stores when there is a food shortage, and it hampers weight loss in a person who fasts or undertakes a very low-calorie diet (less than 1,000 kcal/day).

ENVIRONMENTAL TEMPERATURE.   Both heat and cold raise the body's BMR. Persons living in a tropical climate generally have metabolisms 5–20 percent higher than those living in more temperate areas. Exercising in the heat also raises BMR. Muscular shivering in colder climates can increase BMR.

EXERCISE. Several studies have evaluated the effect of exercise on increasing the BMR. In general, depending upon the intensity and duration, exercise can increase the BMR, and the metabolic rate may remain elevated for several hours after high-intensity activity (Getchell, 1983). On the other hand, some investigators find no relationship between exercise and BMR (Frankle & Yang, 1988). We will have to wait for additional research to fully evaluate the role of exercise on BMR. Currently, the major way to elevate BMR is to increase lean body mass. Adding some form of regular exercise can contribute to this goal.

Determining BMR

An average 20-year-old adult male of 150 pounds burns 1,800 calories a day to sustain BMR, and the average 20-year-old female of 120 pounds burns 1,320 calories a day to sustain BMR. Here is a simple formula for calculating BMR (Deutsch, 1980):

Adult Males. Multiply client's weight by 10; add double the client's weight to this value. For example, for a 150-lb male:

$$1,500 + (2 \times 150) = 1,800 \text{ cal/day BMR}$$

Adult Females. Multiply client's weight by 10; add the client's weight to this value. For example, for a 120-lb female:

$$1,200 + 120 = 1,320 \text{ cal/day BMR}$$

After age 20, BMR should be lowered by 2 percent per decade. That is, estimated BMR should be lowered by 2 percent for clients in their 30s, 4 percent for those in their 40s, 6 percent for those in their 50s, and so on.

PHYSICAL ACTIVITY

Physical activity has a profound effect on human energy expenditure and contributes 20–30 percent to the body's total energy output. During sustained, large-muscle exercises like running and swimming, clients can generate metabolic rates that are 10 times above their resting values. The number of calories needed for an activity depends entirely on the involvement of the muscles. The greater the amount of muscle mass used, the heavier the weight being moved, and the longer the duration of the activity, the more calories burned.

Energy Requirements of Physical Activity.

Estimates for the number of calories (energy) used during physical activity are based on experiments that measure the amount of oxygen consumed during a specific bout of exercise. There is a rather linear relationship between exercise intensity and oxygen uptake. As the intensity level of work increases, so does the amount of oxygen consumed and, therefore, the number of calories expended.

Body size also plays an important role with respect to the energy requirements during exercise. The total energy or calories expended by a heavier client is considerably more than that of a lighter client.

Since energy requirements are affected by both the duration of the activity and the body weight of the participant, both these factors should be taken into account. The energy costs of various activities can be roughly calculated by using the Energy Expenditure values presented in Table 10–1.

Example: What is the energy requirement for a 150-pound individual to walk at a 16 min/mile pace for 30 minutes?

1. Convert lb weight to kg weight.

150 lb ÷ 2.2 lb/kg = 68 kg

2. Multiply the Energy Expenditure by the body weight (kg).

0.08 kcal/min/kg × 68 kg = 5.44 kcals/min

3. Multiply the energy expenditure per minute by the number of minutes.

5.44 kcals/min × 30 min = 163 kcals

Table 10–1   ENERGY EXPENDITURE DURING ACTIVITIES

ACTIVITIES	ENERGY EXPENDITURE (kcal/min/kg)	APPROXIMATE CALORIC EXPENDITURE 30 MINUTES OF ACTIVITY		
		110lb/50kg	150lb/68kg	190lb/86kg
Badminton	0.06	90	122	155
Basketball	0.14	210	286	361
Boxing	0.22	330	449	568
Canoeing				
Leisure	0.04	60	82	103
Racing	0.10	150	204	258
Dancing				
Ballroom	0.05	75	102	129
Choreographed (vigorous)	0.17	255	347	439
Golf	0.09	135	184	232
Running				
9 min/mile	0.19	285	388	490
8 min/mile	0.22	330	449	568
7 min/mile	0.24	360	490	619
6 min/mile	0.28	420	571	722
Swimming				
Crawl fast	0.16	240	326	413
Crawl slow	0.13	195	265	335
Tennis (singles)	0.11	165	224	284
Volleyball	0.05	75	102	129
Walking (level)				
16 min/mile	0.08	120	163	206
20 min/mile	0.07	105	143	181

Adapted from: American College of Sports Medicine: *Guidelines for exercise testing and prescription*, **4th ed. Philadelphia: Lea & Febiger, 1991.**

Table 10-1 provides examples of the energy requirements for individuals weighing 110, 150, and 190 pounds. However, the formulas above can be used to determine approximations for any weight individual.

MET METHOD. Another means for measuring physical energy expenditure is the **MET system** (metabolic energy cost of activities). A **MET** is a unit of oxygen expended, with 1 MET being the energy needed while the body is in a resting state. Classifying an activity at 7 METS, for instance, means it requires seven times more energy than does a state of rest (see Table 10-2). In a strict sense, the energy expenditure during exercise depends on the client's body weight: A heavier client would have a larger resting VO_2 than would a lighter one. The MET method allows trainers to measure the energy expenditure of clients during varying levels of physical activity based on total body weight.

Formula: Calories = Body weight × Oxygen consumption × Activity intensity

1 MET = 3.5 ml O_2/kg/min (amount of oxygen consumed during rest)

1 liter (1,000 ml) O_2 consumed = 5 kcal

Example: What are the energy needs of a 100-pound client walking at 4 mph (5 METS) for 30 minutes?

1. Change body weight from pounds to kilograms: Since 1 kg = 2.2 lb, then

$$100 \text{ lb} \times \frac{1 \text{ kg}}{2.2 \text{lb}} = 45.4 \text{ kg}$$

2. Determine *oxygen cost consumption* at rest per minute by multiplying body weight (in kg) by oxygen cost equivalent:

$$45.4 \text{ kg} \times \frac{3.5 \text{ ml } O_2}{1 \text{kg} / \text{min}} = 159 \text{ ml } O_2/\text{min (1 MET)}$$

3. To get calorie cost, multiply the volume of O_2 by the number of calories per liter (or per 1,000 ml):

$$\frac{159 \text{ ml } O_2}{\text{min}} \times \frac{5 \text{ kcals}}{1,000 \text{ ml } O_2} = \frac{0.795 \text{ kcal}}{\text{min}}$$

4. To determine the approximate total caloric cost for the activity, multiply the kcals per minute by the intensity level (MET level):

$$\frac{0.795 \text{ kcal}}{\text{min}} \times 30 \text{ min} \times 5 \text{ (MET level)} = 120 \text{ kcal}$$

The same client working out at a MET level of 10 for 30 minutes would burn up twice as much energy (240 kcals), and so would the client who continued walking for 60 minutes at the 5-MET level.

There are two factors for trainers to consider in recommending exercise. One is the amount of time it takes, the other is the intensity of the effort. Both factors can vary considerably. For example, two people of the same body size could expend an equal amount of energy performing the same task, one

Table 10–2   COMMON ACTIVITIES GROUPED ACCORDING TO RELATIVE METABOLIC COST

MET Cost	Activity
0.85	Sleeping
1	Awake, resting quietly, reading, watching TV
1.5	Any moving, sitting activity such as eating, writing, sewing, typing, knitting, desk work, driving; also, stationary standing such as showering, dressing
2	Light moving, standing activity, such as cooking, strolling, and light housework
3	Level walking (2.5 mph), cycling (5.5 mph), social dancing, archery, sailing, bowling, golf (using cart), heavy housework
4	Walking (3 mph), cycling (8 mph), badminton singles, tennis doubles, raking leaves, many calisthenics
5	Walking (4 mph), cycling (10 mph), ice or roller skating, digging in garden, shoveling light earth
6	Walking (5 mph), cycling (11 mph), tennis singles, splitting wood, shoveling snow, square dancing
7	Jogging (5 mph), cycling (12 mph), basketball, mountain climbing, canoeing (5 mph), touch football, paddleball
8	Running (5.5 mph), cycling (13 mph), basketball (vigorous), fencing, handball (social), squash (social)
9	Competitive handball or racquetball, ski touring (4.5 mph)
10	Running (6 mph), shoveling 10 shovelfuls per minute (15 lb)

Source: **Adapted from Samuel M. Fox, et al. (1972). Physical activity and cardiovascular health. In *Modern Concepts of Cardiovascular Disease*, pp. 27–28. New York: American Heart Association. Used by permission.**

exerting extreme effort over a short period, the other exerting less effort over a longer period. For example, one client could run the stairs at maximum speed, expending 30 calories in one minute, while the other could move more leisurely, taking two minutes to expend 30 calories. The basic difference in achieving the same output is the time taken and the intensity of the activity. Because these two factors are so closely related, the trainer will often have to adjust one to the other. For instance, high-intensity activity should usually be limited in duration, because fatigue sets in more quickly. The less demanding the activity, the longer the training session can be for the client to achieve the same calorie expenditure.

Food Assimilation: Thermic Effect of Food (TEF)

The third component of energy expenditure has to do with managing food. When food is taken into the body, metabolism (energy expenditure) is increased. The smooth muscles of the intestines speed up their rhythmic contraction to move food through the digestive tract. Specialized cells that manufacture and secrete digestive enzymes increase their output. All these cells, and others, need extra energy to participate in digestion, absorption, and metabolism of food. This assimilation process (digestion) is generally thought to use about 10 percent of the total food energy consumed. The increase in energy required to digest food is referred to as the **thermic effect of food (TEF)**.

FORMULA FOR ESTIMATING TEF. Have the client record food intake for a day and then approximate the total calories. The energy cost of metabolizing food is approximately 10 percent of the total calories in the food consumed. For example, for a total daily food consumption of 2,000 calories:

TEF = Total kcals consumed × 10%
2,000 kcal × 0.10 = 200 kcal

A typical breakdown of the total energy spent by a moderately active male weighing 150 pounds would look like this:

Basal metabolism	1,800 cal
Physical activity	450 cal
Assimilating 2,500 kcal of food	250 cal
Total:	2,500 cal

UNDERSTANDING BODY WEIGHT

Over the course of many thousands of years of human history, survival demanded continual exercise and energy expenditure. Now, over the course of only a few generations, we have come to live in a very different, highly technological society, with a life-style that demands little if any physical activity. Such inactivity has contributed to a host of modern ills, including heart disease, diabetes, hypertension, and widespread **obesity**.

Obesity is one of America's major health problems. It is estimated by the National Center for Health Statistics that over 34 million adults in the United States are obese. Over the past 80 years, Americans on the average have been getting fatter. The prevalence of obesity is generally agreed by researchers to have almost doubled since 1900. Today, the United States leads the world in obesity. The typical overweight person at age 50 has put on one to two pounds each year since age 20—and it shows. Scientists have been studying body composition for the past 40 years, and they believe that body-fat analysis, a method that singles out an individual's level of body-fat, may be a more reliable index of health than is mere body weight, which can't differentiate among a body's fat, muscle, fluid, and bones.

HEIGHT–WEIGHT CHARTS

The standard Metropolitan Life Insurance height–weight charts are not reliable guides for trainers to use in determining whether a client possesses normal body weight for a given age and gender. Since these tables were compiled by measuring a limited population and using distribution curves to establish normality, there are large discrepancies in the norms. According to the height–weight charts, it is possible to be heavy and even overweight yet possess only a moderate amount of body-fat. Many individuals who are muscular are otherwise lean in overall body composition. The distinction is important. For example, a football player can be markedly "overweight" according to the height–weight charts. That is, he can weigh considerably more than the average man of the same height, but much of his greater weight is not fat but muscle tissue. At best, the height–weight charts are just the averages of what others weigh rather than realistic weights for specific individuals. Also, the charts are too liberal in weight variances, especially for young adults, and are often inadequate guides to assessing body leanness. Furthermore, most of the charts allow small increments in body weight with increasing age, a practice that lacks justification. We know that as an individual grows older there is a reduction in total body weight even with an increase in body-fat. This is largely due to the reduction in the quantity of muscle mass as the body ages. Even with all their limitations, however, the tables can be used to draw arbitrary lines between too much and too little body weight. Also, they can help identify the very overweight client when the trainer lacks access to more accurate methods of measuring body-fat.

BATHROOM SCALES

You've often heard it said that you can't judge a book by its cover, so why do individuals attempt to evaluate their body's healthiness by its outward appearance? Unfortunately, many clients have been led to believe that the bathroom scale, which measures total body weight—muscle, organs, bone, and water—is an indicator of good health. However, the scale cannot differentiate between fat pounds and muscle pounds. Clients assume that a loss in scale weight represents a loss in fat. Unmistakably, it is the percentage of fat tissue in the body rather than scale weight that determines good health and fitness.

BODY COMPOSITION

Trainers can be of great assistance to their clients by dispelling the myths regarding body-weight measurements as an indicator of good health. Clients need to know about their **body composition**, that is, how much of their body weight comes from fat mass and how much comes from lean body mass. **Lean body mass**, the major component of active fat-free tissue, is mainly muscle. It accounts for 30–65 percent of the body's total weight. This lean mass is the primary determinant of the body's BMR, and is the major influence on the client's energy requirements and nutrient needs. When a client gains or loses

Table 10–3   NORMS FOR BODY-FAT

CLASSIFICATION	MALE	FEMALE
Very lean	<8%	<15%
Healthy	8–12%	18–22%
Obese	20% and higher	30% and higher

Source: Data from Williams, M. (1988). *Nutrition for fitness and sport* (2nd ed.). Dubuque, IA: Wm C. Brown.

weight owing to dietary changes alone, the loss reflects changes not only in body-fat but also in lean body mass. Table 10–3 presents norms for body-fat. For more detailed information on body composition, see Chapter 6.

ENERGY IMBALANCES: OBESITY

With an increased knowledge of obesity and the factors that contribute to its development, the trainer will be able to assist the client in designing an effective weight-control program. The term **overweight** refers to individuals with body weight 10 percent in excess of the standard height–weight tables. Body weight more than 20 percent over standard is designated as **obese** (Whitney & Hamilton, 1984). In relation to health, however, the term **overfat** would be a more correct designation, because it refers to the percentage of excess body-fat. Experts in the field now define obesity as an excess of body-fat frequently resulting in a significant impairment of health. The excess fat is the end result of an imbalance between the number of calories consumed and the number of calories expended to sustain basal needs and daily activities. Until recently it was believed that the major cause of weight gain and obesity was simply overeating, and that the simplest way to reduce body-fat would be to decrease food intake. However, there are other factors that complicate the obesity issue, including genetic, psychological, and physiological concerns.

GENETIC FACTORS

There is increasing evidence that genetic inheritance probably influences a person's chances of becoming fat more than any other basic factor. Within families, if one parent is obese, an individual has a 40 percent chance of becoming obese. This rises to 80 percent if both parents are obese, and dwindles to 14 percent if neither parent is obese. Studies of twins separated at birth even show that genetic makeup is more important than environment in producing obesity.

PSYCHOLOGICAL FACTORS

Some of our deepest associations with food are emotional. Holidays and social gatherings are interwoven with food and good times. To show love and affection, a person might bake someone's favorite cookies or prepare a special meal. Some people eat more after disappointments or rejections. Using food in this manner, that is, as a means of reestablishing emotional equilibrium, can cause weight gain. What is important for trainers to recognize here is that all food habits are intimately tied up with the client's entire way of life.

PHYSIOLOGICAL FACTORS

FAT CELLS. We are all born with a predetermined number of fat cells. Heredity is the primary factor controlling the number of fat cells in the body, with females inheriting more fat cells than males. In early life, genetic and nutritional factors seem to influence the number of fat cells we gain. It was first thought that after adolescence, only the size and not the number of fat cells could increase to cause obesity. But evidence by Hirsh and Knittle (1970) indicates severe obesity can cause fat cells to proliferate even in adulthood.

BROWN AND WHITE CELLS. There are two types of fat cells in the body— brown and white. **Brown fat cells**, which make up about 1-2 percent of body fat, are metabolically active and are found above the kidneys, surrounding the heart, and between the shoulder blades. Brown fat burns energy like a radiator and serves to regulate body temperature. Brown fat cells contain a high amount of iron and hemoglobin, which are found in red blood cells. However, instead of storing fat, brown fat cells have the capacity to produce as much as 25-50 percent of the body's heat by burning fat. Recent research on the obese has shown that they have less active brown fat. This may be one of the subtle factors that cause the obese not to burn energy as efficiently as others, while other people simply do not gain weight.

The other 98-99 percent of body-fat is composed of **white fat cells**. This is the storage form of fat, the fat we can see on hips and buttocks. The number of white fat cells can be altered during childhood and adolescence. Excessive caloric intake and inactivity tends to promote production of white fat cells in these formative years.

SET-POINT. Several researchers have proposed that the body has an internal control mechanism that drives it to maintain a particular level of body-fat (Keys et al., 1950). This **set-point theory** assumes an individual metabolic regulation of body-fat. The set-point mechanism acts much like a thermostat, turning energy expenditure up or down to avoid either weight gain or weight loss. The weight-regulating mechanism directs the body to maintain the set-point weight when dieting threatens its stability. That is, when clients restrict caloric intake, the body attempts to maintain its weight and fat by lowering the metabolic rate; conversely, the body will lose weight gained in excess of its internally regulated point by increasing metabolism. This may explain why some clients can lie in bed all day and never gain an ounce while others have to exercise a great deal in order not to gain weight. The major way of manipulating the set-point is by increasing exercise, thereby programming the body to store less fat.

EXTREME APPROACHES TO WEIGHT LOSS

Eating disorders typically begin with failed attempts at weight loss through dieting, often with rigid fad diets, unsafe diet gimmicks, and arbitrary weight goals. Affected individuals eventually believe that the combination of severe dietary restriction, excessive exercise, and/or binge-and-purge behavior is the ultimate solution to the problem of weight control. Instead, the pattern of abnormal eating becomes impossible to control, and the clients believe they cannot put a stop to the behavior. Anorexia nervosa and bulimia are eating disorders that are most common among women, but men, especially obligatory runners, may suffer from them as well.

Anorexia Nervosa

Anorexia nervosa is a serious and potentially fatal eating disorder. A typical case involves a young female client who becomes obsessed with the idea that she is fat and uses self-denial as a means of controlling her weight. This starvation approach is then carried to an extreme of undernourishment at which total body weight may reach 70 pounds or less. This condition can become life-threatening, eventually causing malnutrition and requiring hospitalization.

Anorexia nervosa is sometimes difficult to diagnose, because so many individuals are engaged in the pursuit of thinness. Anorexic-like patterns are common among fashion models, dancers, gymnasts, long-distance runners, and jockeys. Early treatment by an experienced physician or a clinic is essential if permanent health damage is to be avoided. Without the proper psychological and medical therapies, approximately 10 percent of anorexics die of starvation (Whitney & Hamilton, 1989).

Some common warning signs of anorexia nervosa include:

- Intense fear of becoming obese or overweight that does not lessen with weight loss.

- Excessive exercising in spite of fatigue.

- Unusual eating patterns, for example, cutting food into small pieces or playing with it on the plate.

- Distorted self image—always feeling fat.

- Wearing multiple layers of clothing and/or baggy clothes.

Denial tends to run high among anorexics, and they are known to effectively deceive their families and friends. Although trainers may feel hesitant about approaching a client they suspect of having an eating disorder, they should be more concerned about the dangers of ignoring the problem. If the disorder remains undiagnosed and untreated, the client may suffer permanent physical injury such as malnutrition, electrolyte imbalance, dehydration, cardiac irregularities, and seizure, among a host of other problems. The trainer who recognizes the symptoms of such a disorder in a client should see that the client is referred to a health professional prepared to deal with the problem. For guidance, the trainer can contact the nearest chapter of ANRED (Anorexia Nervosa and Related Eating Disorders), c/o Headquarters, P.O. Box 19461, Columbus, OH 43229.

Bulimia

Bulimia is characterized by excessive eating. Bulimics gorge themselves on large amounts of food and then follow the binge with vomiting or laxatives. Bulimics can eat as much as 1,000–5,000 calories in a 1–2 hour period. Often the binge consists of high-calorie, easily ingested sweet foods such as cookies, cake, and ice cream. Left untreated, the condition can lead to kidney failure, potassium depletion, urinary tract infections, and ulcers.

Bulimia in many respects is easier to treat than anorexia nervosa, because it seems to be more of a chosen behavior. Clients with bulimia know that their behavior is abnormal, and many are willing to gain control over their eating disorder. Bulimics should be encouraged to eat as many meals as possible with friends, since most binging occurs when eating alone.

Some common warning signs of bulimia include:

- Consuming vast quantities of high-calorie foods.

- Eating inconspicuously during a binge.

- Weight fluctuations due to alternating fasts and binges.

- Preoccupation with food/diet and body-fat/weight.

- Swollen glands (below and in front of ears).

- Tooth discoloration/decay.

Assisting the Client with Anorexia Nervosa or Bulimia

An alert and informed trainer can assist the client with one of these eating disorders in the following ways.

1. Try to form a trusting alliance with clients, to enable them to resolve food fears. Clients may feel too ashamed, embarrassed, or afraid to discuss the problem openly. Working with the trainer may, in fact, be the first step taken toward facing and overcoming the eating disorder. Be supportive and nonjudgmental in collaborating with clients. Aim to establish a climate of mutual respect, and develop a rapport that allows for open discussion of secret behaviors and fears.

2. Outline for clients the basic facts about calories, body-fat, and weight control. Clients may hold distorted views about the ability of particular foods to cause weight loss or weight gain, and to increase or deplete body-fat stores. Clients may suffer from dichotomous thinking, classifying certain foods as "bad" (sweets, sugar, fats) and others as "good" (diet foods, low-calorie foods, lettuce, cottage cheese). An on/off mentality triggers eating binges and causes the overeating/self-starvation cycle to continue. Such absolutist thinking creates food-related guilt and makes it impossible to enjoy eating, which contributes further to the distorted eating cycle.

3. Instruct the client to keep an activity/exercise record, to help in assessing the intensity and frequency of exercise. This record should also reflect the client's usual habits, and can be referred to repeatedly to emphasize the importance of regular but not excessive physical activity.

4. To be effective, permanent changes must be made slowly and gradually. Encouraging rapid weight gain can overwhelm clients. Requesting too many changes too quickly can also reinforce a client's perceived inability to control his/her environment. The client should outline a plan of action with the trainer's support and guidance, then the trainer should allow the client to consider the options and to make comfortable choices.

FASTING

Fasting is not recommended for the client who wants to lose weight. Fasting results in **ketosis**, a process in which the body first depletes its glycogen stores, then breaks down fat incompletely for energy. The incomplete breakdown of fat yields **ketone bodies**. The result is a buildup of ketones in the blood that can upset the body's natural acid–base balance. Since these ketones are excreted into the urine, the fasting client quickly urinates larger amounts of water—and so primarily loses water weight while becoming progressively dehydrated. During a fast, the body breaks down not only fats but also protein tissue to serve as energy. The result is a drastic reduction in energy output—as the body tries to conserve both fat and lean tissue. Organs shrink and muscles atrophy, causing a reduction in energy needs. Extreme weakness and fatigue often accompany the loss of minerals and water from the body. Metabolism slows, and the loss of fat falls to a minimum. Often, less fat is lost than would be on a low-calorie diet. Most of the weight loss that occurs during fasting is from loss of water and lean body tissue. Typically, the fasting client has not learned new eating habits and gains back the lost weight, and often even more weight.

SPECIAL CLOTHING AND BODY WRAPS

"Melts away pounds as you work or play," say the advertisements for garments such as sauna suits, plastic wraps, and rubber jumpsuits. These garments have been on the market for a number of years under a variety of trade names. They are made of a nonporous material that holds in body heat, causing per-spiration. The perspiring leads to dehydration and a temporary body-water weight loss, not a fat loss. This procedure is also potentially dangerous, since it prevents normal evaporation of sweat. The garment retains body heat, and core temperature can rise to a dangerous level.

SPOT REDUCING

Exercising a specific place on the body where fat is deposited—for example, the stomach—will not stimulate the body to use fat from that specific deposit area. The "spot exercise" fallacy assumes that if you have fat deposits on your abdominals, exercising the muscles underlying that fat will make it go away. A client who does 100 sit-ups a day for a flabby stomach will increase muscle endurance for the abdomen, but will not burn off the fat in that area. Fat is burned through prolonged exercise (aerobic activity), not from doing a specific calisthenic exercise.

CELLULITE

Cellulite is a nonmedical name for subcutaneous fat. Nutritional experts agree that all forms of subcutaneous fat are the same and that cellulite is not a special form of fat. Weight-reducing salons and some diet books define cellulite as a gel-like substance made up of fat, water, and wastes trapped in lumpy pockets beneath the skin. Regardless of the terminology, these lumpy deposits tend to be more visible in women than men. A somewhat thicker skin in the upper legs and buttocks keeps the fat deposits from showing through in men.

DIET PILLS/DRUGS

The use of numerous diet pills has been shown to be extremely harmful and sometimes fatal. The various drugs (prescription and patent medicine) em-ployed to lose weight generally attempt to reach that goal through (1) increasing the metabolic rate, (2) curbing the appetite, or (3) causing fluid loss. Over-the-counter amphetamines and hormones such as thyroxine are the most com-monly used diet pills. Amphetamines toy with the thyroid gland, speed up metabolism, and require increasingly strong doses as the body builds up a tolerance. Side effects include nervousness, sleeplessness, and irritability. Currently there are no pills or drugs available that are both safe and effective in producing long-term weight loss. The use of diurectics and laxatives for weight control is also dangerous and should be avoided. They can cause gastrointestinal troubles and serious dehydration, and they have proven to be ineffective as weight-loss aids.

SURGERY

Surgical techniques are usually reserved for severely obese individuals, and only after traditional methods of weight control have failed. Surgical methods include such procedures as wiring the jaws shut, gastric stapling of the stomach, and the insertion of the "gastric bubble" into the stomach. It is important to note that there have been deaths reported from complications of all of these surgeries. One of the more popular surgeries today for control of body-fat is lipo-suction. Introduced in the early 1980s, fat-removal surgery (lipectomy) is performed by inserting a hoselike device through the skin and into the fat tissue to be removed. The surgery is neither a cure for general obesity nor a substitute for healthful eating and exercise. Serious health hazards exist such as infection, depressions in the skin, and blood clots that can lead to kidney failure. It's important for personal trainers to remind clients that there is no fast, easy method or device for losing weight and body-fat.

VIBRATING BELTS AND MUSCLE STIMULATORS

Passive exercise, in which a machine moves your body with little or no effort on your part, is useless for weight reduction. Devices that shake the person or the body part do not break up fat deposits, improve posture, or take off the inches. Electric muscle stimulators placed on specific muscle groups discharge a small electrical current, causing the muscles to contract. While these devices can help rehabilitate injured muscles, they do not increase caloric expenditure to result in the loss of body weight or fat.

FAD DIETS

An array of various weight-loss diets flood the market. Hardly a month goes by without a new miracle diet being revealed in a leading magazine or the Sunday newspaper. They usually sell briefly and then fade away, largely because their "quick fix" does not work. There are over 30,000 diets listed with the Food and Drug Administration. The sheer number of weight-loss plans in existence testifies to the inadequacy of most of them. If the great, magical diet existed, everyone who was overweight would be on it, and there would be no more fat people.

Today, nutritional science finds itself caught in the "diet wars" because there are no magical answers to such a complex problem. The majority of people who go on a diet are unable to keep the weight off for an extended period. The American Dietetic Association states that 90 percent of the individuals who lose 25 pounds or more on any diet gain back that fat weight within a year. The long-term success rate of a diet is less than 5 percent. Most of the fad diets fail for the client either because they are based on scientific inaccuracies and misinformation, and therefore are nutritionally inadequate, or because they do not address the basic behavioral problem involved, that is, the need for lifelong changes in food and exercise habits.

Some clients are always hoping that some new diet will work. They find themselves caught in the trap of "yo-yo dieting," with their weight going up and down. They try one diet after another; at first they lose weight, then they gain it right back. Part of the problem is metabolism. With extremely low-calorie diets, the body adjusts to what it perceives as a state of starvation and tends to stay in this semistarvation mode. This metabolic roller-coastering makes weight loss more and more difficult each time and leaves the body resistant to permanent weight loss.

PLANNING A SUCCESSFUL WEIGHT-CONTROL PROGRAM

Trainers can assist the client in understanding the difference between temporary quick-weight-loss diets and the comprehensive restructuring of eating and exercise habits required for permanent weight control. Clients must be willing to commit time and long-term effort to change life-style habits that have contributed to the weight problem. And lastly, personal trainers can foster the appropriate climate for this change by being nonjudgmental and supportive listeners.

PRINCIPLES OF A SAFE AND EFFECTIVE DIET PLAN

MAINTAIN ENERGY BALANCE. The American Dietetic Association recommends that a minimal number of calories be consumed on a daily basis to meet the body's nutritional needs: 1,000 calories a day for women and 1,200 calories a day for men. Therefore, any diet or eating program that restricts the female client to fewer than 1,200 calories daily and the male client to fewer than 1,400 calories a day is unsafe and ineffective. Severe caloric restrictions will slow down the BMR, making weight loss harder to achieve (American Dietetic Association, 1980).

MAINTAIN NUTRIENT BALANCE. The basic nutrients (carbohydrates, proteins, and fats) need to be included in proportionate amounts. According to the U.S. Dietary Guidelines, about 58 percent of total calories should come from carbohydrates, with emphasis on complex forms such as grains, fruits, and vegetables and a limit on the simple forms such as sugar. Approximately 12 percent of total calories should come from protein, including the lean-food forms such as chicken, turkey, fish, and well-trimmed lean meats. The remaining 30 percent of calories should come from fat.

Many dietitians and sport nutritionists (Clark, 1990) are suggesting for clients in training or those wanting to maintain a high energy level the following nutrient balance: carbohydrates 65–70 percent, protein 15–20 percent, and fat 20–25 percent. The trainer may want to provide the client with information and resources from reputable authorities such as a registered dietitian or exercise nutritionist in planning a program for optimal nutritional benefits.

MAINTAIN CPF BALANCE. CPF refers to the proportion of carbohydrates, proteins, and fats in a given food. Carbohydrates are important not only for endurance events but also for those individuals who train hard day after day and want to maintain high energy. Carbohydrates are the best choice for fueling muscles and promoting a healthy heart. Foods that have higher percentages of carbohydrates are assimilated more efficiently during digestion. For example, a medium-size banana and one tablespoon of peanut butter each contain approximately 100 calories; and yet the banana is composed mainly of carbohydrates, while the peanut butter is primarily fat:

Food	Carbohydrates	Protein	Fat
Banana	96%	4%	0 (trace)
Peanut Butter	12	16	72

Researchers at the University of Massachusetts Medical School have found that the body is able to convert dietary fat into body-fat with greater ease than it can convert carbohydrates into body-fat. Thus, if a client who has been consuming 2,000 calories a day cuts his/her fat intake from 40 percent of calories to 20 percent (exchanging 400 fat calories for 400 carbohydrate calories), his/her metabolic savings would be about 80 calories per day. That could account for a loss of about two pounds in three months, and eight pounds a year.

MAINTAIN A FREQUENCY OF MEALS. Three meals a day is standard in our society. But no law says people can't have four or five smaller meals. It is wise for clients to avoid the all-too-common pattern of no breakfast, little or no lunch, and a huge dinner. Having several mini meals of 400–500 calories ("grazing") instead of three meals of 800 calories will keep the body temperature elevated longer and the body's metabolism elevated. Eating breakfast is one of the most efficient ways to get the body and the BMR off to a good start, even something as simple as a piece of toast or a piece of fruit. Clients who skip breakfast are sabotaging their body's ability to lose weight.

INCLUDE A VARIETY OF FOODS. A good diet allows for a wide variety of foods from all the food groups. A diet is unbalanced if it promotes eating large amounts of one type of food—even if it's a good food—to the exclusion of others. For instance, one popular diet program suggested eating nothing but fruit and rice. Yet this diet was inadequate in protein, vitamins, and minerals. A number of diets provide calories almost entirely in the form of protein, with very little from the main energy sources of carbohydrate and fat. Subsistence on such "liquid protein" diets or other high-protein diets frequently leads to feelings of malaise and weakness. The body, unable to be fueled through carbohydrates and fats, is forced to metabolize protein, producing electrolyte imbalances and, occasionally, disturbances of the heart rhythm. Also, there is no nutritional research to support the idea that a single food or combination of foods will make you lose weight. For example, eating protein only with other proteins or eating fruits by themselves will make no difference.

EMPHASIZE ORDINARY FOODS. A client's food plan should consist of foods available in regular grocery stores. There is no need to buy special, expensive, or unusual foods from health stores or diet centers. The foods we eat should not be so restrictive that we are unable to eat at restaurants and social gatherings.

MAINTAIN A STEADY, GRADUAL PACE. We live in a microwave society that demands instant foods as well as instant weight loss. Claims for producing very large weight losses in a very short time have proven quite attractive to the overweight. Programs that "melt away the fat" as you sleep or that state you can lose 10 pounds in five days are illusionary. Most of this loss, if it occurs at all, involves a loss of water, the water your body is forced to excrete when it relies on the body's protein and fat for energy. When regular eating resumes, the lost water and the lost pounds are regained. Plans that are too fast or too ambitious, or that make ridiculous claims, will usually fail. Most experts agree that a safe weight loss is 1–3 pounds a week. If clients set out to lose one pound a week for the next year, they would lose 52 pounds. This is more than enough for most clients. Dropping 3 pounds a week, an individual would lose 156 pounds in a year. By allowing months, perhaps a year, the weight loss will happen, and it will be more permanent.

FOLLOW A BALANCED EXERCISE PROGRAM.   Physical activity is a key component of any successful weight-loss program. Exercise burns calories, speeds metabolism, and helps offset the dreaded "plateaus" at which weight loss slows down or stops temporarily. Weight loss without exercise can have a negative effect on body composition, especially if the weight is regained. A client who diets without exercising loses both lean and fat tissue. If the client gains weight without exercising, more fat than lean is gained. Fat tissue is less active metabolically than lean tissue, and so client's daily energy expenditure is less. Each time weight is lost and regained without exercise, the metabolism requires fewer calories. When a client returns to eating the same amount as before the last diet, he/she will not maintain weight but will gain weight.

Introducing clients to a balanced program of healthful eating, exercise, and behavior change is not the only consideration for personal trainers, however. In order for exercise to be of maximum benefit to the client, it must involve a balanced program of stretching, strength development, and aerobics.

Stretching achieves and maintains normal range of motion in body joints, may prevent injury, and may improve enjoyment of exercise.

Strength development exercises prevent injury by increasing joint stability, and are specific to weight loss by increasing lean body mass most effectively.

Aerobic exercises increase cardiovascular fitness, enhance the body's ability to use fat as a source of energy, and assist in the maintenance of lean body weight.

Refer to Chapters 7, 8, 9, and 11 for more information on cardiovascular fitness, muscular strength and endurance, flexibility, and designing an exercise program.

PLANNING A SUCCESSFUL WEIGHT-GAIN PROGRAM

Some clients have the opposite energy problem: They weigh less than they should, and have difficulty putting on weight. The first step for the trainer in designing a weight-gain program is to have the client schedule a physical examination, to be sure that a medical disorder is not behind the problem. A check-up is particulary important if the client has previously been of normal weight and has recently lost a significant amount of weight without really trying. Emotional stress is a common cause of involuntary weight loss. Some of the aids to gaining weight are the reverse of techniques suggested for losing weight.

PRINCIPLES OF A SAFE AND EFFECTIVE WEIGHT-GAIN PROGRAM

CONSUME MORE ENERGY.   Starting with a nutritionally adequate diet, the client should eat larger meals, eat more often, and increase the energy density of food. For example, increasing caloric intake by about 500 calories a day will add about one pound a week. Recommend calorie-dense foods (the very ones the dieter is trying to stay away from), for example: dried fruit along with fresh fruit, avocado instead of cucumber, and whole-wheat muffins instead of whole-wheat bread.

CONSIDER STRENGTH TRAINING.   For the client who wants to gain weight, exercise is indispensable to ensure that the majority of the gain will be lean tissue. Moderate aerobic exercise (three times a week) is acceptable. However, have clients avoid more frequent aerobic training, (4–6 times a week) for this may have them burning up more calories and losing weight rather than gaining it. Strength training is recommended as a more efficient way of supporting weight gain. A progressive strength-training program will add body weight in the form of lean tissue (muscles) and strengthen the body. (For more information on strength development see Ch. 8.)

LOOK FOR GENETIC INFLUENCES.   If implementing these suggestions with the client does not achieve the goal weight, the client may need to accept the fact that his/her body is regulated at a lower level of fatness. Maintaining a greater amount of body weight may require more time, effort, and expense than are worthwhile.

Steroids

Certain drugs have been used by some athletes and underweight persons because of their potential to increase muscle mass. The synthetic anabolic androgenic steroids, patterned after the male sex hormone testosterone, can increase muscle mass when used in conjunction with a weight-training program. However, they are not recommended by the ACSM, for there are some inherent medical risks associated with their use. Here are some of the major highlights of the ACSM position on steroids (See ACSM, 1984):

- The prolonged use of steroids has resulted in liver disorders in some persons.

- Steroids given to males may result in a decrease in testicular size and function, and a decrease in sperm production.

- Steroid use does not bring about any significant improvements in strength, aerobic endurance, lean body mass, or body weight.

SUMMARY

Weight control, probably more than any other reason, is the initial motivation for many to begin exercising. Therefore, it is crucial that the personal trainer be an excellent role model, and knowledgeable in the most current factual information that promotes healthful weight loss. The average consumer is bombarded with fictitious information regarding diet and ways to manipulate metabolism. Regardless of the type of exercise program the trainer is developing, issues of weight loss, weight gain, and weight maintenance must be considered.

Scientifically backed theories regarding energy balance, set-point, basal metabolic rate, exercise, genetic considerations, and psychological, and physiological factors have been presented. The trainer must draw on this information and more recent scientifically supported studies when working with the client. Because weight loss is of such importance to many individuals, the trainer must also be on the lookout for signs and symptoms of anorexia nervosa, bulimia, and the use of gimmicks like spot reducing, diet pills, and sauna suits that promise the metabolically impossible. A successful weight-management program requires a long-term approach, one designed to modify the behaviors that brought on the concerns in the first place.

REFERENCES

American College of Sports Medicine. (1984). Position statement: The use of anabolic-androgenic steroids in sports. *Medicine and Science in Sports and Exercise, 9*, xi–xiii.

American Dietetic Association. (1980). Position statement on nutrition and physical fitness. *Journal of the American Dietetic Association, 76*, 437– 443.

Clark, N. (1980). *Nancy Clark's sports nutrition guidebook*. Champaign, IL: Leisure Press.

Deutsch, R. (1980). *Realities of nutrition*. Palo Alto, CA: Bull Co.

Frankle, Reva, & Yang, Mei-Uih. (1988). *Obesity and weight control*. Rockville, MD: Aspen Publisher.

Getchell, B. (1983). *Physical fitness: A way of life* (3rd ed.). New York: Wiley.

Katch, F., & McArdle, W. (1988). *Nutrition, weight control and exercise* (3rd ed.). Philadelphia: Lea & Febiger.

Keys, A., et al. (1950). *The biology of human starvation*. Minneapolis: University of Minnesota Press.

Hirsh, J., & Knittle, J.L. (1980). Increase in adipose tissue lipoprotein lipase activity with weight loss, *Journal of Clinical Investigation*. 67: 1425.

Whitney, E.N., & Hamilton, E.M. (1984). *Understanding nutrition*. St. Paul, MN: West.

Williams, M. (1988). *Nutrition for fitness and sport* (2nd ed.). Dubuque, IA: William C. Brown.

Williams, S.R. (1989). *Nutrition and diet therapy* (6th ed.). St. Louis: Times Mirror/Mosby.

SUGGESTED READING

American College of Sports Medicine. (1991). *Guidelines for exercise testing and prescription* (4th ed.) Philadelphia: Lea & Febiger.

American College of Sports Medicine. (1983). Position statement: Proper and improper weight-loss programs. *Medicine and Science in Sports and Exercise, 15*, ix-xiii.

American Dietetic Association. (1988). Position of the American Dietetic Association: Nutrition intervention in the treatment of anorexia nervosa and bulimia nervosa. *Journal of the American Dietetic Assocation,* Jan. Vol 88, issue 1, pp. 68-71.

Brody, J. (1981). *Jane Brody's nutrition book*. New York: Norton.

Coleman, E. (1988). *Eating for endurance*. Palo Alto, CA: Bull Publishing.

Costill, D. (1986). *Inside runners–Basics of sports physiology*. Indianapolis: Benchmark.

Hamilton, E.M., Whitney, E.N., & Sizer, F. (1988). *Nutrition: Concepts and controversies* (4th ed.). St. Paul, MN: West.

Krepton, D., & Chu, D. (1986). *Everybody's aerobics book* (2nd ed.). Minneapolis: Bellweather.

Pavlou, K., et al. (1985). Effects of dieting and exercise on lean body mass, oxygen uptake and strength. *Medicine and Science in Sports and Exercise, 17,* 466–471.

Rock, C.L., & Coulson, A.M. (1988). Weight control approaches: A review by the California Dietetic Association. *Journal of the American Dietetic Association, 88,* 44.

University of California, Berkeley, wellness letter. (1988, Oct.)

Wood, P. (1983). *California diet and exercise program*. Mountain View, CA: Anderson World Books.

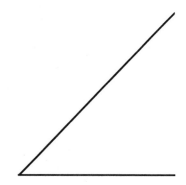

Individualized Program Design **PART IV**

Just as there is an unlimited number of types of potential clients, the variety of exercise programs is equally limitless. Trainers must use their knowledge of exercise science, the client's current fitness level and goals, training principles, and personal experience to design an exercise program that is safe, efficient, and effective. Although every client is different, the chapters in this part provide information on programming for the "apparently healthy adult" and on modifications for certain health conditions and special populations. The case studies provided are only examples of the numerous types of programs that can be developed. The title *personal trainer* implies just that, "personally tailored workouts" designed to meet the needs and desires of the participant. The reader should view the following information as an example of how it all comes together.

Programming for the Healthy Adult

Kathy Alexander and Irv Rubenstein

11

Kathy Alexander, Ph.D., and Irv Rubenstein, Ph.D., are exercise physiologists who own and operate S.T.E.P.S., Inc. (Scientific Training and Exercise Prescription Specialists), a personal fitness training facility in Nashville, Tennessee. Both have taught exercise physiology and other exercise science courses at the university level.

IN THIS CHAPTER:

- Factors to consider when designing an exercise program: muscle-strength and endurance training, cardiovascular training, flexibility training, and body composition.

- Signs of overtraining.

- Designing the workout, including four example routines and three case studies that pull together information on client fitness, life-style, and goals and apply it to the design of specific exercise programs.

The goal of every trainer should be to help each client develop a balanced exercise program that fits that client's specific needs, goals, life-style, and limitations. To accomplish this the trainer must apply knowledge of the exercise sciences, human motivation, and safety. Central to the idea of personal training is the word *personal*, meaning that the trainer will be working with a variety of clients, each with different goals, likes, and dislikes. Thus, it is impossible to design one or even several simple exercise programs and expect them to meet the needs of every client the fitness professional will encounter. But trainers are expected to use their technical knowledge and experience to develop a safe, effective, and enjoyable program for each client.

Every apparently healthy adult client is capable of achieving a level of fitness commensurate with his/her age and health. The trainer is responsible for assessing the client's current fitness status through health screening and fitness evaluation, clarifying measurable and realistic goals, and developing a program that will help the client accomplish those goals. From the beginning, not only must the trainer and the client work together to establish mutually agreed-on goals, but they also must agree on the types of exercises to be used. Without the initial "buy-in" from both the trainer and the client, the program is likely to fail.

In designing a program, the trainer must consider the basic physiological components of fitness: muscular strength and endurance, cardiovascular endurance, flexibility, and body composition. Since each client comes to the trainer with varying degrees of each component, the trainer must design an exercise program that addresses the areas of greatest need while not overlooking the other areas. The trainer is often required to assess not only the client's performance on standardized tests but also the types of sports or hobbies the client likes to engage in. For example, if the client likes to golf, the trainer needs to be aware of exercises and stretching techniques that will affect the client's golfing performance. Keeping these considerations in mind will help the trainer provide quality service.

Finally, the trainer must consider the client's individual goals. Often there is conflict between the client's goals and areas of weakness the trainer has discovered. In such situations the trainer should educate the client, helping him/her understand the importance of accepting and supporting additional goals, while adding the appropriate exercises to the program. The trainer's goal should not be short-sighted, merely placating the client with short-term solutions. Rather the trainer needs to aim to help each client make a lifetime commitment to exercise. This larger perspective will guide the trainer as he/she works with clients.

FACTORS TO CONSIDER WHEN DESIGNING AN EXERCISE PROGRAM

Muscle-Strength and Endurance Training

In designing a comprehensive exercise program for the healthy adult, the personal trainer must consider the development of the musculoskeletal as well as the cardiovascular system. Maintenance of sufficient muscular tone and strength will assist clients with weight control; provide an appealing physique, better posture, and greater endurance for daily and athletic activities; and reduce the risk of certain musculoskeletal injuries. The trainer should consider the following seven principles when designing and implementing the strength-training component of an exercise program.

1. Always make *safety* the primary concern.

2. Train each body segment by working it against a resistance capable of *overloading* the muscles.

3. Plan exercise so it is performed throughout the *full range of motion*.

4. Ensure that training *speed* is always slow and controlled. (There are exceptions, such as training for competitive sports, where faster sport-specific training may be appropriate.)

5. Create an exercise program that is *balanced* between agonistic and antagonistic muscle groups.

6. *Prevent injuries* by training those muscle groups that require special attention because of daily misuse, muscular imbalances, or athletic pursuits.

7. Provide at least one day of *rest* between workouts of the same muscle groups.

The overload principle is the basis for considering the variables of intensity (the amount of resistance encountered), number of repetitions, and number of sets. Although no magical formula exists for determining a specific amount of weight or a precise number of reps or sets, there are generally accepted training principles (see Ch. 8 for greater detail). The trainer must also consider: how many muscle groups need to be exercised and the length of the session; which training methods, such as body-weight exercises (calisthenics), free weight, or weight machines, will be recommended to overload each muscle group; and, finally, how to balance laterally (left–right) and antagonistically (agonist–antagonist).

In designing a strength-training program, the trainer must consider not only initial workouts but the potential progression of the routine as the client begins to accomplish intermediate goals. Progression can take many forms, including adding exercises to the program, increasing the amount of resistance, and altering repetitions, sets, frequencies, and duration. Regardless of the method the trainer recommends, it is imperative that the trainer address the need for change and variety.

Cardiovascular Training

Cardiovascular training is training that increases the functional capacity of the heart, lungs, and blood vessels that transport oxygenated blood to the working muscles. Maintenance of even average levels of cardiovascular fitness can reduce one's risk for coronary heart disease. Other benefits of cardiovascular exercise include weight control, hypertension control, better lipid control, and, possibly, assistance in controlling the stresses of life. The trainer should follow the guidelines of the American College of Sports Medicine (ACSM) as presented in Chapter 7 when designing the aerobic component of the exercise program. The important factors to consider are the mode, intensity, duration, and frequency of the activity. Just as in strength training, the principles of overload and specificity cannot be overlooked. In order for an activity to qualify as aerobic exercise, it must involve a continuous, rhythmical, and sustained movement using large muscle groups. Such activities include brisk walking, swimming, running, cycling, aerobic dance, roller skating, ice skating, rowing, cross-county skiing, rope skipping, stair climbing, and various recreational and game activities if they are performed in a continuous manner with few or no rest periods.

It is important to match the client's aerobic activities to his/her fitness level, exercise goals, orthopedic history, and personal preference. For example, the beginning or overweight client may find walking, swimming, or stationary cycling more comfortable than impact options such as jogging, rope jumping, and some forms of aerobic dance. Clients who are interested in burning calories and improving their aerobic fitness will find any of these exercises suitable. The trainer may incorporate cross training, alternating between two or more aerobic activities, as a way to add variety and fun, and reduce the risk of injuries from overtraining.

Clients training for specific performance, such as a marathon or century (100-mile) cycling, should focus most of their training in that sport (this is an example of the law of specificity). In other words, the runner should run, the cyclist should cycle, and the swimmer should swim. Although any aerobic exercise will enhance cardiovascular fitness, muscles tend to adapt specifically to the type of exercise they perform.

For the cardiovascular component of an exercise program, the trainer should consider frequency, intensity, and duration. Just as in strength training, there are no magic formulas that will work all the time with every client. However, there are a number of physiological principles (see Ch. 7) that provide the backbone for cardiovascular program design.

After designing a program, and prior to implementing it, the trainer must teach the client how to monitor performance intensity. It is often difficult for the beginning client to gauge exercise intensity correctly. Use of individualized exercise target heart rate zones, subjective ratings of perceived exertion, and the **talk test** will assist the client in achieving his/her goals in the safest and most efficient manner possible.

Flexibility Training

Flexibility is an often overlooked or underemphasized component of the exercise program. Clients do not generally think of flexibility in the same way as muscular strength or cardiovascular endurance when they consider their overall fitness level. In addition, because flexibility is specific to each joint, it cannot easily be improved or maintained by simply performing one or two quick stretches. However, adequate muscular flexibility is important in maintaining range of motion as well as in preventing injuries. Trainers should include flexibility training in every exercise program to create a balance between muscle groups that might be overused during physical training sessions or subject to chronic tightness due to daily activity or inactivity. And it is important to consider not only the muscles and subsequent joints being exercised but also the client's limitations (or areas needing attention) and the goals of the program. Flexibility programs should address all major muscle groups.

The following basic information should be considered when incorporating flexibility into the client's exercise program. (Ch. 9 discusses the principles and methods of flexibility training in greater detail.)

1. Muscles and tendons stretch better when warmed up. Have the client stretch after 5–10 minutes of light aerobic warm-up and/or at the end of the training session.

2. Isolate each muscle or muscle group. The client must not stretch in a manner that will put undue or unnecessary strain on ligaments and joints.

3. Slow, passive, static stretching is recommended. Static stretching involves a slow, gradual, and controlled elongation of the muscle. Ballistic or dynamic stretching is generally not recommended, because it incorporates a high-force, short-duration bouncing action.

4. When performing a static stretch, clients should stretch to the point of feeling tension in the muscle, but *not* pain.

5. Have the client hold each stretch for 15–30 seconds.

6. The client should do 3–5 repetitions of each stretch.

Proprioceptive neuromuscular facilitation (PNF) stretching provides an additional stretching option. This involves an initial isometric contraction against maximum resistance for approximately 10 seconds followed by relaxation and a slow and passive stretch to the point of pain-free limitation. This sequence is usually repeated several times.

Although it is important to stretch a wide variety of muscles, the following body parts are particularly susceptible to tension and flexibility-related tightness: the posterior neck, the upper shoulder and back, the low back, the hamstrings, and the calf. Although the reasons for this vary, a properly designed stretching program can improve flexibility, while poorly planned and imbalanced training techniques can exacerbate the problem.

Body Composition

Since one of the most common goals of clients is weight loss, body composition is the final component of health-related fitness that the trainer needs to consider when programming exercise for the apparently healthy adult. **Body composition** can be divided into 2 basic subfractions of body weight—**lean body mass** (or fat-free weight) and body-fat. If the client's primary goal is weight loss (preferably accomplished by fat loss and lean-tissue maintenance or gain), the trainer should design a program that will generate a negative caloric balance so that the client is expending more calories than are being consumed. Although producing a negative caloric balance is not always enough to reduce body-fat, research indicates that the best approach to weight loss is to combine appropriate caloric restriction with exercise. Since aerobic exercise burns the most calories, the client should engage in such activities up to five times a week, expending 300–500 calories per activity session. Theoretically, the client must have a negative caloric balance of 3,500 calories to lose one pound of fat.

Remember, exercise should be a component of any weight-loss program in order to maintain lean tissue. The strengthening component of the workout will increase the lean tissue that has been lost during sedentary activity, dieting alone, injury, or immobilization. Not only does exercise increase lean tissue lost to a sedentary life-style or "yo-yo" dieting, it also improves the client's muscle tone and appearance. If clients like their new appearance after fat loss, they may be more likely to keep up their newly acquired health habits to maintain the new, healthy look.

It is important for the trainer to keep all the physiological factors and personal limitations and goals of the client in mind when designing an exercise program. Once the program has been instituted, however, the trainer's work may not be done. Performing the same routine week after week not only can become boring for the client, it can soon fail to achieve the desired goals. Therefore, the trainer is continually challenged to evaluate the client's progress and goals in order to design new programs that allow the client to progress.

Signs of Overtraining

When assessing a client's progress, the trainer should also look for signs and symptoms of overtraining. While some clients may be challenging to work with because they do not want to work very hard at their program, others may be overzealous, driving their bodies too hard in an effort to achieve their goals more quickly. The trainer must be attentive to this potential problem, and communicate with the client about any noticed signs of discomfort or overtraining.

Some clients believe the "no pain, no gain" approach to exercise and find themselves plagued with injuries or symptoms of overtraining. The trainer needs to educate each client that the most sensible and certainly most enjoyable approach to exercise is to "train, don't strain." The role of proper rest and program intensity, duration, and frequency must continually be evaluated. The trainer must always be looking for the following symptoms of overtraining:

- Insomnia

- Irritability

- Elevated morning pulse (10 bpm higher than normal for several days in a row)

- Consistently elevated blood pressure
- Fatigue
- Loss of appetite
- Depression
- Decreased or lost motivation to exercise
- Increased frequency of colds and influenzas
- Increased frequency of injuries

DESIGNING THE WORKOUT

A client expects (and it is the trainer's responsibility to provide) a program tailored specifically to his/her needs. Information obtained from the client's health screening and fitness evaluation must be considered when planning a program, as should the client's needs, goals, life-style, and time limitations. The trainer must choose a beginning workload that balances frequency, intensity, and duration and that is consistent with the client's health and fitness level. A health history, a fitness evaluation, and in some cases a medical clearance should be obtained before a trainer begins designing the exercise program. This protects both the client and the trainer and facilitates the application of scientific exercise principles. With proper exercise programming, the trainer maximizes the client's benefits and minimizes the risk for injury.

It is also important to consider the equipment and facility options available to the client. Will training take place in the home, at a fitness club or studio, or at an outdoor location? Trainers should also recognize their own limitations. They should never attempt to show a client how to do exercises or use types of equipment that they themselves are not fully skilled in. In addition, since the client views the trainer as a role model, caution must be taken to ensure that the client does not try to do too much too soon in an effort to be "like the trainer." Encourage the client to work at his/her own level, emphasizing that every person has different exercise goals and abilities. If the client and trainer are exercising together, the trainer should work out at the intensity of the client, to reduce the client's urge to overtrain. Never assume that a client knows what to do. It is the trainer's responsibility to educate the client, to spot the client, and to do whatever else is necessary to ensure the client's safety. This also means designing a program that will not put the client at undue risk.

In addition to designing workouts that are safe and effective, the trainer should have a specific goal for each of the client's workouts. They should be varied, to keep both the trainer and the client interested in long-term training. The trainer should be creative, using various options and combinations of exercises when designing each workout. The following four examples of routines, though lacking full detail, are meant to show how trainers can use time and training modalities to accomplish client goals.

Example Routine 1

WARM-UP (15 MIN).   Aerobic activities such as walking, cycling, and rowing. The client could spend the entire time on one piece of equipment, or use several pieces of aerobic equipment, or engage in nonequipment activities such as walking.

STRENGTH TRAINING (35 MIN). Using weight and/or manual resistance, the client might train the upper body first, then the lower body. At the next workout, the order could be reversed. As the client achieves repetition goals, weight could be added and repetitions reduced, or weight could be lowered and additional manual resistance applied by the trainer.

COOL-DOWN (10 MIN). Gentle cycling or walking, and stretching of the exercised muscle groups.

Example Routine 2

AEROBIC TRAINING (30 MIN). Includes gradual warm-up, and focuses on one or more aerobic activities. Depending on equipment availability the trainer could instruct the client to alternate upper and lower body muscles—e.g., cycling (10 minutes), then using the arm ergometer or rowing machine. Or the client could jog on the treadmill for 30 minutes.

STRENGTH TRAINING (20 MIN). The client could perform a variety of body-weight (i.e., push-ups, chin-ups, or dips) and floor exercises. The trainer could assist by adding additional resistance.

FLEXIBILITY TRAINING (10 MIN). Have the client complete the workout with stretches for all the major muscle groups, or the specific muscle groups that were emphasized in the workout. The trainer might also apply resistance and assist with some PNF stretching.

Example Routine 3

WARM-UP (10 MIN). The client works on cardiovascular equipment, with a brief stretching period before starting the next phase of the workout.

CIRCUIT TRAINING (40 MIN). The client progresses from one weight machine to the next, performing 15–20 repetitions at each station and quickly moving on to the next station. The client could alternate between strength-training stations and cardiovascular stations.

COOL-DOWN (10 MIN). Gentle walking or cycling followed by flexibility exercises.

Example Routine 4

Another training variation is to have a *game or play day* in which a sporting activity is substituted for the more traditional strength and cardiovascular exercises. Many clients enjoy a day out of the gym every once in a while. They might ride mountain bikes or jog at a nearby trail or park. Games such as basketball and tennis can be a great workout if arranged properly. Play day can be a fun treat for the client. Such breaks from the norm are also great motivators. Remember to include flexibility exercises, emphasizing to the client that flexibility training needs to be incorporated into every workout.

These examples are just four of the almost limitless number of ways the trainer can manipulate the time spent on each component of fitness to meet the needs of the client. Remember, the focus is on the *personal* aspect of the training program. Each client should be able to understand how the program is tailored specifically to achieve his/her goals.

The trainer not only determines how much time will be spent on each component of fitness, but must then determine exactly what exercises are going to be performed during the time allotted. Again, the options are almost limitless. There are numerous ways to develop safe and effective programs, so the following case studies are not meant as absolute exercise recommendations. Rather they are intended to help the trainer assimilate the information already covered. Each case study presents general information about the client, his/her goals, and a recommended exercise program. It does not present all the information that would normally be obtained through the health screening and evaluation process, but only a sampling, enough to justify the design of each exercise program. Following the exercise program is a brief discussion of variables the trainer should consider for each client.

CASE STUDY 1   LOCATION: FITNESS CENTER

Sex: Male   *Age*: 50   *Blood pressure*: 140/85

Body-fat: 20%   *Resting heart rate*: 69   *Smoker*: No

Flexibility: Tight low back and hamstrings, but no limitations.

Physician clearance: Because of borderline hypertension and age, the client had been referred to his physician. He has been cleared for all forms of exercise. When performing strength-training exercises, care should be taken to avoid the **Valsalva maneuver**.

Goals: The client says he wants to "get in better shape." After further discussion, it is decided that the client wants to reduce his body-fat to 15 percent and increase his stamina so he can comfortably walk all 18 holes while golfing. Long-range goal is to be able to jog the local three-mile exercise course. Additionally, the client wants to improve his strength, in anticipation of spending more time with his grandson and improving his golf game.

Additional information: The client has lived a sedentary life-style for the last 15 years. His only exercise is one round of golf a week in which he rides in a golf cart.

Initial Workout Routine

WARM-UP AND AEROBIC COMPONENT.   A gentle warm-up (5–7 minutes) on a stationary bike with little to no resistance, followed by 15–20 minutes of brisk walking on a treadmill or cycling on a stationary bike. Attention should be given to maintaining target exercise heart rate (120–135 bpm). Ratings of perceived exertion (RPE) of 12–15 may also help the client in the initial exercise sessions. Finish with a 5–7 minute cool-down of slow walking or cycling.

FLEXIBILITY COMPONENT.   10–15 minutes of passive static stretching of all major muscle groups is recommended. Special attention should be placed on the low back and hamstrings.

TIME REQUIREMENTS.   This program is to be performed on Monday, Wednesday, and Friday, with workout time of approximately 90 minutes.

STRENGTH-TRAINING COMPONENT.

Exercise	Muscle Group(s)	Reps	Sets
Leg extension	Quadriceps	10–12	1
Hip extension	Hamstrings, gluteals	10–12	1
Leg curl	Hamstrings	10–12	1
Push-ups (modified if needed)	Triceps, pectorals, anterior deltoids	10	1
Bench press	Triceps, pectorals, anterior deltoids	10	1
Bar dips	Triceps, pectorals, latissimus	4–8	1
Lat pull-downs	Latissimus, biceps	10–12	1
Bicep curls	Biceps	10–12	1
Wrist curls	Forearms	10–12	1
Trunk curls	Abdominals	10–15	3
Twisting trunk curls	Obliques	10–15	3

Program Variables and Special Considerations

CARDIOVASCULAR CONSIDERATIONS. The ACSM recommends a training heart rate of 50–85 percent of heart rate maximum reserve. Because the client has been sedentary, is 50 years old, and has elevated blood pressure, a conservative approach for the initial exercise heart rate of 50–65 percent has been used. As the client progresses through the program, it may be appropriate to increase the recommended target heart rate. The use of perceived exertion can assist the trainer and the client in understanding when it would be appropriate to elevate the exercise heart rate. Changes of the resting heart rate will also need to be considered.

After the first few weeks, if the appropriate cardiovascular equipment is available, the client could try a few minutes of rowing, stair climbing, or cross-country skiing, or the use of an arm ergometer for the last 3–4 minutes of his aerobic workout. This will introduce the client to other cardiovascular training options without sacrificing the benefits of the current workout. The client may find an interest in other training options that will support cross training, reducing the risk of overtraining with one exercise modality while adding variety to the program.

Care should be taken in the early stages of the program not to increase the intensity of the training too fast. Although both the musculosketal and cardiovascular systems adapt to exercise, the trainer must be cautious and not allow the client to progress too quickly. The skeletal system takes time to adapt to high-impact activities, and thus the trainer may want to counsel the client against adding high-impact activities too soon.

Duration of the aerobic component may progress moderately unless there are signs of overtraining. The addition of 3–5 minutes per session every 1–2 weeks would be appropriate. Although the client is meeting with the trainer three times per week, after 6–8 weeks the client could increase the cardiovascular training to 4–5 times a week, performing the additional workouts on his/her own or with a partner.

STRENGTH CONSIDERATIONS. Since the client is sedentary, overfat, and mildly hypertensive, the trainer's program design must take into account caution above everthing else. Attention to the training techniques of proper body alignment, slow and controlled movement throughout the full range of motion, and continuous breathing are mandatory. Progression within each session from the larger muscle groups to smaller or individual muscles will provide a well-rounded workout. This allows the client to first exercise all the muscles that make up a muscle group before exercising the individual muscles of that group. To minimize the risk of injury and muscle soreness, the trainer must determine the amount of weight the client should use on each exercise. A percentage of a one-rep maximum could be used (see Ch. 8), or the trainer could estimate initial starting weights. Because the client has borderline hypertension, determining this one-rep maximum for each exercise is contraindicated. Although it is more subjective, the trainer should make very conservative estimates of appropriate starting weight. The trainer should spot the client on each exercise, making sure the weights are not too heavy. It would be best to start the client out with lighter weights, progressing slowly over 3–5 workouts up to his appropriate workout weights. This approach should help to maintain lower blood pressures during the exercise and reduce muscle soreness afterwards.

This program "preexhausts" the larger muscle groups by exercising the larger muscle groups before exercising the individual muscles that make up each group. One set is sufficient for general conditioning, especially since there is a preexhaustion component for most of the major muscles. Machines, manual resistance free weights, and calisthenics are interchanged. Likewise, various exercises can be alternated among these three modes from session to session. Remember that strength increases quickly during the first few weeks, with most of the early increases the result of neuromuscular adaptations. Some delayed-onset muscle soreness is to be expected, and the trainer should inform the client in advance about this and give suggestions for relief. A day of rest between workouts is important to allow for recovery. As training progresses, the trainer has several options: (1) add resistance by increasing weight, (2) add manual resistance by pressing against the moving segment of the machine or the body in order to make the exercise more difficult, or (3) do multiple sets of the same exercise. With this particular client, the trainer should avoid suggesting excessive low-repetition/high-resistance exercises, eccentric resistance training, and short-rest-period training modalities.

FLEXIBILITY CONSIDERATIONS. Because his neck, shoulder, and back flexibility are not optimal and the strengthening exercises may contribute to tightness, pectoral, anterior deltoid, and latissimus stretching would be appropriate. Special attention should also be given to the hamstrings and low back, to address preexisting tightness. (See Ch. 9 for specific exercises.) The flexibility portion of the exercise program could be performed by the client daily. Additional stretches could be added to assist in stretching the back and shoulders, to assist in the client's golf game. The client should be advised to perform the proper warm-up and stretching before each golf game, including stretching the upper and low back, the shoulders, and the hips. Slow and controlled rotation of the torso would also be helpful.

CASE STUDY 2 LOCATION: CLIENT'S HOME

Sex: Female   *Age*: 40   *Blood pressure*: 122/78
Body fat: 38%   *Resting heart rate*: 78   *Smoker*: 1 pack/day

Flexibility: Tight low back and hamstrings.

Physician clearance: No restrictions. The trainer requested clearance before working with her because of a history of smoking and recurring low-back fatigue.

Goals: Reduce body-fat and quit smoking. Also wants to strengthen back to eliminate the back fatigue she feels at the end of the day and when horseback riding.

Additional information: She has smoked for 15 years and is afraid of gaining additional weight when she stops smoking. She believes that exercise is a necessary first step to quitting smoking. She is a computer operator, and spends the majority of her day sitting. She enjoys horseback riding and gardening as hobbies.

Initial Workout Routine

WARM-UP AND CARDIOVASCULAR TRAINING.   Initial training will focus on a walking program around the client's neighborhood. Warm-up will consist of 10 minutes of walking to a nearby park. At the park she and the trainer will perform 5 minutes of stretching exercises, with special focus given to the low back, hamstrings, and calves. After the client has stretched, the trainer will lead the client through 20–30 minutes of brisk walking, ending at the client's home to transition into the strength-conditioning portion of her program. The client will initially use the talk test in conjunction with heart-rate monitoring to ensure that she maintains the proper intensity during her aerobic training. Initially, the trainer may need to assist the client in the proper use of these monitoring techniques. Tip: tell the client to avoid breathlessness.

STRENGTH-TRAINING COMPONENT.

Exercise	Muscle Group(s)	Reps	Sets
Seated straight leg lifts	Quadriceps, hip flexors	15–20	2
Standing lunges	Quadriceps	15–20	2
Squats to 90%	Hamstrings	15–20	2
Front-lying leg lifts	Gluteals	15–20	2
Side-lying leg lifts using the upper leg	Hip abductors	15–20	2
Side-lying leg lifts using the lower leg	Hip adductors	15–20	2
Heel raises	Gastrocnemius	15–20	2
Front-lying chest lifts	Low back	10–15	2
Push-ups, modified form	Pectoralis major, triceps	5–10	2
Trunk curls	Abdominals	15–20	2
Twisting trunk curls	Obliques	15–20	2

FLEXIBILITY COMPONENT.   10–15 minutes of passive static stretching of all major muscle groups. Special attention should be paid to the hamstrings, upper and low back, and the neck. Additional PNF stretching could be performed, with the assistance of the trainer, to stretch hamstrings.

TIME REQUIREMENTS.   This program is to be performed in its entirety three days per week, with a one-day rest period in between each strength-conditioning session. The cardiovascular and flexibility segments could be performed daily, allowing a minimum of one day of rest per week. Each workout should take approximately 60–75 minutes.

Program Variables and Special Considerations

CARDIOVASCULAR CONSIDERATIONS.   The client's warm-up should be slow and progressive. During her initial walk to the park, she can gradually pick up speed in order to elevate her heart rate slowly while increasing her peripheral blood flow. This will facilitate a safer and more effective pre-exercise stretching routine.

The walk program will allow her to work at her own pace while increasing her caloric expenditure and aerobic capacity. As her cardiovascular conditioning improves, she will be able to increase the intensity, duration, and/or frequency of her aerobic training. With improvements in cardiovascular and musculoskeletal fitness and a desire to increase caloric expenditure, the client may want to transition from walking to walk/jogging to jogging. Ultimately she should be able to perform this program five days a week. In addition, if she desires, she should be able to increase the duration of the walk to 45–60 minutes and transition from walk/jogging to jogging. This gradual approach allows the client to make small but noticeable improvements along the way, thus keeping her interested and motivated. To add variety to the program, she might substitute bicycling for walk/jogging on the days she is not working with the trainer. It is important for her to build duration and intensity slowly, and to choose activities that will allow her to exercise comfortably.

Because the client has been smoking for 15 years, respiratory inefficiencies may inhibit her ability to attain a normally predicted target exercise heart rate comfortably. The trainer has recommended the use of the talk test along with monitoring the exercise heart rate as the means to determine the appropriate initial exercise intensity. This combined method will allow the trainer to determine better the appropriate exercise target heart rate by comparing actual exercise heart rates with the client's exertion, as measured by the talk test. The Karvonen formula might predict a target heart rate that is too difficult for the client to initially maintain. In addition, because the client smokes, she may have an elevated resting heart rate which, when used in the Karvonen formula, increases the chance for error. In addition to using the talk test, the trainer should use ratings of perceived exertion (the Borg Scale). However, when working with a client outdoors, trying to get the client to remember the numerical values of the scale can be difficult.

The client also wants to lose body-fat while quitting smoking. Because of her higher-than-recommended percentage of body-fat, and the metabolic changes she will undergo while quitting smoking, it is recommended that she modify her diet. Additional dietary information is needed to determine the appropriate dietary changes to assist her in achieving fat loss. A diet high in complex carbohydrates, low in fat, and not less than 1,200 calories per day would be a basic suggestion. Research indicates that exercise alone or diet alone is not as effective as exercise and diet together in reducing body-fat and maintaining lean muscle tissue. The trainer should talk to the client about basic dietary concepts. If the client has detailed questions, it would be prudent to recommend that the client meet with a registered dietitian who is familiar with smoking cessation and exercise .

STRENGTH-TRAINING CONSIDERATIONS. The strength-training or conditioning component of her exercise program is equally important. It is reasonable to assume that the client has lost lean tissue due to her sedentary life-style. Increasing muscle mass will improve her muscle tone and boost her basal metabolism because of the increased caloric needs of the additional lean tissue. This will further assist her in her goals to lose body-fat.

Extra attention has been given to the musculature associated with the complaints of low-back fatigue. Because the physician has noted no structural problems, strengthening of the low back and abdominals while stretching the hip flexors and hamstrings should help address this problem. Additional exercises have been added to strengthen the quadriceps, hamstings, and hip adductors. These exercises will strengthen the areas of the legs that fatigue during horseback riding. Muscle fatigue in these areas often results in poor riding form, which can add undue stress and ultimately fatigue in the client's back.

The trainer might also want to discuss proper sitting posture with the client, since both her vocation and her hobby require her to spend excessive amounts of time sitting. Teaching her how to do simple stretching and strengthening exercises while sitting at her desk can further assist in reducing the back fatigue. As with every client, the trainer must evaluate the muscles involved with daily activities and then work with the client to strengthen and stretch those areas.

The program does not currently include an exercise for the latissimus muscles. When working in the home environment, a good exercise to consider is pull-ups. Since most 40-year-old female clients do not have the strength to perform pull-ups, the trainer might suggest that he/she assist the client. The trainer could help lift the client in the up-phase of the pull-up by standing behind her and grasping her at the waist and lifting. Then the client could lower herself under control, getting an eccentric workout of the muscle. If the client is uncomfortable with this hands-on approach, a chair could be used for the client to step up on during the upward phase of the pull-up, followed again by a controlled lowering of the body. The trainer should inform the client that such an eccentric workout might increase initial muscle soreness. Additional exercise for the upper-back musculature could be added by using dumbbells, rubber bands, or tubing.

FLEXIBILITY CONSIDERATIONS. The trainer has recommended a dual approach to flexibility. Because the client is sitting most of the time, she probably begins each workout session with tight musculature. She will benefit by participating in a pre-exercise stretching program that will also help alleviate the chance of injury. Having a second and more in-depth stretching session at the end of the program helps to ensure long-term improvements in flexibility, and provides a relaxing way for the client to cool down after her workout. As with many sedentary 40-year-old women, her hamstrings, psoas, and low-back muscles are tight and probably contribute to her low-back discomfort. If she commonly wears high heels, she may also have a shortened Achilles tendon.

CASE STUDY 3   LOCATION: PERSONAL TRAINING GYM AND OUTDOORS

Sex: Male   *Age*: 25   *Blood pressure*: 115/70

Body-fat: 16%   *Resting heart rate*: 64   *Smoker*: No

Flexibility: Excellent in the low back and hamstrings. Noticeable tightness in the chest and shoulders.

Exercise history: Past competitive gymnast who stopped competing four years ago, after college. Since that time he has been swimming twice a week, jogging one mile twice a week, and stretching his legs and back daily.

Goals: To run in a 10K in six months and possibly a half marathon within a year. Lower his body-fat to 10 percent. Client also wants to increase his upper-body muscle mass in an effort to regain his college physique.

Additional information: He states that he has experienced some mild shin pain in the past after vigorous running and court sport activities. He is highly motivated.

Initial Exercise Program

WARM-UP AND CARDIOVASCULAR COMPONENT. Warm-up consisting of three minutes of easy climbing on the climbing simulator followed by five minutes of stretching the calves, hamstrings, quadriceps, and anterior tibialis. Running on a treadmill at a pace sufficient to elevate and maintain a target heart rate between 156 and 175 for 20–30 minutes.

STRENGTH-TRAINING COMPONENT

Exercise	Muscle Group(s)	Reps	Sets
Leg extension	Quadriceps	8–12	3
Hip extension	Hamstrings, gluteals	8–12	3
Leg curl	Hamstrings	8–12	3
Bench press	Triceps, pectorals, anterior deltoids	8–12	3
Bar dips	Triceps, pectorals, latissimus, anterior deltoids	10–12	3
Lat pull-downs	Latissimus, biceps	8–12	3
Dumbbell bentover rows	Latissimus, rhomboids	8–12	3
Bicep curls	Biceps	8–12	3
Toe raises	Anterior tibialis	8–12	3
Heal raises	Gastrocnemius	8–12	3
Trunk curls	Abdominals	25	3
Twisting trunk curls	Obliques	25	3

FLEXIBILITY COMPONENT. After the warm-up and before the running, stretches of the calves and anterior tibialis muscles should be performed, with an additional 10 minutes of stretching exercises to be performed after the strength-training and running components, to address all major muscle groups. Special attention should be given to the hamstrings, hip flexors, calves, anterior shin, and the arch of the foot, with additional trainer-assisted stretches of the pectoral and anterior shoulder area.

TIME REQUIREMENTS. This workout should take approximately 90 minutes when the strength and cardiovascular training are done together. It is to be performed three days a week, with a day of rest in between.

Program Variables and Special Considerations

CARDIOVASCULAR AND WARM-UP CONSIDERATIONS. This exercise program is designed to utilize the equipment available at the training facility every other day. To achieve his goals and reduce the risk of injury, the client should start out running three days a week. After the first two weeks of exercise, the trainer and the client can begin to vary the intensity of the running by increasing the speed and/or the grade of the treadmill.

The treadmill offers a couple of advantages as an alternative to running on a track, a trail, or the streets. First, most treadmills provide a cushioning effect, absorbing some of the shock normally encountered when running on hard surfaces. Since the client has experienced some leg pain while running in the past, this should be of some benefit. Second, while the client is running on the treadmill, the trainer can analyze his running form. The trainer can then give immediate feedback to the client to assist him in developing a safer, more efficient running style. Finally, the treadmill allows for better control of the intensity of the run because both speed and grade can be easily adjusted.

During the first few weeks, the client should just enjoy running 2–3 miles, taking up to 30 minutes. A slow, conservative approach is warranted, since the client has not run consistently for more than a mile in the recent past. In addition, he has previously experienced some shin pain after running. Starting the program with low mileage will help reduce the risk of musculoskeletal injuries. The trainer and client should also talk about proper footwear for running. If the client is going to get a new pair of running shoes, it is imperative that he break them in during the training phase before the 10K.

The client may be overzealous in his desire to train for his first race, wanting to increase his program too quickly. The client only needs to build his weekly mileage to a maximum of 15–20 miles while training for the 10K. Small, incremental increases such as a half mile per run per week will suffice. The trainer might recommend that the client vary his mileage from workout to workout. This allows for harder and easier days, which seems to reduce boredom and increase the overall training effect. An example would be to run four miles on Monday, three on Wednesday, and five on Saturday. As the 10K approaches, the trainer should have the client start running on a surface similar to that on which the race will be held. In most cases this means hitting the streets. Since the client has begun this program conservatively, he should have little difficulty adjusting to the new and probably harder surface. Because a change in running surface is frequently a precursor to shin or foot pain, the client should reduce his mileage the first few weeks on the streets. Alternating his running between the treadmill one day and the streets the next could also prove helpful in reducing the risk of injury or soreness.

STRENGTH CONSIDERATIONS. The strength-training program is rather aggressive. Although research indicates that clients can achieve good results with one set of exercises, this program is designed to fully exhaust each muscle group. The best approach would be to start out with lighter resistance and perform only one set of 8–12 repetitions for each exercise. As the client responds positively to the training, additional sets can be added. The trainer can also recommend changes in the weight to be used and the number of sets to be performed. Many clients will hit a plateau where they seem to be making no improvement. By adjusting the weight or the number of sets performed, the trainer can often help the client overcome such barriers. The program incorporates both upper- and lower-body exercises. Although the client is primarily interested in upper-body development, it is prudent to include lower-body exercises to help assist with the running goals. Strengthening of the mid-back and stretching of the chest and anterior shoulder will help correct any forward shoulder posture due to poor chest and shoulder flexibility.

FLEXIBILITY CONSIDERATIONS. The trainer has determined that the client has excellent low-back and hamstring flexibility. This is probably a carryover from his gymnastics days and his continual stretching. The trainer should still emphasize the importance of stretching these areas, especially because the client has started running. Additional stretches of the upper body have been emphasized to counter the client's tight shoulders and pectoral muscles. Without attention to these areas, it is likely that flexibility there will worsen because of the strength-training program.

These case studies are not intended as specific exercise programs. Rather, they are meant to show how the information presented in this manual can be pulled together and applied. In the real-life situation the trainer would gather a variety of additional information on the client's fitness, life-style, and goals.

SUMMARY

Fitness professionals working one-on-one with clients have two primary goals: to help clients attain their own fitness goals, and to guide clients toward the acceptance of fitness as a life-style, not just as a means to the end. To accomplish these goals, the trainer must consider the client's health-screening and fitness evaluation information as well as his/her goals, motivational factors, time limitations, and, most importantly, safety.

The trainer should work with the client to incorporate the four components of fitness—muscular strength, cardiovascular endurance, flexibility, and body composition—into the workout program. Additional education about healthful dietary habits may also be appropriate. Designing each program to include an adequate warm-up, exercise session, and cool-down is critical. Finally, the trainer should try to incorporate a variety of equipment, exercise modes, and workout structures in an effort to make each workout session enjoyable.

Personal trainers should remember that exercise programming is an ongoing process that incorporates planned changes to better facilitate the attainment of client goals. People's goals change all the time, and a good trainer will be able to examine these new goals and implement changes in the client's workout to reflect them. It is an exciting opportunity to work with new clients, programming them for a variety of safe and effective exercises. Successful implementation of a well-designed program for a healthy adult is beneficial for both the client and trainer: The client gets a healthier body and exercise habits that last a lifetime, and the trainer gets personal satisfaction and a satisfied client.

Modifications for Health Conditions and Special Populations

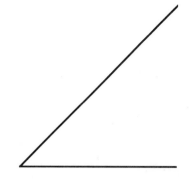

NEIL SOL

NEIL SOL, PH.D., is general manager of *The Houstonian*. Formerly, he served as president of the Medical Products Division of Nautilus Sports Medicine Industries and director of health promotion for Methodist Hospitals of Memphis. He is past president of the Association for Fitness in Business and consulting editor for *Optimal Health: Strategies for the Integrated Health Care System*, which he originated.

12

IN THIS CHAPTER:

- Modifying an exercise program for a variety of health conditions: hypertension, diabetes, arthritis, chronic obstructive pulmonary diseases, obesity, low-back pain.

- Modifying an exercise program for special populations: older clients and pregnant clients.

Every personal fitness trainer will encounter clients across the spectrum of health conditions. Many of these people will come to the trainer for help in managing disabilities or physical conditions that require modification of exercise routines. Although most chronic conditions cannot be cured, fitness training has a place in improving health and quality of life for people with problems such as hypertension, diabetes, arthritis, or low-back syndrome. Whether the client's symptoms are apparent, as in obesity or arthritis, or hidden, as in hypertension or diabetes, it is beyond the scope of practice for the personal trainer to diagnose the client's health condition or dispense medical information. The trainer must rely on the client's declaration of the problem, as well as a careful assessment of personal health history. The fitness evaluations and health histories administered by the trainer in the first sessions with the client (see Chapters 5 and 6) will often identify these special health conditions and alert the trainer to necessary modifications in the exercise program. If evaluation reveals a health problem, the trainer must refer the client to a physician for medical clearance before beginning an exercise program. Often, the trainer will find it helpful to discuss the client's limitations with the physician, as well.

The inherent risks of physical activity may aggravate health conditions in any participant. In people with special medical or health conditions including normal aging and pregnancy, strenuous physical activity may produce injury or disability, even death. On the other hand, a carefully planned exercise program can safely improve physical conditions. This chapter will present the special health conditions that a personal trainer may commonly encounter:

hypertension, diabetes, arthritis, lung disease, obesity, low-back pain, normal aging, colds and flu, and normal pregnancy. The physiology of each condition will be briefly identified so that the trainer can understand appropriate exercise precautions and modifications. A detailed discussion of medical emergencies and first aid may be found in Chapter 17, Emergency Procedures.

Hypertension

Hypertension, or high blood pressure, increases the risk of heart attack or stroke, especially in combination with other risk factors for heart disease, including high cholesterol, smoking, and lack of exercise. Although hypertension is the most common cardiovascular disease, its symptoms are often invisible to the victim. It can only be detected by measuring the client's blood pressure. The American College of Sports Medicine (1986) identifies people with **systolic blood pressure** (upper number) over 140 mmHg or **diastolic pressure** (lower number) over 90 mmHg as having increased risk for heart disease. These people need special modifications to their exercise programs. Because the causes of hypertension are unclear, no cures have been developed. However, blood pressure responds to changes in diet, to certain medications, and to exercise programs. The goal of hyertension treatment is to reduce the blood pressure readings to less than 140 mmHg systolic and less than 90 mmHg diastolic. A blood pressure of 120/80 mmHg is considered normal. If the hypertensive client is not under a physician's care, he/she must be referred for examination before the exercise program begins. Often, the physician will prescribe diuretic medication or salt-restricted diets for clients with mild hypertension. Both diuretics and the other drugs used for high blood pressure will affect the client's response to exercise. Please refer to Chapter 5, Health Screening, for an analysis of the effects of beta blockers, diuretics, and other medications and their effect on the heart-rate response to exercise.

EXERCISE FOR THE HYPERTENSIVE CLIENT. Aerobic exercise has been found to have a beneficial effect on hypertension, often lowering the client's blood pressure. This change can occur with long-term participation in a program that includes a substantial aerobic component. Appropriate activities include walking, jogging, swimming, cycling, rope-skipping, cross-country skiing, stair climbing, and rowing. Hypertensive clients should exercise at low-to-moderate intensity (50–70 percent of maximum heart rate reserve), no matter what their functional capacity. However, clients with above-average fitness capacity, who have controlled blood pressure values of less than 140/90, may exercise at higher intensities (60-85 percent maximum heart rate reserve). Refer to Chapter 7, Cardiorespiratory Fitness, for a discussion of techniques for monitoring exercise intensity.

The personal trainer should measure blood pressure periodically during each exercise session to ensure that the client does not have a hypertensive response. A hypertensive response to exercise may be any of the following:

- Systolic pressure above 250 mmHg.

- Diastolic pressure above 110 mmHg.

- A significant drop (10 mmHg) in systolic blood pressure.

- Failure of systolic pressure to rise with increased exercise workload.

Any of these responses require termination of exercise. Because the hypertensive client is at a higher risk for problems, trainers should be alert to these additional signals for terminating exercise:

- Excess fatigue.

- Light-headedness, confusion, pallor, dyspnea, nausea.

- Onset of angina (chest pain).

- Inappropriate bradychardia (drop in exercise heart rate greater than 10 bpm with increase or no change in workload).

To avoid aggravating the client's blood pressure, the trainer should modify strength-training programs in the following ways:

1. Emphasize lighter resistance and more frequent repetitions per set. For example, keep resistance within 50–60 percent of the client's one-repetition maximum (1 RM), but encourage the client to perform 15–20 repetitions per set, approximately three sets per exercise.

2. Avoid isometric exercise and power lifting for hypertensive clients.

3. As in the aerobic component, periodically monitor the client's blood pressure during weight training.

4. Avoid exercise positions, such as an incline sit-up and a decline bench press, that raise a client's feet above the level of the head.

5. Reduce the load and repetition of exercises, such as shoulder presses or lateral raises, that raise the arms above the shoulders.

6. Caution hypertensive clients not to hold their breath and strain while exercising. This causes a phenomenon called the *Valsalva maneuver*, which increases intrathoracic pressure and blood pressure. Clients most commonly hold their breath when the weights are too heavy or when they are close to the last repetition in a set. Remind clients always to breathe during stretching or exercise movements and to exhale through the mouth on exertion.

7. Use longer and more gradual warm-up and cool-down to allow the body more time to adjust to the physical stress of vigorous physical work.

SIDE EFFECTS FROM BLOOD-PRESSURE MEDICATIONS.   Personal trainers should become familiar with the implications of drugs for their clients' exercise programs. Drugs commonly prescribed for high blood pressure fall into four major categories:

- Diuretics ("water pills").

- Beta blockers.

- Vasodilators.

- Alpha blockers.

Diuretic drugs are used to reduce edema, the build-up of fluid in the body's tissues. Along with the fluids, these drugs leach some of the body's electrolytes, such as potassium. A client with low potassium (**hypokalemia**) may experience muscle cramps during exercise. It is important for anyone taking diuretic medications to see a physician regularly for blood tests to measure potassium levels. Low potassium can also cause heart arrhythmia (a disturbance in the rhythm of the heartbeat) that the client can feel when taking a heart rate. If clients experience either muscle cramps or arrhythmias, they should stop exercising and see their physicians. Arrhythmias can lead to sudden death.

exercising and see their physicians. Arrhythmias can lead to sudden death.

Beta-blocking medications can reduce cardiac output by limiting the heart rate, which reduces blood pressure. Therefore, clients using **beta blockers** will not have normal increases in exercise heart rates and will have difficulty achieving training heart rates. They will also tire sooner because the drug has limited their heart-rate response. Regulating exercise intensity by monitoring the pulse is not appropriate for these clients. Instead, they should use the **ratings of perceived exertion (RPE)** scale (see Chapter 7). The trainer should frequently ask these clients how they are doing, so that they learn to perceive their fatigue accurately and regulate exercise intensity.

Another class of drugs commonly used to reduce high blood pressure is **vasodilators.** **Vasodilators** relax the blood vessels to relieve pressure in the vascular system. During exercise, clients who take vasodilators may experence rapid heart rate or low blood pressure. Cool-down is important to minimize the hypotension that may occur after exercise. Like vasodilators, alpha blockers relax peripheral blood vessels. Unlike beta blockers, they do not affect heart-rate response, so that clients using alpha blockers can appropriately monitor exercise intensity by taking their pulse. As new hypertensive medications are developed and prescribed, the personal trainer must become educated about them and refer to a recent edition of the *Physicians' Desk Reference* for information on unfamiliar medications.

Diabetes

Diabetes mellitus is a chronic metabolic disorder that cannot be cured but can be controlled. Untreated, it can result in vision loss, circulatory problems, kidney disease, and death. There are two types of diabetes: type I, or insulin-dependent diabetes, and type II, or non-insulin-dependent diabetes. Type II diabetes accounts for about 95 percent of all diabetics. Type II diabetics use exercise, diet, and oral medication to control blood glucose (sugar) levels. Type II diabetics typically have developed the disorder during their adult years, and they are frequently obese. Type I diabetics (about 5 percent) are often born with the disease or develop it during childhood. Theirs is a life-long condition, and they must depend on insulin injections.

Diabetes is related to the production and utilization of **insulin**, a hormone secreted by the pancreas that promotes entry of glucose into the body's cells. In a normal person, insulin is released in response to high blood sugar levels (after ingesting a meal, for example) and lowers the blood sugar to acceptable levels. In type I, or insulin-dependent, diabetes, the pancreas produces little or no insulin, and the diabetic must take insulin daily. In type II, or non-insulin-dependent diabetes, the body produces insufficient insulin. This type of diabetes usually develops gradually and may not need to be treated with insulin.

Exercise, along with diet and medication, can help diabetics manage their disease. Because it promotes the entry of glucose into the cells, exercise can lower a diabetic's glucose levels. However, too much exercise, like too much insulin or insufficient food, may bring on an episode of **hypoglycemia**, or low blood sugar. A client experiencing a hypoglycemic episode may feel faint or excessively fatigued, lose consciousness, or have a seizure. Other symptoms are headache, light-headedness, sweating, shakiness, butterflies in the stomach, irritability, slurred speech, and poor coordination. (Refer to Chapter 17, Emergency Procedures, for a more detailed discussion of symptoms and the personal trainer's responsibility for response to a hypoglycemic episode.)

EXERCISE FOR THE DIABETIC CLIENT. Before beginning an exercise program, diabetic clients must consult with their physicians about monitoring and adjusting insulin dosages and injection sites. As explained in Chapter 17, diabetics who have experience with fitness programs and who have become educated in caring for themselves can safely begin an exercise program with a personal trainer. It is prudent to have a diabetic client undergo an ECG-monitored exercise test to rule out cardiovascular abnormalities before starting to exercise.

In designing an exercise program for the diabetic client, the following precautions and recommendations are appropriate:

1. Clients on insulin may need to determine if they should reduce their insulin doses when beginning a regular exercise program. It is important for diabetics to work closely with their physicians to ensure appropriate dosages.

2. Aerobic activity is best suited to use calories, promote weight reduction, and metabolize blood glucose efficiently. Diabetics can best control their blood-sugar levels with exercise that is predictable and consistent in duration, intensity, and frequency.

3. Obese type II diabetics should follow the guidelines for nondiabetic obese clients, which include low-impact, low-intensity aerobic exercise, 3–5 times per week.

4. Diabetics who use insulin should not inject it into the limbs they are about to exercise. The increased circulation in the exercised extremity may cause the insulin to be absorbed quickly enough to bring on hypoglycemia.

5. Exercising in weather extremes could affect insulin absorption. Cold weather may slow insulin absorption, and hot weather may speed up insulin absorption.

6. To help avoid hypoglycemic reactions during exercise, recommend that the diabetic client ingest a complex carbohydrate snack before exercising. If the aerobic exercise duration exceeds 30 minutes, suggest that a carbohydrate snack be ingested every 30 minutes during exercise. Juice or crackers work well in these situations.

7. Have easily digestible carbohydrates, juice, or candy on hand for diabetics who may experience hypoglycemia.

8. Strength and flexibility exercises should be included according to the functional capacity of the client.

9. A client who exhibits diabetic complications such as neuropathy (nerve damage) and peripheral circulation damage should be referred to his/her physician.

10. Diabetic clients should maintain good foot care. Because high blood sugar levels can damage nerves and blood vessels, causing poor circulation and reduced sensation to the legs and feet, foot problems are a major complication of diabetes. Clients should note hot spots, blisters, callouses, cuts, sores, and bunions and receive proper treatment.

Diabetic clients must take responsibility for their own care, including monitoring blood sugars, taking recommended insulin, eating properly, exercising regularly, and keeping medical appointments.

Arthritis

There are two basic forms of arthritis: osteoarthritis and rheumatoid arthritis. The most common form, **osteoarthritis**, is a degenerative disease of the joints and one of the most common causes of chronic physical discomfort and disability, especially with advancing age. During this degenerative process, the joints "wear out." Cartilage gradually breaks down and is worn away, leaving the ends of the bone exposed or unprotected. Without their smooth, normal gliding surfaces, joints become painful to move, and range of motion becomes restricted. Osteoarthritis primarily affects the weight-bearing joints of the hips, knees, spine, and feet, and these joints may be more stiff or painful after overuse or periods of immobility.

The other common form of arthritis, **rheumatoid arthritis**, is a chronic systemic disease. It causes tissue inflammation that leads to destruction of the joints. Characterized by periodic flare-ups and remissions, rheumatoid arthritis is more common among women than men and more prevalent in early middle age. Once a joint becomes affected, the inflammation continues intermittently, leading to swollen, disfigured, and painful joints.

EXERCISE FOR THE ARTHRITIC CLIENT. If a client suffers from stiff or achy joints, avoid planning exercises that add stress to those joints. Clients may experience mild discomfort during exercising, but if the joint pain becomes moderate or severe, the client should stop performing the exercise and see a physician before resuming it. Clients with rheumatoid arthritis should not exercise during an inflammatory episode in which the joints are painful, swollen, red, or hot. The following adaptations will help the arthritic client benefit from an exercise program without damage to the joints.

1. Use an extended warm-up to promote flexibility and range of motion.

2. Use exercises of mild to moderate intensity, especially movements designed to improve joint flexibility through a full range of motion. Exercises should be performed slowly and with good control.

3. Passive range-of-motion exercise, in which the trainer moves the client's limbs, is helpful in warming and loosening joints.

4. Aerobic exercise intensity depends on joint limitations, fatigue, and the client's ability to achieve a training heart rate. The trainer should design the aerobic component to include exercises that keep weight off the affected joints, such as cycling, rowing, swimming, or water exercise. Avoid jogging or high-impact programs.

5. Always use proper body mechanics to ensure appropriate alignment and good posture. Poor posture fatigues the body and can cause joint stress. Exercises should be performed with the joint in its most stable and functional position.

6. Include strength exercises to increase muscle tone and functional strength. Increased strength surrounding the joints often translates into joint protection. Strength training should focus on joint mobility and range of motion. Generally, the arthritic client should use light

weight at a resistance of 40–60 percent 1 RM (one rep-maximum) for 10–20 repetitions in each set.

7. Increase the use of isometric exercises, which increase muscular strength and endurance with no joint movement.

8. Expect clients with rheumatoid arthritis to feel fatigue, which is a side effect of the disease. A client who experiences extreme fatigue at the beginning of a session should not exercise that day.

9. Expect clients to feel discomfort and painful joints. If discomfort is greater than normal, discontinue the exercise or eliminate that particular movement from the workout.

10. Follow the two-hour pain rule, which states that clients have over-exercised if they experience excess joint pain or greater-than-normal pain two hours after the workout.

11. Encourage clients to respect their own limits and to find the proper balance between rest and exercise. In other words, if it hurts, don't do it.

12. The water temperature for aquatic workouts should be 83–88° Fahrenheit. Warm water helps relax muscles and decrease joint stiffness. Buoyancy helps to support the body, decreasing weight on the hips, knees, ankles, feet, and spine.

Chronic Obstructive Pulmonary Disease

Chronic obstructive pulmonary disease (COPD), including asthma, bronchitis, and emphysema, afflicts the sufferer with obstruction to the flow of air in and out of the lungs. **Asthma**, a common form of COPD, results from spasm and constriction of the bronchial tubes. These spasms can be caused by allergic reactions or by exercise itself (exercise-induced bronchospasm). Often, asthmatic symptoms can be controlled by medication and use of inhalers. (See Chapter 17, Emergency Procedures, for a more detailed discussion of symptoms that call for intervention by the trainer.)

Bronchitis, an inflammation of the bronchial tubes, is accompanied by increased mucous secretions that narrow these airways and can result from respiratory infections or from smoking. Clients with bronchitis will cough, wheeze, and produce a lot of sputum. They will have difficulty with physical activity because of the reduced air flow to the lungs.

Emphysema is an end-stage COPD, typically the result of a long smoking habit. Clients with emphysema will have severe limitations to physical activities. Personal trainers should refer clients with emphysema or chronic bronchitis to their physicians or to pulmonary rehabilitation programs. They are not appropriate for private fitness training programs.

EXERCISE FOR THE ASTHMATIC CLIENT. Only clients with controlled asthma, that is, people who take prescribed medication and who use a **bronchodilating inhaler** before, during, or after exercise, should be accepted for training by a personal trainer. These clients can participate in a comprehensive exercise program. They will benefit from aerobic training appropriate to their fitness levels as well as from strength and flexibility exercises. The following modifications will improve the safety of the program for the asthmatic client.

1. Remind clients to take their medications and use their inhalers according to their doctors' directions.

2. Plan an extended warm-up to avoid exercise-induced bronchospasm.

3. Reduce the intensity and increase the duration of the aerobic component to obtain cardiovascular benefits while avoiding asthmatic symptoms.

4. Encourage clients to use purse-lipped and diaphragmic breathing to assist in breathing more fully and exhaling more forcefully.

5. Remind clients to keep well-hydrated to decrease mucous secretions.

6. Control environmental conditions that may increase the likelihood of an attack. Avoid exercising in extremely low temperatures, in areas with a high pollen count, or in heavy air pollution.

Obesity

Many overweight and obese persons will seek out personal trainers to assist them in reducing their body-fat and improving their fitness. Because obesity and overweight are different, the trainer's initial evaluation should determine the body-fat percentage for each client. **Overweight** has been defined as exceeding normal weight for a specific height according to standard height and weight tables. Overweight clients may not be over-fat. They may even have an excess of lean body tissue. **Obesity**, on the other hand, is a condition of excessive body-fat—greater than 25 percent in men or 30 percent in women.* Obesity is associated with a number of medical problems, including hypertension and diabetes, that may affect a client's response to exercise. The trainer must keep these conditions in mind when designing the exercise program.

During the initial fitness evaluation, the trainer should identify eating patterns that may contribute to excess fat and offer help in changing those patterns. Any suspicion of anorexia or bulimia in a client should lead to an immediate referral for psychotherapy and medical treatment. Trainers should caution clients against weight-loss fads and should emphasize the role of a healthy diet combined with an exercise program in attaining the client's goals. A safe weight loss for an obese client on a modified-calorie diet, in combination with low-intensity exercise sessions 3–5 times per week, is 1–3 pounds per week. In the early stages of the program, a client may lose more pounds per week, but the loss will level off as the client approaches target weight. Quick, excessive loss will probably be regained and will produce a yo-yo effect, each loss and gain making it harder to lose the next time. A personal trainer should not accept clients on fasting diets unless they are supervised by physicians. These diets can produce electrolyte imbalances that can lead to dangerous cardiac arrhythmias. They can also reduce lean muscle tissue. Refer to Chapter 10 for a more complete discussion of exercise and weight control.

EXERCISE FOR THE OBESE CLIENT.   Most obese clients are not accustomed to regular exercise and need a program that proceeds slowly. The appropriate training heart rate for these clients is approximately 60–70 percent maximum heart rate reserve with a duration of 30–60 minutes. Exercise sessions should occur 3–5 times per week. To help burn body-fat, emphasize longer duration and lower intensity.

---

* Obesity is both a quantitative and a qualitative measure. Other tests may list slightly different numbers.

Aerobic exercise, which increases metabolism and burns calories more efficiently than weight training, should be the main component of the exercise program. Walking or low-impact aerobic activity will minimize trauma to the musculoskeletal system and reduce the risk of orthopedic injury. Swimming, rowing, and cycling are appropriate because these activities support the client's body weight. Lack of previous exercise and the immobility caused by being overweight may have reduced the client's flexibility, so that stretching and ROM exercises are beneficial. The obese client may participate in weight training for cosmetic reasons, to firm or define specific areas of the body. The weight-training program should touch on all major muscle groups, with emphasis on higher repetitions and low weight sets. By helping to change body contour, weight training can keep the client motivated to continue the fitness and weight-loss program.

If the obese client exhibits shortness of breath, profuse sweating, or dizziness, the personal trainer should slow or stop the exercise until the symptoms dissipate. (Please refer to Chapter 17, Emergency Procedures, for symptoms and appropriate response to clients' fainting, dyspnea (labored breathing), or chest pain.)

Low-Back Pain

The most frequent cause of activity limitations among people under age 45, **low-back syndrome** (pain) is also the most common job disability. It occurs among approximately 80 percent of Americans. Symptoms include pain and muscle spasm in the area of the lumbar spine. Low-back syndrome results from:

- Tight muscles in the low back.
- Tight hamstrings.
- Poor posture.
- Weak muscles in the trunk, particularly the abdomen.
- Structural abnormalities.

Clients who present with pain or discomfort anywhere along the spine should be referred to their physicians for evaluation before beginning an exercise program. Acute back pain requires medical attention and treatment. Any structural abnormality also requires medical treatment to correct the condition. Before any low-back work, clients must have physician evaluations and recommendations, especially if these clients have not previously sought medical attention for their back problems.

An exercise program designed to correct low-back syndrome will include careful warm-up and cool-down before and after activity, as well as emphasis on correct posture and mechanics in performing the exercises. Exercises will require the client to stretch tight muscles, particularly the hamstrings, gluteals, erector spinae muscles, and hip flexors. In addition, the client will need to strengthen weak muscles, especially the abdominal group.

EXERCISE FOR LOW-BACK SYNDROME.   Clients with low-back syndrome should focus on exercises to strengthen and stretch the muscles of the trunk and back to obtain prolonged relief and prevent future problems. Figures 12-1 through 12-11 illustrate several such exercises. The personal trainer should

Figure 12–1 *Back extension:* Lie flat on the floor with hands in a push-up position. Slowly press up with the hands, lifting the shoulders while relaxing the pelvis and hips. Keep thighs on the floor, letting the back sag. Hold the top position for two or three seconds, then lower shoulders back to the floor. Repeat 5–10 times, remembering to hold in the top position.

Figure 12–2 *Knee to nose:* Lie flat on the back with legs extended, and slowly bring one knee toward the chest with hands clasped over the shin. At the same time bring the head forward as if to kiss the knee. Hold for five seconds. Return to starting position and repeat five times on each leg.

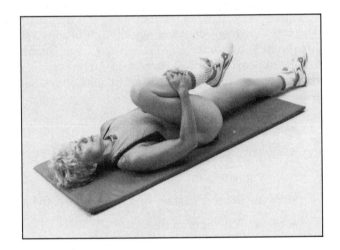

Figure 12–3 *Half sit-ups:* Lie flat on the back with knees bent, feet on the floor, and hands resting on the chest. Slowly raise the head and shoulders while reaching toward the knees. Hold for five seconds, then slowly lower to starting position. Repeat 5–10 times, remembering to exhale while lifting upward.

Figure 12–4   *Knee raises*: Lie flat on the back with knees bent. Clasp both hands around the shin and slowly pull toward the chest. Hold for five seconds. Repeat 5–10 times with each leg.

Figure 12–5   *Pelvic tilt*: Lie on the back with knees bent. Place hands behind the head and contract the muscles of the buttocks (not the lower back), raising the pelvis slightly without the aid of the back or legs. Hold for five seconds.

Figure 12–6   *Hip rotation*: Lie on the back with arms out to the side. Slowly draw the knees to the chest and roll them gently from side to side, keeping the shoulders, head, and arms on the floor. Repeat 10–15 times.

Figure 12–7 *Cat stretch*: Start on the hands and knees with the back flat and the head in a neutral position. Slowly drop the head and arch the back. Hold for five seconds. Reverse the action by raising the head and letting the back drop to a swayed position. Hold for five seconds. Repeat 5–10 times.

Figure 12–8 *Backward stretch*: Start on the hands and knees with the back flat and the head in a neutral position. Then slowly drop backward until the buttocks almost touch the heels, keeping the arms in front to stretch the shoulders and back. Hold for five seconds. Repeat 5–10 times.

encourage the client to perform basic back exercises, or any other exercise that uses low-back muscles, slowly with a static stretching technique instead of bouncing or ballistic movements. The trainer should also remind the client to continue breathing.

Clients with low-back syndrome should avoid exercises that may aggravate their condition, including:

- Standing military presses.
- Sit-ups with toes anchored or straight legs.
- Lifts with straight legs.
- Double leg raises with straight legs.
- Standing or sitting toe touches with straight legs.

The personal trainer should attempt to balance strength between the abdominal and erector spinae muscle groups. The client also needs to maintain equal flexibility in both groups. If clients are not in pain, they can participate in aerobic activities that are appropriate for their functional capacity, especially activities that minimize trauma to the spine. For example, appropriate aerobic exercise could include cycling, swimming, or walking. Weight training may be used, but with extra caution.

The personal fitness trainer should help the client move through the range of motion slowly during each strength exercise and also be prepared to offer spotting support earlier than usual. Emphasize the use of lighter weights and higher repetition sets. Ensure that the client employs proper lifting mechanics, using the legs to lift rather than the low-back muscles. For all clients, but especially those with low-back problems, observe a client's lifting technique, not only during the lift but also just before and just after. Often a client will perform an exercise correctly and then bend at the waist with knees straight to put the weight back on the floor. Clients with low-back syndrome must use extra care in performing strength exercises such as the following:

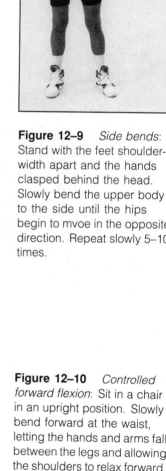

Figure 12–9 *Side bends*: Stand with the feet shoulder-width apart and the hands clasped behind the head. Slowly bend the upper body to the side until the hips begin to mvoe in the opposite direction. Repeat slowly 5–10 times.

Figure 12–10 *Controlled forward flexion*: Sit in a chair in an upright position. Slowly bend forward at the waist, letting the hands and arms fall between the legs and allowing the shoulders to relax forward. Hold for 5–10 seconds and slowly return to the sitting position. Repeat 5–10 times.

Figure 12–11 *Arching the back*: Lie face down on a small pillow placed at the waist, with the arms stretched backward and the hands resting on the back of the thighs. Slowly raise the head and shoulders off the floor and hold for 3–5 seconds. Relax and return to the starting position. Repeat 5–10 times.

- Shoulder press.
- Bentover rows.
- Seated rows.
- Lat pull-downs.

Aging

Medical and physiological research into the process of human aging are demonstrating that disability, weakness, and disease are not inevitable in growing older. People who maintain a healthy life-style—choosing foods wisely, avoiding alcohol and tobacco use, keeping emotionally involved with others, and keeping fit—can forestall most of the disabilities traditionally associated with aging. An active exercise program, wisely adapted to the physical changes the human body undergoes after middle age, is an important part of staying healthy into later life. However, the personal fitness trainer who works with people 50 years and older must be familiar with the normal physiological changes in this age group and be able to adapt a training regimen to these changes.

After age 30, physiological processes begin a subtle decline that becomes more obvious around age 55–60. Vision, hearing, and taste, for example, become less acute over time. The most important changes from the personal trainer's point of view are declines in cardiac output, muscle mass, basal metabolic rate, joint flexibility, and bone mass.

CARDIOVASCULAR SYSTEM. As people age, their heart rate slows and stroke volume decreases, reducing their maximum cardiac output. Maximal heart-rate capacity, calculated as a function of age (220 minus age), drops with each decade, resulting in reduced training rates for older adults. The reduction in cardiac output also reduces maximum oxygen consumption ($\dot{V}O_2$ max.) by about 9 percent per decade after age 30. With a lower $\dot{V}O_2$ max., the older client has less capacity to generate energy and perform work. Activities performed easily when a client was young may be perceived as more difficult after middle age because the cost of the activity has become a higher percentage of maximum. Blood pressure also tends to increase with advancing age. This increase is due to decreased diameter of the blood vessels (atherosclerosis), resulting in increased resistance to blood flow. Increases in the systolic blood pressure of 10–40 mmHg are not uncommon.

MUSCULAR SYSTEM. After age 30, muscle mass decreases, and later, muscle strength decreases. There is a decrease in both the number and size of muscle fibers and a decrease in the number of **fast-twitch fibers** in skeletal muscle. Although muscles do not hypertrophy with training as readily in older adults as in those younger, strength training still provides benefits. For example, a 20-year-old who can press 100 pounds may improve to 200 pounds after 10 weeks of training. In comparison, a 60-year-old who can press 50 pounds may improve to 100 pounds. Both athletes may have a 100 percent improvement, but in absolute terms the 20-year-old is stronger.

Along with the decrease in muscle mass, there is a gradual reduction in **basal metabolic rate (BMR)**. This can lead to creeping obesity and an increase in body weight by ½-pound of fat per year after age 30. Thus, older adults typically have a higher percentage of body-fat. Exercise can help the client compensate for this trend by increasing daily caloric expenditure, maintaining muscle mass and slowing the weight gain.

Aging impairs muscles, tendons, and ligaments, so that they lose elasticity. Although many older adults experience some loss in joint mobility and flexibility after age 65, their flexibility can be restored to youthful levels if there are no complications from disease. Stretching and flexibility exercises are important, even for homebound elderly people or those confined to wheelchairs.

SKELETAL SYSTEM. Both men and women lose bone mass and strength with age, but women are at higher risk because of hormone changes after menopause. Osteoporosis is a potentially life-threatening condition. A high proportion of older people die as a result of complications from fragile broken bones. Older women should consult their physicians about hormone therapy to protect their bones. In addition, adequate calcium in the diet and regular exercise help to maintain bone mass. Weight-bearing and progressive resistance exercise have been shown to be the most effective types of exercise. Simply using light hand weights in muscle endurance exercises will increase bone mass in women over 50.

RESPIRATORY SYSTEM. There will be a decrease in vital capacity and residual volume with advancing age. This decrease occurs as a result of reduced alveoli and gas-exchange area in the lungs. The gas exchange also becomes less efficient and breathing muscles weaken. Chest expansion and breathing exercises may help to keep the breathing muscles strong and elastic and promote a more full inhalation and exhalation.

NERVOUS SYSTEM. With aging, the speed and conduction of the nerve impulses lessen, resulting in slowed reflexes. Delayed reflexes translate into slower movement time than may have been experienced at an earlier age.

EXERCISE FOR THE OLDER ADULT. Before beginning any exercise program, clients over age 50 must have approval of their physicians. Ideally, clients would also undergo ECG-monitored exercise tests so that their physicians could identify cardiovascular abnormalities that may appear during physical activity. This test also establishes the clients' functional capacity, so that the personal trainer can develop an accurate exercise program.

The following are appropriate exercise modifications and recommendations for the older adult:

1. All components of the exercise program should start and progress slowly.

2. Exercise intensity should fall between 40 and 70 percent of maximum heart rate reserve. Exercise sessions should last 15–60 minutes, approximately 3–5 times per week.

3. All types of aerobic activity are appropriate, depending on the client's state of health and fitness. For example, weight-bearing activities are inappropriate for obese or arthritic clients. Such clients will have less risk for orthopedic injury with activities such as rowing, swimming, and cycling.

4. With all clients, the trainer should be alert to signs of distress or overexercising.

5. Weight training is appropriate for older clients who do not suffer from arthritis or orthopedic problems. Weight training should emphasize lighter resistance, approximately 40–50 percent of 1 RM for 10–15 repetitions.

6. Light hand weights (1–3 pounds), surgical tubing, or rubber bands will help build bone mass and strength. Emphasize alignment and balance and ensure that the older client performs all strength exercise slowly and with control. Use extra caution while spotting.

7. Older clients should perform flexibility exercises slowly, warming up first and using static stretching techniques.

8. During stretching, monitor the client for joint pain. If any exercise results in excessive joint ache or pain, the client should stop and see a physician before resuming exercise.

The personal trainer can be especially valuable as an exercise leader for the older client, ensuring adherence to a progressive fitness program. The trainer should encourage the client, emphasizing that it is never too late to begin a fitness program and that the client can expect substantial improvements with training.

Colds and Flu

In their enthusiasm and commitment, clients will often appear for exercise sessions with colds or flu. The best advice a trainer can give a client with a cold or flu is to rest and allow the condition to subside before continuing the exercise program. When the client has recovered, the trainer should guide a slow re-entry into the exercise routine. People develop colds or flu because their resistance was low. Using extra energy to work out will reduce their ability to fight the bacteria or virus, exacerbating the illness. Furthermore, upper respiratory or sinus involvement also limits the clients' breathing and oxygen intake. Clients with sinus problems should avoid swimming because the pool chlorine can aggravate this condition. Colds and flu can produce muscle weakness that increases the risks of injury during weight training.

Medications can also interfere with clients' ability to exercise during bouts of illness. Many over-the-counter cold medications increase both resting and exercise heart rates, making it difficult to assess the proper intensity of the workout. Prescription medications may cause drowsiness, reducing motivation to exercise and increasing risk of injury. However enthusiastic, the sick client should be told to take it easy until the cold or flu has abated.

Pregnancy and Postpartum

Pregnant and postpartum clients need special consideration in their exercise programs. While pregnancy is a normal human condition, it does change women's physiological responses during exercise. The trainer must adjust the fitness program to allow for these changes, including changes in hormone levels and body conformation. During pregnancy and postpartum, the goal of exercise is to maintain the highest level of fitness consistent with maximum safety. Like clients with other special health conditions, the pregnant woman may exercise, but should participate with the permission and, if necessary, the special instructions of her physician. The American College of Obstetricians and Gynecologists (ACOG, 1985) has developed guidelines for safe exercise during pregnancy (see Table 12-1).

Using these guidelines, most pregnant women can exercise safely and obtain optimal benefits. However, certain conditions may limit a woman's physical activity. Pregnant or postpartum women with any of the following require approval from a physician before beginning an exercise program:

- Hypertension.

- Anemia or other blood disorder.

- Thyroid disease.

- Cardiac arrhythmia or palpitations.

- History of sudden labor.

- History of fetal growth retardation.

- Bleeding during present pregnancy.

- Breech position during last trimester.

- Excessive obesity.

- Extreme underweight.

- Extremely sedentary life-style.

ACOG recommends that pregnant or postpartum women with the following conditions should not exercise:

- History of three or more spontaneous abortions.

- Ruptured membranes.

- Incompetent cervix.

- Bleeding or a diagnosis of placentia previa.

- Diagnosed cardiac disease.

A personal trainer whose client has one of these conditions should immediately seek direction of the client's physician.

The normal physical changes caused by pregnancy likewise require adaptations in the exercise regimen. For example, pregnant women have higher basal body temperatures that may cause difficulty exercising in warm environments. Pregnant women may show signs of overheating sooner than other clients; they should be cautioned not to exercise in hot, humid conditions or when they have a fever. The trainer can minimize overheating in pregnant

Table 12–1   ACOG GUIDELINES FOR EXERCISE DURING PREGNANCY AND POSTPARTUM

The following guidelines are based on the unique physical and physiological conditions that exist during pregnancy and the postpartum period. They outline general criteria for safety to provide direction to patients in the development of home exercise programs.

Pregnancy and Postpartum

1. Regular exercise (at least three times per week) is preferable to intermittent activity. Competitive activities should be discouraged.

2. Vigorous exercise should not be performed in hot, humid weather or during a period of febrile illness.

3. Ballistic movements (jerky, bouncy motions) should be avoided. Exercise should be done on a wooden floor or a tightly carpeted surface to reduce shock and provide a sure footing.

4. Deep flexion or extension of joints should be avoided because of connective tissue laxity. Activities that require jumping, jarring motions or rapid changes in direction should be avoided because of joint instability.

5. Vigorous exercise should be preceded by a 5-minute period of muscle warm-up. This can be accomplished by slow walking or stationary cycling with low resistance.

6. Vigorous exercise should be followed by a period of gradually declining activity that includes gentle stationary stretching. Because connective tissue laxity increases the risk of joint injury, stretches should not be taken to the point of maximum resistance.

7. Heart rate should be measured at times of peak activity. Target heart rates and limits established in consultation with the physician should not be exceeded.

8. Care should be taken to gradually rise from the floor to avoid orthostatic hypotension. Some form of activity involving the legs should be continued for a brief period.

9. Liquids should be taken liberally before and after exercise to prevent dehydration. If necessary, activity should be interrupted to replenish fluids.

10. Women who have led sedentary life-styles should begin with physical activity of very low intensity and advance activity levels very gradually.

11. Activity should be stopped and the physician consulted if any unusual symptoms appear.

Pregnancy Only

1. Maternal heart rate should not exceed 140 bpm.

2. Strenuous activities should not exceed 15 minutes in duration.

3. No exercise should be performed in the supine position after the fourth month of gestation is completed.

4. Exercises that employ the Valsalva maneuver should be avoided.

5. Caloric intake should be adequate to meet not only the extra energy needs of pregnancy, but also of the exercise performed.

6. Maternal core temperature should not exceed 38°C.

Source: American College of Obstetricians and Gynecologists. (1985). *Exercise during pregnancy and the postnatal period* (ACOG home-exercise programs). Washington, D.C.: Author. Reprinted with permission.

clients by reducing exercise intensity, extending recovery time, and exercising in air-conditioned rooms.

During pregnancy, the expectant mother uses carbohydrates faster to provide energy to support her baby. Sharing energy with the fetus reduces the energy available for exercise, so the pregnant woman may experience hypoglycemia during physical activity. She may not have enough energy to support prolonged exercise of moderate-to-strenuous intensity and may fatigue earlier than before she was pregnant. A snack of complex carbohydrates 15-30 minutes before exercise will help eliminate hypoglycemic reactions.

Pregnancy affects the positions a woman may use for exercise. For example, hormonal changes relax the connective tissues and may produce joint instability in pregnant clients, increasing their risk for injury. Furthermore, these relaxed connective tissues, combined with the enlarged hips and uterus, may result in back strain and back or hip pain. Women's center of gravity changes as their pregnancy advances, so that all movements must be performed differently. Pregnant clients should not exercise in the supine position after the fourth month because this position allows the fetus to press on the vena cava, impairing blood return to the mother's heart and head. Exercising in the supine position may make the pregnant woman light-headed and cause difficulty for her in proceeding with the activity.

A pregnant woman's blood volume increases approximately 30 percent and as a result resting heart rate and cardiac output will significantly increase. The trainer must take these changes into account in calculating a safe target heart rate, which should be 25-30 percent lower than when the client is not pregnant, or less than 140 beats per minute.

EXERCISE FOR THE PREGNANT CLIENT. The ACOG recommends aerobic activity at a fairly low intensity, 50-60 percent of functional capacity with a training heart rate below 140 beats per minute, for pregnant women. However, the heart rate may not measure exercise intensity accurately during this time. Pregnant women should simply exercise at an intensity that makes it somewhat difficult to carry on a conversation, but below the level at which they feel short of breath. Aerobic exercise sessions should be limited to approximately 15 minutes duration, 3-4 days per week. Pregnant clients should exercise on alternate days so that they rest adequately between sessions.

The personal trainer should expect to see the amount of exercise performed decrease during pregnancy. Progression of exercise should be slow, especially for women who were somewhat sedentary before pregnancy. Physical work capacity decreases in the first and third trimester but may increase in the second, so that exercise will be more difficult, with a higher perceived exertion, in the first and third trimesters. In addition, the risk of fetal growth retardation is highest during the first trimester, and so care should be taken to avoid overheating and overexercising. It is common to see a decrease in exercise progress as a woman's body weight increases, especially in the third trimester. The personal trainer must insist on rest days for the client. In addition, the trainer must observe the client for any of the following unusual symptoms that may result from exercise:

- Fainting.

- Vaginal bleeding.

- Sharp pains in the chest or abdomen.

- Extreme nausea.

- Feeling of disorientation.

- Temperature extremes of very hot or cold and clammy.

- Gush of fluid from the vagina.

- Blurred vision.

- Marked swelling or fluid retention.

- Severe or continuous headache.

If any of these signs or symptoms appear, the client must immediately stop exercise and consult with her physician.

As pregnancy progresses, aerobic activities should be chosen for minimal stress on the joints: swimming, cycling, or walking. Weight training should focus on maintaining muscle tone and improving muscular strength and endurance, which are useful to maintain joint stability as the connective tissues relax during pregnancy. Although strength training is commonly believed to decrease labor and increase the ease of pregnancy, research results are equivocal on this subject. In any case, the personal trainer should ensure that the client does not strain or hold her breath (Valsalva maneuver) during exercise and should plan for light resistance (30–50 percent of 1 RM) and higher repetitions (12–20 per set). The trainer may supplement the normal exercise regimen with Lamaze exercises and with **Kegel exercises** to strengthen the pelvic floor muscles.

Although flexibility is an important component of any exercise program, a pregnant woman's loosening joints will require a modified approach. The fitness trainer should primarily focus on using flexibility movements to abate the muscle soreness that the client may feel because of her postural changes. Stretching should be static; avoiding ballistic movements, the client should avoid deep flexion, any movements in the supine position, and hyperextension of the joints. Pregnant women should also avoid bending forward from a standing position, as in standing toe touches, because this position may cause dizziness or heartburn and place undue stress on the lumbar spine.

Like flexibility and stretching, calisthenic exercises also require modification during pregnancy. For example, during abdominal exercise the client should avoid traditional sit-ups in the supine position, instead performing reverse curls from the seated position. The client may use push-ups in the modified position, with the fulcrum at the knees. The pelvic tilt is one of the most beneficial exercises for pregnant women. It helps maintain abdominal tone and stretches low-back muscles (see Figure 12–5).

EXERCISE FOR THE POSTPARTUM CLIENT. Clients will benefit from regular exercise continued after their babies are born. During the postpartum period, the goal of exercise is the same as during pregnancy, to maintain the highest level of fitness that maintains maximum safety. However, the postpartum client may also be attempting to regain the fitness and body shape she had before pregnancy. The personal trainer must help the client understand that most of pregnancy's physiological changes will continue through postpartum, and that similar precautions and guidelines are necessary.

Postpartum women may begin exercising 4–6 weeks after delivery, or when the bleeding stops. Exercise may increase blood flow. A woman who has had a cesarean should obtain a physician's release before resuming exercise. The intensity of exercise should remain low to prevent accumulation of lactic acid in the mother's milk. Furthermore, because the client has been relatively inactive during the last trimester of pregnancy, she should progress slowly with her exercise program after childbirth.

SUMMARY

As interest in personal training grows, more persons with medical conditions will seek assistance in improving their health and fitness. Such clients typically seek a personal trainer to ensure safety and success in their exercise programs. It is important for the trainer to know how to modify exercise programs for a variety of special conditions, ranging from diabetes, asthma, arthritis, and low-back pain, to the normal states of pregnancy and aging. It is even more important for the trainer to know when to refer clients to their physicians and/or to more specialized clinical programs. Most persons with special health conditions can participate in appropriately modified exercise programs. While an improper exercise regimen can aggravate a disability, an appropriate and carefully planned program can produce safe and positive results for the client.

REFERENCES

American College of Sports Medicine. (1986). *Guidelines for exercise testing and prescription* (3rd ed.). Philadephia: Lea & Febiger.

American College of Obstetricians and Gynecologists. (1985). *Exercise during pregnancy and postnatal period (ACOG home exercise programs).* Washington, D.C.: Author.

Physicians' Desk Reference (44th ed.) (1990). Orodell, NJ.: Edward R. Barnhart Publishing.

SUGGESTED READING

American College of Sports Medicine. (1991) *Guidelines for exercise testing and prescription* (4th ed.). Philadelphia: Lea & Febiger.

de Vries, H. (1986). *Exercise physiology for physical education and athletics.* Dubuque, IA.: William C. Brown.

Howley, E.T. & Franks, B.D. (1986). *Health/fitness instructor's handbook.* Champaign, IL.: Human Kinetics.

Stephens, G.W. (1980). *Pathophysiology for health practitioners.* New York: Macmillan.

Wallace, J.P. (1987). Exercise and pregnancy. In N. Van Gelder & S. Marks (Eds.) *Aerobic dance-exercise instructor manual* (pp. 205-215). San Diego: American Council on Exercise.

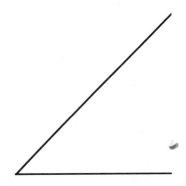

Leadership and Implementation   PART V

Participation is everything: The best-designed program is nothing more than some well thought out ideas until the trainer and the client begin to implement the plan. Today's fitness trainer is more than a designer of programs, he/she is an educator, providing instruction in many facets of fitness, from correct exercise technique to equipment and apparel selection. The chapters on adherence and motivation, communication and instruction, and selecting equipment, apparel, and footwear will assist the trainer in making the client's exercise experience valuable and rewarding. Although often overlooked in favor of the technical aspects of program design, the personal techniques presented make the difference in the long run.

Principles of Adherence and Motivation

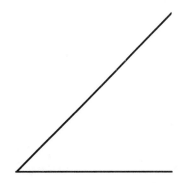

Abby C. King

13

Abby C. King, Ph.D., is a licensed clinical psychologist and senior research scientist at the Stanford Center for Research in Disease Prevention, Stanford University School of Medicine. She has written numerous articles and papers investigating the behavioral and psychological factors influencing adherence to a variety of health regimens, and she is a recent recipient of a National Institutes of Health research career award to study the effects of physical activity on stress-related response in older adults.

IN THIS CHAPTER:

- Identifying factors that influence exercise adherence: personal factors, program factors, and environmental factors.

- Understanding motivation: methods for enhancing and maintaining client motivation to exercise.

In addition to providing ongoing expert advice and instruction about effective training for a client, a major part of the personal trainer's job is motivating the client to stick with a training regimen. Motivation, like other aspects of exercise, is a personal issue; what works for one client may not work for another. Developing strategies to keep each client interested and motivated will often be as important as designing the exercise program.

THE CHALLENGE OF ADHERENCE AND MOTIVATION

Those of us working in exercise or physical fitness find physical activity to be an integral part of our lives. Understanding what it can do for us physically and mentally, as well as the sheer enjoyment we get from working out regularly, keeps us with our exercise regimen regardless of inconveniences or barriers we may encounter from week to week. Indeed, many committed exercisers feel miserable if they can't exercise; the rewards from completing an exercise session, and the negative consequences of not exercising, make the exercise schedule or routine a relatively simple undertaking. For such persons, regular exercise remains a high priority regardless of what life may bring.

Unfortunately, only a relatively small percentage of people in the U.S. and other Western countries share this attitude. While many acknowledge the importance of physical activity to health and well-being, surprisingly few are regularly active enough to receive significant health benefits. Current estimates suggest that at least 40 percent of the American population may be considered completely sedentary, while only 20 percent or less are active at an intensity and frequency recommended for cardiovascular benefit (Caspersen, Christenson, & Pollard, 1986). Citizens of other countries fare no better. The percentage of regularly active persons decreases with age as well as with educational level. Drop-out rates for those beginning an exercise program are alarming. A number of studies report drop-outs from standard exercise programs to reach 50 percent or more by the end of the first six months (Dishman, Sallis, & Orenstein, 1985). In secondary prevention programs such as cardiac rehabilitation, a 50 percent drop-out by twelve months is typical.

Why do so many people find sticking with exercise over the long haul such an arduous task? The answer is complex and multifaceted, influenced by factors associated with each client and his/her environment, as well as the exercise regimen itself.

Definition of Adherence

Adherence has been defined in a variety of ways. For the purpose of this chapter, adherence means the amount of exercise performed during a specified time, compared to the amount of exercise recommended. Exercise refers to the specific regimen developed by the trainer. Amount of exercise, depending on the trainer's goals or preferences, can refer to the frequency, duration (including number of repetitions), or intensity of exercise, or some combination of these three dimensions. The trainer must define what is considered adequate adherence or progress toward goals for each client.

Factors Influencing Exercise Adherence

A growing body of scientific research in exercise adherence has identified a number of factors that may influence initial participation in an exercise program as well as how well someone will stick with the program. These factors are described below.

PERSONAL FACTORS. Surveys undertaken in the U.S. and elsewhere show that those most likely to begin an exercise program tend to be younger men (especially when the activity is vigorous), more highly educated persons, white-collar as opposed to blue-collar workers, nonsmokers, and those not significantly overweight. Attitudes and beliefs about exercise and its perceived value also appear to be influential. Some of these factors are also associated with how well someone may continue to exercise. Smokers and overweight individuals have poorer adherence rates than their nonsmoking and less overweight counterparts. Finding ways to make the exercise regimen less physically demanding or grueling, such as using lower-intensity exercises or building more frequent breaks into the exercise session, as well as using more frequent reminders concerning the physical and mental health benefits of regular exercise, may be particularly important for such clients. For smokers, pointing out how regular exercise may help counteract a number of negative symptoms and side effects associated with quitting (tension, fatigue, depressed mood, weight gain) may be especially helpful. Interestingly, a client's attitudes or beliefs concerning exercise appear to be less influential for longer-term maintenance of an exercise program once he/she has decided to begin to exercise.

Other personal factors found to be associated with exercise adherence include past experiences with exercise; the actual skills (both physical and behavioral/psychological) a client has to exercise appropriately and effectively; the client's ratings of self-motivation or the ability to persevere without external

Read each of the statements below, and circle the number beneath the letter corresponding to the alternative that best describes how characteristic the statement is when applied to you. The alternatives are:

A. *extremely un*characteristic of me.

B. *somewhat un*characteristic of me.

C. neither characteristic nor uncharacteristic of me.

D. *somewhat characteristic* of me.

E. *extremely characteristic* of me.

Please be sure to answer every item, and try to be as honest and accurate as possible in your responses. No one but you will know your score.

SELF-MOTIVATION ASSESSMENT SCALE

A	B	C	D	E		
5	4	3	2	1	1.	I get discouraged easily.
5	4	3	2	1	2.	I don't work any harder than I have to.
1	2	3	4	5	3.	I seldom if ever let myself down.
5	4	3	2	1	4.	I'm just not the goal-setting type.
1	2	3	4	5	5.	I'm good at keeping promises, especially the ones I make to myself.
5	4	3	2	1	6.	I don't impose much structure on my activities.
1	2	3	4	5	7.	I have a very hard-driving, aggressive personality.

To obtain your self-motivation score, simply add together the seven numbers you circled above. If this total summated score is equal to or less than *24,* you are probably drop-out prone. The lower your self-motivation score, the more likely it is that you may eventually discontinue a regular exercise program.

---

rewards; perceptions of program convenience and enjoyability; perceptions that the activity is not overly uncomfortable or difficult; and the client's ability to resolve typical barriers to exercise, such as travel, injury, illness, competing demands on time, boredom, and high-stress periods.

While some of these factors, such as smoking status or ratings of self-motivation, may be difficult to modify, others, such as perceptions of enjoyability and convenience, are much more amenable to change. These latter factors, discussed in this chapter, should be kept in mind in tackling exercise adherence issues. However, assessment tools such as Dishman's self-motivation inventory (see Fig. 13-1) may be helpful in diagnosing early on which clients may need to find external sources of motivation (something other than willpower), as well as which clients might have internal resources.

PROGRAM FACTORS.   Factors related to the exercise program or regimen itself may also affect client adherence. Among such factors, convenience stands out as particularly important to most U.S. clients and those in other Western countries. For instance, does the client have choices of time of day for training sessions, and is there some flexibility in scheduling to accommodate changing circumstances? If the client is someone with a typically large number of time constraints, such as a middle-aged working woman who is also a wife and

Fig.13–1   Self-motivation inventory. (*Source*: Falls, H.B., Baylor, A.M., and Dishman, R.K. (1988). *Essentials of fitness* (pp. 263–265). Dubuque, IA: Wm. C. Brown. Reproduced with permission of Wm. C. Brown, Publishers/ Rod K. Dishman)

mother, can the personal trainer provide some form of childcare service to help ease competing demands? If the exercise program is held away from the client's home, is it reasonably accessible?

Other relevant program-related questions that require consideration include the following:

- Does the exercise mode itself require special, costly, or time-consuming preparation that could reduce participation levels?

- Is the exercise regimen of a reasonable enough intensity so that the client finds it challenging but not punishing or aversive?

- Is the exercise routine varied enough to maintain interest and diminish boredom?

One of the important benefits of the one-to-one relationship between the personal trainer and the client is the large amount of ongoing individualization that can occur. The personal trainer should take advantage of every opportunity for enhancing motivation as well as shaping the actual exercise program.

ENVIRONMENTAL FACTORS. For many clients, environmental factors provide some powerful incentives (and disincentives) for continuing exercise. They include the general ambiance of the locale in which exercise occurs; regular cues or reminders concerning the exercise training sessions, such as writing down, well in advance if possible, dates and times of sessions in a scheduling book or calendar handy to the client; weather conditions that may influence either travel to an exercise setting or willingness to exercise outside; limitation of time (either real or perceived); and the amount of support and feedback about exercise. Ongoing support, in particular, has been found to be extremely important in promoting exercise adherence. Research shows that effective support can come in many different forms. In addition to face-to-face contact by a personal trainer, telephone or mail contacts, as appropriate, can remind clients about upcoming sessions and make them feel part of a larger organization. Lack of a group to which the client can feel he or she belongs may be at least partially offset by using T-shirts, newsletters, or other devices to identify the client as a member of the personal trainer's "team."

Social support also includes finding ways to minimize negative comments from others concerning the client's attempts to exercise. For instance, negative attitudes towards a client's exercise program by the spouse, significant other, or family have a detrimental effect on attempts to stick with the program. Exploring methods to include members of the family in the exercise enterprise may be quite worthwhile. This may mean finding ways to encourage actual exercise participation on the part of the spouse or significant others, such as undertaking the same or different exercise activities at the same time as the client or simply providing that person with information about the exercise program so that he or she feels included. The personal trainer should consider all three factors—personal, program, and environmental—when developing and carrying out exercise programming.

UNDERSTANDING MOTIVATION

Many of us have the notion that motivation is something that we are born with, or that resides entirely within us. This "trait" notion of motivation suggests that whether a client succeeds in engaging regularly in an activity or not is dependent almost entirely on his/her personal resources, abilities, or strengths, rather than on external factors or circumstances. Faced with a nonadherent client or clients, personal trainers subscribing to a trait notion of motivation will often place either the responsibility or the blame for nonadherence entirely on the client. By assuming that only personal factors influence adherence, they often write the individual off as lazy, incompetent, or unmotivated, in essence, engaging in what is known as "blaming the victim."

However, as noted, adherence to health regimens such as exercise is influenced by a host of environmental and situational factors in addition to personal factors. Some of these factors may be out of the client's control. Others may be factors of which the person is completely unaware. Because of the generally complex interrelationships among the factors, a trainer cannot rely solely on a clients' own reports of why they are or are not staying with programs to meet their needs. Rather than simply placing the blame for nonadherence on the client, the personal trainer must view motivation as a joint responsibility shared with the client. It is also helpful to view the motivation process as something dynamic; different strategies may be needed for different clients at different stages in the program. For example, the types of strategies used to enhance adherence or attendance during the initial "critical period" of exercise (first three to six months), when many of the difficulties associated with participation typically occur, may well differ from those most useful in helping to maintain exercise over the long haul.

Because motivating the client is one of the trainer's most important and most difficult responsibilities, the ability to address the motivational needs of the client in an ongoing, effective fashion may well be the single largest measure of a trainer's success.

Leadership Qualities

Exercise leadership by the personal trainer is an important factor in adherence and motivation. Some of the qualities of an effective exercise leader include the following:

- *Punctuality and dependability* about scheduling sessions and communicating with the client. This includes being regularly prepared for training sessions.

- *Professionalism in dress, behavior, and demeanor.* This means treating clients with respect and letting them know (through actions as well as words) that you take the trainer-client relationship seriously. It also means respecting the client's privacy and the confidentiality of what is shared as part of the trainer-client relationship.

- *Dedication to the exercise training endeavor,* as demonstrated through putting continual effort into making training sessions fun, rewarding, safe, and educational. Trainers should be working as hard in their capacity as clients are expected to work in their exercise sessions.

- *Willingness to plan ahead* for things that may interfere with a training session and preparing the client, as much as possible, for any breaks that may occur.

- *Sensitivity to each client's past experiences, current preferences and current and future needs.* This means providing a regular means for evaluating the client's performance as well as your own, and being open to suggestions and alternatives that may enhance training sessions.

- *A commitment to seek additional education for professional growth*, which includes keeping abreast of the latest scientific information about physical activity as well as current exercise fads about which your client may have questions.

- *Recognizing signs of burnout and taking steps to prevent or ameliorate it* by taking time off and enlisting the aid, advice, and support of fellow trainers.

- *Engaging in communication with the client using supportive and empathetic words* to show understanding of what he/she is going through. Approach the training endeavor with an open, nonjudgmental attitude, a sense of humor, and a willingness to listen.

- *Presenting oneself as a role model* for both exercise training and other areas of health.

- *Taking responsibility for problems that may arise* in the course of helping clients reach their exercise goals. Consider issues of motivation, the training regimen itself, and client safety and well-being. As part of this, the conscientious trainer recognizes when the client may be better served by seeking assistance elsewhere, and aids the client in obtaining an appropriate referral.

- *Forming with each client a partnership in the exercise experience*, which includes having the client play an active role in the training program and any decisions that may be needed to pursue the exercise training goals.

Methods for Enhancing and Maintaining Motivation to Exercise

General guidelines listed below for enhancing motivation and promoting exercise adherence should be used to develop a specific plan of action tailored to the motivational needs of each client. They include personal, programmatic, and environmental influences on exercise adherence.

1. *Structure appropriate expectations at the beginning.* As mentioned earlier, a client's personal beliefs about what exercise can and cannot do, as well as past exercise experiences, can influence motivation. Unrealistic expectations ("If I exercise regularly, I should be able to shed all that excess weight within a month or two"; "no pain, no gain"; "exercise will completely change my life"), fueled by the media and at times a somewhat overzealous health community, currently run rampant. Such expectations, when unfulfilled, can lead to frustration, disappointment, or overexercise that make drop-out more likely.

The personal trainer can help to structure realistic expectations by exploring what the client expects to achieve early in the program. The client should be informed about the exercise regimen itself, how it will be generally structured and why. He/she should also be informed about the types of uncomfortable or negative side effects which often accompany initial efforts to increase physical activity levels, such as stiffness, minor soreness or muscle pain, and some fatigue. It is strongly recommended that clients be informed at this juncture about the types of symptoms (chest pain, undue fatigue lasting well after the exercise session) requiring further attention. Clients should be clearly warned about the difficulties that can arise with starting out too quickly or too strenuously at the beginning of an exercise program. Overuse injuries, in addition to endangering the health of the client, are a primary factor leading to early drop-out. Pollock and others (1984) have reported that, when individuals beginning an exercise program are exposed to exercise frequencies of 5 or more days per week, exercise sessions of more than 45 minutes' duration, and/or exercise intensities greater than 85 percent of aerobic capacity, drop-out, and injury rates increase significantly. The negative consequences of such regimes may affect as many as 50 percent of clients.

2. *Prepare the client for inevitable lapses.* In addition to addressing expectations about program structure and reasonable outcomes in health, fitness, and appearance, warnings should also be provided about the pitfalls clients often run across when attempting to exercise regularly. Such pitfalls may include unplanned breaks in the exercise regimen due to illness, work schedule, holidays, and the like, or failure to observe further gains following a period of significant gains or advances. Preparing clients ahead of time for particularly high-risk situations, when breaks in the exercise regimen are likely, may help prevent the full-blown drop-out often seen following such unplanned breaks. (This pattern has sometimes been referred to as the "New Year's Resolution effect," often fueled by guilt, frustration, or disappointment about not meeting a goal—in this case exercising regularly). There is evidence that educating clients, even in a very basic way, concerning the ways to plan for and interpret lapses in their program can foster adherence (King & Frederiksen, 1984).

3. *Find out the client's preferences, needs, and exercise history.* One of the advantages of being a personal trainer is that usually there is time to assess your client thoroughly. You are typically getting paid to do just that. Take advantage of that opportunity to find out not only at what level your clients are physically, but where they are mentally and experientially as well. This is probably best accomplished through a simple questionnaire for all clients to complete at the beginning of their program, either on their own or in an interview. Questions of interest include the types of exercise programs clients have participated in (types of activities; format—with another personal trainer, in a class, or on their own; length of time of participation; reasons for drop-out); reasons for seeking a personal trainer at this particular time; what expectations and goals they hope to accomplish and how quickly; current preferences concerning specific types of exercise; past and current injuries; potential pitfalls they see ahead based on past experiences; constraints with respect to time, and other issues and questions they would like answered concerning working with you, or concerning your particular method.

4. *Decide on the specific types of activities that will best fit the client's objectives, time, commitments, and personal style.* Based on the above information, tailor the exercise program to each client. This may mean using indoor exercises for the client embarrassed to be seen in public; water exercises for clients with knee or hip problems; exercise sports for clients motivated by competitive challenges; racer equipment for the aggressive, goal-oriented client; or relaxed reading time on a reclining cycle for the stressed or exhausted executive. In addition, if a client says that in the past, one of the major reasons why he or she stopped exercising was because of boredom, then building in variety within or across sessions, as well as varying exercise routes or locations on a regular basis, may be helpful.

5. *Set appropriate exercise goals.* Once you have decided on the specific activities that will make up the client's exercise routine, the next job is to set appropriate, realistic goals for each portion of the exercise routine. Realistic goals are important in order to avoid injury and maintain interest. This is particularly true in the beginning, when many persons have the tendency to overdo the activity. Short-term, flexible goals that are set, at least in part, by the client and that are accompanied by individualized feedback have often been found to be particularly useful. Martin and colleagues (1984) have reported that when specific, personalized feedback and praise were provided, it did not matter whether clients were given distance goals or time-based goals; their adherence to exercise was similar. However, when more general feedback was given, some clients did not do as well in achieving their goals. Regardless of what type of goal is used, with the achievement of one goal, the next one should be discussed.

Goals can be formalized in the form of a **contract** (see Fig. 13-2). Contracts are written agreements signed by the client and the personal trainer (and additional third parties, such as a spouse or exercise partner, if deemed appropriate) which clearly spell out the exercise goals (such as regular attendance at the training sessions and the duration, type, and/or intensity of exercise engaged in with the personal trainer), preferable over a short time period (two to four weeks). These serve to increase the client's personal responsibility and commitment. In addition, the potency of contracts can be enhanced by including in them a positive contingency or reward for having met the goal. The contract should specify goals that are somewhat challenging yet realistically achievable to promote success. This means that in the early stages of an exercise program, it may be more useful to establish goals that focus on attendance rather than exercise-related performance. If the habit of regular exercise is not established early in the program, drop-out will ensue and performance issues become moot.

To summarize, a series of prudent goals should be negotiated by the trainer and client that focus on building the exercise habit through gradual increments rather than larger changes which, though more appealing to some clients, can lead to failure, frustration and/or injury. During the first six to twelve weeks in particular, the goals might need to be focused on simply "showing up," no matter how little the client may feel like doing or be able to do. Alternatively, for the zealous overachieving client, goals can aid efforts to diminish overexertion and injury. The important thing is to match the goals to the needs and preferences of each individual talent.

6. *Whenever possible, offer choices.* While some structure is typically welcomed by clients attempting to change or maintain a behavior such as exercise, many will benefit from being offered some choice of alternatives within the general structure of the program. Doing so helps to foster the notion of a partnership between the personal trainer and the client so vital to long-term maintenance. It can also help to stave off boredom which often creeps into an exercise program. Choices may be made available with respect to the exercise regimen itself (types of activity engaged in, frequency, intensity, and/or duration factors), or the types of goals, feedback, and/or incentives used to enhance adherence. An increasingly flexible view is being taken by national organizations such as the American College of Sports Medicine about types of exercise regimens, choice of activities and their frequency, intensity, and duration, suitable for obtaining reasonable health benefits. Personal trainers can now offer clients an increasing number of options for achieving worthwhile health and fitness goals. In some cases, choices can also be offered about where the exercise session occurs. For those clients who typically exercise indoors, taking a training session outdoors on occasion can serve to reenergize them.

7. *Remember that exercise, like other behaviors, is strongly influenced by its imme-*

My Responsibilities:

1. To attend all of my scheduled exercise sessions (three times per week) over the next four weeks.

2. For any sessions that I have to miss due to illness or other unavoidable reasons, I will:

   a. Call my instructor to let him/her know the reason(s) why I had to miss. (Instructor's telephone number = _____).

   b. Plan to make up the missed session by (specify): _____ .

3. To reward myself at the end of each week that I attend all of my scheduled sessions by engaging in thirty or more minutes of reading for my own enjoyment.

My Helper's Responsibilities:

My designated helper is: _____ . He/she has agreed:

   a. To prompt me during work to attend my exercise sessions.

   b. In return, I will prompt him/her concerning a behavior of his/her choice, as desired.

This contract will be evaluated on _____(date)_____ .

Signed:

_____   _____
     (participant)   (date)

_____   _____
       (helper)   (date)

_____   _____
   (trainer/instructor)   (date)

Figure 13–2

Sample four-week contract

diate consequences. Often the immediate feelings and consequences surrounding actions, rather than more abstract or long-term beliefs or views, have the most powerful effect on daily activities. Exercise is no exception. This helps explain why many in the United States and elsewhere, though aware that regular exercise has a number of positive health outcomes, remain sedentary or only irregularly active. Despite the best of intentions, if the immediate or short-term benefits of exercise do not outweigh the time and effort required, it is likely that drop-out or relapse to being sedentary will result. The trainer must work with the client to identify short-term benefits (feelings of accomplishment, stress reduction, better sleep, changes in circumference of the legs or arms) rather than focusing only on longer-term outcomes (better health, reduction in cardiovascular risk, weight loss). While weight control is certainly an important by-product of regular aerobic exercise, for many clients weight loss through increased exercise alone is often a slow process. In addition, in at least some individuals, the loss in fat weight is often compensated for by an increase in lean weight (muscle), resulting in a net effect of no change on the scale. Taking periodic measurements of parts of the body where one would expect to see change might, for some clients, be a better gauge of progress.

8. *Increase the immediately rewarding aspects of the behavior and decrease the negative or punishing aspects.* Analyze both the positive and negative aspects of the exercise session itself to increase enjoyability and decrease discomfort and boredom. For some, providing a means of distraction from the chore of exercise through social interaction, music, or an interesting exercise routine is important. Through regular monitoring of how clients are enjoying the session (using a simple 6-point rating scale, with one equaling "extremely unenjoyable" and six equaling "extremely enjoyable"), the exercise trainer can modify the regimen. The rating can be extended to finding out how the client likes each specific exercise during the training session. For instance, if a client dislikes a particular portion of the exercise routine (such as military presses), the trainer can substitute a different exercise for the same results. Because what is rewarding or punishing about an exercise program differs from person to person, it is important to individualize, as much as possible, strategies for enhancing enjoyment.

For some clients, modifying the exercise session to increase enjoyment will not be enough, especially for those just beginning an exercise program. For them, the uncomfortable aspects of increased exertion (sweating, increased heart rate, sore muscles) may outweigh any positive outcomes. Such clients may need external incentives, such as contracts with the trainer, whereby the client earns points toward a desirable reward once the goal has been reached. For some clients, an external incentive system can be set up in the form of an achievement club, or related activities, with formal recognition in the form of pins, T-shirts, certificates or other rewards for achieving training goals.

Teaching clients how to successfully monitor their own intensity levels can help maintain an enjoyable workout. Beginning exercisers should be encouraged to exercise at an intensity that allows them to talk comfortably without undue sweating, readily monitored by both the client and the personal trainer. Knowing how to accurately monitor their heart rates, through the regular taking of the pulse or through the use of a portable heart monitor, is another skill all clients should master. A heart-rate range individualized to each client will aid adherence efforts. In addition, use of the Borg Scale (Borg, 1970), which involves the **rating of perceived exertion** (RPE), can provide an excellent means for evaluating the client's perception of exercise intensity. In clients trained in its use, the RPE has been found to provide a useful reflection of the work output and, more importantly, how they are feeling about their workout. Individuals consistently rating themselves at the upper range of perceived exertion, particularly early in their exercise program, may be at increased risk for nonadherence or drop-out, or potential injury.

9. *Provide feedback whenever possible.* Regular **feedback** that is specific and relevant to the client can be an extremely powerful reinforcer or incentive, particularly early in the exercise program, when more intrinsic benefits from exercising, such as an increase in muscle tone or reduction in tension, may not yet be present. Feedback can take many forms; physiologically based feedback may include changes in resting or exertional heart rate or perceived exertion with increased activity. Use of a standardized submaximal exercise test, such as the step-test or 12-minute distance test, administered at the beginning of the exercise program and at regular intervals, can provide useful information to both the client and the trainer. Testing clients every three months or so should provide them with enough feedback to reinforce current activities and motivate future adherence. However, if the client has had to lay off training (due to injury, illness, or scheduling problems), it is preferable to allow him/her to build back up to a reasonable workout before initiating further testing. Testing during a plateau or down period in the client's training program can lead to discouragement and frustration, which in turn can result in either dropping out or overtraining.

Behaviorally based feedback can include regular recordings of the amount of activity (frequency, duration, number of repetitions), as well as periodic completion of an exercise balance sheet, in which the client lists both the positive and negative aspects of regular exercise. Through completing such a sheet, clients are often reminded of the reasons they decided to exercise in the first place. For those clients who are amenable to it, regular logging of exercise behavior can be an effective means for enhancing adherence, particularly when they are working toward specific goals. Logging serves as an immediate, visual record of the client's session-by-session accomplishments, helping to bridge the gap between the exercise sessions and more distant rewards of changes in body composition, endurance, or strength, or earning something tangible such as a T-shirt. Having clients maintain their own records also helps to drive home the point that they share responsibility with the personal trainer.

10. *Encourage public expressions of commitment to the exercise program.* Making and periodically reaffirming a commitment to exercise can serve to maintain adherence during periods when the exercise program is temporarily disrupted or motivation has flagged. The use of the written contract as well as encouraging the client to engage in a written cost-benefit analysis of exercise involvement have been found to bolster commitment and improve adherence. Also, encouraging the client to discuss accomplishments or activities with family and friends can provide another means for maintaining interest and commitment.

11. *Teach the client how to use prompts and reminders to set the stage.* Exercise can be only one of a long list of activities vying for our time and attention. To keep exercise prominently placed in the client's list of priorities, set up a system of **prompts**, or reminders, about the exercise sessions. This may be writing the sessions into a daily schedule book, or providing the client with a calendar or schedule to be prominently displayed on the refrigerator or other suitable place in the home or at work. Encouraging the client to ready his or her exercise apparel the evening before a scheduled exercise session and to display it in a prominent place may help get the client to a class or group.

12. *Model the appropriate behaviors for the client.* Appropriate and consistent modeling of exercise-related behaviors can provide motivation in the early as well as later stages of participation. When modeling the actual exercise routines or activities, perform the activity slowly, both as a demonstration as well as along with clients during their execution of the activity. Breaking more complicated routines into easily learned segments can help, especially in the early stages. In addition to modeling the actual exercises, providing an appropriate role model for prudent goal-setting, exercise attire, injury prevention, coping with breaks in the exercise regimen, and other relevant behaviors are particularly useful. Remember that "Do as I say, not as I do" is as ineffective for adults as it is for children. Remember also that, as a health professional, you are in an excellent position to serve as a role-model for other important health behaviors by not smoking or abusing alcohol and by maintaining healthy dietary patterns and prudent weight control activities.

13. *Foster self-management of the exercise regimen.* In order to help clients establish exercise as a lifelong habit, foster a sense of personal responsibility and commitment to exercise. It is critical to realize that we must take charge of our exercise as a lifelong goal, rather than as a time-limited commitment that ends when certain goals have been reached or temporary set-backs occur. To do this, train clients in the use of self-management strategies that will help them keep the exercise habit going when circumstances interfere with their usual routine. For a personal trainer, this may mean equipping clients with strategies to keep them exercising during those periods, such as business travel, vacations, or changes in work hours, when they are unable to make normally scheduled exercise sessions. For a client who will be traveling, this may include packing appropriate exercise attire, being aware of exercises that can be undertaken in a hotel room, and investigating the types of exercise facilities available near the destination. Given that anticipated breaks from an exercise schedule can lead to drop-out, planning for them ahead of time can increase the probability of subsequent resumption of the exercise program.

When illness, injury, or unexpected travel cause unplanned breaks in the exercise regimen, it is particularly important to, first, let the client know that you care and, second, encourage him/her to get back into the regimen as soon as possible. Expect that many clients will feel at least some level of guilt (that they have let you, as well as themselves, down), in addition to frustration and discouragement. Such feelings breed drop-out. Research shows that provision of even a brief supportive, nonjudgmental telephone call during such a period can help clients maintain their exercise programs.

14. *Prepare the client for changes in trainers.* Perhaps the most disruptive event for many clients is the loss of the regular trainer, even for a brief period. Unfortunately, little, if anything, is typically done to prepare clients for this often unsettling circumstance. Planned transition periods (pregnancy leave, travel, permanent relocation) can be smoothed immensely by preparing clients for the upcoming change well ahead of time and, if possible, introducing the instructor who will be stepping in well before the regular instructor takes his/her leave. Having the regular and new instructor team teach several of the exercise sessions can go a long way to allay fears and prevent clients from dropping out. Even the most healthy trainers will have days when they are unable to work, so all trainers should plan for substitutes and, if possible, introduce them to clients ahead of time. If a substitute is not available, following up with clients by telephone may help to keep them from feeling abandoned, betrayed, or discouraged.

15. *Utilize as many types of social support as possible.* Ongoing social support, in all of its many forms, is invaluable both in the early and more advanced stages of an exercise program. While the face-to-face support provided during the session itself can be invaluable for many clients, don't overlook other potentially important avenues that can complement your personal instruction. These include telephone contacts following missed sessions; regular newsletters or other mailed items that can both educate and motivate continued participation; and the encouragement of support on the part of family members or coworkers through mailed newsletters or other informational pieces.

16. *Look for opportunities to promote an overall healthy life-style.* Exercise does not occur in a vacuum, but rather is only one of a number of activities clients engage in throughout the week. Because for many of us our exercise program has a major impact on the rest of our lives, we often assume that those who exercise regularly will automatically change other health behaviors, such as smoking and dietary practices. Unfortunately, very little scientific evidence supports this widely held belief. Many people who exercise maintain a regular smoking habit or eat a diet high in saturated fats and sugar. Indeed, some maintain the inaccurate belief that regular exercise will protect them against the other negative health habits. Sadly, this is not the case. We must help clients recognize that exercise alone is not a panacea for health, but, rather, only one of a number of behaviors that comprise a healthy lifestyle.

The personal trainer, as a trained health professional, is in an excellent position to provide basic accurate information and encouragement for the development of a healthy life-style beyond exercise. Most trainers are deluged by questions on diet, weight control and other health regimens by those concerned about their health and confused by the mixed messages currently being promulgated in the media and by special-interest groups. Regular contact with clients interested in improving their health provides an invaluable opportunity for educating them in a manner not available to many other types of health professionals. The trainer who stays abreast of current scientific information and developments in health promotion can be sure that health information can be responsibly disseminated. Please refer to Chapters 4 and 10 for useful information about nutrition and weight control.

A healthy life-style also involves participating in physical activities beyond the scheduled training session. Look for opportunities to encourage clients to be more active as a way of life (by walking instead of driving or by using stairs instead of elevators or escalators) to provide a means for burning additional calories. Such changes may also help clients maintain a high energy level when more vigorous activity is not possible. Such activities are particularly important for the older client, as well as other subgroups, such as those who are overweight. By encouraging physical activity in all of its forms, the personal trainer can indeed serve as an important teacher and role model for achieving a healthy life-style.

SUMMARY

Drop-out rates for those beginning an exercise program can reach 50 percent or more after only six months. Instead of blaming the client, a trainer must view motivation as a shared responsibility. By analyzing each client's preferences, habits, and circumstances to anticipate blocks to success, the trainer can design a specific approach to motivate each client to achieve mutually determined goals.

Factors affecting adherence to a health regimen can be complex and interrelated. The trainer must understand that motivation is a dynamic process and use a variety of techniques that will help a client achieve and maintain a healthful life-style. These techniques range from structuring appropriate expectations and goals, identifying short-term benefits, and providing specific feedback, to serve as a positive role model and training clients in self-management strategies. Understanding and applying the principles of adherence and motivation will make the trainer a more effective teacher and health professional.

REFERENCES

Borg, G.V. (1970). Perceived exertion as an indicator of somatic stress. *Scandinavian Journal of Rehabilitation Medicine, 2* 92–98.

Caspersen, C.J., Christenson, G.M., & Pollard, R.A. (1986). Status of the 1990 physical fitness and exercise objectives—Evidence from NHIS 1985. *Public Health Reports, 101* 587–592.

Dishman, R.K., Sallis, J.F., & Orenstein, D.R. (1985). The determinants of physical activity and exercise. *Public Health Reports, 100* 158–171.

King, A.C., & Frederiksen, L.W. (1984). Low-cost strategies for increasing exercise behavior: The effects of relapse preparation training and social support. *Behavior Modification, 4* 3–21.

Martin, J. E., Dubbert, P.M., Katell, A.D., Thompson, J.K., Raczynski, J.R., Lake, M., Smith, P.O., Webster, J.S., Sikora, T., & Cohen, R.E. (1984). Behavioral control of exercise in sedentary adults: Studies 1 through 6. *Journal of Consulting & Clinical Psychology, 52* 795–811.

SUGGESTED READING

Pollock, M.L., Wilmore, J.H., & Fox, S.M. (1984). *Exercise in health and disease.* Philadelphia: Saunders.

American College of Sports Medicine. (1988). *Resource manual for guidelines for exercise testing and prescription.* Philadelphia: Lea & Febiger.

Dishman, R.K. (ed.). (1988). *Exercise adherence: Its impact on public health.* Champaign, IL: Human Kinetics.

Communication and Teaching Techniques

Amy P. Jones

14

Amy Jones, M.Ed., has a master's degree in counseling and has been motivating people to health and fitness since 1974. For 12 years she was director of programs for the Aerobics Activity Center in Dallas, and now is an author and lecturer, technical advisor for the Reebok National Aerobic Championship, and consultant to the Greenhouse Spa. She is a member of the American Council on Exercise Board of Directors, a fellow in the Association for Fitness in Business, and is certified with the American College of Sports Medicine.

IN THIS CHAPTER:

- Stages of the trainer/client relationship: rapport stage, investigation stage, planning stage, action stage.

- Nonverbal and verbal behaviors: attending, perceiving verbal and nonverbal messages.

- Planning: setting goals, exploring alternatives, formulating a plan, evaluating the implementation.

- Training: "tell-show-do," modeling, contracting, feedback.

A personal trainer's relationship to a client is clearly the helping relationship of educator to student. The personal trainer is the helper or teacher; the one being helped is referred to as the student or client. Helping relationships differ from most other kinds of relationships encountered in daily routines. Most ordinary experiences are dialogues in which both people seek personal enhancement or the mutual exchange of ideas or information. In the helping relationship, one person comes out of his/her own world and temporarily sets aside personal needs to help another person. The focus of the relationship is on the other's needs and on goals leading to new behavior. Simply put, helping is enabling another person to change. Instead of encouraging dependence, the purpose of helping is to facilitate the client's taking more control and becoming self-sufficient. Helping is an active process of advising, informing, correcting, and directing.

There are many different kinds of helping relationships. Because there is usually a fee for service in personal training, the personal trainer can be classified as a structured, professional helper, like social workers, teachers, school counselors, and legal advisors. In contrast to this professional level are unstructured levels of helping such as friendships and family relationships.

373

The role of the personal trainer is complex because he/she will function as a teacher, a coach, an advisor, a supervisor, a supporter, a counselor, and a negotiator. To illustrate this point:

Teacher: Explaining to clients what they need to know and must do (e.g., outlining and explaining an aerobic exercise program).

Coach: Training clients in desired skills (e.g., coaching during a free-weight workout).

Advisor: Telling clients the wisest course of action to take (e.g., warning about dangers of an unsupervised liquid fasting program).

Supervisor: Focusing clients on the achievement of predetermined goals (e.g., weighing a client in each week).

Supporter: Encouraging clients as they work on specific lifestyle changes (e.g., providing emotional support for a client who has stopped smoking).

Counselor: Helping clients sort through personal problems (e.g., listening to a client's frustrations regarding problems at work).

Negotiator: Bargaining with clients in order to reach an acceptable agreement (e.g., negotiating an exercise contract with a client for a period of travel).

These roles are described only in a general sense. Personal trainers should be acutely aware of their limitations and must not exceed the professional parameters of offering advice or counseling about personal problems. Personal trainers can obviously listen and offer support, but they should know when to refer clients to other qualified professionals.

STAGES OF THE PERSONAL TRAINER/CLIENT RELATIONSHIP

There are distinct stages in the personal trainer/client relationship (see Fig. 14-1). These stages form a general model or framework for the divisions and related skills of the helping relationship. They may not always occur in this exact sequence, nor are all stages always present. The length of the stages may also vary from client to client. Generally, the initial contact between the personal trainer and client is made in the rapport stage. After the relationship is begun, the process of gathering information forms the investigation stage. The investigation stage gives way to the planning stage when the client's goals and steps toward the goals are mapped out. Finally, the action stage begins when the actual training process starts.

Each of the stages requires specific skills and techniques. In the beginning, for example, attentive listening skills can build the working relationship; in the following stages decision-making and behavioral-change skills are needed more. Developing these skills can increase the effectiveness of the personal trainer. Because this personal trainer/client relationship is dynamic and ever-changing, these stages and skills overlap and may not occur in the exact order given. The specific stages and skills are outlined as follows:

Stage 1: Rapport. Interpersonal communication skills.

Stage 2: Investigation. Information gathering skills.

Stage 3: Planning. Problem-solving or decision-making skills.

Stage 4: Action. Behavioral change skills (feedback, contracting, modeling, etc.).

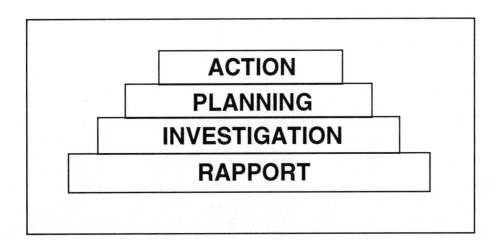

Figure 14–1 Stages of the personal trainer/client relationship.

RAPPORT STAGE

The rapport stage is the foundation for the entire relationship between personal trainer and client. **Rapport** means a relationship of mutual trust, harmony, or emotional affinity. Establishing rapport is building a certain level of comfort or shared understanding into a relationship. The rapport stage begins at first contact. Whether in person or on the telephone, the client is "checking out" the personal trainer and answering the question, "Can this person help me?" Confidence or trust in the personal trainer's skills must be established early because only then will the client be willing to receive guidance.

According to Rogers' (1967) research, people in the helping profession need to communicate three basic attributes or qualities in order for the helping relationship to be successful. These three primary qualities are (1) empathy, (2) warmth, and (3) genuineness. The importance of these qualities has been demonstrated repeatedly in research by Truax and Carkuff (1967) and others. These attributes are the foundation for a successful helping relationship and are key ingredients during the rapport stage.

Empathy is the ability to experience another person's world as if it were one's own. It is understanding the client's point of view or where the client is "coming from." The empathetic personal trainer will be able to respond appropriately to the client's covert feelings and verbal messages by communicating perceptions to the client. The absence of empathy will lead the client to think the trainer does not understand what he/she is experiencing and, therefore, block the entire helping process.

Warmth is an unconditional positive regard or a respect for another person regardless of his/her individuality and uniqueness. It bridges professional distance through friendliness and consideration regardless of a "liking" for another person. Warmth is about caring and understanding rather than judging and impersonalizing. This quality will create a climate which communicates to a client that he/she is safe and accepted even when making mistakes.

Genuineness can be defined as authenticity or being honest and open without putting up a front or facade. It is a state in which the helper's words and actions are congruent. For example, when a personal trainer greets a client with "I'm glad to see you're here today," his/her body language must be consistent with the words of welcome. Genuineness is the ability to relate to people without hiding behind a clipboard or a white coat. It is not necessarily being fully self-revealing, but rather being committed to a responsible honesty with others.

These basic qualities of empathy, warmth, and genuineness are paramount in establishing trust in a working relationship with a client. At first glance, these traits seem to be simplistic because they are the outgrowth of ordinary effective human qualities. However, relevant research and cumulative experience points out the necessity for continuous monitoring of the timing and amount of these facilitating conditions.

Interpersonal communication skills are the primary skills needed to establish rapport and thereby build a trainer/client relationship. These skills are not only important during the rapport stage, but are necessary throughout each stage of the relationship. Interpersonal communication skills can be broadly categorized as nonverbal and verbal. The nonverbal category includes such behaviors as attending, perceiving nonverbal messages, and perceiving verbal messages. The verbal category includes such behaviors as paraphrasing, reflecting, and clarifying. Many of these skills are natural for anyone genuinely involved in helping another person. However, specific communication skills can be learned, practiced, and continuously mastered.

Nonverbal Behaviors

Listening is the primary nonverbal communication skill. Listening is complex and is not the same as hearing. Hearing is perceptions of sound through the ear. Obviously listening involves the physiology of hearing, but is also a more complex psychological procedure of involvement with the other person. It involves skills in attending, perceiving verbal and nonverbal messages, and even verbal responding. All of these skills overlap and are difficult to treat separately.

ATTENDING. Attending behaviors are exhibited by the listener to put the speaker at ease. **Attending** means being attentive or giving physical attention to another person. Instead of interrupting, the listener gives nonverbal acknowledgements during the conversation through posture, eye contact, and gestures. These verbal responses are also a form of attending. The listener may say "yes, I see" to encourage the speaker to continue. Other verbal responses are described later.

Effective attending can build trust and can work wonders in human relationships. Conversely, nonattentive behavior can be devastating. For example, when you are speaking to someone who appears bored and whose eyes are continually distracted to other things, this response leaves you feeling ignored and does not encourage more conversation. The trainer interested in developing good attending behaviors or skills needs to be aware of the following:

1. *Posture*: When both client and personal trainer are seated, specific postures can communicate interest by the personal trainer. To show involvement the trainer faces the client squarely at eye level and leans toward the client in a relaxed manner. To avoid expressing defensiveness, the trainer should maintain an open position with arms and legs uncrossed. This posture says to the client, "I am interested in you and am ready to listen." Research has shown that these postural behaviors demonstrate to the client the traits of empathy, warmth, and genuineness.

2. *Positioning*: Positioning at an appropriate distance from the client demonstrates a respect of spatial distancing and is critical for the personal trainer. Hall (1966) describes an 18-inch or less distance between two people as "intimate space," an 18-inch to 4-foot distance as "personal space," a 4-foot to 12-foot distance as "social distance," and beyond 12 feet as "public distance." Most nor-

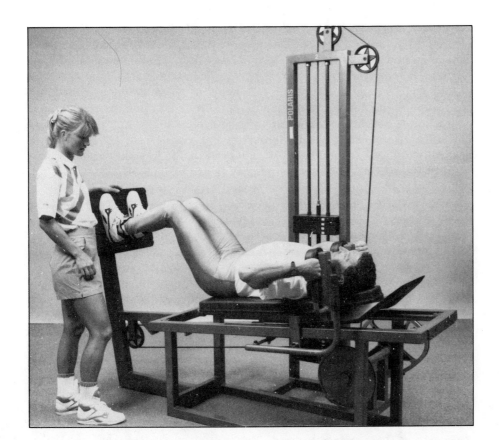

Figure 14–2 Trainer working in a client's personal space.

mal conversation will occur in the personal space (see Fig. 14–2). However, the very nature of the working relationship demands at times that a trainer must enter the client's intimate space. Because of this intimate positioning, a trainer should be sensitive to the client, particularly when hands-on work is being done. Early in the relationship, a trainer may want to ask permission to touch the client and should take care that the client not misconstrue his/her touching or presence in the client's personal space.

3. *Mirroring*: Another technique to establish rapport is mimicking or **mirroring**. Mirroring may be either conscious or unconscious. However, the purpose of mirroring is to establish rapport with another person when previous rapport has not been established. The technique of mirroring involves sensitively matching the posture and gestures of the other person. Mirroring may also involve matching voice tone, voice tempo, and breathing patterns. These techniques often occur naturally as people interact.

4. *Eye Contact*: Eye contact is a key vehicle for indicating interest in a person. Good eye contact is not a fixed stare but rather a relaxed focus on the client's eyes, face, and other body gestures. This posture enables the client to feel safe and comfortable, while at the same time encouraging a feeling of interest on behalf of the personal trainer.

5. *Gestures*: Appropriate body movement is essential in attending. A trainer should respond to the client with relaxed motions instead of appearing rigid and unmoving. Nervous mannerisms such as playing with objects, jingling pocket change, waving to others, and drumming fingers should be avoided.

6. *Environment*: Since much of the personal training process takes place in a gym usually full of talking people, blaring music, and clanging weights, a quiet place is preferable for effective communication. Pleasant surroundings facilitate conversation between people. Therefore, initial sessions should be conducted in a nondistracting environment. To give someone undivided attention when distractions are present is difficult. Distractions may consist of a blaring TV or radio, a ringing telephone, people stopping by to talk, uncomfortable room temperature, and inappropriate lighting. Another type of distraction is seating arrangement. Sitting behind a desk not only puts up a physical barrier, but can be an interpersonal barrier as well. Attempts should be made to limit environmental distractions so that the speaker's thoughts are not interrupted and effective communication can take place.

PERCEIVING NONVERBAL MESSAGES. The saying "actions speak louder than words" is especially true about communications. Mehrabian (1972) determined that 93 percent of communication is nonverbal, leaving only 7 percent for actual content of spoken words. A person's expressions, gestures, posture, and other actions provide a constant source of information. Therefore, improving the interpretation of body language is a most valuable listening skill. Nonverbal messages are usually the means of expressing emotions. We usually search someone's face to determine feelings of anger, sadness, or disgust. Reading nonverbal messages is essential to understanding many of the most important things others are communicating to us. Nonverbal messages tend to be more reliable than verbal messages.

The following listing of nonverbal cues is not by any means exhaustive.

Feature	Nonverbal Cue
Head	Nodding, cocked to side, thrown back, motioning a direction
Facial expression	Frowning, grimacing, animated, distracted
Eyes	Squinting, wide open, closed, winking, blinking, rolling, teary
Mouth	Smiling, pursed lips, lip licking, lip biting, open, closed
Skin	Blushing, paleness, perspiration, rashes
Body posture	Relaxed, rigid, stooped shoulders, leaning forward, leaning backward, chest puffed out
Hands/arms	Fidgeting, tapping, laced fingers, fisted, pointing, touching, crossed arms
Feet/legs	Foot tapping, legs crossed, legs open, knee knocking

Although voice intonation is verbal and is explained in more detail later, it is appropriate to mention as nonverbal behavior. The sound of the voice communicates beyond the specific words spoken. The words spoken may be fast, slow, high pitched, loud, or whispered. These qualities tell much about the mood of the speaker. For example, some people may speak very rapidly or at a high pitch when they are nervous or fearful.

General appearance is also a nonverbal cue. The way in which a person grooms and dresses is a statement to others. A person who wears baggy shorts, a revealing leotard, heavy makeup, or a soiled T-shirt is saying something about himself/herself.

One aspect of interpreting body language is noting discrepancies in the verbal and the nonverbal messages. It is easy to note incongruence in a person who says he is not angry while slamming his fist on a table. When noting a difference between words and nonverbal behavior, it is helpful to search for the meaning of both. Body language can have multitudes of meanings and should be interpreted in context. A single gesture does not stand alone. Gestures should be seen in relationship to other body movements and should be related to a person's words. Misunderstanding often occurs in listening only to words or observing only the body language. Check out the accuracy of your interpretation with the person.

PERCEIVING VERBAL MESSAGES. To understand verbal messages, the listener must be able to recognize both the apparent and the underlying content. The apparent or cognitive content is comprised of the actual words and facts of the message. Cognitive messages are more easily recognized because they are stated. They usually involve talking about things, people, or events and may include one or more themes or topics. The underlying, or affective, content is comprised of emotions, attitudes, and behaviors. Affective messages are communicated both verbally and nonverbally, and these messages are more difficult to perceive and interpret. The client may not be aware of his own feelings and may be surprised when the trainer reveals his/her own perceptions. Generally, emotions can be grouped into four major categories: sadness, anger, fear, and happiness. Often a feeling from one category may cover up a feeling from another category.

Discriminating between cognitive and affective messages will allow the helper to respond appropriately to the client. Many cognitive themes may be communicated at once. Hearing the emotional message will help establish priorities of the cognitive topics. It seems listeners will often respond to the most recent verbal theme instead of the most important one. To illustrate, a client says to a personal trainer in their first meeting, "There is so much going on right now. I have gained 25 pounds since starting school. I'm about to flunk chemistry and if I do, my dad said he would take me out of school. I can't concentrate and I'm not sleeping at night. It seems I just keep gaining weight." In this situation, it is necessary for the personal trainer to listen to the whole message and prioritize the cognitive themes. It may be more helpful for this client to be trained in some stress reduction techniques even before being put on weight control and exercise programs. Certainly, the trainer should keep in mind the particular stress-producing factors when supervising this client's exercise program. If the personal trainer is not knowledgeable in stress reduction techniques or weight management, he/she should refer to a qualified professional.

Verbal Behaviors

Verbal responses are a form of listening and demonstrate to the client an understanding of what he/she is saying and feeling. Appropriate responses encourage the client to continue talking to allow for more exploration. The following are commonly used verbal responses:

- *Minimal encouragers,* brief words or phrases that allow the speaker to continue speaking. These verbal prods let the client know the trainer is with him/her and following what is being said. Example of minimal encouragers are "Mmm-hmmm," "I see," "Yes," and "Go on."

- *Paraphrasing,* a concise response restating the essence of the speaker's content. For example:

Client: I didn't sleep well and don't feel like working out.
Personal Trainer: You're tired today.

- *Probing*, an attempt to gain more information. Statements such as "I'm wondering about..." and "Let's talk about that" will help reveal more information.

- *Reflecting*, restating feelings and/or content in a way that demonstrates understanding. A listener can reflect stated or implied feelings, non-verbal observation, specific content, and even what has been omitted. Examples of reflecting are "You're feeling uncomfortable about starting an exercise program" and "Sounds like you are angry at your husband for insisting that you come today."

- *Clarifying*, an attempt to understand what the client is saying. "I'm confused about..." and "Could you explain that again, please?" are examples of clarification.

- *Informing*, sharing factual information, as when a personal trainer explains the pros and cons of a liquid diet.

- *Confronting*, providing the client with mild or strong feedback about what is really going on. Confrontations are more easily heard when communicated with "I" messages such as "I feel you really don't want to be here today." Another example of confronting is "It seems to me you say...and yet you do...."

- *Questioning*, asking for a response. Questions may be closed or open. Closed questions direct the speaker to give a short response such as "yes" or "no." Open questions provide space for the speaker to explore his or her own thoughts without being hemmed in. "What's on your mind today?" is an example of an open question.

- *Summarizing*, recapping what has been communicated and highlighting major themes. Effective summarizing can tie loose strands of a conversation together at the conclusion. A summary might begin with "Let's recap what we've discussed so far."

As mentioned earlier, the way in which we speak is more important than what we actually say. An effective communicator is aware of the quality of delivery of a message. The elements of voice delivery are intensity, pitch, and pace. The *intensity* or force is an important factor in delivery. Some trainers speak so softly that they cannot be heard, while others speak with such volume that they are annoying. Delivery should be loud enough to be heard, while reserving a range to emphasize important points. Working in the weight room, personal trainers may find an unusual amount of interference from others talking, background music, and weights clanging. This situation provides a challenge to the trainer to determine effective intensity of the voice. Decreasing voice volume in a noisy situation can actually increase the attentiveness of the other person. For example, instead of shouting to a client in a noisy gym, a personal trainer can experiment with lowering his/her voice volume to encourage the client to listen more intently. This technique will also reduce vocal stress.

Pitch is the general level or place of the voice on the musical scale. Everyone has a characteristic pitch. Some speak in a singsong fashion while others speak in a monotone. Some people may end their sentences with an upward inflection while others end with a downward inflection. A noticeable rise in pitch level decreases effective delivery because it usually denotes incompleteness of thought or indecisiveness. Experienced trainers have a wide range of pitch, which they use effectively during delivery.

Rate means the speed of the utterance, the number of words spoken per minute. Most people speak at the rate of 115 to 150 words per minute. Variations in rate depend upon such factors as the importance of the material, the desire for emphasis, and the mood of the content. Speaking too quickly reduces clarity, and can be confusing for those listening. Even though speaking at a slower rate allows others time to absorb what is being said, speaking too slowly may bore the listener. Pausing gives others time to think about what is being said and can accentuate important information.

The rapport stage, which begins at first contact, is critical in establishing a good working relationship between the trainer and client. Sometimes a level of comfort may be quickly established, while at other times more time and energy may have to be expended to win a client's trust. Interpersonal communication skills can be learned and mastered. Merely reading about these skills does not necessarily improve application to everyday situations, but rather these skills must be continuously practiced. Even though the rapport stage is presented as the first stage, there is no end to this stage. The primary qualities (empathy, warmth, and genuineness) and the interpersonal communication skills are important and valuable throughout the entire trainer/client relationship.

INVESTIGATION STAGE

The goal of the investigation stage is to gather information regarding present fitness level, personal goals, and physical and psychological limitations. The process may begin in the initial interview, when the client is encouraged to talk about desires and expectations for the personal training. Health history and life-style questionnaires discussed in Chapter 5 will yield a wealth of information. Additional data can be gathered from fitness assessments (Ch. 6). Historically, health history and life-style questionnaire forms are filled out by the individual client. However, personal trainers are encouraged to ask these questions orally. Understandably, this method requires more time, yet the time spent can be valuable in establishing rapport. In addition, clients will probably reveal more about themselves when they observe the personal trainers's interest. The least that should occur is that the trainer and client discuss the client's written responses to the questionnaire. During the discussion the trainer can probe, question, and clarify in order to gain more information. After all the information is gathered, the personal trainer and client will begin planning by setting goals and making decisions about how they will work together.

PLANNING STAGE

Up to this point, most of the time between the trainer and client has been spent building rapport and gathering appropriate information regarding lifestyle behaviors and current fitness levels. In the planning stage, the trainer and client begin discussing and setting goals according to the client's needs and desires. Because there are usually several ways to reach any goal, the trainer must make use of decision-making skills to determine the best course of action. The outcome will be more effective if the process is done together than if the personal trainer dictates to the client what to do each step of the way.

Decision-making occurs frequently as we go about our daily activities. For example, we must constantly decide how we'll spend our time, money, and energy during any given day. Many of these decisions are second nature for us, and we do not consider the process in determining what is best in a particular situation. Even though there are many decision-making models, the basic process for the personal trainer/client relationship consists of the following steps:

1. Setting the goals.

2. Generating the alternatives.

3. Exploring the alternatives.

4. Making the decision.

5. Formulating the plan.

6. Evaluating the implementation.

SETTING GOALS. Clients seldom approach personal trainers with neatly stated goals. They are usually expressed in vague statements, such as "I want to get in better shape" or "I want to lose some weight." It is, therefore, the personal trainer's responsibility to translate these general aims into precise goals. According to Krumboltz (1966), goals should meet these criteria: (1) the goals are desired by the client and are tailored to him/her, (2) the personal trainer is willing to help the client work toward the goals, and (3) attainment of the goals must be observable and assessable.

The second criterion, willingness of the personal trainer, is significant because the goals of the client must fit the ethical, legal, and competency requirements of the personal trainer. For example, it would be inappropriate for the personal trainer to attempt to teach a client to swim unless he/she possesses knowledge and skill in that area. Personal trainers should recognize their own limitations, both practically and legally, and work together for the overall good of the client, referring to another professional when necessary.

Goals should be written in terms which are measurable. It is difficult to know when a client has obtained a goal that is expressed in terms like "I want to get in better shape." However, both parties would know when the goal is reached when it is stated as, "I want to be able to walk three miles in 45 minutes," or "I'd like to drop 20 pounds." The goals must be ones the client can realistically expect to achieve. It would not be realistic for a non-runner client to say, "I want to run a 10K next week." Realistic goals will help ensure the client's success. Finally, setting both short-range and long-range goals will be helpful. For example, a female client who is 30 percent body-fat may have a long range goal of obtaining 17 percent body-fat in six months. Her short-range goal might be to reach 27 percent in the next four weeks.

GENERATING ALTERNATIVES. This step in decision-making involves proposing all possible alternatives for reaching the goal. This brainstorming process provides more options, giving the client more choices. For example, a client might define his/her goal as "I want to get my thighs stronger for the upcoming ski season." In exploring alternatives to reach this goal, the personal trainer and client might generate the following:

a. I could increase my thigh strength by riding the stationary cycle.

b. I could increase my thigh strength by skiing a couple of hours each day.

c. I could increase my thigh strength by performing squats with free weights.

d. I could increase my thigh strength by climbing stairs.

e. I could increase my thigh strength by stepping up and down on a bench.

The client now has several viable options for obtaining his/her goal.

EXPLORING ALTERNATIVES. After brainstorming the list of options, the next step is to weigh or rank the options. This step evaluates the alternatives for implementation realities and hypothesized consequences. Some options may immediately be thrown out because they are impractical, making it easier for the client to weigh or prioritize the remaining alternatives. From the previous example, a client might discard option b because of its impracticality. With the personal trainer's help, he/she may then rank the rest of the alternatives according to interest, availability, and time.

MAKING THE DECISION. After the previous steps, the client decides on one or more of the alternatives. The decision-making process is to choose the most effective strategy or a combination of the options for this person at this time. For example, our skier may choose to train for skiing by doing squats with free-weights at the gym at least two days a week. In addition, he/she can climb stairs at home when he/she does not have time to get to the gym.

FORMULATING A PLAN. At this point the personal trainer and client determine a specific sequence of actions that likely will result in the accomplishment of the goals. Formulating an action plan includes who needs to do what, when, where, what materials are required, and so forth. This step is further developed as exercise programming, which is covered in Chapter 11.

EVALUATING THE IMPLEMENTATION. This step assesses accomplishment in relation to the predetermined goals and may occur in a formal setting where the client's fitness level is reassessed. The appropriate fitness assessments are described in Chapter 6. The evaluation process may also occur informally during the training sessions as both client and trainer report progress. Either way, together they determine the accomplishment and if necessary determine a new set of action steps.

ACTION STAGE

Once rapport has been established, information has been gathered, and goals have been set, the action stage, or actual training, begins. In the action stage, the personal trainer coaches the client toward his/her goals. As a teacher or tutor, the personal trainer may use many methods of education. In a broad sense, personal training is similar to an individual approach to direct instruction, which is essentially active learning. It consists of the trainer's explaining a new concept or skill to the client. Afterwards, the client demonstrates understanding by practicing under the trainer's direction, while the trainer encourages him/her to continue to practice until the skills become natural. The climate of direct instruction is task-oriented and is high in expectations. The trainer insists on promptness and the client moves from one experience to another with a minimum loss of time.

This teaching theory includes many teaching techniques and methods available to personal trainers. Most of the techniques come from behavior modification theory, one of the oldest and most effective approaches to learning, which gets people to learn new behaviors by means of reinforcement. Selection of techniques will depend upon the styles of the personal trainer and the client. What works for one client may not work for another. Having a variety of teaching techniques is essential to the success of the trainer-client relationship.

"Tell-Show-Do"

> I hear and I forget
> I see and I remember
> I do and I understand
>   —Anonymous

This proverb is at the heart of day-to-day personal training. As early as the 1930s, John Dewey advocated "learning by doing." Probably the most effective systematic method of teaching a skill is by explanation, demonstration, and execution, also known as "tell, show, do." It is based on seeing how something is done correctly and then performing it under the eye of an instructor. (See Fig. 14-3.) This method is most effective because the instructor provides the student with an auditory, visual, and kinesthetic learning experience, thus stimulating all learning pathways.

EXPLANATION. The explanation is a concise verbal description of the skill. It should give a clear understanding of what is to be accomplished. A simple skill may only require one sentence while a more complex skill may require more time. During this time, the client should be told what to watch for during the demonstration. For example, the trainer might say, "I'm now going to show you how to perform the biceps curl. Watch how I control the movement so that I do not use momentum to help lift the weight."

DEMONSTRATION. The demonstration is the visual presentation of the skill. It is critical that it be an accurate representation of the action desired. Therefore, personal trainers must be keenly aware kinesthetically so that proper form is communicated to the client. If a trainer has just explained there should be no use of momentum or swinging during the biceps curl, then the trainer must perform the curl with complete control using no momentum for the lift. Demonstrating the movement slowly will help the client see what is happening. Repeating the demonstration at normal speed while recapitulating main points will also aid learning. The explanation and demonstration steps can be combined effectively in order to save time.

PERFORMANCE. The performance is the client's opportunity to practice the skill. The personal trainer should carefully monitor and supervise the client's performance to correct errors and encourage proper form. Constructive feedback and more practice time complete the learning loop. The problem in many teaching programs is that all the above steps are not followed. Often the explanation or "tell" step is not followed by the "show" and "do" steps. Merely telling a person exactly how to perform a skill does not ensure he/she will be able to do it differently or better. For example, simply telling a client to "stretch the hamstrings after you jog" does not ensure he/she will perform the stretch effectively. To complete the process, the client should be shown how to perform a hamstring stretch properly. Then the client is given an opportunity to practice it while the personal trainer coaches proper form and execution.

Figure 14-3   "Tell, Show, Do." (a) Trainer explaining hamstring stretch, (b) Trainer demonstrating hamstring stretch, (c) Trainer watching client perform hamstrings stretch.

A personal trainer must decide if the skill should be taught as a whole or if it should be broken into parts. These methods of teaching are often referred to as the whole approach and the parts approach, respectively. Less complex skills are practiced as a whole to establish a general idea and feel of the movement. Practicing the biceps curl from start to finish is an appropriate application of the whole approach. More complex skills which require much attention may be divided into parts after the whole concept is presented. Race walking may be demonstrated by the teacher as a whole movement and then broken down into lower torso and upper torso movements so that the student may master each part of the skill. Breaking race walking down into individual parts makes it easier to perform the skill in its entirety.

Modeling

Humans want to identify with other humans. We look to others so we can imitate traits we would like to have. The concept of emulating another's behavior or attitudes is called modeling and the individual demonstrating the behavior is known as the model. We see many examples of modeling in our daily lives. Children adopt parent's language patterns and even nonverbal cues. Children can learn aggressive behavior from watching television. Prestigious models have a profound impact on dress, hair styles, music, and food. Consider the widespread use of leg warmers in exercise classes after Jane Fonda's "Work-out" videotape came on the market. According to Bandura (1977), modeling is probably the most efficient and effective form of learning a new behavior. This places both an enormous opportunity and a responsibility on the teacher.

Two forms of modeling are identified by Good and Brophy (1987). The first is simply imitation or "monkey see, monkey do." The observer adopts the behavior of the model as in the leg warmer example. The second is more complex because the observer infers attitudes, values, beliefs, or personality characteristics as a result of watching the model. The observer draws his/her own conclusions and over time may change his/her behavior. This is a common occurrence in the trainer/client relationship. As a result of observing the trainer's dedication to a healthy and fit life-style, the client may choose a healthier alternative to his/her regular Friday afternoon happy hour. In this form of modeling, people often communicate attitudes unconsciously and are unaware of the effects. Students constantly observe a teacher's approach to a subject, studying the teacher's attitudes and beliefs. They watch the way a teacher interacts with students and other colleagues, and the student may then make inferences regarding the learning process. The way in which a teacher responds to a student's question can affect the learning climate. A teacher responding with "I don't know...let's find out" models enthusiasm for learning and that not knowing the answer is acceptable. This form of modeling is both subtle and powerful.

There are several factors which influence modeling. The first factor is the state of the learner. The more uncertain a learner is, the more significant will be the effects of the model. Therefore, a client is more susceptible to the effects of modeling by the personal trainer at the beginning of the relationship. A second factor which influences modeling is the status of the model in the eyes of the learner. Students are more likely to adopt the behaviors of a teacher they like than of one they do not like.

A personal trainer cannot escape being a model. However, he/she can decide what kind of model he/she will be. Who a personal trainer is and what he/she does sends loud and clear messages to the client about what is important and how the program is really supposed to work. In other words, the way a trainer behaves is more important than what he/she says. The trainer who advocates doing what he/she is unwilling to do will more than likely be unconvincing. It is fruitless for a trainer to tell clients that steroids are bad for their health when it is known that the trainer uses steroids. "Do as I say, not as I do" has no place in the trainer/client relationship. The client views the trainer as an expert and generally believes everything that the trainer says and does. Therefore, it is critical for a trainer to be aware of his/her powerful influence. A personal trainer should be competent and wise in fitness matters and obtain at least a level of fitness which corresponds to the level of teaching. Going beyond mere competence is even more desirable for a trainer.

Contracting

Contracting finds its roots in the behavioral theory of reinforcement, that rewarded behavior tends to be repeated. Contracting systematically arranges the rewards so that the probability of the desired response is increased. Most behavioral contracts are verbal or written agreements between two or more people and consist of two primary parts (see Fig. 14-4). The first part is specifying desired behavior to be achieved. The second part is stating specific reinforcements that will reward the desired behavior. It may take the form of, "If you will do _____ , I will do _____ ." A contract does not necessarily require involving other people. It is possible for a person to make an agreement with him/herself by preparing a self-contract (see Fig. 14-5).

I, the undersigned, agree to the following conditions, which I will follow to the best of my ability:

From _____ to _____ , for a period of one week, I will choose to eat at meal time only.

From _____ to _____ , for a period of one week, I will eat foods recommended by the American Heart Association and the American Dietetic Association.

At the end of the week, as a reward for fulfilling the above conditions, I will attend a movie or another social function with my husband.

Date: _____

Signature of wife: _____

I, the undersigned, agree to take my wife to a movie at the designated time when the above conditions are met.

Date: _____

Signature of husband: _____

Figure 14–4   Example of an exercise contract between two people

I will walk in my target zone a minimum of _____ minutes _____ times per week.

I will record my progress in my personal log.

The following people will help me reach my goal:

Person	Method
1. _____	1. _____
2. _____	2. _____
3. _____	3. _____
4. _____	4. _____

I will reward myself for adhering to the above for _____ weeks with the following: .

_____

_____

I will begin this program ____(date)____ and will reevaluate it on ____(date)____ .

I commit myself to the above.

_____(signature)_____

_____(date)_____

Figure 14–5   Example of a personal exercise contract

All helping relationships have implied contracts or understandings that both people will have responsibilities to carry out. Verbal or informal contracts are used when there is little chance of a misunderstanding of the conditions. The written contract is used to prevent misunderstanding regarding the conditions and to add impact by having the client sign his/her name indicating a commitment.

Several features are necessary for an effective contract. The terms of a contract should be explicitly stated so that the expectations are clearly understood by all parties. An example of an unclear contract is "I agree to lose some weight so I may do something I enjoy." A more clearly stated contract might be, "I will lose five pounds and then I'll be permitted to buy that new dress." Many contracts fail because of impossible terms. Therefore the terms of the contract should be feasible and reasonable. "I will lose 50 pounds this month so I can buy that new dress" is an unreasonable goal. A more reasonable goal is "I will lose 1–2 pounds a week for the next two months." Stating the contract in positive terms rather than negative terms will encourage a more favorable attitude toward the contract. "If you do not quit smoking, I will not work with you" is a negative approach. A more positive approach would be to state a reward upon smoking cessation.

To ensure satisfactory results, contracts need to be evaluated frequently and perhaps renegotiated. This renegotiation can occur any time or during the formal evaluation process. What appeared to be fair and reasonable initially may not be so at a later date. A client may discover he/she cannot meet some specified commitment. The difficulty should be discussed with the personal trainer, and a new contract can be negotiated, drafted, and signed. This evaluation process will help ensure that the contract remains effective.

The following questions will help trouble-shoot and spot problems in writing contracts:

1. Are the terms of the contract clear?

2. Is the contract fair?

3. Is the contract positive?

4. Is the target behavior clearly specified?

5. Does the contract provide for immediate reinforcement?

6. Is the reinforcement frequent and in small amounts?

7. Does the client understand the contract?

8. Is there a time specified for evaluation?

Feedback

Feedback is a powerful contributor to effective learning and client performance. Feedback is any information about current or past behavior that can be used to improve future performance and can be given verbally or nonverbally. It usually occurs after a client has asked a question or done something related to the exercise session. Feedback informs the client of the correctness of his/her performance and recognizes his/her effort. Trainers naturally respond and react to clients' behavior. Clients are greatly influenced by the way trainers behave toward them. They monitor their trainers' reactions and adjust their performance in accord with what they interpret.

In order for feedback to be effective, a clearly defined standard of performance must be given. For example, a trainer defines the standard of performance for proper placement and movement of the arms in race walking during his/her explanation and demonstration of the skill. The client's performance is then measured and corrected according to the demonstrated criteria. The performance standard may need to be set at frequent intervals during instruction by continuing to explain and demonstrate. In order for the feedback to be effective and learning to occur, there must be a practice session. The practice session gives the client an opportunity to correct his/her performance and reach the preset standard.

Research indicates that effective feedback has three characteristics: (1) It is specific, (2) it is contingent on performance, and (3) it provides corrective information for the learner. Specific feedback is clear about what was right and/or wrong in a response. A trainer may watch a client incorrectly perform a lat pulldown on the weight equipment and then exclaim, "That's not right, Susie!" The personal trainer's response does not aid her understanding of the performance, only that it was wrong. By contrast, the personal trainer might respond, "Not quite, Susie, let's reverse the position of the hands." Corrective feedback helps the client know what was wrong with the performance and what to do to get back on track. The number of different cues is infinite. Striving for unique cues requires a trainer's creativity and committed practice.

Feedback should not be given for every single move because too much of a good thing can have a negative effect. People tend to disregard excessive compliments which are overused. To be effective, the feedback should match the achievement and specifically relate the response to the performance. For example, a personal trainer observing a client perform a biceps curl might respond with "That's good" which is only a statement of general praise. However, an even more effective response would be, "That's it, John, you're really isolating the biceps muscle now." This response gives the client specific information as to why the performance is correct. To maximize the effect, cues can be personalized by using a client's name, for instance, "That's the right idea, Jennie." Typical verbal cues are:

Good	Excellent
Right	Correct
All Right	OK
Very Good	Fine

These words are less effective because they have been overused. Examples of other cues trainers might use are:

That's an effective thought.

You've got it.

On the money.

You are really with it today.

I'd give that move a ten.

Nonverbal feedback is far more effective than verbal feedback. Clients tune into facial expressions and gestures. When used properly, nonverbal cues are the epitome of personalization. How else can a "thumbs up" signal and a generous smile be interpreted? Nonverbal *positive* feedback interactions include:

Smiling	Making an "Okay" sign
Nodding	Patting on the back
Shaking hands	Touching
Clapping	Winking
Thumbs up	Applauding

Nonverbal *negative* feedback interactions include:

Frowning	Thumbs down
Shaking head	Drumming fingers
Looking away	Rolling eyes
Grimacing	

A final and important point needs to be made regarding verbal and nonverbal feedback. As in all interpersonal communication, when both verbal and nonverbal cues are given, they must be congruent. For example, when a trainer frowns while telling a client that he/she is doing a great job, the two behaviors are incongruent, and the conflicting messages are confusing. The client will receive a mixed message and will probably believe the frown rather than the words. On the other hand, when verbal and nonverbal cuing are congruently combined, the trainer can have a powerful influence on the client.

SUMMARY

The personal trainer/client relationship is a helping relationship throughout the stages of establishing and building a personal relationship with a client, gathering vital information, developing fitness goals, and implementing a plan to accomplish the goals. As a helper, the personal trainer creates conditions and uses techniques that will help bring about the desired outcomes for the client. Merely possessing a fit body, technical skills, and a wide-based knowledge of health and fitness does not ensure success for personal trainers. Probably the most crucial factor for determining a positive climate for the working relationship is the trainer's repertoire of communication skills. These skills include both verbal and nonverbal behaviors, such as attending, perceiving nonverbal messages, perceiving verbal messages, and verbal responding. These interpersonal communication skills can be learned, practiced, and mastered. They are important not only in the first stage of establishing a rapport but throughout the entire process.

Personal training is about behavioral change, which is the true measure of a successful trainer/client relationship. Every personal trainer is unique and brings into the trainer/client relationship his/her own personal experience and opinions about what brings about life-style changes in people. Each client is also uniquely different. Therefore, personal trainers must be flexible in matching teaching techniques and change strategies to the goals, needs, and personality of the client. A technique that is successful for one client does not ensure the same achievement or change for another. A skilled personal trainer will get to know the client and apply various techniques with wisdom and common sense. One client may relish the structure of a written contract while another may resist to the point of discontinuing the relationship.

The flexibility required of a trainer sometimes demands the trainer to be deeply personal while at other times remain an objective observer. Being able to move freely along the full range of interpersonal skills and teaching techniques will permit a trainer to respond appropriately at various stages of the relationship. On one hand, the process of sizing up and assisting a client toward a healthy life-style is naturally intuitive, and, on the other hand, it needs to be a deliberate, rational process.

REFERENCES

Bandura, A. (1977). *Social learning theory.* Englewood Cliffs, NJ: Prentice Hall.

Good, F., & Brophy, J. (1987). *Looking in classrooms.* New York: Harper & Row.

Hall, E.T. (1966). *The hidden dimensions.* Garden City, NY: Doubleday.

Krumboltz, J. (1966). *Stating the goals of counseling* (Monograph No. 1). Fullerton, CA: California Personnel and Guidance Association.

Mehrabian, A. (1972). *Nonverbal communication.* Chicago: Aldine-Atherton.

Rogers, C.R., Gendlin, E.T., Keisler, D.J., & Truax, C.D. (1967). *The therapeutic relationship and its impact.* Madison, WI: University of Wisconsin Press.

Truax, C.B., & Carkuff, R.R. (1967). *Toward effective counseling and psychotherapy.* Chicago: Aldine.

SUGGESTED READING

Carkhuff, R.R., & Anthony, W.A. (1979). *The skills of helping.* Amherst, MA: Human Resource Development Press.

Jacobson, D., Eggen, P.D., & Kauchak, D. (1989). *Methods for teaching: A skills approach.* Columbus, OH: Merrill.

Kauchak, D.P., & Eggen, P.D. (1989). *Learning and teaching: Research-based methods.* Needham Heights, MA: Allyn & Bacon.

Mosston, M. (1966). *Teaching physical education: From command to discovery.* Columbus, OH: Merrill.

Okun, B.F. (1987). *Effective helping: Interviewing and counseling techniques.* Monterey, CA: Brooks/Cole.

Selecting Equipment, Apparel, and Footwear

MICHAEL D. WOLF
and DOUGLAS H. RICHIE

15

MICHAEL D. WOLF, PH.D., is a partner in New York City–based Fitness Technologies, Ltd., the successor to International Fitness Exchange, a firm Dr. Wolf founded and ran for six years. He is former research coordinator for Nautilus Sports/Medical Industries, Inc., and was assistant professor of exercise science on the graduate faculty of New York University. Receiving his Ph.D. in 1979 from the University of Texas, Austin. Dr. Wolf has written six books and more than 40 articles for fitness, health, and hotel industry trade journals. He has been a contributing editor in fitness at *SELF Magazine* for seven years.

DOUGLAS H. RICHIE, JR., D.P.M., is adjunct professor of physical education at California State University, Long Beach, and associate clinical professor at the California College of Podiatric Medicine. Dr. Richie is on the attending staff at Los Angeles County–USC Medical Center and maintains a sports podiatry practice in Seal Beach, California. He is a member of the board of advisors of IDEA, the Association for Fitness Professionals, and chairs the research committee of the American Council on Exercise.

IN THIS CHAPTER:

- Selecting exercise equipment by assessing client needs, budget, space allocation restrictions, product design, and product value.
- Product features for various categories and models of exercise equipment.

- Selecting apparel, including high-tech clothing and protective gear.
- Selecting footwear: fitness activity purpose, shoe anatomy, types of footwear, guidelines for buying shoes.

With the exercise sophistication of private-training clients seemingly increasing each day, the need for private trainers to bring accurate and broad-based knowledge of exercise equipment and high-tech apparel and footwear to the training situation similarly expands. The job of helping clients to design a home fitness area or choose the proper apparatus when training in a commercial facility can be daunting. Once, the choices in fitness equipment were far more limited, and choosing what to buy or use was simpler. But nowadays the trainer must choose from more than 60 national (and international) manufacturers of bikes, rowers, treadmills, skiers, stair climbers, ladder climbers, and multi-station, single-station, and free-weight strength apparatus. Similarly, the introduction of high-tech fibers to athletic apparel has made it necessary for the trainer who works with competitive athletes or serious amateurs to understand at least the fundamentals of wicking and water transport through fibers. More than ever, trainers and clients need to assess the fit, feel, features, and finish of exercise equipment and apparel–to try before they buy.

SELECTING EXERCISE EQUIPMENT

To objectify and quantify the outfitting of a home fitness facility and the choosing of the right mix of apparatus for commercial settings, a five-step process is presented here along with a 34-item questionnaire that can be used for a side-by-side comparison of competing products. To build knowledge of exercise equipment, a hands-on component is required, so create room in your budget for travel to a fitness-equipment-rich trade show.

The five steps for making intelligent equipment-buying or equipment-using decisions are:

1. Identify the client's *fitness needs*.

2. Determine the *budget*, the funds that are available.

3. Determine how much *space* is available.

4. Examine the *product*: features, design, manufacture, safety, and serviceability.

5. Assess "bang for the buck" with the *Comprehensive Equipment Evaluation Checklist*, a side-by-side comparison tool.

Client Needs

Since interest in the two components of equipment-based training—strength work and aerobic work—will probably never cease to wax and wane with the winds of what's hot and what's not, most clients planning an investment in home fitness equipment should balance their proposed inventory to reflect both. After the initial purchase, which is based on the highest-priority need and on budget and space restrictions, later purchases can fill in with the equipment that you and the client ranked next. Every fitness room—home or commercial—should include both a strength component and a cardiovascular component to serve physiological as well as motivational and enjoyment needs, and equipment purchasing should reflect the anatomy, interests, and fitness level of each client. Only hands-on experience tells you what fits the smaller woman anatomically, what equipment presents unacceptably high initial resistance levels, and what simply feels good and what doesn't—a surprisingly good index of quality of design, components, and manufacture.

In assessing your client's needs—which may be done through unstructured questioning or, more professionally, through oral or written survey instruments—remember that "perceived" needs and "real" needs may not always match. Furthermore the means to meet these needs may be different from what the client thinks. Though true aerobic exercise burns far more calories, and a higher percentage of fat calories, than strength or anaerobic training, those clients seeking body-fat reduction would be best served by the inclusion of a strength component in their aerobic program, to add metabolically active lean tissue. While aerobic exercise burns fat during and briefly after a workout, lean muscle tissue burns calories round the clock. Moreover, body reshaping (as opposed to the reduction of body-fat stores) is more quickly accomplished through the body-sculpting effects of strength training. Don't fall victim to the possible call from clients for cardiovascular equipment to the exclusion of strength apparatus. Be prepared to educate them about the reasons for your final recommendations on purchase or usage.

Budgetary Consideration for the Home Buyer

With fitness equipment currently evolving so rapidly, and with clients seeing commercial fitness facilities that feature the latest high-tech choices, the preparation of a short- and/or long-term buying budget for the client requires thoughtful input from the trainer. You get what you pay for in exercise equipment as with any other product. There are few, if any bargains, because fitness equipment that does its job well, reliably, and under potentially heavy use for several years in a commercial setting cannot be manufactured cheaply. Expect quality fitness apparatus to be found in the following price ranges:

Stationary nonelectronic bicycles	$300–$1,000
Stationary electronic bicycles	$1,200–$3,900
Nonelectronic rowing machines	$700–$1,995
Electronic rowing machines	$2,000–$3,600
Motorized treadmills	$1,200–$9,000
Nonelectronic stair climbers	$350–$1,100
Electronic stair climbers	$2,200–$3,400
Ladder-climbing simulators	$1,395–3,400
Cross-country-ski simulators	$320–$1,395
Upper-body ergometers	$2,200–$3,600
Single-station strength apparatus	$1,300–$4,700 (one person/unit)
Multistation strength apparatus	$1,000–$10,000 (1–12 people/unit)

In the search for equipment, you and your clients are sure to encounter some products that cost surprisingly less than seemingly comparable other products, as well as those that cost surprisingly more. In any case, the following possible explanations should help guide your purchase.

REASONS FOR A SIGNIFICANTLY LOWER PRICE OF A "COMPARABLE" PRODUCT.

- Off-shore vs. domestic manufacture.
- Cheaper components.
- Less rigorous design and assembly.
- Lower profit margin taken by the manufacturer.
- Fewer or less costly built-ins to overhead (e.g., large customer service department).
- Better engineering allowing less-costly assembly.

And conversely, ask these questions about a *higher-priced* product:

- Does it do what it was designed to do *demonstrably* better than lower-priced competitors?

- Does it offer better features?
- Is it likely to last longer?
- Is it likely to require less service?
- Will it be easier and less costly to service?

Affirmative answers to these questions will justify a higher purchase price.

Space Allocation Restrictions

Space allocation is intrinsically linked to a client's home budget and includes the considerations of expected room usage (i.e., which family members), safety, traffic flow, aesthetics, the desired equipment complement, and future expansion opportunities. With fitness equipment having footprints of anywhere from 10 to 300 square feet, formulas for room size are useless. Plan for at least as much open space as equipment space, and use these guidelines:

Treadmills	30 sq ft	Bikes	10 sq ft
Single-station strength apparatus	35 sq ft	Climbers	20 sq ft
Multistation strength apparatus	50–200 sq ft	Rowers	20 sq ft
Free-weight apparatus	20–50 sq ft	Cross-country skiers	25 sq ft

HOW MUCH EQUIPMENT DOES THE CLIENT NEED AT HOME? What you think the client needs physiologically and what he/she has room and/or budget for, can of course be quite different. Considering overall space allocation—budget, space availability, expected usage, traffic flow/safety, aesthetics, and desired equipment complement—these scenarios are possible for home fitness-equipment areas:

Under $500 to spend and 20 square feet:

Stationary upright or inexpensive recumbent bike (user pedals from a bucket seat) ($300–$450), or

Cross-country skier ($395–$500), or

Hydraulic stair-climber ($300–$500)

$500–$1,000 to spend and 20–50 square feet:

Good recumbent or upright nonelectronic bike ($600–$1,000), or

Under $500 bike plus skier; bike plus climber; skier plus climber, or

One or possibly two under-$500 aerobic choices plus one multi-purpose free-weight bench ($250) and a quality set of adjustable dumbbells ($75+)

$1,000–$1,500 to spend and 25–75 square feet:

Entry-level treadmill ($1,200+), or

Two aerobic pieces, free-weight bench and dumbbell or barbell set, or

Three aerobic pieces (for clients with limited-strength programs)

$1,500–$2,000 to spend and 25–100 square feet:

Higher-quality treadmill ($1,995), or

Three aerobic pieces plus free-weight bench and a weight set, or

An entry-level multistation strength apparatus ($1,000) and two aerobic pieces

Obviously, as space and budget increase, the number of options increases beyond the space available for listing them here.

The choices you'll need to help clients make between high-quality, low-sizzle nonelectronic equipment and state-of-the-art simulators, and between inexpensive home multistations that require frequent mechanical changes and those that require none, are difficult, because a low budget can necessitate equipment that falls short in exciting and motivating the user. For some clients, therefore, a balance between home and fitness-center-type equipment may be the answer. Others will require an exercise program that incorporates equipment-based and nonequipment-based exercise. The trainer must be aware of the impact of equipment on the client and devise a program that meets the client's needs and keeps the client motivated while working within budgetary, time, and space limitations.

Product Issues

Questions of product design and manufacture the trainer should be capable of answering include the following:

GENERAL CONSIDERATIONS.

- *Biomechanics*: Is the body required to move in a manner that is correct and safe?

- *Ergonomics*: The interface between man and machine. Is the equipment adjustable? comfortable? easy to teach? easy to learn? able to fit users of various sizes?

- *Intelligence in design*: Are parts easily removed and replaced? Are components the highest possible quality in the price range? Is the equipment space-efficient? Are there any innovations that mark the unit as superior?

- *Advertising claims*: Are the manufacturer's product claims backed up by research or objective consumer publications?

MANUFACTURING CONSIDERATIONS.

- *Excellence in manufacture*: Do moving parts mesh well? How tight are manufacturing tolerances?

- *Bearings*: What types are used? (Are there *no* bearings at pivot points?) Pillow-block, roller, ball, and linear-slide bearings are generally the best; oil-less bronze types are good; polyethylene types are least desirable.

- *Frames*: What is the thickness? (2" x 2" or 2" x 3" is generally best.) Welds should appear clean and smooth; critical joints should have high integrity through combinations of methods such as inside/outside sleeve *plus* welding.

- *Chroming*: Is it done in-house? What's the thickness? Is it nickel-chrome? Is the finish polished or buffed? (The latter stays clean-looking longer, but is less flashy.)

- *Paint*: Electrostatically applied powder-coat paint that is baked on is generally considered best and is less subject to chipping.

- *Weight Stacks*: Are plates cold-rolled steel, for balance? What are the tolerances on guide rod holes? Do plates ride the guide rods smoothly, especially if only one or two plates are selected? Are there bushings in *each* weight stack plate (generally best)?

- *Cable/chain/belt*: What is its rating? adjustability? life expectancy? replaceability? Chain is the most difficult to maintain and keep clean, adjust, and replace. Cable is quiet and quite easy to adjust and replace. (Look for steel cable sealed in teflon, not plastic.) The rubber coating on some "kevlar" belts appears to fray rather quickly under use, and may be difficult to replace should the manufacturer ever go out of business.

- *Pulleys*: Made of what materials? (Bronze is hardest; aluminum, softest; fiberglass/graphite, highest tech.) What is the diameter? (Larger is better.) Inner diameter? (It should match the diameter of the cable, belt, or chain.) What kind of inner bearings? (Ball bearings are best.)

- *Guide rods*: Solid, cold-rolled steel is best; and the bigger the diameter, the better.

- *Upholstery, padding, exposed wood*: What is the quality of materials and workmanship? True stitched upholstery is better than folded edges. One manufacturer has pioneered the use of a high-quality solid foam that requires no outside upholstery skin. Is exposed wood expertly finished?

- *Electronics*: Where do component parts come from? Are they done in-house? Are they user-replaceable ("modular" or snap-out, plug-in)?

SAFETY CONSIDERATIONS.

- Are there obvious or not-so-obvious *design flaws* or weaknesses that increase the chances of injury? For example, escalator-type stair climbing simulators, cross-country skiers with skis that can move simultaneously in the same direction (forward or backward), apparatus with poor stability, which is often associated with poor manufacturing processes.

- Are there features that *enhance user safety*? For example, range-of-motion limiters on strength machines; weight-stack guards or any guards that protect moving parts; side-rail safety switches on treadmills that require both feet on the rails before the belt will start; recumbent bikes for reduced lumbar strain.

Assessing "Bang for the Buck"

"Bang for the Buck" simply means whether a product is truly a value at its price. To objectify making such an assessment, we created the Comprehensive Equipment Evaluation Checklist (see Fig. 15–1). The checklist allows six products at a time to be compared, side-by-side, on the answers to 34 questions relating to the product, the manufacturer, and the dealer. Weight can be assigned to each item, and a single point total will then represent the overall value, or "Bang for the Buck," of each product.

Instructions for Using the Comprehensive Equipment Evaluation Checklist

1. List at the top of the grid on page 401 the names of up to six products you are considering. Use a separate page for each type of equipment.

2. Lay the grid along the left side of the list of questions on page 401.

3. Answer the questions using a 5-point scale with values ranging as follows:

   5 points - Highest score; absolutely true of the product, or true to the best of your knowledge.

   1 point - Lowest (poorest) score; absolutely not true of the product, or false to the best of your knowledge.

4. Use the optional weighting system as follows: Assign a weight to as many of the checklist items as you wish, then multiply the point score for each quetion by its weight. We have left these weights blank so that you (and your staff) may decide which items are most important to you. The weights need not total any specific amount. In our opinion, some of the items that should be weighted due to their importance in the decision-making process are:

   Questions 1, 2, 5, 8, 12, 14, 16, 18, 21, 22, 24, 29, 31-34

5. Total the point scores for each product (multiplying by weights if you choose to use that option).

Comprehensive Equipment Evaluation Checklist

EQUIPMENT SAFETY:

1. Is the equipment safe to use? Are there any obvious design flaws that increase risk?
2. Might any body parts easily exceed a safe range of motion?
3. Do electronic circuits have redundant safety backups?

EQUIPMENT USAGE:

4. Is the equipment self-instructing, or does it come with instructions? Are electronics user-friendly?
5. Is the equipment easy to use? Easy to learn? Are the movements familiar or unusual?
6. Are adjustments sensibly engineered and user-friendly?
7. Does the equipment have inherent motivation? Is it enjoyable?
8. Is it comfortable? Can users of different sizes adapt to it easily and use it for 20 minutes or more?
9. Is the product accompanied by a comprehensive and well-written instruction manual for your staff?
10. Is the product aesthetically appealing?
11. Is the product space-efficient?

DESIGN AND COMPONENTS:

12. Does the product perform the task for which it was designed with fluidity and precision?
13. Is the product quiet during operation? Do moving parts mesh with minimal friction?
14. Does the product appear to be built for the long haul?
15. Are upholstery and paint or surface treatments durable?

DEALER AND WARRANTY:

16. How long and how comprehensive is the product warranty?
17. Will the manufacturer provide a written warranty?
18. Will the dealer provide its own written warranty?
19. Does the local service agent keep parts in stock? How effective are the provisions for warranty service?
20. How easily will service be obtained after the warranty period?

THE MANUFACTURER:

21. How long has the product been on the market? (Especially important for electronic equipment.)
22. What is the past and future of the manufacturer? Are they likely to be around in 3-5 years?
23. Will the manufacturer provide you with documents or numbers on out-of-box failures or warranty repairs?
24. Will the manufacturer or dealer provide instruction? How are the instructors professionally qualified?
25. Will the dealer or manufacturer provide set-up/installation? How soon after delivery can it be done?
26. Does the manufacturer have its own fleet of delivery trucks?
27. Are major component parts manufactured domestically or abroad? Are they built by the manufacturer?
28. Does the manufacturer carry product liability insurance?

AND IN CLOSING:

29. Have your members asked for the product, or will they find it desirable? Is there brand name value?
30. Is the product faddish? Is it likely to be obsolete soon? Can it be upgraded by the manufacturer?
31. Have you formed opinions from personal use of the product?
32. Will the dealer or manufacturer provide a list of users?
33. How do current users rate the product?
34. Is your gut feeling that the price is fair considering the above answers?

Product													
Weight	PTS	PTS X WT	PTS	PTS X WT	PTS	PTS X WT	PTS	PTS X WT	PTS	PTS X WT	PTS	PTS X WT	
													1
													2
													3
													4
													5
													6
													7
													8
													9
													10
													11
													12
													13
													14
													15
													16
													17
													18
													19
													20
													21
													22
													23
													24
													25
													26
													27
													28
													29
													30
													31
													32
													33
Totals													34

Product Features*

STATIONARY BICYCLES.

Nonelectronic models. The basic, entry-level-but-high-quality stationary bike, costing from $300 to $500, offers a resistance (pedaling effort) mechanism of a belt circling a heavy flywheel. (Adding tension to the belt increases pedaling effort.) In this price range are bikes weighing 70–100 pounds, quite capable of lasting years at home, even under heavy use. Feedback can be analog (gauges) or digital (electronic). In the $700–$1,000 range, nonelectronic upright and recumbent bikes offer better feel, comfort, and durability. These are found in home and commercial settings. Recumbent bikes deserve special mention, for they offer greater comfort (which can mean a greater likelihood of use), possibly a higher-calorie burn at the same heart rate as upright cycling (probably due to increased venous return to the heart when the legs and the heart are at the same height relative to gravity), and, for those whose cosmetic interests include work on the buttocks and upper hamstrings, significantly enhanced biomechanical loading on those areas.

Electronic models. Pedaling effort is controlled electronically. These bikes can range in cost from $1,200 to $3,900. This electronic or computer control means that riders will be taken up and down simulated hills, may see exciting computer graphics, and may even have pedaling effort controlled in direct correlation with their heart rate response to the ride. The electronic stationary bike has become de rigeur in commercial fitness centers. The newest generation of electronic bikes uses the "eddy current" braking system, wherein a steel disc rotates in the space between two parallel electromagnets. Its advantage is the promise of a maintenance-free resistance mechanism, since there is no friction between moving and touching parts. Its disadvantage is the feel—uncomfortable or somehow unusual to many because while cycling the resistance lacks the feel of chain meshing with chainwheel. Electronic bikes employ an automobile-type alternator to apply resistance to a chainwheel mechanism. Much of the pleasant feel of the fine meshing of chain and chainwheel is still present, and many users prefer the feel of these bikes to the new generation of eddy-current systems. Alternator-type electronic bikes range in price from $1,400 to $3,900.

ROWING MACHINES. For clients without low-back pain, rowing provides a fine cardiovascular workout with emphasis on major muscle groups of the legs, mid-back, and arms.

Nonelectronic models. Though hydraulic-resistance rowers (using shock-absorber-type pistons) still exist, they simulate rowing so poorly that few buyers use them for very long. They range in price from $200 to $450. Quality rowing simulators using air or actual water for resistance, and therefore without electronic or computer control of rowing effort, range in cost from $700 to $2,000. The source of resistance in the $700 and $1,000 models is air, which is a fluid much like water, and which provides a quality simulation. For $2,000, clients can pull a blade through a small tank of water and get the exact feel and sound of actual rowing. The price—steep for a noncomputerized product—also buys the longest warranty in the business.

---

* The prices listed in the product features were compiled in July 1990.

Electronic models. In the $2,000–$3,600 price range are computerized rowers that place rowing effort under electronic control. The money buys features such as excellent modulation of workout variables (time, speed, computerized competition), and an onboard color TV with added audio effects, but does not, for many, equal the feel of the air- or water-resistance machines.

MOTORIZED TREADMILLS. Since there never has been a nonmotorized treadmill that even remotely simulated walking, jogging, or running, we will discuss only motorized models and refer to them merely as treadmills. Treadmills have been shown in at least one report (Allen and Goldberg, 1986) to burn more calories, and a higher percentage of fat calories, than any other aerobic simulator at heart rates of 65 percent, 75 percent, and 85 percent of age-adjusted maximum. (Other products studied were independent- and dependent-ski cross-country ski simulators, an upright bike, and a hydraulic rower.) The main attraction of treadmills, even to those fortunate enough to reside in warmer climates, is the fingertip control of speed and elevation while in the comfort and safety of home or club. Even in commercial facilities with banked and "tuned" (sprung) indoor tracks, it is not unusual to see more people on treadmills than on the track.

Home treadmills (the motorized version) can be found for as little as $400. But quality models that will last for years rather than months, feel enough like the real thing to be used, and handle larger individuals start at $1,200. Models with manual elevation and substantial drive motors (see next paragraph) range from $1,600 to $2,000, and models with electrical elevation check in at $2,700 and up. Programmable home treadmills range upward from $3,500. Commercial treadmills, which range in cost from $3,200 to more than $9,000, are capable of handling heavy use with proper maintenance and service. Treadmills *must* be built to withstand runners landing approximately 1,000 times per mile with two to four times their body weight, and can be either a club's most popular fixture or its biggest headache. In shopping for treadmills, focus on three items in particular: satisfied local users, the manufacturer's local service capabilities (factory-trained technicians, with a supply of parts, must be nearby), and the electrical nature of the motor. Treadmill pricing turns out to be an excellent guide to quality, as the best brands are also the most expensive. However, opting for simple fingertip control of speed and elevation over computerized control will save you $1,000.

Treadmills are built with motors that are either AC (alternating current) or DC (direct current). AC treadmills, which have been around for over 30 years, are usually less exciting than the newer, computerized DC brands, but currently have an edge in reliability. On the minus side, however, since AC treadmills can, under certain circumstances, be turned on and almost immediately reach the speed at which they were turned off, unwary users can be thrown unceremoniously backward when mounting a treadmill running at 8 mph. In contrast, DC treadmills *always* come on at their slowest speed. Even with the methods that most AC treadmill manufacturers have devised to deal with this problem, AC treadmills are still a slightly higher safety risk. In 1990, three of the premier manufacturers of AC treadmills introduced the first totally-safe-starting AC treadmills. Other manufacturers use electrical strips along the treadmill siderails on which the user must stand to start the running belt; even if the belt starts at high speed, the user will be safely on the siderails.

AC motors turn at only one speed when fed current, and so require a transmission mechanism to alter belt speed. The advantage of constant-speed AC motors is that they are always turning at full torque (turning power). DC motors spin at a speed proportional to the current fed to them—on the one hand eliminating the need for a transmission, but on the other hand meaning that smaller DC motors have low torque at low speeds, bad news for the obese or heavy user who wants to walk at an incline.

STAIR-CLIMBING SIMULATORS. These machines have been grabbing a larger and larger share of both home and commercial equipment budgets. With their excellent aerobic and lower-body effects, stair climbers are now found in over 75 percent of commercial fitness facilities.

Home climbers. Home climbers with foot platforms that do not "articulate" (hinge) to remain parallel to the floor may put greater stress on the ankle and knee than those with platforms that do hinge and may be contraindicated for those with ankle and/or knee problems. Counsel clients to avoid buying cheap (under $300) knockoffs of the quality, home hydraulic climbers. For an extra $50–$100 the newest home climbers that have arm levers linked to the foot levers can be purchased. These models allow for both upper-body and lower-body conditioning.

Electronic models. For $2,200 and more, the stair climber will be computer-controlled, offering more excitement and a more pleasurable exercise experience than home models. It may be independent-step (both steps simultaneously go up or down, increasing learning time), or dependent-step (one goes up when the other goes down). Though the large chain-driven brands have the vast majority of market share, none has been maintenance-free. The climbers that rely on smooth, quiet, and maintenance-free hydraulics have a far smaller market share but are worth considering. Hydraulic climbers lack the feel of the chain-driven brands, but unless the client comes in demanding one of the name brands, you'll do fine with such a product. New climbers that address many of the shortcomings of the existing brands should find receptive audiences. They offer independent action, articulating foot platforms, unusually quiet mechanisms, and excellent feedback and programming. The first research on the comparative mechanics of independent-step and dependent-step climbers should be published soon.

LADDER-CLIMBING SIMULATORS. A market that has been limited to one manufacturer for nearly a decade now sports three manufacturers, but the major player's 10-year lead in product development will be hard to overcome. Ladder climbers, which range in price from $800 to over $3,000, offer more rounded development of the body than do stair climbers. They bring the muscles of the arms and torso into the exercise, but due to the apportionment of workload between upper and lower body, they do *not* burn more calories as a nonexpert might think. The key buying tip? Look for safe foot-holds (foot pedals) and hand-holds (handles), an area where new ladder-climbing products fall short.

Since ladder climbing involves such a high percentage of the skeletal musculature, clients should begin training with short range of motion and slow climbing speeds. Furthermore, stress on the knees, which can be great if the knees are allowed to move forward over the toes during stepping, can be reduced if the client sits back in a semisquat position while climbing.

CROSS-COUNTRY-SKI SIMULATORS. Like stair climbers, cross-country simulators can be found in dependent- and independent-ski models. The latter, though more like true Nordic skiing, are more difficult to coordinate (requiring as they do a slight forward lean), and present a higher safety risk from falls. Skiers offer whole-body aerobic benefits without the trauma of other exercise modalities, because the knees move through a very limited range of flexion and extension and there is no impact at any point. Similar to stair climbers, a plethora of sub-$350 ski simulators is competing for the dollars of uneducated consumers. The major ski-machine manufacturers offer total domestic manufacture, 30-day unconditional trials, and two-year warranties. Clients are again best advised to invest money, rather than throw it away.

UPPER-BODY ERGOMETERS. Resembling bicycles for the arms, these devices were originally intended for the wheelchair-bound, but have found their way into upscale commercial fitness facilities. The three products of the two competitors in this market cost $2,300–$3,600, and differ mainly in the nature of the resistance system: one is mechanical and two are computerized. Clients with access to a recumbent bike may be able to kneel down in front of the chainwheel and work the pedals with their arms, simulating an upper-body ergometer.

FREE-WEIGHT APPARATUS. For the client who needs resistive exercise but has limited space and budget and no access to commercial facilities, the cost of an adjustable dumbbell set, which would include two handles (with revolving sleeves to save the hands), four quick-release collars, and a selection of one-inch-diameter plates (1.25, 2.5, 5, 7.5, and 10 lb), will be under $100. Add a stable, adjustable bench (that can range from flat to nearly upright), at a cost of $150 to $350, and a great deal of strength work can be accomplished. Beware the inexpensive home benches that offer too many things for too low a price. Smart trainers will locate the entry-level products of the top commercial-grade equipment manufacturers and advise clients to skip the feature-laden but poorly made benches available at discount sporting goods stores. A small number of home buyers will have the space, budget, and body size and strength needed for work with so-called "Olympic" free weights. The term *Olympic* refers to bars with one-inch-diameter center shafts but two-inch-diameter weight sleeves, which take, naturally, weight plates with two-inch-diameter holes. Bars come in five-, six-, and seven-foot lengths, and are straight, cambered, or angled for arm-curl work ("EZ-Curl"). Olympic benches are larger, heavier, and more expensive than benches designed for the smaller, one-inch bars and plates.

Keep an open mind about the comparative benefits of free weights and machines. Each has advantages and disadvantages, and neither has the support of unbiased research that it offers dramatically better or faster results than the other. If anything can be said with confidence, however, it is that free weights require greater instruction and supervision and are more likely to cause injuries. Conversely, machines, with their "captured" weight stacks, are both easier to learn and safer. Competitive athletes should train with a broad range of apparatus, including both free-weight and machine components, but the typical adult need not follow such a program.

A complete free-weight area in a commercial setting will have equipment from the following list (and more):

- Dumbbells 5–100 lbs.

- Seven-foot Olympic bars and plates.

- EZ-Curl and cambered bars.

- Olympic incline, flat, decline, and shoulder benches (to allow chest and shoulder work at a variety of angles).

- Squat and power racks for leg work with a seven-foot Olympic bar on the shoulders.

- Weight-stack machines such as the low-pulley and lat pull-down, popular with free-weight enthusiasts for the focus they place on the back and arms.

- Plate-loading machines, a cross between free-weight and weight- stack (selectorized) machines.

MULTIFUNCTION AND MULTISTATION STRENGTH APPARATUS. Inventor ingenuity has brought us numerous multifunction home strength units with countless features for unbelievably low prices. Using rubber bands, springs, hydraulics, or various resistance mechanisms, these devices invariably feel nothing like free-weight or weight-stack training and require more time to be spent on reconfiguring the machine between exercises than on actual training. For $1,100–$2,500, clients can buy a unit that has a single-weight stack and requires no cable changes between exercises. For the client with a family and a fat wallet, a multistation accommodating two to four people training simultaneously can be had for $2,500–$4,000. Counsel clients to invest in the name manufacturers that have withstood the test of time, whose products have far greater value than the more-recent-vintage competitors who claim to do better for less. Commercial multistations are made to accommodate up to 12 simultaneous users. Though they employ various mechanisms to alter resistance to match the changing force output of contracting muscle, only those devices using an actual cam-shaped pulley do so accurately. Devices using sliding fulcrums have the blanket effect, on all stations, of increasing resistance through the range of motion, which is not how most muscles actually work.

SINGLE-STATION STRENGTH APPARATUS. Larger commercial facilities and affluent home buyers will be able to afford single-station strength machines. Each of these stations, ranging in cost from about $1,300 for the simplest machine from smaller manufacturers to $4,700 for the large leg presses from the major manufacturers, accommodates only one user at a time. The advantages of single-station pieces lie in their higher training efficiency, since multistations must make compromises to fit their many exercises into less space at a lower price. Higher training efficiency is operationally effected by the "variable resistance" function of good single-stations (a cam-shaped pulley alters the effective resistance of the weight stack to match the strength curve of muscle), as well as the multiple size adjustments that allow different-sized users to fit comfortably and safely. Multistations generally have few or no adjustments for the body size of the user.

Differences among the major manufacturers exist in the following areas:

Resistance mechanism. Though weight stacks are by far the predominant choice, compressed air and hydraulics are employed quite successfully by two large and stable manufacturers. Both allow something that weight-stack machines cannot: safe, higher-speed training, quite useful for competitive athletes. Without weight stacks to gain inertia, and therefore move "on their own" once imparted a force, air and hydraulic machines are "inertia/momentum-free." After more than a decade on the market, these machines are extremely reliable and nearly maintenance-free. Computers have been employed by several manufacturers in recent years as a source of resistance. Two of the three major brands feature "networked" machines, where performance is sensed and analyzed by a central computer. One of those two brands employs voice-chip technology, by which performance-related spoken feedback is given to the user on each machine. Motivation is, not surprisingly, greatly enhanced with such computerization, and all three brands feature smooth and enjoyable movement.

Weight-stack drive mechanism. The vast majority of single-station machines employ a teflon- or plastic-enclosed stainless steel cable to pull the weight stack along a set of hardened steel guide rods. As just noted, such a system is nearly maintenance-free, and can be quickly shortened in length after stretch with use. Only one manufacturer still uses chain—and boasts of it in its advertising—but chain still requires cleaning and lubrication and is very difficult to shorten once stretched with normal use. High-tech belt drive systems have gotten better over their several years in existence, but still seem guilty of too-rapid stretching. They can be shortened as easily as cable, however.

Accurate variable resistance. All cams do not vary resistance equally (some reflect research into strength curves, some don't; at least one manufacturer tries to use a circular pulley with an offset axis), and trainers must, through hands-on experience, get acquainted with the success of the various manufacturers in effecting *accurate* variable resistance in their machines.

Concentric-eccentric vs. concentric-concentric contraction. All but three manufacturers offer concentric–eccentric-type resistance, where the same muscles raise the weight (the concentric phase) as lower it (the eccentric phase). Single-station hydraulic machines, and two of the computerized systems, offer concentric–concentric work, where the muscle(s) on one side of the joint raise the weight, and the antagonist muscles on the other side of the joint contract to lower it. While concentric–concentric exercise is clearly more time-efficient (half the number of machines are needed), many experts feel that eccentric exercise is an important part of the resistive exercise experience. Beware of overstated claims that downgrade concentric–eccentric exercise because of muscle soreness that is rare with concentric–concentric training; soreness usually disappears one or two weeks into a novice's program, and is rarely an issue again except for high-intensity strength athletes.

Fit and finish. There is a wide range of "fit and finish" on commercial single-station equipment, most obvious if one walks the floor of a large trade show. The top brands look and feel the part, with clean welds, ultrasmooth movement, and tightly stitched upholstery. Lesser-quality equipment is not hard to spot, frequently featuring folded corners on the upholstery, less carefully drawn welds, less than perfectly balanced weight-stack movement, and palpable friction.

Adjustability. Look for machines that can fit the widest range of users with simply performed adjustments. At least one manufacturer now offers width sizing, allowing pullover- and- tricep-extension machines to be sized in or out to fit a variety of users.

Support. Single stations—at least the better ones—need servicing quite infrequently, but many name manufacturers are surprisingly unable to provide parts and service in all but the major metropolitan areas. Make sure the equipment you counsel clients to buy can be serviced quickly and efficiently in your area.

ELASTIC-BAND/CORD RESISTANCE APPARATUS.   Athletes have been using surgical rubber tubing for over 20 years to load muscles during performance simulation. One entrepreneur added handles and an instruction booklet in the early 1980s and spawned an industry of knock-offs. Rubber tubing is portable, versatile, and inexpensive, but has one drawback—the danger of airborne, accidentally released handles. Travelers not fortunate enough to stay at hotels with fitness centers can maintain strength with as little as a $29 investment in rubber tubing.

WATER RESISTANCE APPARATUS.   To take advantage of the low-impact nature of exercising in water, several manufacturers have developed resistance devices to be worn on the wrists, ankles, and even torso to add loading during water exercise. Useful in either strength or aerobic training regimens, these devices range in price from under $10 for gloves to over $200 for the most elaborate creations. Trainers with a swimming background will already know that an old pair of swim fins makes an excellent conditioning tool.

STRETCHING APPARATUS.   It seems to many observers that the reason so few people devote the time they should to flexibility work is the lack of stretching apparatus. The first versatile and smartly designed stretching product, brought to market in early 1990, can be described as a vertical array of stretch cords on which users can place hands and feet in a variety of ways to stretch. At $1,295, the device will not make it to many homes, but early commercial interest has been great.

Maintenance Issues

To ensure user safety, machine longevity, and smoothness of operation, manufacturer maintenance suggestions should be carefully followed. Regarding buyer obligations to perform preventive maintenance procedures, there are currently no manufacturers who specify that failure to perform periodic maintenance will void their warranty. It may be the case, however, that egregious customer failure to maintain equipment could be used by a manufacturer as cause to refuse warranty service or product replacement. In any case, the trainer should counsel clients to maintain a log of all preventive maintenance and repair work, both to back up potential claims for warranty work and for liability reasons.

With high technology lubricants now available for specific uses, no single product fills the needs of all manufacturers. If product literature does not specify lubricants or lubrication points, contact the manufacturer's customer service or parts department for recommendations. Preventive maintenance involves periodic checks (a fixed interval should be chosen and adhered to, probably based on the usage to which the equipment is subjected) on the status of items such as:

- Tightness of all nuts and bolts.

- Integrity and lubrication needs at bearings and bushings.

- Dust/dirt accumulation around moving and electrical/electronic parts.

- Fraying of belts (in treadmills, the running belt and any internal drive belts; in bikes, the friction strap on flywheel bikes; on weight machines, the weight-stack drive belt).

- Stretching or fraying of cable in weight-stack machines. Frayed cables must be replaced immediately for safety and liability reasons. Stretched cable (play in the weight stack) can either be shortened or have the slack pulled out, depending on the machine.

- Integrity of all seat and handlebar posts and their height-locking mechanisms (bikes, strength machines) and rollers (rowing machines).

- Upholstery life. This can be extended through cleaning and treatment with certain commercially available products.

SELECTING APPAREL

High-Tech Clothing

Paralleling the explosive growth in the variety of exercise equipment is the expansion in exercise and competition apparel. Five years ago there was little more to be said than "wear light-colored cotton fabrics in the heat" and "dress in layers in the cold," but there are now high-tech fibers for almost all environmental conditions.

The most widely found fiber property is moisture transport/selectivity—several fibers let perspiration evaporate from the skin outward (water vapor will pass through the fiber; droplets of sweat will not), but do not allow rain droplets to migrate inward. The first such fabric came to market several years back—Gore-Tex™—and now there is a host of competitors— Darlington Fabrics' Superskin™; Du Pont's Microfine™, Cool-Max™, and Thermax™, and 3M's Thintech™. Surely, there will be more to follow. Most fabrics nowadays combine external water repellency with windproofing, and some combine warming properties as well for cold weather exercise or competition.

Swimsuits have been another focus of apparel technology. Suits can now be found that mold to the body when warmed by the skin, and that feature a water-repellent treatment to reduce drag. Triathletes wishing to reduce transition time are frequently using neoprene, a synthetic rubber that does multiple duty during diverse athletic endeavors. For the private training client not competing athletically, not exercising in environmentally extreme conditions, and with a limited budget, the old advice still works: In warm weather, dress in light-colored, 100 percent cotton, open, loose-fitting clothing, and avoid midday sun; in the cold, dress in layers and carry a pack to stash external layers as they are peeled. (Polypropylene, one of the early high-tech fibers, is a good and inexpensive cold-weather fiber. It "wicks" moisture away from the skin and stores it on its external surface—from which it can evaporate—preventing chilling of the skin. It is not waterproof, however.)

Protective Gear

While gloves, knee pads, and elbow pads will surely prevent scratches and dings, the two pieces of protective gear that a trainer should be most familiar with are cycling helmets and lifting belts.

CYCLING HELMETS. According to *Consumer Reports* (Bike Helmets, 1990), of the more than 1,000 bicycling deaths each year, three-fourths are caused by head injuries. Furthermore, one study concluded that wearing a bike helmet can reduce the risk of head injury by 85 percent. Unfortunately, fewer than 10 percent of U.S. cyclist wear helmets, by one estimate. In guiding clients shopping for a helmet, be aware that while there are no safety tests or certificates, there are two private standards-setting organizations: the American National Standards Institute (ANSI) and the Snell Memorial Foundation. *Consumer Reports* (Bike Helmets, 1990) believes the Snell standards to be more stringent and notes that helmets passing the Snell test bear an official green Snell sticker with a serial number. In fitting a cycling helmet, know that a properly fitting model:

- Touches the head at the crown, sides, front, and back.

- Is not movable front–back or side–side.

- Does not allow gaps between the head and pads when the helmet is pulled or tugged.

- Features straps that run (1) nearly vertically down under the chin, and (2) diagonally from the rear of the helmet, under the ear, to meet the other at the hinge of the jaw.

LIFTING BELTS. Not just for muscle-packed, serious weightlifters, lifting belts can dramatically increase intraabdominal pressure and help support the lumbar spine during many strength-training exercises. With a variety of styles and finishes now available, even the fashion-conscious can be protected. The lifting belt, and lifting gloves to protect the hands, should be part of every client's wardrobe.

SELECTING FOOTWEAR

The advice given to a client regarding proper selection of footwear may be the most important information offered by the personal trainer. Inappropriate use of ill-fitting or poorly designed footwear can lead to discomfort, potential injury, and inevitable discontinuation of participation in activity. The credibility of the personal trainer can be greatly enhanced by the information and advice shared with the client that ultimately leads to a satisfactory selection of functional, comfortable athletic footwear.

Purpose of a Shoe for Fitness Activities

The purpose of a shoe for fitness and athletic activities is three-fold:

- Protect the foot from impact and abrasion.

- Support the foot.

- Improve traction.

Do shoes protect the athlete from injury? The answer is a resounding yes! A study of 1,200 aerobic dance students and instructors found twice as many injuries in barefoot dancers compared to shoe-wearing dancers (*Physician and Sports Medicine*, February 1985). Similar studies have also shown the protective nature of shoes in a variety of running sports. In addition to dissipating the vertical impact forces of walking, running, and dance-related activities, the athletic shoe will provide an external support to prevent lateral ankle rollover and instability-related foot, ankle, and knee injuries. In medium-paced long-distance running, vertical impact forces approach three times the body weight of the athlete. In the lateral movements of side-to-side steps in low-impact aerobic dance exercise, lateral forces exerted on the feet and ankles can exceed two times the body weight. A 125-pound human being running at a pace of eight minutes per mile or performing a high-impact aerobic dance segment for 30 minutes will receive over 300 tons of impact on each foot during the 30-minutes of exercise. Obviously, the athletic shoe must provide a significant buffer for shock and impact dissipation between the foot and the ground.

For lower-impact or nonimpact activities such as weightlifting, cycling, and walking, the athletic shoe performs a significant function by supporting the foot to prevent ankle rollover and arch fatigue. In addition, traction of the foot against the sport surface or bicycle pedal is enhanced with the athletic shoe. The human foot has not been conditioned to withstand the shearing forces applied to the foot on weight machines, man-made surfaces, and exotic fitness machines. In short, the human foot must be protected from abrasion, impact and lateral strain. In addition, the athletic shoe can serve as an effective coupler between the human foot and the fitness machine to improve traction and enhance interaction of the subject with the machine.

Shoe Anatomy

Understanding the anatomical features of the athletic shoe will enable the personal trainer to differentiate certain design features and make specific recommendations based on individual needs. The basic anatomy of an athletic shoe is depicted in Figure 15-2. The individual components of the shoe, and the relative function of each, are as follows.

OUTSOLE.   The **outsole** is the outer layer of material that provides the traction component of the athletic shoe. The component materials of the sole as well as the tread design determine the overall traction characteristics and overall durability of the outsole. The two most commonly used compounds are carbon rubber (the black soling common on running shoes) and styrene-butadiene rubber, found on most court, basketball, and tennis shoes.

MIDSOLE.   The **midsole**, the heart of the cushioning system, contains a layer of shock-absorbing foam placed directly over the outsole and underneath the insole of the athletic shoe. The type and quality of midsole material used in athletic shoe construction significantly affects overall performance and durability of the shoe. The two most common midsole materials appropriate for fitness activities are:

> **Ethyl vinyl acetate (EVA).** This chemically blended foam material is used in lightweight midsoles and heel wedges. EVA is probably the most popular material for quality running shoes and aerobic dance shoes because of its lightness, flexibility, and impact resistance. The quality of EVA varies considerably among shoe models. In general, compression-molded EVA is more durable and shock-absorbent than traditional open-cell EVA.

> **Polyurethane (PU).** Polyurethane is a liquid polyester that forms an extremely durable closed-cell foam material used in midsoles and out-

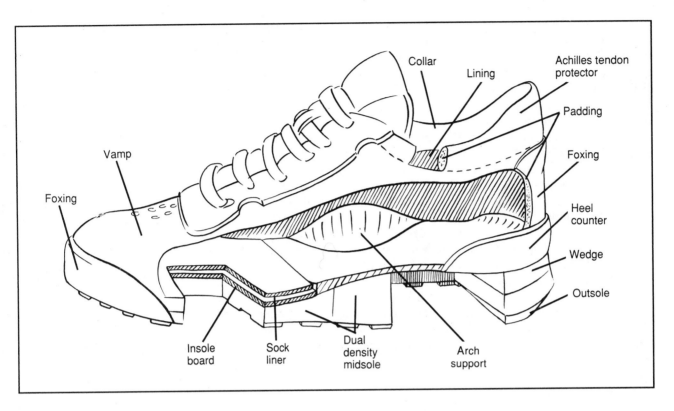

Figure 15–1 Anatomy of a running shoe.

soles. The advantage of PU over EVA is its durability and superior shock-absorbency. However, because polyurethane is generally slightly stiffer and significantly heavier than EVA, it is used less in athletic footwear.

Over the past 10 years, great advances have been made in midsole technology. Specifically, air bags have now been incorporated into midsoles; and visco elastic polymers and tubes of resilient Hytrel® have been embedded in traditional compression-molded EVA to resist compaction. All of these technical advances have improved shock-absorbency while resisting compression and breakdown of the midsole material. These advances have, in some way, justified the near doubling of the cost of the average pair of athletic shoes over the past five years.

THE UPPER. The material sewn into the midsole or outsole comprises the *upper*. The largest pieces of the upper are called the *quarters* (sides of the upper) and the *vamp* (top surface of the shoe upper). The most popular upper materials include leather, woven soft nylon (taffeta), and coarser-grade nylon knitted into a mesh configuration for strength and breathability.

HEEL COUNTER. The *heel counter* is a rigid or semirigid, moldable, external strengthening device in the heel area of the upper. Its purpose is to control and stabilize the wearer's heel inside the shoe and minimize excessive supination or pronation of the foot. Thus, the heel counter is a vital support feature. In general, more expensive athletic shoes have reinforced heel counters with extra "stabilizer bars" made of plastic or polyurethane wrapped outside the heel counter and firmly attached to the midsole of the shoe.

FOXING AND TOE BOX. *Foxing* is extra material, usually suede or rubber, that gives medial and lateral support to the outside of the shoe. In running shoes, the important foxing is at the toe of the upper, forming the *toe box*. In court shoes, the foxing usually includes rubber wrapped around the sole for lateral support. In the popular cross-trainer shoe, foxing can be quite rigid, with stabilizer bars or struts composed of rubber or polyurethane in the forefoot area.

LACING SYSTEM.   Eyestay patterns are often varied, allowing two sets of eyelets that provide a variable-width lacing system. Such a system allows for the adjustment of lacing for wider or narrower feet. The wider- or lower-spaced eyelets allow for greater width variation and are better suited to the wider foot.

INSOLE (SOCK LINER).   Next to the midsole is the second most important feature of the athletic shoe in terms of shock absorption and foot support: the **insole**, or sock liner. The quality and design of insoles vary significantly among manufacturers. Unfortunately, the insole is not often seen or inspected by the consumer before purchase. The insole provides a contoured foot bed and should provide proper arch support. In addition, the foam or polyurethane content of the insole provides a significant amount of shock absorption.

Types of Shoes Worn in Fitness Activities

Wearing an ordinary "sneaker" in fitness-related activities is now obsolete. Shoe technology and biomechanical knowledge have mandated that specific shoes be used for specific sport and fitness activities. The kinetics of running are much different from those of aerobic dance, and the appropriate design of footwear for each activity is unique. For some activities, e.g., running and walking, the biomechanical demands on the feet are fairly similar, so the use of a single shoe for both activities is sometimes appropriate. The average consumer is hesitant to buy a special pair of shoes for each unique fitness or recreational sporting activity. This has led to the so-called "cross-trainer" shoe, theoretically to provide a single shoe suitable for a variety of sporting and fitness activities.

The personal trainer will frequently be asked whether a cross-trainer shoe can be used for any or all fitness activities. The answer varies with specific body type, foot type, and individual activity. As stated earlier, a single shoe suitable for weightlifting, court sports, walking, running, and dance exercise is virtually nonexistent. While a single shoe could be used for all of these activities, there is available a better-designed shoe specific to each activity. The question is whether the benefits of a sport-specific shoe outweigh the expense and possible inconvenience of changing shoes for a particular activity. In general, look at the specific sport or activity and the shoe design peculiar to that sport to determine if crossover between shoes and sports is appropriate. The following discussion of particular sports and their appropriate footwear will help the personal trainer to make decisions based on individual client needs.

RUNNING SHOES.   Today's running shoes demonstrate the highest technical level of athletic shoe design. Most of the recent advances have been in midsole development. Air, gel, and energy-return midsoles are all designed to further dissipate impact shock and provide a more durable shoe with lowered tendency toward compression and midsole breakdown.

Running shoes are suited to running and running only. The elevated heel height of the midsole makes these shoes unsuitable for lateral-movement sports, where instability and ankle rollover can occur. In addition, the traditional carbon-rubber outsoles make these shoes unsuitable for use on specialized floor surfaces in dance-exercise studios. The ample cushioning provided in the shoe is inappropriate for exercise walking and power walking. However, running shoes sometimes can be used for power walking, although they are probably overengineered because their extreme cushioning and stability features are unnecessary for walking. A less expensive running shoe, without the extra cushioning, would probably be just as suitable for power walking.

FITNESS WALKING. The mechanics of walking are quite different from those of running. The vertical impact is only slightly greater, roughly equivalent to 1.2 times body weight, compared to 3 times body weight in running. In addition, there is a purposeful heel-strike followed by forefoot touch-down in exercise walking compared to running, which has the initial force delivered closer to the midfoot. Running shoes tend to elevate the heel too high off the ground, necessitating a greater amount of ankle-joint plantar flexion to allow the forefoot to reach the ground. This can produce unnecessary "foot slap" when a fitness walker wears a pair of traditional running shoes. The ideal walking shoe therefore has minimal cushioning and a low heel profile. At the same time, a strong heel counter is necessary to stabilize the heel during the contact phase of walking. Leather uppers are preferable, with variable-width lacing and foxing reinforcement to the upper to provide additional stability. Strongly recommended are walking shoes that contain polyurethane or compression-molded EVA midsoles, because they are more durable and firmer. Softer midsoles are liable to break down early in fitness walking.

DANCE-EXERCISE. The true aerobic-dance shoe represents a marriage between the running shoe and the court shoe. Since vertical impact forces approach three times body weight in dance-exercise, which is equivalent to those experienced in running, the midsole cushioning properties of an aerobic dance shoe should be similar to those found in a running shoe. In addition, the lateral support features should be similar to those of a well-built tennis shoe or court shoe. With the advent of low-impact aerobics has come a decreasing emphasis on cushioning and greater emphasis on lateral reinforcement in the shoe upper. For this reason, most state-of-the-art aerobics shoes resemble court shoes more than running shoes. The key features to aerobics shoes are flexibility and lateral support. Flexibility in the forefoot of the shoe is of critical importance, to allow freedom of flexion during lateral and jumping movements. A stiff shoe is a known primary contributing factor to plantar fasciitis, which is the single most common foot injury to affect dance exercisers.

SHOES FOR WEIGHTLIFTING AND FOR FITNESS MACHINES. Cross-trainer shoes have become popular, particular among men, for use in weightlifting. They are actually a hybrid of an extremely supportive court shoe and a well-cushioned aerobic-dance shoe. For weightlifting and fitness machines, lateral support of the foot is of paramount importance. The traction quality of the outsole also may be of importance on certain machines. Stair machines require flexibility in the forefoot, and most cross-trainer and court shoes lack significant flexibility in this part of the shoe. Court shoes and aerobic-dance shoes are more than adequate for most weight-training and fitness-machine endeavors. The fit and support of the shoe upper is probably the key feature the consumer should look for in purchasing shoes for these activities. Cushioning should be minimized, since softer midsoles are known to collapse easily under the increased pressures placed on the shoe while lifting weights and pushing machines.

HIGH-TOP VS. LOW-TOP SHOES. Mid-cut or three-quarter-high aerobic-dance and cross-trainer shoes dominate the market today. They offer the potential for increased stability, lowered tendency for heel slippage, and better accommodation of prescription orthotic devices. However, the consumer should not be misled into thinking that mid-cut or high-top shoes offer substantial ankle support. The uppers of these shoes are never strong enough to prevent ankle rollover in the adult of average size. The main advantage of these mid-cut and high-top shoes is the proprioceptive input given to the athlete during lateral movement. The shoe upper provides sensory feedback about the position of the foot and ankle at touchdown, which enables the athlete to correct abnormal alignment quickly, before rollover can occur. Therefore, indirectly, the chance for ankle injuries is minimized.

One caution about mid-cut and high-top shoes: In activities such as dance exercise or possibly on stair-climbers and rowing machines, the posterior (back) portion of the shoe upper can rub the Achilles tendon and cause localized irritation. When buying mid-cut or high-top shoes, look for extra padding.

SOCKS. Socks play an important role in dissipating friction and shearing forces that develop between the foot and the shoe. In addition, properly constructed socks can dissipate significant vertical forces in the foot and serve effectively to transport perspiration from the foot surface to the shoe upper. In this regard, it has been proved that socks composed of 100 percent acrylic fibers (e.g., Orlon and polypropylene) are significantly more effective for athletic use than socks composed of cotton fibers. Contrary to popular belief, cotton lacks the ability to wick moisture off the foot surface and actually loses its shape when it becomes wet. In addition, acrylic-fiber socks tend to remain softer after repeated use compared to socks composed of cotton fibers.

Guidelines for Buying Shoes

When clients consider purchasing shoes for a specific sporting or fitness activity, they must consider their own body type, foot type, and activity level. People with high-arched feet tend to require greater shock absorption than those with average feet. High-arched ("cavus") feet also suffer from lateral instability and are more prone to ankle sprains. Conversely, people with low-arched ("flat") feet require shoes with less cushioning but greater support and heel control.

Most people, however, have no clear-cut foot type that dictates the exact characteristics required for an athletic shoe. Of particular concern is the height and body weight of the participant. Heavier participants in impact-related activities, such as jogging and aerobics, require shoes with firmer midsoles. This is because the heavier person will sink through, or "bottom-out," a shoe with a softer midsole. As heavier persons collapse through a soft midsole, they will hit the bottom of the shoe and receive an inappropriate shock wave into the foot, because no further cushioning is available. Firmer midsoles actually resist bottoming-out and continue to cushion throughout the entire impact phase of running or dancing. Lighter-weight clients can have the luxury of softer midsoles if they so desire. However, the main drawback to soft, highly cushioned midsoles is the potential for instability of the foot. A softer midsole allows greater foot penetration with potential for foot and ankle rollover.

After considering the type of shoe needed for a particular activity and evaluating the individual needs of the person based on foot and body type, the trainer will find the following information of value in the actual fitting of the athletic shoe.

1. Choose an athletic-shoe store or specialty store with trained personnel and a reputation for providing quality fitting and for stocking a large inventory to make a variety of sizes available.

2. Try to get fitted for footwear at the end of the day, when foot size is at its maximum. It is not unusual for an individual to increase up to one-half a shoe size during the course of a single day of standing or walking because of swelling and soft tissue expansion.

3. Wear socks exactly like those worn during the particular sporting activity for which the shoe will be worn. Socks and shoes must be fit together, particularly with the popularity of padded athletic hosiery.

4. Since most people do not have identically matched feet in terms of shoe size, have both feet measured in width (girth) and length.

5. If the shoe does not feel right in the store, don't buy it. If it fits, it fits the first time. Athletic shoes should not be expected to stretch or accommodate to abnormal foot shape.

6. Plan to take at least a half hour to fit your shoes and wear them around the store. You should have an opportunity to simulate the kinetic movements of a particular activity to determine if the shoe will perform properly.

7. Try to compare one brand of shoe to another by placing one model on the right foot and a different model on the left foot. This allows an instantaneous comparison of flexibility and cushioning characteristics as you simulate running or hopping movements in the store.

8. Test the flexibility of the shoes by rolling up on the toes. If the heel slips out of the back of the shoe, the shoe itself is too stiff in the forefoot.

9. Test forefoot cushioning by jumping up and down on the toes. Test rearfoot cushioning by running on the heels.

10. Test lateral stability by standing up on one foot and twisting the foot side to side while balancing on the foot. If the foot slips laterally in the shoe, the upper is unable to control the foot adequately.

11. If the shoe has variable-width lacing, experiment with the narrow and wide eyelets to achieve a better custom fit.

12. Whether a shoe feels superior in terms of flexibility or cushion, the fit characteristics supersede all others in terms of ultimate selection of the proper shoe. If the shoe does not fit properly, it will never perform properly and will cause discomfort and potential injury.

SUMMARY

Helping clients purchase fitness equipment or exercise apparel requires a serious time commitment and a hands-on approach. Trainers should make every effort to try new pieces of equipment as they come on the market. The use of an objective checklist will help the trainer effectively evaluate each product. Although participation in an exercise program doesn't require fancy and expensive apparel, the trainer should be well versed in the use of safety equipment and other types of equipment that might make the exercise experience more enjoyable for the client. Smart buying means greater enjoyability and better adherence.

The importance of proper selection of footwear for sporting and fitness endeavors for both the personal trainer and the client is often overlooked. Remember, the client often looks to the trainer as a role model for shoe selection. Choosing well-designed, properly fitted footwear can assure continued participation and reduce the risk of injury.

REFERENCES

Allen, D., & Goldberg, L., 1986, May. *Physiological comparison of two cross-country skiing machines.* Paper presented at the annual meeting of the American College of Sports Medicine, Indianapolis.

Bike helmets: Unused lifesavers. 1990, May. *Consumer Reports, 55(5),* 348–353.

SUGGESTED READING

American College of Sports Medicine. (1991). *Guidelines for exercise testing and prescription 4th ed.* Philadelphia: Lea & Febiger.

American College of Sports Medicine. (1990). *Position paper on strength training for asymptomatic adults.* Philadelphia. Lea & Febiger.

Cheskin, M. (1987). *The complete handbook of athletic footwear.* New York: Fairchild Publications.

Flect, S. J. & Kraemer, W. J. (1987). *Designing resistance programs.* Champaign, IL: Human Kinetics.

Nigg, B. M. (1986). *Biomechanics of running shoes.* Champaign, IL: Human Kinetics.

Pearl, B., & Moran, B. T. (1986). *Getting stronger.* Bolinas, CA: Shelter Publications.

Segesser, B., & Pofrringer, W. (1989). *The shoe in sport.* Chicago: Yearbook Medical Publishers.

Westcott, W. L. (1983). *Strength fitness.* Newton, MA: Allyn & Bacon.

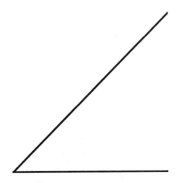

Injury Prevention and First Aid

PART VI

No matter how well designed exercise programs are, the trainer will at some point encounter client injuries. Although the focus should be on proper exercise technique and injury prevention, accidents do happen. The trainer must be ready to respond to minor injuries and major emergencies. The following two chapters focus on recognition of common exercise-related injuries, proper injury management, and how to respond to emergency situations. Client safety is always the trainer's first priority. Careful attention should be given to the material in this section, and the American Council on Exercise encourages all trainers to seek additional education in these areas.

Musculoskeletal Injuries

ALAN H. HALLING

ALAN HALLING, M.S., P.T., A.T.C., is a registered physical therapist and a certified athletic trainer. Currently, he is assistant director of OASIS Physical Therapy and assistant trainer for the San Diego Chargers Football Club. He has worked as physical therapy consultant for the Phoenix Suns and as athletic trainer at the U.S. Olympic Training Centers and the Hula Bowl Football Classic. Halling has developed sports medicine curriculums for high school athletes, and developed and taught a course in joint mobilization for athletic trainers. He is a published author and speaks at various sports medicine seminars.

16

IN THIS CHAPTER:

- The injury cycle.
- Guidelines for recognizing injury, including inflammation.
- Guidelines for the prevention and treatment of injury, including immediate and follow-up care.
- The causes, symptoms, and treatment of the most common injuries and disorders: shin splints, ankle sprains, low-back pain, blisters.
- The causes, symptoms, and treatment of injuries and disorders of the upper extremity: epicondylitis, impingement syndrome, biceps tendon rupture, shoulder dislocation and subluxation, and muscular strains.
- The causes, symptoms, and treatment of injuries and disorders of the lower extremity: plantar fasciitis, Achilles tendinitis/rupture, stress fractures, iliotibial band syndrome, patellofemoral pain syndrome, patellar tendinitis, muscular strains, knee meniscal tears, and tears of the anterior cruciate ligament.

All forms of exercise continue to grow in popularity, and this growth has produced a concomitant increase in the number of injuries. To maximize the benefits of a client's fitness program, the personal trainer must minimize the risk of injury. This is accomplished by recommending exercise appropriate to the client's fitness level, instructing in proper methods and modes of exercise, monitoring and correcting performance, recognizing symptoms of overtraining, and properly applying biomechanical principles. The personal trainer must know his/her limitations in dealing with injuries. If a client is injured, or if the trainer learns of a chronic injury, the client should be referred to a physician.

Figure 16–1 Injury cycle.

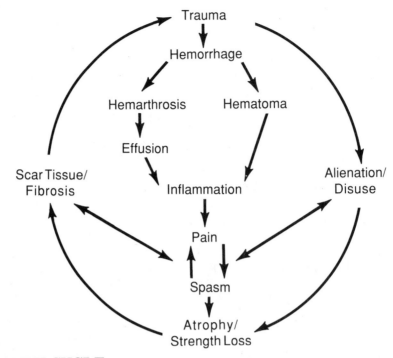

INJURY CYCLE

Most athletic injuries follow the same course, from a traumatic incident to completely healed tissue. Figure 16–1 depicts this cyclical course. A traumatic irritant (direct blow, falling, twisting, overuse) produces *hemorrhage* (bleeding) in the affected part. If the trauma and resulting hemorrhage occur in a joint, the condition is called **hemarthrosis**. If the trauma is to soft tissues (muscle or tendon) and blood pools in these tissues, the condition is referred to as a **hematoma**. In either of these conditions, blood lost from the blood vessels acts as a foreign body and creates an inflammatory reaction. The combination of hemorrhage and inflammation leads to pain and spasm. These two phenomena are related: Pain leads to the onset of protective muscle spasm, and spasm in turn results in increased pain. This vicious cycle of pain and spasm and the possibility of medically prescribed immobilization confront the client with a period of rest, which leads to **atrophy** and strength loss in the affected part. The healing process that follows is commonly characterized by the formation of fibrotic scar tissue. Healing by fibrosis predisposes the damaged area to further injury because of the relative inelasticity of scar tissue as compared with normal tissue.

GUIDELINES FOR RECOGNIZING INJURY

The diagnosis of injuries and illnesses is a science, limited to those adequately trained in the medical profession. However, the personal trainer should be able to recognize certain injuries common in their speciality. A knowledge of injuries not only will prompt proper first aid measures but also will lead to safer and more beneficial training programs.

Initial injury recognition is of utmost importance. The personal trainer should be able immediately to recognize certain symptoms of specific injuries. **Symptoms** are those subjective reactions the client relates to the trainer, such as pain, swelling, stiffness, and numbness. **Signs** of injury are the objective findings from an examination of the client; these fall out of the province of the personal trainer.

Recognizing Inflammation

A tissue's response to injury, no matter what the cause or type, is inflammation. Because of inflammation's obstinate presence, it is extremely important for the trainer to be knowledgeable about its symptoms:

- *Increased temperature* at the injury site, due to dilation of blood vessels and increased blood flow.

- *Redness*, due to increased blood flow.

- *Swelling*, due to movement of a fluid into a restricted area, possibly a hemarthrosis or hematoma.

- *Pain*, caused by swelling that has put pressure on the free nerve endings. (Pain is a protective mechanism of the body and should *not* be ignored.)

- *Loss of function*, which results from the first four symptoms. The client will be less likely to use the part because of the pain.

Steps in Recognizing Injury

Injury recognition is made much easier if the trainer follows a stepped format of some type.

1. *History.* Obtain the history of the injury by questioning the client. Find out what area has been injured and if there is any complaint of pain, tingling, numbness, or stiffness. The pain may be sharp or dull, deep or superficial. Ask the client how it happened. The mechanism of the injury is sometimes the most important information obtained. Find out if the client felt or heard a click or a pop. Ascertain whether this is a first injury of this type or if some preexisting condition led to the current injury. Ask about any changes in training regimen or shoes.

2. *Inspection.* Examine the injured client and the involved body part. Note any variation from the normal position, size, shape, and color, and observe the client's facial expression and the way he/she holds the injured part.

It is critical for personal trainers to stay within their realm of expertise, which includes administering proper first aid and, when necessary, referring clients for further medical care.

PREVENTION AND TREATMENT GUIDELINES

According to O'Donoghue (1976), the prevention of injuries (safety) should be the major goal for anyone designing physical-conditioning programs. There may be differences of opinion concerning the benefits of a fitness program, but most would agree that the only harmful effect is physical injury. If even a small percentage of the time spent devising ways to relieve the effects of injury were devoted to preventing injury, a major portion of the injury problems would be solved. Personal trainers dealing with a daily client load should heed this advice: The best treatment is prevention. Knowing the client before setting up a fitness program will help tremendously. Screening for preexisting conditions, proper warm-up and cool-down techniques, and flexibility and strength programs go a long way toward preventing injury. A knowledge of the extrinsic and intrinsic causes of injury (discussed later) is useful.

No matter how hard we try to prevent injury, some situations are unavoidable. Once a trauma has occurred, the injury cycle is set in motion. The overall goal in any treatment is to get clients back to activity as quickly and safely as possible. To achieve this goal, the components of the injury cycle should be minimized. Inflammation is at the heart of the healing process. As an inevitable part of the injury cycle, inflammation can become self-perpetuating, leading to a chronic condition. Minimizing the inflammatory process will decrease pain and spasm, disuse, atrophy, and strength loss. Ultimately the injury will heal with minimal and mobile scar tissue, thus decreasing the chance of recurrent injury.

Immediate Care: RICE

Immediate management of athletic injuries is most important. Care administered within the first 72 hours is critical to the outcome. Many injuries will respond better and faster if early and appropriate first-aid measures are carried out. These measures can be abbreviated by the acronym *RICE*, which stands for rest, ice, compression, and elevation.

REST.   Rest is necessary to allow the damaged tissue to heal without further injury. In practice, the best form of rest is often a period of "relative" rest. While avoiding activities that stress the injured area, clients can continue other aspects of their training. For example, a weightlifter with shoulder tendinitis should be able to continue training the uninvolved extremities and torso.

ICE.   Ice may be applied in a variety of forms, from commercially made ice packs to ice cubes. A moist ice pack made by wrapping crushed ice in a towel is common. This type of pack should be applied for approximately 20 minutes, four to eight times per day for at least the first three days immediately following injury. The use of ice reduces inflammation, retards swelling, and promotes healing. Prolonged swelling can lead to chronic joint stiffness and secondary joint damage.

COMPRESSION.   Compression, usually with an elastic wrap, aids in reducing swelling by increasing the fluid pressure, forcing the fluid back into the drainage systems of the body. Compression is often used when applying ice.

ELEVATION.   Elevation allows gravity to assist in the movement of fluid toward and into the drainage systems. With the ice pack wrapped in place, the injured area is elevated above the level of the heart.

Follow-up Care

After appropriate first aid has been initiated, some type of follow-up may be necessary. The client may need to be seen at an emergency room or by an orthopedic physician. Once the initial stages of injury have abated, the involved part must be rehabilitated. With proper instructions from someone appropriate in the medical field, the personal trainer may become involved in this rehabilitative process. The injured part must regain any lost range of motion, strength, and balance.

Quite often the most advantageous treatment is ridding the client of the injury cause, whether *intrinsic* or *extrinsic* in nature (see Table 16–1). For example, a runner may have shin splints caused by excessive *pronation* at the foot (see Fig. 16-2). Usually the most successful treatment is to correct this intrinsic biomechanical fault with an *orthotic*, which is a custom-made

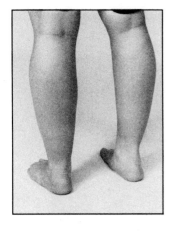

Figure 16–2   Excessive foot pronation.

Table 16–1   INTRINSIC AND EXTRINSIC CAUSES OF INJURY

EXTRINSIC	INTRINSIC
Training errors	Alignment abnormalities
Time	Femoral neck anteversion
Distance	Pronation
Repetitions	Supination
Intensity	Tibial torsion
Hills	Leg length discrepancy
Surfaces	Muscle imbalance
Hard	Muscle weakness
Soft	Flexibility
Canted	
Shoes and equipment	

appliance that fits into the shoe. On the other hand, extrinsic factors such as shoe selection, excessive mileage, and uneven terrain need to be addressed. The personal trainer should know how to handle the extrinsic factors and should have knowledge enough to recognize possible intrinsic factors, apply first aid when necessary, and make appropriate referrals. The personal trainer must stay within the scope of the job in treating injuries and must not assume responsibility for diagnosis or treatment.

MOST COMMON INJURIES/DISORDERS

The most common injuries or disorders a personal trainer will encounter are shin splints, ankle sprains, low-back pain, and blisters. The following are general guidelines for recognizing and treating these injuries.

Shin Splints

The term *shin splints* has been used to mean any pain located in the lower leg, and more specifically a painful syndrome on the inside aspect of the lower leg (see Fig. 16–3). It is an **overuse injury** resulting in an inflammatory reaction at the site of the attachment of deep muscles to the tibia.

CAUSE.   Shin splints are caused by repeated pounding from such activities as running and aerobics combined with extrinsic and intrinsic factors. Biomechanical faults of the foot, such as abnormal pronation, can predispose a client to shin splints.

SYMPTOMS.   The pain present with shin splints is usually along the lower two-thirds of the inner aspect of the tibia, in some instances running the whole length of the tibia as far down as the inside of the ankle. As with most inflammatory conditions, the pain in mild cases occurs only after activity, but it becomes more constant as severity increases. The site will often show some swelling, looking more like puffiness.

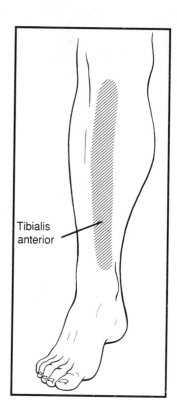

Tibialis anterior

Figure 16–3   Shin splints. The darkened area marks the most common region of pain.

Figure 16–4 Lateral ankle sprain.

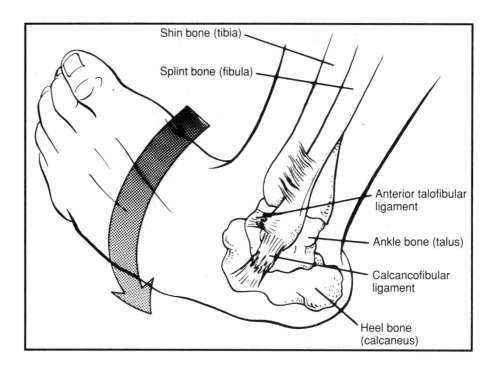

Shin bone (tibia)
Splint bone (fibula)
Anterior talofibular ligament
Ankle bone (talus)
Calcancofibular ligament
Heel bone (calcaneus)

TREATMENT. RICE and ice massage are beneficial. The client must strengthen and stretch the leg muscles to totally rehabilitate the part. Some clients who develop this condition may report a history of many recurrences. In these cases, the cause is most likely more involved, and usually all simple remedies have failed. Recognizing this situation and making the appropriate medical referral will save the client additional aggravation.

Ankle Sprains

The most common **sprains** of the ankle are to the outside (**lateral**) ligaments (see Fig. 16-4). Sprains do occur to the inside (**medial**) ligaments of the ankle, but with much less frequency.

CAUSE. Ankle sprains occur when the ankle is turned inward (**inversion**) with the foot pointed downward (**plantarflexion**). These injuries are common in all weight-bearing athletic activities. The personal trainer might see them often in activities in which clients jump, run, or cut.

SYMPTOMS. Swelling and disability set in rapidly. Within a day or two, discoloration appears around the ankle, and any motion is difficult. Pain is usually present over the outside and front of the ankle, and walking is very difficult.

TREATMENT. It is critical in these situations to use the RICE procedures. Many days can be eliminated from recovery time if proper first aid is applied. Encourage clients who cannot walk without pain and a limp to use crutches. It is always a good idea to refer the client to a physician. An X ray is the only way to distinguish between a sprained **ligament** and a fractured bone. As ankle sprains resolve, it is important that the client regain motion, strength, and balance. A client returning to activity should use caution in exercises that could possibly reproduce the injury mechanism of plantarflexion and inversion.

Swimming and cycling are great alternatives to weight-bearing activities. Have clients discontinue any activity that provokes pain.

Low-Back Pain

Injuries to the spine are complex, even for those trained to deal with them. There are so many kinds of low-back injuries that this chapter cannot expound on each of them. However, a knowledge of some key factors to watch for can be helpful. (See Fig. 2–7 for some of the low-back anatomy important for the personal trainer to understand in any discussion of the back.) Most clients will present back problems that are simply strains or sprains. However, the problem could be more serious, such as a ruptured disc. The personal trainer should never try to diagnose back injuries, but instead should recognize the problem and refer the client to a physician.

CAUSES.   Back injuries have many causes. It is most important for personal trainers to understand those causes common to their profession. Back injuries can stem from or be aggravated by improper weightlifting techniques. Lifting any weight from the floor by using the back and not the legs puts tremendous forces across all structures in the low back, especially the discs. Any lifting that forces the back into end-range **flexion** or **extension** is contraindicated.

SYMPTOMS.   Any complaint of tingling or numbness in the legs signals a major back problem, and all client activity should cease. Even though such symptoms may not always mean a severe injury, such as a ruptured disc, the trainer must still advise caution. Strains and sprains very rarely refer pain or tingling into the legs.

TREATMENT.   Any time a client complains of back pain, all activity should cease and medical care should be advised. Ice can be helpful to quiet the pain and spasm. Rest is usually the treatment of choice. As always, however, the best treatment is prevention. The client should use the stabilization belts provided on many machines to prevent extremes of motion. If weightlifting stations are without stabilization belts, it would be wise to add them. If done improperly, and without stabilization, bench pressing, military pressing, lat-pull-over machines, and squatting can force the back into extreme extension. If a client presents a history of disc problems, it would be best to keep that client away from forced flexion exercises, such as abdominal crunches, and abdominal machines. Usually, but not always, if a disc is involved the client will be better off doing activities that take the spine into controlled extension. Flexion activities tend to make the disc protrude even further, putting additional pressure on the nerve roots. The safest approach is to have clients perform exercises with the pelvis in a neutral position, avoiding excessive flexion and extension.

Blisters

CAUSE.   Blisters are the result of friction between the two top layers of skin. They most commonly occur in the feet, especially when one is breaking in new footwear, but they also occur on the hands in activities requiring gripping. A client will often develop blisters when beginning a new activity.

SYMPTOMS.   It is usually obvious when a blister is beginning to form. The client will notice a hot spot in the area of increased friction.

TREATMENT. Again, prevention is the best treatment. Breaking shoes in beforehand is a smart practice. Wearing two pairs of socks will cause the socks to rub together, thus decreasing the skin friction. Lubricants such as petroleum jelly can reduce friction. If a blister does develop, the best advice is to keep the area clean. Do not remove the skin from the blister, because the skin will protect the injury from infection until a new layer of skin matures. After cleansing the blister, it is best to apply an antibacterial ointment and keep it covered.

UPPER-EXTREMITY INJURIES/DISORDERS

Upper-extremity injuries a trainer will most likely encounter include epicondylitis, impingement syndrome, biceps tendon rupture, shoulder dislocation and subluxation, and muscular strains.

Epicondylitis

Epicondylitis can be classified as an overuse syndrome of the elbow. It is an inflammatory condition that can involve either the medial or lateral epicondyle, which are the prominent bony protrusions on the inside and outside of the elbow, respectively. These conditions are also commonly referred to as *Little League elbow, golfer's elbow,* or *tennis elbow.*

CAUSE. Epicondylitis results from overuse of the forearm muscles. If these muscle groups are not strong enough to handle loads put across them, they will break down and become inflamed. Any activity that uses these muscle groups can be the cause. Improper technique or faulty equipment also can lead to epicondylitis. If, for example, an upper-extremity weightlifting program is set up inappropriately, allowing the client to use too much weight too frequently, an extrinsically caused injury will ensue. Remember to screen clients for any such condition. Continued trauma to an already existing condition will exacerbate the injury.

SYMPTOMS. The client's most common complaint will be pain and tenderness directly over the involved epicondyle with any activity involving use of the wrist and forearm. Swelling can be present; most often it is absent. The client may also complain of weakness of the forearm muscles.

TREATMENT. The best treatment is prevention, using common sense in recommending training techniques. If caught soon enough after the initial onset, the condition can be treated more effectively and rapidly. Initial treatment should always be application of ice and rest from the causative factors. Crushed ice in bags or towels works best and should be applied for 20 minutes, four to eight times per day. Ice massage is also an effective way to apply cold. Paper cups of solid ice can be applied directly to the site, in a circular massaging fashion for six to eight minutes, four to eight times a day. As the condition begins to abate, the strength and flexibility of the forearm musculature must be restored. During this rehabilitation phase, the client should avoid reproducing overuse patterns that might result in reinjury.

Impingement Syndrome

Impingement syndrome, an impingement (or pinching) injury of the shoulder tissues, occurs underneath the coracoacromial arch, which is made up in part by

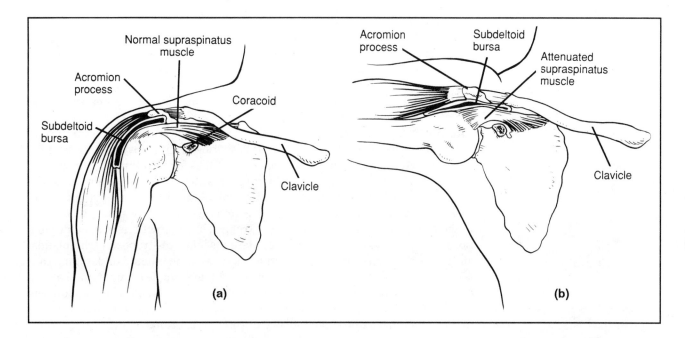

the acromion and coracoid processes (Fig. 16–5) linked by the coracoacromial ligament. The anatomy of this arch is such that the long head of the biceps, the **rotator cuff**, and the subdeltoid/subacromial bursa can all become impinged underneath it. The rotator cuff muscles usually involved in this syndrome are the supraspinatus and infraspinatus. As these tissues are impinged upon, they become inflamed. Biceps tendinitis, rotator cuff tendinitis, and subdeltoid bursitis are often the result of this impingement mechanism. **Tendinitis** and **bursitis** are inflammatory conditions of **tendons** and **bursae**, respectively. If impingement continues and becomes chronic, a tear in the long head of the biceps or in the supraspinatus and/or infraspinatus of the rotator cuff can occur.

CAUSE. The impingement mechanism can occur any time the arm is brought directly overhead. Normally as the arm is raised, the biceps tendon, rotator cuff, and bursa all must ride smoothly underneath the arch. If they don't, they become impinged to some degree. Clients who already have decreased space under the arch are more predisposed to this injury than are others. If the tissues become inflamed from impingement, they swell and decrease the space even further. The usual causes of this syndrome in sports are overhead activities such as tennis, swimming, and weightlifting. Impingement syndrome is also an overuse syndrome, meaning that it usually results from a redundant overhead activity.

SYMPTOMS. The pain from tendinitis at the shoulder is often sharp with various movements, especially those that are overhead. As the condition becomes more **chronic**, the client often feels a constant dull ache. The pain can be localized over the affected tendon, but this is not always the case. Many times the pain is more diffuse, extending into the lateral upper arm and in some cases to the elbow or below. The onset of pain is usually gradual with no recognized trauma. With active overhead movements, there is often pain in the middle and end points of the motion.

Bursitis at the shoulder presents differently from tendinitis. The site of pain is usually in the lateral upper arm. The pain is intense, constant, dull,

Figure 16–5 Impingement of bursa and supraspinatus under the coracoacromial arch with abduction movement: (a) with arm adducted; (b) with arm abducted.

and throbbing. The arm does not feel comfortable in any position, and an attempt at active movement usually shows severe restriction. As mentioned previously, tears in the rotator cuff usually occur in the supraspinatus and/or infraspinatus muscles. Although there can be tears of attrition from constant impingement, they also can result from a traumatic blow or fall. The client will usually complain of weakness, especially in any attempted overhead motions.

TREATMENT. The primary treatment goal should be to stop the irritating cause. This means strict avoidance of activities, such as overhead activities, that may cause impingement. The use of ice packs for 20 minutes, four to eight times per day, will help decrease the inflammation. In cases of tendinitis, the long- range goal after the acute inflammation abates is to restrengthen the involved musculotendinous structure. If it remains weak, any attempt at return to activity will only result in reinjury. Strength in all directions of shoulder motion needs to be restored, and the scapular musculature—trapezius, rhomboids, and levator scapulae—must not be ignored. The trainer should understand that shoulder tendinitis, bursitis, and rotator cuff tears can be brought on in a variety of different fashions, not only as a result of impingement. These conditions may very well be preexisting in some clients, so it is important to be attuned to the symptoms and to take the appropriate precautions.

Biceps Tendon Rupture

The biceps muscle has two different tendons near the shoulder joint, a long head and a short head. The long head, which has its attachment within the shoulder joint, is the tendon that is most commonly ruptured (Fig. 16–6).

Figure 16–6 Rupture of the long head of the biceps brachii.

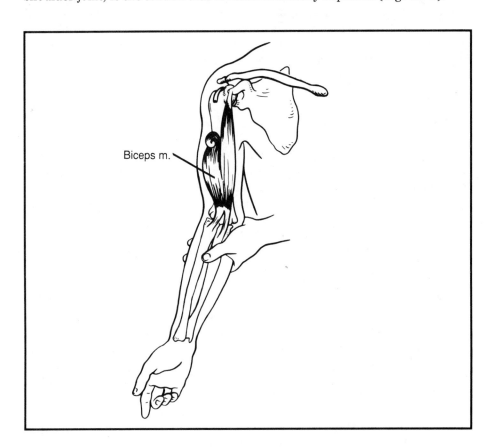

Biceps m.

CAUSE. Rupture of the biceps tendon occurs as a result of either a forceful contraction of the biceps muscle or an external force exerted on the biceps while it is in a shortened state. Weightlifting activities can be a cause during heavy bodybuilding or weight training. Factors such as a history of bicipital tendinitis and/or cortisone injection can predispose the tendon to rupture. Steroid injections do relieve the pain through inhibiting the inflammatory response, but they have an antianabolic effect on connective tissue, which may result in structural weakening of the injected tendon (Kessler and Hertling, 1983). Personal trainers should never recommend an injection of this type. Trainers should be extremely cautious in initiating strength programs that use the biceps with clients who have a history of cortisone injections.

SYMPTOMS. Usually with biceps tendon ruptures, an immediate sharp pain radiates all along the tendon and muscle. There often is a visual defect in the muscle and tendon. After the tendon ruptures, it rolls up like a window shade, forming an abnormal bulge in the biceps region. Swelling is immediate and severe. The client may complain of pain and weakness when bending the elbow.

TREATMENT. Rupture of the biceps tendon is not always preventable, but common sense about training technique can be valuable. When such an injury occurs, apply an ice pack with an elastic compression wrap. Immobilization of the arm by strapping it to the body, with elbow bent, will usually be the most comfortable position for the injured part. The client should seek prompt medical care.

Shoulder Dislocation/Subluxation

The shoulder is a very mobile joint and is one of the most common dislocating or subluxing joints in the body. A **dislocation** of this joint results in a complete separation of the joint surfaces, whereas a **subluxation** is a partial dislocation. In a subluxation of the shoulder, the joint surfaces move apart only partially. Both of these conditions are instability problems.

CAUSE. Dislocations and subluxations can result not only from traumatic forces but also from predisposing factors. The prime predisposing factor is congenitally loose shoulder joints. The looseness can stem from a shallow socket and/or from a loose ligamentous joint capsule. If a traumatic force is the cause, the problem will usually be unilateral, whereas if the joint is congenitally loose, both shoulders are usually involved. Whether it be from trauma or a congenitally loose joint, the dislocation or subluxation most often occurs when the shoulder is externally rotated on an **abducted** arm (Fig. 16–7). The upper arm usually dislocates **inferiorly** (down) and **anteriorly** (front).

Traumatic dislocations should be uncommon when personal trainers are involved. However, clients with a congenital problem can redislocate over and over if they do not take precautions with certain activities. Lat-pull-down or -pull-over machines and wide-grip and deep-bench-press activities put the shoulder into the vulnerable position of external rotation and abduction.

SYMPTOMS. Once the shoulder has dislocated, the dislocation is usually obvious through inspection. The arm is typically held slightly away from the body (abducted), the deltoid muscle appears flatter than normal, and the acromion process (prominence at the top of the shoulder) is quite prominent. There is

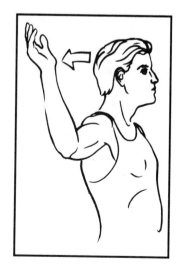

Figure 16–7 Mechanism of shoulder dislocation: abduction/external rotation.

also a bulge in the armpit. There is severe pain, and the injured client will not want to move the arm.

Getting a good history is very important. If a client reports problems with recurrent dislocations or subluxations, the trainer should take precautions in setting up a program that involves the upper extremity. The main precaution is to avoid stressful activities that take the shoulder into a position of abduction and external rotation.

TREATMENT.   If a dislocation occurs, do not try to *reduce* (relocate) it. Further damage can be produced by trying to reduce a dislocation without the proper training. Persons who chronically dislocate can usually reduce their own shoulders without problem. Extreme soft-tissue trauma occurs with first-time dislocations and can include associated damage to surrounding nerves and blood vessels. These situations should be treated as **emergencies**. The arm usually can be easily splinted against the body.

Muscular Strains

A **strain**, that is, an overstretching of musculotendinous tissue, can be classified as mild, moderate, or severe. A *severe* strain involves a complete rupture of the muscle or tendon. *Mild* and *moderate* strains, that is, pulls of muscular tissue, are much more common than complete ruptures. Upper-extremity musculature most commonly strained includes the deltoid, pectoralis major, latissiumus dorsi, triceps, biceps, trapezius, rhomboid, and rotator cuff (supraspinatus, subscapularis, teres minor, and infraspinatus).

CAUSE.   O'Donoghue (1976) describes **acute** strains occurring as a result of a single violent force being applied to the muscle. A strain may be the result of resistance to a force, as when a violent force is applied to a contracted muscle that is greater than the unit's ability to withstand. Strains become **chronic** when the acute injuries are not allowed to heal properly before resuming athletic activity. Chronic strain can also result from overuse of the musculature.

SYMPTOMS.   In cases of acute severe strains, there will usually be a visible defect in the muscle. In giving a health history, such a client will often report a popping or ripping sensation and complain of weakness and pain when trying to use the involved muscle. The onset of swelling is very rapid.

In mild and moderate injuries, the loss of function is not so drastic. The client can usually give a good history of how the injury took place and the site of the injury. Weakness and pain when the muscle is used are also common complaints. Swelling is not as apparent in mild and moderate cases. In some cases **ecchymosis** (discoloration) will appear about the third or fourth day after injury.

TREATMENT.   Immediate treatment should be RICE. An ice pack can be held in place with an elastic compression wrap. Ice should be applied four to eight times per day for approximately 20 minutes. If the strain is in the extremity (forearm or upper arm), then it is advisable to keep the part wrapped with the elastic bandage between ice treatments. Once the initial injury has abated, the involved muscle will need to regain its flexibility and strength. Use caution in returning someone to activity; aggravation of the initial injury will only set the client further behind in the rehabilitation scheme. Again, the best treatment is prevention. Because tighter musculature is more prone to strain, the flexibility component of an exercise program is very important. Proper conditioning techniques and a knowledge of one's flexibility also go a long way in the prevention of muscular strains.

LOWER-EXTREMITY INJURIES/DISORDERS

There are a number of lower-extremity injuries with which the trainer must be familiar: plantar fasciitis, Achilles tendinitis, stress fractures, iliotibial band syndrome, patellofemoral pain syndrome, patellar tendinitis, muscular strains, knee meniscal tears, and anterior cruciate ligament tears.

Plantar Fasciitis

The plantar fascia is the main supporting soft-tissue structure of the longitudinal arch of the foot. It is a dense and tough tissue that runs the whole length of the arch. When it is traumatized and becomes, chronically inflamed, the condition is referred to as plantar fasciitis (Fig. 16–8).

CAUSE.   Plantar fasciitis is an overuse syndrome resulting from repeated trauma to the foot. Activities that most commonly predispose the foot to repeated trauma are running and aerobics. However, almost any activity can be a causative factor. Running and aerobics require the feet to be continually pounded against the ground throughout the activity, and this involves a tremendous force that must be absorbed in part by the feet.

Causes can be intrinsic and/or extrinsic. Biomechanical faults with the foot can be a precursor. If the foot doesn't work correctly when it hits the ground, the forces will not be absorbed sufficiently. In everyday activities this is usually not a problem; however, when the system is tested in a forceful and repetitive fashion, something must break down. Some form of abnormal pronation is usually, but not always, part of the biomechanical fault. It is commonly thought that high-arched feet are more susceptible to strain than low-arched feet, but plantar fasciitis can occur in both situations, regardless of arch height. How the foot functions when in contact with the ground is the determining factor.

Extrinsic factors might include shoes, training regimen, and training terrain. For example, if a distance runner always runs in the same direction, with the right foot on the upward side of a slanted surface, that foot will pronate more forcibly than the left, increasing the stress on the plantar fascia (Fig. 16–9). Overused shoes that have broken down and lend very little support can also be the cause.

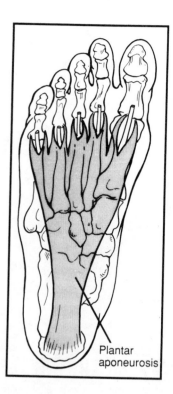

Figure 16–8   Plantar fasciitis. The darkened area marks the most common region of pain.

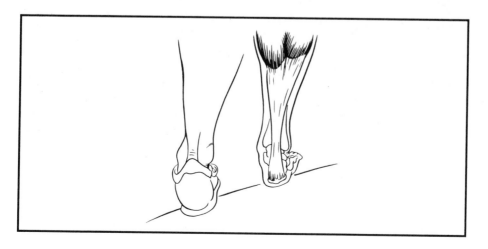

Figure 16–9   Running on uneven ground causes the upside foot to pronate excessively.

SYMPTOMS. Plantar fasciitis is characterized by a low-grade pain along the longitudinal arch, usually starting near its attachment to the heel. As the injury worsens, the pain will get more intense and diffuse, moving down the fascia toward the base of the toes. In mild cases the pain is felt only after exercise, diminishing rapidly. However, as the condition worsens, pain is constant. The pain in such cases is dull and achy during rest, with sharper pain when weight is placed on the foot. Pain is usually much worse when walking barefoot and on a concrete surface, because there is no support and cushion when the foot is in contact with the ground. Swelling is usually not prominent.

TREATMENT. In many cases, the quickest, safest, and most thorough remedy is to eliminate the cause. To treat the condition symptomatically with just rest and ice is usually not enough. High rates of injury recurrence are the result of mismanaged treatment efforts. A personal trainer should be knowledgeable enough to deal effectively with most of the extrinsic factors. Many of the intrinsic causes, however, such as abnormal pronation, should be dealt with by a qualified professional. A custom-fit orthotic is often the answer if a biomechanical fault such as abnormal pronation is the cause. However, orthotics are not the end-all cure for everyone with plantar fasciitis. Supporting the arch with pads gives temporary relief and is certainly an appropriate method of relieving stress to the area. Heel cups or pads also may give temporary relief. But the personal trainer should not go beyond the scope of practice and prescribe orthotics; instead, the trainer should make the proper referral.

Although the most beneficial treatment in the long run will be ridding the client of the cause, it is important to treat the inflammatory signs and symptoms as well. The RICE procedures can be used effectively. Other forms of cold treatment, such as immersion and ice massage, are also very effective. The client can put the affected foot in a bucket of ice water for approximately 10 minutes, four to eight times a day, or use ice-massage techniques such as those described for epicondylitis. As after any injury, once the pain and inflammation subside, strength and flexibility must be restored. With this injury the strength of the foot and ankle musculature are critical to complete rehabilitation, as is the flexibility of the plantar fascia.

It is of utmost importance to screen clients thoroughly to pick up these problems. The longer plantar fasciitis lingers, the harder and longer the recovery period will be. The personal trainer should be able to alter the client's fitness program temporarily to take the stress off the foot by substituting swimming or biking. Chronic plantar fasciitis is a major problem, and the trainer should emphasize prevention by proper medical attention.

Achilles Tendinitis/Rupture

The Achilles tendon is a uniquely strong structure that attaches the gastrocnemius and soleus muscles to the heel. Because of the strength and constant use of this muscle group, the Achilles tendon normally takes a tremendous beating. At times it will break down and become inflamed from overuse. Inflammation of the Achilles tendon can lead to local degeneration, and recurrent injury to a previously damaged tendon can cause partial or even complete ruptures (Fig. 16–10) (Herring & Nilson, 1987).

CAUSE. Tendinitis can result from faulty biomechanics, poorly cushioned or stiff-soled shoes, excessive hill running, or any other activity that demands excessive use of the tendon. Jumping activities such as basketball, volleyball, and aerobics require a great amount of work from the Achilles tendon. It is

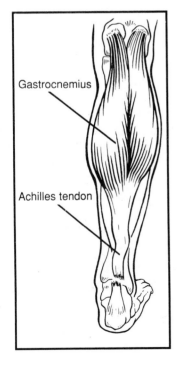

Gastrocnemius

Achilles tendon

Figure 16–10 Total rupture of the Achilles tendon.

thought that tendinitis is, at times, brought on by the tendon's weakness in handling eccentric loads. For example, each time an aerobics participant lands after jumping, the Achilles tendon and gastrocnemius/soleus must contract eccentrically to control the landing motion at the ankle joint. Doing this over and over with eccentric weakness is a plausible cause of tendinitis.

The biomechanical faults discussed with plantar fasciitis and shin splints relate here as well. Abnormal pronation and muscle imbalances can be the problem. Shoes, terrain, training intensity, exercise surface—all must be considered when a client complains of pain in the Achilles region. Remember, a precursor to Achilles tendon rupture is tendinitis. Never ignore an inflamed tendon. Ruptures can happen with any athletic activity as a result of a forceful contraction of the involved musculature. In the case of the Achilles tendon, the gastrocnemius and soleus contract to cause the rupture.

SYMPTOMS. The client will complain of discomfort in the Achilles tendon region, most commonly about an inch above the point of insertion of the tendon into the heel. The onset is usually gradual, with mild cases being painful after activity. The pain can become constant in more severe cases. The tendon can become visibly thickened and swollen, especially in more chronic cases. Sometimes the client will complain of a crackling, squeaking sensation (*crepitus*) in the tendon. When the injured client moves the foot up and down, this crepitus becomes more pronounced. This sensation actually comes from the inflammation of the sheath that surrounds the tendon.

By taking a good history, the personal trainer can recognize ruptures of the Achilles tendon. Most often the client will complain of being kicked in the back of the ankle and will describe a popping sensation. Immediate inspection will show a noticeable gap at the rupture site, but this will quickly fill in with swelling as the tissue bleeds. The client will complain of an inability to use the part, and the pain will progressively become more severe as the swelling increases.

TREATMENT. As with other inflammatory conditions, some form of cold treatment should be initiated promptly. RICE or ice immersion works very well. Eliminating any causative factors will again be the most beneficial long-range treatment. Sometimes felt or foam pads to lift the heel can reduce stress on the tendon and allow the inflammation to subside. These lifts take the stretch off the tendon by moving the ankle out of so much **dorsiflexion** when the foot is in contact with the ground. Clients who use pads should be sure to place one in each shoe.

Achilles tendinitis can become quite stubborn, and thus recognizing and treating it early is best. If the condition lingers even for a short period, it will be wise for the client to seek medical help. In chronic conditions, physicians have immobilized the part and in some cases have resorted to surgery. Be aware of clients who have had several cortisone injections in the tendon. Corticosteroids have a weakening effect on tendinous structures. Use caution in setting up programs for such clients, and avoid heavy calf-press activities.

Tendon ruptures are a medical emergency and should be referred immediately to an emergency room or orthopedic surgeon. Applying an ice pack with an elastic wrap will help control the swelling.

Stress Fractures

Sometimes called "march" or "fatigue" fractures, stress fractures are often observed among foot soldiers. Common sites are the foot (metatarsals) and the lower leg (tibia and fibula). Such fractures are so small that they are not initially detectable on normal X ray. As healing begins to take place, X ray will pick up the new bone formation around the fracture site.

CAUSE.   Repetitive stress is the cause of stress fracture. Long-distance runners seem to be most commonly affected. Repetitive stress on a biomechanically unsound lower extremity is common. The tissues of the body can take only so much stress; if taken past their limit, failure occurs. In some persons the weak link might be the plantar fascia, and in others it might be the bony structures, but, in the end, some tissue will break down if the system is overtaxed. According to Scully and Besterman (1982), stress fractures are frequently encountered two to five weeks following a change in vigorous physical activity. A well-planned training program will diminish the possibility of such injury. The introduction to vigorous physical training should be slow and progressive but, above all, cyclic in nature.

SYMPTOMS.   Aching pain, becoming more severe and remaining localized, is a common symptom of stress fracture. Stress fractures of the tibia are often misdiagnosed as shin splints, and stress fractures of the metatarsals can be misdiagnosed as plantar fasciitis. The distinguishing feature is that the pain associated with stress fractures is usually localized, whereas pain with shin splints and plantar fasciitis is more diffuse. Swelling is often present directly over the fracture site. The trainer should recommend further medical workup if there is persistent pain in the lower leg or foot. Although normal X ray sometimes can't pick these up initially, bone-scan techniques can. Continued trauma to a stress fracture can result in complete fracture of the bone.

TREATMENT.   Rest is the only treatment that will allow the bone to heal. Application of ice may be beneficial in reducing pain and swelling. Sound healing usually takes six to eight weeks. When the client returns to activity, all exercise should be pain-free and remain so. The lack of pain does not always mean the client is ready to return to sport but only to begin rehabilitation with the appropriate medical guidance. Full range of motion, strength, and balance must be restored before returning to activity. Exercise may continue, but in an altered fashion. The runner, for example, can continue a cardiovascular fitness program by switching to swimming. It is important to discontinue any activity that is painful or that stresses the injury. After healing has taken place and the client is ready to return to activity, a thorough biomechanical evaluation might be indicated. If a fault is present and not corrected, the chance of recurrence will be much higher. An orthotic may be appropriate.

Iliotibial Band Syndrome

The iliotibial band (ITB) is a thickened fascial structure on the outer aspect of the thigh and knee. It originates off of the tensor fascia latae muscle and extends down and across the lateral aspect of the tibia (Fig. 16–11). Just before the band crosses the knee, it crosses over a bony ridge of the femur called the lateral epicondyle. This is the spot where the ITB can, and usually does, become inflamed.

CAUSE.   Iliotibial band syndrome is an injury of overuse, especially if the ITB is tight. A tight ITB will predispose one to friction across the lateral femoral epicondyle. As the knee moves into flexion and extension, the band moves back and forth over the bony prominence and becomes irritated. Frequently, clients

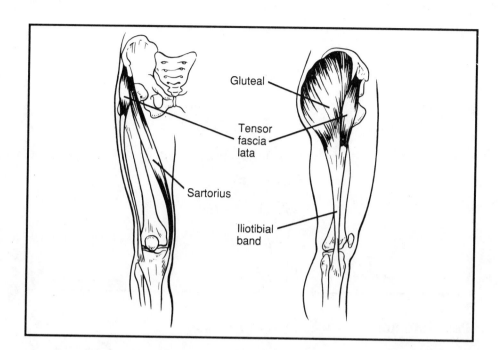

Figure 16–11   Iliotibial band and its epicondylar friction site.

with this problem will have altered their training program. A careful history will often demonstrate that the client has moved into a program demanding either extensive training on unlevel ground or frequent downhill training sessions. Running on banked surfaces for an extended period can create pain in the ITB, especially on the downside leg, which is forced to sway out and stretch the ITB. Abnormal pronation or supination may predispose one to ITB syndrome. Too much supination at heel strike can tend to bow the knee out, putting additional stretch on the ITB, but in a much more complex fashion. A combination of many factors may lead to the development of ITB syndrome. For example, a runner with tight bands who decides to increase the amount of downhill mileage after not having run for two weeks is at a potential risk of developing a problem.

SYMPTOMS.   As with any overuse syndrome, there is a spectrum of discomfort and disability. Initially, the pain may develop only after a long workout. In those mild cases, improvement is noted after a warm-up period. However, in the more severe and persistent cases, the pain begins to be present most of the time. The pain is usually felt just above the knee joint and close to the body epicondylar prominence. As the condition becomes more chronic, the client may begin to experience pain moving up the lateral thigh. Noble (1980) says that the pain is most severe when the foot is in contact with the ground during deceleration activities. As one would expect, walking with a stiff leg on the affected side may provide complete relief. Usually no swelling is associated with this injury.

TREATMENT.   Dealing with the extrinsic factors will often eliminate the problem. That may mean cutting down on mileage or running on flat surfaces temporarily. Sometimes intrinsic factors must be looked at as well, such as abnormal pronation or supination, or tightness of the ITB. Ice in some form should be used to help decrease the pain and inflammation. These conditions rarely warrant surgery; however, they can become quite a nuisance. Every means should be taken to determine the cause and, if it is extrinsic or intrinsic in nature, deal with it immediately.

Figure 16–12 Injuries of the patella. The roughened area on the undersurface marks the region of chondromalacia and patellofemoral pain syndrome. The frayed area is the region of patellar tendinitis.

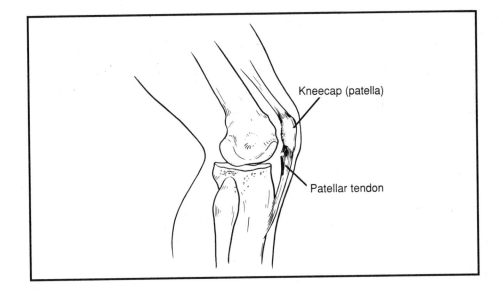

Kneecap (patella)

Patellar tendon

Patellofemoral Pain Syndrome

Patellofemoral pain syndrome is often termed *chondromalacia*, which it may or may not actually be. Chondromalacia patella is a condition on the back of the kneecap (patella) in which the articular cartilage softens and becomes diseased (Fig. 16–12). However, the client can have pain around the patella without actually suffering from chondromalacia.

CAUSE.   Pain around and under the patella often comes from a tracking problem; in other words, the patella does not move normally in its underlying body groove. Usually when the patella tracks abnormally, it does so to the outside (laterally). This patellar pain is often the result of a structural abnormality or imbalance in the lower limb. Such structural deviations are usually of the foot or of the knee itself. How the foot functions biomechanically when in contact with the ground will dictate the function of the entire lower limb, even the knee. Normally, immediately after the heel strikes the ground, a certain amount of foot pronation is necessary to allow adaptation to the ground. Excessive pronation, however, causes the patella to be pulled out of normal alignment. The patella is also more likely to become the focal point of problems in knees that sway inward and/or backward excessively. When the patella is unusually high or lateral in relation to the underlying groove, a potential problem exists.

Muscle imbalances around the knee also can put undue stresses on the patella. Usually, these imbalances tend to pull the patella laterally. For example, tightness of the iliotibial band combined with weakness of the vastus medialis will produce this effect. Training regimen is another factor that may predispose to patellar pain. Sudden increases in intensity or duration of exercise or a change in exercise terrain can produce irritation, especially if an underlying intrinsic factor is present. For example, if a runner who already has knees that sway inward runs on a banked surface, the inward sway will increase on the upside knee. This force causes the patella to track further laterally, causing abnormal compression within the underlying groove.

The knee is a very sensitive joint, and problems can be caused by poor fitness programming. Squatting, leg extension exercises, and stair climbing exercises can all cause patellofemoral problems. Too much resistance or incorrect technique can initiate a problem. Steady progression with certain fitness activities is the key to prevention.

SYMPTOMS.   Typically, the onset of pain in the area of the patella is gradual. It may begin with aching pain behind the patella only after activity; then, as severity increases, the pain will become more constant. With the knee in an irritable state, other activities begin to be painful. Sitting for a long period in a confined environment with the knees bent may cause a stiff/aching sensation. Ascending and/or descending stairs or inclines, squatting, and kneeling are other activities that produce symptoms in clients with patellofemoral pain syndrome.

Swelling and patellar grinding are two symptoms that may be present. If swelling is present, it will occur around and above the patella. Grinding behind the patella is found in some normal knees, and by itself does not mean the knee is diseased. However, when accompanied by pain this is a clear indication that something is wrong.

TREATMENT.   RICE or ice massage is a good cold treatment to help with the pain and inflammation. Some clients may find that neoprene braces help stabilize the patella. The rationale behind these sleeves is that they provide a counterforce, helping to keep the patella properly aligned. However, the most logical method of managing patellofemoral problems is to treat the causative factors. If the foot pronates excessively, a prescription orthotic may be effective. Clients with muscular imbalance often respond to an exercise program designed to strengthen and stretch the appropriate structures. Sometimes evaluation and changing of the exercise terrain or program provide the only treatment necessary.

With a condition of this type, it is important not to have the client work through pain; this will only worsen the condition. Personal trainers can do much to prevent this condition and educate clients about it. If a client has a history of patellofemoral problems, trainers must be cautious with any exercise of the knee, so as not to exacerbate the condition.

Patellar Tendinitis

The patellar tendon runs from the bottom of the patella down approximately one to two inches to a bony protuberance called the tibial tubercle. Through the patella it connects the quadriceps muscle to the tibia. This tendon, like any other tendon, can become overused and inflamed (Fig. 16-12). Sometimes this injury is referred to as jumper's knee, because it frequently occurs in those who participate in jumping activities.

CAUSE.   As just indicated, this injury is another inflammatory reaction of a tendon to repetitive stress. It is most common in activities such as aerobics, basketball, volleyball, and high-jumping. Just as the Achilles tendon is required to help control the landing motion at the ankle joint, the patellar tendon, in conjunction with an eccentric contraction of the quadriceps, is required to control the knee joint while landing. Weakness of the quadriceps and patellar tendon eccentrically can be a predisposing factor in the development of patellar tendinitis.

Patellar tendinitis doesn't seem to be related as much to biomechanical foot problems as do other overuse syndromes of the lower extremity. Extrinsic factors, such as training surface, shoe type, and training intensity and duration can all be involved in the development of patellar tendinitis. Making sure that clients do aerobics on a resilient surface will go a long way to prevent patellar tendinitis as well as any other overuse syndrome in the lower extremity.

SYMPTOMS. The onset of this condition is gradual, as with other overuse syndromes, and with mild conditions pain is present only after activity. As severity and chronicity increase, the pain becomes less intermittent. The tendon can become thickened as the condition worsens, and crepitus can be present just as with Achilles tendinitis. Use of the quadriceps muscle group will usually be somewhat painful, and the client may complain of weakness.

TREATMENT. Ice treatment in some form is appropriate. Some clients will try various kinds of knee sleeves and bands in an attempt to take the pressure off the tendon. These supportive garments may help reduce the symptoms, but in the long run they are not going to eliminate the problem. Rest from the aggravating activity is the most plausible solution, along with correction of any extrinsic factors. As the inflammation abates, the quadriceps and patellar tendon will need to be strengthened, especially eccentrically. It is also important that flexibility be restored to the tendon and associated quadriceps muscle group. Patellar tendon ruptures occur less frequently than do Achilles tendon ruptures. However, it is still important to be cautious with those clients who have a history of patellar tendinitis and/or tendon injections.

Muscular Strains

The advice regarding strains in the upper extremity applies to the lower extremity as well. As with the upper extremity, certain muscles of the lower extremity are more susceptible to strain than others. The gastrocnemius and the hamstring, quadriceps, and groin muscle groups are commonly strained in athletic activities. Causes, symptoms, and treatment are the same as for upper-extremity strains.

Knee Meniscal Tears

The inside (medial) and outside (lateral) cartilages (menisci) of the knee are important structures that add to the stability and cushioning of the joint. They are a part of the weight-bearing surface of the tibia, attached around the perimeter by ligaments (Fig. 16–13). Tears of these structures can interfere markedly with participation in exercise programs.

CAUSE. Most commonly, the menisci are torn in association with a traumatic blow to the knee. However, the traumatic force doesn't always have to be large for a tear to occur. The client often will not be able to recall the exact mechanism and onset of the injury. Rotary forces within the joint are often the cause of the tear. A force causing the knee to bend or straighten too far can also put stress on the meniscus and cause it to tear. These tears can occur in activities such as running, aerobics, and weightlifting, and especially in squatting activities.

SYMPTOMS. The client will usually complain of pain, either intermittent or constant, along the medial or the lateral aspect of the joint. Sometimes clicking and popping are associated with this pain, with the knee even locking occasionally. The client may be unable to squat without pain and may often complain of the knees giving way. Acute cases might involve some swelling, but if this is present, it usually is not pronounced.

TREATMENT. If a meniscal tear exists, the chances of its healing are remote. Usually the only remedy for a torn cartilage in the knee is surgical arthroscopic

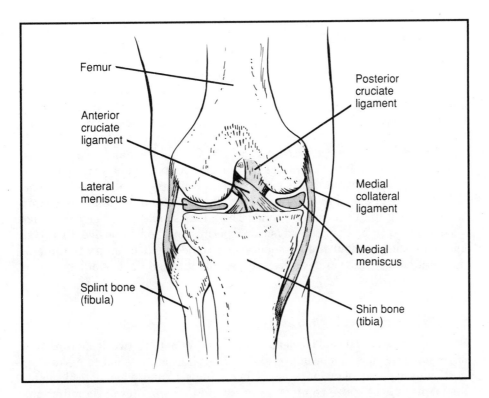

Figure 16–13 Knee joint anatomy depicting the anterior cruciate ligament (ACL) and medial and lateral menisci.

resection. Although many clients with tears continue to exercise, this is not advisable. The joint surfaces begin to erode from the constant friction of the torn meniscal piece, setting one up for arthritic problems later in life. If a client sustains a knee injury, the personal trainer should refer the client to a physician. With those clients who have had meniscal surgery, the precautions to knee exercise should be minimal. Progress slowly, and adjust to the client's tolerance. It is advisable to talk with the client's physician for guidance.

Tears of the Anterior Cruciate Ligament

The anterior cruciate ligament (ACL) lies deep in the center of the knee and gives stability to the joint (see Fig. 16-13). Personal trainers will rarely encounter clients who tear an ACL in their presence. However, it will not be uncommon to have a client with an ACL-deficient knee and/or a surgically reconstructed knee.

CAUSE.   The ACL is usually torn in contact sports such as football. However, tears can occur frequently in sports such as basketball. A blow to the outside of the knee with a rotary component can cause the ACL to tear, and often with this mechanism the medial collateral ligament (MCL) and the medial meniscus are also torn. Injury can also happen without a traumatic blow, for example, getting shoes caught on the playing surface or returning to the surface awkwardly after jumping.

SYMPTOMS.   Within the first few hours after such an injury, swelling, quite often severe, will develop. As the swelling increases, so will the pain. The client will give a history of feeling or hearing a pop in the knee. In cases of chronic ACL deficiency, the knee joint will be very unstable and the client may complain of its giving way with certain activities, some as routine as stepping off of a curb.

TREATMENT. If a client suffers a knee injury in the presence of a personal trainer, the first aid treatment of choice is the same as that for other injuries— RICE. Referral to an orthopedic physician would be wise. If the ACL is indeed torn, and the client wishes to continue with a regular exercise routine, a surgical reconstruction will quite often be the treatment of choice. Activities in which a client feels any giving way, instability, or shifting should be halted. Many clients will wear custom-fit functional knee braces that help to decrease the shear forces somewhat.

Clients with a surgically reconstructed ACL should be handled differently. Always use caution if the client has had surgery less than one year ago. Most physicians believe a year must pass before allowing a client to return to activity. It would be wise to call the client's physician for a written prescription before setting up a fitness program. The client should avoid any explosive quadriceps work without the physician's permission. An explosive, thrusting knee extension without proper supervision could result in injury to the new ligament. Knee extension exercises, especially through the last 30°, put great stress on the ACL.

SUMMARY

Some insight as to musculoskeletal injuries common to the work environment of personal trainers has been presented. The intention was not to make diagnosticians of personal trainers, but rather to impart knowledge that will enable the trainer to recognize common injuries and to begin appropriate first aid. Many of the injuries discussed result from overuse, frequently in conjunction with intrinsic and/or extrinsic causative factors. Recognizing such factors, and attempting to correct them, often will be all the treatment that is necessary. Remember, however, that the province of a personal trainer is limited when it comes to dealing with injured clients. It is always advisable to consult with, or refer clients to, a physician in such circumstances. Helping clients avoid injury in the first place is primary. Always think prevention—it is the best form of treatment.

REFERENCES

Herring, S.A., & Nilson, K.L., (1987). Introduction to overuse injuries. *Clinics in Sports Medicine, 6* (2), 225–239.

Kessler, R.M., & Hertling, D., (1983). *Management of common musculoskeletal disorders.* Philadelphia: Harper & Row.

Noble, C.A. (1980). Iliotibial band syndrome in runners. *American Journal of Sports Medicine, 8* (4) 232–234.

O'Donoghue, D.H. (1976). *Treatment of injuries to athletes.* Philadelphia: Saunders.

Scully, T.J., & Besterman, G.M., (1982). Stress fracture—A preventible training injury. *Military Medicine, 147* 285–287.

SUGGESTED READING

American Academy of Orthopedic Surgeons. (1985). *Athletic training and sports medicine.* Chicago: AAOS.

Daniels, L., & Worthingham, C. (1972). *Muscle testing: Techniques of manual examination.* Philadelphia: Saunders.

Gould, J., & Davies, G. (1985). *Orthopedic and sports physical therapy.* St. Louis: Mosby.

Hay, J.G. (1973). *The biomechanics of sports techniques.* Englewood Cliffs, NJ: Prentice-Hall.

Hoppenfeld, S. (1976). *Physical examination of the spine and extremities.* New York: Appleton-Century-Crofts.

Kendall, H.O., Kendall, F.P., & Wadsworth, G.E. (1971). *Muscles: Testing and function.* Baltimore: Williams & Wilkins.

Klafs, C.E., & Arnheim, D.D. (1977). *Modern principles of athletic training.* St. Louis: Mosby.

Peterson, L., & Renstrom, P. (1986). *Sports injuries, their prevention and treatment.* Chicago: Year Book Medical Publishers.

Roy, S., & Irvin, R. (1983). *Sports medicine.* Englewood Cliffs, NJ: Prentice-Hall.

Williams, P.L., & Warwick, R. (Eds.). (1980). *Gray's Anatomy* (36th Brit. ed.). Philadelphia: Saunders.

Emergency Procedures

Kathleen M. Hargarten

17

Kathleen Hargarten, M.D., FACEP, is assistant professor at the Medical College of Wisconsin. She is board-certified in emergency medicine and is a fellow of the American College of Emergency Physicians. She also serves on the American Council on Exercise's personal trainer examination committee.

IN THIS CHAPTER:

- Emergency equipment and procedures: stocking a first-aid kit, activating the EMS system, conducting primary and secondary assessments.

- Providing first aid for common medical emergencies and injuries.

- Identifying common medical emergencies and injuries: dyspnea, chest pain, syncope, insulin reaction, heat illness, seizures, soft-tissue injuries, fractures, head injuries, neck and back injuries.

A personal fitness trainer encourages clients to realize a healthier lifestyle through exercise and improved nutrition, minimizing the risk of injury. However, no matter how knowledgeable the trainer or how well-designed the program, a medical crisis or acute injury may occur. Although most people actively engaged in regular physical activity are healthy adults with no serious medical problems, some have underlying disease that has not yet manifested itself. Appropriate health screening and fitness testing before an exercise program begins will help identify these persons, and the personal trainer can simply refer them to their physicians for medical clearance, thereby forestalling emergency conditions. But what if the unforeseen happens? Knowing what to do during those first critical moments, or how to access the emergency medical system, can make the difference—between life and death, between temporary and permanent disability, between rapid recovery and a long hospital stay.

This chapter will familiarize the personal trainer with several important procedures for preventing and coping with emergencies. However, the chapter is not comprehensive. Clients should be referred to their physicians for diagnosis of injury or medical condition and for medical advice. The author assumes the reader has taken a course in airway management and cardiopulmonary resuscitation (CPR) and is presently certified in basic life support (BLS) (see the Appendix at the back of this manual).

EMERGENCY EQUIPMENT AND EMERGENCY MEDICAL SERVICES

Whether a trainer works in a health club, out of a home, or in clients' homes, he/she needs a telephone and a first-aid kit near at hand. Rapid access to a telephone is vital for contact with emergency medical personnel if they are needed. The first-aid kit should be stocked completely and systematically maintained. It should contain the following supplies:

For airway management:

- Pocket mask with one-way valve for protected mouth-to-mask ventilations (see Fig. 17–1).

For assessing circulation:

- Sphygmomanometer (blood pressure cuff).
- Stethoscope.
- Penlight or flashlight.

For general wound management:

- Sterile gauze dressings (medium and larger sizes).
- Adhesive tape (1-inch and 2-inch sizes).
- Bandage scissors.
- Liquid soap (if soap is unavailable in workplace).

For suspected sprains or fractures:

- Splinting material (see section on fractures).
- Chemical cold pack, or ice and plastic bag.

Figure 17–1   Mouth-to-mask ventilations: A small pocket mask with a one-way valve prevents contact with a victim's face during mouth-to-mouth resuscitation.

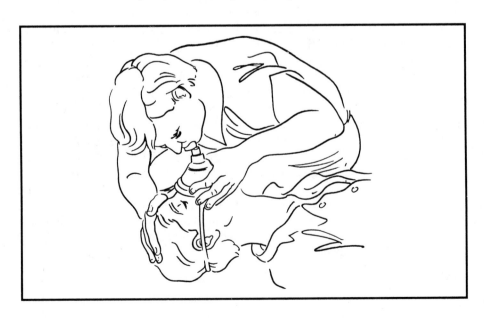

The trainer should check this first-aid kit at least every three months to replace outdated items and become familiar with the contents. Any items used from the kit should be replaced immediately. The trainer can tape a list of contents to the inside of the cover, so that nothing will be inadvertently omitted during restocking.

Accessing the Emergency Medical Services System

Every personal trainer needs a well-thought-out plan of action for any emergency, taking into account services available in the community. When an emergency occurs, the trainer must know how to activate the emergency medical services (EMS) system and whom to call for immediate stabilization of a person in critical condition. Most large cities have a 911 telephone number that will automatically set the EMS system in motion. When someone dials 911, a dispatcher trained in recognizing emergencies will answer the telephone and ask the questions that help determine which medical unit is needed. In communities without centralized dispatch, the caller must choose the police, sheriff, fire department, or ambulance emergency number. For either system, the caller must be prepared with name, location, and telephone number at that location. The dispatcher will ask questions about the sex and approximate age of the victim, the nature of the illness or injury (for example, level of consciousness, respiratory difficulty, location of pain, presence of trauma or bleeding), and past medical history that may affect the victim's condition.

When a centralized dispatch number is not available, it becomes important for the caller to know the difference between emergency medical technicians and paramedics. **Emergency medical technicians** are trained to recognize the nature and seriousness of a patient's illness or injury, and to provide basic care to sustain life and prevent further injury. This basic care includes splinting fractures, handling simple wounds, controlling bleeding, maintaining open airways, and administering CPR. **Paramedics**, on the other hand, are specially trained to administer advanced care and work under direct physician supervision, usually by radio. With approximately 1,000 hours of training, they are qualified to perform many life-saving procedures, such as opening airways by endotracheal intubation, administering medications, starting intravenous fluids for shock, and performing simple life-saving surgical procedures. Clearly, any victim of a potentially life-threatening emergency needs a paramedic's services immediately. When in doubt about which help is needed, the trainer should call the paramedics to be safe.

EMERGENCY ASSESSMENT

Most injuries or illnesses allow enough time for the trainer to obtain a history, perform a brief examination, obtain assistance from emergency systems, and provide reassurance to the victim. Unfortunately, a few situations require prompt action to save a life. Any condition that prevents the victim from breathing adequately or getting enough oxygen could cause death. A few basic principles will help the trainer to identify these situations and act appropriately.

Oxygen, the basic fuel for sustaining life, is required by the cells of all the body's organs to carry out their functions. The three vital organs that must function for life to continue are the heart, the lungs, and the brain. The heart is a pump that supplies oxygen-rich blood to all the cells through the arteries and then returns oxygen-depleted blood back to the lungs. The intricate brain coordinates most of our functions, including movement, sensation, emotion, speech, wakefulness, sleep, and thought. The lower brain level coordinates body functioning, as well as life-support systems such as respiration and arterial blood pressure. Important for sustaining life, these brain cells are so sensitive to oxygen depletion that they will die within minutes after circulation to the brain stops.

Although many types of injuries and medical emergencies may occur, anything affecting the client's airway (A), breathing (B), or circulation (C) must be acted upon promptly. The most obvious example is a person who suffers a cardiopulmonary arrest. An asthma attack, airway obstruction, injury to the trachea, heart attack, or heavy hemorrhage from a wound has the potential to be just as serious a threat to life. When assessing an injury or illness, the trainer may ask the ABC questions:

A. Does this person have a compromised *airway*?

B. Is he/she *breathing* adequately?

C. Is blood *circulation* interrupted to prevent oxygen getting to heart, lungs, or brain?

Once the personal trainer identifies a true emergency, he/she must respond rapidly and appropriately.

The trainer needs two skills to determine the nature of an emergency: (1) ability to extract key information from the victim and other people around, and (2) the trainer's own assessment of the victim. If the victim is awake and responding, the trainer may ask what problems he/she is experiencing and whether these problems have occurred before. Usually, the victim can talk about what is wrong: "My asthma is acting up again," "I'm having chest pain that feels the same as my last heart attack," "I think I broke my ankle," or "I'm having an insulin reaction." The victim may even give information about the help needed: "My inhaler is in the locker room," "If you could get my nitroglycerine pills from my purse, I think I'll be fine," or "I need some sugar to reverse my insulin reaction."

Unfortunately, it is not always this easy. If the victim is unconscious, cannot breathe easily, or has never experienced these symptoms before, the trainer must rely heavily on physical assessment of the victim for answers. The **primary assessment** includes rapid examination to identify life-threatening or disabling circumstances. When help is on the way and the victim is out of immediate danger—breathing without assistance, bleeding controlled, pulses present—the trainer can proceed to a more complete **secondary assessment**.

Primary Assessment

The purpose of the primary assessment, which may take only one or two minutes, is to identify any threats to life or limb that need immediate attention. This examination provides not only enough information to start first aid, but also valuable information for the EMS dispatcher, the paramedics, or a physician.

The first moments after an emergency takes place can be so frightening that logic and experience are insufficient; to be able to respond appropriately and rapidly enough, the trainer needs a rote, systematic approach to assessing the victim. The trainer can recruit other people on the scene to summon the EMS once an emergency has been identified, freeing him/herself to continue assessment and apply first aid.

The trainer starts with the ABCs of basic life support. Although the canned

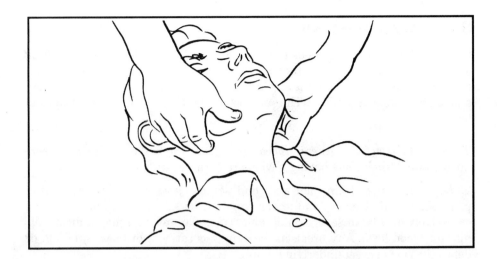

Figure 17–2 The jaw-thrust maneuver: The victim's head is carefully supported, without tilting or turning it in any direction. While kneeling at the head, push the lower jaw forward by exerting pressure with four fingers behind the angles of the jaw.

question from the BLS course, "Annie, Annie, are you ok?" may seem trite, asking the victim a simple question can give an assessment of the ABCs in less than five seconds. If the victim can answer, the airway is patent, breathing is sufficient to sustain life for the moment, and circulation is adequate to supply the brain with oxygen. If the victim is unable to answer a simple question, the trainer must assess airway, breathing, and circulation individually by physical examination.

1. *Assess the airway for patency.* If the victim is not breathing or is making "snoring" respirations, the airway may be obstructed. The trainer should establish a patent airway by using the jaw-thrust maneuver (Fig. 17–2). A simple sweep of the fingers clears foreign debris from the airway. With anyone who has sustained an injury above the clavicle (collar bone), the personal trainer should suspect cervical spine injury and use the jaw-thrust maneuver to avoid extension of the neck. Excessive movement of the neck could convert a cervical spine fracture without neurological damage into a fracture dislocation with paralysis.

2. *See whether the victims's chest rises and falls.* If the chest does not move, and if exhaled air cannot be felt coming from the mouth or nose, the trainer should begin mouth-to-mouth or mouth-to-mask ventilations at 12 breaths per minute (see Fig. 17–1).

3. *After two breaths, check victim's circulation by feeling the carotid pulse.* If pulses are absent and the victim is not breathing spontaneously, the trainer should begin CPR.

4. *Look quickly for signs of bleeding and control hemorrhage with direct pressure over the wound.* Victims who are bleeding profusely will not get enough oxygenated blood to vital organs. Even when they are alert at first, they will go into shock and quickly lose consciousness if appropriate measures are not taken.

5. *Perform a rapid neurological examination.* It is important to ascertain the victim's level of consciousness, pupil size, and pupillary reaction. The trainer can perform this exam by asking the victim to state his/her name, where he/she is, and what day it is. The trainer should also check whether the victim's pupils are equal, as well as whether the pupils contract when a light shines on them. Although this brief exam is somewhat crude, it provides useful information to medical personnel if the victim's condition should deteriorate later.

Secondary Assessment

Once the life-threatening needs of the victim have been addressed (breathing and circulation) and help is on the way, the trainer can conduct a more thorough evaluation. Again, a systematic approach will prevent the trainer from missing a subtle but important injury. The simplest method is to survey the victim from head to toe.

1. *Look at the victim's general appearance.* Does the person look sick or seriously injured? Is he/she having obvious respiratory difficulty?

2. *Look at the skin.* Skin color and condition can give clues about amount of pain, amount of bleeding, and underlying injuries. A victim who is sweating excessively may be in severe pain. Pale, cool, clammy skin may indicate significant blood loss. Any break in the skin (lacerations, bruises, swelling, or deformity) may reveal underlying injury.

3. *Check the head and face.* The trainer should look for lacerations (cuts), hematomas (bumps), or bruises, and then ask whether the victim is having pain in the neck. If any evidence of head or neck injury appears, the trainer should immediately immobilize the victim's neck to prevent spinal-cord damage and permanent disability.

4. *Observe the chest for injury.* The chest should rise and fall evenly with each respiration, and both sides of the chest should be symmetrical. The trainer should look for lacerations or bruising.

5. *Ask whether the victim has abdominal pain.* The trainer should look for signs of obvious trauma, such as bleeding or breaks in the skin.

6. *Protect the spine if a fall has occurred.* The trainer can assess spinal injury by simply asking if the victim is in pain. If the person cannot answer or is unconscious, the trainer must assume a spinal injury until proven otherwise. The victim should not be turned over for examination but should be kept on his/her back and prevented from moving until a physician can perform an examination and order X-rays. Do not move a victim who falls in a side-lying position and is having back pain. Wait for help to arrive so the victim can be properly positioned on a backboard to immobilize the spine. The trainer's actions may prevent permanent paralysis.

7. *Check for injury to arms and legs.* If swelling, discoloration, or deformity are present, prevent the victim from moving until help arrives. If the victim must be moved because of a long delay in getting help or a dangerous situation, the trainer should immobilize the limb with a simple splint.

8. *Perform a more thorough neurological examination.* Now that the more urgent problems have been addressed, the trainer can take a moment to ask whether the victim is noticing any weakness, numbness, or "pins-and-needles" feeling in the extremities. If the victim complains of these symptoms, the trainer should prevent unnecessary movement and then report the symptoms to the emergency medical personnel so that they can take precautions against spinal injury. The trainer may also reevaluate the victim's level of consciousness by repeating the same simple question asked during the primary survey: "Annie, Annie, are you OK?"

9. *Check vital signs.* The trainer should note blood pressure, pulse rate, and respiratory rate. These vital signs provide valuable information about the cardiovascular system, the amount of bleeding, and the severity of respiratory problems.

COMMON MEDICAL EMERGENCIES AND INJURIES

The personal fitness trainer may encounter a variety of injuries and medical emergencies over the course of a career. Here are some of the most common, along with guidelines for treatment.

Dyspnea (Difficult Breathing)

Labored breathing that persists after exercise has ceased—out of proportion to the amount of exertion—may have several causes. The sudden feeling of **dyspnea** may result from emotional excitement, airway obstruction, emphysema, **asthma** attack, or acute metabolic abnormalities. Victims may feel they cannot get enough air ("air hunger") and may display an anxious expression. Their breathing may labor audibly and their nostrils flare, or their neck and chest muscles may retract with each breath, indicating their distress. Cyanosis, a bluish discoloration, may appear around the lips and fingertips. Breathing may be rapid and shallow. If left untreated, the condition may progress to respiratory arrest. Following are the basic first-aid procedures the personal trainer should use with someone who is having respiratory difficulty:

1. *Stop all activity immediately.* Have the victim sit down in a comfortable position. Never urge a victim to lie down if he or she is resisting; the supine position may make the symptoms worse.

2. *Question the victim about any history of medical problems.* However, a victim in severe respiratory distress needs energy for the work of breathing and may not be able to respond to extended questioning.

3. *Administer oxygen* if it is available. Allow the victim to take his/her inhaled medication if it is available.

4. *Administer mouth-to-mouth or mouth-to-mask ventilations* if the victim is unconscious and has no spontaneous respirations.

ASTHMA.   Many asthmatics are active people who do not need to restrict their activities, but some may need occasional modifications to the exercise schedule. During an asthma attack, the smooth muscle surrounding the airway goes into spasm. Mucous plugs or excessive secretions in the airway also contribute to respiratory difficulties. Most attacks result from allergic reactions to things in the environment, such as mold, pollen, dust, trees, grass, animals, and certain foods. Young people often suffer asthma attacks induced by exercise, attacks that are influenced by the type, intensity, and duration of the exercise. Some people also suffer asthma attacks or more intense symptoms if they inhale cold air. During a typical asthma attack, the victim wheezes, breathing with a musical or "whistling" quality. Severe breathing difficulties will produce retracted neck and chest muscles, flared nostrils, cyanosis, and inability to speak. A victim who cannot speak in complete sentences because of the struggle to breathe needs immediate treatment and rapid transport by paramedics. Advanced airway maneuvers may be necessary, and delay could mean the difference between life and death.

The asthmatic client can easily manage mild symptoms by decreasing the intensity of the workout. Other asthmatics may need to use their inhalers to reverse the symptoms quickly. If the symptoms resolve, the client can continue exercising as before. Here are some steps to prevent an asthma attack:

1. Use a prolonged warm-up to prevent or reduce symptoms of **exercise-induced asthma**.

2. Decrease the intensity and increase the duration of the aerobic phase to avoid asthma symptoms while maintaining the cardiovascular benefits of the exercise.

3. Use a medicated asthma inhaler before beginning exercise. The client should consult with a physician before using this strategy.

4. Comply with prescribed medication and follow up with a physician to maintain an active life-style while controlling asthma symptoms.

Chest Pain

Chest pain can originate from any structure in or near the chest, such as the esophagus, aorta, or other large blood vessels, muscles, cartilage, lungs, or heart. The most alarming cause of chest pain, of course, is **coronary artery disease**, still the number-one killer of adults in the United States. In 1989, more than 1.5 million people are estimated to have had heart attacks; approximately 35 percent died. With the population of physically active older persons growing, more personal trainers may find themselves providing first aid to clients complaining of chest pain and showing signs of heart attack.

CORONARY ARTERY DISEASE.   The coronary arteries supply blood rich in oxygen to the myocardium (heart muscle). When plaque build-up or a spasm of the artery wall impedes blood from flowing through the arteries, the victim will feel chest pain. This pain originating from the heart is called **angina**. Someone who has coronary artery disease may experience angina during or immediately following physical exertion. The pain generally goes away when the victim dissolves a nitroglycerine pill under the tongue. However, if the myocardium continues without enough oxygen for a prolonged period, or if complete blockage of the artery stops blood flow to the heart, the muscle will die. This permanent damage to the myocardium is called a heart attack or myocardial infarction.

SYMPTOMS OF MYOCARDIAL INFARCTION.   Victims of a **myocardial infarction** will complain of pain in the middle or on the left side of their chests. Frequently they describe this pain as a pressure sensation over the anterior chest. Others have described this pain as "vise-like," "heavy," or "squeezing." The pain may radiate to the left shoulder and arm, up the neck or around the back. In addition, victims commonly have shortness of breath, nausea and vomiting, palpitations (heart pounding), and lightheadedness. The trainer may observe excessive sweating, difficult breathing, and an anxious expression in the victim. Heart attack patients often describe a feeling of impending doom during the event.

EMERGENCY TREATMENT.   About half of cardiac deaths occur within two hours after the onset of symptoms, often before the victim reaches the hospital. Immediate recognition of symptoms and effective treatment within the first few moments are critical to the victim's survival. Upon observing cardiac symptoms, the personal trainer should immediately activate the EMS system or recruit a bystander to assist with this task. Paramedics are needed because they are trained in advanced life-support and they can begin treatment immediately. If the victim has a cardiac arrest, paramedics can use electric stimulation (defibrillation) to convert an erratic heartbeat into a functional rhythm. Paramedics also have been trained to perform advanced airway procedures and administer intravenous medications to resuscitate the victim. Before paramedics arrive, these first-aid measures should be followed:

1. Place the victim in a comfortable position. Victims frequently ask to sit up, especially if dyspnea (breathing difficulties) accompany the chest pain.

2. Allow the victim to take prescribed medication (nitroglycerine) if he/she requests it.

3. Administer oxygen if available. The myocardium is not getting enough oxygen for the demands made on it.

4. Keep the victim still until help arrives, thereby avoiding excessive exertion and increased demands on the heart. Reassurance that help is on the way will reduce stress and anxiety.

5. If the victim is unconscious, check airway, breathing, and circulation. Begin CPR as needed.

Syncope (Fainting)

Fainting, or **syncope**, is a transient state of unconsciousness during which the person collapses from lack of oxygen to the brain. Some common causes of syncope include rapid or irregular heartbeat, vasovagal reaction, heat illness, and insulin reaction (hypoglycemia). Anything that causes relative decrease in blood volume, such as excessive blood loss or severe dehydration from vomiting or diarrhea, can also cause fainting.

Angina or a heart attack may disrupt the normal electrical activity coordinating the heartbeat. The resulting rapid or erratic heart rhythm can cause the victim to collapse. If the heart loses its ability to pump, quivering instead, the brain may incur irreversible damage within four minutes. Death may occur.

The most common and least serious form of fainting results from an increase in vagal nerve tone combined with dilation of the arteries, a vasovagal reaction. Such an attack typically occurs with the victim in a standing position, and follows an unpleasant or anxiety-provoking event, such as pain, fright, or the sight of blood. The victim typically experiences profuse sweating, loss of skin color, nausea, and restlessness. Heart rate and blood pressure drop dramatically, decreasing blood flow to the brain so that the victim loses consciousness. These symptoms resolve rapidly when the victim lies down.

Insulin Reaction (Insulin-induced Hypoglycemia)

Hypoglycemia occurs when there is a deficiency of sugar in the blood. The most common cause of hypoglycemia is an insulin reaction in a person with diabetes mellitus. **Insulin**, the antidiabetic hormone secreted by the pancreas, is necessary for the utilization of glucose (blood sugar) by the cells and for maintenance of proper blood-sugar levels. Inadequate production or utilization of insulin leads to improper metabolism of glucose and fats for energy production and brings on diabetes. **Diabetes mellitus**, a chronic and incurable disease resulting from poor insulin production or utilization, is characterized by high blood sugars and excretion of glucose in the urine. A diabetic can control the disease's symptoms and prolong life by using insulin injections and by closely monitoring blood sugars.

A diabetic may experience a hypoglycemic episode from too much insulin, too much exercise, or insufficient food. The episode produces fatigue, excessive sweating, headache, trembling, slurred speech, and poor coordination. The diabetic may feel faint, lose consciousness, or have a seizure. Other physical symptoms, such as pale moist skin, full rapid pulse, tremors, and elevated blood pressure, may also appear. Many diabetics are aware of early symptoms and can quickly reverse the process by simply consuming candy, fruit juice, or some other food rich in simple sugars. Other people may have no warning and go into insulin shock suddenly. The personal trainer's prompt response may prevent hospitalization or serious complications. Basic first aid for a diabetic with a hypoglycemic reaction includes the following steps:

1. *If the victim is conscious,* prevent injury by having him or her lie down or sit while someone gets help.

2. Give the victim sugar in the form of fruit juice, soft drinks sweetened with sugar, candy, and so on.

3. Prevent the diabetic client from resuming activity after the insulin reaction.

4. Encourage the victim to eat a meal and consult a physician to prevent further reactions.

If the victim loses consciousness, first-aid treatment changes. Following is a list of procedures in order of priority:

1. *If the victim is unconscious,* check airway, breathing, and circulation. Noisy respirations may indicate an obstruction that requires airway maneuvers. Artificial ventilations may be started as needed. The trainer should take care to protect the victim's cervical spine if a fall has occurred.

2. Telephone for paramedics. They can administer intravenous glucose that will quickly reverse a potentially life-threatening insulin reaction.

3. Protect the victim and prevent injury if he/she has a seizure. During a seizure, avoid restraining the victim. Place a soft object (towel, jacket, blanket) under the head to keep it from banging on the floor during violent muscular contractions.

4. Do not give anything by mouth. An attempt to give sugar by mouth to an unconscious person could cause aspiration of the substance and airway obstruction. If the victim vomits, the trainer should turn the victim on his/her side to prevent aspiration (see Fig. 17–3).

ADAPTING A TRAINING REGIMEN FOR DIABETICS. Most physicians today encourage their diabetic patients to exercise because of the many physical and psychological benefits. In consultation with their physicians, experienced and knowledgeable diabetics can safely embark on a training program, maintain good diabetic control, and avoid hypoglycemic reactions. The following methods will help the diabetic athlete:

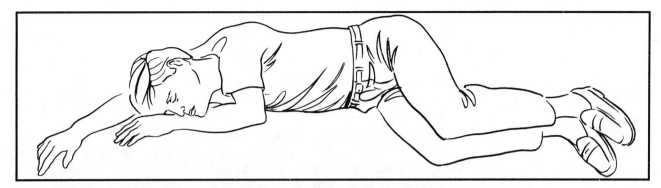

Figure 17–3 Side position for unconscious victim: Placing the victim on the side prevents airway blockage in case of vomiting. This position allows fluids to drain from the nose and mouth.

- Athletes on insulin may need to reduce their doses by 20–40 percent when beginning an exercise program. Diabetics need to work closely with their physicians during this process to ensure appropriate dosage of insulin.

- Diabetics respond best to exercises that have predictable duration, intensity, and frequency. Some examples of exercise that allow consistent and predictable energy expenditure include aerobic activities: walking, running, cycling, dance exercise, and cross-country skiing.

- Diabetics should avoid injecting their insulin into exercised extremities. The increased circulation in the exercised limb may allow the insulin to be absorbed too rapidly, causing hypoglycemia. Abdominal sites may be safer for insulin administration.

- During sustained exercise, a quick source of energy containing 10 grams of carbohydrates should be taken every 15–20 minutes. This could include ½ cup of regular soda, ½ cup of soft drink with sugar, 6–8 hard candies, or ¼ cup of gelatin dessert (Sperling, 1988).

- Several hours before competing in an athletic event, diabetics should eat a meal high in carbohydrates and relatively low in fats and protein. Within one hour before prolonged strenuous exercise, a mixed snack containing 15–20 grams of carbohydrates should be consumed. This could consist of ½ cup of milk and 2 or 3 crackers (Sperling, 1988).

- Diabetics must take responsibility for their own care by closely monitoring blood sugars, taking insulin as recommended, eating properly, exercising regularly, and keeping all medical appointments.

Heat Illnesses

Hot climates present serious health hazards to athletes. Runners, especially enthusiastic novices, are particularly vulnerable to heat illness. Runners may attempt to finish a race by exceeding their training levels or running too fast for their level of fitness. The normal metabolic processes of the body continuously produce heat that is dissipated to a cooler air temperature.

Normal body temperature is about 98.6°F (37°C). When the body gains excess heat—from increased metabolism during exercise, a hot environment, impaired dissipation of heat to the environment, or a combination of these—the brain's temperature regulatory center, the hypothalamus, activates several cooling mechanisms. Sweating, the most important method the body has to release excess heat during exercise, produces heat loss through evaporation. Also the superficial veins in the skin dilate, losing heat through convection (transfer of heat to air currents) and radiation. The amount of evaporation and heat loss depend on the air temperature, humidity, and wind speed. When humidity is high and the air is still, evaporation will diminish or cease completely. Convection of heat will cease when the air temperature approaches 100°F (38°C).

Anyone who exercises in a hot, humid environment—indoors or outdoors—runs a risk for heat illness. Injuries from heat occur in three forms, **heat cramps**, **heat exhaustion**, and **heat stroke**. Although the following description separates them, they overlap a great deal. A person with heat illness may display a combination of symptoms.

HEAT CRAMPS. The mildest heat illness, heat cramps typically occur during or after strenuous physical activity. This disorder is characterized by painful muscle spasm affecting those muscles worked the hardest. For example, runners most often feel heat cramps in their calf muscles, while racquetball players are more likely to have them in their arms. It is not clear what causes heat cramps, although they appear to be related to profuse sweating accompanied by loss of body salt (sodium). Hyperventilation and accumulation of lactic acid in the muscles may also contribute to the condition. The heat-cramp victim exhibits painful muscle cramps, sweating, and a normal body temperature. Treatment consists of drinking a commercially available electrolyte solution and massaging the affected muscle. If the cramps do not respond to these simple measures, the victim should be transported to a hospital for intravenous fluids and, possibly, muscle-relaxing medication.

HEAT EXHAUSTION. The most common heat illness for athletes, heat exhaustion typically follows intense exercise in a hot, humid environment. Profuse sweating with resultant fluid and electrolyte loss and inadequate fluid replacement may produce a dramatic drop in blood pressure. The victim's temperature may be normal or slightly elevated, and he/she will be sweating profusely. Other signs and symptoms vary; they may include early fatigue, lightheadedness, nausea, vomiting, severe headache, decreased coordination and staggering, hypotension (blood pressure less than 90 systolic), tachycardia (heart rate more than 100), and syncope (fainting).

A victim of heat exhaustion needs rest and fluid replacement. Follow these simple first-aid measures:

1. Move the victim to a cool place to reduce further sweating and fluid loss.

2. If the victim is profoundly hypotensive (blood pressure less than 90 systolic), call paramedics to transport the victim to the hospital.

3. If the victim is alert and mildly hypotensive (blood pressure 90-100 systolic), offer oral electrolyte solution until help arrives. The emergency room can rehydrate the victim more effectively with intravenous saline.

4. Victims of heat exhaustion should avoid activity for at least 24 hours afterward and be sure to drink adequate amounts of fluids during that time. Furthermore, they should refrain from exercising in the heat for at least a week because they are especially susceptible to repeat episodes within that period.

HEAT STROKE. The least common but most serious heat illness, heat stroke results from heat overload and impairment of the body's ability to dissipate heat. A true medical emergency, it may result in significant complications or death. The three classic symptoms of heat stroke are high body temperature (106°F or higher), altered consciousness, and lack of sweating. However, in heat stroke induced by exertion, dry skin is not a reliable sign because the victim may be sweating from exercise. People affected by heat stroke have commonly been exercising in hot, humid weather. The conditions that predispose someone to heat stroke include:

- Older age.

- Exercise and exertion.

- Hot, humid weather.

- Dehydration.

- Obesity.

- Heavy clothing.

- Infection and fever.

- Certain drugs: alcohol, amphetamines, diuretics, beta blockers, anticholinergics.

- Cardiovascular disease.

- Poor acclimatization.

- Hyperthyroidism.

Older people and those who have been using drugs (including alcohol) may not be able to protect themselves from a high environmental temperature, leaving them susceptible to heat stroke. Alcohol dilates the blood vessels, facilitating heat gain if the air temperature is higher than the body's. Any condition that increases metabolism can increase heat production and increase susceptibility to heat stroke. The excess thyroid production seen in people with hyperthyroidism, any exercise or exertion, infections, and stimulants such as amphetamines all increase metabolism.

Acclimatization refers to the body's ability to adapt to heat stress over time, resulting in increased capacity to work in hot, humid conditions. On the first day of vigorous exercise in a hot environment, a person may experience severe fatigue, elevated body temperature, and a heart rate near maximum. Over the next 4–8 days of similar exposure, the body will compensate by improving blood distribution and increasing blood volume, sweating at a lower temperature to improve heat loss, reducing urination to preserve body fluids, and reducing salt concentration in the sweat gland. People with inadequate acclimatization tolerate heat poorly and are more susceptible to heat stroke.

Anyone who is dehydrated, who has cardiovascular disease, or who takes diuretics or beta blockers may have reduced skin circulation. Adequate skin circulation is needed to dissipate heat. Anticholinergic drugs, such as certain medications prescribed for depression, can impair the body's ability to sweat and thus impair cooling from evaporation. Many other drugs that affect mood and thinking can also impair the brain's temperature-regulatory center.

Once heat stroke is suspected, the victim needs rapid treatment aimed at lowering the body temperature by whatever means are available. For immediate first aid the trainer should:

1. Call for emergency transportation to a hospital emergency room.

2. At the same time, move the victim to a cool area and remove clothing to expose the skin to air.

3. Immediately apply ice packs to areas of increased blood flow—the groin, underarms, and neck.

4. Apply cool water to the skin surface and then fan the victim by hand or machine to increase evaporation.

5. If the victim begins shivering, remove ice packs and use only cool sponging. Intense shivering increases metabolism, promoting heat production.

After transportation to the emergency room, the victim can receive care to minimize the damage from prolonged and intense heat to various organ systems.

PREVENTION OF HEAT ILLNESS. All heat illnesses may be prevented with proper planning and common sense. To minimize risk of problems with heat, the client should:

- Avoid exercising in extreme heat and humidity.

- Wear sensible, porous, light-colored, loose-fitting clothing while exercising in the heat.

- Train for competition in heat by acclimating slowly, increasing intensity and duration of exercise over eight days.

- Maintain a high level of fitness to work better in the heat and acclimate faster.

- Avoid dehydration by drinking adequate water before, during, and for 24 hours after vigorous exercise. Commercially prepared electrolyte and glucose solutions are unnecessary except for long periods of exertion in the heat, as in running a marathon. In fact, excessive salt intake can cause stomach cramps, weakness, and high blood pressure. Use of solutions containing too much glucose can retard absorption from the gastrointestinal tract by keeping the solution in the stomach longer.

- Use table salt more liberally the day before prolonged exercise (eight hours or more) in heat. Plenty of fluids should be consumed before the event (10–20 ounces about one hour ahead), in anticipation of fluid loss through sweating and breathing. A hypotonic electrolyte solution containing less than 0.9 percent concentration of sodium chloride (salt) should be consumed every 10–20 minutes during a long event. A commercially made or homemade solution, dissolving one quarter teaspoon of salt to a quart of water, can be used. Salt tablets should be avoided.

- Recognize the early symptoms of heat stress—dizziness, cramps, clammy skin, extreme weakness—and don't be too proud to quit if these should occur.

- Take more frequent rest periods and find a cool, shaded area for these breaks.

- Avoid drugs (including alcohol) that predispose to heat injury.

Seizures

A **seizure**, or convulsion, originates from the brain and causes disturbances in movement, behavior, sensation, or consciousness. Symptomatic of another condition, a seizure can result from an irritation in the brain from trauma, infection, blood clot, or hemorrhage. Other causes include decreased oxygen supply to the brain from cardiac or respiratory disturbance; metabolic abnormalities in sodium, calcium, magnesium, or glucose (hypoglycemia); poisons; alcohol withdrawal; high fever (especially in children); and complicated pregnancy. Epilepsy is a seizure disorder without an underlying cause. Epileptic seizures usually appear during childhood and recur spontaneously throughout life. With the use of anticonvulsant medication, epileptics can lead normal lives and control their symptoms. They are the people in whom the personal trainer is most likely to see a seizure occur.

A major motor seizure, called a grand mal episode, presents with violent and uncontrollable muscular contractions. It can be frightening to see for the first time. It has four phases:

- The **aura**, when an unusual sensation of smell, taste, or sound warns the person that a seizure is imminent.

- The **tonic phase**, in which victims lose consciousness, become rigid with all extremities extended, and hold their breath. As a result of not breathing, they appear cyanotic.

- The **clonic phase**, in which the muscles alternate between contraction and relaxation, making the victim appear to jerk. There may be incontinence of urine or feces.

- The **postictal phase**, in which the victim becomes comatose and his/her muscles become flaccid (limp). Consciousness returns slowly, with some initial confusion, headache, and extreme fatigue.

FIRST AID FOR SEIZURES.   The trainer's first task is to protect the victim from injury that might result from the flailing head and extremities. The simplest method is to put something soft under the victim's head and move all objects out of the way. No one should attempt to hold the victim's arms or legs down, because this restraint may inadvertently cause a fracture or dislocation. Facial muscle spasms may cause the victim to bite his/her tongue. If a padded tongue blade or bite block is readily available, it may be gently placed between the victim's teeth to prevent tongue biting. The trainer should avoid placing fingers or a pencil into the victim's mouth for fear of damage. The jaw muscles are creating enormous force that has the potential for serious injury.

It is important not to panic or attempt to force open the jaw during the tonic phase, when the victim may stop breathing and look cyanotic. This phase will pass and the clonic phase will bring renewed breathing and improved skin color.

During the postictal phase, the victim's muscles will become flaccid. A snoring sound during respiration usually indicates airway obstruction. If the victim has fallen to the floor with these noisy respirations, the trainer can make a big difference by protecting the victim's neck from further movement and controlling the airway with jaw-thrust maneuver (see Fig. 17-2). The trainer should also call an ambulance to transport the victim immediately to a hospital emergency room.

Soft-Tissue Injuries

Tissues, such as skin, muscles, and nerves, are composed of groups of cells that act together for a specific function. Bone, the hardest connective tissue in the body, will be discussed later under Fractures. This section will present identification and first aid for common wounds, sprains, and acute strains.

WOUNDS.   A break in continuity of the soft tissue, a **wound** can be open or closed. An open wound is manifested by broken skin, while a closed wound involves injury to underlying tissue without a break in the skin. Types of open wounds are:

- **Abrasion** a scraping away of the skin or mucous membrane. Bleeding from an abrasion may be minimal, perhaps just a little oozing. However, abrasions still have potential for contamination and infection.

- **Incision** a cut in the skin, typically from contact with a sharp object. The amount of bleeding depends on the size, depth, and location of the incision.

- **Laceration** a jagged, irregular cut or tear in the soft tissues, usually caused by a blow. Bleeding may be brisk in a laceration and tissue destruction is greater than with an incision. A laceration has great potential for contamination and resulting infection.

- **Puncture** a piercing wound from a sharp object, such as a nail, pin, or wood splinter, that makes a small hole in the skin. If external bleeding is minimal, the risk of infection is high. Bleeding flushes the area and assists in removing dirt and bacteria. A puncture wound over the trunk (chest, back, abdomen) can damage the underlying organs, causing internal bleeding.

- **Avulsion** a forcible tearing away of tissue from the body. Damage may be small, as when a minor accident tears away a little skin, or extensive, as when a crushing injury tears a limb from the body. In more serious avulsion injuries, significant bleeding may occur and infection may develop if precautions are not taken.

HEMORRHAGE CONTROL.   Wounds usually result from external physical forces, such as falls or mishandling of equipment. First aid for open wounds emphasizes controlling bleeding and reducing risk of infection. If an open wound is bleeding profusely, bleeding control takes precedence over infection control. Once the dressing has been applied and the profuse bleeding controlled, the dressing should not be removed until the victim reaches the hospital. The trainer should attend to the most life-threatening condition first. Following are some simple techniques the personal trainer can take to control bleeding:

1. Elevate above the heart any briskly bleeding wound of the head, neck, arm, or leg. This elevation reduces arterial bleeding from force of gravity, as well as encouraging venous blood return to the heart by draining excess blood from the elevated part.

2. Apply direct pressure over the bleeding point, using a gloved hand over a gauze dressing (see Fig. 17–4). If bleeding is brisk and gauze dressings not readily available, firm pressure with a small towel over the wound may be used. If at all possible, caregivers should avoid using bare hands to keep from further contaminating the wound and to protect themselves from blood-borne infections (such as hepatitis and AIDS).

3. Apply a pressure dressing by elevating the wound, placing a gauze dressing over it, and applying direct pressure over the site of bleeding. If this method controls bleeding, then the trainer may wrap a long bandage or strip of cloth firmly over the gauze pad and tie it with the knot directly over the pad. If the pressure dressing does not control the bleeding, then it must be removed and direct pressure applied until emergency help arrives.

4. Place a victim who has lost a significant amount of blood, looks pale and sweaty, and has a weak pulse, in the shock position. Elevating the legs above the level of the heart assists venous return of blood to the heart.

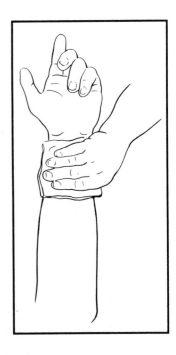

Figure 17–4   Direct pressure for hemorrhage control.

Caution: a tourniquet can be dangerous; it should only be used by medical personnel. Direct pressure and the measures discussed above will control nearly all bleeding wounds. A tourniquet shuts off the down-stream blood supply to the extremity. All viable tissue will die. Medical personnel may consider using a tourniquet only under life-threatening conditions, bearing in mind that its use means saving a life at the cost of losing a limb.

PREVENTING INFECTION.   Contamination of a wound leads to infection, and open wounds are vulnerable to contamination from several sources, including the sharp or blunt object that inflicted the injury, air-borne bacteria and particles, and normal skin bacteria. To minimize risk of infection, the personal trainer may take several measures:

1. Remove all debris, such as wood splinters, pieces of glass, clothing particles, or dirt, by gently flushing the wound with warm water. In a superficial wound, the trainer may remove embedded particles by gently brushing them off with a cotton swab or pulling them out with tweezers. Particles embedded deep in a wound should be left for a physician to remove, because pulling them out could disrupt an artery or sever a tendon or nerve.

2. Encourage the victim to wash a superficial wound with mild soap and warm water, rinsing thoroughly with warm running tap water. The wound may be blotted gently with a clean towel or sterile piece of gauze and covered with a dry sterile bandage. If signs of infection develop—redness, warmth, swelling, tenderness—the victim should seek medical attention.

3. Obtain immediate medical attention for any wound that may need stitches. Delay in closure of the wound increases infection risk.

4. Place a dressing over any open wound to protect it from additional contamination. The dressing may be secured with tape or a gauze strip.

FIRST AID FOR CLOSED WOUNDS.   Closed wounds typically result from external forces, such as a fall or a blow from a blunt object (a racquetball hitting the body or a free-weight falling onto it, for example). Even when the skin has no visible break, injury may still occur to underlying skin and other organs, muscles, tendons, ligaments, and bones.   Internal bleeding may produce a contusion (bruise), hematoma (collection of blood), or bleeding within the body cavity. Closed wounds are much less susceptible to infection than open wounds because the skin keeps out environmental bacteria. Although most closed wounds heal by themselves, some may involve deep structures with significant internal bleeding. Here are some tips for the personal trainer in managing a closed wound:

1. If the wound is minor, apply ice to the area to reduce swelling and slow bleeding within the tissues.

2. If the victim has no outward sign of injury but complains of pain and tenderness, suspect an internal injury. **Call paramedics immediately if the following signs and symptoms appear:**

- Pale, cool, and clammy skin; rapid and weak pulse; victim complains of lightheadedness. These may be signs of shock from internal bleeding.

- Extreme pain and tenderness over the injured area.

- Restlessness, confusion, or coma. These may be signs of head injury or insufficient oxygen to the brain.

- Vomiting or coughing up blood; blood in urine or feces. These may be signs of significant injury to the chest or gastrointestinal tract.

- Rapid, painful, or difficult breathing (dyspnea). Breathing difficulty may result from injury to the chest wall (ribs, cartilage, muscles) or to the respiratory system.

3. Examine the victim's extremities for swelling, discoloration, or deformity that might indicate a fracture or dislocation. If these indications are present, avoid moving that body part. Keep the victim quiet and wait for help to arrive. The limb may be immobilized using simple splinting techniques if the victim *must* be moved before paramedics arrive (see Fractures).

SPRAINS.   When the ligaments that normally stabilize a joint tear, the resulting **sprain** can range from a simple twist that causes minimal symptoms to a complete tearing of the ligaments that produces an unstable joint, severe pain, and swelling. The ankle is the most commonly sprained joint, typically from an inversion injury (turning in of the foot) caused by landing off balance or exercising on an irregular floor surface. When a joint is sprained, the victim may hear a popping sound if a significant tear has occurred. Pain, swelling, discoloration, or inability to bear weight may also be present. It is often difficult to distinguish between a sprain and a fracture without X-rays. Treatment of a sprain consists of RICE (rest, ice, compression, elevation). If a sprain is suspected, the personal trainer should:

1. Stop all activity immediately and have the victim rest the injured extremity.

2. Apply an elastic bandage and ice to the injury. Elevate it to minimize swelling.

3. If pain or swelling is severe, do not allow the victim to walk. Immobilize the extremity with simple splinting maneuvers, and arrange for transportation to a hospital emergency room where the limb can be examined for fracture or other disabling injury.

MUSCLE STRAINS.   A tear in a muscle or its tendon, a muscle **strain** is often called a "pulled muscle." This injury can be minor, involving less than 5 percent of the muscle fibers, or it can be severe, with complete disruption of the muscle or its tendon, and it can result from several sources. The muscle may have been warmed up insufficiently before vigorous use, or it may have been overtrained and fatigued. It may have been weakened by a previous injury. A tense muscle or tendon may be injured in movements that demand flexibility. And muscles exposed to cold weather have less capability of contracting than normal. The following are symptoms of a muscle strain:

- At the moment of injury, a sharp pain is felt; contracting the injured muscle reproduces this pain.

- Localized tenderness and swelling may occur over the damaged muscle or tendon.

- Pain may inhibit the muscle from contracting if it is partially torn; the muscle will not be able to contract at all if completely torn.

- Bruising and discoloration may appear 12–24 hours after the injury.

Treatment of minor muscle strain consists of RICE (rest, ice, compression, elevation). If the injury affects the leg and walking causes discomfort, the victim should use crutches until medical evaluation can be obtained.

Fractures

A **fracture**, a break in a bone, may be closed or open. A closed (simple) fracture has no opening from outside the skin to the broken bone. An open (compound) fracture, which is more serious, results when the broken ends of the bone pierce the skin, or when a sharp object penetrates the skin and fractures the underlying bone. In either case, the opening between the skin and the injured bone brings a high risk of infection. A fracture is a serious injury not only because the bone is broken, but because of the potential injury in the surrounding soft tissue. Tendons, ligaments, muscles, nerves, and blood vessels may be damaged, with a threat of permanent disability. Fractures may result from a direct blow or a more indirect cause, such as a fall. Following are signs of possible bone fracture:

- Audible snap at time of injury.

- Abnormal motion or position of the injured limb.

- Inability to bear weight on the limb (stand or walk).

- Swelling.

Figure 17–5 Splinting the forearm: The bone has been immobilized by newspaper that has been rolled up, padded with a towel, and tied with strips of material to hold the splint in place. Using a sling in combination with the splint will immobilize the joints below the fracture (wrist) and above the fracture (elbow). The sling also elevates the hand slightly above the elbow to minimize swelling.

- Deformity.

- Discoloration.

- Pain or tenderness to the touch.

FIRST AID FOR SUSPECTED FRACTURE. Immediate care for a victim with a suspected fracture has the goals of controlling hemorrhage, preventing further injury to the bone and soft tissue, and providing first aid for shock, if necessary. A personal trainer who suspects a fracture should take the following steps:

1. Keep the victim quiet; do not allow him/her to move the injured part or attempt to put weight on it.

2. Remove or cut away clothing that covers the injury. This step allows more thorough assessment and prevents contamination of an open fracture.

3. Cover an open fracture with a sterile gauze dressing or clean cloth to prevent further contamination. Control hemorrhage by applying pressure over the bleeding site with a gloved hand and a gauze pad. If a protruding bone makes it impossible to apply direct pressure, call for paramedic transport immediately and keep the victim lying down to improve circulation to the heart and brain.

4. Leave the protruding ends of bone in place. Attempting to push them back in will increase risk of infection and further injury to soft tissue.

5. If emergency transportation will be delayed, or if the injury is not too serious, splint the limb to immobilize it. However, if rapid ambulance service is available, or if the extremity is grossly deformed and splinting may be difficult, merely prevent the injured limb from moving until medical help arrives. An untrained person's attempts to move a fractured limb can convert a closed fracture into an open one, or cause nerve and vascular injury in an uncomplicated fracture.

SPLINTING TECHNIQUES. Splinting or immobilizing a fractured limb protects it against further injury during transportation, reduces pain, and prevents bone fragments from injuring arteries or other tissues. Many household objects or pieces of equipment in a health club may be converted to emergency splints—any object that provides support and prevents movement. Some examples include heavy cardboard, newspapers, rolled blankets or towels, exercise mats, and straight sticks. The splint should simply be long enough to extend past the joints above and below the suspected fracture and should be padded to prevent pressure injuries from hard surfaces or sharp edges.

To splint a limb, the personal trainer needs to recruit assistance from a bystander for the following procedure:

- The trainer places one hand above and one below the fracture site, while the helper slips the splint beneath the extremity. Any movement of the fracture site should be avoided. The trainer can then tie cloth strips around the splint to hold it in place.

- The victim's pulse, skin color, and sensation **distal** to the fracture site must be checked before and after splinting. If the splint is too tight, constricting the arteries, the limb may lose its pulse or become cyanotic. If the victim complains of numbness, tingling, or inability to move fingers or toes, the cloth ties must be loosened immediately to prevent permanent nerve damage.

Figures 17–5 and 17–6 illustrate properly applied splints of the forearm and ankle, using materials commonly found in the home or health club.

Head Injuries

Typically the result of a blow or a fall, head injuries are less common than extremity injuries, but their complications can produce long-term disability. Thus, it is important for the personal trainer to be able to identify a potential head injury and take appropriate precautions. When the skull accelerates or decelerates suddenly, the brain can move within the skull, and its impact on the skull may injure the brain. Bleeding may occur within the brain tissue, as in cerebral contusions (bruising of the brain) and hematomas (collection of blood). Bleeding may also occur from vessels between the brain's covering membranes. Because the skull is a rigid bony structure filled with brain tissue, it contains little room for expansion. Any bleeding or tissue swelling exerts compression force against the brain cells, resulting in serious neurological damage.

Symptoms of head injury may be fairly minor, such as headache, dizziness, nausea, and vomiting. They may be severe, including speech disturbance, partial or complete paralysis, seizures, and coma. A force strong enough to cause a temporary loss of consciousness is strong enough to cause serious complications or death. **Any victim of head injury who loses consciousness, however briefly, needs immediate transportation to a hospital emergency department for neurological evaluation.**

Visible signs of trauma to the head or face are further clues that hidden injury to the brain may have occurred. A laceration or large hematoma of the scalp (collection of blood under the scalp that feels like a large bump) needs a physician's attention. Signs of possible skull fracture include discoloration and swelling around the eyes (raccoon sign), visible blood in the ear canals, clear fluid draining from the nose or ears. This seepage may be cerebrospinal fluid, the fluid that surrounds the brain and spinal cord. A fractured skull needs further evaluation that may include a radiological scan or observation in the hospital. The excessive force required to fracture the skull may have also produced injury to the underlying brain.

Head injuries seldom occur in isolation. Damage to the cervical spine (neck) accompanies 15–20 percent of head injuries, so it should always be considered in caring for the victim, especially a victim with altered mental status, unconsciousness, or any of the visible signs listed previously. The personal trainer must take precautions to immobilize the neck, thereby preventing disabling injury. When in doubt, the trainer should always protect the cervical spine until the victim is thoroughly examined by a physician and X-rays are taken. With a comatose victim whose airway is compromised, jaw-thrust maneuver will assist the airflow without moving the neck. Paramedics are needed immediately to open the airway and transport the victim to the hospital.

Neck and Back Injuries

AIRWAY COMPROMISE. Blunt force against the front of the neck, the face, or the jaw can produce airway compromise. For example, a client may bench

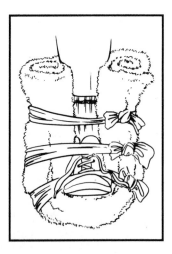

Figure 17–6 Splinting the ankle: Remove the victim's shoe and check circulation and sensation. If the shoe cannot be removed without moving the leg, just loosen the laces. Splint the ankle using a rolled blanket (or exercise mat), applying it around the ankle and sole of the foot and tying it into place with cloth strips.

Figure 17–7 Immobilization of the head and neck: Kneel at the victim's head, place your hands on either side of the head and neck, and hold firmly in place. Keep the victim quiet and prevent movement of the head. Do not try to reposition the victim.

press too much weight, become fatigued, and drop the barbell on the front of his or her neck. Extensive swelling may occur around the trachea, or the larynx may fracture, either of which may result in airway obstruction. Time is critical. Paramedics should be summoned immediately for rapid transport to a hospital, where a surgical airway (tracheostomy) may be necessary. If the victim sustains a respiratory arrest, the personal trainer should begin mouth-to-mouth or mouth-to-mask ventilations while waiting for help to arrive.

SPINAL CORD INJURY. Injuries to the vertebral column occur most frequently when excessive force is applied from the top or bottom, as in a fall or a dive into a shallow pool. The resulting fractures or dislocation of the vertebrae disrupt the ligaments that hold the bones in place. The spinal cord, normally protected within the vertebral canal, may be injured, the blood supply to the cord interrupted, and neurological dysfunction with paralysis may result.

It is extremely important to keep in mind the possibility of a vertebral injury for any victim of head trauma, or for someone with several areas of trauma. It is easy to overlook the neck during the initial assessment when, for example, a large laceration of bony deformity dominates one's impressions. However, many victims of multiple trauma also have spinal cord injuries. Anyone with one or more of the following signs should be considered to have an injured spinal cord for purposes of first aid:

- Altered level of consciousness.
- Obvious numbness, tingling, weakness, or paralysis.
- A fall or injury that might have injured the spinal cord.
- Head or facial injury.
- Pain or tenderness over the spine.
- Swelling or deformity over the spine.

EMERGENCY RESPONSE TO NECK AND BACK INJURY.   Initial management of a neck or back injury is extremely important to the long-term outcome. Improper management may turn a simple bony injury into permanent neurological disability and paralysis. Following are techniques to protect the spinal cord while help is on the way:

1. Handle the victim carefully, avoiding movement of the head and neck or bending of the neck. Simply hold the head and neck stationary to prevent the victim from moving until help arrives (see Fig. 17–7).

2. Do not attempt to move the victim until an ambulance arrives with trained emergency technicians equipped with spinal immobilization devices.

3. If the victim's airway is compromised or he/she requires artificial respirations, keep the victim lying flat on his/her back or side, do not attempt to reposition the victim, and avoid hyperextension of the neck. The most effective and appropriate airway maneuver is the jaw-thrust.

SUMMARY

A personal trainer who will be working closely with clients of various ages and fitness levels needs (1) a basic knowledge of common injuries and medical emergencies, and (2) a well-thought-out plan of action of all emergencies. Although this chapter is not comprehensive, it has presented most of the common medical emergencies the trainer might encounter and first-aid procedures for responding to them.

All trainers should be competent in CPR and should take additional training in first aid. A well-stocked and systematically maintained first-aid kit should always be near at hand, whether the trainer works in a health club or in a client's home. The trainer's ability to recognize a true emergency, as well as the trainer's ability to respond correctly, can play a critical role in the ultimate outcome of an illness or injury. Immediate treatment for such common injuries as sprains and strains can reduce pain and swelling and shorten a client's recovery time. A trainer familiar with the signs of a heart attack, insulin shock, or seizure can save a life. Finally, it is important to remember that a trainer should never attempt to provide medical advice. Instead, the trainer's responsibility is to provide immediate first aid, refer injured clients to their physicians, and, when necessary, call for emergency aid.

REFERENCES

Sperling, M.A. (Ed.). (1988). *Physician's guide to insulin-dependent (type I) diabetes*. Alexandria, VA: American Diabetes Association.

American Red Cross. (1979). *Standard first aid and personal safety* (2nd ed.). Washington, DC.

Kulund, Daniel. (1982). *The injured athlete*. Philadelphia: Lippincott.

Peterson, L., & Renstrom, P. (1986). *Sports injuries: Their prevention and treatment*. London: Year Book Publishers.

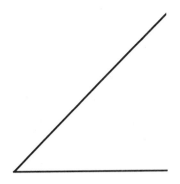

Legal Issues

PART VII

The previous parts of this manual have focused on the design, development, and implementation of quality exercise programs. This final part highlights legal issues, an area often overlooked by the fitness professional. An understanding of legal guidelines, professional responsibilities, and business practices is paramount to the long-term success of the client/trainer relationship. Trainers are not only responsible for the development of high-quality programs; they are also accountable for their actions. Providing fitness instruction is a business, and with it comes all the responsibilities associated with any business. The following should provide the fitness professional with some basic guidelines. In addition, however, it is recommended that the trainer consult both a lawyer and an insurance agent.

Legal Guidelines and Professional Responsibilities

David K. Stotlar

18

DAVID K. STOTLAR, ED.D., teaches sport management and sport law and is director of the School of Kinesiology and Physical Education at the University of Northern Colorado. A consultant, author, and lecturer, he conducts safety audits in conjunction with Fitness Risk Management, Inc., has contributed to numerous publications, and conducts management seminars throughout the world.

IN THIS CHAPTER:

- Employment status: independent contractors vs. employees, contracts.

- Business structure: sole proprietorship, partnership, corporation.

- Legal responsibilities: scope of practice, facilities, equipment, testing, instruction, supervision.

- Legal concepts and defenses: standard of care, assumption of risk (informed consent, waivers, and warnings), negligence.

- Other concerns: liability insurance, music copyright, certification, risk management.

Although personal fitness trainers may be well trained and comfortable with their responsibilities for designing exercise programs and working with clients, they may be far less comfortable with legal concepts important to running a fitness business. This chapter is intended to increase that comfort level and to address some of the legal and business concerns most commonly encountered by fitness trainers. It will also describe the scope of practice in fitness training and summarize the legal responsibilities of trainers. The guidelines offered here, while based on sport law and the experience of fitness professionals, are not intended as legal advice but, rather, as guidance to assist the fitness trainer's understanding. Trainers should always consult lawyers in their own states for specific legal questions and problems.

INDEPENDENT CONTRACTORS VS. EMPLOYEES

Personal trainers who work in clubs may be either **independent contractors** or employees, while self-employed personal trainers are usually independent contractors. This term has evolved from the concept of a leased employee. For example, a homeowner might hire a bulldozer and an operator to move some dirt in the backyard. The bulldozer operator would not legally be considered the homeowner's employee, but rather an employee of the bulldozer company. The driver merely came along with the equipment, making the bulldozer company responsible for any negligent actions of the driver. Similarly, clients who hire personal trainers do not usually intend to hire them as employees but prefer to lease their services for a brief period, to hire independent contractors.

Some owners of fitness clubs use independent contractors so that the club can avoid the expense of training, medical benefits, social security withholding, worker's compensation, or unemployment coverage for these workers. However, most clubs still require independent contractors to follow club rules. Clubs may also prefer to deal with independent contractors because it is harder legally to fire an employee than simply not to renew a contract.

Many personal trainers enjoy the freedom of the independent contractor status, including:

- Choosing when and where to work.
- Charging variable fees for different situations.
- Having professional freedom in conducting work.

These freedoms must be weighed against the disadvantages of having no employer to provide training, benefits, or equipment.

Legal Tests

Both independent contractors and club employees must be certain that all details of their agreements are clear from the beginning of their work with a fitness club or center. Often the legal nature of the relationship is ambiguous, and people have filed lawsuits attempting to collect worker's compensation or unemployment insurance from clubs that consider them independent contractors. Personal trainers, both as employees and as independent contractors, have found themselves without health benefits or insurance coverage. In addition, trainers have discovered the penalties of neglecting payments to tax and social security accounts during the year, assuming that the clubs with which they worked were paying into the accounts for them. Clubs only do this for people they consider employees, not for independent contractors.

Court cases have established 10 legal tests for determining whether someone is an employee or an independent contractor. These tests include the following:

1. How much control can the employer exercise over the details of the work? The right to control indicates an employer-employee relationship.

2. Are people paid by the hour or by the job? People paid regularly by the hour or by the week have generally been considered employees. On the other hand, people who receive a single payment for services rendered can more easily qualify as independent contractors.

3. How long has the person been working in this establishment? People hired for short periods (a few days or weeks) are more easily defined as independent contractors than people employed over several months or years.

4. How much training does the person need? If the worker brings specialized or technical skills to the employer, the worker typically may be considered an independent contractor. On the other hand, if the employer provides training to a recently hired person, the court usually considers the person an employee.

5. Does the person provide services to more than one client or business? If so, this person may be seen more easily as an independent contractor. If the person provides services for only one business or client, he/she would probably be considered an employee.

6. Who provides the equipment? In general, independent contractors provide their own equipment. However, using the club's or client's weights or other heavy equipment, in itself, would not disqualify a trainer from independent contractor status.

7. Is the work integral to the business? If so, the worker will more likely be considered an employee. Supplemental services have been more likely to support the status of independent contractorship.

8. Is the work traditionally performed by an independent contractor or an employee in other clubs? Current practices in the field may help determine if a trainer is an employee or an independent contractor.

9. What did the club and the trainer intend when they made their agreement? If the trainer believed he/she was hired as an independent contractor, and so did the club, the court would attempt to enforce their original intent.

10. Is the employer engaged in business? If a client hires a trainer to perform fitness training, the court will probably consider the trainer an independent contractor. The intent is to protect clients from being construed as employers.

All of these questions have arisen in court cases over employment status, each with varying degrees of authority. Both personal trainers and clubs must understand these issues when they initiate agreements.

CONTRACTS

To perform their work, get paid for it, and avoid costly legal battles with clients and employers, personal trainers need an adequate knowledge of legal contracts. Whether they work as individuals or as employees of a club or fitness center, they must be aware of basic contract law. The following elements are necessary for a binding contract:

- An offer and acceptance, with mutual agreement on terms.

- Consideration—an exchange of valuable items, such as money for services.

- Legality—acceptable form under the law.

- Ability of the parties to enter into a contract, with respect to legal age and mental capacity.

For example, personal trainers may talk to prospective clients and mention the services they can provide, such as designing individualized exercise sessions three days per week to meet the client's goals. Trainers and clients may also agree on dates and times for exercise sessions. This negotiation constitutes an offer and acceptance. Stating a fee of $50 per hour for services sets up an exchange of consideration, training services for money. Once these negotiations have been accomplished, the trainer should prepare a written contract by filling out a basic contract form or by having one specifically written for each agreement. In either case, trainers should consult legal counsel to assure that the written form is valid under contract law. This document becomes a valid contract when signed by both the trainer and the client, if both are of legal age to enter into contracts.

Personal trainers beginning in business may feel that written contracts are unnecessary, that a brief chat—or oral contract—and a handshake are enough. However, in case of misunderstanding or injury, legal complications can arise from such a simple oral contract, which can be enforceable under law. Business matters are less likely to lead to problems when the parties put the contract in writing, spelling out details to avoid potentially expensive misunderstandings. It is useful to pay for the services of a lawyer to develop the basic agreement. The trainer can then personalize this basic agreement for each client, avoiding additional legal fees. Whether the contract is for use with clients or with a fitness club, the trainer and attorney should address the following considerations in developing it:

- Identification of the parties to the contract, such as trainer and client or club.
- Description of services (fitness training and consultation).
- Specification of compensation, payment method, or rate of compensation per hour, day, or month.
- Confidential relationship—an agreement by each party not to divulge personal or business information acquired through the relationship.
- Business or employment status.
- Term and termination, defining the length of the contract and the conditions under which termination will be allowed by either party.

BUSINESS STRUCTURE

Early in their professional lives, personal trainers must decide whether they are acting as individuals, as corporations, or as employees of fitness centers. The fitness trainer who wishes to conduct business independently from a fitness center or club has three types of business structures available: sole proprietorship, partnership, and corporation.

Sole Proprietorship

As the name implies, a **sole proprietorship** is a business owned and operated by one person. This person owns all assets and is responsible for all income, losses, and liabilities. Forming a sole proprietorship establishes a legal right to conduct a business and gives the owner legal title to it. The owner—the personal fitness trainer, for example—has sole control over decisions and profits. This business structure also offers the advantages of ease and low cost when the business is started. Furthermore, profits are taxed at the owner's individual rate, which is typically lower than a corporate rate. The owner reports income and taxes on a schedule attached to the personal income tax form instead of a separate business tax return. Government regulation is minimal compared with other business structures.

However, the risk of liability is a drawback that often convinces people to choose other business structures. In sole proprietorships, the owner is completely responsible for all liabilities, court awards, or damages incurred by the business. An injured person who sues the owner and wins a sizeable judgment can be awarded, if necessary, the proceeds from seizure of the owner's personal savings and property, such as house and auto. If the owner's business liabilities exceed personal assets, the owner could be paying years into the future for today's problems.

Another disadvantage of sole proprietorships is the difficulty the owner has in getting away from the business for vacations, illness, or emergencies. It may be impossible to find someone to watch the shop with the same care and interest as the owner. Often, the owner does not recognize these pressures in the early days of establishing the business, not until the stress and pressure of successful operation suggest a break from the daily routine.

Partnership

When two or more people agree to operate a business, sharing profits and losses, they can form a partnership. For example, two personal trainers could form a company, or a trainer could become a partner in the ownership of a club. Although partnerships may be loosely created without legal documents, serious business relationships benefit from a partnership agreement that establishes rules of operation. This agreement should lay out the structure for authority, the partner's rights, expected performance and contributions from each partner, buy-out clauses, income distribution, and responsibility for debts. The agreement should also stipulate whether the business is a general partnership or a limited partnership.

GENERAL PARTNERSHIP. In a general partnership, all partners are fully liable for the actions of the business. For example, suppose that you and a friend go into business as Metroplex Personal Trainers. You will be the personal trainer, and your friend will run the office as well as do the marketing and promotion. Because the business was your idea, you have put up $50,000 to get started; your friend agrees to work at minimum wage until things get rolling. Early on, a video company approaches your friend to produce and sell videotapes to your clients as part of the fitness package. Your friend agrees to a deal for $25,000, payable in 90 days. Shortly thereafter, your friend suffers a breakdown, gets a divorce, squanders all personal assets, and stops managing the business. After the 90 days, the video company demands its $25,000. Regardless of your profit-sharing agreement, the video company can legally collect from *you* all the money owed. It makes no difference that you owned only 50 percent of the business, or that you had an agreement that each partner would be responsible for only 50 percent of debts. You are also liable for all debts if a court judgment is entered against your partner for activities of the business. You could sue your partner to try to recover your losses, but you might never benefit financially from your suit.

LIMITED PARTNERSHIP. To avoid such devastating personal liability, limited partnerships allow certain partners, usually those who have invested in the business, to limit their liability to the amount of money they have contributed. The law usually prevents these limited partners from taking an active role in managing the business. Although it might seem intriguing to limit financial liability by organizing a business with only limited partners, the law also requires that at least one partner be designated as a *general* partner. The general partner may be anyone in the business, typically the person who runs the day-to-day operations. General partners are personally liable, while limited partners risk only their original investment.

All partnerships have the same tax advantage as sole proprietorships: profits are taxed at personal rates. This advantage makes partnerships attractive to investors because the partnership passes on to them the tax losses, credits, and deductions, while providing the limited partners with many of the legal protections they would ordinarily find only in corporate structures.

Corporations

Regulated by state laws, corporations exist as legal entities independent of their owners. They are taxed separately from their owners, and corporate assets may be easily sold or transferred. In most cases, any number of people may own the corporation through shares issued by the business. Typically, the shareholders elect a board of directors to represent their interests. Fitness trainers who intend to form a corporation will first choose a company name that has not been previously registered and then file a notice of incorporation with their state, paying the appropriate fees and designating a registered agent as a contact for the state. Applicants may retain attorneys to guide them through this process or may call their secretary of state directly. Often a friendly and knowledgeable state clerk can talk applicants through the incorporation procedures, saving them hundreds of dollars in legal fees.

Many businesses decide to form corporations to limit shareholder's financial liability. Creditors can attach assets of a corporation if it owes bills or has a judgment against it, but the personal assets of the corporate officers, board, and shareholders are typically not at risk for liabilities of the corporation. However, taxes can be more burdensome in a corporate structure. As an independent legal entity, a corporation must pay taxes, usually at a rate higher than for individuals. In addition, all corporate profits after taxes are paid as dividends to the shareholders, who in turn must declare them as income and pay taxes on them. This double taxation may be avoided if shareholders play an active part in the corporate management and draw salaries as managers. These salaries may offset the corporate profits, eliminating a tax on corporate earnings. The Internal Revenue Service requires that the salaries be reasonable for the work performed, and, of course, the salaries are subject to individual tax as earned income.

A second method of avoiding double taxation may be a better choice for personal trainers starting out: the S corporation. This structure passes its profits through to shareholders, where the income is taxed at the individual rate. S corporations have certain restrictions attached, such as limiting the number of shareholders to 35.

Few personal trainers will choose to take on the complicated tax structure, government regulations, and legal procedures necessary to begin and maintain a corporation. Most will simply register as sole proprietors at their county courthouses. In most cases, it will be helpful to consult a lawyer when making this choice. Table 18-1 offers a brief summary of the advantages and disadvantages of these business structures.

SCOPE OF PRACTICE

Whether trainers work as employees in fitness clubs or as independent businesspersons, they will find that clients ask for their advice on a variety of problems. Not only is it important for trainers to be well educated and familiar with their own discipline, but it is also important for trainers to understand the limitations of their practice. Personal fitness trainers are not usually licensed or qualified physicians, physical therapists, dietitians, marriage counselors, or social workers. They should avoid practicing these disciplines without appropriate training.

Table 18–1   ADVANTAGES AND DISADVANTAGES OF SOLE PROPRIETORSHIPS, PARTNERSHIPS, AND CORPORATIONS

Sole Proprietorships and Partnerships	Corporations
• Easily formed under the law	• Complicated legal requirements
• Low costs of formation	• High costs of formation
• Unlimited liability (except limited partners)	• Limited liability for corporate acts
• Typically can operate in different states without registration	• Must be registered in each state where business is conducted
• Owners pay taxes, but business does not	• Both corporation and owners are taxed, except for S corporation
• Minimal government regulation	• Extensive government regulation

Health Assessment

According to fitness law expert David Herbert (September 1989), "wellness-assessment documents should be utilized for . . . determination of an individual's level of fitness . . . never for the purpose of providing or recommending treatment of any condition." The personal trainer should use the health history form to screen the client for appropriate placement in a fitness program and to refer the client with potential risks to a physician for clearance before the program begins. The trainer who uses this form to recommend treatment could be accused of practicing medicine without a license. Far better to have a physician sign the form, indicating the types of training suitable for this client, or clear the client for exercise by writing a letter on the physician's letterhead. Some trainers prefer using the physician's letter to forestall the client's forging the doctor's signature on a fitness form. However, if a client fakes a physician's signature without the trainer's knowledge to obtain acceptance in a fitness program, the trainer would probably not be held liable.

Fitness trainers must understand and use the information collected on the personal history, asking only questions they know how to interpret or apply. Trainers who request information about types of medications may be held responsible for knowing the biochemical and physical reactions to these drugs. Trainers must read and fully understand the answers to other questions, as well. One sports administrator required all participants to complete health and physical appraisal forms and then filed them without reading them. When a participant who had noted his heart defect on his form died, the sports administrator had little legal defense in the ensuing lawsuit.

Nutritional Counseling

According to the American Dietetic Association, in 1989 only 26 states regulated or licensed nutritionists. In the other states, anyone can profess to be one. Personal trainers should check the laws in their own states to ensure they are not violating laws by advising clients about food, vitamins, or calorie consumption. Trainers should avoid giving advice on subjects in which they have not received training, in this area as in others. Clients with complex dietary questions should be referred to a registered dietitian (RD).

LEGAL RESPONSIBILITIES

Liability simply means responsibility. Certain obligations and responsibilities arise from the legal relationship between personal trainers and their clients, specifically those responsibilities that a court would recognize as part of a fitness professional's employment. These responsibilities may include facilities, equipment, supervision, instruction, and exercise recommendations and testing.

Facilities

Personal trainers have an obligation to make sure that the facilities they use are free from unreasonable hazards, a big problem for trainers who conduct exercise sessions in their clients' homes or in places of business where the trainer has little control over the setting. The trainer must select the workout area carefully, giving special attention to the following:

- Floor surface. Many exercises require floor surfaces that will cushion the feet, knees, and legs from excessive stress.

- Adequate free space around workout stations.

- Appropriate use of public spaces. Use of public beaches, parks, or public trails for business is illegal in some areas. Check with a local attorney.

- Ethical use of other business establishments. Accompanying a client into a fitness center may violate laws as well as ethical business practice. A local attorney can advise the fitness trainer.

The trainer's ultimate responsibility is the client's safety, so he/she must inspect facilities regularly, using a safety checklist. A trainer who notices unsafe facilities must notify the club management or the client. If a club owner does not repair the problem and someone is injured, the trainer is technically responsible, but juries have often looked favorably on employees who tried unsuccessfully to have management change dangerous conditions. However, a private client may not wish to follow suggestions for making a safer environment if it does not fit his or her home's decor. In this case, the client is assuming responsibility for these decisions. In either case, occasions may arise in which the environment is simply too dangerous for an exercise program, and the personal trainer must make a professional assessment and decision about whether to continue.

Equipment

Fitness programs incorporate a variety of equipment, and injuries by exercise equipment give rise to most of the litigation in the fitness industry. To protect both the client and the trainer, equipment should meet the highest safety and design standards. Homemade equipment should be avoided because it can increase the trainer's liability if it causes injuries. Trainers must be concerned about selection, maintenance, and repair, routinely inspecting equipment they use with clients.

Personal trainers may find a conflict between professional practice and legal protection when it comes to equipment owned by a client. A conservative legal stance would be to avoid any contact or adjustment to the client's equipment, but most personal trainers accept some liability by using their expertise to adjust client's equipment or to recommend maintenance. If a trainer arrived at a client's home for a first fitness session and found a leg extension machine with a frayed cable, for example, the trainer would be wise to inform the client that the equipment needed repairs, to suggest he/she call the company to order a replacement part, and then to conduct sessions without using this equipment until it had been repaired.

RECOMMENDATIONS. If a client asks for recommendations about exercise equipment, clothing, or shoes, the personal trainer should be cautious in giving advice, particularly if the trainer receives payment for endorsing a product or retail store. Before giving advice, the trainer should become completely knowledgeable about the products and equipment available, as well as their advantages and disadvantages. Otherwise, trainers should protect themselves by referring clients to their choice of retail sporting goods stores. Advice based solely on personal experience should be given with that express qualification.

Supervision

Although an instructor conducting a large aerobics class may have difficulty ensuring each client's safety, a personal trainer should always be in direct control, close to each client, to ensure safety. The trainer should never leave the client during an exercise session in which direct supervision is needed. A trainer who is working with a couple should find a position from which to observe both persons during activity without turning his/her back on one. If the trainer asks one client to perform an exercise that requires direct supervision, the other client should not be engaged in the same activity but rather one in which general observation could ensure safety. For example, the personal trainer would not ask one client to do squats with heavy weight while the other is doing a one-rep max in the bench press. The trainer could not spot both clients at the same time. It would be safer to have one client stretching or working out on a stationary bicycle while the other is lifting and being spotted. Proper supervision requires planning to ensure that each client can be monitored all the time.

It also requires adequate planning for emergencies (see Ch. 17). Personal trainers should keep with them during training sessions the emergency medical information each client provides before the first session, so that an emergency will not necessitate calling the office to get critical information about a client. The trainer should also ask each client about location and availability of a telephone for emergency use. Whether in independent practice or in a club, trainers should know how to activate the emergency medical system—in many areas by dialing 911. It is also critical to know the address where the trainer is working. A trainer may find it difficult to recall a client's exact address when telephoning for help during an emergency.

Instruction

To avoid potential litigation, instructional techniques should be consistent with current professional practices. A personal trainer who fails to demonstrate a movement or give proper instructions for use of equipment may be found negligent. Legal standards require that "adequate and proper" instruction be given to a client before and during an activity. In a courtroom, an expert witness could be asked to assess "proper" or factually correct instruction. Adequate and proper instruction also means avoiding contraindicated exercises, or those not recommended by professional peers. Advocating dangerous or controversial exercises puts the trainer at risk for a lawsuit if a client is injured.

A relatively new aspect of instructional liability concerns touching clients. Trainers should avoid touching a client unless it is essential in instruction. Furthermore, trainers should inform clients about the purpose of touching and should substitute a less offensive activity if the client objects. Charges of sexual assault, even if groundless, can have disastrous consequences for a personal trainer's career.

Exercise Recommendations and Testing

Many states allow medical prescriptions to be developed only by licensed doctors, so it is important for trainers to be sure they are providing exercise programs, not exercise prescriptions. Although the difference between these terms may sound like a technicality, it can become important in court. Trainers will be safer if they follow guidelines for exercise programs recommended by professional organizations such as the American Council on Exercise, the National Strength and Conditioning Association (NSCA), the American College of Sports Medicine (ACSM), and the American Heart Association (AHA). Of course, the age, medical history, and previous activity patterns of each client must be taken into consideration.

Personal fitness trainers may administer fitness assessments if the tests are recognized by a professional organization as appropriate for the intended use and are within the qualifications and training of the trainer. For example, the ACSM has established protocols for fitness assessments as well as training and certification in several areas of testing. The personal trainer should carefully follow ACSM procedures when conducting these tests, and should never attempt to administer a test without having been trained to do it. Personal trainers can legally administer tests that do not require maximum effort. However, trainers should not hook up electrodes and administer a maximum capacity test, such as a treadmill stress test, unless a physician is present. Any highly specialized testing should be referred to physicians or exercise physiologists. Some states regulate the administration of such tests as the Graded Exercise Tests (GXTs). In addition, some professional associations, such as ACSM, the American Heart Association, and the American College of Cardiology, provide certification for testing as well as guidelines for the role of physicians in GXTs.

The development of exercise technology has offered several dilemmas for personal trainers, among them the legal concern over monitoring clients who can attach electrodes to their chests and continuously monitor their heart rates while exercising. The personal trainer must make every effort to monitor clients during exercise, even with the fancy technology available. Failure to do so may constitute a breach of legal duty.

LEGAL CONCEPTS AND DEFENSES

As implied throughout this chapter, personal trainers must conduct their professional activities with high standards not only for their professional competence and training but also for their ethical and legal position. In court, certain concepts have special meanings that trainers must familiarize themselves with to protect their clients and themselves. Some of these concepts have been discussed previously. The remainder of this chapter will present several other concepts important to the personal trainer.

Standard of Care

A personal trainer's actions must be appropriate for the age, condition, and knowledge of the client, as well as for the program selected. To evaluate **standard of care**, a court would typically ask an expert witness to describe the current professional standards—what other fitness professionals of similar training would do (or should have done) in the same situation. This manual, for example, constitutes a standard for personal fitness training. In a legal dispute, a court would almost certainly look to the practices described in this manual to evaluate the appropriateness of a trainer's actions.

Assumption of Risk

If a client voluntarily accepts the dangers known to be part of an activity, the trainer can use the **assumption of risk** defense. However, the two important issues here are "voluntarily" and "known danger." If the client's participation was involuntary, this defense cannot be used. Furthermore, if the client was not informed about the specific risks of the program or test, the client cannot be held to have assumed them. Does this defense imply that a trainer must describe every injury that might occur? In general, yes, but the best way to take care of this issue is to use standard forms for informed consent (express assumption of risk) or waiver forms.

Known technically as exculpatory agreements, waivers, informed consents, and warnings fall under contract law and are often used by exercise leaders and fitness centers to absolve themselves of liability. Although many fitness professionals have little faith in the value of these documents, the courts have been increasingly willing to uphold them.

WAIVERS.   A voluntary abandonment of the right to file suit, **waivers** are used to release the personal trainer from liability for injuries resulting from an exercise program. Waivers must be clearly written and must state that the client waives all claims for damages, even those caused by the trainer's negligence (see Figs. 18-1 and 18-3). Occasionally, these documents have been so poorly worded that they had little value in court.

INFORMED CONSENT.   **Informed consent** refers to acknowledgement that one has been specifically informed about the risks in the activity one is about to engage in (see Fig. 18-3). Some personal trainers use an informed consent similar to a waiver (see Fig. 18-2) but primarily intended to communicate the dangers of the program or test procedures to the client. Trainers should obtain informed consent from every person who enters their programs and before every test administered. Nygaard and Boone (1989) recommend that a trainer should let the client know that questions about the program or testing are welcome, and that he/she is free to withdraw consent and discontinue participation at any time. The trainer should inform the client about:

- The exercise program or test, providing a thorough and unbiased explanation of the purpose of each.

- The risks and possible discomforts involved.

- The benefits expected.

- Alternatives that may be advantageous to the client.

WARNINGS. In one Colorado case, a health club's failure to warn a client of the dangers of an activity and a piece of equipment was judged "willful and wanton" misconduct. Personal trainers should obtain signed proof that they have warned their clients about foreseeable hazards and risks. Case law about the validity of waivers, warnings, and informed consent documents is complicated. One such case, *Brown v. Racquetball Centers, Inc.* (1987), shows that the specific wording of the form is critical in the eyes of the court. In this case, the form did not contain language that clearly stated the risks of participating in the program (Herbert, July 1989). Other cases demonstrate support by the courts for well-written waivers (*Gimpel v. Host Enterprises Inc., 1986; Schlobohm vs. Spa Petite (1982); Larsen v. Vic Tanny International, 1984*). Courts prefer to deal with these issues on a case-by-case basis. Personal trainers should consult attorneys in their own states and provide examples to give the attorneys a model.

Negligence

Someone who fails to perform as a reasonable and prudent person would under similar circumstances is considered negligent. This definition has two important components: failure to act, and appropriateness of the action. A person can be sued both for neglecting to do something that should have been done, such as not spotting a client in a free-weight bench press, and for doing something that should not have been done, such as prescribing straight-leg sit-ups for a client with low-back problems. This action may be found inappropriate as compared with what a reasonable and prudent professional would do.

To substantiate a charge of **negligence** in court, the plaintiff must establish four elements:

- The defendant had a duty to protect the plaintiff from injury.

- The defendant failed to exercise the standard of care necessary to perform that duty.

- Damage or injury to the plaintiff occurred.

- This damage or injury was caused by the defendant's breach of duty (proximate causation).

Negligence in personal training could occur, for example, if a personal trainer agreed to provide fitness instruction that included instruction and supervision (*duties*) in weight lifting, and during the first session told the client he/she would spot him/her during a lift but failed to do so (*breach of duty*). Perhaps the client suffered broken ribs and was unable to work for three months, incurring both medical bills and lost wages (*damages*). The damages would not have occurred except for the trainer's failure to spot for the client during the lift (*proximate causation*).

CONTRIBUTORY NEGLIGENCE. If the client played some role in getting injured, a few states provide a total bar to recovery for damages (check your state laws). For example, the client might exceed the recommended heart rate in a recommended exercise program. It would also be important to determine whether the trainer was present when the client was hurt, or whether the client was exercising alone and following the trainer's guidelines. If present, the trainer might have noticed the client's overexertion and warned him/her about exceeding the recommendations.

COMPARATIVE NEGLIGENCE. A court may apportion guilt and any subsequent award for damages, measuring the relative fault of both the plaintiff and

---

AGREEMENT AND RELEASE OF LIABILITY

1. In consideration of being allowed to participate in the activities and programs of _____ and to use its facilities, equipment and machinery in addition to the payment of any fee or charge, I do hereby waive, release, and forever discharge _____ and its officers, agents, employees, representatives, executors, and all others from any and all responsibilities or liability from injuries or damages resulting from my participation in any activities or my use of equipment or machinery in the above mentioned activities. I do also hereby release all of those mentioned and any others acting upon their behalf from any responsibility or liability for any injury or damage to myself, including those caused by the negligent act or omission of any of those mentioned or others acting on their behalf or in any way arising out of or connected with my participation in any activities of _____ or the use of any equipment at _____ .(Please initial _____)

2. I understand and am aware that strength, flexibility, and aerobic exercise, including the use of equipment, is a potentially hazardous activity. I also understand that fitness activities involve a risk of injury and even death, and that I am voluntarily participating in these activities and using equipment and machinery with knowledge of the dangers involved. I hereby agree to expressly assume and accept any and all risks of injury or death. (Please initial _____)

3. I do hereby further declare myself to be physically sound and suffering from no condition, impairment, disease, infirmity, or other illness that would prevent my participation or use of equipment of machinery except as hereinafter stated. I do hereby acknowledge that I have been informed of the need for a physician's approval for my participation in an exercise/fitness activity or in the use of exercise equipment and machinery. I also acknowledge that it has been recommended that I have a yearly or more frequent physical examination and consultation with my physician as to physical activity, exercise, and use of exercise and training equipment so that I might have his/her recommendations concerning these fitness activities and equipment use. I acknowledge that I have either had a physical examination and been given my physician's permission to participate, or that I have decided to participate in activity and use of equipment and machinery without the approval of my physician and do hereby assume all responsibility for my participation and activities, and utilization of equipment and machinery in my activities.

_____   _____
Date   Signature

Figure 18–1   Sample waiver of liability reprinted with permission from Koeberle, B. E., *Legal Aspects of Personal Fitness Training* pages 154-155, Copyright 1990 by Professional Reports Corporation, Canton, Ohio 44718-3629. All rights reserved.

INFORMED CONSENT FOR EXERCISE TESTING PROCEDURES OF APPARENTLY HEALTHY ADULTS

Name _____

1. Purpose and Explanation of Test

It is my understanding that I will undergo a test to be performed on a motor driven treadmill or bicycle ergometer with the amount of effort gradually increasing. As I understand it, this increase in effort will continue until I feel and verbally report to the operator any symptoms such as fatigue, shortness of breath, or chest discomfort which may appear. It is my understanding and I have been clearly advised that it is my right to request that a test be stopped at any point if I feel unusual discomfort or fatigue. I have been advised that I should immediately upon experiencing any such symptoms, or if I so choose, inform the operator that I wish to stop the test at that or any other point. My stated wishes in this regard shall be carried out. **IF CORRECT AND YOU AGREE AND UNDERSTAND, INITIAL HERE** _____.

It is further my understanding that prior to beginning the test, I will be connected by electrodes and cables to an electrocardiographic recorder which will enable the program personnel to monitor my cardiac (heart) activity. During the test itself, it is my understanding that a trained observer will monitor my responses continuously and take frequent readings of blood pressure, the electrocardiogram, and my expressed feelings of effort. I realize that a true determination of my exercise capacity depends on progressing the test to the point of my fatigue. Once the test has been completed, but before I am released from the test area, I will be given special instructions about showering and recognition of certain symptoms which may appear within the first 24 hours after the test. I agree to follow these instructions and promptly contact the program personnel or medical providers if such symptoms develop. **IF CORRECT, AND YOU AGREE AND UNDERSTAND INITIAL HERE** _____.

Before I undergo the test, I certify to the program that I am in good health and have had a physical examination conducted by a licensed medical physician within the last _____ months. Further, I hereby represent and inform the program that I have accurately completed the pre-test history interview presented to me by the program staff and have provided correct responses to the questions as indicated on the history form or as supplied to the interviewer. It is my understanding that I will be interviewed by a physician or other person prior to my undergoing the test who will, in the course of interviewing me, determine if there are any reasons which would make it undesirable or unsafe for me to take the test. Consequently, I understand that it is important that I provide complete and accurate responses to the interviewer and recognize that my failure to do so could lead to possible unnecessary injury to myself during the test. **IF CORRECT, AND YOU AGREE INITIAL HERE** _____.

Figure 18–2   Sample informed consent form

2. Risks

It is my understanding that there exists the possibility of adverse changes during the actual test. I have been informed that these changes could include abnormal blood pressure, fainting, disorders of heart rhythm, and very rare instances of heart attack or even death. These risks include, but are not necessarily limited to, the possibility of stroke or other cerebrovascular incident or occurrence; mental, physiological, motor, visual or hearing injuries, deficiencies, difficulties or disturbances; partial or total paralysis; slips, falls, or other unintended loss of balance or bodily movement related to the exercise treadmill (or bicycle ergometer) which may cause muscular, neurological, orthopedic, or other bodily injury; as well as a variety of other possible occurrences any one of which could conceivably, however remotely, cause bodily injury, impairment, disability, or death. Any procedure such as this one carries with it some risk however unlikely or remote. THERE ARE ALSO OTHER RISKS OF INJURY, IMPAIRMENT, DISABILITY, DISFIGUREMENT, AND EVEN DEATH. **I ACKNOWLEDGE AND AGREE TO ASSUME ALL RISK. IF YOU UNDERSTAND AND AGREE, INITIAL HERE** _____.

I have been told every effort will be made to minimize these occurrences by preliminary examination and by precautions and observations taken during the test. I have also been informed that emergency equipment and personnel are readily available to deal with these unusual situations should they occur.

Knowing and understanding all risks, it is my desire to proceed to take the test as herein described. **IF CORRECT AND YOU AGREE AND UNDERSTAND, INITIAL HERE** _____.

3. Benefits to be Expected and Alternatives Available to the Exercise Testing Procedure

I understand and have been told that the results of this test may or may not benefit me. Potential benefits relate mainly to my personal motives for taking the test, i.e., knowing my exercise capacity in relation to the general population, understanding my fitness for certain sports and recreational activities. Although my fitness might also be evaluated by alternative means, e.g., a bench step test or an outdoor running test, such tests do not provide as accurate a fitness assessment as the treadmill or bike test nor do those options allow equally effective monitoring of my responses. **IF YOU UNDERSTAND, INITIAL HERE** _____.

4. Consent

I hereby consent to voluntarily engage in an exercise test to determine my circulatory and respiratory fitness. I also consent to the taking of samples of my exhaled air during exercise to properly measure my oxygen consumption. I also consent, if necessary, to have a small blood sample drawn by needle from my arm for blood chemistry analysis, and to the performance of lung function and body-fat (skinfold pinch) tests. It is my understanding that the information obtained will help me evaluate future physical fitness and sports activities in which I may engage. **IF CORRECT AND YOU AGREE, INITIAL HERE** _____.

Figure 18–2(cont.)   Sample informed consent form

5. Confidentiality and Use of Information

I have been informed that the information which is obtained in this exercise test will be treated as privileged and confidential and will consequently not be released or revealed to any person without my express written consent. I do, however, agree to the use of any information for research or statistical purposes, so long as same does not provide facts which could lead to the identification of my person. Any other information obtained, however, will be used only by the program staff to evaluate my exercise status or needs. **IF YOU AGREE, INITIAL HERE** _____.

6. Inquiries and Freedom of Consent

I have been given an opportunity to ask questions as to the procedures. Generally these requests which have been noted by the testing staff and their responses are as follows:

_____

_____

_____

_____

IF THIS NOTATION IS COMPLETE AND CORRECT, INITIAL HERE _____

I acknowledge that I have read this document in its entirety or that it has been read to me if I have been unable to read same.

I consent to the rendition of all services and procedures as explained herein by all program personnel.
Date _____

_____   _____
Witness' Signature   Participant's Signature

_____   _____
Witness' Signature   Spouse's Consent

                                   _____
                                   Test Supervisor's Signature

Figure 18–2(cont.)   Sample informed consent form reprinted with permission from Herbert, D.L, and Herbert, W.G., *Legal Aspects of Preventive and Rehabilitative Exercise Programs: Second Edition* pages 281-284, Copyright 1989 by Professional Reports Corporation, Canton, Ohio 44718-3629. All rights reserved.

Please note that this waiver is only a guideline, compiled from the forms upheld in Illinois, Minnesota, and Tennessee. The rules vary from state to state, so do not expect this particular waiver to hold up in your state court. See your attorney for advice.

If your attorney discovers that waivers of liability are not upheld in your state, redraft your waiver to comply with these recommendations anyway. You never know when the law may change.

"I, _____ , have enrolled in a program of strenuous physical activity including but not limited to aerobic dance, weight training, stationary bicycling, and the use of various aerobic-conditioning machinery offered by __[name of business]__. I hereby affirm that I am in good physical condition and do not suffer from any disability that would prevent or limit my participation in this exercise program."

"In consideration of my participation in ____[name of business]____ exercise program, I, _____ , for myself, my heirs and assigns, hereby release ____[name of business]____ (its employees and owners), from any claims, demands and causes of action arising from my participation in the exercise program."

"I fully understand that I may injure myself as a result of my participation in ____[name of business]____ exercise program and I, _____ , hereby release ____[name of business]____ from any liability now or in the future including but not limited to heart attacks, muscle strains, pulls or tears, broken bones, shin splints, heat prostration, knee/lower back/foot injuries, and any other illness, soreness, or injury, however caused, occurring during or after my participation in the exercise program."

_____
Signature

_____
Date

I hereby affirm that I have read and fully understand the above.

_____
Signature

Figure 18–3 Sample waiver of liability/informed consent

the defendant. The court or jury then determines the percentage of responsibility of each party to prorate the award. This defense can be useful if a client is somewhat to blame in injuring him/herself.

OTHER BUSINESS CONCERNS WITH LEGAL IMPLICATIONS

In addition to their legal responsibilities in the areas of scope of practice, facilities, equipment, testing, instruction, and supervision, trainers must be aware of the legal implications of such business concerns as liability insurance, use of musical recordings, and certification.

Liability Insurance

A system that distributes the risk of financial loss over a group of policy holders, liability insurance may be purchased individually or through professional groups, such as the IDEA, ACSM, NCSA, and AFAA. Individual policies are considerably more expensive than policies purchased through a group. Most professional organizations have arrangements that allow members to purchase policies at reduced rates. Alternatively, inexpensive personal liability coverage may be obtained from insurance agents as an extension of coverage on a trainer's residence. These extensions may be called a "business pursuits rider" or "umbrella coverage," and trainers must educate themselves about the services a particular policy provides. It is the insurance agent's responsibility to give a complete explanation and answer any questions. A good policy should cover the cost of legal defense as well as the amount of damages that may be awarded. Policies that cover only the damages leave the trainer responsible for paying legal costs, which can be considerable. Furthermore, each personal trainer should examine policies to ensure that the activities covered are the ones most frequently included in his or her clients' programs.

Music

All the popular recordings on radio and television have been protected by artists and studios with copyrights. Any use of this material for profit is a violation of federal law, even if the trainer has purchased the recording. Recordings sold commercially are intended strictly for the private, noncommercial use of the purchaser. Although two groups, **ASCAP** and **BMI**, will issue licenses for commercial use of recordings, their fees are probably prohibitive for the personal trainer, who will find it more economical to use recordings designed and sold for fitness and aerobic dancing. Another option is for clients to purchase their own recordings for use during workouts. In effect, the clients are then using these recordings for their own private non-commercial enjoyment during exercise.

Certification

Although certification from a professional organization can assist a defendant by providing evidence of competency, it does not protect against findings of negligence. Some trainers believe that juries will hold certified personal trainers to a higher standard of care than noncertified trainers, but, in reality, negligence is negligence, and a competent attorney can expose a substandard performance in either case. Most legal experts acknowledge that certification demonstrates minimal competency in the fitness profession. It will also help the personal trainer assure clients that they are receiving instruction from a knowledgeable and recognized professional.

Risk Management

A process in which personal trainers review their programs, facilities, and equipment to evaluate potential dangers to clients, risk management allows the trainer to decide the best approach for reducing costly injuries in each situation. Following are the most common methods of reducing risk:

- Transfer of risk, as with insurance policies.

- Reduction (through continuing education).

- Retention (budgeting for minor emergencies).

- Avoidance of certain activities or equipment.

A personal trainer can also manage risk by examining procedures and policies and developing conduct and safety guidelines for clients' use of equipment. Strict safety guidelines for each activity, accompanied by procedures for emergencies, are particularly important. Trainers must not only develop these policies but become thoroughly familiar with them, mentally practicing their emergency plans. Once risks are identified, personal trainers should carry out the actions needed to reduce these risks.

SUMMARY

Although often overlooked when considering the technical aspects of providing quality personalized fitness instruction, the legal, ethical, and business concerns are of paramount importance. Fitness instructors accept a tremendous amount of responsibility when they assume the role of personal trainer. Fitness professionals must always be aware of their scope of practice. This chapter touched on the legal, ethical, and business issues that must be considered. The guidelines offered are not legal advice. Rather they are a condensed presentation of the technicalities that the responsible trainer must understand.

REFERENCES

Herbert, D.L. (1989, September). Appropriate use of wellness appraisals. *Fitness Management*, p. 23.

Herbert, D.L. (1989, July). Prospective releases must conform to law. *Fitness Management*, p. 24.

Nygaard, G., & Boone, T.H. (1989). *Law for physical educators and coaches*. Columbus, OH: Publishing Horizons.

SUGGESTED READING

Herbert, D.L. (1989, September). Appropriate use of wellness appraisals. *Fitness Management*, p. 23.

Herbert, D.L., & Herbert, W.G. (1989). *Legal aspects of preventive and rehabilitative exercise programs*. Canton, OH: Professional Reports Corp.

Koeberle, B.E. (1990). *Legal aspects of personal training.* Canton, OH: Professional Reports Corp.

Koeberle, B.E. (1989, October). Personal fitness liability: A trainer's guide to legal fitness. *The Exercise Standards and Malpractice Reporter,* pp. 74-79.

Kooperman, S. (1989, May). Liability waivers: Can they really work? *IDEA Business Today,* pp. 2-3.

Kooperman, S. (1989, August). Should you sign a waiver? *Shape,* p. 99.

Kooperman, S. (1986, September). In defense of health clubs. *Dance Exercise Today,* pp. 29-30.

Stotlar, D.K. (1988, March). The liability crises. *Dance Exercise Today,* pp.26-31.

Stotlar, D.K. (1987, May). The dance-exercise industry and independent contractors: The legal issues. *Dance Exercise Today,* pp. 45-46.

Stotlar, D.K. (1987). Professional responsibilities and liabilities. In N. Van Gelder and S. Marks (Eds.), *Aerobic Dance-Exercise Instructor Manual* (pp. 339-347). San Diego: American Council on Exercise.

Stotlar, D.K. (1986, Spring). Applying legal concepts in the administration of strength and conditioning programs. *National Strength and Conditioning Association Journal,* pp. 77-78.

Stotlar, D.K., & Steward, S.J. (1984, August). Liability in recreation: Sound risk management can prevent litigation. *Athletic Business,* pp. 43-44.

Appendix A

Standards and Guidelines for Cardiopulmonary Resuscitation (CPR) and Emergency Cardiac Care (ECC)

Adult Basic Life Support

Basic life support (BLS) is that particular phase of emergency cardiac care that either (1) prevents circulatory or respiratory arrest or insufficiency through prompt recognition and intervention or (2) externally supports the circulation and ventilation of a victim of cardiac or respiratory arrest through cardiopulmonary resuscitation (CPR). The major objective of performing CPR is to provide oxygen to the brain, heart, and other vital organs until appropriate, definitive medical treatment (advanced cardiac life support) can restore normal heart and ventilatory action. Speed is critical—the key to success. The highest hospital discharge rate has been achieved in those patients for whom CPR was initiated within four minutes of the time of the arrest and who, in addition, were provided with advanced cardiac life support measures within eight minutes of their arrest. Early bystander CPR intervention and fast emergency medical service (EMS) response are therefore essential in improving survival rates and good neurological recovery rates.

INDICATIONS FOR BLS

Respiratory Arrest

When there is primary respiratory arrest, the heart can continue to pump blood for several minutes, and existing stores of oxygen in the lungs and blood will continue to circulate to the brain and other vital organs. Early intervention for victims in whom respirations have stopped or the airway is obstructed can prevent cardiac arrest. Respiratory arrest can result from drowning, stroke, foreign-body airway obstruction, smoke inhalation, drug overdose, electrocution, suffocation, injuries, myocardial infarc-

tion, injury by lightning, and coma of any cause leading to airway obstruction.

Cardiac Arrest

When there is primary cardiac arrest, oxygen is not circulated and oxygen stored in the vital organs is depleted in a few seconds. Cardiac arrest can be accompanied by the following electrical phenomena: ventricular fibrillation, ventricular tachycardia, asystole, or electromechanical dissociation.

THE SEQUENCE OF BLS: ASSESSMENT AND THE *ABC*S OF CPR

The assessment phases of BLS are crucial. No victim should undergo any one of the more intrusive procedures of cardiopulmonary resuscitation, (i.e., positioning, opening the airway, rescue breathing, and external chest compression) until the need for it has been established by the appropriate assessment. The importance of the assessment phases should be stressed in the teaching of CPR.

Each of the *ABC*s of CPR, *A*irway, *B*reathing, and *C*irculation, begins with an assessment phase: "determine unresponsiveness," "determine breathlessness," "determine pulselessness," respectively. Assessment also involves a more subtle, constant process of observing and interacting with the victim.

<u>A</u>irway

1. Assessment: Determine Unresponsiveness. The rescuer arriving at the scene of the collapsed

491

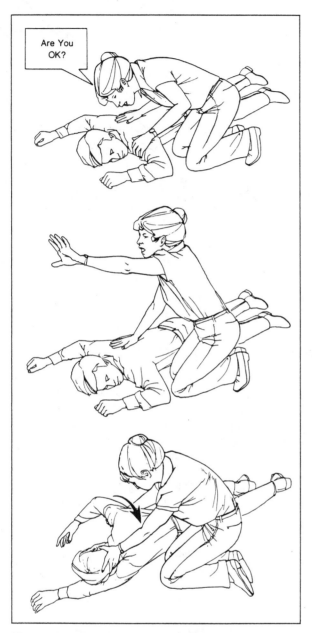

Figure A–1 Initial steps of cardiopulmonary resuscitation. Top, determining unresponsiveness; center, calling for help; bottom, positioning the victim.

victim must quickly assess any injury and determine whether the individual is unconscious (Fig. A-1, top). If the victim has sustained trauma to the head and neck, the rescuer should move the victim only if absolutely necessary because improper movement may cause paralysis in a victim with a neck injury.

The rescuer should tap or gently shake the victim and shout, "Are you OK?" This precaution will prevent injury from attempted resuscitation of a person who is not truly unconscious.

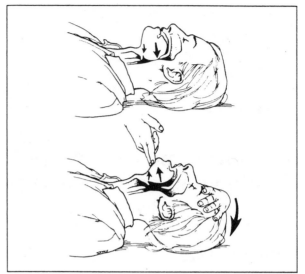

Figure A–2 Opening the airway. Top, airway obstruction produced by tongue and epiglottis; bottom, relief by head-tilt/chin-lift.

2. Call for Help. If the victim does not respond to attempts at arousal, call out for help (Fig. A-1, center). When someone responds, send that person to activate the EMS system.

3. Position the Victim. For CPR to be effective, the victim must be supine and on a firm, flat surface (Fig. A-1, bottom); even flawlessly performed external chest compressions will produce inadequate blood flow to the brain if the head is positioned higher than the thorax. If the victim is lying face down, the rescuer must roll the victim as a unit so that the head, shoulders, and torso move simultaneously with no twisting. The head and neck should remain in the same plane as the torso. Once the body is supine, the victim's arms should be placed alongside the body. The victim is now appropriately positioned for the next step in CPR.

4. Rescuer Position. By kneeling at the level of the victim's shoulders, the rescuer can perform, in turn, rescue breathing and chest compression without moving the knees.

5. Open Airway. The most important action for successful resuscitation is immediate opening of the airway. In the absence of sufficient muscle tone, the tongue and/or the epiglottis will obstruct the pharynx and the larynx, respectively (Fig. A-2, top). The tongue is the most common cause of airway obstruction in the unconscious victim. Since the tongue is attached to the lower jaw, moving the lower jaw forward will lift the tongue away from the back of the throat and open the airway. Either the tongue or the epiglottis, or both, may produce obstruction when negative pressure is created in the airway by inspiratory effort, causing a valve-type mechanism to occlude the entrance to the trachea.

The rescuer should use the head-tilt/chin-lift maneuver described below to open the airway (Fig. A–2, bottom). If foreign material or vomitus is visible in the mouth, it should be removed. Excessive time must not be taken. Liquids or semiliquids should be wiped out with the index and middle fingers covered by a piece of cloth; solid material should be extracted with a hooked index finger. The mouth can be opened by the "crossed finger" technique.

HEAD-TILT/CHIN-LIFT MANEUVER. Head-tilt/chin-lift is more effective in opening the airway than the previously recommended head-tilt/neck-lift. Head-tilt is accomplished by placing one hand on the victim's forehead and applying firm, backward pressure with the palm to tilt the head back. To complete the head-tilt/chin-lift maneuver, place the fingers of the other hand under the bony part of the lower jaw near the chin and lift to bring the chin forward and the teeth almost to occlusion, thus supporting the jaw and helping to tilt the head back. The fingers must not press deeply into the soft tissue under the chin, which might obstruct the airway. The thumb should not be used for lifting the chin. The mouth should not be completely closed (unless mouth-to-nose breathing is the technique of choice for that particular victim). When mouth-to-nose ventilation is indicated, the hand that is already on the chin can close the mouth by applying increased force and in this way provide effective mouth-to-nose ventilation. If the victim has loose dentures, head-tilt/chin-lift maintains their position and makes a mouth-to-mouth seal easier. Dentures should be removed if they cannot be managed in place.

JAW-THRUST MANEUVER. Forward displacement of the mandible can be accomplished by grasping the angles of the victim's lower jaw and lifting with both hands, one on each side, displacing the mandible forward while tilting the head backward. The rescuer's elbows should rest on the surface on which the victim is lying. If the lips close, the lower lip can be retracted with the thumb. If mouth-to-mouth breathing is necessary, the nostrils may be closed by placing the rescuer's cheek tightly against them. This technique is very effective in opening the airway, but is very fatiguing and technically difficult.

The jaw-thrust technique without head-tilt is the

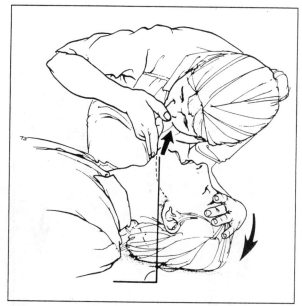

Figure A–3 Determining breathlessness.

safest first approach to opening the airway of a victim with a suspected neck injury because it usually can be accomplished without extending the neck. The head should be carefully supported without tilting it backward or turning it from side to side. If jaw-thrust alone is unsuccessful, the head should be tilted backward very slightly.

Breathing

6. Assessment: Determine Breathlessness. To assess the presence or absence of spontaneous breathing, the rescuer should place his or her ear over the victim's mouth and nose while maintaining an open airway (Fig. A–3). Then, while observing the victim's chest, the rescuer should (1) look for the chest to rise and fall; (2) listen for air escaping during exhalation; (3) feel for the flow of air. If the chest does not rise and fall and no air is exhaled, the victim is breathless. This evaluation procedure should take only three to five seconds.

It should be stressed that, although the rescuer may notice that the victim is making respiratory efforts, the airway may still be obstructed and opening the airway may be all that is needed. If the victim resumes breathing, the rescuer should continue to help maintain an open airway.

7. Perform Rescue Breathing.

MOUTH-TO-MOUTH. Rescue breathing using the mouth-to-mouth technique is a quick and effective way of providing the necessary oxygen to the victim's lungs (Fig. A–4, top). The rescuer's

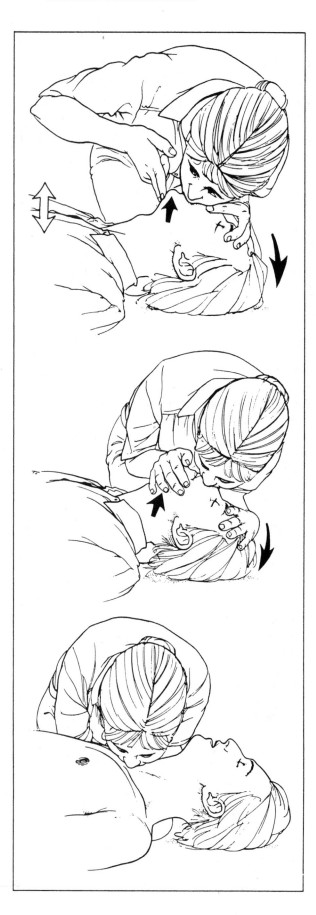

Figure A-4 Rescue breathing. Top, mouth-to-mouth; center, mouth-to-nose; bottom, mouth-to-stoma. (Adapted from *Cardiopulmonary Resuscitation.* Washington, DC, American National Red Cross, 1981, pp 16–17. Used by permission.)

exhaled air contains sufficient oxygen to supply the victim's needs. Rescue breathing requires that the rescuer inflate the victim's lungs adequately with each breath. Keeping the airway open by the head-tilt/chin-lift maneuver, the rescuer gently pinches the nose closed using the thumb and index finger of the hand on the forehead, thereby preventing air from escaping through the victim's nose. The rescuer takes a deep breath and seals his or her lips around the outside of the victim's mouth, creating an airtight seal; then the rescuer gives two full breaths.

Adequate time for the two breaths (1 to 1½ seconds per breath) should be allowed to provide good chest expansion and decrease the possibility of gastric distention. (Measurements of time "per breath" given herein are, more precisely, measurements of the victim's inspiratory time.) The rescuer should take a breath after each ventilation, and each individual ventilation should be of sufficient volume to make the chest rise. In most adults, this volume will be 800 mL (0.8 L). Adequate ventilation usually does not need to exceed 1,200 mL (1.2 L). An excess of air volume and fast inspiratory flow rates are likely to cause pharyngeal pressures that exceed esophageal opening pressures, allowing air to enter the stomach and, thus, resulting in gastric distention. Indicators of adequate ventilation are (1) observing the chest rise and fall and (2) hearing and feeling the air escape during exhalation.

If the initial attempt to ventilate the victim is unsuccessful, reposition the victim's head and repeat rescue breathing. Improper chin and head positioning is the most common cause of difficulty with ventilation. If the victim cannot be ventilated after repositioning the head, proceed with foreign-body airway obstruction maneuvers (see "Foreign-body Airway Obstruction," below).

MOUTH-TO-NOSE. This technique is more effective in some cases than mouth-to-mouth (Fig. A-4, center). The technique is recommended when it is impossible to ventilate through the victim's mouth, the mouth cannot be opened (trismus), the mouth is seriously injured, or a tight mouth-to-mouth seal is difficult to achieve. The rescuer keeps the victim's head tilted back with one hand on the forehead and uses the other hand to lift the victim's lower jaw (as in head-tilt/chin-lift) and close the mouth. The rescuer then takes a deep breath, seals the lips around the victim's nose, and blows into the nose. The rescuer's mouth is then removed, and the victim exhales passively. It may be necessary to open the victim's mouth intermittently or separate the lips (with the thumb) to allow air to be exhaled since nasal obstruction may be present during exhalation.

MOUTH-TO-STOMA.   Persons who have undergone a laryngectomy (surgical removal of the larynx) have a permanent stoma (opening) that connects the trachea directly to the skin. The stoma can be recognized as an opening at the front base of the neck. When such an individual requires rescue breathing, direct mouth-to-stoma ventilation should be performed (Fig. A–4, bottom). The rescuer's mouth is sealed around the stoma and air is blown into the victim's stoma until the chest rises. When the rescuer's mouth is removed from the stoma, the victim is permitted to exhale passively. Other persons may have a temporary tracheostomy tube in the trachea. To ventilate these persons, the victim's mouth and nose usually must be sealed by the rescuer's hand or by a tightly fitting face mask to prevent leakage of air when the rescuer blows into the tracheostomy tube. This problem is alleviated when the tracheostomy tube has a cuff that can be inflated.

Circulation

8. Assessment: Determine Pulselessness. Cardiac arrest is recognized by pulselessness in the large arteries of the unconscious victim (Fig. A–5). The pulse check should take 5 to 10 seconds, and the carotid artery should be used. It lies in a groove created by the trachea and the large strap muscles of the neck. While maintaining head-tilt with one hand on the forehead, the rescuer locates the victim's larynx with two or three fingers of the other hand. The rescuer then slides these fingers into the groove between the trachea and the muscles at the side of the neck where the carotid pulse can be felt. The pulse area must be pressed gently to avoid compressing the artery. This technique is usually more easily performed on the side nearest the rescuer. Adequate time should be allowed since the pulse may be slow, irregular, or very weak and rapid. This is the most accessible, reliable, and easily learned technique for locating the pulse in adults and children. The pulse in the carotid artery will persist when more peripheral pulses (e.g., radial) are no longer palpable. For health care professionals, or in the hospital setting, determining pulse-

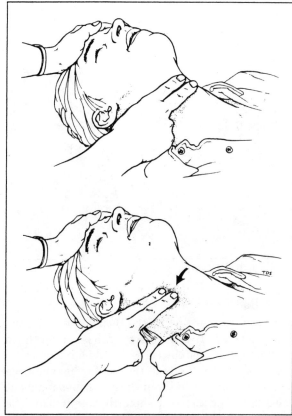

Figure A–5   Determining pulselessness.

lessness using the femoral pulse is also acceptable; however, this pulse is difficult to locate in a fully clothed person.

Proper assessment of the victim's condition must be made since performing external chest compressions on a person who has a pulse may result in serious medical complications. If a pulse is present but there is not breathing, rescue breathing should be initiated at a rate of 12 times per minute (once every 5 seconds) after initial two breaths of 1 to 1½ seconds each.

If no pulse is palpated, the diagnosis of cardiac arrest is confirmed. If not yet done, the EMS system should be activated and external chest compression begun after the initial two breaths.

9. Activate the EMS System. The EMS system is activated by calling the local emergency telephone number (911 if available). This number should be widely publicized in each community. The person who calls the EMS system should be prepared to give the following information as calmly as possible: (1) where the emergency is (with names of cross streets or roads, if possible); (2) the telephone number from which the call is made; (3) what happened—heart attack, auto accident, etc.; (4) how many persons need help; (5) condition of the victim(s); (6) what aid is

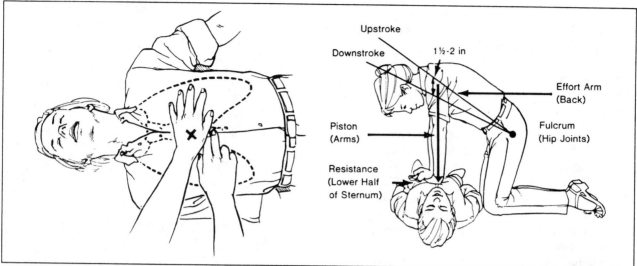

Figure A–6 External chest compression. Left, locating the correct hand position on the lower half of the body; right, proper position of the rescuer, with shoulder directly over the victim's sternum and elbows locked. (Adapted from *Cardiopulmonary Resuscitation.* Washington, DC, American National Red Cross, 1981, p. 25. Used by permission.)

being given to the victim(s); (7) any other information requested. To ensure that EMS personnel have no more questions, the caller should hang up last.

If no one responds to the call for help and the rescuer is alone, CPR should be performed for about one minute and then help should be summoned. The decision when to leave the victim to telephone for help is affected by a number of variables, including the possibility of someone else arriving on the scene. If the rescuer is unable to activate the EMS system, the only option is to continue with CPR.

10. External Chest Compressions. Cardiac arrest is recognized by pulselessness in the large arteries of the unconscious, breathless victim. All the ABCs of CPR are required in rapid succession to optimize the chances for survival.

The external chest compression technique consists of serial, rhythmic applications of pressure over the lower half of the sternum (Fig. A–6). These compressions provide circulation to the heart, lungs, brain, and other organs as a result of a generalized increase in intrathoracic pressure and/or direct compression of the heart. Blood circulated to the lungs by external chest compressions will receive sufficient oxygen to maintain life when the compressions are accompanied by properly performed rescue breathing.

During cardiac arrest, properly performed external chest compressions can produce systolic blood pressure peaks of more than 100 mmHg, but the diastolic blood pressure is low, the mean blood pressure in the carotid arteries seldom exceeding

40 mmHg. The carotid artery blood flow resulting from external chest compressions on a cardiac arrest victim usually is only one-fourth to one-third of normal.

The patient must be in the horizontal supine position when external chest compressions are performed. Even during properly performed external chest compressions, blood flow to the brain is reduced. With any elevation of the head above the heart, blood flow to the brain is further reduced or even eliminated. If the victim is in bed, a board, preferably the full width of the bed, should be placed under the back of the patient. Elevation of the lower extremities, while keeping the rest of the body horizontal, may promote venous return and augment artificial circulation during external chest compressions.

PROPER HAND POSITION. Proper hand placement is established by the following guidelines (Fig. A–6, left):

1. With the middle and index finger of the hand nearest the victim's legs, the rescuer locates the lower margin of the victim's rib cage on the side next to the rescuer.

2. The fingers are then moved up the rib cage to the notch where the ribs meet the sternum in the center of the lower part of the chest.

3. With the middle finger on this notch, the index finger is placed next to it on the lower end of the sternum.

4. The heel of the hand nearest the patient's head (which had been used on the forehead to maintain head position) is placed on the lower half of the sternum, close to the index finger that is next to the middle finger in the notch. The long axis of the heel of the rescuer's hand should be placed on the long axis of the sternum. This will keep the main force of compression on the sternum and decrease the chance of rib fracture.

5. The first hand is then removed from the notch and placed on top of the hand on the sternum so the hands are parallel to each other.

6. The fingers may be either extended or interlaced but must be kept off the chest.

7. Because of the varying sizes and shapes of different people's hands, an alternate acceptable hand position is to grasp the wrist of the hand on the chest with the hand that has been locating the lower end of the sternum. This technique is helpful for rescuers with arthritic problems of the hands and wrists.

PROPER COMPRESSION TECHNIQUES. Effective compression is accomplished by attention to the following guidelines (Fig. A–6, right):

1. The elbows are locked into position, the arms are straightened, and the shoulders of the rescuer are positioned directly over the hands so that the thrust for each external chest compression is straight down on the sternum. If the thrust is other than straight down, the torso has a tendency to roll, losing part of the force, and the chest compression may be less effective.

2. The sternum must be depressed 1.5 to 2 inches (3.8 to 5.0 cm) for a normal-sized adult.

3. The external chest compression pressure is released to allow blood to flow into the heart. The pressure must be released completely and the chest allowed to return to its normal position after each compression. The time allowed for release should equal the time required for compression.

4. The hands should not be lifted from the chest or the position changed in any way, lest correct hand position be lost.

Rescue breathing and external chest compression must be combined for effective resuscitation of the cardiopulmonary arrest victim.

CPR PERFORMED BY ONE RESCUER

A lay person should learn only one-rescuer CPR. The previously recommended two-rescuer technique is thought to cause too much confusion and to be infrequently used by lay people in actual rescue situations. Teaching only one-rescuer CPR should result in better skill retention and possibly better performance. One-rescuer CPR is effective in maintaining adequate circulation and ventilation but is more exhausting than two-rescuer CPR. When trained professionals arrive at the scene of an emergency, they will proceed with two-rescuer CPR and advanced cardiac life support, as appropriate for the situation. The lay rescuer is relieved of responsibility at this point.

One-rescuer CPR should be performed as follows:

A. Airway. (1) Assessment: determine unresponsiveness (tap or gently shake and shout), (2) call for help, (3) position the victim, and (4) open the airway by the head-tilt/chin-lift maneuver.

B. Breathing. Assessment: determine pulselessness. If the victim is breathing, (1) monitor breathing, (2) maintain an open airway, and (3) activate the EMS system (if not done previously). If the victim is not breathing, perform rescue breathing by giving two initial breaths. If unable to give two breaths, (1) reposition the head and attempt to ventilate again, and (2) if still unsuccessful, perform the foreign-body airway obstruction sequence. If successful, continue to the next step.

C. Circulation. (1) Assessment: determine pulselessness. If pulse is present, continue rescue breathing at 12 times per minute and activate the EMS system. (2) If pulse is absent, activate the EMS system (if not previously done) and continue to the next step. (3) Begin external chest compression: (a) Locate proper hand position. (b) Perform 15 external chest compressions at a rate of 80 to 100 per minute. Count "one and, two and, three and, four and, five and, six and, seven and, eight and, nine and, ten and, eleven and, twelve and, thirteen and, fourteen and, fifteen." (Any mnemonic that accomplishes the same compression rate is acceptable.) (c) Open the airway and deliver two rescue breaths. (d) Locate the proper hand position and begin 15 more compressions at a rate of 80 to 100 per minute. (e) Perform four complete cycles of 15 compressions and 2 ventilations.

D. Reassessment. After four cycles of compressions and ventilations (15:2 ratio), reevaluate the victim.

Check for return of the carotid pulse (5 seconds). If it is absent, resume CPR with two ventilations followed by compressions. If it is present, continue to next step.

Check breathing (3 to 5 seconds). If present, monitor breathing and pulse closely. If absent, perform rescue breathing at 12 times per minute and monitor pulse closely.

If CPR is continued, stop and check for return of pulse and spontaneous breathing every few minutes. Do not interrupt CPR for more than seven seconds except in special circumstances.

ONE-RESCUER CPR WITH ENTRY OF A SECOND RESCUER

When another rescuer is available at the scene, it is recommended that this second rescuer should activate the EMS system (if not previously done) and perform one-rescuer CPR when the first rescuer, who initiated CPR, becomes fatigued.

The following steps are recommended for entry of the second rescuer. The second person should identify himself/herself as a qualified rescuer who is willing to help. If the first rescuer is fatigued and has requested help, the logical sequence is as follows: (1) The first rescuer stops CPR after two ventilations. (2) The second rescuer kneels down and checks for pulse for five seconds. (3) If there is no pulse, the second rescuer gives two breaths. (4) The second rescuer commences external chest compressions at the recommended rate and ratio for one-person CPR. (5) The first rescuer assesses the adequacy of the second rescuer's ventilations and compressions. This can be done by watching the chest rise during rescue breathing and by checking the pulse during the chest compressions.

Appendix B

Personal Trainer Exam Content Outline

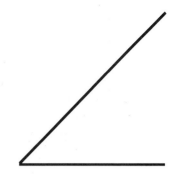

The purpose of this exam content outline is to set forth the tasks, skills and knowledge necessary to perform at a minimum professional level as a personal trainer or fitness center floor staff teaching components of fitness to apparently healthy individuals on a one-to-one basis.

It is the position of the *American Council on Exercise* that the recommendations outlined here are not exhaustive to the qualifications of a personal trainer but represent the minimum level of proficiency and theoretical knowledge essential for personal trainer to (1) screen and evaluate prospective clients, (2) design a safe and effective exercise program, (3) instruct client in correct exercise technique to avoid injury and (4) respond to the typical questions and problems that arise in a one-to-one setting.

These recommendations apply only to personal trainers working within a fitness facility or in and outside the home training healthy individuals who have no apparent physical limitations or special medical needs. It is not ACE's intent to provide recommendations for trainers delivering specialized programs for highly trained athletes, pre/postnatal women, older clients, the physically handicapped, the morbidly obese, or individuals known to have coronary heart disease.

CONTENTS

I. HEALTH SCREENING

Task 1: Identify health problems/risk factors.

Task 2: Obtain lifestyle information.

II. EVALUATION

Task 1: Select and administer fitness tests.

Task 2: Analyze and interpret fitness test data.

Task 3: Emergencies.

III. INDIVIDUALIZED PROGRAM DESIGN

Task 1: Select activities/exercises.

IV. PROGRAM IMPLEMENTATION

Task 1: Instruct the client.

Task 2: Supervise and monitor client.

Task 3: Motivate client.

Task 4: Basic first-aid and/or CPR.

Task 5: Minimization of risk.

V. RE-EVALUATION

Task 1: Reassessment of progress and goals.

VI. PROFESSIONAL/ETHICAL/ LEGAL ISSUES

Task 1: Ethical practice.

Task 2: Professional limitations.

Task 3: Legal issues.

DOMAIN I:
HEALTH SCREENING

TASK 1:
Identify health problems and risk factors by obtaining a health history in order to determine if consultation with health professionals is required.

Knowledges:

1. Elements of a health history (e.g., age, medications, past surgery, past injuries, etc.).

2. Past and present health conditions, risk factors (e.g., diabetes, hypertension, coronary artery disease, pregnancy and musculoskeletal disorders, etc.) and medications (e.g., antihypertensives, insulin, etc.) that may interfere with the ability to exercise safely.

3. Technique for obtaining blood pressure.

TASK 2:
Obtain statement of client's goals and lifestyle information that may effect program planning in order to design an exercise program.

Knowledges:

1. Relevant lifestyle information (e.g., exercise habits and preferences, dietary habits, time limitations, smoking, alcohol consumption, etc.).

2. Role of client's specific fitness goals in program planning.

DOMAIN II: EVALUATION

TASK 1:
Select and administer fitness tests by reviewing health history data and client's goals and administer fitness tests in order to obtain fitness data.

Knowledges:

1. Fitness tests including cardiovascular endurance, muscular strength/endurance, flexibility and body composition.

2. Test selection criteria (e.g., client's age, gender, health and goals, test pros and cons, duration, safety, expense and facilities, etc.).

3. Test administration protocols including protocols for cardiovascular endurance (step test, cycle ergometer, etc.), body composition (skinfold caliper), flexibility and muscular strength/endurance.

4. Warning signs/symptoms that require intervention (e.g., shortness of breath, dizziness, chest pain, etc.).

TASK 2:
Analyze and interpret fitness data in order to establish baseline fitness level and design exercise program.

Knowledges:

1. Test norms.

2. Factors that affect test results (test error and sources of test error, e.g., client, test conditions, etc.).

3. Procedures for converting raw data into fitness measures.

TASK 3:
Recognize emergencies and respond appropriately by activating the EMS system.

Knowledges:

1. Warning signs/symptoms that require intervention (e.g., shortness of breath, dizziness, chest pain, etc.).

2. Cardiopulmonary resuscitation (CPR).

DOMAIN III: INDIVIDUALIZED PROGRAM DESIGN

TASK 1:
Select activities/exercises and determine their appropriate levels of intensity, frequency and duration based on screening and evaluation data in order to achieve fitness goals.

Knowledges:

1. Activities/exercises for each component of fitness (cardiovascular endurance, muscular strength/endurance, flexibility and body composition).

2. Anatomy.

3. Exercise physiology.

4. Applied kinesiology.

5. Nutrition and weight control principles.

6. The effect of environmental conditions on exercise.

7. Exercise-related injuries.

8. Types of exercise equipment (e.g., free weights, stationary bike, adjustable exercise machines, etc.) including their operations, functions, uses and benefits.

9. Advantages and disadvantages of isometric, isotonic and isokinetic exercise.

10. Training methods (cardiovascular endurance, muscular strength, flexibility, etc.) and their applications.

11. Properly balanced fitness program (variety, components of fitness, muscle groups, etc.).

12. Difference between training for general fitness and training for specific performance (e.g., running for cardiovascular fitness vs. training for a marathon).

13. Phases of a fitness workout and their proper order (e.g., warm-up, flexibility, cardiovascular, cool-down, etc.).

14. Ergogenic aids.

15. Modifications made to exercise programs for individuals with physical limitations or health conditions who have been given physician approval to participate, e.g., arthritis, obesity, low back pain, diabetes mellitus, hypertension and pregnancy.

16. Time frames for improvements/reversibility in cardiovascular fitness, muscular strength and endurance, flexibility and body composition based on client participation.

17. Appropriate exercise apparel for a variety of activities and environmental conditions.

18. Benefits of participation in a regular exercise program.

19. Effects of aging relative to: skeletal muscle, bone structure, maximal oxygen uptake, flexibility, heart rate and body composition.

DOMAIN IV:
PROGRAM IMPLEMENTATION

TASK 1:
Instruct client in the proper techniques for performance of selected activities/exercise by demonstrating, assisting, teaching, etc., in order to achieve fitness goals.

Knowledge:

1. Activities/exercises for each component of fitness (cardiovascular endurance, muscular strength/endurance, joint flexibility and body composition).

2. Anatomy.

3. Exercise physiology.

4. Applied kinesiology.

5. Nutrition and weight control principles.

6. The effect of environmental conditions on exercise.

7. Exercise-related injuries.

8. Types of exercise equipment (e.g., free weights, stationary bike, adjustable exercise machines, etc.) including their operations, functions, uses and benefits.

9. Advantages and disadvantages of isometric, isotonic and isokinetic exercise.

10. Training methods (cardiovascular endurance, muscular strength and flexibility) and their applications.

11. Properly balanced fitness program (variety, components of fitness, muscle groups).

12. Difference between training for general fitness and training for specific performance (e.g., running for cardiovascular fitness vs. training for a marathon).

13. Phases of a fitness workout and their proper order (e.g., warm-up, flexibility, cardiovascular, cool-down, etc.).

14. Ergogenic aids.

15. Modifications made to exercise programs for individuals with physical limitations or health conditions who have been given physician approval to participate, e.g., arthritis, obesity, low back pain, diabetes mellitus, hypertension and pregnancy.

16. Time frames for improvements/reversibility in cardiovascular fitness, muscular strength and endurance, flexibility and body composition based on client participation.

17. Appropriate exercise apparel for a variety of activities and environmental conditions.

18. Benefits of participation in a regular exercise program.

19. Effects of aging relative to: skeletal muscle, bone structure, maximal oxygen uptake, flexibility, heart rate and body composition.

20. Instructional techniques (e.g., modeling, feedback, demonstration, etc.).

21. Spotting techniques.

22. Workout routine phases.

23. Principles of good communication skills.

24. Proper techniques for a variety of exercises/ activities (e.g., running, biking, etc.)

TASK 2:
Supervise and monitor client by observing and documenting performance in order to appropriately modify exercise program.

Knowledges:

1. Warning signs/symptoms that require intervention (e.g., shortness of breath, dizziness, chest pain, etc.).

2. Activities/exercises for each component of fitness (cardiovascular endurance, muscular strength/endurance, joint flexibility, body composition).

3. Anatomy.

4. Exercise physiology.

5. Applied kinesiology.

6. Nutrition and weight control principles.

7. Effect of environmental conditions on exercise.

8. Exercise-related injuries.

9. Types of exercise equipment (e.g., free weights, stationary bike, adjustable exercise machines, etc.) including their operations, functions, uses and benefits.

10. Advantages and disadvantages of isometric, isotonic and isokinetic exercise.

11. Training methods (cardiovascular endurance, muscular strength and flexibility) and their applications.

12. Properly balanced fitness program (variety, components of fitness, muscle groups).

13. Difference between training for general fitness and training for specific performance (e.g., running for cardiovascular fitness vs. training for a marathon).

14. Phases of a fitness workout and their proper order (e.g., warm-up, flexibility, cardiovascular, cool-down, etc.).

15. Ergogenic aids.

16. Modifications made to exercise programs for individuals with physical limitations or health conditions who have been given physician approval to participate, e.g., arthritis, obesity, low back pain, diabetes mellitus, hypertension and pregnancy.

17. Time frames for improvements/reversibility in cardiovascular fitness, muscular strength and endurance, flexibility and body composition based on client participation.

18. Appropriate exercise apparel for a variety of activities and environmental conditions.

19. Benefits of participation in a regular exercise program.

20. Effects of aging relative to: skeletal muscle, bone structure, maximal oxygen uptake, flexibility, heart rate and body composition.

21. Equipment maintenance procedures.

22. Monitoring techniques (e.g., heart rate, rating of perceived exertion, momentary muscle failure, respiration, etc.).

23. Signs of technique breakdown.

24. Effects of drugs (e.g., beta blockers, diuretics, caffeine, etc.) on performance.

TASK 3:
Motivate clients by providing feedback, encouragement, education, program variety, etc., in order to ensure adherence to fitness program.

Knowledges:

1. Activities/exercises for each component of fitness (cardiovascular endurance, muscular strength/endurance, flexibility, body composition).

2. Anatomy.

3. Exercise physiology.

4. Applied kinesiology.

5. Nutrition and weight control principles.

6. The effect of environmental conditions on exercise.

7. Exercise-related injuries.

8. Types of exercise equipment (e.g., free weights, stationary bike, adjustable exercise machines, etc.) including their operations, functions, uses and benefits.

9. Advantages and disadvantages of isometric, isotonic and isokinetic exercise.

10. Training methods (cardiovascular endurance, muscular strength and flexibility) and their applications.

11. Properly balanced fitness program (variety, components of fitness, muscle groups).

12. Difference between training for general fitness and training for specific performance (e.g., running for cardiovascular fitness vs. training for a marathon).

13. Phases of a fitness workout and their proper order (e.g., warm-up, flexibility, cardiovascular, cool-down, etc.).

14. Ergogenic aids.

15. Modifications made to exercise programs for individuals with physical limitations or health conditions who have been given physician approval to participate, e.g., arthritis, obesity, low back pain, diabetes mellitus, hypertension and pregnancy.

16. Time frames for improvements/reversibility in cardiovascular fitness, muscular strength and endurance, flexibility and body composition based on client participation.

17. Appropriate exercise apparel for a variety of activities and environmental conditions.

18. Benefits of participation in a regular exercise program.

19. Effects of aging relative to: skeletal muscle, bond structure, maximal oxygen uptake, flexibility, heart rate and body composition.

20. Principles of good communication skills.

21. Motivational techniques (e.g., encouragement, feedback, training logs, etc.) and compliance/non-compliance principles.

TASK 4:
Recognize emergencies and respond appropriately by activating the EMS system and/or applying basic care, first aid and/or CPR.

Knowledges:

1. Warning signs/symptoms that require intervention (e.g., shortness of breath, dizziness, chest pain, etc.).

2. Cardiopulmonary resuscitation (CPR).

3. Basic first-aid procedures for such conditions as sprains, strains, heat illness, etc.

TASK 5:

Minimize the risk of injury by appropriately applying exercise to the client's fitness level, instructing client in proper methods and modes of exercise, monitoring and correcting performance, recognizing symptoms of overtraining, applying biomechanical principles, etc.

Knowledges:

1. Elements of a health history (e.g., age, medications, past surgery, past injuries, etc.).

2. Past and present health conditions, risk factors (e.g., diabetes, hypertension, coronary artery disease, pregnancy and musculoskeletal disorders, etc.) and medications (e.g., anti-hypertensives, insulin, etc.) that may interfere with the ability to exercise safely.

3. Technique for obtaining blood pressure.

4. Relevant lifestyle information (e.g., exercise habits and preferences, dietary habits, time limitations, smoking, alcohol consumption, etc.).

5. Role of client's specific fitness goals in program planning.

6. Fitness tests including cardiovascular endurance, muscular strength/endurance, flexibility and body composition.

7. Test selection criteria (e.g., client's age, gender, health and goals, test pros and cons, duration, safety, expense and facilities, etc.).

8. Test administration protocols including protocols for cardiovascular endurance (step test, cycle ergometer), body composition (skinfold caliper), flexibility and muscular strength/endurance.

9. Warning signs/symptoms that require intervention (e.g., shortness of breath, dizziness, chest pain, etc.).

10. Test norms.

11. Factors that affect test results (test error and sources of test error e.g., client, test conditions, etc.).

12. Procedures for converting raw data into fitness measures.

13. Activities/exercises for each component of fitness (cardiovascular endurance, muscular strength/endurance, flexibility and body composition).

14. Anatomy.

15. Exercise physiology.

16. Applied kinesiology.

17. Nutrition and weight control principles.

18. Effect of environmental conditions on exercise.

19. Exercise-related injuries.

20. Types of exercise equipment (e.g., free weights, stationary bike, adjustable exercise machines, etc.) including their operations, functions, uses and benefits.

21. Advantages and disadvantages of isometric, isotonic and isokinetic exercise.

22. Training methods (cardiovascular endurance, muscular strength and flexibility) and their applications.

23. Properly balanced fitness program (variety, components of fitness, muscle groups).

24. Difference between training for general fitness and training for specific performance (e.g., running for cardiovascular fitness vs. training for a marathon).

25. Phases of a fitness workout and their proper order (e.g., warm-up, flexibility, cardiovascular, cool-down, etc.).

26. Ergogenic aids.

27. Modifications made to exercise programs for individuals with physical limitations or health conditions who have been given physician approval to participate, e.g., arthritis, obesity, low back pain, diabetes mellitus, hypertension and pregnancy.

28. Time frames for improvements/reversibility in cardiovascular fitness, muscular strength and endurance, flexibility and body composition based on client participation.

29. Appropriate exercise apparel for a variety of activities and environmental conditions.

30. Effects of aging relative to: skeletal muscle, bone structure, maximal oxygen uptake, flexibility, heart rate and body composition.

31. Instructional techniques (e.g., modeling, feedback, demonstration, etc.).

32. Spotting techniques.

33. Workout routine phases.

34. Principles of good communication skills.

35. Proper techniques for a variety of exercises/activities (e.g., running, biking, etc.).

36. Equipment maintenance procedures.

37. Monitoring techniques (e.g., heart rate, rating of perceived exertion, momentary muscle failure, respiration, etc.).

38. Signs of technique breakdown.

39. Effects of drugs (e.g., beta blockers, diuretics, caffeine, etc.) on performance.

DOMAIN V: RE-EVALUATION

TASK 1:
Systematic reassessment of client's progress with specific performance measures and consultation with client in order to adjust, refine or reinforce program goals.

Knowledges:

1. Fitness tests including cardiovascular endurance, muscular strength/endurance, flexibility and body composition.

2. Test selection criteria (e.g., client's age, gender, health and goals: test pros and cons, duration, safety, expense and facilities, etc).

3. Test administration protocols including protocols for cardiovascular endurance (step test, cycle ergometer, etc.), body composition (skinfold caliper) joint flexibility and muscular strength/endurance.

4. Warning signs/symptoms that require intervention (e.g., shortness of breath, dizziness, chest pain, etc.).

5. Test norms.

6. Factors that affect test results (test error and sources of test error, e.g., client, test conditions, etc.).

7. Procedures for converting raw data into fitness measures.

8. Cardiopulmonary resuscitation (CPR).

9. Activities/exercises for each component of fitness (cardiovascular endurance, muscular strength/endurance, flexibility, body composition).

10. Anatomy.

11. Exercise physiology.

12. Applied kinesiology.

13. Nutrition and weight control principles.

14. The effect of environmental conditions on exercise.

15. Exercise-related injuries.

16. Types of exercise equipment (e.g., free weights, stationary bike, adjustable exercise machines, etc.) including their operations, functions, uses and benefits.

17. Advantages and disadvantages of isometric, isotonic and isokinetic exercise.

18. Training methods (cardiovascular endurance, muscular strength and flexibility) and their applications.

19. Properly balanced fitness program (variety, components of fitness, muscle groups, etc.).

20. Difference between training for general fitness and training for specific performance (e.g., running for cardiovascular fitness vs. training for a marathon).

21. Phases of a fitness workout and their proper order (e.g., warm-up, flexibility, cardiovascular, cool-down, etc.).

22. Ergogenic aids.

23. Modifications made to exercise programs for individuals with physical limitations or health conditions who have been given physician approval to participate, e.g., arthritis, obesity, low back pain, diabetes mellitus, hypertension and pregnancy.

24. Time frames for improvements/reversibility in cardiovascular fitness, muscular strength and endurance, flexibility and body composition based on client participation.

25. Appropriate exercise apparel for a variety of activities and environmental conditions.

26. Benefits of participation in a regular exercise program.

27. Effects of aging relative to: skeletal muscle, bone structure, maximal oxygen uptake, flexibility, heart rate and body composition.

28. Motivational techniques (e.g., encouragement, feedback, training logs, etc.) and compliance/noncompliance principles.

29. Appropriate intervals for re-evaluation.

30. Effects of changes in fitness measures on continued progression toward fitness goals.

DOMAIN VI: PROFESSIONAL/ LEGAL/ETHICAL ISSUES

TASK 1:
Personal trainer practices are consistent with published codes of ethics that apply to the fitness profession.

Knowledges:

1. The American Council on Exercise Code of Ethics.

TASK 2:
The personal trainer is aware of his/her professional limitation and makes referrals to other qualified professionals when client's needs exceed the scope of practice.

Knowledges:

1. Past and present health conditions, risk factors (e.g., diabetes, hypertension, coronary artery disease, pregnancy and musculoskeletal disorders, etc.) and medications (e.g., anti-hypertensives, insulin, etc.) that may interfere with the ability to exercise safely.

2. Scope of practice of the personal trainer.

TASK 3:
The personal trainer is aware of and conforms to all laws that affect professional practice and recognizes the importance of informed consent, waivers and liability insurance.

Knowledges:
1. Laws pertaining to negligence, copyright and contracts.

2. Uses and components of informed consents, waivers and physician clearances.

3. Liability insurance.

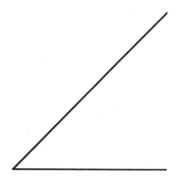

GLOSSARY

Abduction Movement of a body part away from the midline of the body; opposite of *adduction*.

Abrasion A scraping away of a portion of the skin or mucous membrane.

Acclimatization The process whereby the body physiologically adapts to an unfamiliar environment, achieving a new steady state. For instance, the body can adjust to a high altitude or a hot climate, thereby gaining increased capacity to work at high altitudes or in hot conditions.

Actin Contractile protein in a myofibril.

Acute Descriptive of a condition that usually has a rapid onset and a relatively short and severe course. Opposite of *chronic*.

Adduction Movement of a body part toward the midline of the body; opposite of *abduction*.

Adenosine triphosphate (ATP) A high-energy phosphate molecule required to provide energy for cellular function. Produced both aerobically and anaerobically, and stored in the body.

Adherence The amount of programmed exercise a client engages in during a specified time period compared to the amount of exercise recommended for that time period.

Adhesion A fibrous band holding together parts that are normally separate.

Aerobic With or in the presence of oxygen.

Aerobic composite training An individualized combination of numerous training methods characterized by a variety of intensities and modes, primarily for those in the maintenance phase of conditioning. Example: jog 15 minutes to a pool, swim for 20 minutes, and jog home.

Agonist muscle A muscle that is directly engaged in contraction; opposes the action of an *antagonist muscle*.

Alienation The body's rejection of exercise or activity, mainly because of pain.

Alveoli Air sacs in the lungs; site of carbon dioxide and oxygen exchange within the surrounding pulmonary capillaries.

Amino acids Nitrogen-containing compounds that are the building blocks of proteins.

Anabolic androgenic steroids Synthetic derivatives of the male sex hormone testosterone. Used for their muscle-building characteristics.

Anaerobic Without the presence of oxygen; not requiring oxygen.

Anaerobic threshold The point during high-intensity activity when the body can no longer meet its demand for oxygen and anaerobic metabolism predominates.

Anatomical position Standing erect, with the feet and palms facing forward.

Angina Pain, originating from the heart, characterized by a substantial "pressure" sensation within the chest, commonly radiating down the arm, up into the jaw, or to another site. Generally caused by decreased blood flow through the coronary arteries supplying oxygen to the myocardium (heart muscle) secondary to partial occlusion from plaque or clot formation or spasm of the artery itself. Also called angina pectoris.

Anorexia nervosa An eating disorder characterized by an intense fear of becoming obese, a distorted body image, and extreme weight loss. A form of self-starvation. Metabolic abnormalities are commonly associated with this disorder and can sometimes be fatal.

Antagonist muscle The muscle that acts in opposition to the action produced by an *agonist muscle*.

Anterior Anatomical term meaning toward the front. Same as ventral; opposite of *posterior*.

Aorta The largest artery in the body, originating from the left ventricle of the heart. It is the main outflow tract of oxygenated blood from the heart.

Appendicular skeleton The bones of the upper and lower extremities of the human body.

Applied force An external force acting on a system, body, or body segment.

Arteries Vessels that carry oxygenated blood from the heart to the tissues.

Arterioles Smaller divisions of the arteries.

Arthritis Inflammatory condition involving a joint. See *Osteoarthritis* and *Rheumatoid arthritis*.

ASCAP The American Society of Composers, Authors and Publishers. One of two performing rights societies in the United States that represent music publishers in negotiating and collecting fees for the nondramatic performance of music.

Assumption of risk A legal defense used to show that a person has voluntarily accepted known dangers by participating in a specific activity.

Asthma A disease of the pulmonary system, characterized by episodes of dyspnea (difficult breathing) due to narrowing of the airways from constriction of bronchial smooth muscle and overproduction of mucus. See *Chronic obstructive pulmonary disease*.

Atherosclerosis A specific form of arteriosclerosis, characterized by the accumulation of fatty material on the inner walls of the arteries, causing them to harden, thicken, and lose elasticity.

ATP See *Adenosine triphosphate*

Atrium One of the two (left and right) upper chambers of the heart (pl.: atria).

Atrophy A decrease in the cross-sectional size of a muscle resulting from inactivity or immobilization following injury.

Aura An unusual sensation, in the form of a smell, taste, sound, or vision, warning a person that an epileptic seizure is imminent.

Auscultation Listening to sounds (through a stethoscope) arising within the bodily organs (e.g., the heartbeat).

Autogenic inhibition An automatic reflex relaxation caused by excessive stimulation of Golgi tendon organs (GTOs).

Avascular Not vascular; without blood supply.

Avulsion A wound involving forcible separation or tearing of tissue from the body.

Axis of rotation The imaginary line or point about which an object, such as a body or a lever, rotates.

Ballistic stretch A high-force, short-duration stretch using rapid bouncing movements.

Basal metabolic rate (BMR) The energy expended by the body at rest to maintain normal body functions.

Base of support That area beneath the body that is encompassed when you connect, via one continuous line, all points of the body that are in contact with the ground.

Beta-blockers (beta-adrenergic blocking agents) Medications, used for cardiovascular and other medical conditions, that "block" or limit sympathetic nervous system stimulation. They act to slow the heart rate and decrease maximum heart rate.

Blood pressure The pressure exerted by the blood on the walls of the arteries, measured in millimeters of mercury by the sphygmomanometer.

BMI Broadcast Music, Inc. One of two performing rights societies in the United States that represent music publishers in negotiating and collecting fees for the nondramatic performance of music.

Body composition The makeup of the body in terms of the relative percentage of lean body mass and body-fat.

Bodybuilders Persons who use strength training as a means for achieving a better muscular appearance, especially with regard to muscle size, shape, definition, and proportion.

Bronchioles The smallest tubes that supply air to the alveoli (air sacs) of the lungs.

Bronchitis Acute or chronic inflammation of the bronchial tubes. See *Chronic obstructive pulmonary disease*.

Bronchodilating inhaler Medication that can be inhaled before, during, or after an asthma attack to dilate (enlarge) and relax the constricted bronchial smooth muscle. Example: Proventil.

Brown fat cells A special form of fat in the body that is designed to produce heat; small amounts are found around vital organs such as the heart and lungs.

Bulimia An eating disorder characterized by episodes of binge eating followed by fasting, self-induced vomiting, or the use of diuretics or laxatives.

Bursa Saclike structures, located around the joints of the body, that secrete a lubricating fluid that reduces friction, allowing the tissues to slide on one another.

Bursitis Painful inflammation of a bursa, occurring most often in the knees, hips, shoulders, and elbows.

Calorie The amount of heat energy needed to raise the temperature of 1 gram of water 1°C. Also called a small calorie. A large calorie, or kilocalorie (kcal), equals 1,000 small calories and is the amount of heat energy needed to raise the temperature of 1 kilogram of water by 1°C.

Capillaries The smallest blood vessels that supply blood to the tissues, and the site of all gas and nutrient exchange in the cardiovascular system. They connect the arterial and venous systems.

Carbohydrate (CHO) An essential nutrient that provides energy to the body. Dietary sources include sugars (simple) and grains, rice, potatoes, and beans (complex). 1 gm CHO = 4 kcals.

Cardiac output The amount of blood pumped by the heart per minute; usually expressed in liters of blood per minute.

Cardiovascular (cardiopulmonary) endurance The ability to perform large muscle movement over a sustained period; the capacity of the heart-lung system to deliver oxygen for sustained energy production. Also called cardiorespiratory endurance.

Cardiovascular risk factor A condition, a behavior (such as smoking), or a disease that increases one's risk for cardiovascular disease.

Cartilage A smooth, semi-opaque material providing a "frictionless" surface of a joint.

Cellulite A nonmedical term often used to describe subcutaneous fat, commonly found in the thighs and buttocks, that appears dimpled like an orange peel. Nutritional authorities agree that all forms of subcutaneous fat are the same and that cellulite is not a special form of fat.

Center of gravity The center of a body's mass; the actual geometric center in a rigid, symmetrical object of uniform density. In the human body, it is the point about which all parts are in balance with one another; it depends on the body's current position in space, anatomical structure, gender, habitual standing posture, and whether external weights are being held.

Cerebrovascular accident (CVA) Damage to the brain, often resulting in a loss of function, from impaired blood supply to part of the brain. More commonly known as a stroke.

Cervical Regional term referring to the neck.

Cervical vertebrae The seven vertebral bones of the neck.

Cholesterol A fatty substance found in the blood and body tissues and in animal products. Essential for body production of hormones, steroids, and so on. Its accumulation in the arteries leads to narrowing of the arteries (*atherosclerosis*).

Chronic Descriptive of a condition that persists over a long period of time; opposite of *acute*.

Chronic obstructive pulmonary disease (COPD) A condition, such as asthma, bronchitis, or emphysema, in which there is chronic obstruction of air flow. See *Asthma*, *Bronchitis*, and *Emphysema*.

Circuit strength training A strength training program in which one moves immediately from an exercise for one muscle group to an exercise for a different muscle group until each major muscle group has been worked.

Circuit training A form of training that takes the participant through a series of four to ten exercise stations, with brief rest intervals between stations. Can emphasize muscular endurance, aerobic conditioning, or both.

Clonic phase A phase during a grand mal seizure in which the muscles alternate between contraction and relaxation, giving a jerking appearance to the victim.

Collagen The main constituent of connective tissue, such as ligaments, tendons, and muscles.

Concentric contraction A contraction in which a muscle exerts force, shortens, and overcomes a resistance.

Connective tissue The tissue that binds together and supports various structures of the body. Examples: ligaments and tendons.

Contingency The immediate consequence of a particular behavior. Can be either positive (reward) or negative (punishment).

Continuous training Conditioning exercise, such as walking, jogging, cycling, or aerobic dancing, in which the prescribed intensity is maintained continuously between 50 percent and 85 percent of maximal oxygen consumption (functional capacity).

Contract A written agreement signed by the participant and the trainer (and additional third parties as appropriate) that clearly states the exercise goals to be achieved over a given time period. Also, a legally binding agreement stating services, fees, and other pertinent information regarding the trainer/client relationship.

Contracting Systematically providing rewards for positive behavior; stems from the behavioral theory of reinforcement.

Contusion Slight bleeding into soft tissue as a result of a blow, when the skin is not broken. More commonly known as a bruise.

Coronary artery disease (CAD) The major form of cardiovascular disease; almost always the result of atherosclerosis. Also called coronary heart disease (CHD).

Creatine phosphate (CP) A high-energy phosphate molecule that is stored in cells and can be used to resynthesize ATP immediately. One of the phosphagens.

Crepitation A grating sensation found when bones articulate abnormally or when fractured bone ends move against one another.

Deep Anatomical term meaning internal, that is, located further beneath the body surface than the *superficial* structures.

Delayed muscle soreness Muscle soreness that occurs 24 to 48 hours after intense exercise.

Diabetes mellitus A disease of carbohydrate metabolism, in which an absolute or relative deficiency of insulin results in an inability to metabolize carbohydrates normally.

Diastole The relaxation phase of the cardiac cycle during which blood fills the ventricles.

Diastolic blood pressure The pressure exerted by the blood on the blood vessel walls when the heart relaxes between contractions.

Dislocation Displacement of a bone from its normal position in a joint.

Distal Anatomical term meaning away from the attached end of the limb, origin of the structure, or midline of the body. Opposite of *proximal*.

Diuretic Medication that produces an increase in urine volume and sodium (salt) excretion.

Dorsal Anatomical term meaning the top surface of the foot and hands; toward the back; posterior. Opposite of *ventral*.

Dorsiflexion Movement of the dorsum (top) of the foot up toward the shin (proximally). Opposite of *plantarflexion*.

Duration The total time of each exercise session.

Dynamic flexibility Resistance to motion at the joint involving speed during physical performance.

Dynamic (isotonic) constant-resistance equipment Strength training equipment that provides a constant resistance throughout the movement range.

Dynamic (isotonic) variable-resistance equipment Strength training equipment that automatically varies the resistance throughout the movement range.

Dyspnea "Air hunger" resulting in difficult or labored breathing.

Eccentric contraction A contraction in which a muscle exerts force, lengthens, and is overcome by a resistance.

Ecchymosis Tissue discoloration from the movement of blood into tissue spaces; the purple discoloration from contusion.

Economy of movement (exercise economy) Exercise efficiency, or the ratio of external energy production (e.g., running speed) to energy input (e.g., oxygen consumption).

Ectomorph A body type characterized by a light build and slight muscular development.

Edema Swelling as a result of the collection of fluid within the tissues.

Effusion The escape of fluid into a body part.

Ejection fraction The percentage of total volume of blood in a ventricle at the end of diastole that is pumped out in systole.

Elastic property Temporary or recoverable elongation of connective tissue.

Emergency medical technicians (EMTs) Men and women trained to recognize serious emergencies and provide basic care needed to sustain life and reduce further injury.

Emphysema A chronic lung disease characterized by loss of air sacs resulting in decreased ability to exchange gases. Carbon dioxide levels are increased and oxygen levels are decreased, causing rapid breathing and dyspnea.

Endomorph A body type characterized by a heavy, rounded build, often with a marked tendency toward overweight or obesity.

Energy The potential to do work and activity; measured in calories derived from carbohydrates, fat, or protein.

Energy balance theory The principle that body weight will stay the same when caloric intake equals caloric expenditure, and that a positive or negative energy balance will cause weight gain or weight loss.

Enzymes Proteins necessary to bring about biochemical reactions.

Erythema Redness of the skin.

Essential nutrient A nutrient that must be provided in the diet because the body cannot produce it.

Etiology Study of the causes of injuries, diseases, and illnesses.

Eversion Movement of the sole of the foot outward; opposite of *inversion*.

Exercise-induced asthma Intermittent labored breathing precipitated by exertion during exercise. See *Asthma*.

Exercise recording A written record of each exercise session, including such information as repetitions, sets, and resistance.

Extension Movement at a joint, bringing two parts into or toward a straight line, thereby increasing the angle of the joint, such as straightening the elbow. Opposite of *flexion*.

Extrinsic External; not situated within or pertaining exclusively to a part.

Fartleck training A form of training similar to interval training, except the work-rest intervals are not systematically measured but instead are determined by how the participant feels.

Fast-twitch fiber A type II (white) muscle fiber characterized by its fast speed of contraction and a high capacity for anaerobic glycolysis.

Fat An essential nutrient that provides energy, energy storage, and insulation to the body. 1 gm fat = 9 kcals.

Fatty acid The building block of fats. An important nutrient for the production of energy during prolonged low-intensity exercise.

Feedback Verbal or nonverbal information about current behavior that can be used to improve future performance.

Flexibility The range of motion possible about a joint.

Flexion Movement about a joint in which the bones on either side of the joint are brought closer to each other. Opposite of *extension*.

Force A push or a pull that causes or tends to cause a change in a body's motion or shape.

Fracture A break in a bone; classified as "closed" when no opening from the outside of the skin to the broken bone occurs, and "open" when the fractured ends of the bone pierce the skin or an outside object penetrates the skin and fractures the underlying bone.

Frequency Refers to the number of exercise sessions per week.

Frontal plane An imaginary longitudinal section that divides the body into anterior and posterior halves; lies at a right angle to the *sagittal plane*.

Fulcrum The support on which a lever rotates in moving or lifting something.

Functional capacity The maximum physical performance, represented by maximal oxygen consumption.

Glucose A simple sugar; the form in which all carbohydrates are used as the body's principal energy source.

Glycogen The storage form of glucose found in the liver and muscles.

Golgi tendon organ A sensory organ within a tendon that, when stimulated, causes an inhibition of the entire muscle group to protect against too much force.

Graded exercise (stress) test A test that measures exact maximum aerobic capacity.

HDL High-density lipoprotein; a lipoprotein that contains more protein than cholesterol. Labeled "good" cholesterol because it removes excess cholesterol from the body.

Heart rate maximum reserve The result of subtracting the resting heart rate from the maximal heart rate; represents the working heart-rate range between rest and maximal heart rate within which all activity occurs.

Heat cramps A mild form of heat-related illness generally occurring during or after strenuous physical activity and characterized by painful muscle spasms.

Heat exhaustion The most common heat-related illness, usually the result of intense exercise in a hot, humid environment and characterized by profuse sweating with fluid and electrolyte loss, drop in blood pressure, light-headedness, nausea, vomiting, decreased coordination, and often syncope (fainting).

Heat stroke A medical emergency that is the most serious form of heat illness due to heat overload and/or impairment of the body's ability to dissipate heat. Characterized by high body temperature (>105°F), often dry, red skin, altered level of consciousness, seizures, coma, and possibly death.

Hemarthrosis The accumulation of blood in a joint cavity.

Hematoma The collection of blood in a confined soft tissue area.

Hemoglobin The protein molecule in red blood cells specifically adapted to carry (bond with) oxygen molecules.

Hernia   A protrusion of the abdominal contents into the groin (inguinal hernia) or through the abdominal wall (abdominal hernia).

Herniated disc   A condition in which the disc between two vertebrae of the spine bulges backward, often compressing a nerve root and compromising the function of that nerve.

Hypertension   High blood pressure, or the elevation of blood pressure above 140/90 mmHg.

Hyperthyroidism   A condition characterized by increased levels of the hormone secreted by the thyroid gland, causing a higher metabolic rate.

Hypertrophy   An increase in the cross-sectional size of a muscle in response to progressive resistance (strength) training.

Hyperventilation   A greater-than-normal rate of breathing, resulting in an abnormal loss of carbon dioxide from the blood. Dizziness may occur.

Hypoglycemia   A deficiency of sugar in the blood commonly caused by too much insulin, too little glucose, or too much exercise in the insulin-dependent diabetic.

Hypokalemia   A deficiency of potassium in the blood.

Hypokinesis   Lack of activity or energy.

Hypothyroidism   A condition characterized by a reduced level of the hormone secreted by the thyroid gland, requiring thyroid medication to increase metabolism to normal.

Incision   A cut in the skin, frequently from a sharp object.

Independent contractors   People who conduct business on their own on a contract basis and are not employees of an organization.

Inferior   Anatomical term meaning away from the head; situated below. Opposite of *superior*.

Inflammation   An immune response of the body tissues to an irritant.

Informed consent   Voluntary acknowledgement of the purpose, procedures, and specific risks of an activity in which one intends to engage.

Insole   The inside liner or "foot bed" of an athletic shoe that gives the shoe important stability and shock-absorbing features.

Insulin   A hormone, secreted into the bloodstream by the pancreas, that helps regulate carbohydrate metabolism.

Intensity   The physiological stress on the body during exercise. Indicates how hard the body should be working to achieve a training effect.

Internal muscle friction   Frictional forces within muscle tissue that decrease concentric force output and increase eccentric force output.

Interval training   Short, high-intensity exercise periods alternated with periods of rest. Example: 100-yard run, 1-minute rest, repeated eight times.

Intrinsic   Situated entirely within or pertaining exclusively to a part.

Inversion   Moving the sole of the foot inward; opposite of *eversion*.

Ischemia   A local deficiency of blood supply produced by constriction or obstruction of the arteries and resulting in decreased supply of oxygen to the tissues.

Isokinetic equipment   Equipment that provides a fixed speed of movement and varies the resistive force in accordance with the muscle force.

Isometric contraction   A contraction in which a muscle exerts force but does not change in length.

Isometric equipment   Equipment that does not permit joint movement, resulting in static (isometric) muscle contractions.

Isotonic equipment   See *Dynamic constant-resistance equipment*; *Dynamic variable-resistance equipment*.

Karvonen formula   The mathematical formula that uses maximum heart-rate reserve (maximal heart rate minus resting heart rate) to determine target heart rate.

Kegel exercises   Exercises designed to gain control of and tone the pelvic-floor muscles by controlled isometric contraction and relaxation of the muscles surrounding the vagina.

Ketone   An organic compound (e.g., acetone) with a carbonyl group attached to two carbon atoms. See *Ketosis*.

Ketosis   An abnormal increase of ketone bodies in the body, usually the result of an excessive low-carbohydrate diet, fasting, or starvation. See *Ketone*.

Kinesiology   The study of the principles of mechanics and anatomy in relation to human movement.

Kinesthetic awareness   One's sense of one's position and movement in space during various activities.

Korotkoff sounds   Five different sounds created by the pulsing of the blood through the brachial artery. Proper distinction of the sounds is necessary to determine blood pressure.

Kyphosis Exaggerated sagittal curvature of the thoracic spine, often accompanied by a forward head position.

Laceration A jagged or irregular cut or tear of the soft tissues, frequently caused by a blow to the body with a blunt object.

Lactic acid (Lactate) A waste product of anaerobic energy production known to cause localized muscle fatigue.

Lacto-ovo vegetarian A person who consumes milk and eggs but not meat, poultry, or fish.

Lateral Anatomical term meaning away from the midline of the body; pertaining to the side. Opposite of *medial*.

Lateral rotation Movement around an axis and away from the center of the body. Also called external rotation.

Law of acceleration The force F acting on a body in a given direction is equal to the body's mass m multiplied by the body's acceleration a in that direction: $F = ma$, or $a = F/m$.

Law of inertia The tendency of all objects and matter to remain at rest if at rest, or, if moving, to continue moving in the same straight line unless acted on by an outside force. Proportional to body mass.

LDL Low-density lipoprotein; a lipoprotein that contains more cholesterol than protein. Labeled "bad" cholesterol because it deposits cholesterol on the artery walls.

Leader nutrients Key nutrients that, when consumed, assure a balanced diet.

Lean body mass Body weight minus body-fat; composed primarily of muscle, bone, and other nonfat tissue.

Lever A rigid bar that rotates around a fixed support (fulcrum) in response to an applied force.

Liability Legal responsibility.

Ligament A connective tissue that functions to connect two bones.

Line of gravity The mechanical axis of the body as a whole; an imaginary vertical line passing through the body's center of gravity and along the pull of gravity toward the center of the earth.

Linear momentum The force with which a body moves; equal to its mass times its velocity.

Linear motion Movement in a straight line (rectilinear) or curved line (curvilinear) by an object that is not fixed at any point.

Lipoprotein The transport vehicle that transports fat throughout the body. Made up of protein, fat, and cholesterol.

Lordosis An exaggerated forward curvature of the lumbar spine, often resulting in a protruding abdomen and buttocks. Sometimes referred to as a swayback.

Low-back syndrome Pain or spasm in the lumbar spine area of the back.

Lumbar Anatomical term referring to the portion of the back between the abdomen and the pelvis.

Lumbar vertebrae The five vertebral bones of the low back.

Mass The quantity of matter anything contains; the property of a physical body that gives it inertia. Mass is constant and is independent of gravity.

Maximal heart rate (MHR) The highest heart rate a person can attain.

Maximal oxygen consumption ($\dot{V}O_2$ max) The highest volume of oxygen a person can consume during exercise; maximum aerobic capacity.

Medial Anatomical term meaning toward the midline of the body; pertaining to the center. Opposite of *lateral*.

Medial rotation Movement around an axis and toward the center of the body. Also called internal rotation.

Meniscus Semilunar cartilages that are pads of connective tissue that act mainly as shock absorbers and stabilizers at the knee and other joints.

Mesomorph A body type characterized by a husky, muscular build.

MET system A simplified system for classifying physical activities using metabolic equivalents, or METS. One MET is equal to the resting oxygen consumption, which is approximately 3.5 milliliters of oxygen per kilogram of body weight per minute (3.5 ml/kg/min).

Metabolism The chemical and physiological processes in the body that provide energy for the maintenance of life.

Midsole The layer of foam or cushioning material in a shoe that provides shock absorption.

Minerals Organic substances needed in the diet in small amounts to help regulate bodily functions.

Mirroring Imitating another's behavior or attitudes.

Mitochondria Specialized subcellular structures located within body cells that contain oxidative enzymes needed by the cell to metabolize foodstuffs into energy sources.

Momentary muscle failure Exercising to the point where a muscle can no longer contract concentrically.

Momentum See *Linear momentum.*

Monounsaturated A glycerol molecule with one fatty acid attached.

Motive force The force that starts or causes a movement.

Motor unit A motor nerve and all the muscle fibers it stimulates.

Muscle fiber A muscle cell.

Muscle length The actual length of a muscle between its tendon attachments.

Muscle spindle The sensory organ within a muscle that is sensitive to stretch and thus protects the muscle against too much stretch.

Muscular endurance The capacity of a muscle to exert force repeatedly against a resistance, or to hold a fixed or static contraction over time.

Muscular strength The maximum force that a muscle can produce against resistance in a single, maximal effort.

Myocardial infarction (MI) Death of a portion of the heart muscle from interruption of the blood supply. Commonly called a heart attack.

Myofibril Contractile protein in a muscle fiber.

Myosin Contractile protein in a myofibril.

Myotatic stretch reflex Muscular reflex created by excessive muscle spindle stimulation in order to prevent potential tissue damage.

Negligence Failure of a person to perform as a reasonable and prudent professional would perform under similar circumstances.

Neuromuscular system The network of nerves that causes muscles to contract or relax and the muscle fibers to which they attach.

Nutrient density Quantitative analysis of the amount of nutrients versus the amount of calories in a given food. Nutrient-dense foods provide more nutrients than calories.

Obesity An excessive accumulation of body-fat. Usually defined as more than 20 percent above ideal weight, or over 25 percent body-fat for men and over 30 percent body-fat for women.

Orthotic A custom-made appliance that inserts into a shoe to help correct faulty foot mechanics (such as excessive pronation).

Osteoarthritis A degenerative joint disease, found chiefly in older adults, caused by degeneration of the articular cartilage of the joints.

Outsole The outer layer of the athletic shoe that contacts the ground, providing traction.

Overuse injury An injury caused by activity that places too much stress on one area of the body over an extended period.

Overweight Being 10 percent over the average weight according to standard height-weight charts.

Palmar Anatomical term referring to the anterior surface of the hands.

Palpation The use of hands and/or fingers to determine an arterial pulse (e.g., carotid pulse) or to examine an injured area. (Compare with *Auscultation.*)

Paramedics Men and women trained to administer advanced care to victims of medical emergencies or injuries and who work under direct physician control.

Passive stretch A stretch in which the elastic components of the muscle are relaxed and the portion of muscle most likely to be loaded is the connective tissue. A static stretch is an excellent example.

Performance feedback Evidence or information regarding one's physical performance.

Phosphagens Adenosine triphosphate (ATP) and creatine phosphate (CP), two high-energy phosphate molecules that can be broken down for immediate use by the cells.

Plantar Anatomical term referring to the sole or bottom of the foot.

Plantarflexion Movement of the plantar surface of the foot distally. Opposite of *dorsiflexion.*

Plastic or viscous property Permanent or nonrecoverable elongation of connective tissue.

Polyunsaturated Refers to a triglyceride in which two or more carbons have double bonds.

Positive reinforcement Supporting a client's efforts by praise or reward.

Posterior Anatomical term meaning toward the back. Opposite of *anterior.*

Postictal phase The late phase during a grand mal seizure, characterized by flaccid muscles and an altered level of consciousness.

Power weightlifter A person who trains with weights in order to lift heavier-weight loads in the squat, dead lift, and bench press events.

PNF See *Proprioceptive neuromuscular facilitation.*

Primary assessment A rapid examination to identify life- or limb-threatening injuries or illnesses that need immediate attention.

Primary risk factor A characteristic or behavior that, by itself, is significantly associated with a major health problem.

Prime-mover muscle The muscle that contracts concentrically to accomplish the movement in any given joint action.

Prognosis Prediction as to the probable outcome of a disease or an injury.

Progressive resistance Gradually adding more resistance during strength training exercises as one's strength increases.

Prompt A reminder, cue, or other type of stimulus used to set the stage for or encourage performance of an activity.

Pronation A triplanar motion at the subtalar joint consisting of abduction, dorsiflexion, and eversion. Looks a lot like *eversion*. Position of the forearm with the palm facing backward or down.

Proprioceptive neuromuscular facilitation (PNF) A method of promoting the response of neuromuscular mechanisms through the stimulation of proprioceptors in an attempt to gain more stretch in a muscle. Often referred to as a contract/relax method of stretching.

Proprioceptors Specialized nerve endings in muscles, tendons, and joints that are sensitive to changes in tension during activity, giving a body part a sense of where it is in space.

Protein An essential nutrient made up of 22 amino acids. Builds and repairs body tissues. 1 gm = 4 kcals.

Proximal Anatomical term meaning toward the attached end of the limb, origin of the structure, or midline of the body. Opposite of *distal*.

Puncture A piercing wound of the skin from a sharp object, creating a small hole in the tissue.

Range of motion (ROM) The number of degrees that an articulation (joint) will allow one of its segments to move.

Rapport A relationship of mutual trust, harmony, or emotional affinity.

Ratings of Perceived Exertion (RPE) Developed by Borg, this scale provides a standard means for evaluating a participant's perception of his/her physical exertion. The original scale was 6-20; the revised scale is 0-10.

Reactionary force An equal but directionally opposite force applied by a second body on a first body in response to the first body's applied force, which is in accordance with Newton's Third Law: For every action there is an equal and opposite reaction.

Reciprocal innervation (inhibition) Reflex co-acting with stretch reflex to inhibit activity of an opposing muscle group.

Recommended Dietary Allowances (RDA) Recommended vitamin and mineral intake for practically all healthy people to obtain optimum health.

Registered dietitian A professional trained in nutrition and accredited by the American Dietetic Association.

Rheumatoid arthritis An autoimmune disease that causes inflammation of connective tissues and joints.

Risk factor A characteristic, inherited trait, or behavior related to the presence or development of a condition or disease.

ROM See *Range of motion*.

Rotary motion Movement by an object around a fixed point.

Rotator cuff Muscle group of the shoulder made up of the supraspinatus, infraspinatus, teres minor, and subscapularis muscles. Responsible for shoulder strength and stability.

RPE See *Ratings of Perceived Exertion*.

Sagittal plane Anatomical term referring to the imaginary longitudinal line that divides the body or any of its parts into right and left parts.

Sarcomere Repeating unit of a muscle fiber.

Saturated fatty acid A fatty acid that carries the maximum possible number of hydrogen atoms, leaving no point of unsaturation.

Scar tissue An inelastic, avascular, and fibrous tissue that is the result of the body's normal healing process.

Scoliosis A lateral curvature of the vertebral column, usually in the thoracic area.

Secondary assessment After immediate life- or limb-threatening injuries/illnesses have been identified, this more thorough evaluation is performed to identify more subtle, yet still important, injuries.

Secondary risk factor A characteristic, inherited trait, behavior, or condition that, by itself, has a weak association with a disease but that increases the risk when other risk factors are present.

Seizure A disorder originating from the brain in which there is a disturbance of movement, behavior, sensation, or consciousness.

Set-point theory The weight control theory that states that each person has an established normal body weight. Any deviation from this set point will lead to changes in body metabolism to return to the normal weight.

Sign An objective finding during examination of an injured body part.

Sliding filament theory A generally accepted theory explaining the interaction between actine and myosine proteins and ATP to cause muscle contraction.

Slow-twitch fiber   A type I (red) muscle fiber characterized by its slow speed of contraction and a high capacity for aerobic glycolysis.

Sole proprietorship   A business owned and operated by one person.

Spotter   A training partner who gives assistance to an unsuccessful lifting attempt, adds resistance during an exercise, provides encouragement and feedback, and otherwise helps the exerciser train in a safe and effective manner.

Sprain   Overstretching or tearing of a ligament or joint capsule, resulting in discoloration, swelling, and pain.

Stabilizer muscles   Muscles that stabilize one joint so a desired movement can be performed in another joint.

Standard of care   Appropriateness of an exercise professional's actions, in light of current professional standards and based on the age, condition, and knowledge of the participant.

Static flexibility   Range of motion (ROM) about a joint with little emphasis on speed of movement.

Static (passive) stretch   A low-force, long-duration stretch that holds the desired muscles at their greatest possible length for 15 to 30 seconds.

Steroids   See *Anabolic androgenic steroids*.

Strain   Overstretching or tearing of a muscle or tendon.

Strength plateau   In a training regimen, a period of time during which no further strength gains occur, indicating that some aspect of the training should be changed to enable further progress.

Stretch weakness   The weakening effect on muscles remaining in the elongated position for an extended period of time.

Stroke volume   The amount of blood pumped from the left ventricle during one heartbeat.

Subluxation   A partial dislocation of a joint; usually reduces itself.

Substrate   A fuel source for energy metabolism.

Superficial   External; located close to or on the body surface.

Superior   Anatomical term meaning higher or toward the head. Opposite of *inferior*.

Supination   A triplanar motion at the subtalar joint consisting of dorsiflexion, adduction, and inversion. Looks like *inversion*. Position of the forearm with the palm facing forward or upward.

Symptom   A subjective complaint given by an injured person to an examiner.

Syncope   A transient state of unconsciousness during which the person collapses to the floor as a result of lack of oxygen to the brain. Commonly known as fainting.

Synergist   A muscle that assists another muscle in its function.

Synovial fluid   Transparent, viscous lubricating fluid found in joint cavities, bursae, and tendon sheaths.

Systole   The contraction phase of the cardiac cycle during which blood leaves the ventricles.

Systolic blood pressure   The pressure exerted by the blood on the blood vessel walls during ventricular contractions.

Talk test   A subjective method for measuring exercise intensity using observation of respiration effort and the ability to talk while exercising.

Tendinitis   Inflammation of a tendon.

Tendon   Strong, fibrous connective tissue that attaches a muscle to a bone.

Tendon insertion   The point at which a muscle tendon attaches to a bone.

Tensile strength   The greatest longitudinal stress a substance can bear without breaking apart.

Thermic effect of food (TEF)   An increase in energy expenditure due to an increase in cellular activity associated with the digestion, absorption, and metabolism of food.

Thoracic   Anatomical term referring to the portion of the body between the neck and abdomen; also known as the chest (thorax) region.

Thoracic vertebrae   The 12 vertebral bones of the mid-spine.

Tonic phase   A phase during a grand mal seizure in which the victim loses consciousness, becomes rigid with all extremities extended, and displays breath holding.

Torque   A force causing rotation about a fixed axis of rotation; the act or process of turning around on an axis.

Transverse plane   Anatomical term for the imaginary line that divides the body or any of its parts into superior and inferior parts. Also known as the horizontal plane.

Triglyceride   The storage form of fat consisting of three free fatty acids and glycerol.

Underweight   Being 10 percent below the average weight according to standard height-weight charts.

USRDA   United States Recommended Dietary Allowances. Used in food labeling; expresses nutrients of the RDA in percentages.

Valsalva maneuver   Increased pressure in the thoracic cavity caused by forced exhalation with the breath held.

Vasodilator   A nerve or drug that acts to relax (dilate) a blood vessel.

Vegan   A pure vegetarian who excludes all animal-derived foods from the diet.

Veins   Blood vessels that carry blood, usually deoxygenated, to the heart.

Ventral   Anatomical term meaning pertaining to the front. Opposite of *dorsal*.

Venules   Smaller divisions of the veins.

Ventricle   One of the two (left and right) lower chambers of the heart. The muscular left ventricle pumps blood to the body; the smaller right ventricle pumps blood to the lungs.

Viscoelastic   A combination of elastic and plastic properties found in all connective tissue.

Vitamins   Organic compounds that function as metabolic regulators in the body. Classified as water soluble or fat soluble.

$\dot{V}O_2$ max   See Maximal oxygen consumption.

Waiver   Voluntary abandonment of a right to file suit; not always legally binding.

Weight   The force with which gravity pulls a body to the earth; the product of a body's mass and the acceleration of gravity. The weight of a given mass may change, depending on the gravitational pull.

White fat cells   The primary fat in the body; makes up 98 to 99 percent of the body's total fat.

Wound   A break in the continuity of the soft tissue of the body. The five main types of wounds are *abrasions, avulsions, incisions, lacerations,* and *punctures.*

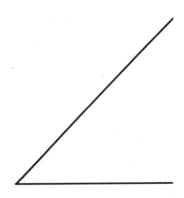

Index

A

132–33, 134, 247; toxicity of, 120–21, 123, 133
vocal stress, reducing, 381
voice, use of, 380–81
V̇O₂ max, 11–12; *see also* maximal oxygen consumption

W

waivers, 481, 483, 487
walking, 214–15, 299, 301; and footwear, 411, 413, 414
warm-up, 287; and arthritis, 340; and asthma, 342; and cycling, 217; examples, 324–25, 326–32; exercises, 197–99; and hypertension, 337; need for, 16–17, 197–99, 244–45; and pregnancy, 352; and rowing, 219; and stair climbing, 219–20; and swimming, 218; and walking, 215

warnings, 481–82
waste products: of ATP production, 9–10; and delayed muscle soreness, 283; elimination of, 7, 33, 34; and fatigue, 28; and stretching, 287
water, 114; and ATP production, 9–10; consumption of, 342; and fatigue, 28, 228; and muscle composition, 246; replacement of, 9–10, 19–20, 129, 133, 228, 229; retention of, 223
weather conditions, and adherence, 362; *see also* cold weather, hot weather
weight-bearing exercise: alternatives to, 216–18; benefits of, 17–18, 349, 350
weight control, 150, 310–12, 321, 394
weight-gain program, 312–13

weightlifting, 245–46; and footwear, 411, 413, 414; and momentum, 72
weight loss fads, 305–310, 342
weight machines, 240–41, 250; exercises on, 263–69; selecting, 395–401, 406–9; and spotting, 246
weight training. *See* strength training
Wolff's Law, 39
wounds, first-aid for, 460–62
wrist joint: exercises for, 59; muscles that act on, 60–61

Y

YMCA sub-maximal tests, 163–69 170